Administrative Law
PRINCIPLES AND ADVOCACY

THIRD EDITION

John Swaigen

CONTRIBUTOR
Jasteena Dhillon

 ▪ Toronto, Canada ▪ 2016

Emond Montgomery Publications Limited
60 Shaftesbury Avenue
Toronto ON M4T 1A3
http://www.emond.ca/highered

Printed in Canada.
Reprinted November 2019.

MIX
Paper from
responsible sources
FSC® C004071

FSC
www.fsc.org

We acknowledge the financial support of the Government of Canada. Canada
Nous reconnaissons l'appui financier du gouvernement du Canada.

Emond Montgomery Publications has no responsibility for the persistence or accuracy of URLs for external or third-party Internet websites referred to in this publication, and does not guarantee that any content on such websites is, or will remain, accurate or appropriate.

Vice-president, publishing: Anthony Rezek
Acquisitions editor: Lindsay Sutherland
Managing editor, development: Kelly Dickson
Developmental editor: Heather Gough
Director, editorial and production: Jim Lyons
Production editor and coordinator: Laura Bast
Copy editor: Cindy Fujimoto
Permissions editor: Lisa Brant
Proofreader: Rohini Herbert
Typesetter: Tara Wells
Indexer: Paula Pike
Cover image: Sophie James/Shutterstock

Library and Archives Canada Cataloguing in Publication

Swaigen, John, 1944-, author
    Administrative law : principles and advocacy / John Swaigen ; contributor, Jasteena Dhillon. — Third edition.

Includes index.
ISBN 978-1-55239-667-4 (paperback)

    1. Administrative law—Canada—Textbooks.   I. Dhillon, Jasteena, author   II. Title.

KE5015 S93 2016   342.71'06   C2015-905568-7
KF5402 S93 2016

To Arel, Julia, and Sarah Lynn

Contents

PART I

PRINCIPLES AND THEORY

1 Introduction to the Legal System 3

2 Administrative Agencies and Tribunals 25

6 Fairness: The Right to Be Heard 147

7 Fairness: Bias 167

PART II

ADVOCACY

8 Advocacy Before Government Departments, Administrative Agencies, and Tribunals 187

APPENDIXES

Preface

In 1951, when Robert Reid, later Justice Reid of Ontario's Divisional Court, was asked to teach administrative law at Osgoode Hall Law School, he discovered that there were no Canadian textbooks on the subject to assist him. Administrative law did not even exist as a heading in Canadian legal encyclopedias. In his foreword to a text on Canadian administrative tribunals, Justice Reid tells how he tried with limited success to scrounge advice and notes that would help him put together a course on administrative law.

Today, 65 years later, there are numerous texts on administrative law. There are practical guides for lawyers, tribunal members, and even expert witnesses. There are scholarly treatises. There are texts on specific issues such as bias, administrative investigations, and delegated legislation. But to my knowledge, until I wrote this book, there was still not one text designed specifically for students in institutions of higher learning (other than law faculties). University and college teachers generally used texts written for other purposes, supplemented by photocopies of materials they had collected. There was, and still is, very little that addresses both theory and practice—and that does so in plain language.

This book attempts to fill this gap. It is designed primarily for students who are studying to be paralegals, community legal workers, or law clerks, and for students who will work for government departments, regulatory agencies, or tribunals. It describes the underlying principles of administrative law and the variety of applications of those principles in a way that engages students and facilitates learning. It also contains practical advice on dealing effectively with departments, agencies, and tribunals.

The structure of this edition largely reflects that of the second, which was revised to reflect the competencies for paralegals identified by the Law Society of Upper Canada, and the Law Society's syllabus for community college courses for paralegals when the Law Society began to regulate paralegals in 2006.

With the help of Jasteena Dhillon, an experienced professor of administrative law, the text has been revised and expanded to improve its pedagogical features, such as the review questions, exercises, fact scenarios, and cases to consider at the end of each chapter.

This edition also reflects the substantial body of Supreme Court administrative law, Charter, and human rights decisions that have been made since the second edition was published, including decisions that have: clarified the standard of review of tribunal decisions (*Alberta (Information and Privacy Commissioner)*); clarified the scope of procedural fairness (*Newfoundland and Labrador Nurses' Union*); clarified the relationship between administrative law and the Charter (*Doré* and *Harkat*); changed the criteria for granting public interest standing in Charter cases (*Downtown

East Side); addressed the ability of tribunals to decide constitutional questions (*Conway*); affirmed the availability of damages as a remedy for violations of the Charter (*Ward*); reconfirmed the test for validity of delegated legislation (*Katz Group Canada Inc*); addressed the application of section 11 of the Charter to administrative proceedings (*Guindon*); interpreted section 15 of the Charter (*Law* and *Withler*); and clarified the jurisdiction of bodies other than human rights tribunals to hear human rights arguments (*Figliola*).

The text has also been revised to address some subjects for the first time or in greater depth, such as the *functus officio* doctrine, legitimate expectations (*Mavi*), tribunal governance and "clustering" (Ontario's *Adjudicative Tribunals Accountability, Governance and Appointments Act, 2009*), delegated legislation, public interest standing, the duty to consult First Nations under section 35 of the Constitution, whether the Charter imposes positive obligations on government, and the mandate and procedures of the Immigration and Refugee Board.

Like the first two editions, this text deals with both theory and practice. It addresses issues ranging from the very concrete and specific—for example, how to conduct research or lead evidence—to more abstract questions of principles, ethics, and courtesy. It suggests ways that representatives might carry out these responsibilities fairly, effectively, and efficiently. It also explains the responsibilities of representatives to their clients and to the regulators and tribunals before which they appear, as well as the obligations of these agencies to parties and their representatives.

The premise of this book is that all administrative departments and agencies are subject to certain common fundamental premises, yet no two government agencies are alike. The fact that each agency has been designed to meet a particular need makes it a challenge to determine in any specific case how the principles of administrative law apply to that agency.

Given this variety in administrative bodies and tribunals and their procedures, a "one size fits all" approach to describing and prescribing appropriate behaviour for advocates and government agents will fit no one perfectly. I hope, however, that the book's double approach to the practice and theory of administrative law will fit most well enough.

Acknowledgments

Jasteena Dhillon is responsible for the improved pedagogical features (review questions, exercises, fact scenarios, and key cases) in this edition.

My thanks to Andy Anstett, Michael Bossin, and Gary Yee, who reviewed my descriptions of the regulatory agencies and tribunals with which they are or have been involved, and provided me with comments and insights into the workings of those entities.

I also want to reiterate my thanks to several chairs, vice-chairs, and members of tribunals, tribunal staff members, staff and members of regulatory agencies, tribunal counsel, and administrative law instructors who provided helpful advice and comments on drafts of the first and second editions: Andy Anstett, Bernie Aron, Judith Goldstein, Donald Hale, Katherine Laird, David Lampert, Genevieve Leslie, Alan Levy, and Gary Yee.

Thanks also to the reviewers, Denise Labelle at Mohawk College, Gurpreet Gill at Conestoga College, and Deirdre Way at Loyalist College, for their helpful feedback.

I owe a debt of gratitude to Lindsay Sutherland and Heather Gough for overseeing and editing this edition, as well as to Cindy Fujimoto for copy editing, Rohini Herbert for proofreading, and Paula Pike for indexing. Thanks also to Paul Emond for his personal involvement in smoothing the way for this edition.

I remain grateful to the staff at Emond Publishing who brought the earlier editions to fruition, in particular Peggy Buchan, Sarah Gleadow, Jim Lyons, Christine Purden, and Paula Pike.

Finally, I would be pleased to receive suggestions for improvement from both students and teachers. Comments can be sent to my attention at help@emond.ca.

John Swaigen
January 2016

About the Author

John Swaigen (BA, LLB, LLM) is a lawyer and author in Ontario, Canada. He received a BA from the University of Toronto, and an LLB and LLM from Osgoode Law School. Since being called to the Ontario bar in 1974, he has served as director of quality assurance at the Ontario Legal Aid Plan, chair of Ontario's Environmental Appeal Board, research associate at the Institute for Environmental Law and Policy, counsel for the Municipality of Metropolitan Toronto and the Ontario Ministry of the Environment, general counsel to the Canadian Environmental Law Association, and legal counsel in the Office of Information and Privacy Commissioner/Ontario. Swaigen has served on several boards of directors, including the Sierra Legal Defence Fund and the Canadian Environmental Defence Fund. Since 2011 he has been a staff lawyer with Ecojustice, a national charitable organization dedicated to defending Canadians' rights to a healthy environment. He has been a member of the Complaints Committee of Professional Engineers Ontario since 2013. Swaigen has written books and articles on environmental law.

About the Contributor

Jasteena Dhillon (BA, JD, LLM) is professor of law at Humber College and adjunct professor in the Faculty of Law, University of Windsor. She graduated from the University of Toronto in 1990 and from the University of Windsor Law School in 1995. She received her LLM from Leiden University in the Netherlands. She was an associate fellow at Harvard Kennedy School's Carr Center for Human Rights Policy, where she focused on informal justice and rights in tribal areas. She now teaches international law at the Faculty of Law in Windsor and administrative law at Humber College Institute of Technology and Advanced Learning.

Dhillon began her career as a community advocate in legal clinics for those unable to access government services. After completing law school she worked as a lawyer with the Office of the Children's Lawyer representing children in welfare and family/civil matters. Her work with vulnerable communities in Ontario and Canada has earned her recognition from her peers in the movement. Dhillon also provides training and advice to government bodies, including the Canadian Armed Forces, Public Safety Canada, and the Privy Council Office. She acts as a consultant on legal, administrative, and policy issues.

She has worked internationally as a legal and development expert in conflict, post-conflict, and transitional crisis areas around the world, and for the United Nations (UN), the North Atlantic Treaty Organization (NATO), the Organization for Security and Co-operation in Europe (OSCE), the International Catholic Migration Commission (ICMC), and the Norwegian Refugee Council (NRC).

PART I

Principles and Theory

Introduction to the Legal System

1

LEARNING OUTCOMES

After reading this chapter, you will understand

- what is meant by the term "law";
- why we need laws, as well as other, less formal rules, to govern our conduct;
- what kinds of behaviour are regulated by laws;
- how laws are made;
- who has the authority to make laws;
- what distinguishes various categories of laws; and
- how different kinds of laws are administered and enforced.

The law is the last result of human wisdom acting upon human experience for the benefit of the public.

Samuel Johnson

What Is a Law?

There are various ways of defining the concept of a law. For the purposes of this book, a **law** is described as a rule made by a body of elected representatives or their delegates or by a court, using procedures that are also prescribed by law. All of the steps set out in the procedural rules must be followed. For example, in the case of laws made by Canada's federal Parliament, a provincial legislature, or the council of one of the territories, the proposed law must be

- read three times in the open assembly,
- debated,
- passed at the second and third reading by a majority of the elected representatives present, and
- assented to by the Queen's representative (the governor general for federal laws and the lieutenant governor for provincial laws).

If any of these steps are missed, the law will not be valid.

Why Do We Need Laws?

People often think of laws as rules that prohibit individuals from doing certain things and that punish those who break them. Although that is the nature and effect of many laws, laws do not just impose duties and punishments; they also create rights. In addition, laws create a framework to ensure that the many complex activities of contemporary society are carried out in an honest, fair, efficient, and effective manner. Laws are, in effect, a blueprint or a set of "rules of the road" for carrying on business, protecting consumers, regulating the use and development of land, conferring government benefits, protecting human dignity and preventing discrimination, and distributing and redistributing wealth. Imagine driving a car in a crowded city if there were no rules governing motor vehicle safety, driver training, when to stop and go, when to make turns, how fast to go, and which side of the road to drive on. Imagine the chaos if half of the drivers chose to drive on the right-hand side of the road and the other half decided to drive on the left!

How Do Laws Differ from Other Rules?

In a democratic society, people have considerable freedom to do what they want in any way they want. However, certain behaviour is restricted, either by formal laws imposed by governments and the courts or by other kinds of rules that are followed by most people but are less strictly enforced. The latter may be imposed through social pressure or by mutual agreement (social norms), or may be accepted as a condition of belonging to some group or organization, such as a school, business, church, or club. Although breaking such rules may lead to penalties—for example, loss of membership in a group—compliance with them is, in a sense, a matter of choice. In contrast, compliance with laws is required.

While governments and the courts can restrain the activities of ordinary people, they can do so only by passing, enforcing, or applying a law. As discussed, in order to be valid as a law, any rule made by a government in the form of a law must be passed by a majority of the elected representatives using prescribed procedures. Similarly, any restraints imposed by tribunals or courts must be authorized by laws passed by governments or made by judges.

> *Law will never be strong or respected unless it has the sentiment of the people behind it.*
>
> James Bryce, *The American Commonwealth*, vol 2 (1888)

Governments and courts must also follow laws that set out the procedures for applying or enforcing laws, and they must limit their activities to those that are **delegated** to them by a valid law. In other words, governments, tribunals, and courts are not entitled to do whatever they want, but only what validly made laws authorize them to do. This limit on the right of governments, tribunals, and courts to control the conduct of citizens is known as the **rule of law**.

According to the rule of law, all law-making is governed by a supreme law called the Constitution. The **Constitution** establishes the basic institutions of government, reflects some of the fundamental values of society, and determines the values or goals that all other laws must reflect. In this way, the Constitution governs the validity of all other laws. The relationship between the Constitution and the creation of other laws is discussed in the next section.

The purpose of the rule of law is to prevent arbitrariness and, at worst, tyranny. By restricting the powers of government and by setting out strict rules for the passing, application, and enforcement of laws, the democratic system deters those who are granted these powers from acting impulsively or capriciously, making up rules as they go along. It also deters individuals or groups from assuming or exercising powers that they do not legitimately possess.

Using the rule of law as a method of curbing the powers of government prevents many abuses. To avoid arbitrariness, the rule of law requires that like situations be treated alike and different situations be appropriately distinguished from each other. In addition, new rules are subjected to a predetermined process of scrutiny by elected representatives. They are not imposed in a dictatorial fashion with no accountability.

A Hollywood take on the meaning and importance of law:

Let me tell you what justice is. Justice is the law. And the law is man's feeble attempt to lay down the principles of decency. And decency isn't a deal, it's not a contract or a hustle or an angle! Decency—decency is what your grandmother taught you. It's in your bones.

Morgan Freeman as Judge Leonard White in *The Bonfire of the Vanities*

The Canadian Constitution and Its Limits on Law-Making

The Constitution of Canada is the supreme law of the land. All other laws must conform to it. The Constitution consists of a combination of principles of democracy inherited from Britain as traditions and two statutes passed by the Parliament of Canada—the *Constitution Act, 1867* (formerly called the *British North America Act, 1867*) and the *Constitution Act, 1982*. A court can declare any law that conflicts with the Constitution to be invalid, or the effect of such a law may be restricted by a court or, in some circumstances, by a tribunal. An invalid law is called "unconstitutional." No one is required to follow an unconstitutional law.

There are two parts of the Constitution that determine the validity of laws passed by the federal and provincial governments and of municipal bylaws. The first is the division of powers. The second is the *Canadian Charter of Rights and Freedoms*.

Division of Powers

The Constitution allocates law-making powers to the federal and provincial governments on the basis of subject matter.[1] If one level of government passes a law that regulates an area granted to the other level by the Constitution, the law is considered invalid. For example, if a provincial government passes a criminal law—an area of jurisdiction that the Constitution grants exclusively to the federal government—that law cannot be enforced.

The Charter

The second part of the Constitution to which laws must conform is the *Canadian Charter of Rights and Freedoms*.[2] The Charter sets out a list of fundamental freedoms, democratic or political rights, legal rights, mobility rights, and equality rights belonging to all persons. Any law or government action that infringes these rights *to a greater extent than can be justified in a free and democratic society* is either invalid or has no effect to the extent that it infringes these rights. That is, the rights set out in the Charter are not absolute.

---

1   The division of powers is found primarily in the *Constitution Act, 1867* (UK), 30 & 31 Vict, c 3, reprinted in RSC 1985 Appendix II, No 5. Some clarification is found in the *Constitution Act, 1982*, being Schedule B to the *Canada Act 1982* (UK), 1982, c 11.

2   The *Canadian Charter of Rights and Freedoms* is contained in Part I of the *Constitution Act, 1982*, *supra* note 1. Before 1982, the civil liberties of Canadians were not part of the Constitution. There were some federal and provincial statutes (such as the federal *Canadian Bill of Rights*, Quebec's *Charter of Human Rights and Freedoms*, and the human rights codes of other provinces) that guaranteed civil liberties, but they did not have constitutional status—that is, they did not override conflicting statutes.

The Charter allows courts (and, in some cases, tribunals) to balance the civil liberties of individuals and corporations against the collective rights of the public as a whole. If a law or the way a law is implemented infringes a person's constitutional rights, the government is required to demonstrate that the infringement is important for the benefit of the community and that the intrusion is no greater than is necessary to achieve this social benefit.

If the government can justify the extent to which the law infringes a right or freedom guaranteed by the Charter, the courts will consider the law to be valid. If the government cannot justify the infringement, the law will not be binding on the person whose right or freedom it infringes.

For more information on the Charter, see Chapter 4, The Charter and Its Relationship to Administrative Law.

Who Makes the Laws?

Our system of government has three basic branches—legislative, executive, and judicial. In general, the legislative branch (such as the federal Parliament or provincial legislatures) makes laws; the executive branch (such as government departments or police forces) enforces laws; and the judicial branch (the courts) interprets laws.

Our system also has three levels of government—federal, provincial (or territorial), and municipal. As discussed, the division of powers between the federal and provincial governments is set out in the Constitution. For example, criminal law is under federal jurisdiction, while employment law is under the jurisdiction of each of the provinces. Some subject areas, such as family law, are shared. The provinces also have the power to delegate authority over local issues to municipal governments. For example, municipalities generally have the authority to pass and enforce bylaws governing land development and public transit within municipal boundaries.

As shown in the chart below, the federal and provincial governments have all three branches of government, while the municipal governments have only legislative and executive branches. All Nunavut judges are appointed by the federal government; judges in Yukon and the Northwest Territories are appointed by the territorial and federal governments.

Level of government	Branch of government		
	Legislative	Executive	Judicial
Federal	✓	✓	✓
Provincial	✓	✓	✓
Territorial (Nunavut, Yukon, and the Northwest Territories)	✓	✓	✓
Municipal	✓	✓	

Each of these levels and branches of government must stay within the authority granted to it by the Constitution or by another statute. This concept of "separation of powers" follows from the principle of the rule of law. It is intended to be a safeguard against any of the three levels or branches becoming too powerful and abusing its authority. One of the challenges of administrative law is to ensure that this safeguard continues to operate while still allowing society to benefit from the flexibility and efficiencies that can result from the delegation of powers.

The Three Branches of Government

The Legislative Branch and Its Law-Making Powers

The legislative branch consists of individuals elected by citizens (the general public) to represent them in the federal Parliament, the provincial legislatures, the councils of the territories, and municipal councils. It is called the legislative branch because under Canada's Constitution its members have a monopoly on the power to **legislate** (pass laws). In fact, passing laws is the main function of this branch of government. These elected representatives as a group pass statutes (or **acts**) or, at the municipal level, bylaws.

The federal and provincial legislatures can also make other kinds of laws called regulations, discussed below, but normally they pass a statute in which the authority to make a regulation is delegated to an official or a body that is part of the executive branch, such as the **Cabinet** or a Cabinet minister. Occasionally, the legislature will pass a statute that delegates the power to make regulations to an unelected body such as an agency, board, or commission. **Regulations** are detailed rules that "flesh out" the meaning and requirements of a statute. They are discussed in more detail below, under the heading "Common Law and Statute Law."

DELEGATION OF LAW-MAKING POWERS TO AGENCIES, BOARDS, AND COMMISSIONS

As stated above, a body of elected representatives, such as a provincial Legislative Assembly, will occasionally pass a law that delegates the power to make binding rules or regulations to an agency created by that assembly. Only in these circumstances does an unelected agency have the authority to make binding rules. Sometimes the rules are procedural; in other cases, they are more substantive. (See the box feature "Delegation of Legislative Functions.")

DELEGATION OF LAW-MAKING POWERS TO TERRITORIES

The three territories are like a hybrid between a province and a municipality. Like municipalities, they have no powers of their own granted by the Constitution, only those delegated to them by federal statutes. In practice, however, each territory has almost the same law-making powers as a province. The federal government has passed statutes giving each of the three territories powers to pass laws, sometimes called **ordinances**, which are similar in content to provincial and federal statutes.

Delegation of Legislative Functions

- **Substantive rules**   Ontario's *Conservation Authorities Act* establishes conservation authorities to protect watersheds from flooding and erosion, and permits them to make binding regulations that govern development of land along riverbanks. Other commissions established by the Ontario government have the right to amalgamate municipalities or close hospitals.

- **Procedural rules**   Ontario's *Statutory Powers Procedure Act*, which sets out various procedural requirements for administrative tribunals, also permits tribunals to make their own rules for the conduct of certain aspects of their proceedings, such as postponement of a hearing, preliminary motions, and pre-hearing conferences.

The Executive Branch and Its Law-Making Powers

The second branch of government is the executive, which consists of the federal or provincial Cabinet or, in the case of municipal government, the executive committees of municipal councils, and their staff—the many civil servants who report to the ministers of Cabinet and to municipal councils and their committees. This branch administers and enforces the laws that the legislative branch passes. However, in the case of the federal and provincial governments, the Cabinet (and sometimes individual Cabinet ministers) also makes the regulations that implement the statutes. This is actually a legislative function, but it has been delegated by the legislators to the executive. For this reason, regulations are sometimes called "delegated legislation."

The federal and provincial cabinets consist of elected representatives chosen by the prime minister or the premier. Committees of municipal councils consist of a group of elected representatives chosen by the mayor or by the council. In theory, this system preserves the accountability of the people who carry out the laws as well as that of the people who make them. However, these elected groups are just the tip of the iceberg. They preside over an extensive network of hired civil servants, as well as members of agencies, boards, and commissions (ABCs, collectively known as **agencies**) appointed by the executive, who are not directly accountable to the electorate. In the federal and provincial governments, each Cabinet minister is responsible for the work of a **department** (called a **ministry** in some provinces). A department consists of hundreds or thousands of civil servants who carry out the laws and administer government programs. In many cases, the minister will also be responsible for several agencies established by the government.

The Judicial Branch and Its Law-Making Powers

The third branch of government is the judiciary. The judiciary consists of the courts and judges, who settle disputes between citizens (individuals or organizations) and between the government and citizens regarding the interpretation or application of the law. They decide whether someone has broken the law, and, if so, what punishment will be imposed, what compensation must be paid, or what other action the violator must take.

Judges are appointed by the executive branch of the federal or provincial government. Once appointed, they are independent and have the right to settle disputes—including disputes between the government and citizens—without fear of losing their job, having their salary reduced, or being subjected to any other form of government interference or pressure. The judiciary therefore provides an important protection for citizens against violations of the law either by the government or by other citizens. The duties of the judiciary include interpreting laws and striking down laws that are passed without proper authority. Moreover, since the passage of the *Canadian Charter of Rights and Freedoms*, the courts can strike down any law that violates the fundamental rights and freedoms set out in the Charter.

Judges also have a legislative function within certain areas of law. The body of law that is made by judges is called "common law." It is discussed later in this chapter under the heading "Types of Law."

The Three Levels of Government

As discussed, in Canada we have three levels of government—the federal government, provincial governments and territorial councils, and municipal governments. Each is presided over by an assembly of elected representatives, which exercises the government's law-making powers.

The federal and provincial governments are permanently established under our Constitution. Municipal and territorial governments have no constitutional status or permanence. The existence of municipalities depends on the will of the provincial government, and their powers are limited to those specifically granted by provincial statute. For this reason, municipalities are often referred to as "creatures of the province." Similarly, territorial councils owe their existence and their law-making powers entirely to the federal government.

Federal laws are laws that apply throughout the whole country. They are passed by the federal **Parliament**, which consists of the House of Commons (whose members are elected) and the Senate (whose members are appointed by the government of the day).

Provincial laws apply throughout a province. They are passed by the provincial **legislature** or **Legislative Assembly**[3] (known in Quebec as the "National Assembly").

Municipal bylaws apply only within the boundaries of a municipality. They are passed by the municipal council, which consists of elected councillors (sometimes called "aldermen"). Similarly, territorial ordinances are passed by the elected councils of the territories and apply only within the territory.

---

3 Provincial legislatures are also known as "provincial parliaments." To avoid confusion, this book will use the term "Parliament" to refer only to the federal legislature.

Each level of government has the constitutional or statutory authority to pass laws in certain subject areas. In some areas, the law-making powers of the different levels may overlap. In such cases, if a higher level of government has the authority to pass a law and has done so, any conflicting laws or bylaws passed by a lower level of government cannot be enforced.

Federal Law-Making Powers

Under section 91 of the *Constitution Act, 1867*,[4] the federal government has the authority to make laws in a variety of areas that were considered at the time of Confederation (1867) to require uniform standards across the country. Generally, federal laws deal with matters of national concern, such as criminal activity, monetary policy, foreign relations, national defence, interprovincial and international trade and commerce, and interprovincial and international transportation.

Provincial Law-Making Powers

Under section 92 of the *Constitution Act, 1867*, provincial governments have the authority to make laws governing matters that were considered in 1867 to be primarily regional or local in nature. These include the regulation of business activities that take place within the province; the regulation of professions; the creation of local infrastructure such as roads, water treatment plants, and sewer systems; the creation of the structure of municipal government; the establishment of municipal boundaries; and land-use planning.

Municipal Law-Making Powers

Municipal councils may make bylaws governing conduct within the municipal boundaries, such as licensing local businesses, zoning, policing, and operating schools and libraries. However, the powers of municipal governments are limited to those specifically granted by laws passed by the provincial legislature.

Overlapping or Unclear Law-Making Authority

For many areas of conduct, the Constitution is silent or ambiguous about which level of government has the authority to pass laws. In some cases, the subject area did not exist in 1867—for example, atomic energy, aeronautics, telecommunications, and the Internet. In other cases, matters that were primarily of local or regional interest in 1867 have since taken on national dimensions. For example, the regulation of salary levels is normally within provincial jurisdiction, but in the 1970s inflation became so widespread that the federal government stepped in to pass a law implementing Canada-wide wage controls.

---

4 *Supra* note 1.

Confusion often arises because a law has aspects that fall within both federal and provincial powers. For example, the provinces have authority to regulate labour relations, but the federal government regulates telecommunications. In the case of a law regulating union activities at a telephone company, it would be unclear which level of government had the authority to pass the law, and a court would have to decide whether the primary purpose of the law was the regulation of labour relations or the regulation of telecommunications.

Types of Law

Laws can be divided into categories in several ways. These categories overlap, so an individual law may fall into more than one category. A body of law, such as administrative law, may be a combination of laws in two or more categories.

It is important to understand how categories of laws are distinguished from each other. Some of the categories to be distinguished are

- common law and statute law;
- public law and private law;
- statutes and subordinate legislation; and
- substantive law and procedural law.

The distinctions between these categories are explained in the following sections.

Common Law and Statute Law

In Canada, we have laws developed by the courts as well as laws passed by governments. The laws made by courts are called "common law." The body of law (**legislation**) made by elected representatives consisting of statutes, regulations, territorial ordinances, and municipal bylaws is called "statute law."

A harmful activity may become the subject of both common law and statute law. Under common law, a person who is harmed by a particular activity (a **tort**, or wrong) has the right to sue the wrongdoer for compensation (**damages**) or for an order to stop carrying on the activity (an injunction). Under a statute, the government may designate the same activity as an "offence" and impose a punishment for it. (See the box feature "Interaction of Common Law and Statute Law.")

Interaction of Common Law and Statute Law

A driver carelessly injures a pedestrian, who sues for compensation under the common law tort of negligence. If the court upholds the claim, the driver will be required to compensate the victim for the harm he has suffered. However, careless driving is also an offence under the provincial highway traffic statutes, and the police may lay a charge against the driver. If the driver is found guilty, he may be required to pay a fine, be sentenced to prison, and/or have his driver's licence or vehicle permit suspended.

Common Law

Common law is the body of rules established by judges over centuries in the course of making decisions in disputes between citizens and between citizens and their government. The common law embodies certain rights and principles on which the courts base their decisions. Among the most important of these are principles of fairness or reasonableness.

There is a hierarchy of courts, and cases that are heard by a lower court may sometimes be appealed to one or more higher courts. (For a diagram of Canada's court structure, see Figure 1.1.) Once a court has established the principles that should apply to a particular type of situation, all courts that are lower than that court in the judicial hierarchy must apply those principles when deciding cases similar to the one in which the principles were established. This is called the requirement to follow **precedent**; in Latin, it is known as the doctrine of ***stare decisis***. It is this requirement to follow precedent that gives the principles the force of law.

Although courts will usually apply the principles established for a particular type of situation by other courts at the same level in the judicial hierarchy, two courts at the same level may reach conflicting decisions about what the proper principle to apply to a particular situation is. Where such conflict arises, a higher court—ultimately, the Supreme Court of Canada—will settle the matter.

> *The judges developing the common law proceed from case to case, like the ancient Mediterranean mariners, hugging the coast from point to point and avoiding the danger of the open sea of system or science.*
>
> Lord Wright, "The Study of Law" (1938) 54 Law Q Rev 185 at 186

FIGURE 1.1   Outline of Canada's Court System

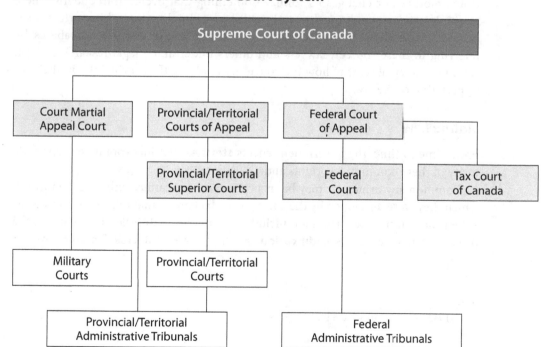

An example of a common law principle and how it developed following the doctrine of *stare decisis* is the doctrine of negligence. During the first half of the 19th century, the courts developed the principle that if a person failed to exercise the standard of care in carrying out an activity that a reasonably prudent person would have exercised in similar circumstances and if this resulted in harm that was foreseeable, this was negligence, and the victim of the harm was entitled to sue for damages. The courts can expand or contract the scope of common law principles such as negligence. For example, until 1932, the courts had ruled that a person injured by the use of a product could not sue the manufacturer unless he or she had purchased the product directly from the manufacturer. In other words, the manufacturer could be sued under the common law principles governing contracts if there was a breach of the contractual obligation to provide a safe product, but not otherwise.

In 1932, however, in the case of *Donoghue v Stevenson*,[5] Britain's highest court established a new principle of product liability. Because it is foreseeable that a person who purchases a defective product might suffer harm from using it, the manufacturer has a duty to take reasonable steps to prevent the harm regardless of whether or not there is a contract between the manufacturer and the consumer. One implication of this is that the manufacturer of a defective product can be held responsible for any injuries suffered by a person as a result of using the product, whether the person purchased the product from the manufacturer, bought it from a store that purchased it from the manufacturer, found it on the street, or received it as a gift.

Because of the requirement that all lower courts follow precedent, this principle of legal liability has been adopted by the courts in jurisdictions—such as Canada and the United States—that inherited the common law system from Britain, and it forms the basis for an expanded scope of the common law doctrine of negligence.

If Canada's highest court, the Supreme Court of Canada, rules that a right exists or a principle applies, all courts must follow this rule unless and until the Supreme Court modifies or changes its ruling—something that occurs infrequently. These principles are gathered together and published in legal texts, and important decisions of the courts are published and also made available on computer databases. By referring to these sources, lawyers and others undertaking legal research or legal action can keep abreast of how the courts are applying these principles in their interpretation of the law.

Statute Law

From time to time, the government enacts **statutes** that incorporate or supersede many of these common law rights and obligations.

Common law principles may be incorporated into statutes either in the form in which they were developed by the courts or with changes that reflect current needs. When the common law rules are included in statutes with little or no change, the process is referred to as **codification**. Examples are Ontario's *Statutory Powers*

---

5 [1932] AC 562, 101 LJPC 119, 147 LT 281.

Procedure Act[6] (SPPA), Alberta's *Administrative Procedures and Jurisdiction Act*[7] (APJA), and Quebec's *Administrative Justice Act*[8] (AJA), which set out basic rules of procedural fairness for tribunals that formerly were part of the common law.

On other occasions, a statute is passed to replace a common law doctrine that the legislature considers to have outlived its usefulness. For example, at common law, jilted lovers could sue their fiancé(e)s for breaking the promise to marry them—a tort that has now been abolished by statute in some provinces.

A statute may be passed to make it an offence to do something that is considered wrong and that requires compensation at common law, so that a person who commits the offence will also be subject to punishment such as a fine or jail time. A statute may also be passed to establish a new procedure or to set up a bureaucracy to enforce certain common law rights, so that people are not required to use the more cumbersome procedures of the courts to address infringement of those rights. Sometimes the purpose of affirming common law rights in a statute is to clarify ambiguities or remove contradictions created when courts are inconsistent in interpreting or applying a principle.

As discussed, **statute law** consists of statutes, regulations, and bylaws. Both the federal and the provincial governments have the authority to pass statutes. These laws usually do not set out all the rules that the public must obey. Instead, they set out a framework for creating the more detailed rules contained in accompanying regulations. Usually, the statute permits the Cabinet of the governing party (referred to in statutes by its formal name—provincially, the lieutenant governor in council, and federally, the governor in council) to make regulations, but occasionally a statute delegates the power to make regulations to an individual Cabinet minister or to a regulatory agency or board. There is no constitutional requirement that regulations be scrutinized by the federal or provincial legislature, although in practice there are often parliamentary committees that review some aspects of these rules before they take effect.

To be valid, the contents of regulations must be explicitly or implicitly authorized by the wording of the statute under which they are made. If regulations set out requirements that go beyond the matters that the statute permits them to address, the regulations are not valid.

As noted, statute law also includes **bylaws**, which are passed by elected municipal councils. Bylaws are often voluminous and very detailed, because municipal councils do not have the power either to make regulations or to delegate such power to committees or boards. As a result, compliance requirements must be included in the bylaw itself. A bylaw is valid only if the provincial statutes granting municipalities the power to pass laws state that the municipality may pass bylaws of that nature.

---

6   RSO 1990, c S.22.

7   RSA 2000, c A-3.

8   CQLR c J-3.

The Relationship Between Common Law and Statute Law in Quebec

The relationship between common law and statute law is somewhat different in Quebec from the rest of Canada. Canada's *Criminal Code* applies to Quebec, but private law in Quebec is governed by a lengthy statute, the *Quebec Civil Code*, which has over 3,000 provisions. The fundamental principles of Quebec private law are codified in this compendious statute. In this sense, the *Civil Code* is like a constitution: it is the foundation of all other Quebec laws governing private relations. Other statutes are passed from time to time to supplement or create exceptions to the *Civil Code*, but judicial decisions are not conceived as setting out the law governing private relations as they are in common law provinces.

Public Law and Private Law

Public Law

Different authors have suggested different definitions of public law. In general, **public law** deals with the structure and operation of government. It regulates how the three branches at each level of government carry out their responsibilities.

Public laws govern the relationship between an individual or private organization and the government, the relationship between one government and another (for example, between the government of Canada and the government of Ontario or of India), and the relationships between departments and agencies within a government. Criminal law, constitutional law, administrative law, and treaties made under international law are all considered part of public law.

Public laws dictate how government bodies may raise money (for example, by imposing taxes or by levying fees or fines), how they may spend money (for example, on building roads or airports, operating schools, providing medicare, giving subsidies to businesses, or hiring police), and what procedures they must follow to account for money spent (financial administration). (See the box feature "How Public Laws Regulate Elections.")

How Public Laws Regulate Elections

In Ontario, the provincial *Representation Act* determines the size and boundaries of electoral districts, which in turn dictates how many seats there will be in the Legislative Assembly. The *Election Act* authorizes the lieutenant governor to decide the length of the election campaign. The *Election Finances Act* describes how much money candidates may spend on their campaigns and on what activities; it also requires them to disclose to the public how much money they raised and the identities of the donors. The *Public Service Act* sets out rules that govern which public servants are permitted to engage in partisan campaigning and what limits are imposed on their activities. Under the *Broadcasting Act*, radio and television stations and networks must make advertising time available to all political parties on an equitable basis during elections. If the political parties cannot agree on how to divide the time among them, a broadcasting arbitrator appointed under the *Canada Elections Act* may allocate the amount of airtime for each party.

ADMINISTRATIVE LAW

As discussed, public law regulates the structure and activities of all three branches of government—legislative, executive, and judiciary. **Administrative law** is a branch of public law that regulates the executive branch.

Until the 20th century, the executive branch at the federal and provincial levels consisted largely of a set of departments headed by ministers and staffed by civil servants. However, as governments became involved in a broader range of activities requiring more expertise, flexibility, and independent advice, a variety of agencies or **administrative agencies** were created to supplement—or, in some cases, replace—the role of the departments in meeting these needs. Administrative law developed as a way of ensuring that these departments and agencies did not exceed their authority, abuse their power, or follow unfair procedures when making decisions.

The fundamental principles of administrative law—procedural fairness or natural justice, and principles related to jurisdiction, discretion, subdelegation, subordinate legislation, and judicial review—are discussed in Chapter 3, The Foundations of Administrative Law.

Private Law

Private law is the body of laws that regulate how individuals or corporations are required to treat each other. Private law includes torts, contract law, property law, and family law.

Both private and public laws can be statutory or can consist of common law rights and remedies. Moreover, a single law may have both public and private aspects or components. For example, Ontario's *Trespass to Property Act*[9] (TPA) prohibits trespassing on both public and private property. Although financial compensation for harm is usually a matter of private law and fines are normally imposed only under public law, the TPA permits a court that convicts someone of trespassing both to impose a fine and to award compensation.

Statutes and Subordinate Legislation

As discussed, although only elected legislatures can pass statutes, these statutes may grant the Cabinet, individual Cabinet ministers, and special interest bodies the authority to make more detailed regulations that flesh out the meaning and requirements of the statutes. These regulations are sometimes called **subordinate legislation** or **delegated legislation**. They are valid only if they conform to the statute under which they are passed.

Substantive Law and Procedural Law

Laws may also be characterized as substantive or procedural. **Substantive law** is concerned with the substance of a problem or the legal issue that the law is designed

---

9 RSO 1990, c T.21.

to solve or address. **Procedural law** sets out procedures for implementing substantive law..

A simple example is the combination of substantive and procedural provisions of the *Criminal Code*[10] dealing with theft. The *substantive* provisions of the Code make it an offence to take someone else's property without the owner's consent. Its *procedural* provisions specify how the police and courts will treat someone who is believed to have committed theft. These procedures deal with the steps taken by police in arresting someone and laying charges (such as fingerprinting); the procedures that the courts will follow before trial, such as granting bail and holding preliminary inquiries; the procedures during the trial, such as reading the charge, entering a plea, and calling evidence; and the procedure for deciding what sentence to impose if the person is convicted of the crime.

The difference between substantive law and procedural law is important because the characterization of a law as substantive or procedural affects whether it can apply to conduct that took place before the law was passed (that is, "retroactively") and how far authorities can stray from following the strict letter of the law and still have their actions upheld by the court. Generally, officials have more flexibility and leeway in applying procedural laws than in applying substantive laws. Also, procedural laws may apply retroactively, but substantive laws may not.

How Various Types of Law Are Administered and Enforced

Different laws are administered and enforced in different ways. Some laws are enforced by police, others by inspectors who are employees of government departments, and still others by the staff of specialized agencies.

Enforcement by Police

Violations of criminal laws, for example, are usually investigated by federal, provincial, or municipal police forces. Charges for such violations are laid by police and prosecuted by federal and provincial Crown prosecutors in the criminal courts. Provincial highway traffic laws and some other regulatory laws are enforced by municipal and provincial police departments. In Ontario, for example, the Toronto Police Service enforces the *Highway Traffic Act* in the city, while the Ontario Provincial Police patrol the highways.

Enforcement by Government Departments and Government Agencies

Breaches of federal and provincial regulatory statutes are sometimes investigated by inspectors in government departments and sometimes by police. Charges for

---

10 RSC 1985, c C-46, as amended.

violating municipal bylaws may be laid by police or by bylaw enforcement officers employed by the municipality. The prosecutors are usually lawyers or prosecution officers hired by the government department or agency responsible for administering the law in question. For example, Ontario's *Environmental Protection Act* is enforced by inspectors employed by the Ministry of the Environment and Climate Change. However, the breach of securities laws is investigated and prosecuted by an independent agency, the Ontario Securities Commission, and child welfare laws are typically enforced by children's aid societies.

Enforcement by the Person Affected

As discussed, common law rights and remedies are considered part of private law rather than public law. That is, although the government or the courts have established the rights and obligations governing certain private relationships and the government provides the court system in which they may be enforced, the government does not consider that there is a sufficient public interest in the outcome of such disputes to justify the government's also providing a staff of investigators, inspectors, and prosecutors. The person aggrieved must pursue a remedy at his or her own expense, which usually involves hiring a lawyer to provide advice and representation in court.

Some statutory rights also must be pursued privately by the person entitled to redress. For example, certain remedies available to consumers under consumer protection statutes must be pursued by the consumer against the seller. The government does not enforce these rights.

Many laws do not create duties whose breach leads to punishment or payment of compensation. Some laws create a set of procedures that must be followed or standards that must be met in undertaking certain activities. For example, where a developer requires the approval of government authorities before proceeding with a project, the developer generally must submit an application, plans, and other specified information to the government agency, which then assesses the proposal against legislated standards and decides whether or not to grant approval.

Other laws confer privileges or benefits (such as social assistance, or compensation for injuries suffered in the workplace or for losses to the victim of a crime) on classes of people who qualify for these benefits. In some cases, the government hires staff or provides resources or funding to assist the person in making a case for receiving the benefits. In other cases, the person must apply for the benefits on his or her own, or with the assistance of an adviser hired at the person's own expense.

In most provinces, for example, the government has staff who represent employees who are challenging decisions to deny them workers' compensation benefits. A few provinces also provide this assistance to small employers. Individuals challenging immigration decisions are often represented by lawyers or legal workers employed by independent community legal clinics that receive funding from the government. In contrast, most governments provide no legal assistance to individuals challenging government decisions to refuse access to records under freedom-of-information laws.

In some cases, government officials within a department make the initial decision whether to issue a licence, approve an activity, enforce a right, or confer a benefit under a statute. In other cases, the government creates an arm's-length agency (that is, an agency with some independence or separation from the government) to make the initial decision regarding how to apply or implement the law. In either case, the person or persons affected may be entitled to appeal the decision to an arm's-length agency or to a court.

Often, the arm's-length agencies that are established for these purposes are administrative tribunals. Administrative tribunals are an important part of our system of government, and they play a significant role in administering our statute laws. Tribunals, as well as other government decision-makers, are regulated by the branch of public law known as "administrative law." Administrative law evolved out of the legal system described above, and the fundamental principles on which it is based are rooted in that broader system. For the purposes of learning administrative law, what is most important to understand is that the principles of administrative law, especially the duty to act fairly, apply to government decisions regardless of whether making those decisions has been assigned to an official within a government department, to an official of an arm's-length agency, or to a tribunal.

The next chapter provides a discussion of these principles.

CHAPTER SUMMARY

Laws are binding rules made by governments. They regulate almost every aspect of human life from birth to death, a vast range of social and economic activities, and formal relationships among citizens (both individuals and organizations) and between citizens and government.

There are three levels of government that make laws—the federal, provincial, and municipal or territorial governments. There are also three branches of government that pass, apply, and interpret laws—the legislature, the executive, and the judiciary, respectively.

Laws take a variety of forms and regulate particular spheres of conduct. They can be categorized in a number of ways—as common law or statute law, as public law or private law, as statutes or subordinate legislation, and as substantive law or procedural law. How a law is administered and enforced, and by whom, depends on the nature of the law and the category into which it falls.

KEY TERMS

act: *see* statute

administrative agency: *see* agency

administrative law: law that governs the organization, duties, and quasi-judicial and judicial powers of the executive branch of government, including both central departments and agencies; a branch of public law

agency: any body, such as a board, commission, or tribunal, established by government and subject to government control to carry out a specialized function that is not an integral part of a government ministry or department

bylaw: law enacted by a subordinate legislative body, such as a municipality, under the authority of a statute

Cabinet: a committee of members of Parliament or the provincial legislature appointed by the prime minister, in the case of the federal government, or the premier of a province to preside over government departments (also known as the "governor in council" federally and the "lieutenant governor in council" provincially)

codification: the collection of the principles of a system or subject of law into a single statute or set of statutes

common law: a body of law set out in court decisions; derives its authority from the recognition given by the courts to principles, standards, customs, and rules of conduct (generally reflecting those accepted in society) in deciding disputes; distinguished from statute law

Constitution: the body of binding fundamental rules that govern the exercise of power by government; to be valid, all other laws must conform to this set of fundamental rules

damages: a sum of money awarded by a court as compensation for harm or loss caused by a violation of the law

delegate: entrust a person or body to act in another's place

delegated legislation: *see* subordinate legislation

department: a unit of the executive branch of government over which a minister presides; usually established to administer a specific set of laws and programs relating to a particular subject area, such as health, protection of the environment, government finance, or stimulation of business activity

law: a rule made by a body of elected representatives or their delegates or by a court, using procedures that are also prescribed by law

legislate: pass statutes and bylaws, and make regulations

legislation: the creation of law; the statutes, regulations, and bylaws passed by bodies of elected representatives or their delegates

Legislative Assembly: the body of elected representatives constituting the legislative branch of a provincial government; in Quebec, known as the "National Assembly"; also called the "legislature" or "provincial parliament"

legislature: in Canada, the body of elected representatives constituting the legislative branch of the federal or a provincial government; *see also* Legislative Assembly, Parliament

ministry: *see* department

ordinances: laws enacted by the northern territories, similar in content to provincial and federal statutes

Parliament: the body of elected representatives constituting the legislative branch of Canada's federal government; also called the "legislature"

precedent: a decision or judgment of a court of law that is cited as the authority for deciding a similar situation in the same manner, on the same principle, or by analogy; *see also stare decisis*

private law: law that governs the conduct of persons other than government; distinguished from public law

procedural law: law that prescribes methods of administration, application, or enforcement of a law—for example, the provisions of the *Criminal Code* that specify the procedures to be followed when a person is believed to have committed an offence; distinguished from substantive law

public law: law that deals with the structure and operation of government; governs the relationship between individuals or private organizations and the government, between governments, and between departments and agencies within a government; includes administrative law; distinguished from private law

regulations: detailed rules that flesh out the meaning and requirements of a statute; made under the authority of a statute, either by Cabinet or by a body to which this power is delegated; also called "subordinate legislation" or "delegated legislation"

rule of law: the principle that governments, as well as individuals and corporations, must follow the law; in particular, governments may take actions that limit the activities of citizens or their access to rights or benefits only in accordance with substantive and procedural requirements prescribed by law

stare decisis: Latin term referring to the principle that courts should decide similar cases in the same way unless there is good reason for them to do otherwise; the rule that courts must follow previous decisions made by higher courts; *see also* precedent

statute: law passed by Parliament or a provincial legislature; also called an "act"; often specifically provides for the authority to make regulations or to delegate this power; distinguished from subordinate legislation; *see also* statute law

statute law: in Canada, the body of laws passed by Parliament or a provincial legislature; generally, the body of laws passed by an assembly of elected representatives of the public; distinguished from common law

subordinate legislation: legislation made by a body other than Parliament or a provincial legislature (such as Cabinet, a Cabinet minister, an agency, or a municipal council), as authorized by statute; generally includes regulations, proclamations, rules, orders, bylaws, or other instruments; also called "delegated legislation"; distinguished from statutes

substantive law: law that is concerned with the substance of a problem or the legal issue that the law is designed to address; for example, the provisions of the *Criminal Code* setting out the elements of the offence of theft; distinguished from procedural law

tort: a wrongful act or omission causing an injury, other than a breach of contract, for which recovery of damages is permitted by law

REVIEW QUESTIONS

1. Laws are created by whom and for what reason? How do laws differ from other rules or customs that people follow?

2. The "rule of law" sets out how society organizes and regulates itself. Explain what function the rule of law plays in society. What major Canadian document encapsulates the rule of law? Using this document, describe the way the rule of law works.

3. What are the three branches of government in Canada, and what are the functions of each? Explain how the branches are related to each other.

4. What are the three levels of government in Canada, and what is the law-making power of each? In what document is the description of each level of government and its powers found?

5. What is the purpose of the Constitution of Canada? What part of the Constitution regulates the rights of citizens? How does it regulate the power of governments to pass or implement laws?

6. Name four ways in which laws can be categorized and distinguished. Explain each way, and explain how the distinction works.

7. What are the consequences of breaking a law? Are the consequences the same for all categories of law? Explain.

8. Who administers and enforces laws? Is the answer the same for all laws? Explain.

EXERCISES

1. In groups with multiples of three people in them (3, 6, 9, 12, etc.), assign each person or group to be a different branch of government—legislative, executive, or judiciary.

   a. Each person or group should prepare a summary of the key responsibilities of their assigned branch of government.

   b. Each group should find 3 to 5 statutes that are frequently used in administrative law. Use Appendix B to find research tools to assist you in looking for legislation.

   c. Each group should explain the intent and purpose of each of the statutes in the answer to question 1.b.

   d. Each group should describe the responsibility of their branch in relation to the operation of the statute.

2. a. Using any of the research tools described in Appendix B, find

   • two examples of statutes that regulate government elections;

   • two examples of statutes that protect consumers;

   • two examples of statutes that establish government agencies;

   • two examples of statutes that prohibit certain conduct and impose penalties for violating the prohibitions;

   • two examples of a statute that regulates a trade, profession, or business;

   • two examples of statutes that provide rights of compensation for harm done by individuals or corporations; and

   • two examples of statutes that provide rights of compensation for a loss resulting from government action.

   b. Categorize each of the above laws as public or private, or substantive or procedural. If the law fits into both of these categories, list them both. (For example, a statute may be public and substantive, or private and procedural.) Explain why you chose the category or categories in each case.

   c. Explain briefly some of the rights and obligations imposed by the above laws.

   d. Explain who administers or enforces these laws.

   e. Discuss briefly some of the procedures that are followed in enforcing or administering these laws.

FURTHER READING

Lisa Braverman, *Administrative Tribunals: A Legal Handbook* (Aurora, Ont: Canada Law Book, 2002) ch 1.

Linda Silver Dranoff, *Everyone's Guide to the Law: A Handbook for Canadians*, revised ed (Toronto: HarperCollins, 2001).

John Fairlie & Philip Sworden, *Introduction to Law in Canada* (Toronto: Emond Montgomery, 2014).

Nora Rock & Valerie Hoag, *Foundations of Criminal and Civil Law in Canada*, 3rd ed (Toronto: Emond Montgomery, 2011).

Administrative Agencies and Tribunals

2

LEARNING OUTCOMES

After reading this chapter, you will understand

- how the system of agencies developed, and how agencies have modified the traditional approach to administering and enforcing laws;

- the issues that agencies raised for government accountability and independence, and how this led to the development of a body of "administrative law";

- where administrative agencies fit into the executive, legislative, and judicial branches of government;

- the kinds of agencies that governments establish and why they establish them;

- what administrative tribunals are and how they compare with other agencies;

- the kinds of decisions that are likely to be referred to tribunals rather than to government officials; and

- how tribunals are similar to courts and how they are different.

Since it deals with the exercise of governmental power, administrative law is itself part of constitutional law. Nor is there any other department of constitutional law which displays such an active conflict of forces. We are here on the most lively sector of the front in the constant warfare between government and governed. Whole new empires of executive power have been created. For the citizen, it is vital that all power should be used in a way conformable to his ideas of liberty, fair dealing, and good administration.

HWR Wade, *Administrative Law* (Oxford: Oxford University Press, 1961) at 3

Introduction

As discussed in Chapter 1, there are three branches of government in Canada: the legislative branch, the executive branch, and the judicial branch. The structure of the legislative and judicial branches of government has remained largely the same over the past century. However, the structure of the executive branch has changed dramatically. Departments presided over by ministers are still the core of the executive branch, and the staff of these departments continue to exercise powers and make decisions that are subject to administrative law. However, many of the former functions of departments are now carried out by a complex network of administrative agencies, boards, and commissions (ABCs; also referred to collectively as "agencies") that are at arm's length from the minister to whom they report and from department staff. This system gradually evolved in response to the growing complexity of Canadian society. There are now so many departmental offshoots or freestanding agencies that they have become recognized as a separate "sector" within the executive branch. Some commentators go so far as to call them the "fourth branch" of government.

This chapter discusses how and why agencies are established, how they function, how they affect the traditional division of powers among the three branches of government, and what issues these "hybrid" entities raise for government accountability and independence. It also takes a closer look at administrative tribunals, and compares and contrasts their roles and functions with those of the courts.

The Traditional Role and Structure of the Executive Branch

In its traditional form, the executive branch of the federal and provincial governments consisted of centralized departments or ministries, each headed by a Cabinet minister who was a member of Parliament or the provincial legislature. This minister was responsible to the legislature both for making policy and for implementing it, including the way in which civil servants in the department (numbering in the hundreds or even thousands) carried out their functions. This system was called "responsible government" because the minister was responsible to the executive branch (the prime minister or premier and his or her Cabinet colleagues), and because the minister and his or her fellow ministers were responsible for the work of the departments to the elected legislature and—through the legislature—to the Canadian public.

Unlike the minister who headed the department, the civil servants who carried out the work of a department were largely insulated from political pressure by a number of mechanisms. First, they reported not to the minister but to another civil servant: the deputy minister of the department, who was appointed by the prime minister or the premier. Second, the rules for hiring and firing civil servants were established and carried out by independent commissions, not politicians. Third, the hiring, remuneration, promotion, and dismissal practices of the civil service, and its operation, were governed by legislation. This system promoted hiring on the basis of ability and expertise rather than political connections, and the security of tenure of civil servants enabled them to "speak truth to power."

The traditional departmental structure thus rested on two cornerstones: accountability of the minister to the public as a member of the legislature, and insulation of the civil service from political influence through an independent system of hiring, remuneration, promotion, and dismissal.

The Development of Administrative Agencies

Over the years, as governments responded to changes in society and as the corresponding demands on governments grew more diverse, the relatively simple structure described above became more complex. To allow the government to carry out civil service functions with greater flexibility, efficiency, and expertise, special-purpose agencies were established outside the traditional structure of the executive branch.

The first administrative agency in Canada was established in 1851, 16 years before Confederation. The Board of Railway Commissioners was set up under the *Railway Act*, primarily to approve rail rates. In 1912, the British Columbia government set up its first administrative agency, the Workmen's Compensation Board. The First World War, the Great Depression, and the Second World War all stimulated the federal and provincial governments to become more involved in regulating the economy and in influencing social and cultural issues.

As Canadian society expanded in population and diversity and became more complex economically, culturally, and technologically, so did the structures that governments created to meet their needs and address their problems; the result was a proliferation of special-purpose bodies. For example, between 1945 and 1984, the number of agencies more than doubled in Saskatchewan and almost doubled in Ontario, with significant growth in other provinces as well. When Robert Macaulay conducted his review of Ontario's ABCs in 1989,[1] he found that there were about 1500 across Canada, and 580 in Ontario alone. By 1990, there were at least 120 federal administrative commissions, boards, and councils. In 2015, despite shutting

---

1   Robert W Macaulay, *Directions: Review of Ontario's Regulatory Agencies Report* (Toronto: Queen's Printer for Ontario, 1989).

down several ABCs in the 1990s and amalgamating others, Ontario still had 560 provincial agencies,[2] and even Canada's smallest province, Prince Edward Island, listed 78 ABCs on its website.[3]

Categorizing Agencies, Boards, and Commissions

Agencies, boards, and commissions perform a wide variety of functions: they give advice, set standards, regulate businesses and professions, coordinate the activities of government departments, and provide goods and services. Ontario's Management Board Secretariat divides the province's agencies into seven categories:

- *Advisory agencies* These agencies provide advice to a ministry and assist in the development of policy or the delivery of programs, but they do not make decisions or carry out programs. The Livestock Medicines Advisory Committee and the Commodity Futures Advisory Board are two such agencies.

- *Operational service agencies* These agencies deliver goods or services to the public, often at a low fee or no fee. The Ontario Tourism Marketing Partnership Corporation is an example of such an agency.

- *Operational enterprises* These agencies sell goods or services to the public in a commercial manner. They may compete with the private sector, or they may be monopolies. Examples are the Niagara Parks Commission, the Liquor Control Board of Ontario, and the Ontario Lottery and Gaming Corporation.

- *Regulatory agencies* These agencies make independent decisions (including inspections, investigations, prosecutions, certifications, licensing, and rate setting) that limit or promote the conduct, practice, obligations, rights, and responsibilities of individuals, businesses, and corporate bodies. Examples include the Ontario Film Review Board and the Workplace Safety and Insurance Board.

- *Adjudicative agencies* (often referred to as "tribunals") These agencies make independent decisions, similar to those of courts, that resolve disputes over the obligations, rights, and responsibilities of individuals, businesses, corporate bodies, and government decision-makers under existing policies and laws. They may also hear appeals from previous government decisions. Two such agencies are the Ontario Labour Relations Board and the Ontario Municipal Board.

- *Crown foundations* These agencies solicit, manage, and distribute donations of money or other assets to support public organizations such as art galleries, museums, amateur sports associations, theatre groups, and universities.

---

2 <http://www.pas.gov.on.ca/scripts/en/faqs.asp#10>. Some of these agencies are ones to which the Provincial government appoints one or more members, while the organization itself appoints the other members, such as the Complaints Committee of the Council of Professional Engineers Ontario, the body that regulates the engineering profession.

3 <http://www.gov.pe.ca/eco/ABC/participate.php3?abbrev=All+Departments+…&action=GO&lang=E>.

Examples are the Art Gallery of Ontario Crown Foundation and the University of Toronto Foundation.

- *Trust agencies* These agencies administer funds or other assets for beneficiaries named under a statute. Examples include the Workplace Safety and Insurance Board and the Ontario Public Service Pension Board.

The Ontario government also recognizes a category of agencies called "non-scheduled agencies," which do not fit into any of the above categories. Examples include university and hospital governing boards, as well as the boards and committees of professions such as engineering, which have a majority of members elected by their peers, but also one or more members appointed by the government.

To this list may be added at least two additional kinds of agencies. The first is "watchdog" bodies, such as the ombudsman and other ombudsman-like agencies. They are established to monitor whether government departments and agencies are carrying out their duties fairly, effectively, and efficiently, and to address individual complaints of unfair treatment. These officials often are appointed by and report to the legislative assembly as a whole rather than to the government. Their independence from the government may be enhanced by security of tenure and salaries that are the same as those of senior officials such as judges or deputy ministers, rather than negotiated with the government. In most provinces these watchdog agencies include the ombudsman, the provincial auditor, the information and privacy commissioner, and the chief electoral officer. Some provinces also have an integrity commissioner, who investigates whether members of the legislature have conflicts of interest. The Government of Ontario and the federal government also have an environmental commissioner. The federal government has no ombudsman, but there is an auditor general, a chief electoral officer, an integrity commissioner, a privacy commissioner, an information commissioner, and a commissioner of official languages.

The second additional kind of agency is royal commissions and other commissions set up to carry out public inquiries. These bodies are usually established by governments to investigate and to make findings and recommendations about a specific problem. Once they have reported their findings, they are dissolved; the government that appointed them may or may not implement their recommendations. Usually, prominent judges or academics who are independent of the government are appointed to conduct the inquiries, but the government sometimes supplies staff from within the civil service. Examples of inquiries include those conducted into the future of medicare; the response of public health authorities to the outbreak of severe acute respiratory syndrome (SARS) in 2003; the cause of the Westray mine disaster in Nova Scotia; the collapse of a shopping mall roof in Elliot Lake, Ontario, which killed two people; the wrongful convictions of several innocent individuals; and racism in various provincial justice systems.

In his 1989 review of Ontario's ABCs, Robert Macaulay divided ABCs into eight categories:[4]

- agencies that investigate and advise, and that may hold hearings in doing so;

---

4 Macaulay, *supra* note 1.

- agencies that deal with appeals from decisions of government or other regulators;
- agencies that resolve problems between individuals or between individuals and the government;
- agencies that monitor and regulate substantial segments of the economy;
- agencies that deal with land-use planning, assessment, and values;
- agencies that deal with employment, wages, pensions, and social assistance;
- agencies that set standards and quotas, including marketing boards; and
- agencies that deal primarily in natural resources, preservation, and conservation.

It is important to understand that some agencies carry out more than one function. An agency may have any combination of advisory, regulatory, investigative, policy-making, adjudicative, and other functions. It may have to follow one set of rules when carrying out one function and another set when carrying out another. Sometimes, the functions of an agency overlap in such a way that the official responsible for carrying out the different functions cannot do so without a conflict of interest or an appearance of bias. In these cases, the conflict of functions or interests is resolved using principles of administrative law (discussed in more detail below, under the heading "Multipurpose Agencies").

Why Governments Create Administrative Agencies

There are numerous reasons why a government may choose to set up an administrative agency rather than delegate a task to a department:

- *To demonstrate independence*   The government may want to ensure that decisions on certain issues are not seen to be "political." An agency that is independent, and that is perceived to be independent, can demonstrate that its function and decisions are free of political influence.
- *To reduce the size, workload, or budget of a department*   The government may establish an outside agency to carry out some of the functions of a department in order to save space, achieve more efficiency in the delivery of services, or reduce costs.
- *To reduce conflicts of interest*   Where one government department carries out two or more functions that may come into conflict, the conflict may be resolved by "hiving off" some of the department's functions to independent bodies. For example, until the 1990s, the Ontario Ministry of the Environment (now the Ministry of the Environment and Climate Change) was responsible for regulating municipal water treatment and sewage treatment plants, but it also designed, built, owned, or operated many of the plants. If one of the plants were in violation of environmental laws, the Ministry might be reluctant to impose stringent operating conditions on one of its own

facilities or to prosecute its own staff. To prevent this conflict, the government created a separate agency, the Ontario Clean Water Agency, in 1993.

- *To provide flexibility in human resources*   The government may want to avoid some of the hiring practices, employment standards, salary and benefits rules, tenure requirements, and reporting requirements that must be followed when employing civil servants. For example, in Ontario, the Civil Service Commission regulates salaries, job classifications, recruitment, benefits, and hours of work for civil servants. Ministries are required to follow these rules when hiring, promoting, setting wage levels, or firing, but the government is not bound by them when appointing members of many agencies, boards, and commissions. The government can set lower wages, appoint members who have no prior experience or qualifications for the job, and limit the length of the appointments or the opportunities for reappointment.

- *To provide expertise and specialization*   The government may want to obtain expertise in a particular subject matter that is not readily available within the civil service. The use of outside bodies to bring expertise to a problem is common in the setting of technical standards, the provision of advice, and the regulation of specialized businesses, trades, and professions.

- *To ensure representativeness*   The government may want to involve members of the general public or particular interest groups in making some decisions.

- *To avoid permanence*   The government may want the flexibility to create a body to deal with a current problem or issue and then to disband or restructure it to reflect changing needs.

- *To reduce labour costs*   Appointment to an agency is usually considered an honour; as a result, highly skilled and dedicated people are often willing to work for fees much lower than they can command in the marketplace. Moreover, many agencies are composed wholly or largely of part-time members. Talented individuals who might not be willing or able to work full time for low wages are often willing to work for a few days or weeks per year at reduced levels of compensation.

- *To signal a new or different approach*   The government may create an outside agency where existing agencies have been found wanting in their approach to a problem, or where a new approach to an existing problem is desired. Similarly, the government may create a new agency to regulate an activity or matter that was previously unregulated. Examples of areas that were once unregulated are human rights, the environment, and rent review. More recent examples include access to government information, the protection of privacy, and genetic engineering.

- *To achieve coordination or uniformity*   Where similar or related functions are carried out by several departments or ministries, the government may create a new agency to carry out those functions, or it may set up an advisory agency to help coordinate the activities of all the departments. The result may be a more consistent approach, greater effectiveness or efficiency, or a pooling of resources. The Canadian Food Inspection Agency is an example of a coordinating agency. It was created in 1997 to bring together food inspection activities previously carried out by four federal government departments—Agriculture Canada, Fisheries and Oceans Canada, Health Canada, and Industry Canada.

Administrative Agencies, Accountability, and Administrative Law

As discussed, the traditional departmental structure of the executive branch balanced accountability and independence, and maintained the separation of powers between the branches of government. However, the development of ABCs challenged the traditional methods of balancing accountability and independence in the civil service, and threatened to undermine the separation of powers.

The heads and members of ABCs were appointed by ministers, not by the legislative assembly, which meant that they were not accountable to the legislature the way that ministers were. Also, because they were often not civil servants, they were not subject to the same methods of accountability or mechanisms to avoid political pressure that civil servants were (for example, they were not protected by civil service staffing rules). In fact, patronage was rife in the selection process. Unqualified individuals were appointed to reward people for their contributions to the party in power. They often lacked the expertise and permanence that contributed to the independence of the civil service.

Some of the new agencies not only carried out the traditional functions of the executive branch—implementing laws, and developing administrative policies and practices—but also performed legislative and judicial functions. In some cases, this led to a blurring of roles that undermined the separation of powers that prevents abuse of authority.

The need for an appropriate balance between accountability and independence required the development of a body of "administrative law" to regulate how government in general—and the executive branch in particular—carries out its functions.

Multipurpose Agencies

Many administrative agencies are multipurpose bodies; that is, they have several functions. In order to ensure fairness, administrative law often requires multipurpose agencies to separate their functions and follow different rules when carrying them out.

For example, provincial law societies are authorized by statute to regulate the practice of law in each province. The statutes require all lawyers to be members of their provincial law society and to comply with the standards it sets. The laws regulating the legal profession require law societies to

- provide professional education;
- set standards for professional conduct;
- randomly audit the records of lawyers to determine whether they are following the rules, even without a complaint of misconduct;

- investigate complaints of misconduct or incompetence; and
- determine the validity of complaints of misconduct or incompetence, and take appropriate disciplinary action or action to improve competence.

In cases of alleged professional misconduct by a lawyer, the law society is investigator, prosecutor, and adjudicator. If an audit or investigation turns up evidence of misconduct, lawyers on the staff of the law society will prepare a case against the alleged offender, which they will present before a panel of members of the governing body. The panel will then decide whether the charges of misconduct are justified and, if they are, what discipline to impose.

Each of these functions may require different procedures to ensure that they are carried out in a manner that is fair to members. For example, the setting of standards for the conduct of lawyers is a "legislative" function, and there is no requirement to give all law society members notice of the process or to allow them to make submissions regarding it. There may or may not be a requirement to show members all of the information and studies that the governing body relied on in formulating the standards.

Similarly, if a member is being investigated for misconduct or incompetence, there may be no requirement to notify the member of the investigation, or to give him or her an opportunity to review the evidence or tell his or her side of the story. The reason for this is that investigation can result only in a recommendation regarding whether or not to take further action, not in a binding decision that will prevent the lawyer from practising law. However, if the prosecuting staff decide to launch a disciplinary proceeding, they must then give the member notice of the specific charges and the opportunity to see and answer the evidence on which the decision was based.

The Key Requirement: Separation of Functions

A key concern when an agency has multiple functions is to structure the agency to avoid any unfairness as it carries out those functions. Particularly when an agency is investigator and prosecutor as well as adjudicator, it is important to keep these functions separate from each other. This may be achieved by ensuring that the investigators, prosecutors, and adjudicators are different people, and by isolating the activities of investigators, prosecutors, and decision-makers to prevent each of them from unduly influencing the others or usurping the others' functions. The investigators, adjudicators, and prosecutors also often obtain their legal advice from different lawyers. Failure to ensure separation of functions may invalidate the process.

Many multifunction agencies are structured to create a "tribunal" to adjudicate disputes that is separate from the investigators and prosecutors in the agency.

A key principle of justice is, "No one shall be a judge in his own cause" (in Latin, *nemo debet esse judex in propria causa*). This means that the prosecutor and the decision-maker may not be the same person, because a person who is responsible for proving a case against someone cannot be expected to be impartial in deciding whether it is proven. (Although the functions of prosecuting and evaluating the evidence of the prosecutor are often incompatible, the legislature does permit the same person to be both investigator and adjudicator in certain situations. This "inquisitorial" process is discussed below, under the heading "Adjudication.")

A Further Requirement: No Delegation of Authority

A further requirement that ensures the separation of functions is that an adjudicator may not delegate his or her decision-making authority (this doctrine, called "sub-delegation," is discussed in Chapter 3, The Foundations of Administrative Law). If the decision-maker is not sufficiently independent of the prosecutor, there is a risk that the decision-maker will inadvertently defer to the wishes of the prosecutor in making his or her decision.

Similarly, it is important to ensure that the prosecutor has a reasonable level of independence from the investigator. The prosecutor should be in a position to objectively and independently assess the accuracy and comprehensiveness of the evidence uncovered by the investigator, and to make an informed recommendation or decision whether the evidence is sufficient to warrant laying a charge. If the evidence is suspect or false in the prosecutor's view, he or she must be able to refuse to support it.

Many agencies that have multiple and potentially conflicting functions aim to reduce the likelihood that problems will occur (if not prevent them altogether) through the creation of internal structures and barriers; if problems do occur, the structures and barriers are intended to moderate their impact. For example, the Saskatchewan Human Rights Commission investigates complaints of human rights violations and makes findings regarding whether or not the complaints are valid. The Commission plays different roles in relation to human rights complaints at different stages in the process. At intake, it plays a "gatekeeping" role, determining whether a potential complaint is within its jurisdiction and whether the complainant has reasonable grounds for believing that the *Human Rights Code* has been violated. If the complaint passes this initial test, the complainant is permitted to file a formal complaint.

During the investigation, the Commission plays a neutral, objective role, including providing the parties with a mediation service. If, after investigating, the Commission finds that the complaint is without merit or that it has been dealt with appropriately in another forum, it dismisses the complaint. If, however, it finds sufficient evidence of discrimination, it does not itself decide whether to uphold the complaint but rather refers the case to a separate tribunal—the Saskatchewan Human Rights Tribunal. At the hearing before the Tribunal, the Commission switches hats and becomes an advocate, presenting the case for a finding in favour of the complainant.

> In summary, the function of the preliminary inquiry committee [of the College of Physicians and Surgeons of Saskatchewan] is to investigate; the function of the discipline committee is to hear and adjudicate; and the function of council is to deal with reports of the discipline committee and to impose penalties for misconduct. ...
>
> It must be added that the division of functions as outlined above is necessary to preserve fairness in a situation where the college, through its agents, committees and governing bodies, in disciplinary matters which can have grave consequences to its members, acts in various stages as investigator, prosecutor, and adjudicator—in more common terms, it acts as policeman,

prosecutor, judge, jury and executioner. The separation of functions ensures that at least two or three different bodies must review the case. It guards against the possibility that knowledge acquired or biases induced by one stage of the proceedings will not [sic] improperly influence a later stage of the proceedings. Furthermore, investigation and adjudication often require quite different approaches. Finally, there are procedural safeguards built into each step of the disciplinary process, and action outside of that process would deprive the doctor under investigation of those safeguards.

Stephen v College of Physicians and Surgeons (Sask)
(1989), 61 DLR (4th) 496 (Sask CA)

Administrative Tribunals in the ABC Scheme

Some agencies are required by statute or by common law to follow procedures similar to those of courts in making decisions. These agencies are called administrative justice tribunals or, more simply, **administrative tribunals** or **tribunals**. Tribunals may also be called boards or commissions, among other names. They are created by special statutes passed by Parliament or a provincial legislature for the purpose of adjudicating (settling) disputes between individuals and/or companies, or between individuals or companies and the government, over statute-based rights, entitlements, and duties.

Tribunals generally use a more formal, court-like process than that followed by government staff when deciding whether to grant approvals or bestow benefits. There is no fixed boundary between tribunals and other government decision-makers. All government decision-making processes that affect people's rights and entitlements fall somewhere on a continuum, from very informal procedures carried out primarily behind closed doors, to procedures similar to those of a court that involve adversarial techniques and are usually conducted in public.

The government creates different kinds of decision-making processes for different kinds of decisions, guided by principles of efficiency, effectiveness, and fairness.

For straightforward administrative decisions, the government usually delegates the decision-making function to an internal decision-maker within a department. Generally, that person must act fairly, in the sense of disclosing what criteria are being used to make the decision, providing an opportunity to address how those criteria apply, and giving a brief explanation of the reasons for the decision, but the decision-maker is generally permitted to use informal procedures in making decisions.

However, where there is a dispute between a person and a government official who has made a decision that adversely affects that person, or where there is a dispute between two or more parties—for example, the kinds of disputes discussed in the box feature "Examples of Quasi-Judicial Tribunals"—the government often establishes a **quasi-judicial** tribunal to resolve the dispute. To ensure fairness to all parties, tribunals are generally required to operate more formally, providing greater safeguards for a fair process, such as an oral hearing and opportunities to cross-examine witnesses. To ensure the appearance of fairness, particularly where one of the parties is a government department or agency, the government often ensures that a tribunal has an arm's-length relationship with the administrative agency to which it reports or which is a party to its hearings; this is often achieved by establishing the tribunal under separate legislation and ensuring independent operation from the agency, such as by giving the tribunal its own staff rather than staffing it with civil servants and providing that the tribunal's members may not be civil servants.

Examples of Quasi-Judicial Tribunals

- Federal and provincial parole boards, such as the Ontario Parole and Earned Release Board, decide whether inmates of jails and prisons may be released before they have served their full sentences.

- Property tax assessment review boards, such as the Alberta Assessment Appeal Board, hear appeals by property owners of their property tax assessments.

- Tribunals, such as Ontario's Social Benefits Tribunal, determine applicants' eligibility for social assistance payments.

- The federal and provincial human rights tribunals determine whether persons have suffered discrimination based on prohibited grounds such as sex, age, race, or religion, and, where appropriate, order remedial action and compensation.

- Ontario's Criminal Injuries Compensation Board determines whether an applicant's injuries were caused by criminal conduct and, if they were, how the provincial government should compensate the injured person.

- Land-use planning tribunals, such as the Alberta Planning Board and the Ontario Municipal Board, hear cases relating to municipal planning and financing, including appeals from municipal government decisions about zoning and official plans.

- The Ontario Child and Family Services Review Board hears applications for release from children being held in secure treatment facilities due to concern that they may harm themselves or others, as well as appeals from refusals of government officials to approve the adoption of a child.

- Federal and provincial energy boards, such as the National Energy Board, the Alberta Energy Regulator (formerly the Alberta Energy and Utilities Board), and the Ontario Energy Board, set the rates that hydroelectric utilities and gas distributors may charge their customers.

- Licensing bodies, such as the Alcohol and Gaming Commission of Ontario, decide whether it is in the public interest to issue liquor licences to restaurants and other facilities that wish to serve alcohol, and may suspend or revoke licences that are abused.

- The federal Immigration and Refugee Board hears appeals from decisions of federal immigration officials to refuse entry to individuals who are not Canadian citizens or remove them from Canada.

Because tribunal decisions often uphold, grant, or take away rights, benefits, or privileges, tribunals are required to follow certain rules to ensure that the decision-making process is a fair one; these rules are discussed in Chapters 6 and 7.

Although many administrative law texts focus on tribunals and the law that governs them, it is important to remember that tribunals are not the only kind of government body regulated by administrative law, and that administrative law also applies to government departments and other kinds of government agencies.

The Place of Tribunals in the Government Structure

Administrative tribunals are often viewed as part of the executive branch, but they also perform functions similar to those of the judicial branch. Because they do not fit neatly into either branch, tribunals are sometimes described as "hybrid" bodies—the reason why some political scientists initially viewed them as illegitimate. In particular, concerns were expressed about tribunals' lack of accountability to the public.

In recent years, however, tribunals have become so integral to our system of government that their legitimacy is no longer questioned, although some concerns do remain. Politicians and civil servants may feel that tribunals are not sensitive enough to government policy or do not understand that the limited resources available make it difficult for the officials to carry out their functions in the way the tribunal feels they should. In contrast, parties appearing before tribunals may fear that an agency whose members were appointed by Cabinet or by the legislature will not be sufficiently independent of politicians and bureaucrats to ensure that everyone receives a fair and impartial hearing. In other words, politicians and civil servants often view tribunals as being too independent, while parties subject to their decisions regard them as not being independent enough.

The Source and Scope of Agency Powers and Duties

Every administrative tribunal and other ABC is governed by its **enabling legislation**—the statute that creates the agency for a specific purpose—and other statutes that set out its powers and duties. The powers and duties of a tribunal or other agency are often supplemented by common law requirements for fair procedures where the statute is silent on the rights of the parties, and by any additional powers that are reasonably necessary to carry out the statutory powers. The powers and duties of tribunals may include holding hearings, requiring witnesses to attend and give evidence, receiving evidence, and deciding a dispute between parties in favour of one or the other.

In some cases an agency may have a mandate not only to decide a dispute but also to perform related tasks, such as investigating, regulating, prosecuting, advising, and/or setting policy. In these cases, to ensure fairness and impartiality, the agency is usually divided into separate bodies with different members or staff to perform different functions. The tribunal that carries out the dispute resolution function may operate as a separate body within the agency, with safeguards to ensure that it operates independently from the other bodies of the agency. In some cases, such as human rights agencies, the tribunal may be a completely separate agency with different personnel, a separate budget, and separate statutory powers and duties.

Why Governments Delegate Decisions to Tribunals

A government often establishes a tribunal in the following circumstances:

- The government wants to create a mechanism to review the decision of a government decision-maker. In many cases an initial decision may be made in an informal manner, so a statutory right to appeal the decision to a tribunal ensures that the decision can be judged objectively and fairly.

- The decision-maker must resolve a dispute between two or more individuals or companies rather than deciding an issue strictly between the government and an individual.

- The decision has serious consequences for a person or for society. An informal decision-making process for decisions that may affect things such as an individual's livelihood or the public's health or safety is inappropriate. The higher the stakes involved, the more likely it is that the agency making the initial decision will be a tribunal, or if the initial decision is made by a department or an agency that is not a tribunal, there will be an appeal to a tribunal.

Advantages of Tribunals over Government Administrators or Politicians

In some ways, the decision-making function of a tribunal is similar to that of an administrator in a government department who decides whether to issue an order, grant a licence, or confer a benefit. In other ways, this function is similar to that of a court that applies relevant laws in a structured forum.

If the decision is essentially political or administrative, then why not have an administrator in a government department or a politician make the decision?

Governments create administrative tribunals for many of the same reasons that they delegate functions to other agencies. For example, the government may create a specialized tribunal

- to demonstrate the impartiality of a decision-making process and avoid any perception that the decision-maker is biased (that is particularly important where the decision of a government official or minister is being reviewed, since an appeal to someone within the same department may not appear to be impartial);

- to ensure fairness of procedure and outcome through the use of a procedure similar to that of a court;

- to send a message to the community that the issue is important to the government;

- to distance the government from potentially unpopular or controversial decisions;
- to allow for citizen participation (to give the public affected by a government decision the opportunity to participate in the decision-making process);
- to involve experts in the decision; or
- to handle cases more efficiently or cost-effectively (where this may be achieved more easily by creating a new agency than by expanding or modifying the structure of an existing ministry).

Advantages of Tribunals over Courts

If the purpose of having decisions made outside of the government bureaucracy is to ensure that the decision is made at arm's length from the government and follows procedures similar to those of a court, then why not delegate the function to the courts? There are a number of possible reasons, some of which are apparent from the discussion above.

- Where it is desirable to have the decisions made by a person's peers or by experts, judges may not be any more appropriate as decision-makers than civil servants or politicians. A panel with some community membership may bring a different sensitivity and personal experience to its tasks from that brought by a court.
- Over time, the members of a specialized tribunal can develop expertise in administering a particular set of laws. This expertise can ensure that an area of law is interpreted in a consistent fashion and that the interpretation reflects certain social values, professional standards, or government policies.
- Tribunals can include representatives of interest groups affected by the tribunal's mandate, or individuals with professional backgrounds relevant to the subject matter covered by the tribunal. In a dispute between competing interest groups, a tribunal that includes representatives from each group in addition to one or more neutral members may ensure that the interests of both groups and those of the general community are all represented. For example, labour relations boards and workers' compensation tribunals often consist of one member selected by a union, one member selected by company management, and one neutral party chosen by the other two members or by the tribunal chair or specified by the enabling legislation.
- Tribunals may have certain structural advantages over courts. They can be less formal and more accessible; it may be possible to ensure fairness with fewer procedural safeguards; and the public may be more comfortable appearing before tribunals. (Although representation by legal counsel before a tribunal is not uncommon, individuals do not always need a lawyer to participate effectively.)

- Tribunals can often hear cases quickly and without delay. The rules and practices of each tribunal can be tailored to meet the specific needs of the parties and to avoid unnecessary "red tape."

The traditional rationale for the establishment of administrative tribunals is cheapness, expedition, and expertise. The objectives are freedom from what is popularly seen as the undue delay and cost of court proceedings and the inexperience of judges trained in the law but not in matters of social improvement.

Roosma v Ford Motor Co of Canada Ltd (1988), 66 OR (2d) 18 at 24 (Div Ct)

Similarities Between Tribunals and Courts

Common law and statutes that govern tribunals often grant tribunals the freedom to be more informal than courts, but there are limits to this informality. These limits have been imposed by the common law doctrine of procedural fairness; by the particular statutes that create particular tribunals; and by statutes such as Ontario's *Statutory Powers Procedure Act*[5] (SPPA) and Quebec's *Administrative Justice Act*,[6] which set out minimum rules of procedure for some tribunals in those provinces.

Like courts, tribunals generally must follow a fair process, which means that affected persons must have the right to be heard, and to be heard by an impartial decision-maker. This entails rules governing notice, disclosure, the presentation of evidence, the questioning of witnesses, adjournments, submissions, and representation by counsel or other agents. (For a detailed description of the fairness rules that apply to tribunals, see Chapters 6 and 7.)

Like courts, tribunals generally must

- ensure that all parties have been given reasonable notice of the proceedings before the hearing begins;
- ensure that all parties have an opportunity to present their case;
- ensure that all parties have been informed of the case they have to meet;
- allow all parties to present evidence and to cross-examine witnesses or test the accuracy of the evidence against them in other ways;
- grant adjournments if a party would otherwise be deprived of a reasonable opportunity to present its case fully;
- allow all parties to be represented by a lawyer or agent;
- avoid any statements or actions that would suggest that the tribunal has prejudged issues or harbours a bias for or against a party;
- apply the law that governs the proceedings and take into account considerations that are relevant under that law;
- give all parties a chance to make final submissions; and
- give reasons for their decisions that are reasonably clear.

---

5   RSO 1990, c S.22.

6   CQLR c J-3.

Differences Between Tribunals and Courts

The rules and procedures of tribunals are generally less formal and more flexible than those of courts. This can be an advantage or a disadvantage to the parties.

The differences between tribunals and courts in matters of substance and style are summarized in Tables 2.1 and 2.2.

Similarities and Differences Between Tribunal Members and Judges

For the most part, the responsibilities of tribunal members, their requirements for impartiality, and the scope of their decision-making powers are similar to those of judges. There are differences, however, and the extent of the similarity or difference is open to debate and may vary from tribunal to tribunal.

Like judges, tribunal members are expected to render impartial decisions that are not influenced by political pressure or by connections to any of the parties that appear before them. However, some of the safeguards afforded to judges to assist them in withstanding political pressures are not afforded to many tribunal members; unlike judges, tribunal members have no security of tenure, and the government may terminate their appointments at any time.

Like judges, tribunal members are expected to avoid interests and associations that may suggest that their decisions are not impartial. However, many tribunal members serve in a part-time capacity, and may be involved in business, professional, volunteer, and social activities that might be unacceptable for judges and that may bring their impartiality into question.

Like judges, tribunal members are required to apply and interpret the law, and may not substitute their own view of what the law should be for the decisions of the legislators. Unlike judges, however, tribunal members may have considerable discretion (power to choose a course of action from among a variety of options) in applying the law, or they may be expected to apply, interpret, or follow government policies.

Like judges, tribunal members are expected to decide cases on the basis of the evidence put before them. But while judges are required to decide cases using only the evidence presented by the parties, tribunal members with specialized knowledge and expertise may have some latitude in applying their knowledge or understanding of professional standards and norms in making a decision.

Adjudication

Adjudication is the process of receiving and considering the evidence and arguments presented by both sides in a dispute and making a binding decision by applying the relevant law to the issues in the case.

In our tribunal system, the adjudicator is often relatively passive, for the most part weighing and evaluating the evidence and arguments submitted by opposing parties, and generally playing only a limited role in deciding what evidence will be sought out and brought before the tribunal. The adjudicator's role is to watch and

TABLE 2.1   Substantive Differences Between Tribunals and Courts

Tribunals	Courts
Tribunal members are not required to follow previous tribunal decisions. Two decisions of the same tribunal can interpret the same provision in a law in different ways.	Lower courts are bound by the decisions of higher courts. All judges must interpret the law in the same way that a higher court has interpreted it.
Tribunals can accept any evidence that is reliable, including some evidence that courts would disallow. Tribunals vary greatly in what they will accept as evidence. Some tribunals will accept virtually any evidence.	Courts require parties to follow complicated rules of evidence that are designed to prevent misleading information from coming before the court. These rules of evidence are difficult to understand and apply correctly, even for lawyers.
Tribunals sometimes require little or no advance disclosure of evidence. This results in an earlier hearing and lower initial costs, but can also result in "trial by ambush" and delay resulting from requests for adjournment to make up for surprises during the hearing. It can also result in arguments and objections that new information has "prejudiced" a party (unduly harmed its ability to prepare or present its case).	Courts generally require parties in civil cases to disclose their evidence before the hearing. (In criminal cases, only the prosecutor must disclose evidence in advance.) This results in lengthy delays and substantial costs before the hearing begins, but it reduces surprises and improves the efficiency of the hearing. Disclosure also facilitates settlements and may reduce or eliminate the need for a hearing.
Some tribunals have staff who investigate, prepare a case, present evidence, and argue for a particular outcome, either alongside or instead of the parties.	Courts rely entirely on the parties to present the evidence and the arguments on which the court will base its decision.
Some tribunals are permitted to follow less formal or less adversarial procedures.	Courts usually follow a formal and adversarial process.

TABLE 2.2   Style Differences Between Tribunals and Courts

Tribunals	Courts
Tribunal members often identify themselves at the start of a hearing, and may have nameplates in front of them.	Judges do not identify themselves at a hearing, and court clerks do not identify them either.
Seating arrangements may vary from tribunal to tribunal. At some tribunals, all participants, including the adjudicator, sit around the same table.	Seating arrangements in courts are standardized. The judge often sits on a dais at the front of the courtroom, elevated above the participants.
The practice regarding sitting or standing varies from tribunal to tribunal, but bowing is uncommon and robes or gowns are never worn.	Courts have more ceremonial trappings. Everyone stands when the judge enters. The lawyers and agents always stand when they are addressing the judge and when examining or cross-examining witnesses. The lawyers and the judge bow to each other when the judge enters the courtroom, and the lawyers bow to the judge when they leave. In certain courts, lawyers and judges wear robes or gowns.
The practice of oath swearing varies from tribunal to tribunal. Under Ontario's SPPA, the oath is optional, and tribunals may require it or dispense with it.	Witnesses must swear an oath or solemnly affirm that they will tell the truth.

judge. He or she is like a referee who makes sure that the parties follow the "rules of the game" but is not permitted to favour one party or the other. (In some tribunals, adjudicators may have the right to take a more active role in investigating and collecting evidence and information; see the description of inquisitorial systems in the next section.)

Adjudication may be contrasted to other methods of resolving disputes, such as mediation and conciliation. In these methods of dispute resolution, often called **alternative dispute resolution**, the facilitator or decision-maker interacts with the parties in ways that may be quite different from the techniques used by an adjudicator. By employing various techniques and tools, the facilitator seeks to help the parties reach an agreement without the need for a formal hearing by someone who issues a binding order.

Adjudication and the various forms of alternative dispute resolution both have their strengths and weaknesses. Chapter 9, Tribunal Procedures Before Hearings, includes a brief discussion of which approach works best in which circumstances.

The Adversarial and Inquisitorial Systems of Adjudication

There are two different approaches to the conduct of hearings: the adversarial and the inquisitorial.

In the **adversarial system**, the parties themselves determine what evidence is brought before the tribunal, and the tribunal is not permitted to actively seek out evidence beyond that presented by the parties. It is required, though, to give each party extensive opportunities to put forward their case and to challenge the case put forward by the other parties. In Ontario, this approach is driven by the requirements of the SPPA,[7] which sets out numerous rules of procedure for most tribunals. Because Canada's common law principles of natural justice were developed within the adversarial system, many of these rules are based on the adversarial approach and the tribunals therefore take a more passive role (for a discussion of natural justice, see Chapter 3, The Foundations of Administrative Law).

The adversarial system is based on a number of related assumptions: that the parties are in the best position to decide what evidence is useful, that both parties have adequate financial resources and access to information to participate effectively in the process, and that there is no substantial power imbalance between the parties. In disputes between government officials (who have access to substantial expertise and resources) and individuals (who frequently have limited financial resources and limited expertise), a purely adversarial process may not be the best way to bring out the truth and ensure that the individuals involved are able to articulate their goals and interests clearly.

In contrast to the adversarial system, the **inquisitorial system**, which is often found in Europe, requires the tribunal to conduct the investigation and collect the evidence. Adjudicators have much greater latitude to examine and cross-examine the parties and witnesses, and may call witnesses on their own initiative. An inquisitorial system can help re-establish the balance between "weak" citizens and "strong"

---

7 *Supra* note 5.

government, particularly if the adjudicator's authority to obtain information does not prevent the parties from playing a substantial role in bringing forward evidence and making representations.

In an adversarial system, one of the parties usually has the burden of proof. In an inquisitorial system, the tribunal itself may have the burden of finding enough evidence to determine whether a party is entitled to a remedy. In other words, in an inquisitorial system, a party could win even if he or she doesn't show up for the hearing!

> *The role of adjudicators in an adversarial system is quite limited. Adjudicators do not investigate. They do not introduce evidence. They do not cross-examine. They do not advocate. Adjudicators act like neutral sponges that absorb all of the evidence and submissions. Then, at the end of the hearing, the sponge is squeezed and out flows the truth.*
>
> Steinecke Maciura LeBlanc, "The Adversarial
> System," *Grey Areas* (February 2006)

Adversarial or Inquisitorial?

Some tribunals are permitted by their governing legislation to be more inquisitorial than adversarial. If a tribunal's enabling legislation contains one or more of the following provisions, it is likely that the tribunal has some leeway to follow an inquisitorial process:

- the statute refers to the decision-making process as an "inquiry" rather than a "hearing";
- the statute says the tribunal "may" hold a hearing or inquiry rather than "shall" hold one;
- the statute gives the tribunal power to collect evidence independently of the parties;
- the statute requires the tribunal to determine what constitutes the public interest or is necessary to protect public health or ensure public safety, rather than to resolve a dispute between individuals about property or money; or
- the statute requires that the adjudicators have special expertise in the subject matter.

As mentioned, Ontario's SPPA establishes the minimum procedural safeguards that most tribunals must follow, and these reflect the adversarial approach. Therefore, if an enabling statute in Ontario limits the application of the SPPA to the decision-making process or excludes it, this may be a sign that the statute expects (or does not prohibit) a more inquisitorial process.

Examples of Inquisitorial Tribunals

Federal and provincial parole boards and information and privacy commissioners often follow an inquisitorial approach. In Ontario, the Information and Privacy

Commissioner is an example of a tribunal that is authorized to follow an inquisitorial procedure. The Commissioner decides whether to require the government to disclose documents to individuals and companies as requested under the *Freedom of Information and Protection of Privacy Act.*[8]

If the government refuses to disclose a document and an individual has appealed this refusal, a traditional adversarial hearing—where everything is done in public and the parties have the right to see all the relevant information that the other party has—would defeat the purpose of the process. Through the hearing, the requesting party would learn what is in the document that the government is refusing to disclose. He or she would win by default, and the process would be unfair to the government.

Therefore, instead of giving the parties full access to each other's information in a hearing open to the public, the Commissioner conducts hearings in writing. If the government provides any information to the Commissioner that would reveal the contents of the document, the Commissioner does not share this information with the requester, despite the usual requirements of fairness that all evidence be available to all parties.

Since the requester does not know what is in the document being withheld, his or her ability to ask probing questions or to argue that the document should be disclosed is limited. To reduce the potential unfairness of this barrier to the requester, the Commissioner plays an active role in ensuring fairness by setting out for the parties what he or she considers to be the relevant legal and factual issues to be resolved, by questioning both parties, and by actively seeking additional information not provided by parties where such information would be helpful in reaching a decision.

Combining Adversarial and Inquisitorial Techniques

Not all tribunals follow a purely adversarial or purely inquisitorial approach; some combine elements of both processes. In tribunal proceedings, the extent to which adjudicators are permitted to conduct an investigation, intervene in the parties' presentation of evidence and argument, or withhold information provided by one party from another depends on the tribunal's mandate, the wording of the enabling legislation, and what is fair in the circumstances.

> [T]he traditional advocacy skills of the lawyer are generally inapplicable to appearances before the National Parole Board. Parole hearings are inquisitional rather than adversarial, which indicates that Parliament intended that there be many differences between this and other tribunals. For example, there are no parties in the sense of adversaries between whom a lis [a legal dispute between two or more parties] may be said to exist. Similarly, although those institutional and parole personnel most familiar with the prisoner's case do attend parole hearings, they are not usually present as witnesses, and

---

8 RSO 1990, c F.31.

questions may only be put to them through and with the permission of the attending Board members. Again, counsel does not lead the client through his version of events; rather the Board members closely question the prisoner as to what, in their opinion, is important.

David P Cole, "The Bridge of Sighs: Appearing Before the National Parole Board" in Franklin R Moskoff, ed, *Administrative Tribunals—A Practice Handbook for Legal Counsel* (Aurora, Ont: Canada Law Book, 1989) 67 at 69

Agency Reform and Tribunal "Clustering"

Over the past few decades, several academic studies and government reports have been published recommending changes to the structure, staffing, and operation of agencies, particularly tribunals. Some studies have analyzed the operation of specific agencies.[9] Others have looked at agencies in general or specific agency sectors.[10] These studies have been done in response to the perceived need to improve the transparency, accountability, effectiveness, efficiency, and fairness of agencies.

In many cases, these studies have led to structural, administrative, and operational reforms implemented through policy rather than changes in the law. In a few cases, such as Ontario's *Adjudicative Tribunals Accountability, Governance and Appointments Act, 2009* (the ATAGA Act),[11] studies have even resulted in legislated reforms. The purpose of the ATAGA Act is "to ensure that adjudicative tribunals are accountable, transparent and efficient in their operations while remaining independent in their decision-making."

The Act requires all prescribed tribunals to develop and follow a memorandum of understanding between the tribunal and the minister to whom the tribunal reports. The Act also requires these tribunals to publish a business plan; an annual report containing an account of its activities, including member recruitment activities, in the previous year; and a financial statement for that year.

All prescribed tribunals must also have a mandate and mission statement; a consultation policy that describes whether and how the tribunal will consult with the public when contemplating changes to its rules and policies; a policy that sets out a process for receiving and responding to complaints from the public; and an ethics plan dealing with matters such as conflict of interest.

---

9   For example, Paul C Weiler, *Reshaping Workers' Compensation for Ontario* (Toronto: Ministry of Labour, 1989); Cam Jackson, Minister Without Portfolio Responsible for Workers' Compensation Reform, *Report on New Directions for Workers' Compensation Reform* (Toronto: Government of Ontario, 1996); Ontario Human Rights Code Task Force, Mary Cornish, Chair, *Achieving Equality: A Report on Human Rights Reform* (Toronto: Ministry of Citizenship, 1992); Ontario Human Rights Commission, *Reviewing Ontario's Human Rights System*: Discussion Paper (2005).

10 *Report of the Royal Commission Inquiry into Civil Rights*, JC McRuer, Commissioner (Toronto: Queen's Printer, 1968); *Report of the [Quebec] Working Group on Administrative Tribunals*, Yves Ouellette, Chair, 1987; Robert Macauley, *Directions: Review of Ontario's Regulatory Agencies* (Toronto: Queen's Printer for Ontario, September 1989); Law Reform Commission of Nova Scotia, *Reform of the Administrative Justice System in Nova Scotia—Final Report*, January 1997.

11 SO 2009, c 33, Schedule 5.

Every six years, the minister responsible for a tribunal must appoint a public servant to review that tribunal's mandate and whether it continues to be relevant; whether the tribunal's functions would be better performed by another entity; and whether the tribunal's governance structure and management systems continue to be appropriate.

The Act also deals with the proliferation of tribunals. The creation of more and more tribunals, many of which are inefficient and under-resourced because of their small size and small caseload, has frequently been identified as a concern. Some jurisdictions, such as Quebec and Australia, have addressed this problem by merging numerous smaller tribunals into one large tribunal with several smaller divisions within it to deal with different subject matters.

In the ATAGA Act, the Ontario legislature took a slightly different approach. Instead of merging tribunals, it created the framework to combine groups of tribunals into "clusters." The Act provides that Cabinet may, by regulation, designate two or more tribunals as a "cluster" if these tribunals can operate more effectively and efficiently as a cluster than alone. Cabinet may appoint an executive chair to be responsible for a cluster and an associate chair for each of the individual tribunals within the cluster. All tribunals included in a cluster must jointly develop and adopt the "public accountability documents" and "governance accountability documents" described above.

The purposes of clustering are to promote the best use of resources through cross-agency cooperation and coordination of operations and administration, as well as to enhance consistency in tribunal practices, procedures, and decision-making. Tribunals maintain their separate identities and legislative mandates, but they can coordinate their operations. This coordination can improve access to justice and foster consistency in the application of principles of procedural fairness.

However, clustering may also have downsides. For example, cross-appointment of members of one tribunal to which they were appointed because of a particular subject matter or legal expertise to another tribunal that deals with matters outside their expertise or familiarity with the law can potentially lead to poorer decisions rather than better ones. In some cases, two sets of rules of procedure may be required—a set of common rules to be followed by all tribunals in the cluster and a separate set of rules that apply to a single tribunal within the cluster. Instead of simplifying procedure, this could complicate it.

How successful Ontario's experiment with clustering will be remains to be seen. Bigger is not necessarily better.

Tribunal members are to be selected by a competitive, merit-based process, in which the criteria for selecting members must include:

- experience, knowledge, or training in the subject matter and legal issues dealt with by the tribunal;
- aptitude for impartial adjudication; and
- aptitude for applying alternative adjudication practices.

The minister to whom the tribunal reports is required to make public the recruitment process. Important for the independence of the tribunal and the quality of its appointments is the fact that the tribunal's chair plays a pivotal role in the recruitment process. No member may be appointed or reappointed unless the chair recommends this.

As of June 2015, the government had created three tribunal clusters. They are:

- the Environment and Land Tribunals Ontario (ELTO), which brings together the Assessment Review Board, Board of Negotiation, Conservation Review Board, Environmental Review Tribunal, and Ontario Municipal Board;
- the Social Justice Tribunals Ontario (SJTO), which brings together the Child and Family Services Review Board, Criminal Injuries Compensation Board, Custody Review Board, Human Rights Tribunal of Ontario, Landlord and Tenant Board, Ontario Special Education (English) Tribunal, Ontario Special Education (French) Tribunal, and Social Benefits Tribunal;
- the Safety, Licensing Appeals and Standards Tribunals Ontario (SLASTO), bringing together the Animal Care Review Board, Fire Safety Commission, Licence Appeal Tribunal, Ontario Civilian Police Commission, and Ontario Parole and Earned Release Board.

CHAPTER SUMMARY

Traditionally, the regulation of social and economic activities in Canada was a responsibility shared by three separate branches of government: the legislative branch, which passed laws; the executive branch, which implemented and enforced them; and the judiciary, which interpreted laws and resolved disputes by applying them to the facts of a particular case. As society became more complex and government regulation became more pervasive, governments established a new kind of organization to carry out some of the functions traditionally carried out by the three branches: the administrative agency.

For the most part, these agencies were responsible for certain functions of the executive branch. However, they sometimes combined the functions of two or more branches of government. One kind of agency, the tribunal, has duties very similar to those of a court, although tribunals usually carry out these duties in a less formal manner. The development of ABCs challenged the traditional methods of balancing accountability and independence in the civil service, and threatened to undermine the separation of powers. The body of administrative law was developed to regulate how government in general—and the executive branch in particular—carries out its functions.

Although tribunals are technically part of the executive branch of government, their adjudicative function resembles that of the judicial branch. They are required to follow many of the same procedures that courts follow to ensure that all parties receive a fair hearing. Tribunals differ in their practices, and their procedures range from the purely adversarial, in which the tribunal is passive and the parties control the presentation of evidence, to the inquisitorial, in which the tribunal plays an active role in collecting information and presenting evidence.

Both tribunals and courts apply the law, but tribunals also apply government policy and often base their decisions on their interpretation of the public interest as well as on the rights or interests of the parties. Like courts, they must be independent from the executive branch in order to remain impartial. However, they are not as independent as courts, and their members lack the security of tenure that secures the independence of judges.

KEY TERMS

adjudication: the process of receiving and considering the evidence and arguments presented by both sides in a dispute and making a binding decision by applying relevant law to the issues in the case

administrative tribunal: *see* tribunal

adversarial system: a system of resolving disputes by holding a hearing in which the judge or adjudicator does not actively seek out the truth or investigate but relies on opposing parties or their representatives to present evidence and challenge each other's evidence; the adjudicator's decision is based on the evidence presented, regardless of how complete or incomplete the evidence is

alternative dispute resolution: methods of resolving disputes without adjudication, such as conciliation or mediation, in which a facilitator seeks to assist the parties in reaching an agreement without a formal hearing

enabling legislation: a statute that sets out the powers of an agency; it is often, but not always, the statute that establishes the agency; some agencies are established by one statute but carry out functions under several statutes, each of which may give it powers for the purpose of the functions governed by that statute

inquisitorial system: a system of resolving disputes through holding a hearing in which the judge or adjudicator plays an active role in investigating, collecting facts, putting forward evidence, and questioning witnesses

quasi-judicial: similar to that of a judge; often used to describe the functions of a tribunal when it must make a decision regarding the substantive rights of a person

tribunal: a type of agency that is not a court but operates like a court in deciding disputes between individuals and/or companies, or between individuals or companies and the government, over statute-based rights, entitlements, and duties

REVIEW QUESTIONS

1. Explain the relationship between the administrative agency, board, or commission and the centralized department or ministry. How does the function of the agency, board, or commission affect how the department or ministry traditionally operated?

2. Explain how administrative law became its own area of law. What role did the development of agencies, boards, and commissions play in the growth and development of administrative law within the broader category of public law? What are two goals that administrative law achieves?

3. What are seven categories into which agencies, boards, and commissions may be divided, and what is the function of each? Provide examples of agencies, boards, and commissions for each category listed.

4. List as many reasons as you can why a government might set up a separate agency instead of having a department carry out a function.

5. What are the adjudicative bodies in administrative law called?

6. Give examples of areas of dispute that are typically delegated to tribunals for resolution.

7. Under what circumstances does the legislature delegate the job of making a decision to a tribunal rather than to a body such as a ministry or a court?

8. List as many similarities between courts and tribunals as you can.

9. List as many differences between courts and tribunals as you can.

10. What are the two main systems of adjudication used by tribunals? How do they differ from each other, and what are the advantages and disadvantages of each?

11. When you read a statute that governs the operation of a tribunal, what "clues" should you look for to determine which model of adjudication the tribunal follows?

EXERCISES

1. **a.** Using the tools described in Appendix B, find an example of each of the following anywhere in Canada (do not use examples mentioned in this text):

    - a government department or ministry that reports to a Cabinet minister;
    - an advisory agency;
    - an agency that regulates the sale or distribution of a product or commodity;
    - an agency that gives grants to individuals or to businesses, charities, or other bodies;
    - an agency that operates a business or provides a service to consumers; and
    - a tribunal.

    b. For each organization, briefly describe (where applicable)

    - how its members are appointed and by whom;
    - its main functions;
    - whether its members and staff are members of the public service;
    - what statutory steps, if any, the agency must take before making decisions that affect the public; and
    - what procedures the legislature has put in place to ensure that the agency is accountable for its activities (for example, the requirement to produce an annual report, undergo audit by a government auditor, submit its budget to the government for approval, or have its individual expenditures approved by the government before or after they are made).

2. The Information and Privacy Commissioner of Ontario is an example of a body that has both regulatory and adjudicative functions. It is governed by Ontario's *Freedom of Information and Protection of Privacy Act* (RSO 1990, c F.31), which gives individuals the right to obtain copies of all records in the custody or under the control of ministries and other agencies of the Ontario government, subject to certain exceptions listed in the Act. Answer the following questions. Library or online research is recommended.

    a. How does an individual obtain access to information under the Act?

    b. What is the process for appeal if a request is denied under the Act?

    c. The Act sets out the method by which the Commissioner must process this appeal. On the basis of the Act's description of the Commissioner's powers and procedures, do you think the Act establishes an adversarial or an inquisitorial process? Explain.

    d. Which of these processes—inquisitorial or adversarial—is better suited to the function that the Commissioner must carry out, and why?

    e. Compare the process used to challenge an institution's decision to refuse access to documents under Ontario's *Freedom of Information and Protection of Privacy Act* with the process under the federal *Access to Information Act* (RSC 1985, c A-1). How do the two systems differ?

    f. Which system is preferable, and why?

FURTHER READING

Jerry V DeMarco & Paul Muldoon, *Environmental Boards and Tribunals in Canada: A Practical Guide* (Toronto: LexisNexis, 2011).

Robert W Macaulay, *Directions: Review of Ontario's Regulatory Agencies Report* (Toronto: Queen's Printer for Ontario, 1989).

Robert Macaulay & James Sprague, *Practice and Procedure Before Administrative Tribunals* (Toronto: Carswell) (loose-leaf), ch 1–4.

Manitoba Law Reform Commission, *Improving Administrative Justice in Manitoba: Starting With the Appointments Process*, Report No 121 (November 2009).

Murray Rankin, "Cabinets and Courts: Political Tribunals and Judicial Tribunals" (1990) 3 Can J Admin L & Prac 301.

The Foundations of Administrative Law

3

LEARNING OUTCOMES

After reading this chapter, you will understand

- the six fundamental principles of administrative law;

- the kinds of individuals and bodies that must observe the principles of administrative law, and the kinds of exercises of power that administrative law governs;

- the meaning of "jurisdiction" and why agencies must act within it;

- the meaning of "discretion" and how it must be exercised;

- the rule against subdelegation;

- what makes subordinate legislation valid or invalid;

- the requirement that officials and tribunals follow fair procedures when deciding disputes;

- the relationship between procedural fairness and natural justice;

- the components of procedural fairness;

- the main statutes that set out the rules of fair procedure;

- the application of the rules of fair procedure in different contexts; and

- the role of the superior courts in ensuring, through judicial review, that the executive branch of government follows the principles of administrative law.

The effect of agencies on the lives of Canadians is pervasive. They impact almost every aspect of our daily lives morning through night. Behind the waking sounds of the clock radio is the CRTC, the licensor of the radio station. The electricity powering the radio is provided by Ontario Hydro. The furnace, hot water heater and the stove may all run on natural gas which is provided under federal and provincial regulation. The eggs and the milk in the morning omelette are subject to grading and production quotas set by provincial egg and milk marketing boards.

… This plethora of governmental agencies is a reflection of the increase in government services and responsibilities since the Second World War. There are now about 1,500 agencies in Canada, of which 580 are in Ontario. They range widely in size and nature from the Wolf Damage Assessment Board to the Ontario Labour Relations Board. They also vary in the way they function and in their relations with the government and the public. …

Administrative agencies have evolved in the years since the Second World War into a significant and important manifestation of government. Because each agency has been created individually and on an ad hoc *basis, there is extraordinary variety and inconsistency in their powers, methods of operation, relations with their ministries, etc.*

Robert W Macauley, *Directions: Review of Ontario's Regulatory Agencies Report* (Toronto: Queen's Printer for Ontario, 1989) at 1-1, 1-2

What Is Administrative Law?

Administrative law primarily regulates the activities of the executive branch of government, rather than the legislative or judicial branches. It is the body of rules and principles that regulate how the government departments and agencies that administer and enforce our laws, and other bodies created or given powers by statute, must behave when carrying out their functions. Administrative law also encompasses the authority of the superior courts to supervise how these departments and agencies carry out their powers, the procedures that these courts follow, and the remedies that the courts can provide when departments or agencies act outside their authority or exercise their powers in an unreasonable or unfair manner.

Fundamental Principles of Administrative Law

Administrative law is founded on six fundamental principles:

1. Decision-makers who exercise powers granted by statute ("administrators") must stay within their legal authority, or jurisdiction.

2. Administrators must exercise their judgment in a reasonable manner when they have discretion in making decisions.

3. Administrators must follow fair procedures when making decisions that affect a person's rights or interests. This principle is known as "procedural

fairness" or, in some cases, "natural justice." It protects the rights and interests of persons affected by a decision by providing for

   a. the right of persons to be given notice of intended decisions that may affect them and the right to be heard before such decisions are put into effect; and

   b. the right to an impartial decision-maker.

4. A person to whom the legislature has delegated authority to carry out a function may not delegate it to someone else. There are some exceptions to this principle, which is known as "the rule against subdelegation" and which is important but less central to administrative law than the first three principles.

5. To be valid, subordinate (or delegated) legislation must conform to the statute under which it is passed. In other words, regulations and bylaws must be consistent with the objectives of their enabling statutes and the scope of the regulatory powers set out in those statutes. This is an important check on the power of the executive branch of government to make laws that are not subject to review by the legislature.

6. If decision-makers violate any of the above principles, the superior courts have an inherent power to intervene to rectify this failure. This intervention is called "judicial review." It is an important mechanism for preventing abuse of executive power because it is available even when the legislature has made no provision for an appeal of executive actions. As well, any law that a legislature passes to prevent judicial review is unconstitutional and therefore invalid.

These six principles are discussed in this chapter. For a more detailed discussion of procedural fairness, see Chapters 6 and 7; for a more detailed discussion of judicial review, see Chapter 16.

Why Did Administrative Law Develop?

Chapter 2 described the evolution of the executive branch of government to include, in addition to government departments, a new sector of administrative agencies. The main reason for the creation of these agencies was that governments were taking on a much larger role in regulating social and economic activities. As well as moving into new areas of regulation, governments were applying stricter or more detailed requirements or standards. To support this expanded role, the powers of central departments were increased, and the new agencies were given wide-ranging responsibilities intended to complement—or, in some cases, replace—various functions otherwise performed by departments. Their responsibilities included legislation, enforcement, administration, and adjudication.

The more the government intervened in the daily lives of citizens, and the broader the powers granted to its departments and agencies, the more important it became to implement a system of rules for scrutinizing and regulating these activities. In particular, it was essential to maintain the separation of powers among the three branches of government by preventing departments and agencies that were part of the executive branch from encroaching on the functions of the legislative and judicial branches. It was also necessary to promote the accountability of departments and agencies; to ensure that they acted fairly; and, at the same time, to protect their independence.

These objectives were achieved by developing a body of law that constrained the actions of government departments and agencies. Initially, the courts took the lead by developing a set of fairness principles. Later, these and other principles and rules were codified in statutes. This body of principles and rules is what we now know as "administrative law."

Who Is Subject to Administrative Law?

Administrative law governs the exercise of powers granted by statute. Thus, any individual or body exercising a power granted by statute or regulation is subject to the principles of administrative law. This means that, in addition to government entities, organizations such as universities, hospitals, and self-regulating professions that are established or given powers by statute must follow the principles of administrative law when exercising those powers. In other words, "it is not the nature of the body but the source of the power it is exercising that determines whether it is subject to those principles."[1]

Although administrative law applies primarily to bodies created by statute when they make decisions authorized or required by statute, this general description is incomplete. For example, the courts will intervene from time to time to ensure that statutory bodies act properly even when they are carrying out functions that *do not* involve statutory decision-making, such as investigation or the making of non-binding recommendations.

In addition, the same principles of law apply to ensure that non-government, non-statutory voluntary organizations—such as trade associations, clubs, and churches—abide by their own rules and apply those rules fairly when they are taking action that affects the interests or rights of their members. That is, the organizations must stay within their jurisdiction as set out in their own rules (rather than in a statute), and must follow a fair procedure when, for example, they wish to revoke a membership or fire a staff member.

There is some disagreement among writers on administrative law as to whether the application of administrative law principles, such as fairness and the requirement to stay within their jurisdiction, means that administrative law itself applies to voluntary organizations. While many maintain that administrative law does apply to voluntary organizations, a few writers treat the application of administrative law principles to clubs and other voluntary organizations as a similar but separate and unnamed area of law, or as a part of employment law.

---

1   The Law Society of Upper Canada, *Public Law—Reference Materials*, 45th Bar Admission Course Materials (Toronto: Law Society of Upper Canada, 2002) ch 1 at 1-1.

Evolution of Administrative Law

Fairness as a Guiding Principle

As mentioned, in response to concerns about the expansion of powers of government bodies, the courts began to develop rules of fairness in decision-making. Initially, these rules applied only to decision-makers who made quasi-judicial decisions that affected people's rights. Later, they were expanded to apply whenever departments and agencies made any administrative or quasi-judicial decision—other than a legislative or policy decision, or a minor administrative decision—that affected an individual's rights, privileges, or interests. More recently, the courts have extended the application of fairness principles to require decision-makers to consult individuals who have come to rely on a policy or a procedure before they change the policy or procedure where those individuals have been led (by a promise or other administrative action) to have a "legitimate expectation" that the policy or procedure would continue to apply.

THE DISTINCTION BETWEEN PROCEDURAL FAIRNESS AND NATURAL JUSTICE

Historically, the courts drew a rigid line between quasi-judicial functions—the kinds of functions that tribunals typically carry out—and other functions characterized as legislative, policy-making, investigative, or administrative. They took an all-or-nothing approach to rights to challenge the fairness of procedures used by government bodies.

If the decision-maker was a tribunal, the affected parties had a wide variety of procedural fairness rights, such as the right to a hearing; this included the right to receive notice of the proceedings, to be represented by a lawyer or agent, to have an oral hearing, to call and cross-examine witnesses, and to make arguments at the end of the hearing. However, if the decision-maker was an administrator, affected persons had no right to notice or to an opportunity to be heard before or after the decision was made.

Until the late 1970s, if a decision was considered quasi-judicial, the official responsible for making the decision was required to give the affected individual a hearing before making the decision. This requirement was known as **natural justice**. Generally, if a government administrator denied a right or entitlement, the decision was considered quasi-judicial, and the rules of natural justice had to be followed. Refusal of a business licence or approval to carry out some regulated activity (such as the construction of a building) usually fell into this category. For example, an applicant who was denied a business licence would usually be entitled to a hearing before a tribunal, at which the applicant had the right to be told the reasons for the refusal, be represented by a lawyer or agent, give testimony, call and cross-examine witnesses, and make final arguments before a decision was rendered.

If the decision was considered administrative, however, there were no minimum procedures that had to be followed to ensure a fair process except for those that were explicitly or implicitly set out in the statute that authorized the decision-making process—that is, the decision-making process was not subject to any common law rights of natural justice. Cases in which an administrator denied a privilege or benefit—for example, where an administrator denied an individual the government-funded services of a homecare provider because the administrator decided that the individual did not qualify—were considered administrative decisions. Similarly, if a tribunal made a binding ruling, the ruling was considered quasi-judicial, but if it made a recommendation to government, the process was generally considered administrative, and natural justice was not required.

In practice, the line between administrative and quasi-judicial decisions was "sometimes dim and the consequences of drawing it [were] sometimes uncertain."[2] In the 1979 case *Minister of National Revenue v Coopers and Lybrand*,[3] the Supreme Court of Canada attempted to clarify the difference between quasi-judicial and administrative processes and reaffirmed the traditional approach of denying procedural rights except in relation to quasi-judicial decisions. The Court ruled that if a body was making a decision that was "required by law to be made on a judicial or quasi-judicial basis," it must apply certain procedures.

In deciding whether a process was quasi-judicial, the Court said that the following factors should be considered:[4]

- whether anything in the language of the statute suggests that a hearing is contemplated before a decision is reached;
- whether the decision directly or indirectly affects the rights and obligations of a person affected by the decision;
- whether an adversarial process is used in making the decision; and
- whether there is an obligation to apply substantive rules to many individual cases rather than an obligation to implement social and economic policy in a broad sense.

If the answer to all of these questions was "yes," the person affected by the decision was entitled to be given notice of the decision and had a right to a hearing. If the answer to any of the above questions was "no," the decision would not be considered quasi-judicial. In this case, the courts would not consider the fairness of the process, meaning that the body was largely free to make the decision without consulting those who would be affected by it, much less providing the other rights associated with a quasi-judicial decision. On this basis, a wide variety of executive or administrative decisions were not subject to the rules of natural justice.

However, in another case decided in the same year, the Supreme Court changed its position. In *Nicholson v Haldimand-Norfolk Regional Police Commissioners*,[5] the Court decided that the requirement to follow fair procedures did not depend on

---

2   Robert F Reid & Hillel David, *Administrative Law and Practice*, 2nd ed (Toronto: Butterworths, 1978) at 119.

3   [1979] 1 SCR 495 [*Coopers and Lybrand*].

4   *Ibid* at 504.

5   [1979] 1 SCR 311 [*Nicholson*].

whether a decision was quasi-judicial or fell into some other category, such as an administrative decision. Instead, certain basic procedural rights applied to *any* government decision that would affect a particular individual or group more than it would affect the general public. Six years later, in *Cardinal v Director of Kent Institution*,[6] the Supreme Court reaffirmed that any administrative decision that affects "the rights, privileges or interests" of an individual triggers the duty of fairness.

At a minimum, anyone adversely affected by such a decision must be told the reasons for it and given an opportunity to respond, or at least to "be heard" by an unbiased decision-maker, if not to have a full "hearing."[7] Affected persons were entitled to be given notice of the decision and the reasons for it, and an opportunity to respond; this principle or doctrine was called **procedural fairness**.

> *[T]he purpose of the participatory rights contained within the duty of procedural fairness is to ensure that administrative decisions are made using a fair and open procedure, appropriate to the decision being made and its statutory, institutional, and social context, with an opportunity for those affected by the decision to put forward their views and evidence fully and have them considered by the decision-maker.*
>
> L'Heureux-Dubé J in *Baker v Canada (Minister of Citizenship and Immigration)*, [1999] 2 SCR 817

The courts have described the right bestowed by the doctrine of procedural fairness as a *right to be heard*. This is not the same as a *right to a hearing*—the kind of formal proceeding that must be held by a court or tribunal according to the rules of natural justice. Thus, one way to describe the difference between natural justice and procedural fairness is that natural justice requires that a person affected by a decision be given a right to a formal hearing, while procedural fairness requires that the person be consulted before a final decision is made.

Today, the standard of treatment required of all agencies, including tribunals, is generally referred to as "procedural fairness," even though the duties that this entails differ depending on several factors, including whether the body making the decision is a tribunal or some other body or an individual. "Natural justice" is still sometimes used to describe the particular kind of procedural fairness that applies to tribunals.

Gradually, the right to receive procedural fairness has also been extended from the person most directly affected by a decision to others who may be less directly affected (see the box feature "Entitlement to Procedural Fairness"). In addition, principles of procedural fairness are increasingly being applied to legislative, investigatory, and advisory functions, although the requirements for fairness are much more rudimentary in these contexts.

---

6   [1985] SCR 643 at 847.

7   *Supra* note 5 at 328.

Entitlement to Procedural Fairness

The owner of a restaurant applies for a licence to sell liquor under provincial liquor control legislation. According to the rules of procedural fairness, the decision-maker is required to notify the restaurant owner's neighbours of the application and to give them an opportunity to present their objections before the final decision is made. If the neighbours oppose the application, they have a right to bring their concerns, and the evidence supporting those concerns, to the attention of the decision-maker.

If the decision-maker refuses to grant the licence, the rules of procedural fairness (as well as the rules of natural justice) entitle the restaurant owner to an opportunity to challenge the decision. If the applicant decides to challenge the decision, the neighbours are also entitled to notice of this challenge and an opportunity to participate in the appeal proceedings.

LEGITIMATE EXPECTATIONS

In 1990, the Supreme Court of Canada ruled that procedural fairness requires government agencies to consult affected individuals in cases that involve expectations rather than rights.[8]

Where a person has no right to continue receiving the benefit of a government practice but has come to rely on it, he or she will sometimes be entitled to an opportunity to comment before the practice is changed. Even if a person claiming some benefit or privilege has no legal right to it, he or she may still have **legitimate expectations** of receiving the benefit or privilege, and the courts will require some consultation before it is removed. A person may have legitimate expectations based on reassuring statements that the government has made about the continuance or availability of the benefit or privilege, or based on a pattern of conduct that implies that the benefit or privilege will continue.

In its 2011 *Mavi* decision,[9] the Supreme Court elaborated on the scope and application of the legitimate expectations doctrine:

> [68]   Where a government official makes representations within the scope of his or her authority to an individual about an administrative process that the government will follow, and the representations said to give rise to the legitimate expectations are clear, unambiguous and unqualified, the government may be held

---

8   The concept of "legitimate expectations" originated in the United Kingdom in the late 1960s and early 1970s. In particular, Lord Denning laid the foundation for the acceptance of this doctrine in *R v Liverpool Corporation, Ex parte Liverpool Taxi Fleet Operators' Association*, [1972] 2 QB 299 (CA). The doctrine was soon being referred to in Canadian courts, and throughout the 1980s legitimate expectations were increasingly claimed with varying degrees of success. However, it was not until the early 1990s that the Supreme Court recognized the doctrine (*Old St Boniface Residents Assn Inc v Winnipeg (City)*, [1990] 3 SCR 1170) and ruled on its scope in Canada (*Reference Re Canada Assistance Plan (BC)*, [1991] 2 SCR 525).

9   *Canada (Attorney General) v Mavi*, [2011] 2 SCR 504.

to its word, provided the representations are procedural in nature and do not conflict with the decision maker's statutory duty. Proof of reliance is not a requisite. ... It will be a breach of the duty of fairness for the decision maker to fail in a substantial way to live up to its undertaking.

In *Mavi*, the federal minister of citizenship and immigration sought to be reimbursed for social assistance payments from sponsors of immigrant relatives who had become dependent on social assistance. These sponsors had signed an agreement to reimburse the government if this occurred. In the Court, the sponsors challenged the demand to pay these debts on several fairness grounds, including their legitimate expectations that the government would not take steps to collect the money "in appropriate circumstances." This expectation was based on statements by the government in writing to that effect.

The Court found that the government's statements supported the sponsors' contention of a government representation to them that there was discretion not to take enforcement action and therefore, it was not open to the bureaucracy "to proceed without notice and without permitting sponsors to make a case for deferral or other modification of enforcement procedures" (even though the Court found there was, in fact, no discretion to forgive repayment, only to defer it).

(In addition, see the box feature "Legitimate Expectations: The Exception to the Rule" later in this chapter.)

Other Central Principles

The principles most frequently dealt with in texts on administrative law are those of procedural fairness or natural justice. However, as mentioned, there are several other fundamental principles of administrative law that apply to government generally, including departments and administrative agencies. These principles relate to jurisdiction, discretion, subdelegation, subordinate legislation, and judicial review.

Jurisdiction

What Is Jurisdiction?

Jurisdiction is a central concept of administrative law. Simply defined, it refers to the scope of the authority or powers conferred on a government body or official by legislation or by common law. The concept of jurisdiction is expressed in the principle that government bodies and officials must always act within their legal authority or powers. If an administrator does something outside his or her jurisdiction, that action is invalid because it is *ultra vires* (Latin for "outside his or her powers"), and the decision may be struck down by a court.

Sources of Jurisdiction: Statutes and Common Law

Government departments and agencies are created by statute. Their jurisdiction, therefore, is generally limited to the powers granted explicitly to them in the relevant statutes. In addition to this, there are two other, very limited sources of jurisdiction for departments and agencies.

First, at common law, agencies have whatever additional powers are necessarily incidental to their explicit powers. A court will find these additional powers by **necessary implication** only where the jurisdiction sought is necessary to accomplish the objectives of the legislative scheme and is essential to the body fulfilling its mandate.

For example, suppose the statute that regulates a particular type of business requires all operators of such businesses to submit a financial statement prepared by an accountant to the regulator each year. An operator who is an accountant submits a financial statement and claims to have complied with the requirement. However, even though the statute does not state that the financial statement must be prepared by someone independent of the operator, it may be interpreted to mean this. The power to require an independent accountant can be implied because this is necessary to fulfill the purpose of the provision, which is to monitor the financial transactions of these businesses in order to ensure that the public is protected.

This **implied powers doctrine** is a source of *substantive* jurisdiction.

Second, agencies may have unwritten *procedural* powers at common law. Agencies have common law authority to create and follow procedures not provided for in their statutes, but only to the extent that these procedures are reasonably necessary to allow them to carry out their statutory obligations. For example, even without explicit power, a tribunal will be considered to have the power to grant or refuse an adjournment or to grant a stay of an administrative action appealed to the tribunal until the tribunal has held its hearing on whether to uphold the action, since these powers are necessary for the tribunal to exercise its other powers effectively.

This common-law source of jurisdiction is known as the **inherent powers doctrine**, and is expressed as a rule that "every agency is the master of its own process."

Requirement to Act Within Jurisdiction

As discussed in Chapter 1, when making any decision, government bodies and officials are bound by the rule of law. This has two important consequences related to jurisdiction:

1. The powers and duties of any government department, agency, or official are limited to those established by a law.

2. Any department or agency that has powers and duties under legislation must follow the procedures set out in the legislation when exercising those powers and duties.

Agencies, departments, and their officials do not have the right or the authority to ignore provisions of the law even if they believe that they are justified in doing so. Their task is not to determine what the law *should* be; that function belongs to the elected members of the legislature or the municipal council. The role of agencies and officials is to interpret and apply the law as it is written, in every case that comes before them.

An agency acts outside its jurisdiction if it does something that its statutory or common law powers do not authorize it to do, or if it fails or refuses to do something that it is legally required to do. In these cases, a superior court may require the agency to take an alternative action that *is* within its jurisdiction. As mentioned, this inherent right of superior courts is called "judicial review" and is discussed later in this chapter.

Jurisdiction and Procedural Fairness

As mentioned, the requirement to stay within jurisdiction means both that departments and agencies, and their officials may not act outside the statutory or common law authority granted to them *and* that they must do everything that a statute or common law requires them to do. If a statute requires an agency to make a decision and the agency fails to do so within a reasonable time, the agency is said to be **declining jurisdiction**. (Alternatively, failing to make the required decision may be treated as a breach of procedural fairness.)

Similarly, if a statute requires an agency to follow a particular procedure in making decisions, the agency may be acting outside its jurisdiction if it follows a different procedure, even if this departure does not prejudice anyone. If the unauthorized procedure has the effect of depriving someone of a fair opportunity to present his or her case, it may also be a breach of procedural fairness.

"Jurisdiction" may also have a broader meaning in certain contexts. For decision-makers who determine the rights and obligations of others, and for tribunals that resolve disputes, there is also the duty to exercise those powers in accordance with the common law rules of procedural fairness. Consequently, some courts and writers on administrative law also describe the failure to follow a fair procedure as "exceeding jurisdiction," "acting outside jurisdiction," or "making a jurisdictional error." Courts and writers have differed in their opinions as to whether failure to follow procedural fairness should be treated as a question of jurisdiction or whether procedural fairness is a separate rule from the requirement to act within jurisdiction.

Fairness also comes into play in interpreting an agency's powers. An agency must interpret the powers given to it by legislation in the context of these rules of fairness. That is, even if the wording of a statute appears to authorize a tribunal to do something, if taking that action would involve a breach of the rules of procedural fairness and if the statute is open to interpretation, the proper interpretation of the statutory power is the one that does not violate fairness requirements.

Discretion

What Is Discretion?

The role of an administrator becomes most interesting when the law does not provide the answer. In many cases, the law grants **discretion** to an official, or the right to choose from a variety of options.

Most statutory authority is discretionary. Legislators cannot contemplate all of the circumstances and conduct to be regulated within a field of activity. Someone must be given the responsibility of applying the legislation to each situation as it arises. Also, legislation may be ineffective if no one is appointed to ensure compliance. Such a person is granted discretion to determine whether a specific situation is covered by the legislation and whether a compliance order or other remedy is warranted. Discretion may be conferred so that considerations of public policy and the public interest may be taken into account when applying the statute to specific circumstances.

Sara Blake, *Administrative Law in Canada*, 5th ed
(Toronto: LexisNexis Butterworths, 2011) at 99

Requirement to Exercise Discretion in a Fair or Reasonable Manner

When an official is granted discretion, just applying the law to the facts often will not provide the "right" answer; it may also be necessary to determine which of several possible applications of the law is the most fair or reasonable in the circumstances. However, this does not mean that officials are free to do whatever they think is fair or reasonable. The rule of law requires that decisions be based on the intent and purpose of the statute granting the discretion, not on an official's personal beliefs and values. Otherwise, the exercise of discretion in decision-making would lead to perpetual inconsistency and uncertainty—a situation contrary to the purpose of laws.

The courts have therefore developed a rule that discretion must be exercised reasonably (although the word "fairly" would be equally appropriate). There are several principles that govern whether the exercise of discretion is reasonable or unreasonable. Among these are principles requiring decision-makers to avoid looking at options either too broadly or too narrowly.

Limits on the Right to Choose Among Options

There are four limits on a decision-maker's right to choose among options:

1. Discretion must be exercised within the "four corners" or boundaries of the statute (in other words, within the decision-maker's jurisdiction). The fundamental rule in the exercise of discretion is that the choices made must be both consistent with the purpose of the statute and with its wording. In recent years, the courts have stated that not only must discretion be exercised in accordance with the purpose and wording of the statute that grants the discretionary power, but "administrative decision-makers must act consistently with the *values* underlying the grant of discretion, including *Charter* values."[10] [Emphasis added]

---

10 See, for example, *Doré v Barreau du Québec*, 2012 SCC 12, [2012] 1 SCR 395 at para 24. See Chapter 4 for further discussion of the relationship between administrative law and the Charter in challenges to discretionary decisions.

2. In making choices, officials must consider only relevant factors—those that are consistent with the purpose and wording of the statute and relate to the issues they are to decide. They must not take into account extraneous or irrelevant factors (those that are outside the scope of the statute or have no relevance to the issues in the particular case). This rule is closely related to the first rule.

3. Similar cases should be treated in a similar way, and different cases should be treated differently from each other. There must be no discrimination between persons on the basis of irrelevant considerations.

4. Discretion must be exercised in good faith. Officials act in bad faith when they deliberately ignore the limits set out above for an improper purpose. For example, if the exercise of discretion is influenced by outside pressure or by the official's personal feelings toward a party, the choice is made not only on the basis of an irrelevant factor, but also in bad faith.

Limits on the Authority to Rule Out Options: The Rule Against Fettering Discretion

While the principles set out above require officials to rule out irrelevant or inappropriate options, there are also principles that require them *not* to rule out other options. When officials rule out options that the law requires them to consider, they are said to be **fettering their discretion**.

In certain situations, officials may have statutory authority to refuse to deal with matters over which they have jurisdiction. For example, a statute may give an official authority not to process a request where it is obvious that the request has no possibility of success. Similarly, a tribunal may have statutory authority not to hear a case where the documents submitted indicate that the case has absolutely no merit.

Generally, however, the authority to rule out options is subject to two limitations:

1. An official with a power to exercise discretion cannot refuse to exercise that discretion. If an official has discretion, he or she must use it to make a decision on a matter within his or her jurisdiction when called upon to do so by a member of the public entitled to a ruling. The official cannot say, "I don't like any of the options, so I refuse to make a decision." The official is required to select one of the available options. These options often include granting the request, refusing the request, or granting the request subject to appropriate terms and conditions. The official cannot say, "I am not going to consider whether I should exercise my discretion favourably or not."

2. An official with a power to exercise discretion cannot refuse to consider any factor that is relevant in deciding which option to choose. For example, some environmental protection laws permit government officials to order the current owner and all past owners of a property to pay for cleaning up pollution associated with the property, regardless of whether

they contributed to causing it; in other words, an official has discretion to order a person who has not owned a property for ten years to clean up pollution caused by the current owner just recently. However, this does not mean that the official can disregard the fact that the previous owner had nothing to do with causing the pollution. This is a relevant factor that must be considered in deciding whether to order that person to pay for the cleanup.

Officials have no authority to refuse to exercise their discretion in the ways described above. As long as the law allows them choices, they are required to give genuine consideration to each of those choices.

In practice, the rule against fettering discretion means that tribunals, for example, cannot make any binding rules that would require different panels to make consistent decisions in similar cases or that would prevent panel members (adjudicators) from considering all options. Consequently, tribunals can never ensure that their decisions are entirely consistent. Nevertheless, adjudicators, as well as other government administrators, should attempt to minimize the degree of inconsistency in their own decisions and between their decisions and those of other panel members or officials without fettering the discretion of their officials. The next section discusses several ways that this may be accomplished.

> [D]iscretion must still be exercised in a manner that is within a reasonable interpretation of the margin of manoeuvre contemplated by the legislature, in accordance with the principles ... of administrative law governing the exercise of discretion, and consistent with the Canadian Charter of Rights and Freedoms.
>
> L'Heureux-Dubé J in *Baker v Canada (Minister of Citizenship and Immigration)*, [1999] 2 SCR 817 at 853–54

Ways to Minimize Uncertainty and Inconsistency Without Fettering Discretion

Policies and Guidelines

Where inconsistency in the exercise of discretion is a potential problem, it is advisable for the government department or agency to develop policies or guidelines to promote both consistency and fairness in decision-making. However, these must never be treated as binding rules or be used to justify the exclusion of choices provided by the law. A requirement to follow such directives slavishly would be a fettering of discretion.

Sometimes, a government department will establish policies for its administrators to apply in carrying out their functions, including the exercise of discretion. If a tribunal is called upon to review how those administrators did their job and if it has the power to substitute its own views as to how the regulatory regime should apply, it is usually also appropriate for the tribunal to consider those government policies. However, the tribunal may not treat the policies as strict requirements, or this too will constitute a fettering of discretion.

The original decision-maker or the tribunal reviewing the decision must follow ministerial directives only when required to do so by statute. If there is no statutory requirement, the directives should be considered, but both the original decision-maker and the reviewing tribunal can refuse to follow the directives, provided that the facts of a particular case justify their choice.

Consultation

When an official is considering making a decision that would be inconsistent with an earlier decision of the department or agency, consultation with others may be helpful. Government officials are generally free to consult other staff members when making decisions, and they are not generally required to disclose those consultations. Tribunal members, on the other hand, are more constrained in their ability to consult outside the hearing.

Except where a statute governing a tribunal excludes or places stricter limits on the right to consult, it is acceptable for an adjudicator to seek advice from other tribunal members, staff, counsel, or the chair as long as

- the adjudicator makes the final decision,
- the consultation is voluntary on the adjudicator's part,
- no one who is consulted puts pressure on the adjudicator to make a particular decision, and
- no new issues or facts are introduced without the parties being notified and permitted to comment.

Caution in Overturning Discretionary Decisions

In some cases, a tribunal reviewing discretionary decisions of a government official has statutory authority to overturn a particular decision only if the official was clearly "wrong," in the sense of acting outside his or her mandate, ignoring relevant evidence, or deciding on the basis of irrelevant factors. In other cases, however, the tribunal is given broad discretion to substitute its own decision for that of the official.

This kind of broad discretion must be exercised with caution. In the civil courts, higher courts will usually refuse to overturn a lower court's discretionary decision where the only basis for doing so is that the higher court prefers its own discretionary decision. The same is true of tribunals. The reason for this is obvious: when a tribunal superimposes its discretion on the discretion of another administrator, even though the first decision was one that a decision-maker could reasonably make, this undermines the certainty and predictability of outcome that a legal system is expected to provide. Therefore, even if there are no explicit limits on a tribunal's exercise of discretion, discretionary decisions by other administrators are usually overturned only if they are unreasonable or unfair, or if the administrator followed an improper procedure in reaching the decision. In either case, the tribunal should make its reasons for overturning the decision clear.

Reviewing Discretionary Decisions

Government departments and agencies do not always provide their administrators with policies or principles to assist them in discretionary decision-making. When a tribunal reviews a decision made under such circumstances, it is helpful if the tribunal has established its own guidelines for deciding whether or not to overturn the decision.

Guidelines may either emerge from the decisions of individual tribunal members or be developed by the tribunal as a whole. Both approaches are appropriate as long as the guidelines are not used to fetter discretion.

If guidelines are developed by the tribunal as a whole, they should generally be published. Parties to cases brought before the tribunal are entitled to know in advance what criteria the tribunal will apply in exercising its discretion.

Subdelegation

In general, an official to whom the legislature has delegated decision-making power may not delegate that power to someone else. Such delegation is called **subdelegation**. The rule against subdelegation is expressed in the Latin phrase *delegatus non potest delegare*, which means "a delegate cannot delegate."

The purpose of the rule against subdelegation is to preserve the quality of decisions and ensure the fairness of decisions. The presumption behind the rule is that the legislature has chosen the delegate carefully, and another person may not possess the same knowledge, skills, or qualifications. Equally important is the fact that accountability for decisions may be compromised when decision-making takes place outside the established structure for the exercise of statutory powers. The rule against subdelegation is another example of the more general rule that a body must stay within its jurisdiction; if the legislature has delegated to someone jurisdiction to do something, this does not confer jurisdiction on some other person to do that thing.

Subdelegation is permitted in certain circumstances. For example, the rule against subdelegation does not apply to a minister delegating statutory powers to public servants in his or her ministry. Where a statute says that the ministry "may" do something, this is sufficient to allow the minister to delegate even discretionary decisions to ministry staff.

Subdelegation is also permitted in circumstances where it is specifically authorized by a statute. In addition, the power to subdelegate can sometimes be implied from the statutory context, even though it is not expressly granted. Where there is no express or implied statutory authorization, whether subdelegation is allowed may depend on whether the power being delegated can be described as purely administrative (often requiring little or no exercise of discretion) or as quasi-judicial.

Courts are more willing to uphold the subdelegation of purely administrative functions than the authority to make decisions involving the exercise of discretion or the determination of substantive rights.

Where a delegate is required to follow a specific procedure in making a decision or setting standards, the delegate is not allowed to circumvent these requirements by delegating the decision to a different official who is not subject to the same restraints.

In practice, delegation of decision-making authority occurs across a wide spectrum of activities, and it is difficult to determine in any given case whether a delegation not explicitly authorized by a statute is valid or not.

Validity of Delegated Legislation

There are two types of delegated legislation—regulations made under statutes, usually by Cabinet or a Cabinet minister, and bylaws passed by municipalities.

The fact that these regulations are not passed by Parliament or a provincial legislature raises concerns about fairness and accountability that are similar to those raised in relation to the exercise of other statutory powers. Some jurisdictions have attempted to address these concerns by providing for public consultation before regulations are finalized or by bringing proposed regulations before a parliamentary committee for discussion. The main control over regulations and bylaws, however, has been the requirement that everything in them be authorized by statute.

The basic principle governing delegated legislation is that regulations and bylaws must be consistent with the objectives of their enabling statutes and the scope of the regulatory powers set out in those statutes. As one text put it, "Regulations should not contain provisions initiating new policy, but should be confined to details to give effect to the policy established by the statute."[11] This is just another way of requiring regulators to stay within their jurisdiction.

Generally, compliance with this principle requires the statute under which a regulation or bylaw falls to contain an explicit provision allowing the executive or municipality to make a regulation or bylaw dealing with a particular subject matter. However, if there is no explicit power to make the particular regulation or bylaw, the power may be read into the statute where it is necessary to the exercise of other powers that are explicitly set out in the statute.

> *A successful challenge to the vires of regulations requires that they be shown to be inconsistent with the objective of the enabling statute or the scope of the statutory mandate. ... Regulations benefit from a presumption of validity .... This presumption has two aspects: it places the burden on challengers to demonstrate the invalidity of regulations, rather than on regulatory bodies to justify them ... ; and it favours an interpretative approach that reconciles the regulation with its enabling statute so that, where possible, the*

---

11 Denis Holland & John McGowan, *Delegated Legislation in Canada* (Scarborough, Ont: Carswell, 1989) at 93.

regulation is construed in a manner which renders it intra vires .... *Both the challenged regulation and the enabling statute should be interpreted using a "broad and purposive approach ... consistent with this Court's approach to statutory interpretation generally" .... This inquiry does not involve assessing the policy merits of the regulations to determine whether they are "necessary, wise, or effective in practice."*

Katz Group Canada Inc v Ontario (Health and Long-Term Care), 2013 SCC 64 at paras 24–27

Since statutes always take precedence over regulations and bylaws, a regulation or bylaw is generally invalid if it conflicts with its enabling statute or any other statute. However, a regulation that conflicts with its enabling statute or other statutes may be valid if the statute explicitly provides that its regulations are intended to amend, abrogate, enlarge, or abridge that statute or other statutes.

A regulation may also be *ultra vires* if the legislature fails to follow a procedure that is mandatory in making the regulation. This is known as failure to meet a mandatory condition precedent. For example, Ontario's *Endangered Species Act, 2007*[12] states that certain regulations that may weaken the protections of endangered species set out in the Act may be made by Cabinet only if the minister of natural resources has first obtained an expert opinion on whether the proposed regulations are likely to jeopardize the survival of threatened or endangered species of plants or animals. That the minister obtain this opinion is a mandatory condition precedent to Cabinet exercising its authority to make the regulations in question. Therefore, the minister's failure to comply with this condition would presumably deprive Cabinet of its jurisdiction.

Regulations and bylaws are also not permitted to be discriminatory unless the enabling statute explicitly or implicitly authorizes the discrimination. A regulation or bylaw is not considered discriminatory if it treats individuals or groups differently who are in different situations in relation to the subject being regulated. However, a regulation or bylaw that treats individuals or groups in the same situation differently from each other will be invalid unless its enabling statute authorizes such treatment.

Whether a bylaw treats two different groups differently or treats similar groups differently can depend on how one characterizes the groups. For example, if a bylaw prohibits street vendors from setting up their displays on the sidewalk but permits store owners to display their wares on the sidewalk outside their stores, is the bylaw discriminatory or not? The answer depends on whether the bylaw is treating individuals or groups differently who are in different situations or whether it is treating individuals or groups in the same situation differently.

In this case, it could be argued that, because street vendors and store owners are in the same situation—that is, both are merchants—allowing store owners to display goods on the sidewalk but prohibiting street vendors from doing the same discriminates against the street vendors. However, it could also be argued that, while street

---

12 SO 2007, c 6, s 57.

vendors and store owners are both merchants, they are in different situations in relation to the subject being regulated. Store owners pay property taxes on their stores, are responsible for removing snow from the sidewalks in front of their stores, and have other costs flowing from maintaining a permanent facility (such as paying rent), while street vendors do not have these responsibilities. Because store owners and street vendors are in different situations, they may be legitimately subject to different treatment.

> *Parliament alone must possess this delicate power which consists in disad-vantaging one category of citizens in relation to another. … The obvious corollary of this principle is the illegality of any discriminatory regulation which is not authorized by a legislative provision.*
>
> Dussault & Borgeat, *Administrative Law*, 2nd ed,
> vol 1 (Toronto: Carswell, 1985) at 436–37

Finally, a power in a statute to make regulations or bylaws to *regulate* an activity cannot validly be used to *prohibit* the activity. For example, if a statute authorizes a municipality to pass bylaws to control traffic flow on the sidewalks of a town, a bylaw that prohibits street vendors from carrying on their business everywhere in the town (rather than restricts them to areas where they will not impede pedestrian traffic) would be invalid because it is beyond the municipality's jurisdiction.

Procedural Fairness or Natural Justice

As discussed, historically, the courts imposed fairness requirements only in relation to quasi-judicial decisions affecting rights, not in relation to administrative decisions or decisions affecting privileges or other interests. This fairness requirement for quasi-judicial decisions made by tribunals was known as "natural justice." After decades of criticism of this often arbitrary distinction, in 1979, the Supreme Court ruled that certain minimal rules of fair procedure apply to the exercise of *any* statutory power that may result in the deprivation of a right or the denial of a benefit. The courts called this "procedural fairness." Today, "procedural fairness" is usually the term used to encompass both "natural justice" before tribunals and the duty of administrative decision-makers to follow fair procedures.

What Is the Duty of Procedural Fairness?

The duty of procedural fairness—also known as the duty to act fairly or the "fairness doctrine"—states that whenever a public body (or, in some cases, a private one) makes a decision that affects a person's interests more directly or substantially than it affects the general public, that body has two obligations:

1. a duty to notify the person of the intended decision and the reasons for it, and to provide the person with an opportunity to challenge that decision if it is unfavourable; and

2. an obligation to provide an impartial decision-maker.

Although it is easy to state, the fairness principle is not so easy to apply. It is a procedural rule rather than a substantive rule, which means that it does not provide a right to a fair decision, but a right to a decision reached through a fair *process*. What constitutes a fair process will vary from case to case. It will depend on the character of the body making the decision (for example, whether it is a tribunal or a regulator), the kinds of functions that the body carries out, the nature of the decision, and the importance of the decision to the persons who will be affected by it.[13]

Which Bodies Must Act Fairly?

The duty to act fairly can apply to all kinds of regulatory bodies as well as to many kinds of decisions. However, the procedural safeguards to be applied may be more rigorous for some agencies than for others. In particular, tribunals are required to follow formal procedures similar to those that the courts must follow. In addition, the second component of the duty to act fairly—the obligation of impartiality—applies more strictly to tribunals than to other government decision-makers.

Decisions Subject to the Requirement to Act Fairly

The Supreme Court has said that procedural fairness obligations arise when a department or an agency makes "any administrative decision which is not of a legislative nature and which affects the rights, privileges or interests of an individual."[14] Statutes that have codified this fairness right describe the types of decisions to which the requirement applies (see the box feature "Decisions Requiring Procedural Fairness").

Decisions Requiring Procedural Fairness

Alberta's *Administrative Procedures and Jurisdiction Act* applies when a person's "rights" are affected (s 1(b)). More particularly, the Act refers to decisions that grant or revoke permission to do something, affect a status provided for under a statute, approve an act that would otherwise be illegal, prohibit someone from doing something that would otherwise be legal, or impose a duty on someone (s 1(c)).

Ontario's *Statutory Powers Procedure Act* applies to decisions that affect a person's legal rights, powers, privileges, immunities, duties, or liabilities, including eligibility to receive a benefit or a licence (s 1(1)).

Quebec's *Administrative Justice Act* applies generally to "decisions made in respect of a citizen," but specifically mentions indemnities and benefits (s 1).

The kinds of decisions that typically attract a duty to act fairly include the following:

- *Licensing*   "Licensing" is the approval of some ongoing activity, usually professional or commercial in nature, such as permission to practise law or

---

13   *Baker v Canada (Minister of Citizenship and Immigration)*, [1999] 2 SCR 817.

14   *Cardinal v Director of Kent Institution*, [1985] 2 SCR 643 at 653.

medicine, sell real estate or cars, own or drive a taxi, operate a waste disposal site, or run a trucking firm. All of these are regulated activities, subject to specific criteria for qualification and to standards or rules of conduct.

- *Issuing permits*   The issuing of permits usually involves approval of individual projects. Building a house, constructing a septic system, installing a dock at the cottage, or damming a stream are all activities that require an application to government for permission to proceed with the project.

- *Granting or denying a benefit*   Government administrators decide whether individuals qualify for financial allowances such as social assistance, insurance benefits, pension payments, and tax relief.

- *Determining eligibility to receive a service*   Government officials also decide whether individuals qualify to receive certain publicly funded services. For example, some individuals with disabilities are entitled to a specialized transportation service provided by the local public transit authority, and an official in a government office or agency may be responsible for determining whether a particular applicant has the extent or type of handicap that qualifies him or her for this service. Similarly, a community care access centre may assess the circumstances of an elderly person living at home to determine whether he or she qualifies for the assistance of a nurse, cook, or cleaner in order to remain at home and avoid institutional care.

Decisions Not Subject to the Requirement to Act Fairly

Generally, government bodies and officials are not required to engage in public consultation before they make legislative or policy decisions, or decisions that address minor administrative matters. (However, see the box feature "Legitimate Expectations: The Exception to the Rule.")

Legislative or policy decisions establish rules or guidelines that apply to a particular group of persons. Often, the group is very large. Although the decision may have a substantial impact on any particular person, because everyone in the group is affected by the decision, no one has a right to be consulted. For example, when statutes are passed by elected assemblies, the proposed legislation is scrutinized by the entire body of elected representatives, and any representative may vote against the measure. However, the legislators have no additional duty to inform the persons who will be affected or to seek public input before the proposed statute becomes law.

Legitimate Expectations: The Exception to the Rule

Although there is generally no duty for government bodies and officials to consult with the public or with individuals for policy or minor administrative decisions, there is an exception under the rule of legitimate expectations. Where a department or agency raises expectations of a certain result or that a certain procedure will be followed, either by promises or by a course of action on which people have come to rely, the department or agency may not change its practice or procedure where the change will have an adverse effect without first notifying the persons who will be affected and giving them an opportunity to comment on the proposed change.

In practice, such consultation often does take place, through discussion papers and invitations to make submissions to committees of the legislature or municipal council. Similarly, when Cabinet or a minister makes a regulation, although there is no common law duty to consult those affected or the general public, sometimes discussion does take place, and a few statutes now require it.

In addition, where an employment relationship between a government body and an office holder is completely governed by an employment contract, the government has no duty to follow procedural fairness requirements before terminating employment (such as providing a hearing). Although the Supreme Court had ruled—in *Nicholson*[15] and in *Knight v Indian Head School Division No 19*[16]—that public employees were entitled to procedural fairness, in *Dunsmuir v New Brunswick*[17] the Court stated that where a public employee is employed under a contract of employment, the applicable law governing his or her dismissal is the law of contract, not administrative law.

Components of Procedural Fairness

Duty to Give Notice and an Opportunity to Be Heard

The kind of notice that must be given and the nature of the opportunity to be heard vary according to the authority responsible for making the decision and the impact of the decision on the person affected.

The responsible authority is determined by the legislature. A particular type of decision may be delegated to an individual official or to a more formal tribunal.

Where the decision is delegated to an official, the duty of fairness is relatively simple. Often, the official need only give notice of the intended decision, explain in writing the rationale for it and the facts on which it is based, and provide affected persons with an opportunity to respond. An opportunity for a written response is usually sufficient, and seldom is a chance to respond orally considered necessary. Rarely is it necessary to provide the kind of hearing held by a court.

Where the decision is delegated to a tribunal, much more stringent requirements apply. They often include the opportunity to be heard in person, to be represented by an advocate or lawyer, to summon witnesses to appear and testify, and to cross-examine the witnesses of the government. In addition, there is often an opportunity for others who may be affected by the decision, such as business competitors or neighbours, to participate in the proceedings.

> The categories of administrative bodies involved range from administrative tribunals whose adjudicative functions are very similar to those of the courts, such as grievance arbitrators in labour law, to bodies that perform multiple tasks and whose adjudicative functions are merely one aspect of broad duties

---

15 *Supra* note 5.

16 [1990] 1 SCR 653.

17 2008 SCC 9, [2008] 1 SCR 190.

and powers that sometimes include regulation-making power. The notion of administrative decision-maker also includes administrative managers such as ministers or officials who perform policy-making discretionary functions within the apparatus of government. The extent of the duties imposed on the administrative decision-maker will then depend on the nature of the functions to be performed and on the legislature's intention. In each case, the entire body of legislation that defines the functions of an administrative decision-maker, and the framework within which his or her activities are carried on, will have to be carefully examined. The determination of the actual content of the duties of procedural fairness that apply requires such an analysis.

Imperial Oil Ltd v Quebec (Minister of the Environment),
2003 SCC 58, [2003] 2 SCR 624 at para 31

Obligation of Impartiality

The duty of impartiality applies to all who carry out decision-making functions within the structure of government. However, it applies in different ways to different administrative authorities—for example, it has a very different application in decision-making by government officials than it has in relation to tribunals. In addition, the Supreme Court of Canada has stated that impartiality does not apply to ministers in the same way that it does to tribunals.[18]

The right to an impartial decision-maker entails two requirements:

1. the decision-maker must approach the decision with an open mind, and
2. the decision-maker must be independent.

Only the first requirement applies to government administrators. These officials are not expected to act independently; indeed, their very purpose is to carry out government policy. However, they are still expected to be unbiased, to act in good faith, and to avoid conflicts of interest. For example, a person who is responsible for purchasing equipment for a government department and is closely related to the owner of a company competing for a contract should not take part in the decision-making process because there would be an appearance of partiality.

Tribunals, on the other hand, often hear cases in which the government is one of the parties. To be able to provide a hearing that both *is* fair and *appears* fair, they must have sufficient structural separation and independence from the government to enable them to make decisions without fear of reprisals as well as without any appearance of bias.

A tribunal may appear to have a built-in bias where one of the parties that appears before it is a government department that approves its budget, appoints its members, provides its staff, or exercises control in other ways that may suggest that the

---

18 *Imperial Oil Ltd v Quebec (Minister of the Environment)* 2003 SCC 58, [2003] 2 SCR 624 at paras 31–39.

department has influence over the tribunal's decisions. This kind of built-in bias is called **institutional bias**. If an agency's independence is restricted by the statutory framework that governs it, the appearance of bias does not prevent the tribunal from hearing the case, since the legislature has the right—subject to any violation of the Constitution—to impose such restrictions. However, if institutional bias results from administrative arrangements that are not required by law, the entire tribunal could be disqualified from hearing a case.

Importance of Separation of Functions

Some government agencies are multipurpose bodies responsible for a variety of functions. Where individuals or groups within a multipurpose agency carry out conflicting functions, there is a risk of bias in decision-making.

Agencies should be guided by the maxim: "No one shall be judge in his own cause." A person who examines the basis for a dispute and forms an opinion on the correct outcome should not also act as the prosecutor and make the final decision. If the person has already reached a conclusion and is arguing that it be accepted, that person cannot be impartial in deciding whether the decision is correct and fair.

For this reason, Crown prosecutors in criminal cases are independent of the police who conduct the investigation, and they have the power to drop charges even if the police believe that the case should proceed to trial. Similarly, it is improper for a prosecutor to have any discussion with a judge outside the courtroom about a case that he or she is arguing.

The same kinds of restrictions apply to agencies. When an agency undertakes an investigation, carries out a prosecution, holds a hearing, and renders a decision, it is important to avoid conflicts of interest between the individuals or groups carrying out these different functions. This is achieved in multi-function agencies by ensuring that the investigators, prosecutors, tribunal members, and others involved in the decision-making function operate at arm's length from each other as well as from the government to which the agency reports.

The duty of impartiality ranks among the fundamental obligations of the courts. The Canadian Charter of Rights and Freedoms *recognizes the right of any person charged with an offence to be tried by an independent and impartial tribunal (s. 11(d)). In the matters which fall within the legislative jurisdiction of Quebec, s. 23 of the* Charter of Human Rights and Freedoms, *[CQLR] c C-12, recognizes the right to a fair hearing by an independent and impartial tribunal as a fundamental human right. The concept of impartiality refers to the decision-maker's state of mind . . . . The decision-maker must approach the issue submitted to him or her with an open mind, not influenced by personal interests or outside pressure. It is not sufficient that the decision-maker be impartial in his or her own mind, internally, to the satisfaction of his or her own conscience. It is also necessary that the decision-maker appear impartial in the objective view of a reasonable and well-informed observer.*

The duty of impartiality, which originated with the judiciary, has now become part of the principles of administrative justice.

Imperial Oil Ltd v Quebec (Minister of the Environment),
2003 SCC 58, [2003] 2 SCR 624 at para 28

Where Fairness Obligations Are Found

In addition to any policies, rules, or guidelines that an agency might voluntarily impose on itself, there are five main sources of fairness obligations that bind agencies:

1. common law,
2. individual enabling statutes,
3. statutes of general application to agencies or tribunals,
4. the *Canadian Charter of Rights and Freedoms*,[19] and
5. Section 35 of the *Constitution Act, 1982*.

For the most part, the rules of fair procedure have been developed by judges as part of the common law. A number of these fairness principles have been incorporated into provincial statutes that establish tribunals, while others have been set out in the Charter. (The relationship between the Charter and administrative law is discussed in Chapter 4, The Charter and Its Relationship to Administrative Law.)

In practice, procedural fairness requirements for an agency usually consist of the following:

- a few statutory rules;
- rules of procedure, guidelines, and practice directions developed by the agency; and
- supplementary requirements that courts have "read into" the agency's enabling statute in their decisions in order to ensure fairness.

For a more detailed discussion of procedural fairness, see Chapters 6 and 7.

Enabling Statutes for Individual Tribunals

Quebec's *Environment Quality Act*[20] (EQA) is a typical example of an enabling statute that codifies fairness procedures. It permits the minister of the environment to issue pollution-prevention and pollution-cleanup orders, sets out the procedures that the minister must follow to ensure fairness, and provides for an appeal of the order to the Administrative Tribunal of Quebec (ATQ). The fairness procedures that

---

19   Part I of the *Constitution Act, 1982*, being Schedule B to the *Canada Act 1982* (UK), 1982, c 11.

20   CQLR c Q-2.

the tribunal must follow are set out in a separate statute, the *Administrative Justice Act*[21] (AJA), and are discussed in the next section.

The EQA permits the minister to order a person who has caused contamination to the environment to arrange for studies to be conducted to determine the nature and extent of the contamination; for the preparation of a remediation plan; and, ultimately, for decontamination of the polluted soil or water. The EQA also sets out rules for procedural fairness in issuing these orders. At least 15 days before the order is to take effect, notice and a copy of the order must be sent to the person who will be required to carry it out. The order must include a statement of the minister's reasons for issuing it, while the notice must tell the recipient when the order will take effect and offer him or her an opportunity to make "observations." The notice must also be accompanied by a copy of every analysis, study, or other technical report considered by the minister in deciding to make the order (s 31.44).

Notice must also be given to the owner of the property, if this is someone other than the person ordered to carry out the work, and to the clerk of the municipality where the contamination is located (s 31.44). The municipality, the owner of the property, and any other persons affected by the order have the right to appeal it to the ATQ (s 96).

Statutes of General Application: Ontario, Alberta, Quebec, and British Columbia

As discussed, the concept of procedural fairness is based on common law principles developed and applied by the courts. Once common law principles are well established, governments often codify them by setting them out in statutes.

At various times, the federal government and the governments of several provinces have considered proposals to set out in a statute some minimum rules of fair procedure based on the common law principles, which all agencies—or at least all tribunals—would be required to follow unless specifically exempted. This approach has the benefit of promoting consistency in the application of fairness procedures among tribunals and of making the rules available in one place. Despite these advantages, only Ontario, British Columbia, Alberta, and Quebec have passed statutes incorporating such general codes of procedure.

Ontario's *Statutory Powers Procedure Act*[22] (SPPA) and British Columbia's *Administrative Tribunals Act*[23] (ATA) apply only to tribunals, not to government officials. The SPPA sets out procedures that all tribunals must follow (unless exempted by another statute) when they are required by law to hold a hearing or to give parties an opportunity for a hearing before the tribunal exercises "a statutory power of decision" (s 3(1)). The ATA applies to tribunals, but only to the extent that the tribunal's enabling statute explicitly provides for this. Thus, a statute that establishes or governs a tribunal may not state that the ATA applies, or it may provide that only some of the provisions of the ATA apply to the tribunal. When the ATA was passed in June

---

21   CQLR c J-3.

22   RSO 1990, c S.22.

23   SBC 2004, c 45.

2004, it amended 25 enabling statutes to make the ATA apply, at least in part, to a number of tribunals dealing with matters such as health, transportation, housing, labour relations, employment standards, property assessment, and preservation of farmland.

Unlike the SPPA and ATA, which apply only to tribunals, Alberta's *Administrative Procedures and Jurisdiction Act*[24] (APJA) also applies to other persons authorized to exercise a "statutory power" (ss 2 and 1(a)). However, in contrast to the SPPA, which applies to all tribunals that are not specifically exempted, the APJA applies only to seven agencies designated by a regulation under the APJA and to a few others designated under other statutes.

Unlike the SPPA and the ATA, the APJA does not apply only when the law requires a hearing before a tribunal; instead, its provisions apply before a designated agency makes any statutory decision affecting rights or interests. The APJA requirements, however, are less stringent and formal than those imposed by the SPPA. They reflect the limited and flexible requirements of procedural fairness that the courts have imposed on internal government decision-makers, rather than the stricter rules of natural justice that tribunals are required to follow. Thus, although the APJA covers both formal, adversarial hearings and more informal, internal decision-making processes, its requirements are geared toward the latter and may not always be adequate to cover the former.

The SPPA and the APJA use different words to describe the kinds of decisions to which the specified hearing procedures do and do not apply. However, the results are similar. Both statutes apply to decisions authorized by a statute or a regulation under a statute that affect the legal rights, powers, privileges, immunities, duties, or liabilities of a person, or a person's eligibility to receive some benefit, licence, or approval. The required procedures do not apply to hearings held by a court, legislative activities, or investigations or inquiries that result in non-binding recommendations. The ATA, on the other hand, applies to all decisions of the tribunals to which it applies.

Because the SPPA and the APJA apply to persons who have been authorized under a statute to make decisions that affect the rights of individuals, and not more restrictively to government or public authorities, their procedural requirements must also be followed by non-governmental organizations whenever such organizations are making a decision that they have been empowered to make by a statute. Therefore, entities such as hospitals, universities, self-governing professions, and even private clubs and churches may sometimes have to follow the procedures set out in the SPPA or the APJA. For example, whenever Ontario's association of professional engineers intends to hold a hearing to decide whether to discipline a member, the member is entitled to details of the allegations against him or her prior to the hearing, as required by section 8 of the SPPA.

Both the APJA and the SPPA require the decision-making body to give notice to anyone whose rights will be affected by its decision. Under section 3 of the APJA, this is notice of the intention to make a decision, since the statute does not apply

---

24 RSA 2000, c A-3.

only to bodies that hold hearings. Under section 6 of the SPPA, the tribunal must give the parties to a proceeding reasonable notice of the hearing. Both statutes leave it up to the decision-maker to decide the timing of the notice, although section 10 of the APJA gives the provincial Cabinet authority to establish deadlines. With respect to the content of the notice, other than stating that the notice must be "adequate," the APJA leaves this to the decision-maker; however, section 10 of the APJA gives the Cabinet authority to make regulations specifying the information to be provided in a notice.

Section 6 of the SPPA requires that the notice include

- the statutory authority for the hearing;
- the time and purpose of the hearing;
- whether the hearing will be held orally, electronically, or in writing; and
- other requirements specific to each type of hearing.

The ATA also requires that notice be given of the intention to hold a hearing and specifies information that must be included in all notices, as well as appropriate methods of delivering the notices. However, it does not specify who shall be considered a "party" to a hearing or otherwise sufficiently affected by the proceedings to be entitled to notice. That is left to the enabling statute for each tribunal.

The APJA, the SPPA, and the ATA all require the decision-maker to give parties an opportunity to provide relevant evidence. However, under section 10.1 of the SPPA and under the ATA, the tribunal must permit reasonable cross-examination at an oral or electronic hearing, while section 5 of the APJA requires the decision-maker to provide a party with an opportunity for cross-examination only if information adverse to the interests of the party cannot be adequately contradicted or explained by other means.

The ATA and the SPPA give parties the right to be represented by a lawyer or other agent, but section 6 of the APJA states that the right to make representations to the decision-maker does not include the right to be represented by a lawyer.

Under the SPPA, the "default" position is a requirement for an oral hearing. Any departure from this format to a written or electronic hearing must be justified (ss 6(4)(b) and 6(5)(c)). In contrast, section 6 of the APJA states that the right to make representations does *not* include the right to make them orally unless written representations are not adequate.

The APJA, the ATA, and the SPPA all make it optional for the tribunal to require an oath before a witness or other party provides evidence, and permit the decision-maker to receive evidence that would be inadmissible in court—for example, "hearsay" evidence (for a discussion of this kind of evidence, see Chapter 11, Presenting Evidence at a Hearing).

Although the APJA is less specific than the SPPA and the ATA about the information that must be given in a notice of intention to make a decision, it does impose a duty on the decision-maker to inform the party whose rights will be affected by its decision of any facts in its possession or allegations contrary to the interests of the party in sufficient detail to permit the party to understand those facts or allegations, and to explain or contradict them (s 4). The SPPA permits tribunals to establish disclosure rules (s 25.1) and, if the character or conduct of a party is in issue, grants the party the right to be given reasonable information about the allegations before the hearing (s 8). The ATA permits the tribunal to make rules specifying what information will be provided to parties (s 11).

Finally, the APJA and the ATA require the decision-maker to give all parties a written decision, including the reasons on which a decision is based (APJA, s 7; ATA, ss 51 and 52). The APJA goes even further, requiring that the decision include the decision-maker's findings of fact. In contrast, the SPPA requires a written decision with reasons only at the request of a party, and no statement of facts is required (s 17(1)).

The SPPA and ATA deal with many issues that are not addressed in the APJA—primarily, issues that arise in the context of a formal hearing of the type required for tribunals but not in the context of the kinds of informal decision-making processes covered by the APJA. Other matters covered by the SPPA and the ATA include the authority of the tribunal to make rules of procedure, the summonsing of witnesses and their presentation of evidence, penalties for the failure of a witness to obey a summons, disclosure of evidence by parties, pre-hearing conferences, the correction of errors in tribunal decisions, enforcement of decisions, the effect of appeals on the operation of decisions, and the powers of the tribunal to control its process.

Quebec's *Charter of Human Rights and Freedoms*[25] states that every person has a right to a full and fair public hearing by an independent and impartial tribunal when that person's rights are to be determined. What is "full and fair" is left to be decided by the courts in their interpretation of this provision, and to be fleshed out in other statutes, such as the AJA.

Quebec's AJA sets out minimum rules for all administrative decisions, followed by more stringent rules for the ATQ and other bodies set up to resolve disputes. The ATQ (which, as noted above, was established by the AJA) replaces numerous individual tribunals with one large tribunal that has several divisions and makes decisions in various areas of regulation. The tribunal has a social affairs division, a territory and environment division, an immovable property division, and an economic affairs division.

Under the AJA, all administrative decision-makers are required to act in a manner that is consistent with a duty to act fairly (s 2). This includes giving citizens an opportunity to provide the decision-maker with any information that may be useful in making the decision, making the decision expeditiously, communicating the decision clearly, and providing the person affected with any information needed to permit the person to communicate with the decision-making authority (s 4).

Also under the AJA, when an authority intends to order someone to do something, it must first inform the person of its intention and the reasons for the proposed order, advise the person of the substance of any complaints against him or her, and give the person the opportunity to present observations and produce documents (s 5.5).

---

25 CQLR c C-12.

Adjudicative agencies are required to act not only fairly but also impartially. Procedures specified under sections 10 to 13 of the AJA include

- holding hearings in public (except where a hearing behind closed doors is necessary to maintain public order);
- rejecting evidence that is obtained improperly or that is privileged;
- giving the parties the opportunity to prove facts and present arguments;
- providing assistance to parties where doing so is necessary and fair;
- allowing parties to be represented by lawyers or agents; and
- providing parties with a final decision in writing, including the reasons on which the decision is based.

Section 35 of the Constitution Act, 1982

The Charter is not the only part of Canada's Constitution that requires the government to follow fair procedures. The *Constitution Act, 1982* includes recognition of Aboriginal rights under section 35, which provides, in part:

> 35(1) The existing aboriginal and treaty rights of the aboriginal peoples of Canada are hereby recognized and affirmed.

In *Delgamuukw v. The Queen*,[26] the Supreme Court of Canada interpreted this section to impose on government a duty to adequately consult First Nations before approving projects that may impact lands and resources subject to native land claims and to provide compensation. The Court ruled that aboriginal title to lands and resources such as trees and minerals exists. It said that Aboriginal rights are not absolute. They can be infringed by both the federal and provincial governments. However, any infringements must be justified. The infringement must be in furtherance of a compelling and substantial legislative objective, and it must be preceded by adequate consultation and accompanied by compensation.

The Court did not discuss what kind or amount of consultation would be "adequate" and it did not provide any examples. This was left to be resolved on a case-by-case basis, developing a common law of Aboriginal consultation rights. In one case involving the fishing practices of an Aboriginal group, the British Columbia Supreme Court ruled that the duty of consultation on proposed fishing restrictions required the BC government to "fully inform itself of the fishing practices of the aboriginal group and their views of the conservation measures," seek advice, provide relevant information, afford time for full consideration, and formulate a reasonable response to any objections.[27]

The scope and nature of the duty to consult will vary with the circumstances and the limits will develop through future court rulings. As one pair of commentators have said:

---

26 *Delgamuukw v The Queen*, [1997] 3 SCR 1010.

27 *George v Marczyk* (1998), 53 BCLR (3d) 1 (SC).

In some cases, when the breach is relatively minor, it will be no more than a duty to discuss important decisions that will be taken with respect to lands held pursuant to aboriginal title. Of course, even in these rare cases when the minimum acceptable standard is consultation, this consultation must be in good faith, and with the intention of substantially addressing the concerns of the aboriginal peoples whose lands are at issue. In most cases, it will be significantly deeper than mere consultation. Some cases may even require the full consent of an aboriginal nation, particularly when provinces enact hunting and fishing regulations in relation to aboriginal lands.[28]

In its 2014 decision in *Tsilhqot'in Nation v British Columbia*,[29] the Supreme Court raised the bar for consultation. The Court stated that to justify infringing on Aboriginal title on the basis of the greater public good, the government must show, among other things, that it discharged its procedural duty to consult and accommodate. The Court went on to say that the duty to consult applies both where Aboriginal title has been established by agreement or court decision and where the claim has not yet been decided. The level of consultation and accommodation required is proportional to the strength of the land claim and to the seriousness of the adverse impact that the contemplated government action would have on the claimed right: "A dubious or peripheral claim may attract a mere duty of notice, while a stronger claim may attract more stringent duties."[30]

The duty to consult must be discharged *before* carrying out the action that could adversely affect the Aboriginal right. Where consultation or accommodation is found to be inadequate, the government decision can be suspended or quashed.

Judicial Review

If an official or body is alleged to have violated any of the other fundamental principles of administrative law, the superior courts have the power to review the alleged violation and rectify it as necessary. This process is known as **judicial review** and is an inherent power of the superior courts, meaning that it exists even where no statute authorizes it.

Anyone who is directly and substantially affected by an administrative body's action and believes the body acted unfairly or outside its jurisdiction has the right to make an application to a superior court for judicial review, even where a statute provides no right of appeal. The right to judicial review is an aspect of the rule of law because it ensures that government decisions are made in accordance with the law, and not the personal preferences or biases of decision-makers. It is constitutional in nature, meaning that it cannot be taken away by a provision in a statute that seems to prohibit review of a body's decisions. As a result, it is available even where a statute states that it prohibits courts from reviewing an administrative body's decisions.

28 Michael Bryant & Lorne Sossin, *Public Law* (Toronto: Carswell, 2002) at 32.

29 2014 SCC 44, [2014] 2 SCR 257.

30 *Ibid* at para 79.

In addition to the inherent right of the superior courts to hear judicial review applications, some specialized courts have been established by statute specifically to hear judicial review applications or have been given statutory authority to carry out this function. The Federal Court of Canada has statutory authority to conduct judicial reviews of the actions of federal government departments and agencies. In Ontario, the Divisional Court, a branch of the Superior Court of Ontario, hears judicial review applications.

Generally, courts hearing judicial review applications can

- declare that an action taken by a public official or agency is contrary to the law;
- quash a decision already made by an official or agency (in this case, the court may substitute its own decision or order, or may send the matter back to be decided again, following the correct procedures or principles);
- order an official or agency to take any action that he, she, or it is required by law to take;
- forbid a public official or agency from taking or from continuing any action that he, she, or it is prohibited by law from taking;
- require an official or agency to follow a fair procedure in making a decision; and
- order an agency to free a person who is illegally imprisoned.

For a more detailed discussion of judicial review, see Chapter 16, Challenging Decisions of Tribunals and Administrative Agencies.

CHAPTER SUMMARY

As the functions of government increasingly came to affect Canadians' lives, and because the new administrative agencies were not directly accountable to the public, it became apparent that a legal structure was needed to prevent government departments and agencies from exceeding their authority or acting in an arbitrary manner. This represented the beginning of administrative law.

Over time, the courts developed several principles of administrative law to guide and restrict the exercise of statutory powers by departments and agencies of government. Today, the fundamental principles of administrative law include procedural fairness or natural justice, and principles related to jurisdiction, discretion, subdelegation, the validity of subordinate legislation, and judicial review.

The powers granted to a government body by statute constitute its jurisdiction, and administrative law prohibits an agency from straying beyond those powers in carrying out its functions. In addition, where government agencies have the right to choose between options in making a decision, they must exercise this discretion within their jurisdiction and in a reasonable manner; they must not fetter their discretion—that is, rule out options that the law requires them to consider—but they may promote consistency in the exercise of discretion. The rule against subdelegation prohibits a person to whom the legislature has delegated a function from delegating that function to someone else unless the legislation explicitly or implicitly authorizes such subdelegation, while the rules governing subordinate legislation—that is, regulations and bylaws—require that, for such legislation to be valid, it must be consistent with the objectives of its enabling statute and the scope of the regulatory powers set out in that statute.

Most importantly, all government decision-makers must follow a fair procedure when making decisions that affect individuals' rights, privileges, or interests. At a minimum, decision-makers must consult affected parties and provide them with an opportunity to present their views before a final decision is made. In the case of tribunals, there are more rigid rules of procedural fairness, sometimes called the rules of natural justice, which require a full hearing before the tribunal makes its decision. In addition, procedural fairness requires that decision-makers be impartial. Members of the administrative body must not be biased for or against a person seeking to exercise a right, or obtain a privilege or benefit (or, in the cases of tribunals, a party to their proceedings); must keep an open mind; and must not have a conflict of interest. In addition, a tribunal must be structured in a way that ensures the independence of its members, particularly from other government bodies or officials.

Procedural fairness rules are found in agencies' enabling statutes, in other statutes under which agencies make decisions, in common law principles applied by the courts, and in the *Canadian Charter of Rights and Freedoms* and Quebec's *Charter of Human Rights and Freedoms*. Several provinces have statutes that create uniform procedural fairness requirements for a variety of tribunals, and, in some cases, other agencies. In addition, section 35 of the *Constitution Act, 1982* imposes a duty on governments to adequately consult Aboriginal people potentially affected by resource development and regulatory decisions on lands to which they hold or claim title.

If any of the other principles of administrative law are violated, the final principle provides that the superior courts have an inherent power to supervise the actions of departments and agencies. Through judicial review of government action, the courts can overturn any act or omission by which a department or agency acts outside its jurisdiction or follows an unfair procedure in making a decision.

KEY TERMS

declining jurisdiction: failure of an official or agency to carry out a statutory function that it has a duty to perform

discretion: the power of a government official or agency to choose a course of action from among a variety of options available under the law

fettering discretion: in relation to the actions of a statutory decision-maker, refusing to consider an option that is available under the law, or refusing to consider any factor that is relevant to the choice of an option, when making a decision that affects a person's rights or interests

implied powers doctrine: the common law rule that agencies have whatever additional powers are necessarily incidental to their explicit powers; a court will find these powers by necessary implication only where the jurisdiction sought is necessary to accomplish the objectives of the legislative scheme and is essential to the body fulfilling its mandate; *see* necessary implication

inherent powers doctrine: the common law rule that an agency has an inherent power to utilize a procedure that is reasonably necessary to carry out its statutory functions even if that power is not explicitly set out in a statute

institutional bias: bias or the appearance of bias on the part of a group of decision-makers in an agency, or of the agency as a whole, arising from aspects of the agency's structure or functions that suggest a lack of independence from a government official or body affected by a decision of the agency

judicial review: the exercise by a superior court or other court granted authority by statute of its supervisory authority over ministries and other government agencies by reviewing whether they have carried out their functions in accordance with the principles of administrative law

jurisdiction: the scope of the authority or powers conferred on a government body or official by legislation or by common law

legitimate expectations: the principle that public officials who create the expectation of a certain result, or an expectation that a certain practice or procedure will be followed, should not be able to change that result, practice, or procedure where the change will have an adverse effect without first notifying those who will be affected and giving them an opportunity to comment on the proposed change

natural justice: a body of rules or set of principles of fair procedure that tribunals must follow; *see* procedural fairness

necessary implication: an implication so probable that it would be unreasonable to draw any other inference from the facts; *see* implied powers doctrine

procedural fairness: the requirement that a decision-maker acting under a statutory power of decision must give any person whose rights, privileges, or interests may be affected by a decision reasonable notice of the intended decision and the reasons for it, and an opportunity to respond, and must be impartial, even if the function of the decision-maker is not quasi-judicial in nature; *see* natural justice

subdelegation: in relation to a power or authority that a statute has delegated to a particular person, the act of delegating that power or authority to another person

CASES TO CONSIDER

Procedural Fairness

Nicholson v Haldimand-Norfolk Regional Police Commissioners, [1979] 1 SCR 311

FACTS: Nicholson was hired as a constable under an employment contract that included a 12-month probationary period. After 11 months, Nicholson was promoted. Three months later, the municipality terminated Nicholson's employment. A provision of a regulation under the *Police Act* provided that no police officer was subject to any penalty except after a hearing on appeal, subject to exceptions including the authority of the board "to dispense with the services of any constable within 18 months of his appointment to the force."

ISSUE: Was Nicholson entitled to procedural fairness?

DECISION: Nicholson could not claim the procedural protections of a constable who had worked for longer than 18 months. However, regardless of whether his dismissal was an administrative function or a quasi-judicial function, he had the right to be treated fairly. He should have been told why his employment was being terminated and allowed the chance to respond. If this had been done, and the board's decision was not arbitrary and was made in good faith, his termination would not have been reviewable by the courts. (However, see *Dunsmuir v New Brunswick*, 2008 SCC 9, [2008] 1 SCR 190. Why was Mr. Nicholson entitled to procedural fairness while Mr. Dunsmuir was not?)

Procedural Fairness and the Appearance of Impartiality

Imperial Oil Ltd v Quebec (Minister of the Environment), 2003 SCC 58, [2003] 2 SCR 624, 231 DLR (4th) 577

FACTS: There was environmental contamination at a site once operated by Imperial Oil, and the minister of the environment ordered Imperial to pay for and submit a site-characterization study. Imperial refused to do the study, and asked the Administrative Tribunal of Quebec to quash the minister's order. One of Imperial Oil's arguments was that the rules of procedural fairness were violated because the minister was in a conflict of interest because the minister had been involved in earlier decontamination work and was being sued concerning contamination of the site by the present owners of the land. This case was heard by the tribunal, then by the Superior Court, then by the Quebec Court of Appeal, and eventually by the Supreme Court of Canada.

ISSUE: Did the minister have the appearance of impartiality required by the rules of procedural fairness?

DECISION: The minister had the authority to issue this kind of order under the *Environment Quality Act*, which allows for broad ministerial discretion. The minister's decision under the statute was mainly political, involving his duty to serve the public interest; he was not performing an adjudicative function. While the minister did have to comply with procedural fairness rules—such as providing notice to interested persons and providing reasons for the decision—the principle of impartiality did not apply to this decision. The minister was representing the public interest, not his own personal interests. His decision was upheld.

Rule Against Subdelegation

Can-Du Air Ltd v Canada (Minister of Transport) (1994), 25 Admin LR (2d) 231 (FCTD)

FACTS: Can-Du Air Ltd. applied to the minister of transport for a certificate allowing it to operate a heliport. Can-Du passed all safety, operational, and environmental inspections. However, the minister of transport refused to approve the certificate based, in part, on the opposition of the city council and the deputy minister of municipal affairs, who claimed that the heliport was against the public interest.

ISSUE: Did the minister of transport make an unauthorized delegation of her decision-making power by relying on the opinions of the city council and the deputy minister of a different ministry?

DECISION: The minister of transport did not improperly subdelegate her power. Neither the city council nor the deputy minister of municipal affairs made the final decision. Rather, the minister of transport considered their opinions and agreed with them that the heliport would not be in the public interest.

Legitimacy of Subordinate Legislation

Katz Group Canada Inc v Ontario (Health and Long-Term Care), 2013 SCC 64, [2013] 3 SCR 810

FACTS: In 1985, Ontario passed two statutes to reduce the cost to consumers of purchasing prescription drugs, the *Drug Interchangeability and Dispensing Fee Act* and the *Ontario Drug Benefit Act*. The first statute authorizes the minister to designate a cheaper generic drug as interchangeable with a more expensive brand-name drug. Pharmacists are required to sell to customers the cheaper drug if they arrive with a prescription for the brand-name drug. The second statute prohibits drug manufacturers from giving pharmacies a substantial rebate to induce them to buy their products. The price that manufacturers charged and that customers paid was artificially increased to the extent of the rebates. So the expected savings did not occur, and manufacturers continued to charge high prices for generic drugs. Instead of the rebates, manufacturers started paying pharmacies $800 million a year in "professional allowances." As a result, the acts were amended to eliminate the payment of professional allowances.

The regulations were also amended to prevent pharmacies from controlling manufacturers who sell generic drugs under their own name but do not fabricate them. Under the regulations, these "private label" products cannot be listed in the Formulary or designated as interchangeable.

ISSUE: Were the regulations inconsistent with the purpose of the statutes under which they were made, and therefore *ultra vires*?

DECISION: The intent of the two statutes was to control the cost of prescription drugs in Ontario without compromising safety. This included promoting transparent pricing and eliminating price inflation along the drug supply chain, both with the objective of lowering drug costs. The purpose of the regulations was to prevent a possible mechanism for circumventing the ban on rebates that had kept drug prices high. If pharmacists were permitted to create their own affiliated manufacturers whom they controlled, they would be directly involved in setting the Formulary prices and would have strong incentives to keep those prices high. Therefore, the regulations were consistent with the statutory purpose of reducing drug costs. The regulations were *intra vires*.

REVIEW QUESTIONS

1. In Chapter 1 you learned that laws can be divided into several categories: common law and statute law, public law and private law, statute law and subordinate legislation, and substantive law and procedural law. Into which of these categories does administrative law fit, and why?

2. What are the six fundamental principles of administrative law?

3. What is the difference between procedural fairness and natural justice, and to what kinds of bodies does each apply?

4. What are the two components of procedural fairness?

5. What is "jurisdiction," and why is it important that agencies not act outside this?

6. What is "discretion," and what considerations must a decision-maker bear in mind when exercising discretion?

7. What kinds of action or inaction constitute an abuse of a decision-maker's discretion?

8. What is subdelegation? Why is it often not permitted, and in what circumstances is it allowed?

9. What kinds of decisions must be made using procedures recognized by the courts as fair?

10. What kinds of decisions, if any, are exempt from the requirement to act fairly?

11. What are the components of impartiality, and how do they apply to tribunals and other agencies?

12. Where would you look to find the principles of procedural fairness that apply to

    a. agencies in general,

    b. a particular agency, and

    c. the Aboriginal and treaty rights of Aboriginal peoples?

13. Which courts have a power to conduct a judicial review of the decisions of administrative bodies, and what kinds of orders can they make?

EXERCISES

1. Choose one principle of administrative law other than judicial review. Define and describe the principle, and explain how it applies in practice. Use case law to support your explanation.

    1. Principle: Decision-makers who exercise powers granted by statute ("administrators") must stay within their legal authority, or jurisdiction.

2. Principle: Administrators must exercise their judgment in a reasonable manner when they have discretion in making decisions.

3. Principle: Administrators must follow fair procedures when making decisions that affect a person's rights or interests. This principle is known as "procedural fairness" or, in some cases, "natural justice." It protects the rights and interests of persons affected by a decision by providing for

   - the right of persons to be given notice of intended decisions that may affect them and the right to be heard before such decisions are put into effect; and

   - the right to an impartial decision-maker.

4. Principle: A person to whom the legislature has delegated authority to carry out a function may not delegate it to someone else. There are some exceptions to this principle, which is known as "the rule against subdelegation" and which is important but less central to administrative law than the first three principles.

5. Principle: To be valid, subordinate (or delegated) legislation must conform to the statute under which it is passed.

6. Principle: If decision-makers violate any of the above principles, the superior courts have an inherent power to intervene to rectify this failure. This intervention is called "judicial review."

2. Pick a tribunal that is excluded in whole or in part from the *Statutory Powers Procedure Act*. Why do you think the legislature decided not to require these tribunals to comply with the SPPA? How does the legislation for the tribunal that you chose comply with the principles of administrative law that you defined during Exercise 1?

FACT SCENARIO

A law society is an association established by a statute of the Legislative Assembly of a province (the *Law Society Act*). Law societies are not government agencies; rather, their membership consists of all lawyers in the province. A law society's board of directors consists of 40 lawyers (called "benchers") elected by the members from among their ranks, as well as four "lay benchers" appointed by the provincial government. Elections are held every four years.

The statute gives the Law Society authority to regulate the legal profession in the province. The purpose of the Law Society is to ensure that anyone who practises law in the province is knowledgeable and competent, and to protect the public against incompetent and dishonest lawyers.

The Law Society administers a course that all law students must pass before they can practise law. If a professor fails a student, the student has a right to appeal his or her mark to a committee of the Law Society. If a law student passes the course, the Law Society issues a licence authorizing that person to practise law.

The Law Society specifies standards of conduct that all lawyers must meet and practices that must be followed in maintaining a law office, such as keeping certain books and records, particularly financial records. It sets these standards through regulations under the *Law Society Act* and through binding rules that it can make under that Act, as well as policies and guidelines that are not binding. The benchers make these regulations, rules, policies, and guidelines.

Through its benchers, the Law Society also makes recommendations to the provincial government about changes to the *Law Society Act*; new regulations that the government, rather than the benchers, may enact; and other changes to practices and legislation that are favourable to its members—for example, increases in the rate of payment for legal aid cases, and regulation of paralegals and others who are not lawyers but do certain kinds of legal work.

The Law Society also provides continuing education programs that lawyers are encouraged to attend.

All practising lawyers in a province are required to carry malpractice insurance provided by a corporation established by the Law Society. The *Law Society Act* prohibits the practice of law without payment of the insurance premiums.

The Law Society carries out random audits of law firms' financial records to ensure that they are being kept properly. It also carries out random reviews of lawyers' files to ensure that lawyers are providing satisfactory services to their clients.

In addition, the staff of the Law Society investigate complaints of malpractice brought by clients and by other lawyers. If the staff find that there has been a breach of any regulation or rule of the *Law Society Act* or that a lawyer has fallen below an appropriate standard of conduct, a hearing is conducted before a panel of benchers to determine whether the lawyer should be disciplined.

Lawyers on the staff of the Law Society act as prosecutors, bringing forward the evidence collected by other staff during the investigation. At the end of the hearing, the panel may find the lawyer guilty or not guilty of professional misconduct. If the lawyer is found guilty, possible disciplinary measures include a reprimand, mandatory re-education, a suspension of his or her licence to practise, or a permanent revocation of the licence.

1. Which of the functions described above are subject to the rules of procedural fairness, and which are not? Explain.

2. Of the functions that are subject to the rules of procedural fairness, which ones are subject to the more stringent requirements of natural justice? Explain.

FURTHER READING

Sara Blake, *Administrative Law in Canada*, 5th ed (Toronto: LexisNexis Canada, 2011) ch 2, 3, 5.

Denys Holland & John McGowan, *Delegated Legislation in Canada* (Scarborough, Ont: Carswell, 1989).

John Mark Keyes, *Executive Legislation*, 2nd ed (Toronto: Butterworths, 2010).

Robert Macauley & James Sprague, *Practice and Procedure Before Administrative Tribunals* (Toronto: Carswell) (loose-leaf) ch 2, 3, 5B.

David J Mullan, *Administrative Law*, 3rd ed (Scarborough, Ont: Carswell, 1996) ch 3.

The Charter and Its Relationship to Administrative Law

4

LEARNING OUTCOMES

After reading this chapter, you will understand

- the rights and freedoms guaranteed by the Charter;

- the limits to which these rights and freedoms may be subject;

- how Charter rights can augment or enhance administrative law procedural fairness;

- who is bound by the Charter;

- what remedies are available for breaches of the Charter; and

- which remedies can be granted by tribunals and which are available only from courts.

The Canadian Charter of Rights and Freedoms

As discussed, the purpose of administrative law is to prevent administrators from abusing their powers and from acting unfairly. It accomplishes this by controlling the power of the executive both to make regulations and bylaws, and to implement and enforce laws.

The *Canadian Charter of Rights and Freedoms*[1] is the part of the Constitution that guarantees Canadians certain basic rights and freedoms. Although administrative law generally does not apply to the statute-making power of legislatures or the decision-making powers of courts, the rights and freedoms found in the Charter limit the law-making power of the legislative branch, and, in some cases, the procedures and decision-making powers of the courts. In addition, the Charter can be used to prevent abuse and unfairness in administrative actions and delegated law-making. In this respect, its requirements supplement those of administrative law.

While the reach of administrative law is limited to striking down the unfair or unauthorized actions of administrators, unfair policies or procedures, and unauthorized delegated legislation, the Charter can be used to strike down or amend statutes themselves if they violate Charter rights.

The Charter can also provide those who deal with government agencies with a higher level of procedural protection than is traditionally required by common law and statutes. The rights and freedoms of the Charter can impose fairness requirements on agencies in two ways:

1. If a statutory provision weakens the fairness protections provided by the common law in a way that violates rights under the Charter, the courts can strike down that provision.

2. If a statute or common law procedural fairness requirement does not require a procedure that gives effect to a right or freedom set out in the Charter, the courts can read into the statute a requirement to follow such a procedure.

Who Is Bound by the Charter?

Section 32 of the Charter states that the Charter applies to the Parliament and government of Canada as well as to the legislature and government of each province. This means that it also applies to the ministries and departments of government, as well as to the agencies, boards, and commissions (ABCs) created (by statutes passed by Parliament and the provincial legislatures) to carry out delegated government functions such as regulation and adjudication.

It is less clear whether the Charter applies to other bodies established by statute that regulate trades and professions (such as those that govern lawyers, paralegals,

---

1 Part I of the *Constitution Act, 1982*, being Schedule B to the *Canada Act 1982* (UK), 1982, c 11.

engineers, architects, doctors, and nurses) or that carry out public functions and rely on public funding (such as hospitals and universities). To decide whether the Charter applies to a body, the courts must determine

1. the extent to which the government exercises control over the body; and
2. the extent to which the body is carrying out functions that are essentially governmental in nature.

If a body is carrying out a public policy or program,[2] it will be considered part of government for Charter purposes, even if it is a private body, and the Charter will therefore apply to it. For example, the Supreme Court of Canada found that a community college was subject to the Charter because the system of community colleges was established by the government to implement a government policy of providing an alternative to university education, and because the board of the college was appointed by the government and was removable by the government.[3] In contrast, the Court found that universities are not subject to the Charter because universities appoint their own boards of governors and have greater latitude to establish their own goals.[4] However, those cases may not be the last word on whether the Charter applies to universities. The issue in the cases in which the Court found that the Charter did not apply was whether the university had infringed the section 15 rights of professors by imposing a mandatory retirement age. However, subsequent cases at lower courts have suggested that these cases did not rule out Charter applicability to universities for all purposes. For example, a judge of the Alberta Court of Appeal has ruled that section 2 of the Charter applies to disciplinary proceedings taken by a university against its students.[5] In a case in which the University of Calgary had used anti-trespassing legislation to prevent individuals from distributing pamphlets on campus without the university's permission, the Alberta Court of Queen's Bench ruled that the Charter applied to the university's action.[6]

If the court determines that a body is essentially part of the fabric of government, the Charter will apply to it even when it is carrying out activities that might normally be considered "private." An example might be a government agency contracting with its employees or carrying on a business, such as the Ontario Lottery and Gaming Corporation selling lottery tickets or Atomic Energy of Canada Limited marketing nuclear reactors.

Sometimes the Charter applies to courts, and sometimes it does not. The Charter applies to the activities of courts in relation to certain Charter rights that necessarily

---

2   "Public policy" refers to principles that are, according to the view of the legislative or judicial branch, of primary concern to society. Accordingly, a "public program" is a program designed to put these principles into practice.

3   *Douglas/Kwantlen Faculty Assn v Douglas College*, [1990] 3 SCR 570.

4   *McKinney v University of Guelph*, [1990] 3 SCR 229; *Harrison v University of British Columbia*, [1990] 3 SCR 451.

5   *Pridgen v University of Calgary*, 2012 ABCA 139. Only one judge applied the Charter. The two other members of the panel felt that the case could be decided on administrative law principles without the need to rely on the Charter.

6   *R v Whatcott*, 2012 ABQB 231.

require or prohibit action by a court, such as the right to a trial within a reasonable time, the right of a defendant not to be compelled to testify in a trial, the right to be presumed innocent until proven guilty and to have a fair and public trial, the right to be granted reasonable bail if charged with an offence, the right against self-incrimination, the right not to be subjected to cruel and unusual treatment or punishment, and the right to an interpreter. If a court violates any of these rights—for example, by unreasonably delaying a criminal trial or refusing access to an interpreter in a civil or criminal trial—a higher court may overrule the court's decision because it violates the Charter.

The Charter also applies to courts when they are applying the common law to a case in which the government is relying on a common law rule to justify its action. If the rule on which the government is relying violates the Charter, the courts may find the rule invalid. For example, the Crown cannot rely on the common law rule that a wife may not testify against her husband to prevent a woman who is separated from her husband without any reasonable possibility of reconciliation from testifying against her husband if she wishes to. In this situation, the common law rule interferes with the woman's freedom of expression as protected by the Charter, while not serving its purpose of preserving marital harmony.

However, because the Charter does not regulate private activity by private persons, such as individuals and corporations, in a dispute between private individuals or organizations, the courts will not find a common law rule invalid on the basis that it violates the Charter. For example, the common law rule prohibiting defamation may restrict freedom of expression, which is a Charter right, but the courts can still apply the rule against defamation in a dispute between individuals because the Charter does not apply to such private disputes.

> *Where the principles underlying a common law rule are out of step with the values enshrined in the Charter, the courts should scrutinize the rule closely. If it is possible to change the common law rule, so as to make it consistent with Charter values, without upsetting the proper balance between judicial and legislative action ... then the rule ought to be changed.*
>
> Iacobucci J in *R v Salituro*, [1991] 3 SCR 654 at 675

Although the courts will not use the Charter to *invalidate* common law rules in deciding private cases, a court may make use of the Charter to *modify* common law rules in such cases, even if the Charter does not apply directly to the case before it. In deciding how to interpret or apply a common law rule, the court may look at whether the rule complies with **Charter principles** or **Charter values**—that is, the principles and values that underlie the specific rights and freedoms guaranteed by the Charter. For example, the Charter value of privacy, which preserves human dignity and autonomy, underlies the section 8 right of individuals to be free from unreasonable search and seizure.

Sometimes, values now recognized as Charter values underlie common law doctrines, while at other times these doctrines conflict with Charter values. In a civil action between private persons, a court may modify a common law rule to the extent necessary to reflect Charter principles and values. For example, when interpreting the scope of a common law doctrine such as defamation, the courts may consider the Charter value of privacy and the Charter principle of freedom of expression and modify the doctrine as necessary to ensure that the law of defamation achieves a proper balance between these principles and values.

Rights and Freedoms Guaranteed by the Charter

The Charter protects several categories of rights and freedoms, including political rights, mobility rights, legal rights, language rights, and minority educational rights.

In relation to administrative law, the most important of these rights and freedoms are the fundamental freedoms of religion, expression, peaceful assembly, and association found in section 2, as well as some of the legal rights set out in sections 1 to 14. The equality rights found in section 15 may also have some impact on administrative law.

The Charter provides for two classes of rights and freedoms pertaining to procedural fairness:

1. In the first class are rights addressed by sections 9, 11, and 13. These rights are available primarily or only with respect to penal matters, which are usually decided by courts rather than by tribunals or agencies. They impose duties on courts to act fairly when dealing with criminal or regulatory offences subject to punishment. Generally, these provisions cannot be used to enhance common law or statutory fairness requirements for agencies (although sections 11 and 13 may apply in some circumstances).

2. In the second class are rights addressed by sections 7, 8, and 14, which do not refer to the penal context. These are the principal provisions that may apply where administrative law principles apply—namely, where government conduct affects a person's right to fair treatment, whether or not a punishment is involved.

In addition to these provisions, sections 2 and 15, which establish substantive rights, may also have some potential to enhance common law and statutory procedural fairness requirements.

Section 2

Section 2 of the Charter guarantees the freedoms of expression, religion, peaceful assembly, and association. The courts have given a particularly broad interpretation to the first of these—freedom of expression. In addition to the right to speak freely, this freedom guarantees individuals the right to receive information they need to form sound opinions. As a result, the Supreme Court of Canada has found that section 2 guarantees the traditional common law requirement that courts conduct their proceedings in public (known as the "open court" or "open justice" principle), except where a court order limiting access is necessary to prevent a serious risk of substantial harm to another right or interest that outweighs the public interest in open government.[7]

---

7 *Dagenais v Canadian Broadcasting Corp*, [1994] 3 SCR 835; *R v Mentuck*, 2001 SCC 76, [2001] 3 SCR 442.

Although it has not yet been established that the open justice principle applies to all tribunals, courts have held that the principle applies to *some* tribunals, and there is language in a leading Supreme Court decision on open justice that suggests that many more—if not all—tribunals may be required by the Charter to hold open hearings.[8] The right to a public hearing before a tribunal would be an important new procedural fairness right guaranteed by the Charter.

Section 7

Section 7 has the potential to add new procedural safeguards to the list of those that administrators and tribunals must follow under the common law principles of procedural fairness, and to expand existing procedural fairness requirements to new contexts. Section 7 provides protection against government interference with individuals' rights to life, liberty, and security of the person except in accordance with principles of "fundamental justice" (see below). For a government action to be found invalid on the basis of section 7, two conditions must be met: first, the action must violate principles of fundamental justice, and second, the action must threaten the life, liberty, or security of the person affected by the action.

The Charter does not define the term "fundamental justice"; however, the courts have described it as encompassing "the basic tenets of the legal system." What this means is rather vague, and the explanation of it in subsequent Supreme Court decisions doesn't make it much clearer. In *R v Malmo-Levine*,[9] the Court explained that to be a basic tenet of the legal system, a rule must meet three tests: first, it must be a "legal principle"; second, there must be "a significant societal consensus that it is fundamental to the way in which the legal system ought fairly to operate"; and third, the rule must be capable of being "identified with sufficient precision to yield a manageable standard."

Like the principles of procedural fairness, the principles of fundamental justice depend on the context. The more serious the consequences of a government action are for an individual or individuals, the more stringent are the protections required for the action to meet the requirement of being "in accordance with the principles of fundamental justice."

At minimum, **fundamental justice** incorporates the common law rules of procedural fairness. Therefore, to comply with the requirement to provide fundamental justice, the procedure followed by administrators and tribunals generally will, at the very least, have to conform to the requirements of common law procedural fairness. However, fundamental justice is not limited to common law procedural fairness requirements. In cases where the life, liberty, or security of a person is at issue, fundamental justice may require protections beyond those traditionally required by procedural fairness, such as full disclosure of evidence or a decision without delay.

While procedural fairness is purely procedural, fundamental justice can also include substantive rights, such as an indigent person's right to be represented by a lawyer paid for by the government in certain situations. Another example of

---

8   *Edmonton Journal v Alberta (Attorney General)*, [1989] 2 SCR 1326 at 1336.

9   2003 SCC 74, [2003] 3 SCR 571.

substantive fundamental justice is the rule that a person should not be convicted of any offence for doing things that he or she could not avoid. For example, it would offend fundamental justice to convict a person of illegal parking when a blizzard has buried his or her car in snow and it is not possible to move it due to the conditions. A law that is arbitrary, excessively vague, or "over-broad"—that is, broader than necessary to achieve its purpose—will offend the principles of fundamental justice.

The second condition necessary for section 7 to apply is that the government's action must threaten an individual's life, liberty, or security. Since the abolition of capital punishment, no government body in Canada has the power to take a person's life. However, tribunals and courts do have the power to deprive individuals of their liberty—for example, by ordering that they be confined to mental hospitals, requiring them to accept medical treatment against their will, or refusing to grant them parole—and government actions may affect individuals' security. Because courts have held that security of the person is affected when government action results in serious psychological stress, acts that might adversely affect a person's security include denial of access to abortion services, removal of a child from a parent's custody, and proceedings that could result in deportation to a country where an individual would be at risk of torture.

As a result of the above, section 7 is potentially available whenever a government authority deprives a person of liberty or threatens a person's security. Although the Supreme Court has confirmed that section 7 can apply to tribunals and other government decision-makers, to date the courts generally have not extended the degree of fairness required by fundamental justice beyond what the common law doctrine of procedural fairness would require in a particular situation. However, the Supreme Court has established that section 7 provides a right to disclosure of evidence in certain administrative proceedings.

THE EFFECT OF SECTION 7 ON DISCLOSURE OF EVIDENCE IN ADMINISTRATIVE PROCEEDINGS

The Supreme Court has interpreted section 7 to include a right of anyone charged with a criminal or regulatory offence to "full answer and defence" in his or her trial. This in turn has been interpreted to include a right to full disclosure to the accused of the evidence against him or her. In recent years, however, the Supreme Court has expanded this disclosure right to certain administrative proceedings that have serious consequences for a person's life, liberty, or security, even though procedural fairness does not generally require full disclosure in proceedings before tribunals.

In *Canada (Justice) v Khadr*,[10] the Supreme Court ruled that the duty of disclosure required by section 7, which usually applies only to criminal and regulatory offences committed in Canada, extends beyond the duty to disclose evidence in those proceedings. When Mr. Khadr, a Canadian citizen, was held illegally in a US prison on murder charges under US law, the Supreme Court held that section 7 required disclosure to him of the evidence obtained from him and passed on to the US government by Canadian officials who were participating in a process that was

---

10 2008 SCC 28, [2008] 2 SCR 125.

contrary to international law. The Supreme Court also held that when the federal government holds a hearing to remove a suspected terrorist from the country using a "security certificate," which prohibits him from seeing some of the evidence against him on the grounds that disclosure of the evidence would threaten national security, "it becomes necessary to recognize a duty to disclose evidence based on s. 7."[11] In a more recent decision, the Supreme Court confirmed that there is "an incompressible minimum" of disclosure that the person whom the government seeks to remove from Canada must receive in order for the security certificate scheme to comply with section 7 of the Charter.[12]

Any statutory or common law procedure that does not entail a level of fairness appropriate to the circumstances may violate fundamental justice;[13] if the violation could result in the deprivation of a person's life, liberty, or security, this is a violation of section 7. However, it is generally not necessary to apply section 7 in the context of decisions of tribunals because applying the common law principles of procedural fairness will usually accomplish the same end.

The section 7 requirement for fundamental justice has expanded the implications of the right to representation guaranteed by common law procedural fairness. At common law, parties to tribunal proceedings have a right to be represented by a lawyer or agent of their choice, but this right does not extend to requiring the government to pay for a party's representation if the party cannot afford representation. Under section 7, however—that is, in cases where representation is necessary to ensure a fair hearing and where the lack of adequate representation could result in harm to a party's security of the person—the right to representation may require that the government pay for a party's representation where the party cannot afford to. An example of such a case would be a hearing to determine whether a child should be taken away from his or her parents.

> *I am of the view that s. 7 is implicated when the state, by resorting to the justice system, restricts individuals' physical liberty in any circumstances. Section 7 is also implicated when the state restricts individuals' security of the person by interfering with, or removing from them, control over their physical or mental integrity. Finally, s. 7 is implicated when the state, either directly or through its agents, restricts certain privileges or liberties by using the threat of punishment in cases of non-compliance.*
>
> Lamer J in *Reference re ss 193 and 195.1(1)(c) of the Criminal Code (Man)*, [1990] 1 SCR 1123 at 1177–78

Section 8

Section 8 of the Charter prohibits unreasonable search or seizure. It prevents government authorities from searching premises, seizing property, or demanding that

---

11   *Charkaoui v Canada (Citizenship and Immigration)*, 2008 SCC 38, [2008] 2 SCR 326 at para 53.

12   *Canada (Citizenship and Immigration) v Harkat*, 2014 SCC 37, [2014] 2 SCR 33 at para 54.

13   *Blencoe v British Columbia (Human Rights Commission)*, 2000 SCC 44, [2000] 2 SCR 307; *New Brunswick (Minister of Health and Community Services) v G (J)*, [1999] 3 SCR 46.

individuals produce or provide documents, property, or information unless they have grounds to believe that an offence has been committed. Even then, if a search or seizure is conducted for the purpose of investigating an offence, it is considered "reasonable" only after authorization has been obtained from a court.

The above restrictions do not apply to routine inspections or audits of regulated businesses and industries. The reason the courts have given for requiring a warrant where government officials are investigating an offence but not for a routine inspection or other administrative action is that the right to be free from such scrutiny arises only where there is a reasonable expectation of privacy. The Supreme Court has decided that it is not reasonable for people carrying on businesses to expect to be free from routine inspections and inquiries.[14]

This does not mean that regulatory agencies have unrestricted powers to demand information, enter premises, and/or remove property. The courts have decided that the procedural fairness required by the Charter compels a regulatory agency, once it has found evidence of an offence that may lead to charges being laid, to cease asking questions and making searches, and obtain a search warrant for further searches or demands.[15]

> In a modern industrial society, it is generally accepted that many activities in which individuals can engage must nevertheless to a greater or lesser extent be regulated by the state to ensure that the individual's pursuit of his or her self-interest is compatible with the community's interest in the realization of collective goals and aspirations. ... It follows that there can only be a relatively low expectation of privacy in respect of premises or documents that are used or produced in the course of activities which, though lawful, are subject to state regulation as a matter of course.
>
> La Forest J in *Thomson Newspapers Ltd v Canada (Director of Investigation and Research, Restrictive Trade Practices Commission)*, [1990] 1 SCR 425 at 506–7

Section 11

As mentioned, section 11 generally applies in the context of penal matters. It provides certain procedural safeguards for individuals, including a person's right to be informed of the allegations against him or her, the right to a hearing within a reasonable time, the right not to testify against oneself, the right to be presumed innocent until proven guilty, the right to a fair hearing held in public before an independent and impartial tribunal, the right not to be denied reasonable bail without good reason, and the right not to be punished more than once for the same offence. A precondition for the application of section 11 is that a person must be "charged with an offence."

---

14 *Thomson Newspapers Ltd v Canada (Director of Investigation and Research, Restrictive Trade Practices Commission)*, [1990] 1 SCR 425; *R v McKinlay Transport Ltd*, [1990] 1 SCR 627.

15 *R v Inco Ltd* (2001), 54 OR (3d) 495 (CA), 146 OAC 66, leave to appeal denied by the Supreme Court of Canada, 7 March 2002. See also *R v Jarvis*, [2002] 3 SCR 757 and *R v Ling*, 2002 SCC 74, [2002] 3 SCR 814.

Although it is generally courts rather than tribunals that deal with offences, certain kinds of conduct brought before tribunals are referred to as "offences"—for example, serious violations of professional standards by lawyers, police officers, doctors, and other regulated professionals. However, the Supreme Court has ruled that section 11 applies to administrative action only when a proceeding is, "by its very nature, criminal," or when a finding of guilt for committing the offence can lead to a "true penal consequence."[16]

A proceeding is criminal by its very nature when it is aimed at promoting public order and welfare within a public sphere of activity. Proceedings of an administrative nature, on the other hand, are primarily intended to maintain compliance or to regulate conduct within a limited sphere of activity. The focus of the inquiry as to whether a proceeding is criminal or administrative is not on the nature of the act that is the subject of the proceedings, but on the nature of the proceedings themselves, taking into account their purpose as well as their procedure. Hallmarks of a proceeding that is criminal rather than administrative include the following: the laying of a charge, an arrest, a summons to appear before a court of criminal jurisdiction, and a finding of responsibility that leads to a criminal record. A "true penal consequence" is imprisonment or a fine that, by its magnitude, appears to have been imposed for the purpose of remedying a wrong to society at large rather than disciplining an individual. Because there are few circumstances in which an agency has the power to impose such punishments or follows criminal procedures, section 11 has had virtually no impact on administrative law.

Section 12

Section 12 of the Charter provides for the right of an individual not to be subjected to cruel and unusual treatment or punishment. In the context of administrative agencies, a decision to deport an immigrant to a country where he or she may be tortured, to require students to undergo random tests for drugs, or even to ban smoking in prisons might be argued to be cruel and unusual treatment. However, this is primarily a substantive right rather than a procedural one.

Section 13

Section 13 protects the right of witnesses who testify in proceedings not to incriminate themselves. This includes proceedings before tribunals in addition to before courts. In contrast to the United States, where a person can refuse to testify before courts and tribunals if the testimony would reveal that the person has committed an offence, a witness called before a Canadian court or tribunal *must* testify, even if this means providing evidence that he or she has committed a criminal or regulatory offence. However, this evidence, and any further evidence obtained as a result of the witness's testimony, may not be used against the witness in any future prosecution of him or her.

Although the right against self-incrimination is not a common law rule of procedural fairness, it was incorporated into many statutes governing procedures before tribunals before it was recognized as a fundamental right under the Charter.

---

16 *R v Wigglesworth*, [1987] 2 SCR 541 at 559; *Guindon v Canada*, 2015 SCC 41 at paras 44–46, 63.

Section 14

Section 14 provides for the right to an interpreter in any proceeding where a party or witness does not understand or speak the language used, or is deaf. This section applies to proceedings before courts as well as tribunals.

Section 14 may not apply at the first level of decision-making—for example, when a government official is making a decision that may be appealed to a tribunal—because the process is generally not considered a "proceeding." However, where a decision-maker holds a hearing and the consequences are significant (as in the case of a deportation hearing or a hearing before the Immigration and Refugee Board to determine whether a person is eligible for refugee status), the affected individual would probably be entitled to an interpreter if he or she did not have a good grasp of English or French.

Section 15

As discussed in Chapter 3, administrative law prohibits the making of regulations or the passing of bylaws that discriminate, unless the enabling statute explicitly or implicitly authorizes the discrimination. In addition, where a decision-maker has discretion, he or she must exercise it in a non-discriminatory manner, treating similar cases in a similar way. Section 15 of the Charter extends the rule against discrimination to the contents of statutes and to all governmental actions subject to the Charter:

> Every individual is equal before and under the law and has the right to the equal protection and equal benefit of the law without discrimination and, in particular, without discrimination based on race, national or ethnic origin, colour, religion, sex, age or mental or physical disability.

This provision applies to administrators, not just courts. It transforms human rights that were previously part of human rights codes—and thus considered "quasi-constitutional"—into constitutional rights. Not all distinctions between groups are discriminatory in the constitutional sense, and not all discrimination is prohibited. In *R v Kapp*, the Supreme Court of Canada ruled that to convince a court that an administrative rule or action violates section 15, an applicant must demonstrate the following to the court's satisfaction:

1. that the statute, program, policy, or activity results in a disadvantage being imposed on a listed or analogous ground; and
2. that this disadvantage results from discrimination, which the Supreme Court has identified as "the perpetuation of prejudice or stereotyping."

In deciding whether there is discrimination, a court is to consider four factors:

- the existence of pre-existing disadvantage, stereotyping, prejudice, or vulnerability;
- the correspondence between the distinction and the claimant's characteristics or circumstances;

- the existence of ameliorative purposes or effects on other groups; and
- the nature of the interest affected.[17]

The Supreme Court has continued to elaborate on what the two-part *Kapp* test means and how the factors apply. The Court unanimously reaffirmed its emphasis on prejudice and stereotyping as key factors in *Withler v Canada (Attorney General)*,[18] which states that stereotyping occurs where government action imposes a disadvantage "based on a stereotype that does not correspond to the actual circumstances and characteristics of the claimant." However, in its subsequent decision in *Quebec (Attorney General) v A*,[19] the Court splintered into four separate judgments, each attempting to explain the test for discrimination and how the various factors apply. Abella J, writing one of the majority judgments, noted that reference in *Kapp* to prejudice and stereotyping was not intended to create a new section 15 test nor to impose any additional requirements on those claiming equality. LeBel J, writing one of the minority judgments for himself and three other judges, agreed that prejudice and stereotyping are crucial factors but not the only factors in determining discrimination.

Although section 15 has had little, if any, impact on procedural fairness requirements to date, it may have some potential in that regard—for example, by requiring tribunals to accommodate the religious customs or observances of a party or a witness.

Limits to Charter Rights

As mentioned in Chapter 1, Charter rights and freedoms are not absolute. The two key limits on them are set out in sections 1 and 33.

Section 1

Section 1 of the Charter states that the rights and freedoms set out in it are guaranteed "subject only to such reasonable limits prescribed by law as can be demonstrably justified in a free and democratic society."

If a law or practice is found to violate a Charter right, the onus is on the government to establish that the violation of the right is "demonstrably justified in a free and democratic society." To succeed, the government must meet the requirements of each part of the following four-part test:[20]

1. *Sufficiently important objective*   The objective of the law or action must be sufficiently important to justify limiting a fundamental right. That is, the problem to be solved must be "pressing and substantial."

---

17   *R v Kapp*, [2008] 2 SCR 483. In *Kapp*, the Supreme Court reversed its earlier decision in *Law v Canada (Minister of Employment and Immigration)*, [1999] 1 SCR 497 that a claimant must also prove that the different treatment had the effect of demeaning the applicant's human dignity.

18   2011 SCC 12, [2011] 1 SCR 396.

19   2013 SCC 5, [2013] 1 SCR 61.

20   *R v Oakes*, [1986] 1 SCR 103, as articulated and applied in *Schachter v Canada*, [1992] 2 SCR 679.

For example, saving the government money or achieving administrative efficiency is not usually considered a sufficiently important objective to justify violating Charter rights, but in at least one case where upholding a Charter right would have cost the government a huge amount of money, saving money was accepted as a sufficiently important objective to justify curtailing a Charter right.[21]

2. *Rational connection*   The law or action that the government seeks to defend must be rationally connected to the objective of solving the pressing and substantial problem in the first part of the test. For the law or action to be rationally connected to its objective, it must be carefully designed to achieve that objective, and it must not be arbitrary, unfair, or based on irrational considerations.

   For example, a *Narcotic Control Act* provision that stated that an individual found to be in possession of an illegal drug would be deemed to be a drug trafficker was struck down because there is no rational connection between the basic fact of possession of a drug and an intention to traffic in it. Similarly, more stringent requirements for Canadian citizenship for a person born outside of Canada to a Canadian mother than to a Canadian father were struck down because the Court could see no rational connection between the goal of keeping dangerous individuals out of Canada and the means chosen to achieve this—namely, distinguishing between birth to a Canadian mother and birth to a Canadian father.

3. *Least drastic means*   The law or action chosen must be the least drastic *means* available to solve the problem. The test for this is whether the law or action "minimally impairs" the Charter right. The law or action should impair the right no more than is necessary to achieve the objective.

   For example, section 213(d) of the *Criminal Code*[22] originally said that if a person was in possession of a weapon during the commission of certain crimes, such as robbery, during which his or her accomplice murdered someone, that person was guilty of murder just for participating in the crime. The Court held that this was too drastic a means of discouraging the use of weapons by criminals. Similarly, a rule against lawyers in one province becoming partners with lawyers in other provinces was considered too drastic a means of ensuring that lawyers maintain high professional standards.

4. *Proportionate effect*   The law or action must have a proportionate effect on the Charter right, not an effect that is disproportionately severe. That is, the degree to which individual rights are impaired must not be disproportionate to the benefit achieved by the impairment; the more severely a government measure impairs a Charter right, the more important the object of the measure must be for the effect to be considered proportionate.

---

21 *Newfoundland (Treasury Board) v NAPE*, 2004 SCC 66, [2004] 3 SCR 381.

22 RSC 1985, c C-46.

In practice, the proportionate effect test is largely redundant, since a measure that fails any of the other three tests is likely to be disproportionate as well. There have been no instances of a law or action passing the first three tests but failing the proportionality test.

Section 33: The "Notwithstanding" Clause

Section 33 of the Charter gives Parliament or the legislature of a province the right to override section 2, which guarantees fundamental freedoms, and sections 7 to 15, which protect the legal rights that are most connected to procedural fairness. Parliament or a provincial legislature can do this by amending any statute to state expressly that the Act or a provision of the Act continues to operate "notwithstanding" a provision in one of the above sections of the Charter.

Unlike the limitation prescribed by section 1 (that is, that the rights and freedoms are guaranteed subject to such reasonable limits prescribed by law as can be justified in a free and democratic society), section 33 does not require any proof that overriding the right or freedom is justified by the need to solve some important social problem. The only limit on **notwithstanding clauses** is their shelf life; to stay in effect, they must be renewed every five years.

Quebec, which was bound by the new Constitution in 1982 despite its objections, responded by introducing a notwithstanding clause into each of its existing statutes and every new statute passed after the Charter came into effect. In practice, this meant that the Charter didn't apply to Quebec. Although a new government discontinued the practice in 1985 and notwithstanding clauses were no longer inserted automatically into all new statutes, the new government did insert such clauses into 12 more statutes, the most controversial of which prohibited the use of English on outdoor commercial signs. That notwithstanding clause overrode a decision of the Supreme Court that had ruled that a Quebec law banning the use of languages other than French on such signs violated the freedom of expression guaranteed by section 2(b) of the Charter.[23] After the Supreme Court struck down the language law, Quebec re-enacted the prohibition of English on external signs while allowing bilingual interior signs, and protected the new prohibition with a notwithstanding clause.

Only two other provincial legislatures have used a notwithstanding clause. Saskatchewan employed one to protect back-to-work legislation that was contrary to the guarantee of freedom of association in section 2(d) of the Charter, while Alberta used one in 2000 to protect from Charter scrutiny a law that prohibited the marriage of same-sex couples. While the courts of other provinces ruled that laws prohibiting same-sex marriage violated section 15 of the Charter, Alberta used a section 33 override to get around any such decision that might be made by the Alberta courts.

A declaration that a statute overrides a provision of the Charter automatically expires after five years. The declaration may be re-enacted, but the renewed declaration also expires after five years; whether the declaration can continue to be renewed after this first renewal is not clear. The Alberta law prohibiting same-sex

---

23 *Ford v Quebec (Attorney General)*, [1988] 2 SCR 712.

marriages expired in 2005 and was not renewed, leaving same-sex couples free to wed in Alberta.

The Charter and Positive Obligations

Another limit to the reach of the Charter is the determination by the courts to date that while the Charter can prevent government from doing things that take away people's rights, the Charter doesn't require government to take positive steps to give people new rights or benefits to which existing laws and policies do not otherwise entitle them.

If government passes a law or makes a policy that grants social assistance benefits or other funding to one group, but provides for less money for another group, the latter group cannot argue that they have a right to the same benefits as the former group. Litigants have argued, so far unsuccessfully, that the right to freedom of expression in section 2(b), the right to liberty and security of the person in section 7, and the equality rights in section 15 impose a positive obligation on government to provide benefits such as funding, social assistance, and access to government documents. However, the Supreme Court has not ruled definitively that the Charter can never impose positive obligations on government.

In *Gosselin v. Quebec (Attorney General)*,[24] it was argued unsuccessfully that section 7 imposed a positive duty on government to provide more adequate welfare benefits to certain people who were entitled to lower payments under the scheme enacted by the Quebec government. The Supreme Court ruled that while section 7 of the Charter imposed a duty not to deprive individuals of life, liberty, or security, it had never been interpreted to impose positive obligations on the state to ensure that every person enjoyed life, liberty, and security. However, McLachlin CJ was careful not to close the door completely on the possibility that in future the Charter might be interpreted more expansively.

The Charter and Discretionary Administrative Decisions

In exercising discretion, administrative decision-makers must act consistently with Charter values. When an individual does not challenge a law or other rule, but rather challenges a discretionary decision made to implement that rule, the correct approach to deciding whether the discretion was properly exercised is not to determine whether the decision violates the Charter, but to apply administrative law principles for deciding the validity of the exercise of discretion, taking into account whether sufficient consideration was given to Charter values in making the decision.

The Supreme Court of Canada has refused to apply the *Oakes* test, developed for evaluating the compliance of laws with the Charter (see below), to determine the propriety of discretionary administrative decisions. The alternative approach chosen by the Court was to analyze whether the administrative decision was reasonable overall. Included in this analysis would be a consideration of whether the decision took Charter values sufficiently into account. This involves weighing whether the

---

24   2002 SCC 84, [2002] 4 SCR 429. See paras 77–80.

CASE IN POINT

Doré v Barreau du Quebec, 2012 SCC 12, [2012] 1 SCR 395

FACTS: In *Doré*, the applicant, Mr. Doré, a lawyer, was disciplined by his regulatory body for conduct that allegedly violated a rule of professional conduct requiring speech by lawyers to exhibit objectivity, moderation, and dignity. He had written a private letter to a judge that contained intemperate criticism, calling the judge "loathsome," "arrogant," and "fundamentally unjust." Initially, Mr. Doré argued that the rule against intemperate statements violated the Charter because it violated his right to freedom of expression under section 2 of the Charter. However, at the Supreme Court of Canada, he abandoned his challenge of the rule itself, but continued to allege that the tribunal's decision violated his right to freedom of expression.

ISSUE: Did the decision of the tribunal violate Mr. Doré's section 2(b) right to freedom of expression?

DECISION: The Supreme Court found that the disciplinary panel had a duty to balance competing interests to decide whether the exercise of discretion was proper:

> We are, in other words, balancing the fundamental importance of open, and even forceful, criticism of our public institutions with the need to ensure civility in the profession. Disciplinary bodies must therefore demonstrate that they have given due regard to the importance of the expressive rights at issue, both in light of an individual lawyer's right to expression and the public's interest in open discussion.

decision achieves a reasonable balance between furthering the objectives of the statutory regime under which the decision is made and the values underlying the Charter. This balancing exercise must ensure that the Charter protections are limited no more than is necessary to achieve the statutory objectives that the discretionary decision-maker is required to pursue.[25]

What Remedies Are Available for a Charter Violation?

It is often said that "where there is a right, there is a remedy." There are two sources of remedies for violations of the rights and freedoms guaranteed by the Charter: section 24(1) of the Charter and section 52(1) of the *Constitution Act, 1982*.[26]

Section 24

Section 24(1) of the Charter allows an individual to apply for a remedy for any breach of a Charter right or freedom; this includes the right to challenge any administrative action that allegedly violates a right under the Charter. Section 24(2) allows

---

25 *Loyola High School v Quebec (Attorney General)*, 2015 SCC 12.

26 Schedule B to the *Canada Act 1982* (UK), 1982, c 11.

a court to exclude evidence obtained through a breach of a Charter right. However, section 24 does not provide for remedies for other constitutional violations, such as a provincial legislature passing legislation that can only legally be passed by Parliament, or vice versa; the remedies for these violations arise from section 52(1) of the *Constitution Act, 1982* (see below). Under section 24(1), a court or tribunal may declare a law to be inapplicable in a particular situation, but a law can only be declared void or invalid under section 52(1).

To protect an individual against a violation of his or her Charter rights, section 24 allows a court of competent jurisdiction to provide any remedy that it considers "appropriate and just in the circumstances." While this is potentially broad, if the individual applies to a tribunal rather than a court, the remedies may be limited in practice—as creatures of statute, tribunals can only award the remedies provided for in their enabling statutes. For example, although remedies for a breach of the Charter can potentially include damages for the harm suffered, many tribunals have no statutory power to award compensation. Similarly, awarding costs might be an appropriate remedy for Charter breaches that cause inconvenience or delay to a party to a tribunal hearing, but many tribunals have no statutory power to award costs and, therefore, this remedy is not available from these tribunals.

Typically, in providing a remedy under section 24(1), a tribunal may overrule a decision-maker who has made a decision or followed a procedure that is contrary to the Charter, or refuse to follow such a procedure itself; grant an adjournment; stay proceedings; or refuse to apply a law that contravenes the Charter.

Courts of Competent Jurisdiction

The Charter provides that only a court "of competent jurisdiction" can grant remedies under section 24. Until 2010, the courts held that a tribunal had to meet three requirements to be considered such a court. The Supreme Court of Canada said that a **court of competent jurisdiction** was a body that (a) possesses jurisdiction over the parties, (b) possesses jurisdiction over the subject matter, and (c) has jurisdiction to grant the remedy requested.[27] Because tribunals are creatures of statute, it was necessary to examine a particular tribunal's enabling statute to determine whether the statute either explicitly provided the tribunal with these three attributes or, if not, whether the context and purpose of the statute required that it be interpreted in a way that would grant these powers to the tribunal.

In 2010, in *R v Conway*,[28] the Supreme Court of Canada set out a new approach for deciding whether a tribunal can grant remedies for Charter breaches under section 24(1) of the Charter. The new approach does not consider whether the tribunal can award the particular remedy as a component of whether the tribunal is a court of competent jurisdiction. Instead, the question of jurisdiction to grant the particular remedy is decided *after* it has been decided that the tribunal is a court of competent jurisdiction.

---

27   The test was set out in *Mills v The Queen*, [1986] 1 SCR 863.

28   2010 SCC 22, [2010] 1 SCR 765.

Where a statute governing a tribunal states that a particular remedy sought under section 24(1) is available, it is simple to conclude that the tribunal has jurisdiction to grant the remedy. However, statutes are frequently silent on this point. In such cases, *Conway* states that determining whether a tribunal can grant a particular remedy is an exercise in discerning legislative intent. Relevant considerations in discerning legislative intent will include the tribunal's statutory mandate, structure, and function.

When a remedy is sought from a tribunal, the initial question to be answered is whether the tribunal can grant Charter remedies generally. To make this determination, the first question is whether the tribunal has jurisdiction—explicit or implied—to decide questions of law. If it does, unless it is clearly demonstrated that the legislature intended to exclude the Charter from the tribunal's jurisdiction, the tribunal is a court of competent jurisdiction and can consider and apply the Charter.

Once the threshold question is decided in favour of Charter jurisdiction, the remaining question is whether the tribunal can grant the particular remedy sought. As indicated above, where the statute is silent on this point, this is a question of statutory interpretation, requiring consideration of the tribunal's statutory mandate and functions to determine whether the kinds of remedies sought are the kinds of remedies that the legislature appears to have anticipated would fit within the statutory scheme governing the tribunal.

It is likely that under this approach, more tribunals will be able to grant Charter remedies, and a wider variety of remedies will be available from tribunals than under the previous approach to determining section 24(1) jurisdiction.

Damages for Charter Breaches Under Section 24(1)

In *Vancouver (City) v Ward*,[29] the Supreme Court of Canada clarified the circumstances in which courts and tribunals that have jurisdiction to grant Charter remedies can award damages for a Charter breach. The Court also provided guidance as to the appropriate amount of damages. The decision is likely to expand the availability of damages as a remedy for Charter violations.

Mr. Ward's Charter right to be free from unreasonable search and seizure was violated by Vancouver and British Columbia officials who detained him, strip-searched him, and seized his car without cause. He sued for damages for these breaches of his Charter rights.

The Supreme Court noted that even though the Charter was 28 years old, there were few court rulings on whether damages were an available remedy under section 24(1). Therefore, the Court conducted an extensive analysis of the purposes served by granting damages for Charter breaches and the considerations that guide their award. The Court ruled that damages are available for Charter breaches of a serious nature, even if the breaches are not tortious or in bad faith.

The decision addressed the power of courts, rather than tribunals, to award Charter damages. However, the decision sets out tests that tribunals as well as courts

---

29 2010 SCC 27, [2010] 2 SCR 28.

would apply in deciding whether to award damages, provided that a tribunal has jurisdiction to award Charter damages under the rules established in *Conway*.

The Court ruled that the language of section 24(1) is broad enough to include the remedy of damages for breach of Charter rights if damages are found to be appropriate and just in the circumstances of a particular case. Charter damages are a just and appropriate remedy if they fulfill one or more of the related functions of compensation, vindication of the Charter right, or deterrence of future breaches.

Once the claimant has established that damages are justified because they fulfill these functions, the state has the opportunity to demonstrate that compensation should not be awarded because countervailing factors override the factors that justify a damages award. These factors may include the availability of alternative remedies and the need to support effective government. For example, in some cases, the state might establish that awarding damages would have a "chilling effect" on desirable government action.

In determining what amount of damages would be "appropriate and just," the court must consider what amount of damages would represent a meaningful response to the seriousness of the breach and the objectives of compensation, vindication, and deterrence. The more egregious the breach is and the more serious the repercussions on the claimant are, the higher the award for vindication or deterrence will be.

However, the amount of damages must also be fair to the state. The court may take into account the public interest in good governance, the danger of deterring governments from undertaking beneficial new policies and programs, and the need to avoid diverting large sums of funds from public programs to private interests.

Section 52(1)

In contrast to section 24 of the Charter, which provides a remedy for the administration of a statute in a manner that infringes the Charter, section 52(1) of the *Constitution Act, 1982*[30] provides a remedy where the law itself—whether a statute, regulation, bylaw, or common law principle—is inconsistent with the Charter. It also applies where a legislative body passes a law that it is not permitted to pass under the division of legislative powers in the Constitution (for example, where a province passes a criminal law, which is within the exclusive jurisdiction of the federal government).

The remedy provided by section 52 is to declare the unconstitutional law to be void—that is, "of no force or effect."

Unlike the power of courts in section 24 to provide various remedies, the power of courts or tribunals in section 52 to declare laws to be void does not depend on whether the body is a "court of competent jurisdiction." Rather, whether a tribunal has the power to strike down an unconstitutional law or provision depends on whether the legislature intended to grant the tribunal the power to interpret and apply the Charter. Because tribunals are creatures of statute, a court

---

30 *Supra* note 26.

will determine the legislature's intention with regard to this by looking at the tribunal's enabling statute.

If the statute does not explicitly grant the tribunal authority to decide the constitutional validity of statutes, the court will consider the statute as a whole to determine whether this power is implied. If the power of the tribunal to decide questions of law is expressly stated in or can be implied from the tribunal's enabling statute, there is a presumption that this power includes the power to decide constitutional questions, including Charter questions; the presumption may only be rebutted by showing that the legislature clearly intended to exclude Charter or other constitutional questions from the tribunal's jurisdiction to decide questions of law. Because most tribunals have either explicit or implicit jurisdiction to decide questions of law—at least those they must answer in order to resolve the dispute before them—the result is that most also have the power to strike down unconstitutional laws.

CHAPTER SUMMARY

The *Canadian Charter of Rights and Freedoms* is the part of the Constitution that guarantees Canadians certain basic rights and freedoms in various categories, including political rights, mobility rights, language rights, and minority educational rights. The Charter applies to the Parliament and government of Canada as well as to the legislature and government of each province, including the ministries and departments of the government, and the ABCs. In some cases, it also applies to courts, and to other bodies established by statute that regulate trades and professions or that carry out public functions and rely on public funding.

The rights and freedoms in the Charter limit the law-making power of the legislative branch, and, in some cases, the procedures and decision-making powers of the courts. The Charter can also be used to prevent abuse and unfairness in administrative actions and delegated law-making, and to strike down or amend statutes that violate Charter rights. Finally, it can provide those who deal with government agencies with a higher level of procedural protection than is traditionally required by common law and statutes.

If a law or government action is found to violate a Charter right, the onus is on the government to establish that the violation of the right is justified in a free and democratic society. To demonstrate this, the government must prove that the objective of the law or action is sufficiently important to justify limiting the right, that the law or action is rationally connected to the objective of solving the problem, that it is the least drastic means available to do so, and that its effect on the Charter right is not disproportionately severe. Parliament or a provincial legislature may override the procedural fairness rights outlined in the Charter by amending any statute to expressly state that the statute or any of its provisions continues to operate "notwithstanding" those rights.

Individuals are entitled to remedies for violations of their Charter rights. A court of competent jurisdiction may grant any remedy that it considers appropriate under the circumstances; the remedies that tribunals may grant are limited to those provided for in their enabling statutes. Where a law itself is inconsistent with the Charter, it may be struck down by any body that has the authority to answer questions of law.

KEY TERMS

Charter principles: *see* Charter values

Charter values: the values that underlie the specific rights and freedoms set out in the Charter; for example, the value "privacy" underlies the right to be free from unreasonable search and seizure in section 8 of the Charter; also called "Charter principles"

court of competent jurisdiction: in respect to the power to grant a remedy under section 24 of the Charter, a body that (a) possesses jurisdiction over the parties, (b) possesses jurisdiction over the subject matter, and (c) has jurisdiction to grant the remedy requested

fundamental justice: the basic tenets of the legal system; includes the right to procedural fairness in criminal proceedings and administrative decision-making, as well as certain substantive principles of fairness

notwithstanding clause: a clause in a statute that states expressly that a provision of the statute continues to operate notwithstanding that it violates a right or freedom guaranteed by section 2 or sections 7 to 15 of the Charter

CASES TO CONSIDER ▶

Compelling Testimony: The Right to Remain Silent and the Right Against Self-Incrimination

Thomson Newspapers Limited v Canada (Director of Investigation and Research, Restrictive Trade Practices Commission), [1990] 1 SCR 425

FACTS: Thomson Newspapers and some of its representatives were ordered to appear before the Restrictive Trade Practices Commission to testify and produce documents as required by section 17 of the *Combines Investigation Act*.[31] The orders were issued in connection with an inquiry to determine whether the company had engaged in predatory pricing. If the company refused to comply with the orders, it could be punished.

Thomson Newspapers applied to the court for a declaration that section 17 of the *Combines Investigation Act*, under which the orders were issued, violated the right in section 11(c) of the Charter of an individual charged with an offence not to have to testify against himself or herself, and the right in section 13 that self-incriminatory evidence given by a witness in one proceeding cannot be used against that witness in another proceeding. The company also argued that section 7 of the Charter created a "right to remain silent" during an investigation under the *Combines Investigation Act* above and beyond the rights in sections 11(c) and 13, based on an argument that silence under these circumstances was a "fundamental right."

ISSUE: Did a corporation or its representatives have a right to refuse to comply with an order to testify and produce documents before a regulatory body when under investigation for a trade violation?

DECISION: Section 17 of the *Combines Investigation Act* did not breach the Charter. Unlike the United States, Canada does not provide individuals with a blanket right to remain silent. Where a corporation is under investigation for a regulatory offence, a blanket right to remain silent would thwart the aims of the Act, since investigation would be virtually impossible. The power to compel testimony is important to the overall effectiveness of an investigation under the Act; an absolute right of a corporation to refuse to answer questions would represent a dangerous and unnecessary imbalance between the rights of an individual or a corporation and the public's legitimate interest in discovering the truth about trade practices. Section 17 strikes an appropriate balance. The investigation would not ultimately result in a criminal conviction for either the corporation or its representatives, since there could be no conviction unless charges were laid and further proceedings were held. Therefore, there was no risk of self-incrimination from cooperating in the investigation. Moreover, although the Charter protects individuals from self-incrimination in certain circumstances, corporations have no right against self-incrimination, since they cannot testify against themselves.

Section 11(c) of the Charter, which provides that a person charged with an offence is not a compellable witness against himself or herself, was not applicable because no one had been charged with an offence. Section 13, which provides that a person who does testify in a proceeding has the right not to have any incriminating evidence given used to incriminate him or her in a subsequent proceeding, was not applicable because this inquiry was the first proceeding; it would apply only if the government attempted

---

31 RSC 1970, c C-23.

to use the evidence in a subsequent proceeding. Finally, section 17 of the *Combines Investigation Act* did not contravene section 7 of the Charter. Section 7 may, in certain contexts, provide residual protection to the interests protected by specific provisions of the Charter (such as sections 11(c) and 13), but it does not give an absolute right to silence or a generalized right against self-incrimination on the American model.

Disclosure of Evidence and Procedural Fairness

Canada (Justice) v Khadr, 2008 SCC 29, [2008] 2 SCR 143

FACTS: Omar Ahmed Khadr was apprehended by the American military in July 2002. Mr. Khadr was detained in a US military facility in Afghanistan, and then subsequently at the US naval station in Guantanamo Bay, Cuba. In the course of his detention, the Royal Canadian Mounted Police (RCMP) travelled to Cuba to question Mr. Khadr. The subject of this case is the status of the evidence that was obtained by the RCMP from the interrogation.

ISSUES: Is the information obtained from Mr. Khadr by the RCMP subject to the duty of disclosure, required by section 7 of the Charter?

DECISION: In *Khadr*, the Supreme Court ruled that the duty of disclosure required by section 7, which usually applies only to criminal and regulatory offences committed in Canada, extended beyond the duty to disclose evidence in those proceedings. When Mr. Khadr, a Canadian citizen, was held illegally in a US prison on murder charges under US law, the Supreme Court held that section 7 required disclosure to him of the evidence obtained from him and passed on to the US government by Canadian officials who were participating in a process that was contrary to international law.

In further cases on this issue, the Supreme Court also held that when the federal government holds a hearing to remove a suspected terrorist from the country using a "security certificate," which normally prohibits him from seeing some of the evidence against him on the grounds that disclosure of the evidence would threaten national security, "it [now] becomes necessary to recognize a duty to disclose evidence based on s. 7."[32] In a more recent decision, the Supreme Court confirmed that there is "an incompressible minimum" of disclosure that the person whom the government seeks to remove from Canada must receive in order for the security certificate scheme to comply with section 7 of the Charter.[33]

Any statutory or common law procedure that does not entail a level of fairness appropriate to the circumstances may violate fundamental justice;[34] if the violation may result in the deprivation of a person's life, liberty, or security, this is a violation of section 7.

Unreasonable Delay and Procedural Fairness

Blencoe v British Columbia (Human Rights Commission), 2000 SCC 44, [2000] 2 SCR 307

FACTS: In 1995, Blencoe was serving as a minister in the government of British Columbia when he was accused of sexual harassment. The premier removed him from Cabinet and

---

32 *Supra* note 11.

33 *Supra* note 12.

34 *Supra* note 13.

dismissed him from caucus. After an investigation by the British Columbia Council of Human Rights (now the British Columbia Human Rights Commission), hearings were scheduled before the British Columbia Human Rights Tribunal in 1998—over 30 months after the initial complaints were filed.

Following the allegations, media attention was intense, and Blencoe suffered from severe depression. He considered himself "unemployable" in British Columbia due to the outstanding human rights complaints against him. He commenced judicial review proceedings in 1997 to have the complaints stayed, claiming that the Council had lost jurisdiction due to an unreasonable delay in processing the complaints. Blencoe alleged that the unreasonable delay caused serious prejudice to him and his family, and deprived him of his rights under section 7 of the Charter to liberty and security of the person contrary to the principles of fundamental justice.

ISSUE: Were Blencoe's constitutional rights to liberty and security of the person under section 7 of the Charter violated by the delay?

DECISION: The Supreme Court held that the Charter applied to actions of the British Columbia Council of Human Rights, and that section 7 could theoretically be applicable. However, because there is no constitutional right outside of the criminal context to be "tried" within a reasonable time, this case did not trigger section 7. The state had not violated Blencoe's liberty, because it had not prevented him from making "fundamental personal choices," nor did the delay caused by the Council infringe his right to security of the person. The direct causes of the psychological harm to Blencoe were the loss of his position, the allegations, and the negative publicity—all of which occurred before the complaints to the Council—not the state-caused delay in the human rights process. At best, Blencoe was deprived of a speedy opportunity to clear his name.

Right to Counsel and Procedural Fairness

New Brunswick (Minister of Health and Community Services) v G (J), [1999] 3 SCR 46

FACTS: The New Brunswick minister of health and community services had temporary custody of three children and sought to extend the custody order. The children's mother was indigent and receiving social assistance. Her application for legal aid was denied because custody applications were not covered under the legal aid guidelines. She then sought an order directing the minister to pay for counsel to represent her in the custody proceedings, and she sought a declaration that the legal aid guidelines violated section 7 of the *Canadian Charter of Rights and Freedoms*.

ISSUE: Do indigent parents have a constitutional right to state-funded counsel when a government seeks to suspend custody rights?

DECISION: There was a constitutional obligation, under section 7 of the Charter, to provide state-funded counsel in this case. The minister's application to extend the custody order threatened to restrict the mother's right to security of the person guaranteed by section 7. When an indigent parent wants the government to provide him or her with a lawyer to defend custody against the government, the judge must ask whether the parent applied for legal aid or other state-funded legal assistance; the parent must first exhaust all possible avenues for obtaining state-funded legal assistance. The judge must then ask whether the parent can receive a fair hearing if unrepresented, giving consideration to the seriousness of the interests at stake, the complexity of the proceedings, and the capacity of the parent to effectively present his or her case (considering, for example, the parent's intelligence, education, communication skills, composure, and familiarity with the legal system). If the judge is not satisfied that the parent can receive a fair hearing unrepresented, the government must provide state-funded counsel.

REVIEW QUESTIONS

1. How do the courts assess whether a public policy or program is subject to Charter scrutiny and oversight? Are private bodies treated differently when they are carrying out a public policy? If so, explain how and why.

2. What are the courts obligated to do with common law rules that are used by government to justify actions and that violate the Charter? What is the exception to this rule?

3. Define the *open justice principle*. Explain its application to tribunals and the justification upon which that application is based.

4. Section 7 of the Charter offers procedural guarantees to those involved in legal matters, as well as some substantive protections. What is the only reason, embodied in a principle, that a section 7 right can be curtailed? How is a section 7 right applied? What are the two conditions that must be met? How does application of the conditions intersect with procedural fairness?

5. The Constitution provides for remedies should a law, policy, or procedure be found to violate the Charter. What are the two remedies and how do they work?

EXERCISES

1. The protection of privacy is a Charter value that underlies section 8 of the Charter. What other Charter principles or values underlie

   a. the Charter as a whole, and

   b. specific Charter provisions?

2. Identify the three categories of rights under the Canadian Constitution. Answer the following questions about each category:

   a. Define and describe the category;

   b. Explain the legal tests involved in applying these rights;

   c. Find examples of cases to illustrate the application of the rights.

3. Using *Canada (Justice) v Khadr*, describe how the notion of *fundamental justice* under section 7 has been expanded. Use a contextual analysis that takes into account societal and global issues to explain your answer.

FACT SCENARIOS

Scenario 1

Ontario's *Legal Aid Services Act, 1998* provides for Legal Aid Ontario, an organization funded by the Government of Ontario, to pay for lawyers to represent litigants who cannot afford to pay a lawyer and to retain expert witnesses in certain circumstances. Legal Aid is available for defence of criminal charges; for civil actions in the courts, such as tort and contract cases; and for some family law cases, such as child support applications.

The *Legal Aid Services Act* does not provide for the provision of legal aid to support individuals appearing before environmental tribunals.

The Ministry of the Environment has ordered a wealthy multinational corporation to clean up pollution that is migrating from its factory property into neighbouring farm wells and into the well that provides water for the town of Arimle. The order was issued under section 18 of the *Environmental Protection Act*. The corporation challenges the order before the province's Environmental Review Tribunal (ERT).

The ERT hearing is scheduled to last several months. The Ministry and the corporation are each represented by several experienced lawyers, and both call several expert witnesses.

Some residents of the town where the factory is located and of the surrounding farmland form a group called Preserve Our Water (POW), and the tribunal grants them status as parties to the proceeding. POW has raised several thousand dollars to pay experts and their lawyers, but after many weeks of hearings the funds are depleted. Unless POW obtains additional funding, they will have to represent themselves for the remainder of the hearing or even withdraw from it entirely.

POW asks the ERT to rule that the lack of a provision for funding for participation in this kind of hearing in the *Legal Aid Services Act* and the *Environmental Protection Act* violates the Charter. It asks the ERT to rectify these omissions by providing funding itself or by ordering the Ministry, Legal Aid Ontario, or the corporation to provide funding for its lawyers and expert witnesses.

1. If you were representing POW, what Charter provisions would you base your argument for their request on?

2. Does the ERT have jurisdiction under section 24(1) of the Charter to provide a remedy? Explain.

3. Does the ERT have jurisdiction under section 52(1) of the Charter to provide a remedy? Explain.

Scenario 2

Polygamy is illegal under Canada's *Criminal Code*.

A woman who follows a religion that endorses polygamy applies to the clerk of her municipality for a marriage licence to wed a man who already has a wife, both of whom follow the same religion as the woman. When the clerk refuses to issue the marriage licence on the grounds that doing so would constitute aiding the commission of a crime, the woman makes an application for judicial review of the clerk's decision.

The woman asks the court to declare the prohibition against polygamy in the Code inapplicable to her and to order the clerk to issue a marriage licence. She argues that the prohibition offends the Charter because it violates her freedoms of religion, expression, and association under section 2 of the Charter.

The government concedes that the prohibition against polygamy in the Code and the clerk's refusal to issue a marriage licence violate section 2 of the Charter. However, it claims that the infringement is justified in a free and democratic society under section 1 of the Charter.

What tests will the court apply in determining whether the violation of section 2 of the Charter is "saved" by section 1? Apply these tests to the fact situation.

FURTHER READING

Colleen Flood & Lorne Sossin, *Administrative Law in Context*, 2nd ed (Toronto: Emond Montgomery, 2013) ch 12.

Peter Hogg, *Constitutional Law of Canada*, 5th ed (Toronto: Carswell, 2007).

Guy Régimbald, *Canadian Administrative Law*, 2nd ed (Markham, Ont: LexisNexis, 2008) ch II.

Human Rights Codes and Other Quasi-Constitutional Laws

5

LEARNING OUTCOMES

After reading this chapter, you will understand

- the characteristics that make a law "quasi-constitutional";

- the effect of quasi-constitutional status on how a law is interpreted;

- the kinds of behaviours prohibited by human rights codes, and why these behaviours are prohibited;

- the scope of an employer's duty to reasonably accommodate limitations or differences arising from an applicant or employee's race, religion, sex, or other personal attributes protected against discrimination under human rights codes;

- the bona fide occupational requirement test, and its role in determining whether certain kinds of discrimination are permissible under human rights codes;

- how human rights codes are administered and enforced, and the remedies available for violations of human rights;

- rights to access government information under freedom-of-information laws, and how these laws are administered;

- rights to privacy under privacy statutes, and how these statutes are administered;

- the current status of the *Canadian Bill of Rights*, and its key provisions for ensuring procedural fairness; and

- the purpose, effect, and enforcement of official languages laws.

What Are Quasi-Constitutional Laws?

In the hierarchy of laws, **quasi-constitutional** laws rank somewhere above ordinary administrative law but below the Constitution. These laws were developed to ensure fair treatment of the public, and are called "quasi-constitutional" because, like the Constitution, they embody important—even fundamental—rights and freedoms, but, unlike the Constitution, they do not always override other laws that conflict with them.

Quasi-constitutional laws often embody values recognized throughout the world, not just in Canada. These values, as well as related rights and freedoms, are often expressed in international **conventions**, which are signed by all nations that support the values. Countries that sign such conventions usually agree to pass laws that give effect within their borders to the rights and freedoms outlined in the conventions.

Quasi-constitutional laws are similar to both the Constitution and administrative law. Like these laws, quasi-constitutional laws are intended to prevent abusive behaviour, uphold human dignity and autonomy, and ensure fair treatment of individuals. However, unlike these laws, quasi-constitutional laws often regulate the conduct of individuals and businesses as well as that of government.

Some common law principles, such as solicitor–client privilege (the right of a lawyer's client to have all communications between the client and the lawyer kept confidential), are considered quasi-constitutional. Other quasi-constitutional laws are statutes. The most important laws in the second category are probably the human rights codes passed by the federal government and each of the provinces and territories. Other quasi-constitutional laws include the *Canadian Bill of Rights* (not to be confused with the *Canadian Charter of Rights and Freedoms*), freedom-of-information laws, privacy laws, and laws guaranteeing language rights.

The Effects of Quasi-Constitutional Status

The recognition of a law as "quasi-constitutional" has three effects on its interpretation:

1. The protected rights receive a broad interpretation, while exceptions and defences are narrowly construed.

2. Although quasi-constitutional statutes do not automatically prevail over other statutes, some quasi-constitutional statutes explicitly state that they prevail over other statutes in the event that there is a conflict between them. There is also a rule of statutory interpretation such that, if there are two ways of interpreting a statute, one of which is consistent with upholding the rights granted by a quasi-constitutional statute and one of which is not, the consistent interpretation will prevail. In cases of conflict or inconsistency of a quasi-constitutional statute with other types of legislation, the fact that the other legislation was enacted first will not necessarily mean that it will prevail over the quasi-constitutional statute.

3. When quasi-constitutional laws are interpreted, the key provisions are to be adapted not only to changing social conditions but also to evolving conceptions of the quasi-constitutional right.

Human Rights Codes

Human rights codes typically prohibit discrimination or harassment based on grounds such as race, ancestry, place of origin, colour, ethnic origin, citizenship, creed or religion, sex, sexual orientation, age, marital status, family status, disability (formerly called "handicap"), or the receipt of public assistance. Human rights laws exist in provinces and states through North America and Europe.

Discrimination

Laws prohibiting discrimination have existed in Canada since the turn of the 20th century. The earliest of these laws focused on specific types of discrimination, such as racial discrimination, or on specific areas in which discrimination was prohibited, such as employment or accommodation. These earlier laws were later replaced by more comprehensive human rights codes, which grew out of international conventions such as the Universal Declaration of Human Rights (passed by the United Nations in 1948) and the International Convention on the Elimination of All Forms of Racial Discrimination (adopted by the United Nations in 1965).

In some jurisdictions, human rights commissions and tribunals also administer pay equity and employment equity programs. **Pay equity** is the right of women to receive the same pay as men for work of equal value; human rights codes and pay equity statutes often require employers to develop and implement plans to achieve pay equity. **Employment equity** refers to the elimination of the underrepresentation of individuals in designated groups—such as women, Aboriginals, members of visible minority groups, and people with disabilities—in the workplace. Human rights commissions may require employers to develop and implement employment equity plans to identify and eliminate barriers to the hiring and promotion of individuals in designated groups that result from the employer's employment systems, policies, and practices. They may also require employers to take positive steps to increase the representation of such groups in the workplace.

Unlike section 15 of the *Canadian Charter of Rights and Freedoms*,[1] which only prohibits discrimination by government, human rights codes also apply to the private sector, meaning that they cover the actions of individuals such as landlords, employers, and vendors of goods and services.

> *Anyone can live without voting, but it is extremely difficult to live without a job or without decent accommodation. It is denial of equal access to jobs, homes and public accommodation that most seriously affects a person's dignity, self respect and ability to provide for himself. This is why in the last two or three decades it has been increasingly recognized on this continent that a "shield" against government is not sufficient, what is required is a "sword" against private individuals and groups who practise discrimination.*
>
> Professor Walter Tarnopolsky, quoted in Judith Keene, *Human Rights in Ontario*, 1st ed (Scarborough, Ont: Carswell, 1983) at v

---

1 Part I of the *Constitution Act, 1982*, being Schedule B to the *Canada Act, 1982* (UK), 1982, c 11.

Circumstances Where Discrimination Is Prohibited

In addition to setting out the *grounds* on which discrimination is prohibited, human rights statutes set out the *circumstances* in which discrimination is prohibited. Usually, they mandate equal access to employment, accommodation, government services, education, facilities, and membership in trade unions, professional associations, and similar kinds of organizations.

In many cases, human rights codes provide for exceptions to the rule against discrimination—for example, despite the general right to access to education and employment, a school run by a religious society may be permitted to accept only students who follow that society's religion and hire only teachers who are members of the religion. Other exceptions are discussed below.

The complaints most frequently received by human rights commissions and tribunals relate to discrimination and harassment in employment. Provisions against discrimination in employment generally prohibit a prospective employer from refusing to hire an applicant on grounds such as the applicant's race, age, or sexual orientation. Other provisions prohibit employers from harassing their employees on any of the prohibited grounds, and make employers responsible for taking reasonable measures to prevent their employees from being harassed by other employees, suppliers, or customers. Exceptions to the rule against discrimination in employment include preferential treatment for individuals over 65 or where a law requires Canadian citizenship as a condition of employment.

Although human rights codes usually provide that all persons seeking services, goods, or access to facilities must be given equal treatment, some apply only to services provided to the public generally, to goods provided in public places, and to access to public facilities. Other codes do not make this public/private distinction, instead setting out more specific exceptions—for example, section 10(1) of the Ontario *Human Rights Code*[2] specifies that "service" does not include a levy, fee, tax, or periodic payment imposed by law.

Human rights codes also provide for a right to enter into contracts without discrimination. While the provision of goods, services, and facilities would generally involve making contracts, the right to contract without discrimination also covers such matters as purchasing a franchise; partnership agreements; loans, grants, and guarantees from lending institutions; and the purchase and sale of real estate. As with the other categories, there are exceptions to the right to contract without discrimination. For example, businesses may give preferential treatment to people over the age of 65 (for example, by giving a "seniors discount" on movie tickets), even though this discriminates against younger individuals.

Many human rights codes also prohibit individuals from discriminating in providing accommodation. The right to accommodation would prohibit a landlord from refusing to rent residential, commercial, or industrial property (including a hotel room or vacation cottage) to someone on the basis of, for example, that person's race, and from harassing someone who has already rented the property on such a basis. There are some exceptions. For example, the Ontario *Human Rights*

---

2   RSO 1990, c H.19.

Code recognizes the futility of attempting to force a bigot to share part of his or her home even if it is available to rent; it allows landlords to refuse to rent part of a house where the owner or the owner's family reside in the house and the tenants would share the bathroom or kitchen with the owner's family.

Equity Programs

One of the key exceptions to the rules against discrimination found in human rights codes are **equity programs**, sometimes known as "affirmative action" programs. These programs are designed to "level the playing field"—for example, by removing factors that militate against the acceptance of minorities into post-secondary institutions. To this end, universities may vary application criteria to facilitate higher acceptance levels of individuals who belong to communities historically underrepresented in such institutions, such as by considering non-educational achievements for a certain percentage of new entrants or for applicants who have been in the workforce for a minimum number of years. At the Saskatchewan College of Nursing, for example, some seats are designated for First Nations students once these students have passed entrance examinations.

Educational equity programs may also include accommodating measures such as bridging programs and mentoring. Although critics view affirmative action programs as "reverse discrimination," people in the human rights field see them not as an exception to the rule against discrimination, but as an additional systemic method of pursuing equality.

Finally, human rights codes often prohibit discrimination by trade unions, professional associations, and similar kinds of organizations. For example, a trade union cannot refuse membership to an individual because of that individual's race, and a self-regulating profession cannot subject a member who breaches professional ethics to more severe discipline than it would impose on other members for a similar offence because of the member's sexual orientation.

Intentional and Unintentional Discrimination: The Simpsons-Sears Approach

Although human rights codes have always prohibited *intentional* discrimination against or harassment of individuals, in 1985 the Supreme Court of Canada ruled that such codes also prohibit actions taken in good faith that have an *unintentional* discriminatory effect. In *Ontario Human Rights Commission v Simpsons-Sears*,[3] the Court recognized two types of discrimination: **direct discrimination**, where a standard is discriminatory on its face, and **constructive discrimination** or **adverse effect discrimination**, where an individual or organization imposes an apparently neutral requirement that disproportionately affects a particular individual or group in a negative way. Thus, discrimination can consist not only of treating individuals

---

3   [1985] 2 SCR 536.

differently who are similar, but also of treating individuals similarly who require different treatment to avoid discrimination against them on one of the prohibited grounds.

Consider an employer that requires all male employees who serve customers to be clean-shaven because the employer believes (correctly, in this case) that customers prefer to be served by clean-shaven men. The employer is giving similar treatment to all of its employees, so the policy is not discriminatory on its face. However, even though the employer does not intend to discriminate, the effect of this policy is to exclude all practising male Sikhs from the job, since their religion requires them to wear beards. Therefore, the policy is discriminatory because of its adverse effect on prospective Sikh employees.

In the *Simpsons-Sears* ruling, the Court imposed different requirements on employers depending on whether a discriminatory standard or practice constituted direct discrimination or adverse effect discrimination. In the case of direct discrimination, the employer had the onus of establishing that the practice constituted a bona fide occupational requirement. If it established this, there was no duty to change the practice to meet the needs of affected applicants or employees; if it did not, the practice had to be struck down.

Unlike with direct discrimination, in the case of adverse effect discrimination, the court would not strike down the practice or standard. Rather, it was the employer's duty to modify its practices in relation to the affected employee or prospective employee—to the point of undue hardship to the employer—in order to accommodate him or her. The employee could be denied a job or dismissed only if, after accommodation to the point of undue hardship, he or she could still not perform the job safely and efficiently.

INTENTIONAL (DIRECT) DISCRIMINATION: THE BONA FIDE OCCUPATIONAL REQUIREMENT TEST

In *Simpsons-Sears*, the Court held that an employer could refuse to hire an individual or could terminate an individual's employment because the individual was unable, on grounds recognized by human rights codes, to meet a requirement or condition imposed on other employees *only if* the requirement was a bona fide occupational requirement or qualification. A **bona fide occupational requirement** (usually referred to as a "BFOR") is a requirement that would be essential for anyone to do a particular job successfully. Once a *prima facie* case of direct discrimination has been established, the employer has the legal onus to establish that "the requirement, qualification or factor is reasonable and *bona fide* in the circumstances" (Ontario *Human Rights Code*, s 11(1)(a)).

For the requirement to be a BFOR, it must be necessary for the successful performance of the particular job. For example, a requirement to be able to carry a certain weight over a specified distance may be a bona fide requirement for prospective firefighters because firefighters must be strong enough to carry individuals out of and away from burning buildings. However, for a weight requirement to be a bona fide job requirement, it must be tailored to the requirements of the job. A requirement that applicants be able to carry a weight greater than the weight of the individuals they would need to carry away from the scene of a fire over a distance greater than that over which they would need to carry them in the course of their work—which would exclude all women, including those who have the strength to carry individuals at a fire scene—would not be a BFOR.

To take an extreme example, although it is illegal to discriminate on the basis of disability, a trucking company would not be required to hire a blind driver, since eyesight is a necessary requirement for the job. However, a company could not refuse to hire an individual who was blind for a receptionist position on the basis of this disability, since sight is not necessary to do this job.

UNINTENTIONAL (INDIRECT OR ADVERSE EFFECT) DISCRIMINATION: THE DUTY OF REASONABLE ACCOMMODATION

In the case of the blind applicant for a receptionist position, since sight is not a BFOR, the employer would have a duty to hire the applicant (if he or she was otherwise more qualified for the position than the other applicants) and to provide the equipment and other supports necessary for him or her to perform the job efficiently. An employer's refusal to hire a person because he or she is blind is *direct* discrimination.

To return to the other example above, an employer's refusal to hire a sales clerk because he has a beard is *constructive* or *adverse effect* discrimination. The employer does not intend to discriminate on the basis of the applicant's religion, but prohibiting facial hair has that effect. In such cases, an employer has a duty to reasonably accommodate an employee or applicant who is or who may be a sales clerk and whose religion prevents him from shaving his beard. The doctrine of **accommodation** or the **duty of reasonable accommodation** provides that, where a seemingly neutral qualification or requirement (such as being clean-shaven) has a disproportionately negative impact on a group protected by human rights legislation, the onus is on the employer either to find a way to accommodate the special needs of the affected candidates or employees—including taking all measures that can be taken without causing undue hardship to the business—or to demonstrate that it is unable to reasonably accommodate the employee's needs without undue hardship to the business.

In determining whether a particular accommodation would result in "undue hardship" to an employer, a court or tribunal will focus on the particular circumstances of each case and consider factors such as the cost of accommodating the individual, whether there are outside sources of funding for the measures that will need to be taken, and the potential impact of accommodating the individual on the health or safety of the individual and others.

The duty to accommodate often arises where an employee suffers an injury or illness, or develops an addiction, that prevents the employee from continuing to do his or her job. Despite this, the employer may not fire the employee without first providing reasonable opportunities for rehabilitation or assigning the employee alternative work.

Intentional and Unintentional Discrimination: The "Unified Approach" in BCGSEU

If these distinctions between direct and adverse effect discrimination and between BFORs and the duty to accommodate seem confusing, it's because they are. The

Supreme Court tried to clear up this confusion in its 1999 decision in *British Columbia (Public Service Employee Relations Commission) v BCGSEU*,[4] commonly known as the *Meiorin* case.

In that case, the Court held that although the *Simpsons-Sears* approach represented a significant step forward (because it recognized that, in addition to deliberate discrimination, adverse effect discrimination was illegal as well), it was not reasonable for dramatically different results to follow from classifying a requirement as direct discrimination or adverse effect discrimination. An individual or group that suffers discrimination should be entitled to the same protection regardless of the nature of the discrimination.

The Court therefore held that, regardless of whether the discrimination was intentional or unintentional, the standard causing the discrimination is justified only if the employer establishes

1. that the employer adopted the standard for a purpose rationally connected to the performance of the job;

2. that the employer adopted the standard in an honest and good-faith belief that it was necessary to the fulfillment of that legitimate work-related purpose; and

3. that the standard is reasonably necessary to the accomplishment of that legitimate work-related purpose. (To be found "reasonably necessary," a rule or standard must accommodate individual differences to the point of undue hardship to the employer. If the employer can still make additional accommodations before it reaches the point of undue hardship, the standard is not a BFOR in its existing form and remains a case of discrimination.)

To illustrate the above test, suppose that an employer imposes a requirement for random drug and alcohol testing of all employees in safety-sensitive jobs in an oil refinery, and has a policy of dismissing employees who do not pass the tests based on the belief that these measures are necessary to prevent impaired employees from endangering other employees and the public. Would this requirement of testing and dismissal be a BFOR? Because alcohol and drug impairment may lead to accidents, and because an accident at a refinery could have disastrous results for employees, the public, and the environment, the testing would pass the first and second parts of the three-part *Meiorin* test. However, drug testing would not meet the third requirement of a BFOR. Because a drug test does not measure present impairment but shows only that an individual used a drug within a period of days before the test was administered, a positive drug test provides no evidence of impairment or likely impairment on the job and, therefore, does not demonstrate that an individual is incapable of performing the essential duties of the position.

---

4   [1999] 3 SCR 3.

In contrast, Breathalyzer testing—which measures the amount of alcohol in an individual's blood *at the time of testing*—will show actual impairment of an individual's ability to perform the essential duties of the job; in this case, therefore, requiring all employees in safety-related jobs to undergo and pass random Breathalyzer tests is a BFOR. However, a policy of firing all employees who do not pass the test is *not* a BFOR. Instead, the employer has a duty to accommodate individual differences and capabilities to the point of undue hardship, which would require consideration of sanctions less severe than dismissal, as well as the provision of support to enable employees to undergo treatment or rehabilitation programs.

Harassment and Sexual Harassment

In addition to provisions that prohibit discrimination, many human rights codes have provisions that deal with harassment generally and sexual harassment in particular. The areas in which harassment is prohibited include employment and accommodation.

Harassment consists of vexatious comments or conduct directed at a person because of his or her race, ancestry, or other prohibited ground of discrimination. **Sexual harassment** is any unwelcome sexual solicitation or advance either by someone in a position of power in relation to the victim (such as an employer or landlord) or by someone whose conduct a person in a position of power has the ability to control (such as a co-worker or fellow tenant of the victim). Human rights tribunals do recognize that supervisors or landlords will sometimes become socially involved with employees or tenants, and they differentiate between harassment and normal social contact. As one tribunal put it, "An invitation to dinner is not an invitation to a complaint."

If an employee who is harassing others is in a supervisory position, the employer will generally be held liable for the employee's actions. However, if the harassing employee does not have supervisory functions and is harassing his or her co-workers, the employer may still be held responsible, depending on the circumstances.

Reprisals

Discrimination and harassment are not the only offences against human rights laws. It is also an offence to make or threaten to make a reprisal against a person for attempting to assert or enforce his or her human rights. A reprisal is any unpleasant consequence imposed in retaliation for an action. For example, it would be an offence to fire a worker, refuse to grant a deserved promotion, withhold benefits that are available to other workers, or assign a worker demeaning tasks because he or she rejects an unwanted sexual advance or makes a complaint to a human rights commission.

Enforcement of Human Rights Codes

Human Rights Commissions and Human Rights Tribunals

Most human rights laws establish a human rights commission that has a variety of powers and functions. These powers and functions may include public education;

promoting or establishing policies, guidelines, and programs to create systemic change that will reduce discrimination; and investigating and attempting to resolve allegations of discrimination or harassment, either on the commission's own initiative or at the request of a complainant.

Human rights laws also usually establish a tribunal that will decide the merits of complaints that the human rights commission fails to resolve through conciliation or mediation. These tribunals hold formal hearings in which they hear witnesses, assess their credibility, and decide whether the human rights code has been breached.

The relationship between the human rights commission and the human rights tribunal varies from jurisdiction to jurisdiction. In some cases, the commission decides whether a complaint has sufficient merit to be heard by the tribunal. If the commission brings a complaint before the tribunal, it may also act as "prosecutor," representing the complainant or what it considers to be the public interest against the alleged discriminator at the hearing. Some commissions have a veto power. If they decide that a case does not warrant a hearing, the complainant has no standing to bring the complaint before the tribunal.

In other cases, the complainant can initiate proceedings before the tribunal without the consent or assistance of the commission. The advantage of this system is that complainants are not subject to the whims of a "gatekeeper" or prevented from proceeding by delays in the investigation process. The disadvantage is that complainants may not have publicly funded professional support in investigating the complaint or presenting their case before the tribunal, and may have to hire and pay for their own investigators and lawyers. British Columbia, for example, abolished its human rights commission and gave complainants direct access to a tribunal; however, it provided complainants with no support to assist them in investigating, preparing, or presenting their case before the tribunal.

The Ontario Human Rights Commission primarily carries out public-education and policy-making functions. It no longer investigates complaints, decides whether they warrant a hearing, or prosecutes them before the human rights tribunal. However, the Ontario government has established a Human Rights Legal Support Centre to assist and represent complainants before the Human Rights Tribunal of Ontario. In addition, the Ontario Human Rights Commission has the right to initiate cases on its own and to intervene in cases before the Tribunal. The Tribunal itself has proactive powers to conduct its hearings in a way that will ensure that it can hear and decide the true issues in dispute. For example, regardless of whether the parties are represented and whether they have conducted their own investigations, the Tribunal has the power to order an investigation if one would be helpful, and may order that the results be entered into evidence at a hearing.

Other Methods of Enforcing Human Rights Codes

Although specialized human rights commissions and human rights tribunals have been established specifically to enforce human rights codes, this does not mean that they are the only forum, or even the most appropriate forum, for resolving human rights complaints. The Supreme Court of Canada has ruled that human rights claims do not have to be decided by bodies that have human rights expertise.

Discrimination and harassment occur in relation to matters such as employment, education, and rental agreements. Therefore, specialized bodies set up to resolve disputes in those areas of law, such as the Labour Relations Board, Special Education Tribunal, and Landlord and Tenant Board, as well as some courts, may also have jurisdiction to make a ruling on whether the statutes they enforce have been violated. Where the alleged violation of the employment law, education law, or landlord and tenant law is also a violation of the human rights code, both the tribunal or court with jurisdiction over the subject matter and the human rights commission or tribunal may have jurisdiction to hear the case and provide a remedy. This is known as **concurrent jurisdiction**.

Therefore, when deciding whether to bring a case before a human rights body, a court, or a tribunal that has jurisdiction over the subject area in which the discrimination arose, the first question to ask is whether the court or other tribunal has jurisdiction to decide the human rights issue and grant a remedy for violation of the human rights code, or whether the human rights agency has exclusive jurisdiction. In some cases, such as with arbitrators under Ontario's labour relations laws, a statute gives them explicit power to decide human rights issues. In other cases, a statute will explicitly state that a court or tribunal *cannot* decide human rights issues. When a statute does not explicitly address this question, the Supreme Court of Canada has ruled that any administrative decision-maker that has the power to decide questions of law has the power to apply the human rights code.[5] Since most tribunals have authority to decide questions of law, this means that most tribunals have authority to apply human rights codes.

When the human rights commission or tribunal and another tribunal or court have concurrent jurisdiction, the next question that arises is which forum is the most appropriate for deciding the human rights issue and who decides this question? Can the applicant bring the case before both bodies? If not, can the applicant choose which body to apply to? If the applicant raises the human rights issue before, for example, a landlord and tenant board or a labour arbitrator and obtains an unfavourable result there, can he or she still ask the human rights agency to rule on that issue? The answers are found, at least in part, in the Supreme Court's ruling in *British Columbia (Workers' Compensation Board) v Figliola*.[6]

Mr. Figliola and other workers suffering from chronic pain challenged the British Columbia Workers' Compensation Board's chronic pain policy before the Board's Review Division. There, they raised several issues, including an allegation that the policy was discriminatory under the British Columbia *Human Rights Code*.[7] When the review officer ruled that the policy did not offend the *Human Rights Code*, Mr. Figliola and his co-workers filed new complaints, raising the same human rights issue, before the province's Human Rights Tribunal.

---

5   *Tranchemontagne v Ontario (Director, Disability Support Program)*, 2006 SCC 14, [2006] 1 SCR 513.

6   2011 SCC 52, [2011] 3 SCR 422; see also *Penner v Niagara (Regional Police Services Board)*, 2013 SCC 19, [2013] 2 SCR 125.

7   RSBC 1996, c 210.

The Workers' Compensation Board argued that, having raised the human rights issue and lost before the Board's Review Division, the complainants could not relitigate the same issue before the Human Rights Tribunal of Ontario.

The Supreme Court of Canada ruled against Mr. Figliola, finding that the principles of finality, the avoidance of multiplicity of proceedings, and protection for the integrity of the administration of justice are to be considered in such cases, all in the name of fairness. In this case, the Court found, these principles weighed against allowing the applicants to relitigate before the Human Rights Tribunal of Ontario an issue that had already been decided before the Workers' Compensation Board.

The situation is different, however, when another tribunal has not yet decided a human rights issue brought before both a tribunal and a human rights body. In such cases, a statute may determine which case should proceed (for example, the Ontario *Human Rights Code* provides that where a human rights violation is alleged as part of a civil action, an application may not also be made before the Human Rights Tribunal of Ontario).[8]

Where a statute does not determine who goes first, the human rights body will often defer its consideration of the application until the other proceeding dealing with the same facts is completed. However, a deferral is not automatic. When there are other proceedings pending, the Tribunal will decide whether to defer on a case-by-case basis, having regard to the purposes of the Code and the need to achieve a fair, just and expeditious resolution of claims.[9]

Remedies for Discrimination and Harassment

Human rights codes often give human rights commissions and tribunals wide latitude to fashion remedies to compensate for past violations or to prevent future violations that are appropriate to the circumstances of the particular case. For example, a store owner might be ordered to apologize to a victim; an employer or landlord might be ordered to offer the complainant an opportunity to apply for the next job opening or vacancy in a rental unit; an employer found to have sexually harassed employees might be ordered to notify the human rights commission every time an employee leaves his or her job; a harassed employee might be awarded money to pay for counselling; an unfairly fired employee might be reinstated and compensated for lost income, hurt feelings, humiliation, and so on.

In addition to these remedies for individuals, human rights bodies often have the power to order governments to change practices and policies that result in systemic discrimination against a group of individuals. It remains unclear whether these bodies also have jurisdiction to order government agencies not to apply or enforce statutory provisions that have a discriminatory effect. Although only a violation of the Charter allows a court or tribunal to *strike down* a statute or regulation, some courts have ruled that human rights bodies can still order a regulator to *cease*

---

8   *Supra* note 2, s 34(11).

9   Cornish, Faraday & Pickel, *Enforcing Human Rights in Ontario* (Aurora, Ont: Canada Law Book, 2009) at 108–10.

applying laws that violate human rights codes. At least one court, however, has ruled that human rights tribunals cannot make such an order because it is tantamount to striking down a law, which is a remedy available only for a Charter violation, not a violation of a human rights code.

Freedom-of-Information and Protection-of-Privacy Statutes

The provincial, territorial, and federal legislatures have all passed laws requiring governments to provide the public with access to general government records while protecting the privacy of "personal information"—that is, information that governments have collected about individuals. These access and privacy laws are quasi-constitutional because they foster democracy and government accountability.

> *The overarching purpose of access to information legislation, then, is to facilitate democracy. It does so in two related ways. It helps to ensure first, that citizens have the information required to participate meaningfully in the democratic process, and secondly, that politicians and bureaucrats remain accountable to the citizenry. ... Rights to state-held information are designed to improve the workings of government; to make it more effective, responsive and accountable.*
>
> La Forest J in *Dagg v Canada (Minister of Finance)*,
> [1997] 2 SCR 403 at paras 61, 63

The right to privacy was recognized by the United Nations in its Universal Declaration of Human Rights in 1948, in the 1950 European Convention for the Protection of Human Rights and Fundamental Freedoms, and in the 1966 International Covenant on Civil and Political Rights. The Supreme Court of Canada has explained that privacy is considered a fundamental right because "the protection of privacy is necessary to the preservation of a free and democratic society."[10] The Court went on to explain why privacy is essential to democracy:

> An expression of an individual's unique personality or personhood, privacy is grounded on physical and moral autonomy—the freedom to engage in one's own thoughts, actions and decisions.

Freedom-of-information and protection-of-privacy laws generally provide citizens with a broad right of access to all information in the custody or under the control of government bodies unless the information falls within specific exemptions, which are to be narrowly construed.

Exemptions from the right of access generally include Cabinet documents, advice and recommendations from public servants to their superiors, law enforcement records, information received in confidence from other governments, information

---

10   *Lavigne v Canada (Office of the Commissioner of Official Languages)*, 2002 SCC 53, [2002] 2 SCR
     773 at para 25.

received from businesses in confidence, and information whose disclosure would harm the government's economic interests. Much of the personal information held by governments is also exempted from this broad right of access to preserve personal privacy.

In addition to the government's duty to keep personal information in its possession confidential, privacy laws usually require governments to give individuals records that contain information about them on request and to correct inaccurate personal information about individuals in documents in their possession.

When a government body receives a request for information, access and privacy laws generally require that it decide whether to provide access within a specified time period (usually 30 days) and limit the amount of money that it can charge for this service.

If a government body refuses to provide access to information, denies that a document exists, delays making a decision, refuses to correct inaccurate information in documents containing an individual's personal information, or charges excessive fees to process a request, this decision can usually be appealed to an independent tribunal operated in some cases by the provincial ombudsman and by an information and privacy commissioner in others. In some cases, the commissioner or ombudsman has the power to overrule the government body and order it to release the records; in other cases, such as that of the Information Commissioner of Canada, the commissioner can only recommend disclosure. In those cases, if the government body ignores the recommendation, the applicant or the commissioner may be able to apply to a court for a binding ruling.

In addition to laws to preserve the privacy of government records, the federal government and some provinces have passed statutes restricting the collection, use, and disclosure of the personal information of customers in the course of commercial activities, such as the purchase and sale of goods and services, without the customers' consent. These laws also regulate non-commercial organizations such as non-profit groups when they carry out commercial activities such as fundraising.

In Alberta, Manitoba, Saskatchewan, and Ontario, institutions and individuals subject to privacy laws specific to personal health information that require them to maintain the confidentiality of patient records include hospitals, medical clinics, doctors, and members of other health professions such as dentistry, physiotherapy, and naturopathy.

The Canadian Bill of Rights

Before the Constitution was amended to include the Charter, Canada had (and still has) a quasi-constitutional statute that codified many of the common law rules of procedural fairness and contained rights similar to those now found in the Charter. This statute is the *Canadian Bill of Rights*.[11] The *Bill of Rights* dictates that all other federal laws must be interpreted and applied, wherever possible, in a manner that does not deprive a person of the right to a fair hearing. It also provides that every

---

11 SC 1960, c 44.

other law of Canada must be interpreted so as not to infringe the rights or freedoms recognized in it, unless the law expressly said otherwise.

The *Bill of Rights* protects the right of individuals to a fair hearing in accordance with the principles of fundamental justice in order to determine their rights and obligations, as well as their right not to be deprived of life, liberty, security of the person, and enjoyment of property except by due process of law when decisions are made by federal government bureaucrats and tribunals.

Although the *Bill of Rights* has largely been superseded by the Charter, it is still in force, and courts occasionally rely on its provisions to ensure procedural fairness. For example, in *Singh v Minister of Employment and Immigration*,[12] three of the six Supreme Court judges who heard the case ruled that the failure of the *Immigration Act* to permit the Immigration Appeal Board to give refugee complainants an opportunity to have an oral hearing violated section 2(e) of the *Bill of Rights*, which states that "no law of Canada shall be construed or applied so as to deprive a person of the right to a fair hearing in accordance to the principles of fundamental justice for the determination of his rights and obligations." The other three judges applied section 7 of the Charter to reach the same result.

Official Languages Laws

Language rights are considered a class of fundamental human rights because of the importance of language in preserving cultural identity and institutions. Although Canada has two founding peoples, one English-speaking and one French-speaking, the Constitution provides for the right of individuals to speak and be spoken to in the language of their choice (English or French) only in certain contexts. Quasi-constitutional laws have therefore been passed to extend language rights beyond what the Constitution grants.

> The importance of language rights is grounded in the essential role that language plays in human existence, development and dignity. It is through language that we are able to form concepts; to structure and order the world around us. Language bridges the gap between isolation and community, allowing humans to delineate the rights and duties they hold in respect of one another, and thus to live in society.
>
> *Re Manitoba Language Rights*, [1985] 1 SCR 721
> at para 46, 19 DLR (4th) 1 at 19 (SCC)

The *Constitution Act, 1867* permitted either French or English to be used in debates in the Parliament of Canada and the Quebec National Assembly, and required the records of these debates to be published in both languages. It also required federal and Quebec statutes to be published in both languages, and gave litigants the right to use either language in the federal courts and the courts of Quebec. However, it did not impose these requirements and rights in any of the other provinces.

---

12 [1985] 1 SCR 177.

Language rights have been expanded by the Charter. Section 14 gives any party or witness in proceedings before a court or tribunal who does not understand or speak the language of the proceeding a right to an interpreter. This right is not limited to service in English or French.

The Charter also expands French and English language rights beyond legislatures and courts to other government services. For example, section 20 imposes an obligation on the Government of Canada to provide bilingual services to the public, but only in areas where there is a "significant demand" or where it is reasonable to expect service in French due to the nature of the office. However, the Charter requires that federal offices provide services in both languages throughout New Brunswick.

In all of the provinces that have English-speaking majorities, section 23 provides that a Canadian citizen whose mother tongue is French has the right to have his or her children educated in French.

Where the Charter does not guarantee the right to use the French language in provinces with an English-speaking majority or the right to use English in Quebec or in French-speaking areas of a province (such as those around Ottawa and northeastern Ontario), quasi-constitutional statutes and equality-enhancing provisions in other statutes sometimes fill this gap. For example, in Ontario, the *French Language Services Act*[13] guarantees the use of both languages in the proceedings of the Legislative Assembly; in bills, statutes, and regulations; and in the provision of government services. The Ontario Court of Appeal used the last of these rights to overrule a decision of the Ontario government to reduce the services provided by a French-language community hospital in an area where the primary language spoken is French.[14] Section 530 of the *Criminal Code*[15] gives accused persons the right to a trial before a judge or a judge and jury who speak the official language spoken by the accused.

Quebec's *Charter of the French Language*[16] was passed in 1977 to preserve the use of French as the primary language of that province. Its goal is to make French the everyday language of work, instruction, communication, and business. To this end, it declares French to be the official language of Quebec, and affirms that every person in Quebec has the right to have the government, health services, social services, public utilities, professional corporations, unions, and all enterprises doing business in Quebec communicate in French. Its best-known requirement is the requirement that signs, posters, product labels, manuals, warranty certificates, restaurant menus, and wine lists be in French, although they may also be in another language provided that the French wording has greater prominence.

Canada's *Official Languages Act*[17] (OLA), first passed in 1969, recognized English and French as the official languages of all federal institutions in Canada. After this right was guaranteed by the Charter in 1982, the OLA was amended in 1988 and

---

13 RSO 1990, c F.32.

14 *Lalonde v Ontario (Commission de restructuration des services de santé)* (2001), 56 OR (3d) 505 (CA).

15 RSC 1985, c C-46, as amended.

16 CQLR c C-11.

17 RSC 1985, c 31 (4th Supp).

again in 2005 to flesh out the federal government's responsibilities for promoting bilingualism in the federal civil service and to strengthen the remedies for failure to comply with the Act.

Among other things, the Act requires

- that federal institutions provide services in both languages in areas designated "bilingual";
- that federal public service employees in a designated bilingual region have the opportunity to work in their chosen language;
- that choice of language does not prevent an applicant for a federal public service job from obtaining employment or preclude an employee from advancement;
- that decisions made by the federal government do not have a negative impact on the vitality of an English-speaking community in Quebec or a French-speaking community in a primarily English-speaking province; and
- that the federal government respect the equal status of both languages.

The areas to be designated as bilingual for the purposes of providing service and working are determined by applying rules set out in regulations under the Act. The National Capital Region, some parts of northern and eastern Ontario, the region of Montreal, parts of the Eastern Townships, the Gaspé region and western Quebec, and New Brunswick have been designated as bilingual for such purposes.

The OLA establishes a Commissioner of Official Languages, who is a kind of ombudsman, to oversee the implementation of the OLA. The Commissioner may investigate complaints of violations of the Act. If the Commissioner finds that the complaint is valid, the Commissioner may recommend that the government change its practices.

A complainant who is not satisfied with the Commissioner's findings or recommendations may seek a remedy in the Federal Court. The complainant may also initiate action in court if an institution refuses to follow the Commissioner's recommendations. The Commissioner may also intervene in the proceedings when a complainant claims a violation of the OLA in court.

CHAPTER SUMMARY

Quasi-constitutional laws encompass rights that are recognized nationally, and usually also internationally, as being of fundamental importance to society, such as freedom from discrimination, access to government information, and privacy and language rights. Unlike the Constitution, these laws do not automatically override ordinary laws, but they often contain clauses that provide that they prevail over other laws in the event of a conflict. Even in the absence of such provisions, quasi-constitutional laws will often be interpreted as overriding laws with which they conflict. In addition, while the Charter only protects people from government actions, quasi-constitutional statutes also often apply to businesses and individuals.

The most important quasi-constitutional laws are probably the federal and provincial human rights codes, which prohibit discrimination or harassment on grounds such as race, ancestry, place of origin, colour, ethnic origin, citizenship, creed or religion, sex, sexual orientation, age, marital status, family status, disability, or the receipt of public assistance. Other quasi-constitutional laws are the *Canadian Bill of Rights*, which largely duplicates the rights and freedoms now found in the Charter; freedom of information laws, which give individuals a right of access to government-held information subject to certain exemptions; privacy laws, which require governments, businesses, and the healing professions to keep information about individuals confidential and to give individuals access to their own personal information; and official languages laws, which are intended to protect the cultures of official language minorities by preserving their rights to communicate in the official language of their choice.

KEY TERMS

accommodation: *see* duty of reasonable accommodation

adverse effect discrimination: the act of imposing an apparently neutral requirement that disproportionately affects a particular individual or group in a negative way based on a ground of discrimination prohibited under a human rights code

bona fide occupational requirement: a requirement or qualification for employment that is essential to the successful carrying out of the duties of a position, and therefore justifies discriminating against an individual who cannot meet the requirement based on one of the grounds of discrimination prohibited under a human rights code; also called a "BFOR"

concurrent jurisdiction: two or more courts or tribunals having authority over the same matters

constructive discrimination: *see* adverse effect discrimination

convention: an agreement among nations, such as a multilateral treaty

direct discrimination: discrimination resulting from a standard that is discriminatory on its face, rather than from a standard that is neutral on its face but has a discriminatory effect; *see also* adverse effect discrimination

duty of reasonable accommodation: where a requirement or qualification has a disproportionately negative effect on an individual because of a ground prohibited by human rights legislation, the duty of an employer to take all reasonable steps to the point of undue hardship to accommodate the special needs of that individual

employment equity: the elimination of the underrepresentation of individuals in designated groups—such as women, Aboriginals, members of visible minority groups, and people with disabilities—in the workplace

equity program: program designed to "level the playing field" for disadvantaged groups—for example, an employment, educational, or pay equity program

harassment: vexatious comments or conduct directed at a person because of his or her race, ancestry, or other prohibited ground of discrimination under a human rights code

human rights: the freedoms, immunities, and benefits generally recognized nationally as well as internationally as rights to which all individuals should be entitled in the society in which they live

pay equity: the right of women to receive the same pay as men for work of equal value

quasi-constitutional: in relation to a law, a law that is below a country's Constitution but above ordinary laws in the hierarchy of laws because it protects rights that, although they may not be explicitly recognized in the Constitution, are very important to society

sexual harassment: any unwelcome sexual solicitation or advance either by someone in a position of power in relation to the victim (such as an employer or landlord) or by someone whose conduct a person in a position of power has the ability to control (such as a co-worker or fellow tenant of the victim)

CASES TO CONSIDER

Adverse Effect Discrimination and the Duty of Reasonable Accommodation

Ont Human Rights Comm v Simpsons-Sears, [1985] 2 SCR 536

FACTS: A store required its full-time sales clerks to work Friday evenings on a rotating basis and on two Saturdays out of every three. A sales clerk became a member of a religion that required observance of the Sabbath from sundown Friday to sundown Saturday. When she notified her employer that she could no longer work on Saturdays, she was fired as a full-time employee. She was rehired as a part-time employee and the employer told her she would be considered for any jobs for which she might be suited that did not require working on her Sabbath.

The employee brought a complaint of discrimination on the basis of creed contrary to section 4(1)(g) of the Ontario *Human Rights Code*. The Human Rights Commission represented the complainant in arguing before a board of inquiry that this was discrimination. The board held that the Code prohibited not only employment conditions that are on their face discriminatory, but also those that are innocuous in their terms but result in discrimination against an employee. The board also held that even though the Code does not say so explicitly, an employer has a duty to reasonably accommodate employees affected by employment conditions that have a discriminatory effect.

However, as the employer had taken steps to lessen the adverse impact of its policy, the board held that the employer had acted to reasonably accommodate the employee. Therefore, the complaint was dismissed.

The Commission appealed the dismissal of the complaint to the Divisional Court. The court upheld the dismissal of the complaint on the grounds that the Code prohibited only intentional discrimination. The Court of Appeal also upheld the dismissal of the complaint. The Commission appealed to the Supreme Court of Canada.

ISSUES: Was a policy requiring all full-time employees to work some Friday evenings and Saturdays discriminatory even though it was made for sound business reasons, applied to all employees, and was not intended to be discriminatory? Did the Ontario *Human Rights Code* require an employer to take reasonable steps to accommodate the religious needs of an employee even though there was no explicit language in the Code describing or referring to such a duty?

DECISION: The Supreme Court drew a distinction between direct discrimination and adverse effect discrimination. It found that if the effect of a policy is discriminatory, the policy violates the Ontario *Human Rights Code* even if the purpose of the policy is not discriminatory. The Court also found that even though the Code does not refer to a "duty to accommodate," this duty can be derived as a corollary of the general principles embodied in the legislation. The Court stated that a natural corollary of the right to be free from discrimination in employment must be the social acceptance of a general duty to respect the right and to act within reason to protect the right. "In this case, consistent with the provisions and intent of the *Ontario Human Rights Code*, the employee's right requires reasonable steps towards an accommodation by the employer."

Rejection of the Distinction Between Direct Discrimination and Adverse Effect Discrimination

British Columbia (Public Service Employee Relations Commission) v BCGSEU, [1999] 3 SCR 3

FACTS: Tawney Meiorin was a female forest firefighter who was dismissed after failing an aerobic test imposed by the BC government. The test was intended to measure whether an employee was in good enough physical condition to effectively carry out the duties of a forest firefighter.

Meiorin's union filed a grievance against her dismissal alleging that her dismissal constituted discrimination in employment on the basis of sex. The arbitrator accepted evidence that, due to physiological differences, women have a lower aerobic capacity than men and, unlike men, most women could not pass the aerobic test even with practice. Therefore, requiring a female employee to pass this test constituted adverse effect discrimination because the requirement had a disproportionately negative impact on female employees. The arbitrator also found that the employer had not established that Meiorin's inability to pass the test meant that she constituted a safety risk to herself, her colleagues, or the public. Therefore, the employer had a duty to accommodate her to the point of undue hardship. The arbitrator ordered the employer to reinstate Meiorin and compensate her for lost wages and benefits.

The employer appealed to the Court of Appeal, which held that, as long as the standard was necessary to the safe and efficient performance of the work, and was applied through individual testing, there was no discrimination. Meiorin's union appealed this decision on her behalf to the Supreme Court.

ISSUES: Did the imposition of a standard intended to protect the safety of the public and other workers, and applied through individualized testing, that had a disproportionately negative effect on women discriminate on the basis of sex, contrary to the BC *Human Rights Code*? If so, was the standard justified as a BFOR? If the standard was not justified, what remedies were available?

DECISION: The Supreme Court rejected the distinction between direct discrimination and adverse effect discrimination that it had adopted in *Simpsons-Sears*. The Court stated that, while the distinction may have served well in the past, it was too complex and artificial and should be replaced by a simplified and unified analysis. It was open to the Court to adopt an interpretive approach that reflected the evolution of human rights law and would better fulfill the objectives of that law.

Whether the discrimination was intentional or unintentional, the standard causing the discrimination is justified as a BFOR only if the employer establishes

1. that the employer adopted the standard for a purpose rationally connected to the performance of the job;

2. that the employer adopted the particular standard in an honest and good-faith belief that it was necessary to the fulfillment of that legitimate work-related purpose; and

3. that the standard is reasonably necessary to the accomplishment of that legitimate work-related purpose.

A rule or standard must accommodate individual differences to the point of undue hardship if it is to be found reasonably necessary. Unless no further accommodation is possible without imposing undue hardship, the standard is not a BFOR in its existing form and the standard remains a case of discrimination.

Because the testing disproportionately affected women in a negative way, it was, on its face, discriminatory. Therefore, to be acceptable, the discrimination had to meet the three-part BFOR test. In this case, the testing satisfied the first two steps of the test; however, the employer failed to establish that the aerobic standard in question was reasonably necessary to the determination of whether an individual was able to perform the duties of a forest firefighter safely and efficiently. The employer did not establish that it would experience undue hardship if a different standard were used. The Court reinstated Meiorin to her former position and awarded her compensation for lost wages and benefits.

Privacy Rights and Publication of Tribunal Decisions on the Internet

Germain v Automobile Injury Appeal Commission, 2009 SKQB 106

FACTS: An individual injured in a motor vehicle accident in Saskatchewan is entitled under the *Automobile Accident Insurance Act* (AAIA) to benefits for bodily injury. If the individual does not agree with the amount of benefits that an adjuster for the insurance plan determines he or she is entitled to, the individual may appeal the adjuster's decision to the Automobile Injury Appeal Commission. The Commission publishes its decisions on its website and on the website of the Canadian Legal Information Institute (CanLII).

Elaine Germain was injured in a motor vehicle accident. In an appeal before the Commission, she claimed that she was wrongfully denied benefits under the AAIA. Because she did not want her medical, income, and other personal information made public (stating that this would cause her embarrassment), Germain asked the Commission not to publish any decision about her on its website, or, if it did, to remove her name, age, occupation, and other personal details from the decision. She made the same request of the Commission regarding her personal information in its publications generally. The Commission decided to continue publishing its full decisions on its website, including Germain's personal information.

Germain applied to the Court of Queen's Bench for an order prohibiting the Commission from publishing the results of her appeal on the Internet or otherwise unless her personal information was removed.

ISSUES: Did the Commission's governing legislation give it the authority to publish its decisions generally or on the Internet? Did provincial privacy legislation preclude the Commission from doing so? Would the publication of the decision in Germain's case before the Commission that included her personal information violate her section 7 or section 8 Charter rights?

DECISION: The AAIA does not explicitly authorize the Commission to publish its decisions. However, the Commission does not require explicit authority. The publication of decisions is incidental and necessary to the proper functioning of the tribunal. Moreover, the Commission is part of the administration of justice, and the open court principle mandates openness and accessibility with regard to its decisions. Therefore, the Commission has authority to publish its decisions, including on the Internet, despite the absence of statutory or regulatory provisions specifically allowing it to do so.

The court's inquiry, however, did not end there. The court then sought to determine whether the Commission's powers were circumscribed by other legislation—specifically, whether privacy legislation prevented the Commission from publishing decisions that identified parties. It considered several provisions of the *Health Information Protection Act* (which protects the privacy of personal health information) and the provincial *Freedom of Information and Protection of Privacy Act* (which protects the privacy of other personal information, such as financial information), and found that neither precluded the Commission from publishing decisions on the Internet containing personal health information and other personal information.

Section 8 of the Charter protects the public from unreasonable search and seizure. The information that Germain provided to the Commission was for the purpose of assisting the Commission in assessing the merits of her appeal, not to gather evidence with a view to laying criminal or regulatory charges. This collection of information was not a search or seizure, and there was, therefore, no violation of section 8.

Section 7 of the Charter provides that everyone has the right to life, liberty, and security of the person, and the right not to be deprived of these rights except in accordance with the principles of fundamental justice. Security of the person includes a right to privacy where the violation of privacy is sufficient to interfere with an individual's psychological integrity. However, the Commission's practice of publishing its decisions and any associated stress do not meet this standard because the level of psychological stress produced is not believed to be sufficiently high. In addition, the only principle of fundamental justice alleged to have been violated was Germain's alleged right to be given notice, when she initiated her appeal, that the appeal decision would be published. The lack of notice in this case did not violate the principles of fundamental justice, since Germain's privacy interests must also be weighed against the Charter right of freedom of expression and the open courts principle.

The Scope of Language Rights in Criminal Trials

R v Beaulac, [1999] 1 SCR 768

FACTS: Beaulac was charged with murder. Five days into his trial, he applied to the trial judge for an order that his trial be heard before a judge and jury who speak both official languages of Canada. The request was made pursuant to section 530 of the *Criminal Code*. Section 530(1) provides that if an accused whose language is one of the official languages of Canada applies in a timely manner, the court must direct that the trial be held before a justice of the peace, judge, or judge and jury who speak the official language that is the language of the accused, or, if the circumstances warrant, who speak both official languages.

If an accused fails to apply for an order within the time frame set out in section 530(1) but the court is satisfied that it is in the best interests of justice that the accused be tried by a justice of the peace, judge, or judge and jury who speak the official language that is the language of the accused, section 530(4) permits the court if it does not speak that language, to order that the trial be conducted by a justice of the peace, judge, or judge and jury who speak that language or, if the circumstances warrant, who speak both official languages.

The trial judge refused Beaulac's application.

Subsequently, there was a mistrial, and a retrial was ordered. Beaulac applied for the retrial to be before a judge and jury who spoke both official languages. The judge who heard the application decided that while Beaulac's English "was not the most refined … his message gets across clearly and forcefully." He concluded that no injustice would result from a new trial in English, and refused the application. Beaulac made further applications under section 530(4), and all were refused. On appeal of one of these refusals, the Court of Appeal upheld the refusal to grant a trial before a judge and jury who speak both official languages, based on Beaulac's ability to speak English. Beaulac appealed to the Supreme Court of Canada.

ISSUES: What is the meaning of the phrase "the language of the accused" in section 530 of the *Criminal Code*? What is the meaning of the phrase "the best interests of justice" in section 530(4), and what is the scope of the discretion granted to a court to refuse a trial before a judge and jury who speak both official languages?

DECISION: To understand the language rights and the scope of section 530, it is necessary to interpret them in the context of the objective of protecting official language minorities, as set out in section 2 of the *Official Languages Act*. Language rights must be interpreted purposively, in a manner consistent with the preservation and development of official language communities in Canada. Language rights are a fundamental tool for the preservation and protection of official language communities.

The phrase "the language of the accused" should be interpreted in light of the purpose of section 530, which is to provide equal access to the courts to accused persons speaking one of the official languages of Canada in order to assist official language minorities in preserving their cultural identity, not just to ensure a fair trial. Therefore, for the purposes of sections 530(1) and (4), an accused's own language is either of the two official languages to which that person has a sufficient connection; it does not have to be the person's dominant language. If an accused has sufficient knowledge of an official language to instruct counsel, the accused will be able to assert that that language is his or her language, regardless of whether the accused can speak the other language.

Once it has been determined that the language that the accused wants the judge and jury to speak and understand is "his language," under section 530(4) the judge must determine whether the best interests of justice will be served by granting the application. Since the rule is that access to a trial in one's official language is automatic when an application is made in a timely manner and discretionary when it is not, in an application under section 530(4), in determining the "best interests of justice" the trial judge should consider, foremost, the reasons for the delay in making the application. Other relevant factors are: whether the accused is represented by counsel, the language in which the evidence is available, the language of witnesses, whether a jury has been chosen, whether witnesses have already testified, whether the witnesses are still available, whether proceedings can continue in a different language without the need to start the trial afresh, whether there are co-accuseds (which would indicate the need for separate trials), whether changes will need to be made in the accused's counsel, whether the Crown will need to change prosecutors, and the language ability of the presiding judge. Mere administrative inconvenience is not a relevant factor.

The Court granted Beaulac's application for a new trial to be held before a judge and jury who spoke both French and English.

REVIEW QUESTIONS

1. What characteristics make a law "quasi-constitutional"?

2. What are the effects of characterizing a law as quasi-constitutional?

3. What are the typical grounds upon which human rights codes prohibit discrimination?

4. To what areas of activity do human rights codes generally apply?

5. Is an employer permitted to fire an employee who can no longer perform the job in a satisfactory manner because of an illness, injury, or addiction? Explain.

6. How are human rights codes enforced?

7. What rights do freedom-of-information and protection-of-privacy statutes confer?

8. What rights found in the *Canadian Bill of Rights* have the potential to enhance common law and statutory procedural fairness requirements for administrative actions?

9. What are the obligations of the federal government under the *Official Languages Act*?

10. How does Quebec's *Charter of the French Language* affect the use of English in that province?

EXERCISES

1. Find four court decisions since 2000 that have considered the application of the *Canadian Bill of Rights*. For each case, provide its name and citation, the relevant facts, the issues raised that related to the *Bill of Rights*, and how the court resolved those issues.

2. Compare sections 7 and 11(d) of the *Canadian Charter of Rights and Freedoms* with sections 1(a) and 2(e) of the *Canadian Bill of Rights*. How do they differ from each other?

FACT SCENARIO

An employee has asthma, which is recognized as a disability under the province's human rights code. The employee says that he has difficulty breathing at certain times of the year, including in the spring, when there is pollen in the air, and on very cold days in the winter. In fact, the employee has so much difficulty breathing that he is frequently absent from work. He asks permission to work from home on days when it is difficult for him to breathe. However, this would require him to take confidential materials out of the office, which raises security concerns.

The employer is willing to accommodate the employee within reason. The employer asks for a letter from the employee's doctor explaining what work the employee is capable of, and the prognosis and expected timeframe for improvement of the employee's condition, if applicable. The doctor provides a letter stating simply that the employee must work from home until further notice from the doctor.

The employer asks the employee to provide a more detailed letter from his doctor so that he can assess whether the doctor just accepted what the employee told her or conducted tests and formed an independent diagnosis or prognosis. The employee refuses, saying that disclosing additional details would violate his privacy. The employer then asks the employee to see a doctor selected by the employer. The employee refuses on the same grounds.

Does the employer still have a duty to accommodate the employee's disability under these circumstances? If the employer has a duty to accommodate, does the employee have a corresponding duty to cooperate with the employer? If not, why not? If so, to what extent?

FURTHER READING

Mary Cornish, Fay Faraday & Jo-Anne Pickel, *Enforcing Human Rights in Ontario* (Aurora, Ont: Canada Law Book, 2009).

James D'Andrea, *Illness and Disability in the Workplace* (Aurora, Ont: Canada Law Book) (loose-leaf).

Michel W Drapeau & Marc-Aurèle Racicot, *Federal Access to Information and Privacy Legislation Annotated 2014* (Toronto: Carswell, 2013).

David Goodis & Allison Knight, *The 2013 Annotated Ontario Freedom of Information and Protection of Privacy Acts* (Toronto: Carswell, 2013).

Jeffrey Kaufman, *Privacy Law in the Private Sector: An Annotation of the Legislation in Canada* (Aurora, Ont: Canada Law Book, 2007) (loose-leaf).

Judith Keene, *Human Rights in Ontario*, 2nd ed (Scarborough, Ont: Carswell, 1992).

Barbara McIsaac, Rick Shields & Kris Klein, *The Law of Privacy in Canada* (Toronto: Carswell, 2000) (loose-leaf).

Fairness: The Right to Be Heard

6

LEARNING OUTCOMES

After reading this chapter, you will understand

- the sources of fairness procedures for departments and tribunals and other agencies;

- the factors that determine the appropriate level of procedural fairness to be provided by a department or a tribunal or other agency;

- the two main principles or "pillars" of common law procedural fairness;

- the rights and duties entailed by the first principle of procedural fairness—the right to be heard;

- what constitutes adequate notice of a tribunal's proceedings; and

- the exceptions to and limits on the duty of departments and tribunals and other agencies to ensure that parties receive the rights entailed by the right to be heard.

The Islands Protection Society is an environmental body that is comprised of approximately 1200 members. It concerns itself with matters of environmental interest in the Queen Charlottes. The society has filed a notice of appeal with respect to [two permits to spray pesticides on 300 hectares of timber on the Queen Charlotte Islands]. The society has requested that the appeals be conducted by way of oral public hearings. The [Environmental Appeal] Board denied this request and concluded that the appeals would be determined solely on the basis of written submissions. ... It is agreed that generally, in the absence of legislation, there is no absolute obligation upon an administrative tribunal to hold oral hearings in order to comply with the rules of natural justice. However, in this case the clear implication from the legislation is that an oral hearing is required. ... The legislation in this case contemplates the holding of open public hearings with full participation by interested parties. The Lieutenant Governor in Council has deemed the spraying of pesticides to be of such significance that it has given concerned members of the community who are not parties to the action the right to appeal or intervene. The issue of whether the board ought to either set aside or uphold the granting of the permits is of obvious public importance. It would be fundamentally wrong and against the rules of natural justice to hear and determine matters of such public importance without holding public hearings in which oral evidence and representations can be heard.

Islands Protection Society v Environmental Appeal Board (1986), 8 BCLR (2d) 30

As discussed in Chapter 3, today all government decision-makers must follow fair procedures when making decisions that affect people's rights, privileges, and interests. Unlike in the past, the distinction between administrative and quasi-judicial decisions no longer governs whether procedural fairness is required. However, what specific procedures *are* required still depends to some extent on the nature of the decision, including where it falls on the decision-making spectrum, from purely administrative to quasi-judicial.

For officials and bodies that follow an informal decision-making process, the duty to be fair often only entails giving notice of the intended decision and an opportunity to respond to the individual or individuals who will be affected by the decision. For tribunals that hold formal hearings, however, fairness often requires more elaborate procedures; these apply to tribunal staff as well as to tribunal members, and they apply both inside and outside the hearing room.

Where Procedural Fairness Rules Are Found

Procedural fairness rules are found in agencies' enabling statutes, in other statutes under which agencies make decisions, in common law principles applied by the courts, and in the *Canadian Charter of Rights and Freedoms*, the *Canadian Bill of Rights*, and Quebec's *Charter of Human Rights and Freedoms*. As discussed in Chapter 3, section 35 of the *Constitution Act, 1982* also requires adequate consultation with First Nations before development decisions are made that may affect Aboriginal land claims. Several provinces have statutes that create uniform procedural fairness requirements for a variety of tribunals, and, in some cases, for other agencies.

While the procedures that tribunals must follow to ensure fairness are usually set out in their enabling statutes, the statutes that grant powers to internal government decision-makers are often silent about the procedures that those decision-makers must follow. These procedures may be set out in departmental guidelines or policies. For the minimum requirements that a bureaucrat *must* follow in a particular case, it is often necessary to look to common law fairness principles and try to apply them to that case.

Procedural fairness is "contextual," not absolute. That is, the amount of fairness required depends on the context. The more serious the consequences of a procedure, the greater the fairness required. In *Baker v Canada (Minister of Citizenship and Immigration)*,[1] the Supreme Court said that in determining the appropriate level of fairness and the specific procedures that must be followed by a tribunal or other agency, one should look at

- the nature of the decision (where it falls on the spectrum from administrative to quasi-judicial decision-making processes);
- the nature of the statutory scheme (for example, where the statute does not provide for an appeal from an administrator's decision, more fairness safeguards may be warranted in making the initial decision than if an appeal were available);
- the importance of the decision to the affected person;
- the extent to which the person affected has legitimate expectations of a particular process; and
- the extent to which the legislature intended the decision-maker to have discretion to choose its own procedure.

Permissible Departures from Common Law Procedural Fairness Requirements

If a statute or regulation sets out a more specific fairness requirement than the common law in a particular situation, the statutory requirement takes precedence, regardless of whether it is more onerous or less onerous than the common law requirement.

For example, in Ontario, a person is entitled to refuse medical treatment unless a doctor convinces the Consent and Capacity Board that the patient lacks the mental capacity to make an informed decision. The *Health Care Consent Act, 1996*[2] requires that the hearing take place within seven days of a patient application to the Board to overturn a doctor's decision that the patient lacks capacity. This short time frame

---

1   [1999] 2 SCR 817 [*Baker*].

2   SO 1996, c 2, Schedule A.

takes precedence over the general rule that each side must be given adequate notice of the hearing. In other circumstances, under other statutes, "adequate" notice might be a month; in this case, adequacy is determined by the fact that the hearing itself must be held within seven days.

Similarly, although the evidence and arguments presented by one party must usually be shared with other parties, some statutes permit an adjudicator to scrutinize the information provided by one party without sharing it with the other parties in cases where allowing others to see the information would result in serious harm or loss to the party who provided it. Statutes that give the public a right of access to government records while protecting personal privacy generally fall into this category. If the government refuses an applicant access to a document, this decision can be appealed to a tribunal. The tribunal will scrutinize the document to determine whether to order the government to release it, but the applicant will not be permitted to see the document, even though this would help the applicant argue his or her case effectively. If the applicant saw the document, he or she would win by default, the government would lose by default, and the proceedings would, effectively, be unnecessary.

The Common Law Principles of Procedural Fairness

As mentioned in Chapter 3, the basic principles of procedural fairness may be reduced to just two: the right to be heard and the right to an unbiased decision-maker. Each of these pillars of procedural fairness has a number of components. This chapter discusses the components of the right to be heard. The components of the right to an unbiased decision-maker are discussed in Chapter 7, Fairness: Bias.

The Requirement to Provide a Hearing: The First Pillar of Procedural Fairness

Whenever a government decision-maker intends to make a decision that will substantially affect a person's individual rights, privileges, or interests, that person must be given an opportunity to be heard. However, this does not always mean that the person must be given a "hearing," in the sense of a formal procedure like that of a court, where witnesses are sworn in, asked questions, and cross-examined. Rather, it means that all the information necessary for the decision-maker to make a fair decision must be received and considered. In this chapter, the term "hearing" is used to denote both the opportunity to be "heard" by an administrator and the more formal hearing required when the decision-maker is a tribunal.

There is no single formula for a **hearing**. In some cases, the presentation of the necessary information in writing will be considered a hearing; in other cases, the presentation of oral evidence and cross-examination of witnesses will be considered a hearing. In general, the higher the stakes are, the more procedural safeguards are necessary for a procedure to be considered a "hearing."

There is often a decision-making "ladder." On the bottom rung is a decision such as a decision to issue a licence or permit or to grant a benefit, made by a departmental official. Procedural fairness is required, but will often be fulfilled by very informal procedures. There is sometimes a middle rung between the initial decision and a formal hearing before a tribunal—a relatively informal review by a different official of the department. If this review does not resolve the conflict, there is often a third rung on the ladder: an appeal to an independent tribunal. It is at this stage that the most rigorous procedures for fairness are required, such as disclosure of all relevant documents and evidence, an oral hearing, cross-examination, a right to be represented by a lawyer or agent, and a right to reasons for the tribunal's decision.

In proceedings before a tribunal, the complexity and comprehensiveness of the procedures required for a hearing depend on the nature and complexity of the issues involved and the seriousness of the consequences of the decision to the parties and the public. For example, suppose that two parties oppose each other and the credibility of witnesses is in issue. A process that does not allow parties to know what witnesses have said about them and does not provide an opportunity for cross-examination will not be considered a hearing—or it will be considered an unfair hearing. Where there is only one party, a less formal process will sometimes meet the procedural fairness requirements of a hearing.

If a court conducting a judicial review or appeal of a decision-making process is not satisfied that the process was fair, it may say that the decision-maker failed to hold a hearing, or it may characterize the process as an unfair hearing. "Hearing" and "fair hearing" are sometimes used interchangeably.

As mentioned, the administrative statutes that govern provincial tribunals specify the minimum procedures that will be considered a "hearing" or a "fair hearing": in Ontario, the *Statutory Powers Procedure Act*[3] (SPPA); in Alberta, the *Administrative Procedures and Jurisdiction Act*[4] (APJA); in Quebec, the *Administrative Justice Act*[5] (AJA); and, in British Columbia, the *Administrative Tribunals Act*[6] (ATA).

In Ontario, the requirements for a fair hearing before tribunals subject to the SPPA are generally more stringent than the requirements for hearings before tribunals that are not subject to the SPPA. Historically, one of the most significant differences between tribunals subject to the SPPA and other tribunals was that tribunals under the SPPA were generally required to hold oral hearings—hearings in which the parties, witnesses, and tribunal members were all physically present—and to permit cross-examination of all witnesses. Amendments to the SPPA in the 1990s changed this, allowing tribunals to hold written and electronic hearings without parties' consent as long as such hearings do not prejudice any of the parties. In electronic hearings, some form of cross-examination of witnesses may still be required; in written hearings, the exchange of written questions and answers may be substituted for oral cross-examination.

---

3 RSO 1990, c S.22.

4 RSA 2000, c A-3.

5 CQLR c J-3.

6 SBC 2004, c 45.

Some tribunals that are not subject to the SPPA are specifically authorized by legislation to hold their inquiries in writing—for example, hearings by a board of review under sections 14(3) and (5) of Ontario's *Family Benefits Act*.[7] Others can do this without legislation because the courts accept that the issues they deal with can be addressed in writing without creating unfairness, or because any potential unfairness in holding a written hearing is outweighed by the negative effects of holding a hearing where all parties are present. For example, a victim of crime may apply to the Criminal Injuries Compensation Board for compensation for injuries resulting from a crime. The Board must be satisfied that the crime really occurred and that the damage was real, but the potential trauma to the applicant from allowing the perpetrator of the crime to be present and cross-examine the victim could outweigh the value of permitting the evidence to be tested in this manner.

The Requirement to Give All Parties an Opportunity to Be Heard

In addition to the duty of fairness it owes to the person who initiates the process or from whom rights or privileges may be taken away, a tribunal has a duty to ensure that all other parties and persons who may be substantially affected by the decision are given an adequate opportunity to present their cases. This principle is expressed in the Latin phrase *audi alteram partem*, which means "hear the other side."

> *One man's word is no man's word; we should quietly hear both sides.*
>
> Johann Wolfgang von Goethe

An adequate right to be heard usually implies a measure of equality, although precise equality is not always necessary. As mentioned, for all parties to be "heard," it is not always necessary for all parties to present oral evidence in the presence of the tribunal and for witnesses to be cross-examined. In some cases, as long as each party has had an opportunity to submit written material and to respond to the other parties' written material, the hearing will be considered a fair one. In other cases, nothing less than a right to be present, give testimony orally, and cross-examine opposing witnesses will conform to the *audi alteram partem* principle.

Components of the Right to Be Heard

The Right to Notice

All parties and other persons whose rights, privileges, or interests may be substantially affected by a tribunal's decision are entitled to **notice** of the proceeding. This includes an explanation of the reason for the hearing, which usually involves setting out the decision or proposed decision that will be reviewed by the tribunal, the reasons for the decision, and the legal and/or policy basis for the decision. The notice must also state the date, time, and location of the hearing.

---

7 RSO 1990, c F.2.

The purpose of notice is to give the parties sufficient information about the subject matter of the hearing to allow them to prepare their case, and to give them enough time to do so. The notice should also give the parties a reasonable opportunity to make any arrangements necessary to allow them to attend the hearing themselves, and to allow their representatives and witnesses (if any) to be present as well. If persons other than the parties may be affected by the tribunal's decision, these individuals must also be given notice; the notice should provide these other persons with information about their right to apply for party status or to participate in the proceeding in other ways.

Thus, to be considered adequate, the notice must

1. provide participants with an explanation of what the hearing is about that is sufficient to allow them to prepare to address the issues, and
2. provide them with sufficient time to prepare.

Adequate notice also involves scheduling the hearing at a time when affected persons can participate.

Sometimes the tribunal is responsible for drafting the notice explaining what the hearing is about and giving notice to the appropriate individuals, and sometimes the notice is drafted by the decision-maker whose decision the tribunal will review. For example, when a person appeals a municipality's land-use planning decision to the Ontario Municipal Board, the Board sets the date for the hearing but the municipality is responsible for sending out the notices.

Although the first element of adequate notice is particularly important, it is not always followed. Decision-makers whose decisions are being reviewed by a tribunal do not always explain their decisions in a form that allows the person challenging their decision to know exactly what they decided or why. This leads to confusion at hearings, as well as to unnecessary complexity, cost, and delay. For example, it may be necessary to grant an adjournment in order for the person affected by a decision to be given further details regarding what was decided and why before the hearing can proceed.

Limits on the Right to Notice

In the absence of a statutory or Charter requirement, the right to notice does not always include a requirement for disclosure of evidence beyond the bare minimum required to inform a party of the case it must meet. **Disclosure** of evidence means providing parties with all relevant information in the other side's possession that may be useful as evidence at the hearing. The purpose of disclosure is to give all parties, before the hearing begins, a reasonable opportunity to know the evidence that will be produced against them, as well as evidence in the possession of other parties that may help them. It gives a party an opportunity to produce, at the hearing, evidence that supports its position that is in the possession of an opposing party but that the other party may not put before the tribunal because it would not help that party's case. Disclosure thus prevents "trial by ambush."

At common law, traditionally there was no general procedural fairness requirement for advance disclosure of evidence in proceedings before tribunals, only the right of parties to know the basic substance of the proceeding. Instead, the common law required that, on the presentation of surprise evidence by one party, a request by the other party for an adjournment be granted to allow the other party to prepare a response.

Although the courts have traditionally been unwilling to recognize advance disclosure of evidence as generally being a component of procedural fairness, they have stated that there may be circumstances where disclosure is necessary to ensure procedural fairness. Courts have held that procedural fairness requires disclosure of evidence beyond the minimum requirements for notice in certain cases where the proceedings have serious consequences for an individual, such as disciplinary proceedings and human rights adjudication. The right to disclosure is also enhanced when a Charter right is involved.[8]

In its 2005 decision in *May v Ferndale Institution*, the Supreme Court of Canada expanded the common law requirement for disclosure. The Court held that the duty of procedural fairness generally requires a statutory decision-maker to disclose the information that he or she relied on in reaching a decision.[9]

Section 5.4(1) of the SPPA gives tribunals the power to require disclosure of particulars in addition to evidence as long as the tribunal has made rules governing this process. **Particulars** are details that explain or clarify matters related to evidence, arguments, or remedies disclosed before or in the course of a proceeding—for example, details and clarifications of allegations made by one party against another or, where the tribunal staff presents the case, details of allegations made by the tribunal staff against a party.

The Requirement to Retain Evidence

In *Charkaoui v Canada (Citizenship and Immigration)*,[10] the Supreme Court established a new procedural fairness requirement that an investigator must retain evidence that it may be necessary to disclose to a tribunal or party in the future in order to ensure a fair hearing at that time. The Court initially expanded procedural fairness to include a requirement to retain evidence only in cases where the evidence may have an impact on a proceeding with serious consequences—for example, a deportation hearing that may result in the deportation of a party to a country where he or she may face torture or death.

The Right to Be Present

Parties have the right to be present at a hearing before a tribunal throughout the entire hearing process. This allows them to participate effectively in the process leading up to the decision, and to respond to all evidence and arguments brought by another party (or, in cases where tribunal staff are the "prosecutors" or accusers, by the tribunal). No part of a hearing should be conducted without all parties being

---

8   *Charkaoui v Canada (Citizenship and Immigration)*, 2008 SCC 38, [2008] 2 SCR 326.

9   2005 SCC 82, [2005] 3 SCR 809 at para 92.

10   *Supra* note 8.

present, unless a party has voluntarily given up his or her right to attend or has engaged in conduct that justifies depriving him or her of this right. (Barring a party from being present is limited to extreme circumstances—for example, where a party's conduct is so disruptive that it is impossible for the tribunal to conduct a hearing with that party present.)

One implication of the right to be present is that tribunal members may not discuss the matter with a party in the absence of any of the other parties.

The right to be present includes the right to attend any site visit that the tribunal might hold. (Site visits, or "taking a view," as they are sometimes called, are discussed in Chapter 11, Presenting Evidence at a Hearing.)

In a written hearing, the right to be present takes the form of a right to receive all relevant information presented to the tribunal and to be given a reasonable opportunity to respond to it.

In an electronic hearing, the right to be present is satisfied if all parties are able to hear each other and the adjudicator in a teleconference, or to see and hear everyone else in a video conference.

Limits on the Right to Be Present

There are several circumstances in which a tribunal may proceed in the absence of a party:

- If a party has been served with notice of a hearing and does not attend, a tribunal may proceed in the party's absence. If a party does not attend, the adjudicator must be satisfied that the party was properly served with notice of the hearing. If there is satisfactory evidence that the party was served, the hearing may proceed in the party's absence. (It is usually reasonable to expect a tribunal to wait at least 30 minutes and to ask one of the other parties or tribunal staff to contact the party and find out the reason for the party's absence before proceeding.)

- Where a party persists in disrupting proceedings, the tribunal may exclude the party to maintain order.

- If a party "walks out" of a hearing as a form of protest, the party has waived his or her right to be present.

- In rare circumstances, the sensitivity of evidence may justify allowing a party's representative, but not the party, to have access to the evidence—for example, where the tribunal rules that the evidence must be kept confidential and there is compelling reason to believe that the party will not maintain confidentiality.

The Right to Be Represented

Parties have the right to present their own case or to have their case put forward by a lawyer or other representative. Moreover, parties have a right to choose who will represent them, and the tribunal must make reasonable efforts to accommodate the schedule of a party's representative. This right of representation generally includes the right to have the representative question the client's own witnesses and cross-examine the witnesses called by other parties, to raise objections to procedures or the admissibility of evidence, and to make submissions.

Generally, the right to be represented before a tribunal does not include the right to have the government pay for a lawyer where a party cannot afford one. However, as mentioned in Chapter 4, the Charter has expanded the right to representation to include a right to state-funded legal assistance where an individual is indigent and the interests at stake are so serious and the proceedings so complex that the individual would not receive a fair hearing without legal representation.[11]

Limits on the Right to Be Represented

It is good practice for the tribunal or its members to advise parties as early as possible of their right to be represented, to inquire whether parties intend to be represented, and to ask how much time they will need to find representation and what efforts they will make. If the tribunal has taken these steps, it is in a much better position to establish whether a party has taken reasonable steps to obtain representation and to refuse an adjournment that it believes is being requested for the purposes of creating delay.

Parties are not always entitled to their first choice of representative. If a hearing date has been set, lawyers and agents have a responsibility to the tribunal and to their clients not to accept retainers if they know that they will not be available on that date. There may be exceptional cases where a representative is justified in accepting a case even though he or she is not available on the date set for the hearing (for example, where a party's efforts to find other counsel have been unsuccessful, or where the lawyer or agent has an intimate knowledge of the case that other representatives do not possess). In some circumstances, however, the tribunal may be justified in refusing to adjourn a hearing when a party chooses a representative who is not available on the date scheduled for the hearing, even if this will result in the party losing the opportunity to be represented. Obviously, any step that will deprive a party of his or her right to be represented should be taken only if the party is first given a reasonable opportunity to find a representative who will be available on the date of the hearing, and only after considering all the implications for the parties and the public purse.

In some cases, a tribunal may also have the power to refuse to allow a party to be represented by someone who is incompetent or unethical. At common law, the inherent right of a tribunal to control its own process may be a sufficient basis for a tribunal choosing to bar such representatives from appearing before it. Under section 23(3) of the SPPA, tribunals may refuse to allow any representative who is not a lawyer or a paralegal licensed by the Law Society to take part in the proceedings if the conduct of the representative demonstrates that he or she is not competent to perform the task, or if he or she does not comply at the hearing with the duties and responsibilities of an advocate or adviser. If the tribunal prevents a representative from participating, under some circumstances, fairness may require the tribunal to adjourn the proceedings to afford the affected party an opportunity to find another

---

11 *New Brunswick (Minister of Health and Community Services) v G (J)*, [1999] 3 SCR 46.

representative. In other circumstances, however, it may be reasonable to require the party to continue without a representative. Parties must sometimes accept responsibility for their choice of representatives.

The right to be represented does not give a party an absolute right to an adjournment to obtain representation. A party is entitled to a *reasonable* opportunity to find a lawyer or other suitable representative. However, if the tribunal finds that the party has not taken advantage of the opportunity and a delay will cause serious inconvenience to other parties and raise the cost of the hearing, the tribunal may be justified in refusing an adjournment to allow a party to find a lawyer or agent.

The Right to Present Evidence

Before a tribunal, parties have the right to present evidence in order to establish the facts in a case. Only after the facts are clear is it possible to determine how the law should apply to them.

Parties must have a reasonable opportunity to produce relevant information in an attempt to prove the facts they want the tribunal to accept and to disprove unfavourable allegations by other parties. Usually, the main witnesses are the parties themselves. However, parties often call others as witnesses and may also present documents, pictures, and physical objects as evidence.

A corollary of the right of a party to present evidence is that there must be an appropriate mechanism to enable a party to require other persons who have relevant information to provide it to the tribunal. Usually, this mechanism is a **summons** (sometimes called a "subpoena") issued by the tribunal to a witness that requires the witness to attend the hearing, bring relevant documents, and present evidence. Failure to comply with a summons issued under the SPPA is an offence. For Ontario tribunals that are not subject to the SPPA, their governing statute may make it an offence to ignore a summons.

Limits on the Right to Present Evidence

The right to present evidence does not always mean that a party has the right to present evidence orally in the presence of tribunal members. In some circumstances, an electronic or written hearing may be sufficient. Moreover, a tribunal may refuse to receive information for various reasons—for example, because the information was not disclosed in advance of the hearing in compliance with the tribunal's rules of procedure, or because it is irrelevant or unreliable. (For a more detailed discussion of the reasons why a tribunal may refuse to receive evidence, see Chapter 11, Presenting Evidence at a Hearing, and Chapter 12, Management and Control of the Hearing Process.)

The Right to Cross-Examine

In a hearing before a tribunal, parties have the right to know the evidence being brought against them and to respond to it. They must have a fair opportunity to learn of any information that is unfavourable to them and to correct or contradict it.

In an oral hearing, the second part of this right—that is, the opportunity to respond—generally requires the tribunal to provide each party with an opportunity to cross-examine the other party's witnesses, unless there is some other, equally effective method of testing a witness's evidence. The purpose of cross-examination is to give parties an opportunity to challenge the evidence given by the other side's witnesses. The right to cross-examine witnesses in adversarial proceedings has been described as "fundamental" and "a vital element" of the system.[12] It may show that the evidence is untrue, bring out additional significant facts, or shed a different light on a witness's testimony.

Where a tribunal is permitted to hold a written hearing or inquiry, or is not subject to the SPPA or some other statutory duty to allow cross-examination, the tribunal may meet the requirements of procedural fairness by giving a party access to all the written evidence and submissions on which the tribunal may rely, as well as the opportunity to respond in writing to the evidence and submissions.

Limits on the Right to Cross-Examine

The right to cross-examine does not mean that a party or a party's representative is allowed to ask irrelevant, inflammatory, abusive, or repetitive questions. Ontario's SPPA and British Columbia's ATA give members of tribunals to which these statutes apply the right to place reasonable limits on cross-examination, and it is likely that the inherent right of tribunals not governed by these statutes to control their process gives them the same authority.

Whether a tribunal has the right to disallow cross-examination in order to ensure an inexpensive and expeditious hearing may vary from case to case. The Workplace Safety and Insurance Appeals Tribunal allows a limited form of cross-examination in some circumstances, which it calls "cross-questioning." (For a discussion of the limits on "friendly" cross-examination, see Chapter 11, Presenting Evidence at a Hearing.) Ontario's Information and Privacy Commissioner requires parties at oral hearings to direct questions to witnesses through the adjudicator.

The Requirement That the Person Who Hears Must Decide

The person who hears a case is the only person who may decide the case. This has two implications. First, it is generally improper for an adjudicator who was absent for any part of a hearing to take part in making the decision. (There may, however, be exceptions, such as when all parties consent and there is an effective way of informing a new or substitute tribunal member of the evidence heard in his or her absence.) Second, it is improper for anyone associated with a tribunal—such as the chair, other tribunal members, or tribunal staff—to put pressure on a hearing panel to make the decision in favour of one party or another or to change an intended decision.

---

12 *Howe v Institute of Chartered Accountants of Ontario* (1994), 27 Admin LR (2d) 118 at 137 (CA), per Laskin JA (dissenting); *Innisfil (Township) v Vespra (Township)*, [1981] 2 SCR 145 at 166.

Exceptions and Limits to This Requirement

Subject to certain statutory restrictions,[13] if one member of a panel of adjudicators cannot complete a hearing (for example, as a result of prolonged illness or death), the remaining members may complete the hearing and render a decision. Generally, a new member or adjudicator cannot take the place of the member who cannot complete the hearing partway through the hearing unless all parties consent to the replacement, and it is improper for the tribunal to put any pressure on the parties to accept such an arrangement.

In some cases, however, the parties may agree that, rather than continuing with fewer members, it would be better to have a new member join the panel and to permit that member to rely in part on a transcript or agreed statement of the evidence given earlier in the hearing. In a case where the hearing is held by a single tribunal member, the member's departure would mean that the hearing had to start over. To avoid this, the parties might prefer to have the member's replacement read transcripts or agreed statements of the evidence and complete the hearing using this information.

The rule that only a member who hears a case can decide it does not prohibit that member from seeking the advice of other tribunal members, tribunal counsel, or tribunal staff (a practice sometimes known as "collegial decision-making"). However, there are limits on the scope of such consultation. First, unless the consultation is required by statute, it must be voluntary; it is improper for the tribunal chair or other members to put pressure on the adjudicator to consider their views. Second, the consultation should be limited to questions of law and policy. If new issues or legal arguments are raised as a result of consultation, the parties should be given an opportunity to address them. Finally, the tribunal member must not rely on evidence or facts provided by his or her colleagues without taking precautionary steps. The member must notify all parties that he or she is considering relying on other evidence, and must give the parties an opportunity to challenge not only the accuracy of the evidence but also the member's right to consider it. (The right to consultation is discussed in more detail in Chapter 14, Tribunal Decision-Making Procedures.)

The Requirement to Base the Decision Solely on the Evidence

Unlike decisions made by administrators—who generally have no duty to disclose all the information they have relied on in making a decision—parties before a tribunal have the right to expect that the tribunal's decision will be based on the facts established at the hearing, and not on other information. An adjudicator who relies on facts within his or her own knowledge or on facts learned outside the hearing compromises the integrity of the hearing process. Not only is there a possibility that

---

13 For example, the remaining members may not be permitted to render a decision where a statute requires that the panel include representatives of groups opposed in interest (such as management and a labour union) and the remaining members do not include a representative of each interest group, or where the statute specifies that a panel must consist of a certain number of members.

such information is incorrect, but parties would not have an opportunity to respond to it or to influence how the adjudicator uses it.

Exception to This Requirement

There is an exception to the rule that an adjudicator must rely solely on the facts established at the hearing in making a decision. The exception is known as **judicial notice** or **administrative notice**. Adjudicators are entitled to "take notice" of facts that would be known to a well-informed member of the community (for example, that Ontario is a province of Canada) or that would be known by a well-informed member of a professional group, particularly when the tribunal consists of members of that profession. (This exception is described in more detail in Chapter 14, Tribunal Decision-Making Procedures.)

The Right to Be Heard in a Timely Manner and to Receive a Decision Without Undue Delay

A basic tenet of our legal system is, "Justice delayed is justice denied." The right to be heard within a reasonable time and to receive a decision without delay is now recognized as an aspect of procedural fairness, although traditionally it was not. (It was, however, sometimes recognized as an instance of the decision-maker declining jurisdiction.) A person subject to an administrative action, whether before a tribunal or by a bureaucrat, has a common law right to completion of proceedings and receipt of a decision without undue delay. Where the delay prejudices a person—for example, by impairing his or her ability to receive a fair hearing—it will be considered a breach of procedural fairness if it is longer than necessary, if the individual is not responsible for it, and if the agency has no good explanation for the delay.[14]

The Requirement to Give Reasons for the Decision

It is now established at common law that procedural fairness requires tribunals and other decision-makers to provide reasons for their decisions, at least in situations where the decisions may seriously affect an individual's rights, privileges, or interests, or where reasons are necessary for the exercise of a right of appeal. This duty is also reflected in Alberta's APJA (s 7), Quebec's AJA (ss 5 and 13), and British Columbia's ATA (s 51). Section 17(1) of Ontario's SPPA requires decision-makers to provide reasons where requested by a party.

Although decision-makers must now provide reasons, the courts did not initially require that these be detailed or well thought out. In *Baker*,[15] the case in which the Supreme Court first ruled that providing reasons for a decision is a component of procedural fairness, the Court accepted the mere notes of an administrator as Citizenship and Immigration Canada's "reasons" for a decision to deport a woman

---

14 *Blencoe v British Columbia (Human Rights Commission)*, 2000 SCC 44, [2000] 2 SCR 307.

15 *Supra* note 1.

under the *Immigration Act*. In another case, a court accepted checking a box on a prescribed form as sufficient to fulfill the requirement to provide reasons.[16]

The courts have since described what constitutes sufficient or adequate reasons. Where reasons are required for procedural fairness, but no reasons are given, this omission is a breach of procedural fairness. However, where reasons are given, but are inadequate, this is not a breach of procedural fairness. In other words, deficiencies or flaws in the reasons given do not fall under the category of a breach of the duty of procedural fairness.[17]

This is not to say, however, that inadequate reasons have no legal consequences. Although inadequacy of reasons is not a "stand-alone" basis for quashing an administrative decision, a judicial review of a decision may succeed where the reasons for the decision do not support the decision. Where reasons for a decision are provided, for the decision to be upheld on judicial review, it is necessary for the reasons to clearly explain how that decision was reached.

To be sufficient, reasons do not need to include all the arguments, statutory provisions, jurisprudence, or other details the judges presiding over the judicial review might have preferred. A decision-maker is not required to make an explicit finding on each element, however subordinate, leading to its final conclusion.[18] It has been said that in the context of administrative law, reasons must be sufficient to fulfill the purposes required of them, particularly to let the individual whose rights, privileges, or interests are affected know why the decision was made and to permit effective judicial review. The basis of the decision must be explained, and this explanation must be logically linked to the decision made.[19]

16 *Liang v Canada (Minister of Citizenship and Immigration)*, [1999] FCJ No 1301 (TD).

17 *Newfoundland and Labrador Nurses' Union v Newfoundland and Labrador (Treasury Board)*, 2011 SCC 62, [2011] 3 SCR 708.

18 *Ibid* at para 16.

19 *Clifford v Ontario Municipal Employees Retirement System*, 2009 ONCA 670 at para 29.

CHAPTER SUMMARY

Traditionally, agencies were required to follow fair procedures, known as principles of natural justice, only when exercising their powers in a quasi-judicial manner. Today, all agencies must, at a minimum, give individuals who may be affected by their decisions an opportunity to comment before they make them.

All government decision-makers must follow fair procedures when making decisions that affect people's rights, privileges, and interests. However, what is "fair" depends on the nature and function of the decision-making body. Tribunals must apply the rules of procedural fairness more rigorously than other agencies, and their procedures resemble the procedures followed by courts more than those of other bodies do. While the requirements of natural justice for tribunals were dictated originally by the courts, today many of the rules of procedural fairness are prescribed by statute—either a statute that establishes a tribunal or other administrative body or sets out its powers, or, in some cases, a statute that has general application to a variety of tribunals.

One of the basic components of procedural fairness is the right to a hearing. The right to a hearing before a tribunal includes the right of parties to reasonable notice; to be present throughout the proceedings; to be represented by a lawyer or agent; to present and to challenge evidence; to have the decision made only by the person who heard the case, without interference by others; to have the decision based solely on the evidence; to be given reasons for the decision; and to be heard in a timely manner and receive a decision without undue delay.

KEY TERMS

administrative notice: *see* judicial notice

disclosure: a procedure in which parties before a tribunal present to each other evidence in their possession that may be relevant to the proceeding in advance of the hearing; provides all parties with a reasonable opportunity to know the evidence that will be produced against them at the hearing

hearing: refers both to the opportunity to be "heard" by an administrative decision-maker, in the sense of being notified of an intended decision and given an opportunity to respond, and to the more formal hearing required when the decision-maker is a tribunal, including the various procedural safeguards that are appropriate given the nature and complexity of the issues involved and the seriousness of the consequences of the decision to the parties and the public

judicial notice: the exception to the rule that an adjudicator must rely solely on the facts established at the hearing in making a decision; the acceptance by a court or tribunal of certain facts that would be known to a well-informed member of the community or by a well-informed member of a professional group; also called "administrative notice" or "official notice"

notice: a document that informs a person of a legal proceeding that may affect the person's interests or in which the person may have a right to participate

particulars: details that explain or clarify matters related to evidence, arguments, or remedies disclosed before or in the course of a proceeding—for example, details and clarifications of allegations made by one party against another, or, where the tribunal staff presents the case, details of allegations made by the tribunal staff against a party

summons: a document issued to a witness by a tribunal or court that requires the witness to attend the hearing, bring relevant documents, and present evidence; sometimes called a "subpoena"

CASES TO CONSIDER

Disclosure and Fairness

Howe v Institute of Chartered Accountants (Ontario) (1994), 19 OR (3d) 483, 27 Admin LR (2d) 118 (CA)

FACTS: Howe was a chartered accountant who was charged by the Professional Misconduct Committee of the Institute of Chartered Accountants of Ontario with breaching the *Rules of Professional Conduct*. An investigation report was written by J., who was advised by the Committee that the report would be kept confidential. The Committee therefore refused to disclose the report to Howe. Howe then applied to the Discipline Committee, which was to hear the case against him, for disclosure. That committee also refused disclosure. Howe applied to the Divisional Court for an order compelling disclosure. The Divisional Court refused the application, ruling that the application for judicial review was premature because there was an appeal remedy still available.

ISSUES: Was judicial review of a preliminary ruling appropriate? Was the refusal to disclose the report to Howe a breach of procedural fairness?

DECISION: The majority ruled that a court should interfere with a preliminary ruling, such as the tribunal's refusal to order disclosure of the report, only where the tribunal did not have jurisdiction. The panel of the Discipline Committee chosen to hear the case would have full authority to consider the request for disclosure when the hearing was convened, and a complete remedy for any decision it might make at the hearing would be available through an appeal. Moreover, the majority ruled that it was not clear that a refusal of a tribunal to order disclosure of evidence was a breach of procedural fairness.

Justice Laskin dissented. In this case, denying Howe access to the report impeded his ability to make full answer and defence, which meant that the Committee's duty to act fairly required disclosure of the report unless it was privileged.

Would this case be decided differently today? See *May v Ferndale Institute*; *Charkaoui v Canada (Citizenship and Immigration)*; *Ontario (Human Rights Commission) v Dofasco Inc* (2001), 57 OR (3d) 693 (CA); and *Ruby v Canada (Solicitor General)*, 2002 SCC 75, [2002] 4 SCR 3.

Procedural Fairness and Legitimate Expectations

Baker v Canada (Minister of Citizenship and Immigration), [1999] 2 SCR 817

FACTS: Mavis Baker, a Jamaican citizen with Canadian-born children, was ordered deported and told to make her application for permanent resident status from outside Canada, as is normally required. She then applied for an exemption from this requirement, based on humanitarian and compassionate considerations. A senior immigration officer refused her request by letter, without providing reasons for the decision. However, she received the notes of the investigating officer, which were used by the senior officer in making his decision. Baker's application for judicial review was first heard by the Federal Court Trial Division, then by the Federal Court of Appeal, and finally by the Supreme Court of Canada.

ISSUE: What was the appropriate duty of procedural fairness in this case?

DECISION: The duty of procedural fairness depends on the particular statute and the rights affected. Factors that will affect the content of the duty of fairness include the nature of the decision and the process used to make it, the provisions of the relevant statute, the importance of the decision to the people affected, the legitimate expectations of the person challenging the decision, and the agency's choices of procedure.

There was no legitimate expectation affecting the content of the duty of procedural fairness in this case. Important interests were affected, but the lack of an oral hearing did not constitute a violation of the requirement of procedural fairness; the opportunity to produce full and complete written documentation was sufficient.

Nevertheless, the immigration officer's notes gave the impression that the decision might have been swayed by the fact that Baker was a single mother with several children and had been diagnosed with a psychiatric illness. This raised a reasonable apprehension of bias. Also, the notes did not indicate that the decision was made in a manner that properly considered the interests of the children. The immigration officer's decision was quashed.

REVIEW QUESTIONS

1. What factors determine the appropriate level of procedural fairness to be provided by a tribunal or other agency?

2. What three sources of law would you review to determine the procedures that a particular tribunal or agency must follow to ensure a fair hearing?

3. Explain what is meant by the phrase *audi alteram partem*.

4. What are the two characteristics of an adequate notice of a hearing?

5. Under what circumstances, if any, can a tribunal receive evidence or hear submissions in the absence of a party?

6. Does a party always have the right to be represented by a lawyer? If so, is the party always entitled to his or her first choice of lawyer? Does a party have a right to be represented by someone who is not a lawyer? Explain.

7. Does a party always have a right to cross-examine other witnesses? What methods other than cross-examination may a party use to challenge the evidence of an opposing party?

8. If a tribunal member is absent during the presentation of some of the evidence, under what circumstances may he or she participate in making the decision in the case?

9. List and briefly describe the various rights that a "fair hearing" entails.

10. What are the limits or exceptions to the duty of a decision-making body to ensure that parties receive all of the rights to which they are usually entitled in a hearing?

EXERCISES

1. The provincial government proposes to establish a fund to compensate travellers who do not get what they pay for after arranging a vacation through a travel agency. For example, if construction of their hotel is incomplete, the hotel is infested with cockroaches, and the chartered flight doesn't arrive to take them home, travellers would apply to the fund to be reimbursed for their losses.

   The fund would be established by amending the *Travel Agents Act*, which regulates this industry. The amendment would permit the government to make regulations determining who must pay into the fund, how much they must pay, how and under what circumstances travellers may make claims, and what criteria will be used in determining whether and how much to compensate travellers.

   Do the principles of procedural fairness require the government to provide any individuals or groups with an opportunity to be heard before it amends the statute?

   If so, who is entitled to procedural fairness and what kind of consultation or hearing would satisfy the requirements of procedural fairness that apply in this case?

2. The legislature passes the amendments to the *Travel Agents Act* and the minister of tourism proceeds to draft regulations to establish the compensation fund. The regulations provide that all licensed travel agencies must pay a specified amount into the fund each year. Every agency must pay the same amount, regardless of size and income. However, the amount may be increased or decreased based on the number of past claims against the agency. The minister announces the amount that each travel agency will be required to pay into the fund each year.

   The Consumers' Association of Canada complains that the amount of the payment is too low and that the criteria for compensation are too narrow to provide travellers with fair compensation. The travel agencies, on the other hand, claim that it is unfair to increase the amount of contribution based on claims against travel agencies because problems that travellers encounter are often beyond the agency's control. In addition, small agencies claim that the proposed contribution is too high and will put them out of business. They feel that it would be fairer to base the contributions of individual agencies on their annual incomes.

   a. Is the government required by principles of procedural fairness to provide any individuals or groups with an opportunity to be heard before making the regulation? If not, why not?

      If so, who is entitled to procedural fairness and what kind of consultation or hearing would satisfy the requirements of procedural fairness under these circumstances?

   b. Would your answer be any different if, in a letter to the Travel Agents' Association, the minister of tourism had stated two years earlier that he understood the need to take into account the size of travel agencies in setting fees and would consult with the association before making a regulation, but did not consult? Explain.

3. The regulation establishing the compensation fund has been made. It provides for aggrieved travellers to make claims to the fund. It states that a customer is entitled to be reimbursed for travel services paid for but not provided. The registrar of travel agencies, an official of the ministry, is designated to decide whether to approve claims.

   The registrar develops criteria for determining who is eligible—for example, the kind of information that customers must provide to support their claims—and guidelines and procedures governing the application process.

   Does procedural fairness require that the registrar provide an opportunity for consultation or a hearing before finalizing these criteria, guidelines, and procedures? If not, why not?

   If so, who is entitled to procedural fairness and what kind of consultation or hearing would satisfy the requirements of procedural fairness under these circumstances?

4. Amelia X applies for compensation from the fund. She alleges that she paid the Wings of a Dove Travel Agency for a vacation in a four-star hotel, but the hotel turned out to be a two-star hotel. The registrar is concerned about whether the information she has provided supports her claim and is considering refusing the claim.

   Does procedural fairness require that the registrar provide an opportunity for consultation or a hearing before refusing the claim? If not, why not? If so, who is entitled to procedural fairness and what kind of consultation or hearing would satisfy the requirements of procedural fairness under these circumstances?

5. If the registrar refuses Amelia's claim, does procedural fairness require that she have a right to appeal the decision? If not, why not?

6. Suppose the *Travel Agents Act* does provide Amelia with a right to appeal the registrar's decision to a tribunal, the Travel Compensation Fund Appeal Board. Do the principles of procedural fairness apply to this tribunal? If not, why not?

   If so, what appeal procedures would satisfy the requirement for procedural fairness under these circumstances?

   Would the principles of procedural fairness require that anyone other than Amelia have an opportunity to participate in the appeal?

FURTHER READING

Sara Blake, *Administrative Law in Canada*, 4th ed (Toronto: LexisNexis Butterworths, 2006) ch 2.

Colleen Flood & Lorne Sossin, *Administrative Law in Context*, 2nd ed (Toronto: Emond Montgomery, 2013).

Julie Maciura & Richard Steinecke, *The Annotated Statutory Powers Procedure Act* (Aurora, Ont: Canada Law Book, 1998).

Guy Régimbald, *Canadian Administrative Law* (Markham, Ont: LexisNexis, 2008) ch VI.

Fairness: Bias

LEARNING OUTCOMES

After reading this chapter, you will understand

- the meaning of impartiality and bias in the context of administrative agencies;

- why impartiality is an essential component of procedural fairness;

- the relationship between conflict of interest and bias;

- the difference between individual bias and institutional bias;

- the kinds of interests and conduct that may lead parties to believe that an adjudicator is biased;

- the relationship between an agency's independence and its impartiality; and

- factors that a court will take into account in determining whether an agency has an institutional bias.

> *[I]n considering whether there was a real likelihood of bias, the court does not look at the mind of the justice himself or at the mind of the chairman of the tribunal, or whoever it may be, who sits in a judicial capacity. It does not look to see if there was a real likelihood that he would, or did, in fact, favour one side at the expense of the other. The court looks at the impression which would be given to other people. Even if he was as impartial as could be, nevertheless if right-minded persons would think that, in the circumstances, there was a real likelihood of bias on his part, then he should not sit. And if he does sit his decision cannot stand. Nevertheless, there must be a real likelihood of bias. Surmise or conjecture is not enough. There must be circumstances from which a reasonable man would think it likely or probable that the justice, or chairman, as the case may be, would, or did, favour one side unfairly at the expense of the other. The court will not inquire into whether he did, in fact, favour one side unfairly. Suffice it that reasonable people might think he did. The reason is plain enough. Justice must be rooted in confidence: and confidence is destroyed when right-minded people go away thinking: "The judge was biased."*
>
> Lord Denning in *Metropolitan Properties Co (FGC) Ltd v Lannon*, [1969] 1 QB 577 at 599

7

Impartiality: The Second Pillar of Procedural Fairness

As discussed in Chapter 6, the first pillar of procedural fairness is the right to be heard. The second pillar of procedural fairness is impartiality. Parties have a right to have their case heard by an adjudicator who is impartial. An impartial decision-maker is one who is *not* biased for or against any of the parties and who would not be *perceived* as biased by a reasonable and well-informed observer.

The Two Elements of Impartiality: Individual Impartiality and Institutional Impartiality

Impartiality has two elements. First, the decision-maker must be free from individual **bias**. Second, the tribunal or other agency to which the decision-maker belongs must not be structured in a way that suggests that its decisions will be biased in favour of one party or another. The impartial, unbiased adjudicator will not have prejudged the issues or have a predisposition in favour of one side or the other.

In the case of tribunals, the impartiality requirement has two components. First, the decision-maker must start the hearing with an open mind and must reserve judgment until all evidence and arguments have been presented. If he or she is inclined to support one party's position over the other's, and if this bias is not institutional (see below), the decision-maker is said to be influenced by *personal* bias.

Second, to be perceived as impartial, the tribunal itself must be reasonably independent of any government agency that is a party to its hearings. If the tribunal is structured in a way that does not permit its members to decide freely between the parties in accordance with the applicable law, the decision-makers are said to be influenced by *institutional* bias.

Actual Bias and Reasonable Apprehension of Bias

A decision-maker is biased when he or she does not approach a decision with an open mind. A decision-maker may not have an open mind for various reasons. For example, the decision-maker may stand to benefit financially from the outcome of a decision, or may have a close personal relationship with or strongly dislike a person who will be affected by the decision.

Where a decision-maker has a predisposition to decide one way or the other because of some personal interest, it is improper for the decision-maker to participate in making the decision. However, even if a decision-maker does not believe that a relationship or interest causes him or her to have an *actual* bias in deciding a case, a decision-maker should not hear a case where a reasonable and well-informed observer of the situation would assume that he or she would *probably* be biased. This appearance of bias is called a **reasonable apprehension of bias**.

> [T]he apprehension of bias must be a reasonable one, held by reasonable and right-minded persons, applying themselves to the question and obtaining thereon the required information. ... [W]hat would an informed person, viewing the matter realistically and practically—and having thought the matter through—conclude. Would he think that it is more likely than not that [the judicial officer], whether consciously or unconsciously, would not decide fairly.
>
> de Grandpré J in *Committee for Justice and Liberty v Canada (National Energy Board)*, [1978] 1 SCR 369 at 394

> It is clear from the authorities that the reasonable person is very well-informed, right-minded, practical and realistic. The person must be knowledgeable of all of the relevant circumstances, including "the traditions of integrity and impartiality that form a part of the background and apprised also that impartiality is one of the duties that judges do swear to uphold" ... .
>
> If the words or conduct, no matter how inappropriate or troubling, do not amount to reasonable apprehension of bias, then the findings of the judge will not be affected ... .
>
> In summary, there is a strong presumption of judicial integrity that may only be displaced by cogent evidence establishing a real likelihood of bias. It is trite to note that this burden is higher than a simple balance of probabilities, but lower than proof beyond a reasonable doubt. The burden lies with the person alleging a reasonable apprehension of bias. A reasonable apprehension of bias

is determined by the well-informed, right-minded individual who is aware of all of the circumstances, including the nature of the case, its surrounding circumstances and the presumption of judicial integrity.

Bennet J in *HMTQ v Pilarinos and Clark*,
2001 BCSC 1690 at paras 141–143

In addition to an appearance of individual bias, the entire agency may appear to be biased when it is structured in such a way that a well-informed person would have a reasonable belief that the agency is likely to favour a particular party or class of parties in a substantial number of cases. The extent to which the tribunal is independent of the parties—whether they are individuals or companies, or government officials or bodies—is not conclusive evidence of whether there is institutional bias. However, independence or a lack thereof is one of the most important factors in determining whether there is institutional bias or a reasonable apprehension of institutional bias.

Elements of Individual Bias

The Relationship Between Bias and Conflict of Interest

The terms "bias" and "conflict of interest" are often used interchangeably. However, conflict of interest is only one source of bias or perceived bias; other sources include friendship with a party, a dislike of one of the parties, or prior knowledge of facts that are prejudicial to one of the parties. **Conflict of interest** is a specific kind of bias—a financial interest in the outcome of a particular case, or, more generally, any interest that is incompatible with an individual's function as a member of a tribunal.

Indicators of Possible Bias

As mentioned, an adjudicator must approach each case with an open mind. Certain kinds of behaviour toward the parties during a hearing may suggest that an adjudicator does not have an open mind. However, additional considerations—for example, particular activities, conduct, interests, relationships, and associations—may also cast doubt on an adjudicator's impartiality and raise a reasonable concern about possible bias. These considerations include whether the decision-maker

- meets with one party in the absence of other parties;
- has a close friendship with a person whose interests may be affected by the outcome of the case;
- has a close relative whose interests may be affected by the outcome of the case;
- has a financial interest in the outcome of the case;
- belongs to an association that has taken a position on an issue or issues that must be decided by the tribunal;
- expresses opinions about the issues in the case before all the evidence and arguments have been heard;

- intervenes in the hearing process in a way that persistently favours one party over another;

- expresses a strong like or dislike for a party or its witnesses;

- is in or has been in litigation against a party or witness in a proceeding;

- has or has had in the recent past a significant business or professional relationship with a party or witness;

- has played a part in the case at any stage (for example, the adjudicator may have been consulted about some minor point years earlier);[1] or

- accepts gifts or favours from a party or witness.

Elements of Institutional Bias

Impartiality Versus Independence

As discussed, there is a difference between institutional impartiality and institutional independence. The Supreme Court of Canada has stated that the impartiality of a decision-maker is determined by examining his or her state of mind, whereas the independence of a tribunal is a matter of its status:

> The status of a tribunal must guarantee not only its freedom from interference by the executive and legislative branches of government but also by any other external force, such as business or corporate interests or other pressure groups.[2]

The duty of a tribunal to be impartial is not a duty to be independent from the government. The Supreme Court has made it clear that while the Constitution requires that courts be independent of the other branches of government, there is generally no similar requirement for tribunals, although it is possible that independence could be found to be a constitutional requirement in limited circumstances.[3] Tribunals are generally required to be independent only where a statute provides for this. For example, section 23 of Quebec's *Charter of Human Rights and Freedoms*[4] explicitly states that Quebec tribunals must be independent.

In deciding whether a tribunal is impartial, the courts will consider the degree of independence as one indication of impartiality or institutional bias.

What Constitutes Independence?

To meet the constitutional requirement of judicial independence, judges must have security of tenure, financial security, and control of the operations of their courts.

---

1   See e.g. *Wewaykum Indian Band v Canada*, 2003 SCC 45, [2003] 2 SCR 259.

2   *R v Généreux*, (1992) 88 DLR (4th) 110 at 128, [1992] 1 SCR 259, 70 CCC (3d) 1.

3   *Ocean Port Hotel Ltd v British Columbia (General Manager, Liquor Control and Licensing Branch)*, 2001 SCC 52, [2001] 2 SCR 781. The Court held that the close ties between the BC Liquor Appeal Board and the BC Liquor Licensing Branch were authorized by statute, and that in this case the Charter did not require that the Board be independent of the Branch. (See the description of this ruling in Cases to Consider at the end of this chapter.)

4   CQLR c C-12.

The courts will look at these same factors when considering whether a tribunal is impartial.

As agencies of the executive branch of government, tribunals are not expected to have the same degree of independence as courts. Whether a tribunal's lack of independence will be enough to create an appearance of institutional bias will depend on the types of decisions the tribunal is required to make and the degree to which it is expected to implement government policy.

Factors to Consider in Determining Whether There Is Institutional Bias

The most important considerations in determining whether there is institutional bias are:

- the closeness of the relationship between an agency or tribunal and a government department that is affected by its decisions; and
- where an agency has multiple functions, the extent to which these functions overlap in a manner that suggests that some employees have inappropriate influence over others.

Determining Whether the Agency–Government Relationship Contributes to Institutional Bias

In deciding whether the relationship between an agency or tribunal and the government is so close that there is an appearance of institutional bias, the courts may look at a number of factors. Usually, no single factor is conclusive; it is the overall impact on independence or the appearance of independence that matters. To determine this overall impact, the courts may ask the following questions:

- Are agency or tribunal members appointed for a fixed term, or do they hold their offices at pleasure? (The term "at pleasure" means that an appointment may be terminated whenever the government pleases.)
- If the appointment is for a fixed term, how long is the term? (The longer the term is, the greater will be the appearance of independence.)
- Are members' salaries fixed, or can the government raise or lower them at will? (Fixed salaries will contribute to the appearance of independence.)
- Are the appointments part time or full time? (A part-time appointment raises a greater concern that an agency or tribunal member might be denied work if he or she makes a decision that is unsatisfactory in the eyes of the government or the chair of the agency.)
- To what extent does an agency chair have discretion over which members to appoint to hearing panels? (If the selection process is not random, this increases the ability of the chair to influence the outcome of hearings by appointing members whom he or she feels, from experience, are likely to be sympathetic to one side or the other.)
- Are the staff of an agency selected or employed by the agency, or by the government? (Where the government is sometimes a party to proceedings, the

fact that tribunal staff owe their livelihood to the government rather than the agency can create an appearance of bias.)

- To what extent is an agency required by government rules to follow government policy? (The more an agency must follow policy, the less will be the appearance of independence.)

- Does the minister to whom an agency chair reports conduct the performance evaluation of the chair, and what criteria are used in evaluating the chair's performance? (If the agency makes decisions that can adversely affect the government, the possibility of an unfavourable performance appraisal can be perceived as interfering with the ability of the agency to be impartial, particularly if the criteria used involve an assessment of the wisdom of the decisions that affect the government.)

- Does the government department to which an agency reports determine the agency's annual budget? (If the department controls the budget, there may be an appearance that it is able to reduce the budget to punish unfavourable decisions and increase it to reward favourable ones.)

Changes at the Immigration and Refugee Board—Decision-Makers

On December 15, 2012, the Immigration and Refugee Board announced a change to its hearing procedure: decision-makers will now come from the public service rather than being appointed by the Governor in Council. The release on the IRB website stated:

> Hearings at the independent Immigration and Refugee Board of Canada (IRB) will be conducted by public servant decision-makers rather than people appointed by the Governor in Council (GIC).*

This change in the status of the decision-makers from being independently appointed adjudicators to public service employees was initiated after budgetary changes. These shifts in budget were instituted in order to make the decision-making process more cost efficient.

Courts must consider a number of factors to determine the nature of the relationship between a tribunal and a department or agency that is a party to proceedings before that tribunal. When the tribunal receives its funding from the same department or agency (in the case of the IRB, the Ministry of Citizenship and Immigration) that appears before it, having the decision-makers employed by the public service directly calls into question the ability of the institution to maintain its independence in relation to all of the factors mentioned above. With adjudicators being part of the public service, the type of contract offered, the nature of work (full- or part-time), the level of salary, the scope of duties, the method of evaluation, and the allocation of resources through budgets and policy direction may all be under the control of the Ministry or the civil service rather than the tribunal, which might be viewed as indicating the existence of potential institutional bias.

---

* Government of Canada, "Changes at the Immigration and Refugee Board of Canada (IRB)" (15 December 2012), online: <http://www.cic.gc.ca/english/refugees/reform-irb.asp>.

Determining Whether Overlapping Functions Contribute to Institutional Bias

As discussed in Chapter 2, many regulatory agencies carry out multiple functions. The concentration of a number of functions within a single agency is not necessarily a problem. However, a multifunctional structure creates an appearance of bias when those who are responsible for recommending or prosecuting proceedings against a person are also involved in deciding whether to take away the person's rights, privileges, or benefits. The tribunal that makes the final decision will not be considered impartial if those who recommended or pursued charges can influence its decision—for example, by providing additional information that is not known to all parties, or by providing private legal advice to the tribunal.

To avoid an appearance of institutional bias, there should be a clear separation of roles between those who investigate and recommend administrative action, those who argue the case before the tribunal, and those who make the decision. There will be a perception of institutional bias when, for example, an agency lawyer who is responsible for approving proceedings against a person, or for arguing a case before a tribunal, privately advises the tribunal as to how it should decide the case. A perception of institutional bias will also arise where an official recommends action against an individual and then appoints or serves as a member of the panel that will decide whether to take the action.

Statutory Exceptions to the Requirement of Institutional Impartiality

Despite a tribunal's general duty to be impartial, a lack of independence or impartiality will not disqualify a tribunal from deciding a case if its partiality is clearly mandated by statute, as in the examples below. The only exception to this is where the statutory provisions that curtail independence or impartiality violate a person's rights or freedoms under the Charter.

If the built-in bias is "necessary" in the sense of being required by statute and being not unconstitutional, the bias will be acceptable. For example, a statute may provide

- that a tribunal must follow government policy,
- that the chair must report to the minister of a department that appears as a party before the tribunal,
- that the minister has the right to approve the tribunal's rules of procedure,
- that the chair must provide any information about the tribunal's operations that the minister requests, and
- that the agency's budget must be approved by the minister.

Together, these requirements might raise doubts about the tribunal's impartiality. However, any bias resulting from these requirements is immune from attack in the courts because it is clearly authorized by statute and is not unconstitutional.

Raising an Allegation of Bias

Alleging that a tribunal member or other decision-maker is or appears to be biased is a serious matter, and bias allegations should not be made lightly. Aside from any other reasons to exercise caution, the first rule of good advocacy is to not alienate the decision-maker. Moreover, the courts have made it clear that restraint must be exercised when making such allegations.

Where it *is* necessary to raise the question of whether there is an appearance of bias, it is important to do so as early as possible. The courts will consider a party that does not raise an allegation of bias *during* a hearing to have waived the right to argue it in court. In addition, if a party knows of facts that may give rise to an appearance of bias before a hearing begins, the party should seek to raise the matter discreetly with the tribunal chair or tribunal member and resolve it at that time; in this way, the party will avoid having to raise the matter during the hearing in a public forum, which could embarrass the tribunal and the member. Moreover, it is more convenient and less expensive for everyone if a tribunal assigns a different member before the hearing begins than if a member is forced to withdraw from the hearing partway through. (Recall the rule that the person who hears must decide, and the discussion in Chapter 6 of the difficulties caused by an adjudicator leaving a hearing partway through.)

If a party or advocate becomes aware of facts that may create an appearance of bias after a hearing has begun and believes it is necessary to raise the issue, how this is best done will depend on the circumstances of each case.

In many cases, it will be appropriate to raise this issue with the tribunal member or the tribunal chair outside the hearing and give the member an opportunity to stand aside without a public spectacle. Any such discussion should take place in the presence of all the parties or their representatives.

If the member does not step down following the discussion and the advocate still believes the member should not continue, it will then be necessary to raise the question in the open hearing, make a formal application to the member to step down, and ask for a ruling by the tribunal member. (Even though the adjudicator has a personal interest in the outcome of a bias application, he or she is still the appropriate person to rule on whether there is a reasonable apprehension of bias. Normally, this would not be decided by someone else—for example, the tribunal chair.)

If the member does not agree that his or her participation will result in a reasonable apprehension of bias, it is not necessary to immediately seek judicial review of the member's decision to continue. A party's continued participation in the hearing will not be considered a waiver of the right to raise the issue in later court proceedings, since the issue was raised during the hearing.

Tribunal Response to an Allegation of Bias

How a tribunal or tribunal member should respond to a bias allegation is a difficult and sensitive question, and tribunal members should take steps to prevent such allegations from being raised during a hearing.

If a tribunal member becomes aware of facts that he or she is concerned may give rise to an appearance of bias before the hearing begins, the simplest solution is for the member to ask the chair of the tribunal to assign a different adjudicator; alternatively, the adjudicator may informally disclose the facts that may give rise to an appearance of bias—as well as any facts that the adjudicator feels will show that he or she is *not* biased—to the parties, and volunteer to stand aside. If the parties do not accept the adjudicator's offer to stand aside, the adjudicator may proceed without fear of his or her decision on the hearing being challenged. By accepting the adjudicator's participation, the parties waive their right to raise the issue either during the hearing or after unless further evidence of bias comes to light.

If some parties believe that there is no bias but others argue that the adjudicator should stand aside, the adjudicator faces a difficult decision. If it will not cause substantial cost or inconvenience to the parties, it is best for the adjudicator to stand aside under these conditions regardless of his or her own views as to whether there is any reasonable apprehension of bias.

Even after a hearing has begun, the simplest approach may be for an adjudicator to step down if the adjudicator or a party raises the issue of bias. However, if standing aside after a hearing has begun will lead to substantial delay or expense for the parties, and the adjudicator feels that he or she has no actual bias or conflict of interest and any appearance of bias will not constitute a "reasonable apprehension" of bias, he or she may decide that it is in the public interest for him or her to continue.

To what extent an adjudicator is permitted to defend himself or herself against allegations of bias during a hearing has been the subject of controversy. If the adjudicator raises the issue of bias with the parties during the hearing, he or she might bring forward not only the facts that may suggest a bias but any facts that he or she feels will show that there is no bias. However, if any of the parties dispute or demand proof of the mitigating facts, the adjudicator and the parties are both in a difficult position. In effect, the adjudicator is giving evidence, and an adjudicator is generally not permitted to become a witness in the proceeding over which he or she is presiding. This raises the issue, for example, of whether the parties should then be able to cross-examine the member on his or her explanations.

For example, in an Ontario case in which a party raised the issue of bias during a hearing and brought out facts that supported the allegation, the judges disagreed about whether the adjudicator could present facts in his or her own defence,[5] as this raises the same problematic issues as when an adjudicator raises the bias issue and provides information on his or her own initiative. However, this question may have been put to rest by the Supreme Court in *Wewaykum*.[6] In that case, Justice Binnie wrote the unanimous decision of the Supreme Court in a dispute between two Indian bands. After the decision was released, one of the bands discovered that Justice Binnie had played a role in the strategy discussions that preceded the litigation some fifteen years earlier. On a motion to reopen the case on the grounds that Justice Binnie's involvement raised a reasonable apprehension of bias, the Court permitted Justice Binnie to file a statement saying that he had no recollection of any involvement in the case.

---

5   *Dulmage v Ontario (Police Complaints Commissioner)* (1994), 30 Admin LR (2d) 203 (Ont Div Ct), described in Cases to Consider at the end of this chapter.

6   *Supra* note 1.

CHAPTER SUMMARY

The impartiality of the decision-maker is the second essential element of procedural fairness. Decision-makers must not only *be* unbiased, but must also *appear* to be unbiased. Even if an adjudicator is not actually biased, if a reasonable and well-informed observer would believe that the adjudicator was biased, this constitutes a reasonable apprehension of bias, which disqualifies the adjudicator from participating in the decision-making process. There are two kinds of bias: individual and institutional. A biased individual is one who does not approach a decision with an open mind because he or she is influenced by preconceived views of the merits of a case or has a personal interest in the outcome of the case. Institutional bias arises, or appears to arise, when the structure or functioning of an agency or tribunal leads it to favour, or appears to lead it to favour, one party or class of parties over another in a substantial number of cases.

Institutional bias is likely to be perceived when an agency is too close to a government department that is a party to its proceedings, or where the overlapping functions of agency staff result in an appearance that those who investigate or prosecute are also involved in making the final decision on someone's rights, privileges, or interests.

Although the rules of procedural fairness require impartiality, these rules can be (and sometimes are) overruled by statutory requirements that require decision-makers to act in a way that seems unfair—for example, when a statute requires a tribunal to follow policies established by a regulator, even though the regulator is one of the parties to a dispute before the tribunal. These statutory requirements are overruled by common law fairness requirements only where they violate a person's rights or freedoms under the Charter.

Allegations of bias or reasonable apprehension of bias should be raised as early as possible, and preferably before a hearing begins. Failure to make a bias allegation in a timely manner may disqualify a party from later challenging an adjudicator's participation in a hearing through an appeal to a court or a judicial review application. Ideally, an adjudicator who becomes aware that his or her conduct or interests may raise an apprehension of bias should stand aside before the hearing begins. If an adjudicator or a party raises the issue of the adjudicator's bias during a hearing, the adjudicator is responsible for deciding whether to step down, even though the adjudicator is the subject of the allegation. The extent to which an adjudicator may produce evidence at a hearing to defend himself or herself remains somewhat unclear.

KEY TERMS

bias: an interest, attitude, relationship, or action that leads a decision-maker to favour one party over another

conflict of interest: a situation in which a decision-maker has a personal or financial interest in the outcome of the proceeding that can affect his or her ability to make a fair decision

reasonable apprehension of bias: the appearance of bias to a reasonable and well-informed observer; also called an "appearance of bias" or "perception of bias"

CASES TO CONSIDER

Individual Bias

Committee for Justice and Liberty v National Energy Board, [1978] 1 SCR 369

FACTS: The National Energy Board was considering competing applications for a pipeline in the Mackenzie Valley. The Board was to determine whether there was a need for such a pipeline, and, if so, which of the competing applicants should be permitted to build it. Marshall Crowe, the chair of the three-member panel, had involvement with one of the companies competing for the application in his previous position as president of a federal government agency, the Canada Development Corporation (CDC). In that capacity, Crowe had been an active participant in a study group formed by the CDC for the purpose of considering the economic and physical feasibility of a northern natural gas pipeline to bring natural gas from the Arctic to southern markets. The CDC had brought together several companies that were separately considering building such a pipeline to participate in the study group. During the study, those companies had decided to pool their efforts and had jointly formed a company that was now one of the competing applicants before the Board for the pipeline.

As a member of the study group, Crowe had helped plan the terms of a contemplated application to the Board, which later culminated in the application made by the company formed through the amalgamation of the companies in the study group.

ISSUES: Was the chair biased? Should the chair be rejected from the panel based on a reasonable apprehension of bias?

DECISION: There was no actual bias because Crowe did not have anything to personally gain or lose from his participation in the panel. However, his participation in the study group, which ultimately led to the joint application of the companies, gave rise to a reasonable apprehension of bias because he had played an active role in helping plan the terms of a contemplated application to the Board. There must be no lack of public confidence in the impartiality of adjudicative agencies, particularly where the function of an agency, as in this case, is to further the public interest.

Institutional Overlap

2747-3174 Québec Inc v Quebec (Régie des permis d'alcool), [1996] 3 SCR 919

FACTS: Under the *Act respecting liquor permits*, the Quebec Ministry of Public Security may apply to the Régie des permis d'alcool to revoke a company's permits to sell liquor. After a hearing, the Directors of the Régie des permis d'alcool revoked a company's liquor permits on the ground of disturbance of public tranquility. The company sought to have the decision quashed because the Régie did not comply with the guarantees of independence and impartiality set out in the Quebec *Charter of Human Rights and Freedoms*. The company alleged that the Régie was not independent and impartial, and therefore had an institutional bias, for three reasons.

First, the company alleged that the close ties between the Régie and the Ministry, together with the lack of security of tenure and financial security of Régie members, constituted institutional bias. The Ministry is responsible for administering the Act under which the Régie operates, but is also a party to the Régie's permit revocation proceedings. In its argument, the company relied on, among other grounds, the limited terms for which Régie members are appointed, the government's ability to revoke members' appointments without notice on certain grounds, the requirement that the Régie submit a report to the minister each year, the authority of the minister to require the Régie to provide information about its activities, the requirement that the minister approve the Régie's rules for internal management and regulations made by the Régie, and the fact that the minister conducts a yearly evaluation of the chair's performance. Second, the company pointed out that the same Directors could intervene at various stages of the permit cancellation process—for example, a Director could initiate a review of a licensee's conduct, participate in the decision whether to hold a hearing, and then act as an adjudicator in the hearing. Third, the company pointed out that a lawyer may review investigation files and then advise the Régie regarding what action it should take, prepare files for adjudication, draft notices of summons, present arguments to the Directors at a hearing, and advise the Directors how to decide the case.

ISSUES: Did the close relationship between the Ministry and the Régie, and the Ministry's control over the Régie, result in institutional bias? Where the same people might be involved in prosecuting and adjudicating, did this raise a reasonable apprehension of bias in a sufficient number of cases that it constituted institutional bias?

DECISION: Flexibility must be shown toward administrative tribunals with respect to impartiality. The Régie's structure and multiple functions, its relationship to the Ministry, and the limited security of tenure and financial security of the Régie and its members did not in themselves raise a reasonable apprehension of institutional bias. The fact that the Régie, as an institution, participated in the process of investigation, the summoning of witnesses, and adjudication was not a problem. However, a separation among the Directors and lawyers involved in the various stages was necessary to eliminate the apprehension of bias arising from their overlapping roles. The fact that a particular Director might decide whether to hold a hearing to determine whether to revoke a permit and then participate in the hearing constituted institutional bias because this practice would cause an informed person to have a reasonable apprehension of bias in a substantial number of cases. Similarly, the ability of the Régie's lawyers to review files in order to advise the Directors on whether to hold a hearing and then present arguments to the Directors and draft opinions during the hearing represented institutional bias. Prosecuting counsel must never be in a position to participate in the adjudication process. The Régie's decision was quashed.

Individual Bias

Dulmage v Ontario (Police Complaints Commissioner) (1994), 30 Admin LR (2d) 203 (Ont Div Ct)

FACTS: A board of inquiry panel was established under the *Police Services Act* (RSO 1990, c P.15) to investigate allegations that a woman had been strip-searched in public by a police officer. One of the appointed members of the three-person panel was Frederika Douglas. Ms. Douglas was president of the Mississauga chapter of the Congress of Black Women of Canada both at the time of the alleged strip search and at the time of the hearing. Counsel for the police officer made an application to disqualify Ms. Douglas on the basis of reasonable apprehension of bias as a result of the vice-president of the Toronto chapter of the same organization having made inflammatory public statements concerning the events, including demanding the suspension of the police officers involved in the incident. The panel adjourned the hearing to consider the application.

When the panel reconvened following consideration of the motion, the chair of the panel disclosed further facts to the parties that tended to support the position that Ms. Douglas was not biased, including the fact that the Mississauga and Toronto chapters of the Congress are separate incorporations and that Ms. Douglas was not aware of any involvement of her chapter in discussions or actions concerning the alleged strip search or any other complaint about strip searches. Counsel for the police officers alleged that the fact that the chair was making these disclosures on behalf of the panel raised a reasonable apprehension that the other panel members were also biased, and asked all the panel members to disqualify themselves. They refused, and the matter was brought before the Ontario Divisional Court for review.

ISSUES: Was the test for establishing reasonable apprehension of bias on the part of Ms. Douglas met? Did the panel's presentation of evidence in defence of one of its members against allegations of that member's bias raise a reasonable apprehension that the other panel members were also biased?

DECISION: There was a reasonable apprehension of bias on the part of Ms. Douglas. Although she belonged to the Mississauga chapter and the public statements were made by the vice-president of the Toronto chapter, the combined effect of the fact that the alleged incident had received significant attention in the media, the inflammatory nature of the comments made by the vice-president, and the fact that Toronto is "closely adjacent" to Mississauga was sufficient to create a reasonable apprehension that Ms. Douglas was biased. Moreover, the court ruled (with one judge dissenting) that the procedure used by the chair of the panel—that is, considering the motion to disqualify one of its members and then presenting evidence to support her—resulted in a reasonable apprehension that the chair and the other panel member were biased as well. An order was granted directing that the hearing take place before a different panel.

Institutional Bias

Ocean Port Hotel Ltd v British Columbia (General Manager, Liquor Control and Licensing Branch), 2001 SCC 52, [2001] 2 SCR 781

FACTS: Investigations of a hotel and pub led to allegations that it had committed five infractions of the *Liquor Control and Licensing Act* (RSBC 1996, c 267) and regulations under the Act. Following a hearing, the Liquor Control and Licensing Branch imposed a penalty that included a two-day suspension of the hotel's liquor licence. The hotel appealed to the Liquor Appeal Board by way of a hearing *de novo*. Four of the five allegations were upheld, and the penalty was confirmed.

The hotel applied to the courts to overturn the Board's decision on the grounds that the structure of the Board did not leave it independent enough to be impartial.

Pursuant to section 30(2)(a) of the *Liquor Control and Licensing Act*, the chair and members of the Board "serve at the pleasure of the Lieutenant Governor in Council." Members are appointed for a one-year term and serve on a part-time basis. All members but the chair were paid on a per diem basis. The chair established panels of one or three members to hear matters before the Board "as the chair considers advisable." The BC Court of Appeal held that the members of the Board lacked the necessary independence and set aside the Board's decision.

ISSUE: Were the members of the Liquor Appeal Board sufficiently independent to make fair decisions on violations of the Act and to impose penalties?

DECISION: The Supreme Court of Canada allowed the appeal. Generally, the degree of independence required of a particular government decision-maker or tribunal is determined by the tribunal's enabling statute. The legislature's intention that Board members should serve at pleasure was unequivocal. The statute was not ambiguous.

There is a fundamental distinction between administrative tribunals and courts. Unlike courts, administrative tribunals are not constitutionally required to be independent. They are created precisely for the purpose of implementing government policy. Although tribunals may sometimes attract Charter requirements of independence, as a general rule they do not. The Board is not a court, it is a licensing body. The suspension of the hotel and pub's liquor licence was an incident of the Board's licensing function. Licences were granted on condition of compliance with the Act, and could be suspended for non-compliance. The exercise of power fell squarely within the executive power of the provincial government.

REVIEW QUESTIONS

1. What is the relationship between bias and conflict of interest?

2. What is the difference between an actual bias and a reasonable apprehension of bias?

3. Explain the difference between individual bias and institutional bias.

4. What is the difference between impartiality and independence? What might an agency's independence indicate about its members' impartiality, and vice versa? What else might the degree of independence indicate?

5. What factors will a court consider in determining whether an agency is independent?

6. What factors will a court consider in determining whether a lack of independence makes an agency institutionally biased?

7. What are some circumstances that might lead a reasonable and well-informed observer to assume that a decision-maker is biased?

8. When is the appropriate time to raise an allegation of bias, and what procedure should be followed?

9. What steps should an adjudicator take if a question of bias or conflict of interest arises

    a. before a hearing begins?

    b. during a hearing?

EXERCISE

The Ministry of Consumer Relations, headed by the minister, is responsible for regulating used car dealers. The registrar, an employee of the Ministry, has the right to recommend that a tribunal, the Licence Appeal Board, revoke the business licences of dishonest car dealers.

A customer of Active Auto Sales, managed by Mr. James, complained to the Ministry that the company had turned back the odometer on a vehicle that it had sold to him. After investigating this complaint, the Ministry determined that turning back odometers was standard practice for this dealership. The company was charged and convicted of fraud, but no charges were laid against Mr. James. Despite this, the registrar recommended to the Board that it revoke Mr. James's licence to sell cars, as well as the licence of his employer, on the grounds that Mr. James had to be involved in the fraudulent activity given his position in the company.

The Board holds a hearing to decide whether to accept the registrar's recommendation to revoke the two licences. In addition to arguing that he was unaware of the illegal activities, Mr. James argues that the Board is disqualified from deciding whether to revoke his licence because it is not independent of the Ministry and therefore has an institutional bias.

The *Consumer Protection Act* establishes the Board. It states that the Board will report to the minister of consumer relations; that the chair and members of the Board will not be civil servants; that the premier will appoint the chair and members of the Board; and that the chair will decide which members and how many members will be assigned to each appeal. The Board is required by the statute to follow rules of natural justice, such as giving notice of hearings, hearing evidence, allowing parties to be represented by counsel or agents, permitting cross-examination, and giving written reasons for its decisions. The statute also provides for the Board to summon witnesses, hold pre-hearing conferences, and conduct mediation. The statute allows the Board to make rules of procedure that are approved by the Ministry. It may make practice directions and issue guidelines for hearings without the Ministry's approval. The statute also states that the Board must have regard to any relevant ministry policies when making its decisions.

Each year the chair of the Board proposes a budget for the following year. Because the Board reports to the minister, the minister is responsible for approving the Board's budget. The chair hires the Board staff, but the practice is that a human resources officer from the Ministry is involved in the interviews and takes part in making the decisions. The Ministry establishes the salary range for each Board staff member, but the chair decides what salary to offer within that range and whether employees receive a raise each year. The chair cannot terminate the employment of a Board staff member without approval from the Ministry.

It is the government's policy that each minister enter into a memorandum of understanding (MOU) with the chair of the Board, governing the relationship between the Board and the Ministry. Each time the minister or the chair changes, a new MOU is to be signed by both parties. The current chair was appointed one year ago, but the minister has not signed a new MOU.

Although the Act says that the premier appoints the members, in practice this is done on the recommendation of the minister. The MOU between the minister and the previous Board chair provides that the minister will consult with the chair before deciding which members to recommend for appointment.

The members are appointed "at pleasure" for a fixed term of two years. Traditionally, appointment at pleasure means that an employee may be terminated without any notice. The MOU provides that the minister will seek the advice of the chair when deciding whether to reappoint members at the end of their term. However, there is a government policy that members may not be reappointed for more than one two-year term, regardless of the quality of their performance. About 60 percent of the members are appointed on a part-time basis. One of them is a former investigator of the Ministry.

The salary levels for the chair and members are established by the government.

The current chair was once the director of the legal branch of the Ministry. He left the Ministry three years ago. Before being appointed chair, he was in private practice as a lawyer for one year, then was the director of the Policy Branch of the Ministry of Finance in the provincial government.

Is there an institutional bias that would prevent the Board from hearing this case?

Play the role of Mr. James's lawyer and argue that the Board has no jurisdiction to hear this case.

Then play the role of counsel for the registrar and argue that the Board has no institutional bias.

FURTHER READING

Sara Blake, *Administrative Law in Canada*, 4th ed (Toronto: LexisNexis Butterworths, 2006) ch 3.

Canadian Judicial Council, "Report of the Canadian Judicial Committee to the Minister of Justice After Inquiring into the Conduct of Justice P. Theodore Matlow" (Presented in Ottawa, 3 December 2008), online: <http://www.cjc-ccm.gc.ca/cmslib/general/Matlow_Docs/Final Report En.pdf.>

Colleen Flood & Lorne Sossin, *Administrative Law in Context*, 2nd ed (Toronto: Emond Montgomery, 2013) ch 7.

Robert D Kligman, *Bias* (Toronto: Butterworths, 1998).

PART II

Advocacy

Advocacy Before Government Departments, Administrative Agencies, and Tribunals

8

LEARNING OUTCOMES

After reading this chapter, you will understand

- what steps you should follow in preparing to represent a party before a government department or an agency that is not a tribunal;

- how to represent your client effectively in this administrative process;

- how to obtain the information you need where processes are not transparent;

- what steps you should follow in preparing to represent a party before a tribunal; and

- how to be an effective advocate before a tribunal.

It is not easy or particularly useful to write a general section on how to prepare a case to be presented to an agency mainly because each agency is a world unto itself.

Robert Macaulay & James Sprague, *Practice and Procedure Before Administrative Tribunals* (Toronto: Carswell) (loose-leaf) ch 19 at para 19.1

Introduction

Part I provided you with an understanding of administrative law, and a foundation for carrying out legal research and interpreting laws that may apply in a particular case. Part II will focus on the application of this knowledge

1. in **advocacy**, or representations on behalf of a client, before tribunals and other administrative agencies, as well as government departments; and

2. in the conduct of hearings and decision-making processes by tribunals.

This chapter describes the fundamentals of effective advocacy. It outlines the basic steps that should be followed in most situations. Subsequent chapters provide a more detailed discussion of the procedures involved in preparing for and participating in hearings before tribunals.

Advocacy Before a Department or an Administrative Agency

Understanding the Decision-Making Structure

Many important decisions—such as issuing a licence, approving an income tax return, or authorizing coverage of a medical procedure under health insurance—are initially made by government departments or agencies called "regulators" rather than by tribunals. As discussed in Part I, the procedures that apply to decision-making by tribunals differ from those that apply to other administrative agencies or departments.

While tribunals are required to hold public hearings and follow quasi-judicial procedures, other agencies make their decisions behind closed doors. They often do not describe in detail the procedures that they will follow. They may obtain information from many sources and do not always reveal what information they have relied on, or what policies, guidelines, or criteria they have applied. Officials at several levels in the organization's hierarchy—and even in several different departments—may play a role in reaching the final decision, and officials from other agencies also may be consulted. (See the box feature "Bureaucratic Decision-Making.") Often, there is no blueprint that sets out the responsibilities or functions of these various participants.

Bureaucratic Decision-Making

A developer wants to tear down several houses that he owns and build a complex of apartment buildings and a shopping mall. Before it can proceed, the developer must apply to the municipality's planning department for rezoning of the property from "single-family residential" use to a combination of "multi-unit residential" and "commercial" use.

Several departments and agencies will likely provide input before a decision will be made on the application. The roads department will advise whether the existing network of roads can handle the additional traffic that the new development will generate. The school board will consider whether the local schools can accommodate the children who may live in the apartment complex. The environment department may require proof that the soil is not contaminated. The parks department may want land set aside for recreation. Other considerations will include the impact of the development on the sewage and water supply systems, whether the public transit system can accommodate the additional riders, noise levels, and aesthetic considerations such as the visual impact of the buildings and whether their design is consistent with that of surrounding buildings.

The developer will be required to submit studies and plans to address these concerns. The objective of the developer, and the representative who acts on its behalf, is to persuade the authorities involved that the proposed development will be beneficial to the community. At the same time, others—such as residents of the neighbourhood and competing businesses—may try to persuade those same authorities that the negative effects of the project should cause them to reject it.

The winning side will be the side that provides the most effective advocacy. Ultimately, the planning department—taking into account input from other departments, consultants, lobbyists, and other interested parties—will make a recommendation to the municipal council, and the municipal council will make a binding decision. The losing side may be able to appeal the council's decision to a tribunal. However, different approaches are required in presenting an application to municipal departments and councillors and presenting a case before a tribunal.

This decision-making structure can make the job of the **advocate**, or **representative**, a difficult one. A great deal of detective work, along with some guesswork, may be needed to find out who is involved in making decisions, and when and how decisions are made. Because much of the information that the advocate needs may not be written down anywhere, or, if documented, may not be public, the process of shepherding an application through the bureaucracy consists mainly of asking questions and finding out the points in the process at which recommendations and decisions will be made, who will make them, and what internal policies and criteria those officials will apply in arriving at their decisions.

To me, a lawyer is basically the person who knows the rules of the country. We're all throwing the dice, playing the game, moving the pieces around the board, but if there is a problem, the lawyer is the only person who has read the inside top of the box.

Jerry Seinfeld, *Seinfeld*, "The Visa," episode 56, broadcast 27 January 1993

Steps in the Advocacy Process

A representative advocating before an agency that is not a tribunal must take some or all of the following steps.

Determine What Laws and Policies Apply

As discussed in Part I, government decision-makers exercise powers granted by statute. The statute or regulation that delegates those powers generally sets out broad rules for decision-making, including the nature and scope of the decision, the persons responsible for making the decision, the general procedures to be followed, and the criteria to be applied. The details of the process are often left to be determined by the decision-making body. They are found in written policies or guidelines, or in informal administrative practices.

Determine Stages in the Process and Deadlines

There are often stages in the decision-making process at which recommendations and interim or tentative decisions are made. At some or all of these stages, there may be an opportunity for the advocate to provide input. Therefore, it is important to identify those stages and to find out the deadlines for making comments and suggestions or providing information.

Determine Who Makes the Decision or Recommendation at Each Stage

As mentioned, several departments or branches will often be consulted during the decision-making process. Each will bring to bear its own perspective and will want to ensure that its particular areas of concern are addressed. Consequently, the advocate will need to find out who is involved at each stage and make contact with the various participants.

Determine Concerns of the Department or Agency and Other Stakeholders

As well as determining who is involved, it is important to understand the particular concerns of each participant. For example, certain issues related to an application may be raised internally by agency staff. Other stakeholders may raise additional concerns with politicians and agency officials. For example, if a client is applying for a licence to open a casino and neighbours wish to block the application, the client's advocate should try to find out the details of their concerns both from the neighbours themselves and from agency officials. Unlike in a hearing before a tribunal, where the parties are identified and the evidence of each party must usually be disclosed to the other parties, the concerns and views of officials and stakeholders will not necessarily be disclosed to other stakeholders in other kinds of decision-making processes.

Tailor Submissions

Submissions on the client's behalf should focus specifically on the issues identified by the decision-makers and by external opponents to the application. The arguments should be presented within the framework that the agency will use in making the decision. For example, when representing an applicant for an approval, the submissions should refer to any policies, guidelines, and criteria that support the application and explain why those that do not support it should not be given weight in the circumstances of the case or what steps will be taken to bring the development into conformity with those policies and guidelines. The advocate for the opponents, on the other hand, should emphasize the policies that do not support the application and explain why the agency, in this particular case, should not follow or rely on the policies that do support the application.

Ideally, preparing and delivering submissions should be done within the framework of a communications strategy (see the box feature "Formulating a Communications Strategy").

Formulating a Communications Strategy

- *Decide whether it is best for you as a representative or your client to deliver the message you want the regulator to receive*   The client is often the best person to tell his or her story. Moreover, while clients can deal directly with government officials, lawyers and other representatives often must deal with the regulator's counsel. This can add an unnecessary layer of communications and complications.

- *Figure out how to best deliver your message*   Face-to-face meetings between clients and decision-makers are crucial. Get your (well-prepared) client before the decision-maker to tell his or her story.

- *Develop relationships with officials and legal counsel*   Be cooperative, not adversarial. It is important to foster collegiality and preserve an ongoing relationship. Meet early with officials and their legal counsel to understand parameters of process. Keep up communications. Keep track of the status of the file and where it is heading.

Source: Martin G Masse, Lang Michener LLP, "Advocacy Before Regulators: When the Tribunal Isn't a Tribunal" (The 4th Annual National Forum, Administrative Law & Practice, Osgoode Hall Law School, 20–21 October 2008; paraphrased from a combination of Mr. Masse's PowerPoint slides and his oral presentation).

Obtain Access to Information

In arriving at a decision, a department or an agency other than a tribunal is not always required to disclose the information on which the decision will be based. Consequently, it is often necessary for the applicant's representative, and other outside parties, to take steps to obtain this information.

The decision-makers and support staff involved in the process will usually maintain a file containing the application, internal and external comments on it, analysis of issues, expressions of concern, studies, and other related facts. It is important for the advocate to collect as much of this information as possible, beginning at an early stage in the decision-making process, in order to be able to anticipate and respond to decision-makers' concerns.

Tips for an Effective Advocacy Strategy

- Participate early and often in the agency's decision-making process.
- Target individuals lower in the decision-making chain and work your way up.
- At all stages of the process, ask staff for information about issues identified by the agency, policy concerns, and options under consideration.
- Propose solutions to issues and concerns that agency staff can build into the documentation that will be considered by the ultimate decision-makers.
- Avoid being overly aggressive or hostile.
- Be diplomatic but firm.
- Insist on your client's rights, including the right to access information and the right to procedural fairness.

FORMAL AND INFORMAL ACCESS ROUTES

The first task is finding out what is in the file maintained by the decision-makers and support staff. There are two routes to obtaining this information. The formal route involves an application under freedom-of-information laws. The informal route involves direct contact with the agency itself—for example, keeping in touch with officials by telephone and email, arranging face-to-face meetings, writing letters, and attending any public meetings.

A Useful Starting Point

Some governments maintain lists of the kinds of information available from various departments. For example, the Ontario government maintains an electronic directory of records maintained by ministry branches and by other agencies that are subject to the *Freedom of Information and Protection of Privacy Act*. This directory is found on the website of the Office of the Chief Information and Privacy Officer at <https://www.ontario.ca/page/how-make-freedom-information-request>.

The federal government and each of the provinces and territories have legislation that requires government departments, agencies, tribunals, municipalities, and, in some cases, universities and hospitals to provide access to many of the records in their possession on request. The federal statute is called the *Access to Information Act*.[1] In Ontario, the *Freedom of Information and Protection of Privacy Act*[2] requires

---

1   RSC 1985, c A-1.

2   RSO 1990, c F.31.

disclosure of provincial government information as well as records under the control of hospitals and universities, while the *Municipal Freedom of Information and Protection of Privacy Act*[3] covers municipalities and their agencies. Under these statutes, a person can make a formal request for documents. If access is denied, the applicant has a right to appeal the decision to the federal or provincial information commissioner or to the courts.

Obtaining records from agencies through formal access-to-information procedures can be costly and time consuming. The informal route—that is, speaking, emailing, or writing directly to individuals who may have the requested information at hand—is often faster and cheaper than a formal application to the agency's freedom-of-information (FOI) coordinator, and is particularly useful for identifying what documents are available and which officials are likely to have possession of them. If the informal route does not produce the information that the advocate seeks, knowing where to find the necessary documents will make it easier for the advocate to use the formal procedures under FOI laws.

REQUESTS UNDER FREEDOM-OF-INFORMATION STATUTES

If documents cannot be obtained through informal channels, a formal request can be made under FOI legislation. The request must be made in writing, and, in some jurisdictions, a fee must accompany the application (see the box feature "Information Requests Can Be Expensive"). There is often a standard request form, which is usually available from the agency holding the documents. In Ontario, the form can also be obtained through the website of the Office of the Information and Privacy Commissioner (<http://www.ipc.on.ca>). However, in Ontario and most other jurisdictions, it is not necessary to use the form; instead, the request can simply be sent to the agency's FOI coordinator.

Information Requests Can Be Expensive

In addition to an application fee, a freedom-of-information agency may charge fees in amounts set out in a regulation for time spent

- searching for documents and looking through them to decide whether any part of them must be kept confidential;

- preparing a document for release by blacking out confidential portions that are exempt from disclosure; and

- other functions, such as photocopying.

These fees may be substantial or even prohibitive.

In some jurisdictions, the agency is required to provide the applicant with an estimate of fees before it begins to retrieve the records, and it may require payment of up to half of the estimated cost before it conducts the search or prepares the documents for release. The applicant can request that the fee be waived in some circumstances or, if it appears excessive, that it be reduced.

---

3   RSO 1990, c M.56.

The FOI coordinator is usually well informed about the records held by the agency, their location, and their availability. Under Ontario's FOI laws, the coordinator is required to assist applicants in clarifying their request if it is unclear. The agency must respond to a request within 30 days by advising that it will or will not provide the information requested. However, the agency is entitled to a 30-day extension if a large number of records are requested, if it is necessary to search through many records to find the documents requested, or if it is necessary to consult someone outside the agency before fulfilling the request.

In Ontario, an agency's refusal to provide documents, its failure to decide whether or not to disclose documents within the specified time limit, its failure to conduct a thorough search for records, and the fee it charges for searching for and retrieving records can all be appealed to the Information and Privacy Commissioner (who is independent of the government). The Commissioner has the authority to order the government to provide information that is not specifically exempt from disclosure.[4]

In the case of documents in the possession of federal government departments and agencies, under the *Access to Information Act*[5] a person refused information may complain to the federal Information Commissioner. The Commissioner cannot order the government to disclose information, but may recommend that it do so. If the government refuses to follow the recommendation, either the Commissioner or the applicant may appeal to the Federal Court.[6]

Obtain Reasons for the Decision

Once the department or agency has made its final decision, it is part of the advocate's job to ensure that the client is informed of the reasons for the decision. Generally, the department or agency will have either a statutory or a common law duty to give reasons.

Under section 7 of Alberta's *Administrative Procedures and Jurisdiction Act*[7] (APJA), administrators must provide written reasons for their decisions. In contrast, under section 13 of Quebec's *Administrative Justice Act*[8] (AJA), there is no requirement for departments or agencies other than tribunals to provide their reasons in writing. These agencies are, however, required to communicate their decisions "in clear and concise terms" and, if they are making an unfavourable decision on an application for a licence or permit, they must give reasons. Ontario's *Statutory Powers Procedure Act*[9] (SPPA) and British Columbia's *Administrative Tribunals Act*[10] (ATA) do not require departments and agencies other than tribunals to provide reasons.

---

4   *Freedom of Information and Protection of Privacy Act*, *supra* note 2, s 54.

5   *Supra* note 1.

6   *Supra* note 1, ss 41–42.

7   RSA 2000, c A-3.

8   CQLR c J-3.

9   RSO 1990, c S.22.

10   SBC 2004, c 45.

Appeal Rights

In many cases, there is a statutory right to a review or appeal of administrative decisions, and in cases where no statutory appeal is provided, judicial review may be available. If your client has received an unfavourable decision, advise him or her of any right to have a review of the decision or to appeal it, as well as the time limits for filing an appeal or a request for review. (The time limits for appealing administrative decisions are often very short, and frequently the review officer or tribunal has no power to extend the deadline.)

Many statutory decision-makers routinely include a notice of appeal rights with their written decisions. However, the duty to provide notice of appeal mechanisms has not been recognized as a common law procedural fairness obligation, although it should be.

Advocacy Before a Tribunal

When appearing before a tribunal, an advocate should not make any of the following three erroneous assumptions:

1. *Assuming that, because a tribunal performs quasi-judicial functions, it will follow the same rules or procedures as a court*   The fact that a court will not allow the presentation of hearsay evidence, for example, does not necessarily mean that such evidence will also be inadmissible before a tribunal.

2. *Assuming that, because a tribunal is less formal than a court, a different standard of behaviour and preparation applies*   A tribunal should be treated with the same respect as a court, and the advocate's preparation should be as thorough and the analysis as rigorous as they would be if the advocate were appearing before a court.

3. *Assuming that all tribunals are alike*   Although tribunals are similar in some respects, there are often important differences in procedures, policies, and functions that will affect the advocate's preparation and presentation before a particular tribunal. For example, some tribunals may have adopted an informal approach to the admission of evidence; for other tribunals, the advance disclosure of evidence may be mandatory.

There are three ways to avoid making the above assumptions: prepare, prepare, and prepare. An advocate should learn as much as possible about the particular tribunal before which he or she will appear. If the advocate is familiar with other tribunals, how is this tribunal similar to or different from them? In what ways is the tribunal like a court, and in what ways is it different?

Every tribunal is both similar to and different from a court. However, since no two tribunals are alike, the nature of these similarities and differences varies from one agency to another. Advocates must clearly understand the expectations and procedures of the particular tribunal involved rather than make assumptions that may, for example, cause them to present irrelevant evidence or fail to submit relevant evidence.

As those who have appeared before administrative tribunals know only too well, familiarity with court practice provides only limited comfort when one is confronted with the vagaries of the practice and procedure developed by specialized tribunals in an attempt to carry out their particular mandates in a fair and efficient manner.

Michael I Jeffery, Book Review of *Effective Advocacy Before Administrative Tribunals* by Andrew J Roman, (1989–90) 3 Can J Admin L & Prac 376

Steps in the Advocacy Process

Advocacy before a tribunal involves the steps set out below.

Decide Which Tribunal (or Court) Is Best

In most cases, the appeal or review route is clear. However, as discussed in Chapter 5, in some cases, two or more tribunals or courts may have concurrent jurisdiction to hear a case. For example, if a landlord illegally retains a prospective tenant's rent deposit, the tenant can make an application to the province's landlord and tenant board to return the money. However, if that landlord happens to be a real estate agent, it may also be possible to make a complaint to the governing body of the real estate profession because a realtor renting apartments is considered to be practising real estate.

Similarly, if your client hires an engineer to design a building and a wall collapses, your client may sue in court, but at the same time your client may be able to complain to the discipline committee of the association of professional engineers of your province. In court, your client could get damages for the harm suffered, but at a much higher cost than obtaining a ruling as to the engineer's competence from the discipline committee. The discipline committee can't award damages, but the engineers' association will carry out at its own expense the investigation that you would have to carry out yourself for court, and a finding of professional incompetence by the discipline committee may put pressure on the engineer to compensate your client rather than proceed to court.

The first step, therefore, is to determine which tribunals and courts have jurisdiction and which of the tribunals and/or courts are most effective and efficient in your case.

Find Out About the Tribunal

Before appearing before a tribunal for the first time, an advocate must become familiar with

- the legislation under which the tribunal operates,
- the tribunal's rules of procedure and practice guidelines, and
- decisions that the tribunal has made in similar cases.

This basic information is an essential starting point for the preparation of a case. Today, most tribunals post this information on their websites.

Be Clear About the Tribunal's Jurisdiction and Remedial Authority

Representatives (including lawyers) often make incorrect assumptions about particular tribunals' authority and powers. Most representatives wouldn't ask a criminal court to award damages or a civil court to impose a fine, but many do not take the time to find out what remedies tribunals can and cannot grant. For example, it is surprising how often tribunals are asked to award costs, even though most do not have the authority to do so.

Additional information about the tribunal may be found in its most recent annual reports, and sometimes in papers in conference proceedings written by members of the tribunal or by lawyers familiar with the tribunal's practices.

It is often helpful for an advocate to attend one or two hearings as an observer, and to talk to other representatives who have appeared before the tribunal, in order to get a sense of how the tribunal operates. Tribunal staff are also often helpful in explaining a tribunal's practices.

It is particularly important to find out the time limits for applying to the tribunal. Tribunals often have shorter limitation periods than courts. Sometimes, an application to appeal a decision of a government official must be made within a period as short as 15 to 30 days after the decision is made. While many tribunals have the right to extend this time limit, not all do. The client of an advocate who misses the deadline may lose the right of access to the tribunal, and the advocate may be open to a lawsuit for negligence.

Determine the Standing Requirements

Every tribunal has rules that determine who may appear before it as a party or an intervenor (for more information, see Chapter 9, Tribunal Procedures Before Hearings). An advocate whose client does not automatically have standing (that is, the right to participate in a hearing as a party or intervenor) should determine how and when to apply for standing. Advocates should also find out whether anyone opposed to their client will be seeking standing, and consider whether to oppose those individuals' or groups' applications or seek to limit the scope of their standing. Finally, advocates should consider whether there are individuals or groups that support their client's position that might be encouraged to seek standing.

Identify Issues

The **issues** are the questions that the tribunal must answer in order to arrive at a decision. They are the matters that are in dispute. They may be

- **questions of fact** (that is, questions that are not answered by determining what the law is on a given point—for example, whether a product advertised as performing a function or producing a result is capable of performing the function or achieving the result);

- **questions of law** (that is, questions about what law applies, or how to apply or interpret the law in the circumstances of the case);

- **questions of mixed fact and law** (that is, questions of how to apply a legal standard to a set of facts); or

- questions regarding what the correct policy to apply is, or how to interpret or apply the policy.

For example, suppose that a rural homeowner applies for a permit to install a new piece of equipment to treat his or her domestic sewage rather than installing the usual septic system. The Ministry of the Environment refuses to issue a permit because it has a policy of not approving alternatives to a septic system unless installing a septic system on a property is impossible (for example, because the soil is unsuitable or the lot is too small). If the homeowner appeals the refusal to a tribunal, the appeal might raise issues of fact, such as whether the alternative sewage treatment system will perform adequately; questions of law, such as whether the Director has jurisdiction to make the policy in question; or questions of policy, such as how to apply the policy most fairly and effectively in the circumstances of the case or whether the Ministry should have applied other policies that suggest a different result.

The issues should become apparent through the notice issued by the tribunal; through preliminary procedures such as pre-hearing conferences, motions, and disclosure; and through legal research. Discussion with other parties and representatives is also helpful in determining what the issues are.

Issues: Real and Apparent

Sometimes the real issues in a case are not what they appear to be on paper. Through discussions, you may find out that while the proceedings appear to raise many legal and factual questions, only a few of these are important. For example, a building owner may raise several legal objections to compliance with an order to make repairs, based on allegations that the building inspector exceeded his jurisdiction or followed an unfair procedure. The "real" issues may be that the owner needs more time to look into less expensive repairs and that the building inspector is convinced that the owner is flouting the law.

Determine Burden of Proof and Standard of Proof

Textbooks and reported decisions of courts elaborate on which party has the burden of proof and what is the standard of proof in various circumstances. The **burden of proof** or **onus of proof** is the obligation to provide sufficient evidence to prove a point in dispute. The **standard of proof** refers to the quantity and kind of evidence that will be considered sufficient to prove the point.

In a particular case, is it the government authority that made the decision that must prove that the decision was correct, or is it the client who is appealing the decision who must prove that the decision was wrong or unfair? Is expert evidence or documentation necessary to resolve the issue, or will the tribunal accept the observations and opinions of ordinary people? Answers to these questions can often be found in past decisions of the tribunal or other authorities, and tribunal staff can sometimes provide assistance in this area.

Collect Evidence and Identify Witnesses

Once the issues have been identified, it is necessary to determine what evidence is needed to resolve them and which documents or witnesses can prove the points in issue. Expert witnesses are a valuable resource in tribunal hearings. Their use may require more lead time to identify individuals with the appropriate experience and to prepare their reports and share them with other parties. The tribunal may also have special notice requirements and may request procedures to ensure their presence at a hearing. (For more information about expert witnesses, see Chapter 11, Presenting Evidence at a Hearing.)

Secure Attendance of Witnesses

The advocate should ensure that the witnesses will attend, or that he or she can successfully argue for an adjournment if they fail to attend, by serving each witness with a summons. This should be done as early as possible to avoid potential conflicts in scheduling.

The advocate should also find out the tribunal's procedure for issuing a summons to a witness. Under section 12(2) of Ontario's SPPA, all summonses must be signed by the chair of the hearing panel unless the legislation establishing the tribunal provides for someone else's signature. Some tribunals will issue a blank signed summons for advocates to fill in, while others will demand evidence that the witness has relevant testimony to give.

Research the Law

It is surprising how many advocates will propose an interpretation of the law on disputed points without doing the research and citing cases that support their statements. When a point of law is in issue, it is essential that the representative carry out the necessary research and document the relevant case law.

Organize Materials

Tribunals appreciate professionalism. There are several ways for representatives to make their own jobs easier, as well as the jobs of tribunal members and staff:

1. Ensure that witnesses have been served with subpoenas, in order to avoid having to ask for an adjournment because of the failure of witnesses to appear, and be prepared to show the tribunal proof of service.
2. Prepare a binder of documents to be tendered and distributed to all participants at the beginning of the hearing. In preparing the binder,
   a. arrange documents in the order in which they will be introduced;

b. number all pages consecutively and/or use tabs to facilitate easy location of particular documents;

c. provide a table of contents listing every document included in the binder, with page or tab references;

d. make sure that all documents listed are included, with no missing pages, and with all the pages in order; and

e. prepare enough copies for all tribunal members and other participants in the hearing.

3. Provide all participants with copies of tribunal and court decisions that the representative will rely on in arguing the client's case. If there are many decisions, it is helpful to organize them in a book of authorities with a table of contents and tabs. A **book of authorities** is a binder containing the cases, statutory provisions, and excerpts from legal texts that a representative will rely on in support of his or her position before a court or tribunal.

These suggestions may sound trivial, but they can make the difference between a case that proceeds quickly and smoothly and one filled with interruptions and delays. The client's case is not helped if witnesses, representatives, and panel members have to fumble through a poorly organized binder searching for a particular document, or sit around waiting while someone looks for a photocopier to replace documents that were included in one participant's binder but are missing from others.

Plan an Effective Presentation

The steps described above are all necessary, but not sufficient, steps in planning an effective presentation to the tribunal. All this planning must be bolstered by proper preparation for an effective presentation. Advocacy skills are of key importance at this stage of the case. The following are ways in which the presentation can be made most effective.

BUILD CONFIDENCE AND TRUST

Representatives have three things to offer a tribunal: their intelligence, their preparation and presentation skills, and their integrity.

Trustworthiness is a matter of integrity. When a representative appears before a tribunal, he or she soon gains a reputation as an advocate who either can or cannot be trusted. The following are some of the ways in which an advocate can build trust:

• *Never mislead the tribunal*   While advocates will want to emphasize the strengths of their case, they should also acknowledge the weaknesses. Pretending that these do not exist does not build trust or respect.

• *Do not take extreme positions or positions that clearly are not supported by the evidence or by the law*   Advocates should make the tribunal aware of any cases that do not support or that appear to refute their position, and explain why those decisions should not be followed in this case.

- *Make reasonable concessions and accommodations*   It may be possible to agree with opposing parties on many of the facts of a case, which will shorten the hearing. Similarly, if a party requests an adjournment for a good reason, such as illness, a responsible advocate will not oppose the request.

- *Focus on the most important issues and the most persuasive arguments*   When advocates raise many issues, whether peripheral or not, or present an overwhelming array of arguments, there is a risk that the tribunal will lose sight of the merits of the client's case.

> *Chief Justice Taft used to tell of the lawyer from behind the cactus plants of Texas who explained his presence before the Supreme Court of the United States as follows: "May it please the court, I know that this case should never have come here, but I was afraid it was the only chance I would ever have, and as the jurisdictional grounds were present, I thought I would like to come up and argue one case before you, so that I could tell the boys back home about the time I appeared before the Supreme Court of the United States. I don't know exactly how an argument should be made before you, but I have endeavoured to divide mine in three very common-sense divisions. First, I shall argue to the court the law of the case. I shall then argue the law as applicable to the facts, and in conclusion, I will make one wild pass at the passions of the court."*
>
> John G May, *The Lighter Side of the Law*
> (Charlottesville, Va: Michie, 1956) at 163

APPLY A LIGHT TOUCH

A hearing is not a battleground. Although some tribunal proceedings are more adversarial than others, tribunal members appreciate representatives who treat witnesses, parties, and opposing representatives with respect; who do not raise unnecessary objections; and who do not get into time-wasting arguments with other representatives.

There are times when it is necessary for representatives to be forceful and occasionally even somewhat abrasive, but in general this will not help a client's cause. Tribunals find honey easier to digest than vinegar.

SHOW RESPECT

Advocates should show tribunals the same respect they would show a court.

Because tribunals are generally supposed to be less formal and less legalistic than courts, some advocates may be tempted to behave as they never would in a courtroom. They may think that they are entitled to

- arrive late;
- ask for last-minute adjournments;
- rely on evidence that may be inflammatory, prejudicial, or unreliable;

- make submissions on the interpretation of the law without doing legal research or producing authorities; or
- provide documents to the tribunal but not bring copies for the other parties.

On all these points, they are wrong.

Advocates should never argue with the tribunal members after the tribunal has made a ruling or demand that the members change their ruling, as this is disrespectful. The time for arguing a point is before the tribunal reaches its decision.

As well, advocates should not carry on arguments or debates with opposing representatives; instead, they should address their arguments to the tribunal. Similarly, they should not interrupt other representatives or witnesses, or distract the tribunal members. Whispering to clients, making faces, drumming fingers, and tapping feet are all inappropriate behaviours for representatives to engage in during a hearing.

> *A convicted con man was found to be impersonating a lawyer. Upon learning this, the judge remarked, "I should have known he wasn't a lawyer. He was always so punctual and polite."*
>
> Anonymous

Obtain Reasons for the Decision

The Supreme Court of Canada made it clear in *Baker v Canada (Minister of Citizenship and Immigration)*[11] that tribunals must give reasons for their decisions, at least when important issues are at stake.

Under section 17(1) of Ontario's SPPA, a tribunal must provide written reasons for its decision only if a party requests that it do so. In contrast to this, section 7 of Alberta's APJA requires all administrators and tribunals to provide written decisions with reasons regardless of whether these are requested or not. Section 52 of British Columbia's ATA requires certain tribunals to provide written reasons, while section 13 of Quebec's AJA requires all administrators to communicate their decisions clearly and concisely, but only requires tribunals to give written reasons.

Written reasons for the decision are more important to the party against whom a case is decided than to the party in whose favour it is decided. They are often needed to determine whether there are grounds for a successful appeal or an application for judicial review, such as errors that the tribunal made in reaching its decision. If the tribunal does not provide reasons for its decision, the advocate should ask it to do so.

---

11 [1999] 2 SCR 817 at 844–48.

CHAPTER SUMMARY

The key to effective advocacy before tribunals and other agencies is thorough preparation. Government agencies are less transparent than tribunals. The criteria they will apply, the information they will use, and the bureaucrats or other parties who will provide advice and input to their decisions are not always set out in writing or available to the public. Much of the deliberation and decision-making goes on behind the scenes. Effective advocacy requires, first, learning as much as possible about the rules and procedures of agencies, and the policies, criteria, and guidelines they will apply in reaching a decision; and second, applying this knowledge at every point in the process where there is an opportunity for the advocate to affect the outcome.

Thorough preparation is also the key to successful advocacy before tribunals. It is important to understand that tribunals are similar to courts in some respects but different in others, and that no two tribunals are alike. In addition to solid research and a clear understanding of the rules and practices of a tribunal, other essential components of effective advocacy include building trust, making reasonable compromises and accommodations, and treating the tribunal and other participants with respect.

KEY TERMS

advocacy: the act of pleading for or supporting a position or viewpoint

advocate: a person who pleads for or represents the position or viewpoint of another; also called a "representative"

book of authorities: a binder containing the cases, statutory provisions, and excerpts from legal texts that a representative will rely on in support of his or her position before a court or tribunal

burden of proof: the obligation to provide sufficient evidence to prove a point in dispute; also called "onus of proof"; *see also* standard of proof

issues: matters that are in dispute in a hearing; the questions that a court or tribunal must answer in order to make a decision; may be questions of fact, questions of what law applies, or of how to apply or interpret the law in the circumstances of the case, or questions of what is the correct policy to apply, or of how to interpret or apply the policy

onus of proof: *see* burden of proof

question of fact: a question that is not answered by determining what the law is on a given point

question of law: a question of what law applies, or how to apply or interpret the law in the circumstances of a case

question of mixed fact and law: a question of how to apply a legal standard to a set of facts

representative: *see* advocate

standard of proof: the quantity and kind of evidence that will be considered sufficient to prove a point that is in dispute; *see also* burden of proof

REVIEW QUESTIONS

1. How would your approach to preparing and presenting a case to an administrator differ from your approach to preparing and presenting a case before a tribunal? In what ways would it be similar?

2. What are "issues," and how do you identify them?

3. How do you ensure that your witnesses show up for a hearing before a tribunal?

4. When would you make use of freedom-of-information statutes in representing your client? What are some advantages of obtaining evidence through an informal approach rather than making a formal application under freedom-of-information statutes?

5. In advocating a position before an administrator or a tribunal, "the best defence is a good offence." True or false? Why?

6. "You should prepare and present a case before a tribunal in the same way as if you were appearing before a court." True or false? Why?

EXERCISE

Using the website of the Ontario Government (ServiceOntario), find out whether the Ministry of Community and Social Services maintains statistics on its Ontario Disability Support Program. If it does, what part of the Ministry keeps these records, and what kinds of statistics are collected?

FACT SCENARIO

You are representing a client at a hearing before a tribunal that will last several weeks. Before the hearing, you prepare a book of authorities containing court decisions that support your interpretation of the law. At the beginning of the hearing, you provide copies of the book to the tribunal members and the other parties, with the intention of using the cases to support your argument at the end of the hearing.

1. Shortly after the hearing begins, you discover that one of the decisions in your book of authorities has been overturned on appeal to a higher court. Do you do anything, and, if so, what and when?

2. Shortly after the hearing begins, you discover that a court in a different province has come to the opposite conclusion about the interpretation of a law in a case that is almost identical to one of the decisions in your book of authorities on which you intend to rely.

   a. Do you do anything, and, if so, what and when?

   b. What if the conflicting decision is in relation to a similar law, but was made by a court in a different country?

3. Shortly after the hearing begins, you discover the following with regard to a case on which you intend to rely: a different judge of the same court has come to the

opposite conclusion in a later and similar case. Do you do anything, and if so, what and when?

FURTHER READING

Arlene Blatt & JoAnn Kurtz, *Advocacy for Paralegals* (Toronto: Emond Montgomery, 2009).

Colleen Flood & Lorne Sossin, *Administrative Law in Context*, 2nd ed (Toronto: Emond Montgomery, 2013) ch 6.

Marvin J Huberman & Alvin B Rosenberg, *Appellate Advocacy* (Scarborough, Ont: Carswell, 1996).

Robert Macaulay & James Sprague, *Practice and Procedure Before Administrative Tribunals* (Toronto: Carswell) (loose-leaf) ch 19.

Ronald D Manes & Valerie A Edwards, *Manes Organized Advocacy: A Manual for the Litigation Practitioner*, 2nd ed (Toronto: Carswell, 1988) (loose-leaf).

Andrew J Roman, *Effective Advocacy Before Administrative Tribunals* (Toronto: Carswell, 1989).

Lee Stuesser, *An Advocacy Primer*, 3rd ed (Toronto: Carswell, 2005).

Tribunal Procedures Before Hearings

9

LEARNING OUTCOMES

After reading this chapter, you will understand

- what is required in a tribunal's notice of a hearing;

- what procedures a tribunal may use before the hearing to identify participants and issues;

- how a tribunal may help the parties settle a dispute voluntarily before a hearing;

- how a tribunal determines the form of the hearing; and

- how a tribunal may resolve procedural and other issues before a hearing.

The legislature has left it to the arbitrator charged with deciding a collective agreement dispute to judge whether and to what extent there should be any compelled pre-hearing exchange of information. In my view, one of the considerations to be taken into account in making that judgment is the possibility that an order intended to expedite the hearing and disposition of the matter may have the opposite effect. Once there is an order compelling a party to do something it has not agreed to do, there is then the possibility of disputes about what the order means, how it applies to unanticipated circumstances, whether it has been complied with and what the consequences of non-compliance should be. The resolution of such disputes may consume the very hearing time and expense which the order was intended to save, and more, without advancing the resolution of the underlying dispute even as much as it would have been had no order been made. That will not always be so, but it is a risk which must be weighed against the possible benefits of a more structured and onerous pre-hearing disclosure process.

OV Gray, arbitrator, in *Re Thermal Ceramics and
USWA* (1993), 32 LAC (4th) 375 at 380

Balancing Informality Against Efficiency and Fairness

Tribunals differ greatly in their use of pre-hearing procedures. Some go directly from issuing a notice of hearing to holding the hearing itself, while others engage in a variety of pre-hearing processes designed to identify participants in the proceeding, to focus and narrow the issues, and to establish the procedures to be followed at the hearing. For tribunals whose hearings range from short and simple ones, with few parties and issues, to long and complex proceedings, the pre-hearing processes will vary according to the type of hearing.

As the decision of O.V. Gray, above, suggests, there are many different views with regard to how formal or informal tribunal procedures should be. In the past, one of the main differences between courts and tribunals was that courts used lengthy pre-hearing procedures and tribunals did not. As a result, in simple cases, tribunals provided parties with a cheaper and easier way to settle disputes. However, the lack of pre-hearing disclosure and of processes for clarifying and resolving issues before a hearing could also lead to unfairness, adjournments once the hearing began, and unnecessarily long and complex proceedings.

In order to improve efficiency and fairness, many tribunals have built into their decision-making process a variety of pre-hearing procedures, which are described in the sections that follow. Some of the procedures may be initiated by representatives of parties, while others may be initiated by the tribunal, with representatives invited or required to participate. The procedures include techniques that may be used by parties or by the tribunal

- to clarify or resolve issues,
- to promote settlement, and

- to ensure that all participants have the information necessary to prepare their case for presentation at the hearing.

Notice of Hearing

As discussed in Chapter 6, procedural fairness requires that anyone who will be affected by a proposed decision must be given notice of the decision and an opportunity to challenge it. Therefore, once someone has initiated a proceeding, one of the first actions of the tribunal will be to give notice to anyone who might have a right to participate. This will always include the person who will be most directly affected by the decision—such as the applicant for a licence, privilege, or benefit—but it may also include others with an interest in the outcome of the proceeding. For example, if a prisoner applies for parole, the parole board may notify the victims of the crime to give them an opportunity to present their views.

The notice should include, at a minimum,

- the date, time, and location of the hearing, or of a preliminary procedure such as a pre-hearing conference;
- the purpose of the hearing;
- information about the hearing or pre-hearing procedure; and
- any steps that the interested person must take in order to participate.

In Ontario, section 6 of the *Statutory Powers Procedure Act*[1] (SPPA) also requires the inclusion of a warning that if a person receiving the notice does not attend the hearing, the tribunal may proceed in the person's absence and need not give the person any further notice. There is a similar requirement in section 127 of Quebec's *Administrative Justice Act*[2] (AJA).

Party Status (Standing)

The right to participate fully in a hearing before a court or tribunal as a **party** is called **party status** or **standing** (in Latin, *locus standi*). This is different from intervenor status (discussed under the heading "Intervenor Status," below), which confers a more limited right to participate in a hearing.

The tribunal's enabling statute usually specifies that certain persons are "parties." For example, the *Residential Tenancies Act, 2006*[3] specifies that, in an eviction hearing, the landlord and the tenant are parties. However, tribunals often have discretion to grant standing to others who may be affected by the decision.

An individual's entitlement to be a party to a hearing depends on the nature of the issue to be addressed. In some situations, only the decision-maker and individuals directly affected by the decision are parties. For example, in professional

---

1   RSO 1990, c S.22.

2   CQLR c J-3.

3   SO 2006, c 17.

discipline cases, normally only the body seeking to impose discipline and the professional who may be subject to discipline are parties.

Other types of proceedings, however—such as a decision about what rates a telephone company or Internet service provider may charge—affect a wide variety of stakeholders. For example, when land is being rezoned, in addition to the owner and the decision-maker, individual neighbours and ratepayer groups may be given party status.

Where a statute permits a tribunal to add parties but does not specify the criteria for granting party status, it is appropriate for the tribunal to develop such criteria, whether through individual decisions or in the form of written guidelines. Generally, in order to be a party to a proceeding, a person must demonstrate that his or her interests will be directly and substantially affected by the outcome of the hearing. If the impact on the person's interests is less immediate, he or she may still be allowed to participate as an intervenor.

Rights Commonly Attached to Party Status

Some tribunals have the power to grant rights to certain participants that are not available to other participants. For example, the tribunal may allow some persons to give oral evidence but restrict others to the submission of evidence in writing. However, party status usually gives a person and his or her representatives the right to participate fully in the proceeding.

Full participation rights typically include

- the right to any disclosure of evidence to which parties are entitled under the statute or at common law;
- the right to give evidence;
- the right to call witnesses;
- the right to cross-examine;
- the right to make submissions and participate in final argument;
- the right to notice of the tribunal's decision and reasons, if any; and
- the right to appeal the tribunal's decision under an applicable statute or to apply for reconsideration or judicial review of the decision.

Identification of Parties

In some cases, legislation specifies the individuals who will be considered parties to a particular proceeding. In addition to this, the common law principle of procedural fairness may require the tribunal to grant party status to other affected individuals. In other cases, particularly where the tribunal has a mandate to protect a broad public interest (for example, in land-use planning, human rights, consumer protection, and environmental cases), the tribunal may have discretion to recognize additional parties.

Individuals and organizations other than the statutory parties may seek standing where a wide range of interests beyond those of the statutory parties will be affected directly by the tribunal's decision, or where a hearing raises an issue that will affect many future cases. For example, coroners' inquests are held to determine the cause of death of individuals who have died in a nursing home, prison, or psychiatric hospital, or in police custody. The purpose of such inquests is to prevent similar deaths in the future. Therefore, advocacy groups representing the rights of the elderly, prisoners, and the mentally ill often participate to raise systemic issues and urge the coroner's jury to recommend practices that will improve the treatment of affected groups.

For parties other than those identified in a statute, the tribunal may have a procedure for determining well in advance of the hearing whether there are persons with a sufficient interest to be included as parties to the proceeding. In this case, the tribunal will notify any such persons of the proceeding and provide them with an opportunity to bring a motion (an oral or written application) requesting party status before the hearing date.

Anyone who wishes to participate in a hearing should request party status at the earliest opportunity because preparation for the hearing will take time. It is also important for the tribunal to identify the parties as early as possible because some steps in the tribunal's process, such as setting a date for a hearing or determining disclosure deadlines, may be appropriate only after all parties have been identified. The determination of party status may be made at a pre-hearing conference (discussed below) or on approval of an applicant's formal request submitted before the hearing date.

Intervenor Status

In some cases, a tribunal may want the option of allowing certain persons to participate, but not with the full range of rights to which parties are entitled. For example, the tribunal may want to grant someone permission to participate only in relation to certain issues, or the tribunal may want the person's input on all issues but prefer to limit the extent of that person's participation on each issue (for example, permitting only written submissions). Tribunals will allow such individuals the right to participate as **intervenors**.

Some statutes may provide tribunals with the explicit power to grant "participant" or "intervenor" status as an alternative to party status. Ontario's SPPA does not. In such a case, and if the tribunal's enabling statute also is silent on this point, the tribunal may have to consider whether it has the authority to make rules of procedure governing the granting of **intervenor status**. If it has, the tribunal must then decide whether to set out in those rules some factors that it will consider in deciding whether to grant intervenor status, or whether to provide guidelines listing the criteria for obtaining this status instead of putting the criteria into its rules.

If the tribunal decides that it can recognize intervenors, one of the functions that members may carry out in advance of a hearing is to determine who shall be given this status and what limits, if any, will be placed on their participation. Often, similar criteria are used in determining party status and intervenor status. Like party status, intervenor status may be determined at a pre-hearing conference or through a motion brought by an interested person.

In the absence of any rules, guidelines, or previous tribunal decisions relating to the granting of intervenor status, a tribunal may have to balance the need for public participation against the costs associated with additional participants. Factors to consider include

- the nature of the case,
- the nature of the person's interest in the proceeding,
- the extent to which the person is likely to be affected by the outcome of the proceeding, and
- the likelihood that the person can make a useful contribution to the resolution of issues raised by the proceeding without causing injustice to the immediate parties (for example, undue expense or delay).

Pre-Hearing Conferences

Pre-hearing conferences (PHCs), sometimes called **preliminary hearings**, can be very useful to both tribunals and participants. They allow tribunals to make procedural orders and obtain agreements from parties and other participants that will help resolve issues, promote settlement, and allow the hearing to run more smoothly. Ontario's SPPA, British Columbia's *Administrative Tribunals Act*[4] (ATA), and Quebec's AJA all provide for PHCs.

In Ontario, the matters that can be addressed at a PHC are spelled out in section 5.3(1) of the SPPA. A tribunal may direct the parties to participate in a PHC in order to consider

(a) the settlement of issues,

(b) the simplification of issues,

(c) facts or evidence that can be agreed upon,

(d) the dates for required procedures,

(e) the estimated duration of the hearing, and

(f) any other matter that the tribunal considers appropriate (such as the identification of parties).

The purpose and format of PHCs may vary among tribunals, and the focus or emphasis may differ among members. In some tribunals, the panel that will hear the case conducts the PHC, while in others, a different panel or member conducts the PHC. Under the SPPA, the tribunal may assign a non-member such as a staff member or mediator to conduct a PHC (s 5.3(2)); however, a non-member may not issue any binding directions or orders (s 5.3(3)).

What a party can realistically expect to accomplish at a PHC depends on the nature of the tribunal's process and the circumstances of each case, including the timing of the conference. For example, if the PHC is held very soon after the proceeding is

---

4 SBC 2004, c 45.

initiated, the participants may be able to set dates for disclosure of evidence but may not be in a position to disclose their evidence or to address substantive issues.

Some tribunals require parties to be represented at the PHC by individuals who have the authority to make binding decisions. If the representatives attending cannot make commitments to basic procedural decisions, such as dates for disclosure of evidence or for the hearing itself, the PHC may not be useful. Parties or their representatives are expected to come prepared to set hearing and disclosure dates, articulate the issues, and provide a list of witnesses. However, it may not be reasonable to expect that the representatives will have the authority to make or accept settlement offers without further discussion with their clients, particularly if the PHC is held before disclosure of evidence.

If, at the time of the PHC, parties or their representatives are not prepared to deal with all the matters necessary to promote an efficient hearing process, or if there are many issues to be addressed, the tribunal may extend the conference until more progress has been made, or it may set aside portions of the agenda to be dealt with at a later date.

While PHCs are very useful for dealing with procedural issues, caution must be exercised in attempting to use them to resolve substantive issues or to achieve settlement. Under section 5.3(4) of the SPPA, if the PHC is used for settlement discussions, the presiding member may participate in the hearing only if all parties consent. If the member expresses any views on the merits of the case, there may be an appearance of bias that may disqualify the member from participating in the hearing. In addition, the member at the PHC may hear evidence that will not be put before the hearing panel. If the member participates in the hearing, the parties may be concerned that he or she may consciously or unconsciously rely on evidence that the other members of the panel have not heard.

Disclosure of Evidence

Before a hearing begins, tribunals usually require the parties to disclose the evidence that they will present in support of their respective positions in the case. **Evidence** is information that a party seeks to use in a legal proceeding to prove or disprove a contention or allegation. A tribunal's authority to order the **disclosure** of evidence may be set out in a statute of general application or in the tribunal's enabling statute (see the box feature "Disclosure Orders"), or, in rare circumstances, may arise from the tribunal's common-law procedural fairness duties or be required as a matter of fundamental justice under section 7 of the *Canadian Charter of Rights and Freedoms*.[5] Where a statute does not explicitly provide for disclosure, procedural fairness may still require disclosure; in cases where lack of disclosure could prevent a fair hearing, threatening a person's life, liberty, or security of the person, disclosure may be required as a matter of fundamental justice under section 7 of the Charter.

---

5 Part I of the *Constitution Act, 1982*, being Schedule B to the *Canada Act 1982* (UK), 1982, c 11.

Disclosure Orders

Section 5.4 of Ontario's *Statutory Powers Procedure Act* gives tribunals the authority to order

(a)   the exchange of documents,

(b)   the oral or written examination of a party,

(c)   the exchange of witness statements and expert witness reports,

(d)   the provision of particulars, and

(e)   any other form of disclosure,

provided that the tribunal has made rules governing the procedure for disclosure. This power is subject to any other statute that applies to the tribunal's proceedings. In addition, tribunals cannot require the disclosure of privileged information. (For a more detailed discussion of privileged information, see Chapter 11, Presenting Evidence at a Hearing.)

Disclosure of evidence may take the following forms:

- *Exchange of documents*   The parties are often required to exchange documents that each intends to rely on in support of his or her position. Examples are contracts or written agreements and correspondence relating to the matter in dispute.

- *Oral or written questions and answers*   Some tribunals permit disclosure through oral questioning of a party (**examination for discovery**) or through the submission of written questions (**interrogatories**). (See the box feature "Examination for Discovery.")

- *Witness statements*   These are written statements (sometimes called "will says") setting out the testimony that a witness is expected to give at the hearing. Often, tribunals require that the **witness statement** be accompanied by a list of any documents to which a witness may refer during testimony.

- *Expert witness reports*   Some witnesses present expert evidence on scientific or technical matters. An expert witness report sets out the witness's opinions and the facts on which they are based. The witness may also be required to disclose in the report all studies, texts, or tests upon which he or she will rely in testifying at the hearing.

- *A list of other documents*   The parties may also be required to identify other documents in their possession or under their control that are relevant but on which they do not intend to rely.

- *Access to other evidence*   It is not always possible to bring relevant evidence to the hearing room (for example, where a building or site is at the centre of a dispute). In such cases, the parties may be required to provide access to the relevant evidence as part of the disclosure procedure.

Examination for Discovery

In an examination for discovery, the persons named in the disclosure order must attend at a specified time and place and answer questions put to them by the representatives of opposing parties. Those questions and answers are recorded and transcribed.

Although Ontario's *Statutory Powers Procedure Act* does not specifically provide for examinations for discovery, the provision for oral examination of a party at any stage of the proceeding (s 5.4(1)(b)) appears to contemplate this technique for obtaining evidence. Therefore, a tribunal may require examination for discovery through its rules of procedure, either in all cases or by permitting a party to apply to the tribunal to require this procedure in a specific case.

Timing of Disclosure

Many tribunals require disclosure of evidence well in advance of a hearing.[6] The time at which disclosure is required may be determined in several ways:

- through statutory or procedural rules that set predetermined disclosure dates applicable to all hearings,
- by the requirements set out in the notice of hearing,
- through discussion at a PHC,
- by a request for disclosure in the form of a motion brought by a party to the proceeding, or
- by a combination of these methods.

When timing and other disclosure requirements are decided on a case-by-case basis, all parties should be given an opportunity to make submissions as to what conditions are reasonable before the tribunal issues the disclosure order.

Use of Disclosed Evidence at the Hearing

A question that often arises is whether the information obtained through disclosure may be used as evidence at the hearing or whether parties are only allowed to use the information to help them prepare for the hearing. Some tribunals leave it to the member presiding at the hearing to determine which disclosed material can be used as evidence, while others have rules of procedure providing that all disclosed information is automatically part of the hearing record. Some tribunals

---

6   However, tribunals may have no power to require pre-hearing disclosure unless a statute specifically provides them with this authority or common-law procedural fairness requires it (see *Ontario (Human Rights Commission) v Dofasco Inc* (2001), 57 OR (3d) 693 (CA) at 708), or where s 7 of the Charter requires disclosure (see *Charkaoui v Canada (Citizenship and Immigration)*, 2008 SCC 38, [2008] 2 SCR 326).

treat witness statements, expert witness reports, or answers to written or oral questions as evidence that is admissible at the hearing, while others permit the use of this information at the hearing only if it contradicts evidence given orally at the hearing. In the latter case, a tribunal member may be required to rule, either before or during the hearing, on the admissibility of information obtained through the disclosure process.

If the tribunal's procedural rules do not state whether the information disclosed automatically becomes evidence at the hearing, a representative should consider asking the tribunal to clarify its position, either at a PHC or through a motion.

Both approaches—making disclosed material automatically part of the hearing record and leaving the question to be decided by the hearing panel—have advantages and disadvantages. For example, the treatment of disclosed information as evidence can shorten the hearing because written statements can be substituted for oral testimony. However, if participants know that their statements at disclosure will be used as evidence at the hearing, they may be less forthcoming; they may make preliminary motions objecting to the disclosure of some information; or they may object to the admission of information disclosed by the other party as evidence. As a result, the length and complexity of the proceeding may be increased.

Disclosure of Particulars

Ontario's SPPA allows a tribunal to order parties to disclose particulars, provided that this requirement is set out in the tribunal's procedural rules (s 5.4(1)(d)). As discussed in Chapter 6, "particulars" are details that explain or clarify such matters as the grounds for a party's case, the remedy or decision that the party is seeking, and the evidence or facts on which a party is relying. If the legal theory or argument presented by a party is not sufficiently clear to permit other parties to prepare their response, clarification of this could also fall within the definition of "particulars."

Tribunal members may be required to rule on motions demanding particulars, or they may decide on their own initiative that particulars are needed to ensure an efficient hearing process (after inviting submissions on whether such an order should be made).

Issues that a member may be required to decide in dealing with particulars include

- whether the particulars requested from one party will be provided only to the other parties in order to assist them in preparing their case or whether they will also be provided to the tribunal, and will become part of the hearing record; and
- whether the particulars should be considered binding on the party that provided them.

The second question is especially important. If particulars are treated as binding, they may narrow the grounds upon which a party relies or the issues before the tribunal.

Settlement Before the Hearing

One of the advantages of pre-hearing procedures such as PHCs, motions, and disclosure is that they give the parties an opportunity to learn the strengths and weaknesses of their own case and of the positions taken by other parties. They provide parties and their representatives with an indication of the likelihood that they will succeed, and with an indication of the probable duration and cost of the hearing if it proceeds.

Representatives should use this information to help their clients assess whether it is in their interests to settle, and, if so, on what terms. The main advantages of settling are that

- parties resolve the dispute on their own terms instead of handing over responsibility for the outcome to a third party, and
- parties and the tribunal are saved the costs of a hearing.

Parties who have reached a settlement should notify the witnesses and the tribunal as soon as possible, especially when a hearing has been scheduled and will have to be cancelled. The tribunal members and staff in particular will appreciate this consideration, and it will serve the interests of the representatives in the event of future appearances before the tribunal.

Power of the Tribunal to Proceed Despite a Settlement

In some cases, the tribunal may have the power to overrule a settlement between the parties and proceed with the hearing. A tribunal may be granted this authority by statute, or the case law may support such a decision by a tribunal in some circumstances. Although tribunals generally may not proceed where all parties have reached a settlement, there are some exceptions, usually in cases where the tribunal's role is to protect the public interest rather than the interests of the parties alone.

In addition, if some of the parties settle and others do not, the settlement may not bind the other parties or participants, and the tribunal may order that the hearing proceed. The courts have suggested that, in these cases, the following considerations are relevant in determining the tribunal's authority:[7]

- whether the proceedings are intended solely to resolve a dispute between the parties to the hearing or are part of a regulatory regime designed to protect a broader public interest; and
- whether a withdrawal or settlement by some parties may be contrary to the interests of other parties or potential parties to the proceeding.

---

7   *NSP Investments Ltd v Ontario (Joint Board)* (1990), 72 OR (2d) 379 (Div Ct); *Re Cloverdale Shopping Centre Ltd and Etobicoke (Township)*, [1966] 2 OR 439, 57 DLR (2d) 206 (CA).

Assistance to Parties in Settling Issues

Tribunal members or staff may use a number of mechanisms to encourage parties to settle some or all of the issues before the hearing. The following are some techniques intended to motivate parties to settle:

- Disclosure is often a prerequisite to settlement negotiations.
- The setting of a firm hearing date provides a deadline for settlement. Parties and their representatives often leave settlement negotiations to the eleventh hour. In many cases, parties do not make a serious effort to settle in the absence of a looming hearing date.
- Where the parties request an adjournment of the hearing because they are close to settlement, the adjournment should be for a short and specified settlement period. Otherwise, the pressure to settle will be relieved and the parties may *not* settle. **Sine die adjournments** (adjournments for an indefinite period) are the enemy of settlement.

PHCs and mediation are two other important aids to a pre-hearing settlement.

PRE-HEARING CONFERENCES

PHCs can be used as settlement conferences. While a PHC dealing with procedural matters should usually be public (because the transparency of tribunal proceedings is crucial to their legitimacy), serious settlement negotiations are often impossible in a public setting.

To facilitate settlement at a PHC, the tribunal may separate or "sever" the settlement portions of the conference from the procedural portions and hold the settlement conference behind closed doors. In addition, the tribunal may require the participants to agree to keep the discussions at the settlement conference confidential. If the tribunal does not automatically take these steps, a representative should consider asking the tribunal to do so.

MEDIATION

The members or staff of a tribunal may also attempt to facilitate resolution of issues through a variety of alternative dispute resolution (ADR) mechanisms, such as mediation, conciliation, and arbitration.

Mediation is the intervention in a dispute of an impartial person (a "mediator"), who has no decision-making power, in order to assist the parties in reaching a settlement. It is the primary method used in facilitating settlement before hearings.

The mediator's role usually includes

- structuring the negotiation process,
- helping the parties clarify their needs and interests,
- assisting in identifying and clarifying issues, and
- facilitating constructive discussion between the parties.

In addition, the mediator may offer an opinion on the likely outcome of a formal hearing or make recommendations on settlement terms or other concerns.

Typically, the parties themselves participate directly in the mediation process. Their representatives may or may not be present.

In some circumstances, mediation may have the following advantages over formal adjudication by a tribunal:

- It can be less time consuming and less costly than a hearing.
- It can preserve or strengthen relationships between the parties.
- It can lead to a settlement that is tailored by the parties themselves rather than imposed by an outsider, and is therefore more acceptable to the parties.
- It may offer a broader range of solutions than the tribunal has the power to impose.

On the other hand, mediation may not be suitable in many situations—for example,

- where there is a significant power imbalance between the parties,
- where the law is clearly on one party's side, or
- where it is in one party's interest to maximize delay or cost to the other party (that is, where a party may wish to participate in mediation in bad faith).

In the above cases, mediation may simply lead to more cost and delay before the inevitable hearing. An effective tribunal will not impose mediation in all cases, but will analyze the particular facts and circumstances of a dispute in order to determine whether mediation is likely to be useful in that case.

If a settlement is reached through mediation, the parties set out the agreement in writing, sometimes with the assistance of the mediator. The parties may make the agreement binding by signing a contract. In some cases, the tribunal has the power to put the agreement into the form of a binding order so that the agreement can be enforced in the same manner as any other decision or order of the tribunal. (See Chapter 17, Enforcement of Tribunal Orders.)

The use of mediation and other ADR techniques can raise a number of issues, including:

- whether a tribunal has the power to use ADR techniques where this authority is not explicitly provided by a statute;
- if a statute grants a tribunal authority to use ADR techniques, whether the tribunal may make the participation of parties mandatory;
- whether the agreements made by parties are binding on the parties to the agreement or on other parties to the proceeding who did not sign the agreement;
- whether, and to what extent, information revealed during ADR is privileged; and
- whether a tribunal member who conducts an ADR session may later participate in a hearing involving the parties who were involved in the session.

Some of these issues may be addressed in a statute, as is the case for tribunals governed by Ontario's SPPA (ss 4.8 and 4.9) and British Columbia's ATA (ss 28 and 29). For matters related to the use of ADR that are not covered by statutory provisions, the tribunal should establish a set of procedural rules. This is one of the prerequisites under the SPPA for the use of ADR mechanisms; the second is that all parties consent to participation in the ADR process (s 4.8(1)).

The Tribunal's Authority to Reject an Assisted Settlement

Another issue that arises is whether the tribunal is bound by an ADR settlement or whether, instead, it has the authority to reject the settlement and hold a hearing. This question is particularly important when the tribunal's mandate goes beyond the interests of the parties and permits a decision based on the public interest.

Unless the question is addressed by a statute governing the tribunal, the tribunal will determine the scope of its authority according to its interpretation of its mandate. The tribunal's position may be found in a decision in a particular case, which other members of the tribunal follow as a matter of course, or it may be expressed in procedural rules or practice directions developed by the tribunal over time.

In general, if the involvement of tribunal members or staff in facilitating settlement does not imply acceptance or approval of the settlement by the tribunal, the tribunal should make this clear to the parties. Even if a tribunal does have the authority to approve or reject a settlement, it should not approve any settlement that deals with matters that are outside its jurisdiction.

Determining the Choice of Hearing Format: Oral, Electronic, or Written

A hearing may take one of three forms:

1. an oral hearing (the traditional form), in which the tribunal and all other participants are present in the same location and at the same time;
2. an electronic hearing, held through a teleconference or a video conference; or
3. a written hearing, in which all the evidence and arguments are distributed to the tribunal and to the other parties in written form.

The tribunal may propose the form of the hearing to the parties to the dispute, or the parties may ask the tribunal to consider their preference before making its decision.

Ontario's SPPA sets out specific rules relating to the choice among the three alternatives (s 6). In all cases, the parties must be given notice of the form of the hearing. If the tribunal is considering holding a written or an electronic hearing, the parties must be provided with an opportunity to object and request an oral hearing instead.

Before a tribunal proposes a hearing in any form other than the traditional oral form, it should consider whether the alternative is a fair and efficient method of conducting the hearing. A written hearing may be most appropriate where the facts are largely undisputed and credibility does not appear to be in issue. Where facts and credibility are in dispute, an oral or electronic hearing will usually be required. A written hearing may also be inappropriate where any of the parties is illiterate or poorly educated, or has limited fluency in English or French.

An oral hearing may be more appropriate than a written hearing or a teleconference

- when it is desirable to visit an outside location, such as the site of a building;
- when witnesses must refer to maps, charts, and other visual aids; or
- when observing witnesses is important in assessing their credibility.

An oral hearing may also be preferable to an electronic hearing if, for example, the video conferencing facilities and technology are not of sufficient quality to permit such observations.

Other factors that parties and the tribunal may consider in determining the most appropriate hearing format include:

- convenience to the parties;
- the cost, efficiency, and timeliness of the proceeding;
- which format would provide the degree of fairness and transparency appropriate under the circumstances; and
- the desirability or necessity of public participation in or public access to the conduct of the hearing.

The differences between—as well as the advantages and disadvantages of—oral, written, and electronic hearings are discussed in more detail in Chapter 10, Tribunal Procedures During Hearings.

Preliminary Motions

There are certain issues related to the conduct of the hearing that it is useful to resolve before the hearing begins. These may range from matters of procedure to more fundamental questions of jurisdiction. While the responsibility for resolving such issues rests with tribunal members and staff, it is important that when any question affects the parties involved, all have an opportunity to present their views before a final decision is made.

If a tribunal holds PHCs or settlement conferences, or has an ADR process, many of these issues may be resolved through these procedures. However, there is an additional method of permitting all parties to be heard on preliminary issues: the motion. A **motion** is an oral or written request by one party for a ruling by the tribunal. The party making the request is often called the **moving party**.

Notice of the moving party's request (a "notice of motion") must be served on all other parties. The notice of motion sets out the date, time, and place at which the motion will be heard; the remedy that is requested; and the grounds for the request. Sometimes the moving party provides the tribunal with all the information needed for a motion, and the tribunal serves all the other parties with notice. However, in many tribunals, the tribunal staff give the moving party the information about the hearing of the motion, and that person is then responsible for serving notice on the other parties.

The evidence to be used in support of a pre-hearing motion is usually restricted to written statements, often in the form of an affidavit. An **affidavit** is a sworn statement setting out facts supporting the request. The moving party files this written evidence with the tribunal. Many tribunals require that this evidence also accompany the notice of motion.

The moving party must provide the tribunal with evidence that notice has been served on all the other parties. This evidence is called **proof of service**. Proof of service may take one of two forms:

1. a written statement by the moving party (sometimes in the form of an affidavit), affirming that the notice of motion was served on each of the other parties, and indicating how and when it was served; or
2. a statement acknowledging service written on a copy of the notice and signed by the receiving party.

The tribunal will generally provide an opportunity for other parties, known as **responding parties**, to serve and file responses to the issues raised by the moving party, also consisting of written evidence supporting their positions. In addition, the parties may be entitled to cross-examine each other's witnesses to determine the accuracy of their written statements. The transcripts of any cross-examinations are provided by the parties to each other and to the tribunal.

The reliance on written evidence in deciding pre-hearing motions is an important difference from the procedure followed at many hearings. At an oral or electronic hearing, most of the evidence is typically provided orally by witnesses.

If any party fails to attend the hearing of the motion, the presiding member of the tribunal must check whether that party was properly notified of the motion. If the party seeking a remedy cannot provide proof of service of the notice, the hearing should not proceed.

The following sections discuss some motions that may be presented before a hearing.

Motion for Directions

A motion for directions requests clarification of a procedural matter, usually one that is not addressed in the tribunal's rules of procedure.

An Example of a Motion for Directions

The Wild Peonies Protection Tribunal was established to allow the public to challenge a government land-use planning decision that would permit destruction of wild peony habitat. The tribunal's rules of procedure state:

> On the request of a party at any time before a hearing, another party must provide written answers to written questions that are relevant to the proceedings where this would simplify or shorten the hearing.

The applicant, a naturalist group, claims that the respondent, a developer, should not be permitted to build a condominium because it will harm a rare species of peony. Under this rule, the developer asks the naturalist group for details of how it determined that the flowers growing on his property are the rare peonies rather than a more common variety that is almost identical in appearance. The naturalist group answers the question, but adds that this information is only for the developer's use in briefing his expert witness, a botanist, and the written response is not to be used as evidence at the hearing.

The developer responds that he has every intention of submitting the written response at the hearing because there is nothing in the tribunal's rules to prevent this.

Rather than wait to have the tribunal make a ruling during the hearing, the naturalists make a motion asking the tribunal to specify whether the rule requiring a party to provide written answers is intended to permit the admission of the written response as evidence at the hearing, or whether the developer can use the information only to prepare his witness.

Motion for Summary Determination (Dismissal of the Application or Appeal or Granting It Without a Hearing)

The courts have the power to dismiss a case without a hearing where there is clearly no possibility that the case will succeed. The reason may be either that there is no remedy available under the law or that there is no evidence on which a remedy can be granted. Some tribunals also permit a party to request early dismissal of a case on this basis. Tribunal rules may also permit motions to grant summary judgment in favour of the party challenging the validity of the government action that is the subject of the proceeding, for example, where it is clear on the face of an order that the government had no jurisdiction to issue it.

For a tribunal, permitting parties to bring such motions is a two-edged sword. On the one hand, if a case clearly cannot succeed, it is difficult to justify the time and cost involved in proceeding with a hearing. On the other hand, parties will frequently bring a motion for dismissal or summary judgment even when they cannot provide sufficient evidence to support the request. In these cases, the length, cost, and complexity of the proceeding are increased.

An additional concern is that the hearing of a motion for dismissal or summary judgment may turn into a hearing of the main issue in the case on its merits.

Motion for Summary Determination: British Columbia

Under section 31 of British Columbia's *Administrative Tribunals Act*, a tribunal may dismiss all or part of an application if

(a) the tribunal has no jurisdiction over the application;

(b) the applicant missed the time limit for filing;

(c) the application is frivolous, vexatious, trivial, or gives rise to an abuse of process;

(d) the application was made in bad faith or for an improper purpose;

(e) there was excessive delay in the applicant's pursuit of the application or the applicant did not comply with an order of the tribunal;

(f) there is no reasonable prospect that the applicant will succeed; or

(g) the application has been appropriately dealt with in another proceeding.

However, the tribunal must abide by the following two conditions:

1. before dismissing an application for any of the above reasons, the tribunal must give the applicant an opportunity to make submissions; and

2. after dismissing all or part of an application, the tribunal must notify all the parties of its decision in writing and give reasons for its decision.

Motion to Decide a Jurisdictional Issue

A party may bring a preliminary motion that the tribunal has no jurisdiction to hear the case or to rule on a particular issue in the case. An example of a jurisdictional issue is whether the tribunal has the authority to decide constitutional questions. Tribunals may prefer to address and resolve such issues before proceeding with a full hearing rather than invest time and money in reaching a decision that may later be overturned by a court (as a result of the tribunal having exceeded its jurisdiction).

Motion to Decide a Constitutional Question

Constitutional questions fall into two broad categories:

1. challenges to the constitutional validity of a federal or provincial statute, a municipal bylaw, or a common law rule; and

2. questions as to whether the Constitution affects how such laws or rules apply in a particular case.

For example, a law that denies access to certain services on the basis of an individual's sexual orientation may be challenged as invalid, or it may be considered valid but not applicable in certain circumstances.

Constitutional questions are generally decided with reference to the division of powers between the federal government and the provincial governments, or with regard to the effect of the Charter on the tribunal's process or decisions. Such questions are often raised in the form of a preliminary motion before the date set for the hearing. However, they may also be raised at the beginning of the hearing or at any time during the hearing.

AUTHORITY OF THE TRIBUNAL TO DECIDE CONSTITUTIONAL QUESTIONS

Not all tribunals have authority to decide constitutional questions or to grant the remedies requested by parties or their representatives. In some cases, only a court has the jurisdiction to hear a constitutional question.

The authority of a particular tribunal to decide constitutional questions may be set out in a statute governing the tribunal. If there is no statutory reference, it can be difficult to determine whether the tribunal has this power.

In the 1990s, the Supreme Court of Canada established tests for determining whether tribunals can decide constitutional questions; however, these tests were complex and created much uncertainty. In its 2003 decision in *Nova Scotia (Workers' Compensation Board) v Martin; Nova Scotia (Workers' Compensation Board) v Laseur*,[8] the Court reduced the confusion by ruling that if a tribunal has authority to interpret laws generally, this authority will be presumed to include the ability to decide constitutional issues unless the context requires the opposite conclusion.

The tests are still evolving. As discussed in Chapter 4, in *R v Conway*[9] in 2010 the Supreme Court set out a new approach for deciding whether a tribunal can grant remedies for Charter breaches under section 24(1) of the Charter. The change that *Conway* makes in the analysis of whether a tribunal can grant a section 24(1) remedy is that whether a tribunal can award the particular remedy sought is no longer a component of whether the tribunal is a court of competent jurisdiction. Instead, the question of whether the tribunal has jurisdiction to grant the particular remedy is decided *after* the tribunal has been declared to be a court of competent jurisdiction. The analysis involves two questions: first, whether the tribunal has jurisdiction, explicit or implied, to decide questions of law. If it does, unless it is clearly demonstrated that the legislature intended to exclude the Charter from its jurisdiction, the tribunal is a court of competent jurisdiction and can consider and apply the Charter. In that case, the second question arises: can the tribunal grant the particular remedy requested? This is a matter of interpreting the tribunal's statutory mandate and functions to determine whether the kinds of remedies sought are the kinds of remedies that the legislature appears to have anticipated would fit within the statutory scheme governing the tribunal.

---

8   2003 SCC 54, [2003] 2 SCR 504.

9   2010 SCC 22, [2010] 1 SCR 765.

Authority of the Tribunal to Decide Constitutional Questions: A Case

In the *Martin/Laseur* case, Mr. Martin suffered from chronic pain caused by work-related injuries. He received benefits and rehabilitation from the Workers' Compensation Board of Nova Scotia, but regulations prevented him from receiving these benefits for more than four weeks. Martin appealed the Board's decision to end his benefits to the Nova Scotia Workers' Compensation Appeals Tribunal on the grounds that the regulations infringed his right to equality under section 15 of the *Canadian Charter of Rights and Freedoms*.

Before the Appeals Tribunal, the Board argued that, under a complex test that the Supreme Court had established in previous cases to determine which tribunals have the power to hear Charter arguments, the Appeals Tribunal had no authority to hear a Charter argument; the Appeals Tribunal ruled that it *did* have authority. The Board appealed this ruling to the Nova Scotia Court of Appeal, which held that, under the test established by the Supreme Court, the Appeals Tribunal could not decide Charter questions. Mr. Martin appealed to the Supreme Court.

The Court clarified and simplified the test it had previously developed, ruling that administrative tribunals that have implicit or explicit jurisdiction to decide other questions of law are presumed to have the power to decide constitutional questions unless the context requires the opposite conclusion. In this case, the statute under which the Appeals Tribunal operated gave it explicit authority to decide questions of law, and the resulting presumption that it could decide Charter questions was not rebutted as there was no clear implication arising from anything in the statute that the legislature intended to exclude the Charter from the scope of the Appeals Tribunal's authority.

An example of a context that would rebut the presumption that a particular tribunal can decide constitutional questions is where a statute provides for a tribunal to determine questions of law and does not expressly exclude constitutional questions, but that statute or another statute expressly confers the right to decide the particular kind of constitutional question at issue on a different administrative body and establishes a straightforward procedure for redirecting the issue to the other body.

If the tribunal does not have explicit authority to decide constitutional questions and has not previously ruled on its authority, it may take one of two approaches when asked to hear an argument about the constitutional validity of a practice or action:

1. the tribunal may ask the parties to address whether such authority exists and, if so, what is the scope of that authority, before deciding whether to hear the constitutional question; or

2. the tribunal may assume that it has jurisdiction to decide constitutional questions and proceed to do so, unless one of the parties questions its authority.

If the tribunal decides—after inviting arguments as to its jurisdiction in the first case or after a party challenges its jurisdiction in the second case—that it has no jurisdiction to decide constitutional questions, then it will not agree to consider the constitutional question that has been raised.

The tribunal may develop internal or published guidelines as to which approach its members should take.

WHEN CONSTITUTIONAL QUESTIONS SHOULD BE DECIDED

It is often convenient for a tribunal to decide constitutional questions before a hearing. However, the stage at which a constitutional question should be addressed depends on the nature of the question and the kind of information needed for the decision.

If the question is purely a question of law, the tribunal may choose to decide it before hearing evidence. If the question is more complex, involving an analysis of facts and evidence, the tribunal may either

- hear the constitutional arguments before hearing evidence, but reserve its decision until the end of the case; or

- hear the constitutional arguments at the end of the hearing, along with the final arguments on the other issues raised, and make its decision at that time.

PROCEDURE FOR BRINGING A MOTION

The requirements for bringing a motion on a constitutional question vary widely among federal and provincial tribunals.

In some cases, any person who intends to raise a constitutional question before a tribunal is required by statute to give notice to the attorney general of Canada or the attorney general of the province, or both, before arguing the issue. For example, the *Federal Courts Act*[10] requires notice to both attorneys general before a constitutional question is presented to a federal tribunal. Similarly, Ontario's *Courts of Justice Act*[11] (CJA) prohibits Ontario tribunals from considering constitutional questions without prior notice to the two attorneys general. In some provinces, such as Saskatchewan and New Brunswick, the statutes apply only to arguments before courts; in others, such as Newfoundland and Labrador, it is unclear whether the statutory requirements apply only to courts or also to tribunals.

The notice to an attorney general should set out the facts relating to the constitutional question and the issues that will be raised. In Ontario, the form that the notice must take is specified in the CJA. Although the attorneys general have the right to participate in the argument, they will frequently decline, preferring to become involved only if the tribunal's decision is appealed to a court.

The tribunal should ensure that notice has been served to the attorney or attorneys general before hearing the arguments of the parties. If notice has not been given, a party may object to the hearing of the arguments. Moreover, the tribunal may not grant any remedy requested unless proper notice has been served.

---

10 RSC 1985, c F-7.

11 RSO 1990, c C.43.

CHAPTER SUMMARY

One of the key reasons for establishing tribunals is that they can settle disputes in a more time- and cost-efficient manner than courts. In the past, these savings were achieved in part by the fact that hearings were held without the preliminary procedures used in the courts. However, through this approach, tribunals often sacrificed fairness and thoroughness to speed and convenience. In recent years, the trend has been toward the increased use of pre-hearing procedures as a means of improving both efficiency and fairness.

Some procedures are basic and may be required by statute—for example, identifying participants in the proceeding and notifying them of the hearing. Many tribunals also require parties to disclose at least some of their evidence before the hearing.

Tribunals may encourage the parties to engage in pre-hearing negotiations aimed at resolving issues or settling the case, and some tribunals assist the process through mediation. In addition, procedural matters may be addressed at pre-hearing conferences and through preliminary motions brought by parties to the proceeding. Tribunals may also provide for motions of various kinds before the hearing, such as motions to add parties or intervenors, motions for disclosure, motions for directions, and motions to determine constitutional questions.

Ideally—through disclosure, mediation, and rulings on motions—the issues can be resolved without a hearing or the hearing can be shortened. These mechanisms, along with pre-hearing conferences, also increase the transparency—and therefore the fairness—of the tribunal's proceedings.

KEY TERMS

affidavit: a statement, sworn before an authorized person such as a lawyer, in which the person signing the statement sets out facts that he or she affirms to be true

disclosure: a pre-hearing procedure in which parties are required to present evidence relevant to the proceeding to each other (and sometimes to the tribunal) for use in preparing their cases and, in some cases, to be used as evidence at the hearing

evidence: information that a party seeks to use in a legal proceeding to prove or disprove a contention or allegation

examination for discovery: a form of disclosure in which one party orally questions another party under oath or affirmation

interrogatory: a form of disclosure in which one party submits written questions to another party; that party is required to answer the questions in writing

intervenor: a person who, because he or she may be adversely affected by the outcome or can provide assistance to the tribunal in deciding the dispute, is granted the right to participate in a proceeding, but without the full range of rights granted to a party

intervenor status: the right of a person to participate in a proceeding without the full range of rights usually granted to a party; a tribunal's power to grant individuals such status may be authorized by statute or provided for in a tribunal's procedural rules

***locus standi*:** *see* party status

mediation: a method of alternative dispute resolution in which an impartial person who has no decision-making authority intervenes in a dispute in order to assist the parties in reaching a settlement

motion: an oral or written application to a court or tribunal to rule on an issue in a proceeding

moving party: a party who brings a motion; *see also* responding party

party: a person who has a right to participate fully in a legal proceeding

party status: usually, the right of a person to participate fully in a proceeding; may be granted by statute or at the discretion of the tribunal; also called "standing" or "*locus standi*"

pre-hearing conference (PHC): an informal meeting or formal hearing in advance of the main hearing in a proceeding for the purpose of making procedural decisions or resolving issues

preliminary hearing: *see* pre-hearing conference (PHC)

proof of service: a written statement affirming that a notice of motion has been served on all parties to a proceeding and indicating how and when the notice was served

responding party: a party who is required to respond to a motion brought by another party; *see also* moving party

***sine die* adjournment:** adjournment for an indefinite period

standing: *see* party status

witness statement: a written statement provided by a party to other parties or to a court or tribunal, or both, setting out the expected evidence of a person the party expects to call as a witness; also known informally as a "will say"

CASES TO CONSIDER

Intervention Before Courts and Tribunals

Peel (Regional Municipality) v Great Atlantic & Pacific Co of Canada Ltd (1990), 74 OR (2d) 164 (CA)

FACTS: The People for Sunday Association of Canada, a non-profit group with members from religious groups, trade unions, and small retail businesses, applied to intervene in the appeal of a decision that held that the *Retail Business Holidays Act* (RSO 1980, c 453), which limited Sunday shopping, was unconstitutional and contrary to the *Canadian Charter of Rights and Freedoms*.

ISSUES: Did the People for Sunday Association of Canada have a right to intervenor status? What was the test for intervenor status?

DECISION: When determining whether to grant intervenor status, the court had to consider the following: the nature of the case; the issues in the case; and whether granting an individual or a group the right to participate as an intervenor would likely result in the individual or group making a useful contribution without causing injustice to the principal parties. Allowing intervenor status in a Charter case is often particularly desirable because Charter decisions tend to have a significant effect on people other than the litigants. In this case, the People for Sunday Association represented a large number of people with a direct interest in the outcome of the appeal; its members had special knowledge and expertise of the subject matter; and, even though the attorney general would be making similar arguments in support of the Act, the Association had a different perspective from the attorney general, so its contribution would not duplicate that of the attorney general. The Association met the criteria established by the court and was granted intervenor status.

Jurisdiction to Hear Charter Arguments

Nova Scotia (Workers' Compensation Board) v Martin; Nova Scotia (Workers' Compensation Board) v Laseur, 2003 SCC 54, [2003] 2 SCR 504

FACTS: Donald Martin suffered from the disability of chronic pain caused by work-related injuries. He received temporary disability benefits and rehabilitation from the Workers' Compensation Board of Nova Scotia. However, the regulations excluded chronic pain from the regular workers' compensation system, and Martin's benefits were discontinued after four weeks. Martin argued before the Nova Scotia Workers' Compensation Appeals Tribunal that this infringed his right to equality under section 15(1) of the *Canadian Charter of Rights and Freedoms*.

ISSUE: Did the Appeals Tribunal have jurisdiction to hear the Charter argument?

DECISION: The Appeals Tribunal had jurisdiction to consider the constitutionality of the challenged provisions of the Act and the regulations. Administrative tribunals that have jurisdiction to decide questions of law arising under a legislative provision are presumed to also have jurisdiction to decide the constitutional validity of that provision. In this case, the provisions violated the Charter, and the Nova Scotia government was directed to amend them.

Jurisdiction of Tribunals to Grant Section 24(1) Charter Remedies

R v Conway, 2010 SCC 22, [2010] 1 SCR 765

FACTS: Mr. Conway was found not guilty by reason of insanity of a charge of sexual assault with a weapon, and was detained in a mental health facility. Prior to the mandatory annual review before the Ontario Review Board to determine whether there continued to be a need for his detention, Mr. Conway sent a notice of constitutional question, alleging that he was entitled to an absolute discharge under section 24(1) of the Charter.

ISSUE: Is the Ontario Review Board a body that has jurisdiction to grant remedies under Charter section 24(1)?

Section 24(1) provides:

Anyone whose rights or freedoms, as guaranteed by this Charter, have been infringed or denied may apply to *a court of competent jurisdiction* to obtain such remedy as the court considers appropriate and just in the circumstances. [Emphasis added.]

DECISION: The Board is a court of competent jurisdiction because it has the power to decide questions of law. Therefore, the question that must be answered is whether the Board has jurisdiction to grant the particular remedy requested. The Supreme Court ruled that an absolute discharge was not a remedy available from the Board in the circumstances because the statute governing the proceedings (the *Criminal Code*) states that the Board only has jurisdiction to grant this remedy if it finds that the patient is not a significant threat to public safety and, in this case, the Board found that Mr. Conway continued to be a threat to public safety.

REVIEW QUESTIONS

1. Why do tribunals use pre-hearing procedures?

2. What is "disclosure," and what forms does it take?

3. What is a "pre-hearing conference," and what kinds of issues may be addressed at a PHC?

4. Explain the difference between a "party" and an "intervenor."

5. Explain the difference between "evidence" and "particulars."

6. If some of the parties reach a settlement, what is the effect of this on the parties who do not wish to accept the settlement?

7. What is "mediation," and what are its advantages and disadvantages compared with adjudication of a dispute?

8. What is a "motion," and how do procedures for preliminary motions differ from those for motions at the main hearing?

9. Give four examples of issues that may be resolved through preliminary motions.

EXERCISES

1. The *Residential Tenancies Act, 2006* (RTA) (SO 2006, c 17) regulates all aspects of residential tenancies in Ontario, including the duties of landlords and tenants to each other and their respective rights, the amount of rent that landlords are permitted to charge, and permissible rent increases.

   Ontario's Landlord and Tenant Board was established under the RTA. Your client, a landlord, wants to make an application to the Board to evict a tenant for not paying rent.

   The Board's website at <http://www.sjto.gov.on.ca> contains information regarding such matters as:

   - what form should be used to make such an application;

   - what information should be included in the application;

   - how notice of the application should be served, and to whom;

   - the time frame within which the application must be served;

   - how a representative must satisfy the tribunal that he or she has properly served the notice on everyone entitled to it;

- who is entitled to receive notice of the hearing once the Board has established a date for the hearing;
- what information should be contained in the notice of hearing; and
- who is responsible for serving the notice of hearing.

   a. Draft the application to the Board to evict the tenant. Explain what documents on the Board's website were helpful in drafting the application.

   b. Draft the notice of hearing of the application. Were any documents on the Board's website helpful in drafting the notice of hearing? If not, where did you find information about the necessary contents of a notice of hearing of this application?

   c. Explain what material you or your client will have to file with the Board in order for the Board to be able to proceed with the application.

2. Describe and compare the rules of practice for three tribunals dealing with the following subjects:

   a. how to raise a constitutional question before the tribunal

   b. the conduct of a pre-hearing conference

   c. how to bring a motion in advance of a hearing

   d. disclosure of evidence by parties to each other and/or to the tribunal before a hearing

   e. the use of mediation, conciliation, or other forms of alternative dispute resolution.

3. Name three Ontario statutes that provide that documents that will be used as evidence at a hearing must be provided to a party before the hearing begins. In each case, describe the subject matter of the proceeding, the type of body holding the hearing, who is required to produce the documents, and who is entitled to receive them.

FURTHER READING

Andromache Karakatsanis, "Problem-Solving with ADR: The Tribunal Perspective" (1995–96) 9 Can J Admin L & Prac 125.

Robert Macaulay & James Sprague, *Practice and Procedure Before Administrative Tribunals* (Toronto: Carswell) (loose-leaf) ch 11, 12.

Jerry V DeMarco & Paul Muldoon, *Environmental Boards and Tribunals in Canada: A Practical Guide* (Toronto: LexisNexis, 2011).

Tribunal Procedures During Hearings

LEARNING OUTCOMES

After reading this chapter, you will understand

- the differences between an oral hearing, an electronic hearing, and a written hearing;

- the advantages and disadvantages of each of these hearing formats;

- the roles of various participants in a hearing; and

- the stages of a hearing and the procedures usually followed at each stage.

> *[I]t is of fundamental importance that justice should not only be done, but should manifestly and undoubtedly be seen to be done.*
>
> Lord Hewart in *R v Sussex Justices*, [1924] 1 KB 256 at 259

Introduction

Like pre-hearing procedures, the conduct of hearings varies greatly among tribunals. Some of the differences flow from statutes governing particular tribunals, while others reflect the tribunal's preference for more formal or less formal procedures, or the complexity of the cases brought before the tribunal. Examples of differences in hearing procedures include the following:

- Most tribunals hold their hearings in public; a few hold them in private.[1]
- Some tribunals follow the strict rules of evidence established by the courts; others provide much greater latitude in the kind of information that the parties may present.
- Some tribunals require witnesses to give testimony under oath; others do not.
- Some tribunals permit intervenors; others do not.

Even within a tribunal, the conduct of hearings may vary, depending on the nature of the issues and the number and sophistication of the participants.

Hearing Formats

There are three possible formats for a hearing: oral, electronic, and written. The advantages and disadvantages of each are described in the following sections.

Oral Hearings

In an **oral hearing**, all the participants are physically present in the same place, receiving the same information at the same time. This offers several advantages, in particular:

- Oral presentation of arguments and testimony reduces the need for documentation and therefore saves preparation time and costs.
- Communication is direct and efficient.
- The physical presence of participants allows the tribunal, parties, and representatives to assess the credibility of parties, witnesses, and representatives, and allows parties and representatives to observe the tribunal's responses.

---

1   For example, the Refugee Protection Division of the Immigration and Refugee Board holds hearings in private to protect the applicant for refugee status, whose life, because of the nature of the claim, might be at risk; keeping the hearing private provides safety.

- Procedures such as cross-examination, presentation of arguments, and responses can be carried out more efficiently than in other hearing formats.
- The tribunal has direct control of the hearing process and can intervene as necessary.
- The oral format facilitates observation of proceedings by the public and the media, which promotes tribunal transparency and accountability—both of which are necessary to creating a perception of procedural fairness.

The main disadvantages of an oral hearing are the cost of the hearing space; the difficulty of finding a time when all tribunal members and participants can attend in person; and, in some cases, the time and cost involved in travel to and from the hearing location, and the cost of accommodation.

Electronic Hearings

An **electronic hearing** is generally held through a telephone conference call (a teleconference) or a video conference. These offer the following advantages:

- Particularly in the case of a teleconference, and sometimes for a video conference, there are savings in time and costs if tribunal members and participants do not have to travel to the hearing location.
- As in the case of an oral hearing, there is reduced reliance on written documents and therefore a saving in preparation time and costs.
- A video conference allows for observation of participants and tribunal members, as well as for direct responses.
- A video conference is transparent and often procedurally efficient, and it gives the tribunal reasonably good control of the hearing process.

Disadvantages of electronic hearings include the following:

- For a video conference, there may be costs for using video conferencing facilities. In addition, because these facilities are not available in many areas, some tribunal members and participants may need to travel to a video conferencing facility that is some distance from their homes, although advances in technology have reduced the need to rely on access to videoconferencing facilities.
- Documents must be transmitted in advance of the hearing, and delays may occur in any necessary updating of evidence.
- A teleconference does not allow for observation and may be procedurally inefficient (for example, if participants talk for too long or talk over each other).
- In a teleconference, the tribunal may have difficulty identifying the speakers and controlling the hearing process.
- A teleconference provides less assurance of transparency and procedural fairness than is possible with an oral hearing or a video conference because,

although the parties and the adjudicators (and, if they are permitted to listen in, the public and the media) can hear each other, they cannot see each other.

- For both teleconferences and video conferences, the sound quality of communication may not be either predictable or reliable. For teleconferences, picture quality may be an issue. For example, machines may malfunction, mobile phone batteries might die, or a participant may be in an area where reception is poor or non-existent. Again, however, technological advances have improved the reliability and quality of electronic communications, so this may be less of a concern than in the past.

Written Hearings

In a **written hearing**, all the information—evidence, arguments, and responses—must be prepared in written form and exchanged between the tribunal members and other participants. This format offers four possible advantages:

- It eliminates the travel time and costs that may be incurred for an oral hearing or a video conference.
- It reduces the difficulty of finding a time and hearing location acceptable to all participants.
- It eliminates the cost of providing hearing facilities.
- There is no need to hire a court reporter to record and transcribe the proceedings.

Against these advantages are a number of disadvantages. As one former tribunal chair has noted, "written hearings are not necessarily faster, cheaper or simpler."[2] The main disadvantages are as follows:

- The parties, representatives, and tribunal all incur significant costs for the preparation of documents.
- Further costs, in time and/or money, are incurred for the distribution of documents. Email and fax are the cheapest and fastest forms of delivery, but neither is secure. In addition, some participants may not possess or have access to the technology for transmitting material electronically. Mail is relatively inexpensive, but may be slow and also not secure. Couriers are fast and secure, but expensive.

---

2   Margot Priest, "Amendments to the Statutory Powers Procedure Act (Ontario): Analysis and Comments" in Philip Anisman & Robert F Reid, eds, *Administrative Law Issues and Practice* (Scarborough, Ont: Carswell, 1995) 85 at 93.

Distribution of Documents by Fax: Security Concerns

"Good evening. We begin with a *CTV News* exclusive that goes to the heart of one of those worst nightmare scenarios. Private banking information that you thought was safe and secure is instead out there floating around. In a stunning breach by the Canadian Imperial Bank of Commerce, financial information from customers at hundreds of CIBC branches that was supposed to have gone to bank offices was being faxed mistakenly to a scrap yard in Ridgeley, West Virginia. Despite pleas from a frustrated scrap yard owner, the faxes kept coming right up to this week."

— Lloyd Robertson, *CTV News and Current Affairs*, broadcast 25 November 2004

- There is also a heavy cost in time for the preparation and processing of documents. Evidence and arguments must be distributed in advance of the hearing, then the parties must prepare and distribute their questions and counterarguments, the tribunal panel must prepare and distribute its own questions, and the tribunal must finally write and deliver its decision. In addition to the time spent preparing written materials, delays are possible at all these stages. As a result, the hearing may take much longer than it would in another format.

- The quality of the documentation provided by parties may vary. Further delays will occur if points need to be clarified.

- Written communication is indirect, and there is no opportunity for observation of the demeanour of witnesses. This is a concern if credibility is an issue.

- Updating of evidence takes additional time.

- The tribunal's control of the hearing process relies on the drafting and distribution of clear procedures for document preparation and distribution. Time limits may be set out in the notice of hearing or in separate procedural rules. The difficulty of enforcing deadlines for various stages of the process may further complicate the conduct of the hearing.

- Since a written hearing provides no opportunity for oral cross-examination, the tribunal may use interrogatories to obtain clarification and reach a decision. These too can extend the hearing process.

- A written hearing lacks transparency and may provide little assurance of procedural fairness.

Choice of Hearing Format

Oral Versus Electronic or Written Hearing

Oral hearings have traditionally been the most common form of hearing. For many years, the enabling statutes or common law fairness rules did not permit the use of an alternative format. In Ontario, for example, the *Statutory Powers Procedure Act*[3] (SPPA) did not allow written or electronic hearings until 1994.

---

3   RSO 1990, c S.22.

Comparison of Hearing Formats*

Factors to be considered	Oral hearing Adv	Oral hearing Dis	Electronic hearing Adv	Electronic hearing Dis	Written hearing Adv	Written hearing Dis
Time						
Travel		X	X (TC)	X (VC)	X	
Documents	X			X		X
Procedures	X		X			X
Cost						
Travel		X	X (TC)	X (VC)	X	
Facilities		X	X (TC)	X (VC)	X	
Documents	X		X			X
Communication						
Quality	X			X		X
Directness	X		X			X
Observation	X		X (VC)	X (TC)		X
Efficiency (immediacy/updating)	X		X			X
Conduct of hearing process						
Control	X			X		X
Efficiency	X		X (VC)	X (TC)		X
Fairness/transparency	X		X (VC)	X (TC)		X

*Adv = Advantage   Dis = Disadvantage   TC = Teleconference   VC = Video conference

Oral hearings are still often preferred because they enhance transparency and permit cross-examination, both of which are important to the perception of fairness. However, tribunals that are not constrained by legislation may hold a hearing in any format that facilitates a fair process.

Electronic Versus Oral Hearing

Section 5.2 of Ontario's SPPA permits a tribunal to hold an electronic hearing unless a party satisfies the tribunal that holding an electronic hearing rather than an oral hearing is likely to cause significant prejudice to that party. The notice of the electronic hearing must state that, where the tribunal is satisfied that such risk of prejudice exists, it will hold an oral hearing instead.[4]

In choosing between an electronic and an oral hearing, the tribunal may consider which format is better suited to the public interest. For example, in a case where

---

4 *Ibid*, s 6(5)(c).

many members of the public may be affected by the outcome of the hearing and may wish to attend, either as participants or as observers, an electronic hearing may not be as appropriate as an oral hearing. However, it may be possible to satisfy the public interest through a video conference if a facility can be made available where members of the public can view the proceedings on a screen.

For an electronic hearing, documents must generally be in the hands of all participants and the tribunal panel before the hearing begins. It is usually difficult to transmit documents to the parties and the panel once the proceedings are under way, and it is inefficient to interrupt the hearing while other parties read a document for the first time or listen to a party read it to them. The tribunal may therefore specify in the notice of the hearing the dates by which the parties must exchange and file all documentary evidence.

A tribunal may conduct an electronic hearing largely as it would an oral hearing. However, teleconference hearings in particular involve some variations in procedure. For example, before the hearing, the tribunal should provide directions to the participants with regard to who will speak and the order of speakers. During the hearing, it should require each speaker to identify himself or herself before speaking, and should discourage interruptions.

Witnesses may be examined and cross-examined in the usual manner. However, if a witness will be questioned about the contents of numerous or lengthy documents, the pace will have to be adjusted to ensure that all participants and the panel can follow the documentary references. In these circumstances, an oral hearing may be more appropriate than an electronic hearing.

Written Versus Oral Hearing

Some tribunals are authorized by statute to hold written hearings. Except when prohibited by statute or common law fairness requirements, tribunals may hold written hearings in certain circumstances even without express statutory authority. The courts have held that written hearings do not necessarily violate the rules of natural justice or procedural fairness, and have allowed federal tribunals to hold written hearings despite objections where the proceedings would not infringe common law fairness principles.[5]

In Ontario, section 5.1 of the SPPA allows a tribunal to hold a written hearing unless a party satisfies the tribunal that there is good reason not to do so. The notice of the hearing must state that, where a party objects on this ground and satisfies the tribunal that the objection is justified, the tribunal will hold an electronic or an oral hearing instead.[6] Since the tribunal must then choose between these alternatives, the notice may also invite the objecting party to identify a preferred format. If an oral hearing is preferred, the party should indicate how an electronic hearing would likely cause him or her significant prejudice.

---

5 *Hoffman-La Roche Ltd v Delmar Chemicals Ltd*, [1965] SCR 575; *National Aviation Consultants Ltd v Starline Aviation Ltd*, [1973] FC 571 (CA).

6 SPPA, *supra* note 3, s 6(4)(b).

Instead of notifying parties of its intention to hold a written hearing, and then receiving and considering objections, a tribunal may find it more practical to determine in advance whether the parties consent to a written hearing. If all parties consent, it is likely that a tribunal can hold a written hearing even without explicit statutory authority. For example, Ontario's Workplace Safety and Insurance Appeals Tribunal holds written hearings on consent and without any express statutory authority other than a general power to control its own procedure.

Combining Oral, Electronic, and Written Hearings

Sometimes, the most efficient process is to hold part of a hearing orally, part electronically, and part in writing. For example, in an oral hearing, if an expert witness lives in another jurisdiction and the witness's schedule makes personal attendance difficult, or if the cost of travel and accommodation is too high, the witness might testify electronically or in writing, particularly where credibility is not an issue.

Section 5.2.1 of the SPPA permits a tribunal to hold "any combination of written, electronic and oral hearings" in one proceeding.[7] As long as the appropriate notice is given and there is no prejudice to any party, it is unlikely that a court would rule against the use of a combined format.

Procedures in an Oral or Electronic Hearing

The conduct of an oral or electronic hearing usually consists of the following sequence of procedures (discussed in more detail below):

1. The tribunal presents introductory comments.
2. The tribunal addresses preliminary matters, such as motions on jurisdictional issues, disclosure, or procedural issues.
3. The parties present opening statements.
4. The parties present their evidence.
5. The parties cross-examine each other's witnesses.
6. Re-examination takes place.
7. Reply evidence is called.
8. The parties present closing arguments.

After closing arguments have concluded the proceeding, the tribunal either gives ("renders") its decision or postpones ("reserves") the decision to a later date.

Procedures in a Written Hearing

Different procedures apply to the conduct of a written hearing, usually consisting of the following:

---

7   *Supra* note 3.

1. The tribunal sends a notice to the parties setting out the issues to be addressed and specifying the next step and the deadline for its completion.

2. The party who is required to prove the issue in dispute sends documentation of the evidence and arguments to the other parties and the tribunal.

3. The tribunal requests written responses, including both evidence and arguments, from the other parties by a specified date.

4. The responding parties send their responses to the tribunal and to the other parties.

5. If the responses raise questions or request further clarification, the tribunal may grant the first party to present evidence an opportunity to respond in writing.

6. The tribunal arranges for members of the public to be able to obtain access to all documents in the hearing should any requests be made.

7. The tribunal notifies the parties that the hearing has been completed.

8. The tribunal begins writing a decision.

9. When the decision is complete, the tribunal sends it to the parties.

Participants in the Hearing and Their Roles

The principal participants in the hearing are the **adjudicator** (the presiding tribunal member or a panel of members) and the parties. The hearing may also include intervenors, representatives, witnesses, tribunal staff, agency and tribunal counsel, and a court reporter. The roles of these participants are briefly described in the following sections.

The Parties

The parties include the person who initiated the proceeding and any other person or persons specified by statute, entitled by common law to respond to the initiator, or recognized as a party by the tribunal. In Ontario, sections 10 and 10.1 of the SPPA set out the rights of parties to a tribunal proceeding. Parties may

- be represented by counsel or an agent,
- call and examine witnesses,
- present evidence and arguments, and
- conduct cross-examinations of witnesses as reasonably required for a full and fair disclosure of all relevant matters.

In Quebec, sections 12(4), 102, and 132 of the *Administrative Justice Act* (AJA)[8] give parties the right to be represented before all adjudicative bodies and the right

---

8   CQLR c J-3.

to examine and cross-examine witnesses to the extent necessary to ensure fair proceedings before the Administrative Justice Tribunal.

Sections 4 and 5 of Alberta's *Administrative Procedures and Jurisdiction Act* (APJA)[9] give parties the right to furnish evidence and make representations, and to contradict or explain allegations made against them by an authority. The right to contradict or explain includes a right to cross-examine only where cross-examination is the only way to provide a fair opportunity to do this. The APJA does not provide a right to counsel.

Under British Columbia's *Administrative Tribunals Act* (ATA),[10] parties have the right to summon and examine witnesses and to cross-examine other parties' witnesses, to be represented by counsel or an agent, and to make submissions (ss 38 and 32).

Parties have additional rights under common law principles—for example, the right to be present throughout the hearing and the right to an unbiased tribunal.

The Applicant or Appellant

The person who has set the proceeding in motion is known as the **applicant**. If the proceeding is an appeal of a decision of a government official or agency or of another tribunal, this person may be known as the **appellant**.

The applicant may be a private individual, a group, or an organization. In disciplinary or regulatory proceedings, the applicant may be the agency staff.

The Respondent

The **respondent** is the party who is required to reply to the application, allegation, or appeal brought forward by the applicant. Usually, the respondent opposes the remedy sought by the applicant.

Respondents, like applicants, may be private individuals, groups, or organizations. For example, when a developer seeks approval for an official plan amendment or applies for a building permit or other permit, the respondents may include neighbours, ratepayer groups, the municipal council, and provincial or federal government departments. When a regulated business such as a telephone company or cable provider asks a regulatory agency to grant an increase in rates or access to a new market, the respondents may include competitors, subscribers, and other consumer groups, as well as agency staff.

---

9   RSA 2000, c A-3.

10   SBC 2004, c 45.

Agency Staff as Parties

Agency staff may be the applicant in a proceeding. For example, if the governing body of a self-regulating profession receives a complaint about the conduct of a member, the staff of the agency may investigate the complaint. If they find supporting evidence, the staff may lay charges against the individual. They will then be responsible for proving the charges before the governing body's tribunal.

Agency staff may also be respondents in a proceeding. For example, in the example above, if the professional involved has had his or her licence to practise suspended or revoked, the professional may apply to the governing body to be reinstated. The respondents may then be the agency staff if there are grounds for opposing the application.

In some proceedings, such as an application by a regulated business for approval of an increase in rates, agency staff may play a neutral role, providing unbiased expertise to the hearing panel. Often, however, when agency staff are parties to a proceeding, their role is to represent one side in the case.

Since the tribunal is required to be unbiased, it must treat the evidence provided by staff with the same impartiality that it brings to consideration of the evidence of the other parties. Similarly, the tribunal should not give agency staff preferential treatment or communicate privately with them about any aspect of a case.

Intervenors

As described in Chapter 9, Tribunal Procedures Before Hearings, intervenors play a more limited role in the proceeding than parties. They have an interest in the outcome sufficient to warrant their participation, but not sufficient to merit party status. When intervenors are allowed to participate, any restrictions that may apply to their participation are usually set out in the tribunal's procedural rules. For example, the tribunal may accept written evidence from an intervenor but not oral evidence, or it may permit an intervenor to provide testimony on some but not all of the issues in the case.

Representatives

Parties and intervenors are generally represented in a proceeding by a lawyer (also known as **counsel**) or by a paralegal, law clerk, or other **agent**. The role of a representative, or advocate, is to assist his or her client in preparing and presenting the case and to take any further action that may be necessary after the tribunal has rendered its decision.

Preparing the case usually consists of

- researching the law;
- obtaining information about the tribunal's practices and procedures;
- explaining the hearing process to the client;
- locating and interviewing witnesses and compiling documentary evidence;
- setting a hearing date convenient to the client and the witnesses;
- preparing, serving, and filing documents required by the tribunal;

- advising on strategy;
- deciding what evidence to present; and
- deciding the order in which the client's witnesses will be called.

Presenting the case involves some or all of the following:

- making preliminary motions,
- making opening statements,
- questioning the client and his or her witnesses,
- cross-examining the witnesses of other parties,
- raising reasonable objections to questions asked of the client or witnesses,
- making motions during the hearing,
- presenting arguments about procedural and evidentiary issues that arise during the hearing, and
- making closing arguments.

The role of a lawyer differs in some respects from that of an agent. Generally, under rules of professional conduct established by provincial law societies, a lawyer is not permitted to testify at a hearing in which he or she is representing a client. An agent, on the other hand, may sometimes be a witness. For example, a real estate appraiser may argue the case for a property tax reduction on behalf of a client while also giving evidence about his or her own research into the value of the client's property.

Differences in the status of lawyers and agents in a proceeding are also recognized by some statutes and regulatory bodies. For example, in the event of abuse of a tribunal's process, section 23(3) of the SPPA gives the tribunal authority to bar an agent, but not a lawyer or an agent who is a paralegal licensed by the Law Society, from the proceeding. However, a lawyer or licensed paralegal who abuses the tribunal's process may be subject to disciplinary action by the provincial law society. Agents, on the other hand, are unregulated in most provinces. The ATA permits a tribunal to exclude any person from participation in a proceeding when it is done to maintain order at a hearing. It does not distinguish between lawyers and agents in this regard. For rules that apply to both lawyers and agents in tribunal proceedings, see the box feature "Respect for the Tribunal's Rules of Process."

Respect for the Tribunal's Rules of Process

- Both lawyers and agents have a duty of courtesy and honesty to the tribunal. While they are expected to defend their client's interests vigorously, they may not mislead the tribunal or disrupt its proceedings.
- A lawyer or an agent may not intervene in a proceeding with the sole intention of creating a delay.
- A lawyer or an agent may not give evidence under the pretense of questioning witnesses or making submissions to the tribunal.

Violation of any of these rules may be considered an abuse of process.

Witnesses

Witnesses provide the factual information—and, in some cases, the expert opinions—that the tribunal considers in arriving at its decision. The evidence of witnesses is obtained through questioning by the parties or their representatives, and sometimes by the hearing panel.

Witnesses may be called upon by representatives of the parties to give evidence at the proceeding. In addition, some statutes, such as Ontario's SPPA (s 12), give the tribunal authority to require witnesses to attend an oral or electronic hearing. The summons issued by the tribunal lists any documents or other things that the witness must bring to the hearing.

Section 11 of the SPPA gives a witness the right to be represented by counsel or an agent, but only for the purpose of advising the witness of his or her rights, such as the right to refuse to disclose privileged information. Quebec's AJA, Alberta's APJA, and British Columbia's ATA do not give witnesses a right to a representative.

Section 49 of British Columbia's ATA states that if a witness refuses to attend a hearing, answer questions, or produce documents, a court may punish him or her for contempt of the tribunal. Under section 13(1) of Ontario's SPPA, witnesses are required to answer any question put to them unless a party objects and the tribunal excuses the witness from answering the question. Section 133 of Quebec's AJA states that witnesses before the Administrative Justice Tribunal may not refuse to answer questions put to them by the parties or by the administrative tribunal. Section 13 of the *Canadian Charter of Rights and Freedoms*[11] gives witnesses broad protection from having their testimony used against them in any subsequent proceeding. In Ontario, similar protection is provided under section 14 of the SPPA, which prohibits the use of such testimony against witnesses in subsequent civil proceedings or prosecution against the witness.

Tribunal Staff Providing Administrative Support

Although courts always have their own staff (registrars or clerks) present in the courtroom to assist the judge, many tribunals do not provide this support to their adjudicators. However, at some tribunals, agency staff will assist the adjudicator with tasks such as handling exhibits and swearing in witnesses.

Agency Counsel and Tribunal Counsel

Counsel for a tribunal may play one of two distinct roles:

1. presenting a case to the tribunal on behalf of a party such as the tribunal staff or the staff of a related agency that acts as a prosecutor or as an advocate; or

2. providing legal advice and assistance to the adjudicator.

---

11   Part I of the *Constitution Act, 1982*, being Schedule B to the *Canada Act 1982* (UK), 1982, c 11.

Lawyers performing the first role are referred to as "agency counsel" and those performing the second are called "tribunal counsel."

The reason for making this distinction is that, when agency lawyers represent the agency as a party, the interests of the agency are not the same as the interests of the tribunal. The interests of the agency are to prove its case, while those of the tribunal are to make an impartial and independent decision. Usually, when an agency is a party, the tribunal and the agency are separate bodies or the tribunal members are separated structurally from other functions of the agency. Recognition of this separation in the conduct of the proceeding reduces the possibility of bias and conflict of interest by distinguishing the tribunal in its role as adjudicator from the agency acting as a party in the case. The role of agency counsel is therefore restricted to representation of the agency as a whole or some part of the agency other than the tribunal.

On the other hand, the tribunal members often require their own legal adviser to assist them in making an impartial decision. This function is clearly different from that of agency counsel.

Agency counsel may play an adversarial role—that is, opposing the positions of other parties. They should have no communication with the adjudicator outside the hearing room, and the tribunal should give them no access to information in its possession unless other parties have the same access.

In contrast, tribunal counsel provide direct assistance to the tribunal on matters of procedure and legal interpretation. In an inquisitorial hearing in which the tribunal itself calls witnesses, tribunal counsel will choose the witnesses to be called, prepare them to testify, and conduct the examination of them in the proceeding. If the parties (including agency counsel) also call witnesses, tribunal counsel may question those witnesses, but usually only to clarify rather than challenge their testimony.

Unlike agency counsel, tribunal counsel are permitted to assist the panel behind the scenes. Unless a statute requires that legal advice given to an adjudicator be shared with the parties, the advice given by tribunal counsel to the panel may be treated as privileged; that is, it need not be revealed to the parties. However, this question is open to some debate.[12]

In giving legal advice, tribunal counsel must be careful not to infringe on the adjudicator's decision-making role or to favour one side in the dispute over the other. The kind of assistance that an adjudicator may expect from tribunal counsel is discussed in more detail under the heading "Consultation with Tribunal Counsel."

The Court Reporter

A court reporter (sometimes referred to as a "verbatim reporter") may be present at the hearing to record all the testimony, and sometimes the arguments, in the exact words of the speaker. The reporter may create the record either by simultaneously

---

12   See the discussion of *Pritchard v Ontario (Human Rights Commission)*, 2004 SCC 31, [2004] 1 SCR 809, under the heading "Consultation with Tribunal Counsel."

repeating the spoken proceedings on audio recording equipment or by typing them in shorthand on a word processor. The reporter may later transcribe the recorded information into document form.

Some tribunals are required by statute to record their proceedings. Where recording is optional, because of the high cost of court reporters, tribunals often provide transcripts of audio recordings only upon request. However, it is difficult for a person who was not present to produce an accurate transcript from a recording. Using a trained, certified court reporter provides some assurance that the transcription will be accurate.

In some cases, the tribunal will not pay for a court reporter but will permit parties to provide one at their own expense. Some tribunals also permit parties to tape-record the proceedings to assist them in reviewing the evidence and preparing arguments. However, a transcription of a tape made by a party will not be accepted by a tribunal or a court as a complete and accurate record of the proceedings in a subsequent appeal or judicial review of the decision.

The Adjudicator

The role of the adjudicator is to

- establish procedures for the conduct of the hearing;
- implement those procedures in a fair and flexible, but efficient and effective, manner;
- listen attentively and make detailed notes of evidence and arguments;
- maintain control over the hearing process; and
- make a fair and reasoned decision that reflects the evidence, the law, and the merits of the case.

Adjudicators usually act as passive umpires, calling the plays but not significantly helping any party make its case. However, some tribunals play a more active role in investigating, presenting witnesses, and questioning witnesses.

Parties, intervenors, representatives, and witnesses are entitled to punctuality, attentiveness, patience, courtesy, and respect from tribunal members. At the same time, tribunal members are entitled to these things from the other participants. Participants who are late, long-winded, repetitive, or rude invite a negative response from adjudicators.

Hearing Procedures

Introductory Remarks

Tribunals often open their proceedings with introductory comments about the purpose of the hearing and the process. The information presented generally depends on the nature of the hearing and the experience of the participants. A shorter briefing will be required for counsel who are familiar with the hearing process than for unrepresented parties, who are unlikely to have an in-depth understanding of how tribunals in general, and this tribunal in particular, work.

At the beginning of the hearing, the adjudicator (or, if there is more than one adjudicator, the panel chair) will often

1. introduce himself or herself and any other members of the panel;

2. state the names of the parties and briefly describe the purpose of the hearing;

3. confirm that all parties or their representatives are present, and verify the representatives' names and qualifications (that is, whether they are lawyers or agents);

4. ask whether there is any other person present who wishes to participate in the proceedings, and, if so, give all parties an opportunity to make submissions as to whether the person (or persons) should be given standing to participate as a party or intervenor;

5. describe the hearing process—for example,

   a. whether the parties will be invited to make opening statements,

   b. whether evidence is to be presented under oath or unsworn, and whether orally or in writing,

   c. the order in which the parties will present their case,

   d. the right of parties to cross-examine and re-examine witnesses,

   e. whether the parties will have an opportunity to submit reply evidence, and

   f. whether the parties will be entitled to present closing arguments;

6. ask whether anyone has any questions about the tribunal's procedure; and

7. ask whether any of the parties wish to raise preliminary matters before the hearing begins (for example, requests for adjournment, clarification of procedures, or jurisdictional issues).

The panel chair may also

- inform the parties of any past tribunal or court decisions that may be relevant to the issues in the hearing;

- explain the limits of the tribunal's jurisdiction (that is, its authority to hold the hearing and the kinds of remedies that it can and cannot provide);

- explain whether the parties might expect an oral decision at the end of the hearing or a subsequent written decision, and advise the parties of any tribunal guidelines as to how soon after a hearing decisions should be released; and

- inform the parties of procedures for appealing the tribunal's decision.

Appendix C includes a sample opening statement similar to the kind used by many tribunals.

Preliminary Matters

Some tribunals encourage parties to bring motions well in advance of the hearing for the tribunal's decision on any preliminary matters, such as requests for adjournment, requests for additional disclosure of evidence, recognition of additional parties or intervenors, challenges to the tribunal's jurisdiction, and procedural issues. Nevertheless, at the commencement of the hearing, parties may ask the adjudicator to make rulings on one or more preliminary matters before hearing opening statements and evidence.

The adjudicator's first task is to determine whether these matters should be decided before the hearing proceeds or whether they should be dealt with during or after the hearing. If the adjudicator cannot decide the issue without first hearing extensive evidence, it will be more appropriate to address the issue at the end of the proceeding.

If there are several preliminary motions, the adjudicator's second task is to determine the order in which they should be heard. For example, if a party brings a motion to adjourn and another person brings a motion to be recognized as a party, it may be appropriate to decide the party status motion first. If the person is made a party, he or she will be entitled to support or oppose the request for adjournment.

Jurisdiction

The parties may ask the adjudicator to determine whether the tribunal has jurisdiction to hold a hearing or to grant the remedy requested. If the adjudicator decides that the tribunal has no jurisdiction, the hearing should not proceed unless a party obtains a court ruling that the tribunal does have jurisdiction. If the adjudicator decides that the tribunal does have jurisdiction, the hearing may proceed even if a party subsequently challenges this ruling in a court or before another tribunal.

It is within the adjudicator's discretion whether to adjourn the hearing until the issue has been decided or to continue the proceeding. In exercising that discretion, the adjudicator may consider a variety of factors, including the possible consequences of delaying the hearing and the seriousness of the challenge to the tribunal's jurisdiction.[13]

Absence of a Party or Representative

If a party or a party's representative is not present at the start of the hearing, the adjudicator may proceed, provided that he or she is satisfied that the party or the party's representative was properly notified of the date, time, and place of the hearing. The tribunal's procedural rules may state the appropriate means of notifying a party or a party's representative, and the method of establishing that notice has been served.

In many cases, the person responsible for giving notice of the hearing proves that notice was given by providing the tribunal with proof of service—that is, a copy of

---

13   For a discussion of the factors that may be relevant in deciding whether to proceed, see *Prassad v Canada (Minister of Employment and Immigration)*, [1989] 1 SCR 560, 57 DLR (4th) 663 at 687.

the notice and a signed or sworn statement setting out how and when the notice was given, and to whom. The parties and the adjudicator should check the notice to ensure that it correctly states the date, time, and location of the hearing. They should also check the proof of service to verify how and when the person was served. In addition, if the person who served the notice is present, he or she may testify to having served the document.

If the adjudicator is not satisfied that the absent person received proper notice, he or she will adjourn the hearing and either ensure that the person is served with notice or make further inquiries to determine the reason for the person's absence.

Even if the adjudicator is satisfied that the absent person was properly notified, it is still possible that the tribunal to inquire into the reason for the person's absence before proceeding. The adjudicator may ask the tribunal staff or one of the parties to phone the person to determine whether the person is running late or has forgotten that he or she must appear.

If the adjudicator is still unable to determine why the person is absent but has sufficient evidence that the person was properly notified, the hearing will proceed. If the case is the only one on the adjudicator's docket for the day, it is appropriate to wait a reasonable time (30 minutes is often considered reasonable) before proceeding. The adjudicator will state for the record how he or she established that the person was notified, what steps he or she took to find out the reason for the person's absence, and how long he or she waited before beginning the hearing.

If there are several cases on the docket, the adjudicator may decide to proceed with other cases and defer the hearing until later in the day. By the time the adjudicator has dealt with some of the other cases, the person may have arrived or may have sent an explanation of his or her absence that will help the adjudicator to decide whether to proceed or adjourn.

Request for Adjournment

Adjournments raise the cost of proceedings, create more work for tribunal staff, and sometimes seriously inconvenience the tribunal members and other participants, particularly if the adjournment occurs at the last minute. Many people have busy schedules, and some may have to travel long distances to attend the hearing. If the case is one in which the community has an interest, observers also may be inconvenienced.

For these reasons, tribunals do not like unnecessary requests for adjournment, and representatives who make such requests do not endear themselves to adjudicators.

Generally, if a hearing date has been set well in advance and with the consent of the parties, a party should request an adjournment only because of matters beyond his or her control, such as the sudden illness of the party, the party's representative, or a key witness. Representatives should avoid double-booking and should ensure that they, their client, and their client's witnesses are available before agreeing to a hearing date.

If an adjournment is requested, the adjudicator must grant it if a failure to do so would deprive a party, through no fault of the party, of the right to a full and fair hearing. However, if a party has brought problems on himself or herself—for example, by retaining a representative who is not available on the scheduled date, by retaining a representative at the last minute, or by leaving insufficient time for preparation of the case—the adjudicator may be justified in refusing an adjournment.

Adjournments have been granted so liberally in the past that many lawyers and agents have come to expect that the first request for adjournment will be approved almost automatically. However, government demands for tribunals to work more efficiently have resulted in closer scrutiny of adjournment requests. If a tribunal considers that it can no longer afford the luxury of frequently adjourning and rescheduling hearings, it may issue rules of procedure or practice directions setting out the tribunal's policies and expectations. Both the adjudicator and the parties can use such rules or guidelines to assist them in determining when fairness requires an adjournment and when it does not.

Request for a Stay of Proceedings

Before the main part of the hearing begins, a party may request a **stay of proceedings**. This term has two meanings. First, a stay of proceedings may refer to permanent suspension of a hearing because holding the hearing would result in serious wrongdoing or harm to a party. In effect, the case is dismissed or "quashed," or decided in the party's favour without a hearing. Second, a stay of proceedings may refer to temporary suspension of the hearing until other proceedings have been completed. It is this second use of the term that is addressed here.

There are two situations in which a temporary stay of proceedings may be requested:

1. where a party is subject to civil or criminal proceedings arising out of the same conduct that is the subject of the tribunal's proceeding; and

2. where the party is seeking judicial review of some aspect of the tribunal's proceeding—for example, a procedural ruling or interim order issued by the tribunal.

There is no requirement that tribunals must grant a temporary stay in either of these situations. One of the purposes of setting up specialized tribunals is to provide for the expeditious resolution of disputes. This purpose would be defeated if tribunals were required to stay their proceedings for an indefinite period while a criminal or civil court dealt with a matter, particularly when the court proceedings might take several years.

In deciding whether to grant a stay, a tribunal may consider the same factors that it would apply to an adjournment, such as balancing the possible consequences of proceeding to the party requesting the stay and the possible consequences to other participants and the tribunal of delaying the hearing. Where the stay is requested to allow a party to seek judicial review, the tribunal may also consider the seriousness of the challenge and its likelihood of success.[14] One important factor that the tribunal will take into consideration is whether the court dates have been set for any other trial or judicial review, and whether this is likely to proceed in the near future. If not, granting a stay would cause the tribunal's proceeding to be suspended indefinitely.

---

14 *Ibid.*

If a party requests a stay of proceedings because the issues to be determined by the tribunal are identical to those that the court will decide, this may be a good reason to grant the stay. However, the issues are seldom the same, and the standard of proof in court is often higher. If the issues are the same but the standard of proof is different, the outcome of the court proceedings may not determine the tribunal's decision. (See below for a discussion of the burden and standard of proof.)

Another reason for requesting a stay because of anticipated or pending court proceedings is to reduce the risk that evidence given during the tribunal's proceeding will be used against a party in court. As discussed, both section 13 of the Charter and section 14 of the SPPA provide protection against such use of evidence. However, there is a danger that, even though the evidence itself cannot be used in future court proceedings, it may lead to other incriminating evidence against the party in those proceedings. In general, this is not a sufficient reason to suspend the tribunal's hearing because courts often have the power to exclude such evidence. There may nevertheless be circumstances where the potential prejudice to a party from permitting disclosure is so great that it justifies a stay of proceedings.

Hearing of the Case on the Merits

Once the preliminaries are complete, the adjudicator will call on the parties to present their cases. Depending on the length and complexity of the hearing and the sophistication of the parties, the adjudicator may invite the parties to give opening statements, or the adjudicator may skip this procedure and move directly to the presentation of evidence.

Opening Statements

Opening statements can help focus the hearing. In short hearings involving simple issues, asking the parties to give opening statements may not be an efficient use of time. However, opening statements can be useful in some circumstances, particularly where the tribunal has required little advance disclosure of evidence and the parties are hearing the theory or details of each other's case for the first time.

Opening statements may deal with such matters as the witnesses who will be called, the number and order of witnesses, the nature of their evidence, the probable duration of the hearing, and—most importantly—the issues to be addressed. Identification of the issues can help the adjudicator, other parties, and intervenors to concentrate on the evidence that is most relevant to the resolution of the dispute. Stating the issues and describing the evidence can also help the parties streamline their cases. Sometimes, opening statements reveal to the parties that they agree on matters that they thought were in dispute, or that the matters in issue are different from those they had assumed were in issue. Occasionally, the revelation of each party's case to the other party will lead to the withdrawal of all or part of an application or appeal, or to an early settlement.

Opening statements are usually optional, and one or more of the parties may wish to waive the right to "open." In the courts, a responding party often has the right to defer its opening statement until it begins its case. Unless the tribunal has a rule to the contrary, it will usually respect the wishes of parties who prefer to waive or defer their opening statements.

Evidence

After any preliminary issues have been dealt with and any opening statements have been made, the parties present their evidence. Unless the tribunal sets other requirements, the usual order of presentation is as follows:

1. evidence of the party or parties who initiated the proceeding,
2. evidence of any other parties with a similar interest in the outcome, and
3. evidence of the opposing party or parties.

This stage of the hearing includes the questioning of witnesses by the parties or their representatives. The procedures for the examination of witnesses and the presentation of other evidence are discussed in detail in Chapter 11, Presenting Evidence at a Hearing.

BURDEN OF PROOF AND STANDARD OF PROOF

The burden of proof and the standard of proof are central to the adjudicator's assessment of the evidence and the arguments, and the ultimate decision in the case, as well as to some procedural decisions.

The burden, or onus, of proof is the obligation to establish a particular fact or present a particular kind of evidence. Often, the party who initiated the proceeding has the overall burden of persuading the adjudicator of the correctness or merit of his or her position. However, where evidence is in the hands of a different party, that party may have the obligation to produce the evidence.

The standard of proof is the degree of certainty of a fact that a party must establish in satisfying the burden of proof. In a criminal case, the standard of proof is proof "beyond a reasonable doubt." That is, the person who has the onus of proving a fact must establish it as a near certainty. In tribunals, unless a statute provides for a higher or lower standard, a fact may be proven on a "balance of probabilities." That is, a fact is considered established if it is shown to be more likely true than false.

Sometimes, the statute governing the tribunal specifies the burden and standard of proof. In many cases, however, the statute is silent and the tribunal will be required to decide these matters on the basis of what is fair and reasonable. There may be several burdens and standards of proof relating to different issues that may arise. In addition, the manner in which these requirements are met will depend on whether the tribunal follows an adversarial or an inquisitorial process in arriving at the truth.

If the tribunal relies on an adversarial process, it is the party who bears the burden of proving a fact who must provide evidence establishing that fact to the degree of probability required by the applicable standard of proof. In contrast, if a governing statute authorizes the tribunal to follow an inquisitorial process, the tribunal itself may have the onus of collecting sufficient evidence to resolve the issue. For example, in a hearing dealing with a request for release from custody, the tribunal may be required to determine whether the release of the person will pose a threat to public safety. If there is insufficient evidence for the tribunal to answer the question to the required level of certainty, the statute will indicate, explicitly or implicitly, what course of action the tribunal must take.

QUESTIONING OF WITNESSES BY THE ADJUDICATOR

The authority of an adjudicator to question witnesses may depend on the provisions of the statute governing the tribunal and the nature of the hearing process (for example, whether it is adversarial or inquisitorial). Some statutes permit the adjudicator, implicitly or explicitly, to ask most of the questions, either directly or through tribunal counsel. However, many tribunals, including those governed by the SPPA, are expected to follow the adversarial approach to questioning.

As discussed in Chapter 2, in an adversarial hearing, the parties are responsible for bringing out the relevant information through examination of their own witnesses and cross-examination of the witnesses of other parties. The adjudicator usually asks questions for the purpose of clarifying evidence rather than helping a party to fill in gaps in its case. Nevertheless, adjudicators generally may question witnesses directly, provided that they do not intervene to an excessive extent—that is, to an extent that interferes with the conduct of a party's case or suggests a bias for or against one or more of the parties.

When adjudicators question a witness, they should give all parties an opportunity to ask further questions arising from the witness's responses.

APPROPRIATE TIME FOR TRIBUNAL QUESTIONS

Sometimes it is appropriate for adjudicators to ask a question as soon as it comes to mind, especially if it is a minor point of clarification. However, some adjudicators believe that it is better to hold back their questions until both the examination-in-chief and the cross-examination are complete. Delaying questions reduces the possibility that the adjudicator will inadvertently interfere with a party's presentation of its case, and it may also reduce the need for intervention. Adjudicators often find that, if they wait, one of the parties will ask the question that the adjudicator had in mind.

> ### One commentator on the proper conduct of judges has noted:
>
> *"Do not too soon assume that you know more about the case than counsel—he may have planned all along to ask the very question that springs to your lips but to defer it to a later time in his examination or cross-examination."*
>
> JO Wilson, *A Book for Judges* (Ottawa: Supply and Services, 1980) at 48

Closing Arguments

After all the evidence has been heard, each party is usually entitled to an opportunity to present closing **arguments** or **submissions** (also called "summing up"). With one exception, failure to provide this opportunity is a breach of procedural fairness that may provide grounds for striking down the tribunal's decision. The exception is that, if the person who has the burden of proof has given his or her final arguments and has not convinced the adjudicator, the adjudicator may decide the case in favour of the opposing party without having to hear the opposing party's arguments. In other words, the adjudicator must always hear a party's arguments before finding against that party, but if those arguments are unconvincing, the adjudicator need not hear the arguments of the party in whose favour he or she will decide.

The purpose of final arguments is to permit each party

1. to summarize its case in the manner most favourable to it without distorting the evidence, referring to facts that were not part of the evidence, or misleading the tribunal as to the law; and
2. to attempt to persuade the adjudicator to find in its favour.

Arguments usually summarize the significant evidence as the party sees it, set out the inferences that the party would like the tribunal to draw from the evidence, provide that party's view of the law, and describe the remedy or order that the party would like from the tribunal. In most cases, adjudicators specify the order in which arguments are to be presented. Usually, the parties present arguments in the same order in which they presented evidence, and after all parties have made their submissions, each party may be permitted a brief reply to the arguments made by all opponents who preceded them.

Arguments will usually be given orally, but sometimes may be presented in writing. It is not clear whether tribunals have authority under the SPPA to require parties to give their closing arguments solely in writing. Although adjudicators sometimes prefer to receive arguments in writing because it may make their work easier, representatives may object to this because of the added cost to their client, because of delay while written arguments are exchanged between parties, or because representatives feel that they are more persuasive when they can state their arguments face-to-face before the decision-maker.

On the other hand, some representatives prefer to present written submissions as well as, or instead of, oral ones. Well-organized and clearly expressed written submissions can leave the tribunal with a well-organized road map to use in writing a decision; reduce the risk that the tribunal will forget or misunderstand an important legal point or piece of evidence; and, if judicial review becomes necessary, form part of the record before the court and establish that a party or representative raised an issue before the tribunal that the tribunal failed to take into consideration in its decision.

When the adjudicator has heard the closing arguments and replies, the hearing ends. The adjudicator then reviews all the evidence and arguments, and either renders or reserves the tribunal's decision. The procedures followed at that final stage of a case are discussed in Chapter 14, Tribunal Decision-Making Procedures.

Consultation with Tribunal Counsel

Tribunals may either have their own in-house counsel or they may retain outside counsel to provide legal advice and assistance with respect to a particular case.

There are two stages at which a tribunal must determine what help it can get from its own counsel: during the hearing and after the hearing. At each stage, the kind of help will depend to some extent on whether counsel is neutral or is taking the side of one of the parties against the other. This section focuses on the role that tribunal counsel may play up to the end of the hearing—that is, until all parties have made their final submissions. The role that tribunal counsel may play once the hearing is over is discussed in Chapter 14, Tribunal Decision-Making Procedures.

Where a tribunal exercises a disciplinary function over a profession or licensed business, agency counsel may act as prosecutor. In this situation, counsel is in an adversarial role in relation to one of the parties to the hearing.

In such cases, counsel typically does not represent the tribunal itself but rather the tribunal's staff who have prepared the case against the person alleged to have violated standards. The process is generally structured in a way that ensures that neither the counsel presenting the case nor the tribunal staff have any communication with the adjudicator outside the presence of the opposing party and that the staff receive no preferential treatment from the adjudicator. Moreover, it is improper for agency counsel who has acted as prosecutor to advise the tribunal privately after the hearing with respect to the case, or to take part in the drafting of the tribunal's decision.

In other cases, there may be two or more adversaries with no connection to the tribunal or its staff. In these circumstances, tribunals generally rely on the evidence and arguments presented by the parties and do not obtain any assistance from their own counsel. However, from time to time, an adjudicator may require independent legal advice; or, where permitted by statute and not prohibited by the rules of natural justice, the tribunal may want to call its own witnesses. In these cases, legal assistance may be provided by in-house tribunal counsel or outside counsel.

When the tribunal seeks such assistance, it is important that tribunal counsel not be perceived to be allied with any of the parties to the dispute. As the adjudicator must be seen to be impartial, so too must its legal representative. The adjudicator must maintain an open mind until all the evidence and arguments have been presented, regardless of the participation of counsel. Even if the adjudicator requests the assistance of independent counsel because he or she is dissatisfied with the quality of legal argument or evidence provided by the parties, the adjudicator must not accept or appear to accept the legal arguments of tribunal counsel, or the evidence of witnesses called by tribunal counsel, automatically.

In instructing counsel, tribunals emphasize that counsel's conduct should not be overly aggressive or interventionist, or appear to infringe on the adjudicator's control of the proceedings and decision-making responsibility. Whenever the conduct of counsel gives an impression that counsel has undue influence over the hearing panel, the adjudicator will take whatever steps are necessary to dispel this impression, assert the panel's independence, and demonstrate its impartiality.

A question that arises is whether a tribunal should reveal to the parties the legal opinions given to it by tribunal counsel. Sometimes, the answer is provided by the tribunal's governing statute; otherwise, it is left to the tribunal to decide. One school of thought is that such information is subject to solicitor–client privilege and need not be disclosed. Another is that it is inappropriate for the tribunal to rely on private legal advice unless it is given at the hearing, where all parties have an opportunity to respond. The decision of the Supreme Court of Canada in *Pritchard v Ontario (Human Rights Commission)*[15] appears to have confirmed the tribunal's right not to share legal advice with the parties, although in that case, the body receiving the advice was carrying out an investigatory function rather than an adjudication.

The obligation to disclose legal advice may depend to some extent on whether the advice is given during or after the hearing. Legal advice on procedural, evidentiary, and jurisdictional issues might best be given in the open hearing, if only because frequent private contact between the adjudicator and tribunal counsel while a hearing is in progress raises concerns about counsel's influence on the adjudicator's assessment of the evidence and ultimate decision.

On the other hand, in the case of advice of tribunal counsel provided after the hearing on the ultimate issues of law and policy to be decided, private consultation may be acceptable. In that situation, whether the parties should be informed of counsel's advice may depend on the extent to which this advice raises new concerns or legal issues not addressed during the hearing. The courts have stated that if a new legal or policy issue is raised during any consultation between a hearing panel and others—such as other tribunal members, tribunal staff, or tribunal counsel—it should be disclosed to the parties and they should be given an opportunity to address it.[16]

---

15 2004 SCC 31, [2004] 1 SCR 809.

16 *Re Consolidated-Bathurst Packaging Ltd and International Wood Workers of America, Local 2-69* (1986), 56 OR (2d) 513 (CA) at 517, aff'd [1990] 1 SCR 282, 68 DLR (4th) 524 at 565; *Ellis-Don Ltd v Ontario Labour Relations Board* (1994), 16 OR (3d) 698 (Div Ct), leave to appeal denied by CA and SCC.

CHAPTER SUMMARY

The formality and the format of hearings vary among tribunals, and may vary within a tribunal from case to case, depending on the complexity of the issues and the sophistication of the parties. A hearing may take place orally, with everyone present receiving the same information at the same time; electronically, by teleconference or video conference; or in writing. Each format has its advantages and disadvantages, and a tribunal, in consultation with the parties, should choose the format most conducive to fairness, efficiency, and effectiveness.

Usually, the panel chair begins the proceeding by introducing the panel and explaining the purpose and process of the hearing. Next, the panel addresses any preliminary issues and invites the parties to present opening statements. The parties then call witnesses, who give evidence and may be cross-examined. When all witnesses have been heard, the parties are given an opportunity to make final submissions and the hearing ends. The tribunal either renders or reserves its decision after the hearing, depending on factors such as the complexity of the case and the excitability of the parties.

KEY TERMS

adjudicator: the tribunal member or panel of tribunal members responsible for conducting a hearing and deciding the matter in dispute

agent: a person appointed by a participant in a proceeding to represent him or her; usually distinguished from counsel; also called a "representative" or "advocate"

appellant: a person who appeals a decision of a government official, a tribunal, or a court

applicant: a person who applies for a hearing before a tribunal to obtain a decision on a matter in dispute; *see also* appellant

arguments: presentation to a court or tribunal of reasons to accept a party's point of view, including a summary of the evidence and the law that support this point of view; also called "submissions"

counsel: a lawyer who represents and advises a participant in a proceeding; usually distinguished from an agent; also called a "representative" or "advocate"

electronic hearing: a hearing held through a teleconference or video conference

oral hearing: a hearing in which all the participants are physically present in the same place, receiving the same information at the same time

respondent: the party against whom a claim is brought or who is required to respond to an application, allegation, or appeal by another party

stay of proceedings: the temporary or permanent suspension of proceedings before a court or tribunal by order of that court or tribunal or of a higher court

submissions: *see* arguments

written hearing: a hearing conducted through the exchange of written evidence and arguments

CASES TO CONSIDER

Questioning of Witnesses by Adjudicator

Majcenic v Natale, [1968] 1 OR 189 (CA)

FACTS: Majcenic was hit by a car while crossing a street. She was seriously injured and sued the driver of the car. At trial, the judge questioned several of the witnesses, especially the doctors, frequently interrupting the lawyers in their questioning.

ISSUE: Was the judge allowed to question witnesses?

DECISION: A trial judge may ask the witnesses questions, but the questioning should be kept to a minimum. The purpose of such questioning should primarily be to clarify something that the judge does not understand. The judge should not interrupt the flow of the lawyer's examination or cross-examination, or take over the examination of the witness. Lawyers often plan their examinations carefully, and when the trial judge interrupts too frequently or asks too many questions, the lawyer's strategy with that witness may be destroyed. Also, when a trial judge questions a witness in a manner that appears to be a cross-examination, the jury, if there is one, may think that the judge is challenging the credibility of that witness. As well, the parties may feel that the judge is no longer impartial. A new trial was ordered.

Although this case involves a court, the same principles apply to tribunals.

Burden and Standard of Proof

Coates v Ontario (Registrar of Motor Vehicle Dealers and Salesmen) (1988), 65 OR (2d) 526 (Div Ct)

FACTS: A used-car company controlled by Mr. Coates and employing about 60 employees pleaded guilty to several charges of criminal fraud and tampering with vehicle odometers under the *Weights and Measures Act* (SC 1970-71-72, c 36). Charges against Coates personally were dropped, but the Registrar of Motor Vehicle Dealers and Salesmen proposed to revoke the licences of Coates and the company to buy and sell used cars as a result of these events. Coates appealed this proposal to the Commercial Registration Appeals Tribunal, which ordered the Registrar to revoke Coates' and the company's licences. The Tribunal's reason for revoking Coates' licence was that the convictions of a company controlled by Coates raised a presumption that Coates was personally involved in the company's wrongful conduct and therefore he, as well as the company, should not be allowed to deal in cars.

ISSUE: What are the appropriate burden and standard of proof in a licence revocation appeal before the Commercial Registration Appeals Tribunal?

DECISION: There was no presumption of Coates' guilt arising from conviction of the companies. There was no burden on Coates to prove that he was unaware of the companies' wrongful acts. The burden of showing that Coates' licence should be revoked was on the Registrar. The standard of proof necessary to support the revocation of Coates's licence was clear and convincing proof based on cogent evidence that Coates was personally involved in the wrongful acts. It was not enough that a company controlled by him was convicted. There were many employees of the company, and it was not reasonable to presume that Coates had knowledge of all of their actions. The court set aside the Tribunal's order that Mr. Coates's licence be revoked.

In contrast, in *FH v McDougall* (2008 SCC 53, [2008] 3 SCR 41), Justice Rothstein stated, "I think it is time to say, once and for all in Canada, that there is only one civil standard of proof at common law and that is proof on a balance of probabilities. ... [E]vidence must always be clear, convincing and cogent in order to satisfy the balance of probabilities test." Although *McDougall* was a tort case rather than a tribunal decision, this ruling on the standard of proof has been applied in administrative law decisions (for example, see *Osif v College of Physicians and Surgeons of Nova Scotia*, 2009 NSCA 28).

REVIEW QUESTIONS

1. List and briefly describe the three main formats for a hearing before a tribunal.

2. Under what circumstances might a tribunal combine different formats in the same hearing, and what requirements must be met in order for a combined format to be appropriate?

3. Who are the principal participants in a hearing, and what are the rights and responsibilities?

4. Who else may participate in a hearing, and what are their roles?

5. What is meant by "onus" or "burden of proof"? Who usually has the burden of proof before a tribunal?

6. What is meant by the "standard of proof"? What is the usual standard of proof in a proceeding before a tribunal, and how does this differ from the standard of proof in a criminal case?

7. What are "agency counsel" and "tribunal counsel," and how do their roles differ?

8. What kinds of help may tribunals receive from tribunal counsel and at what stages in a proceeding? What limits should be placed on that help to ensure fairness to the parties?

9. What kinds of issues are best raised or decided before the tribunal proceeds with the hearing on the merits?

10. What considerations may lead a party to request an adjournment of a hearing? Under what circumstances will a tribunal usually grant an adjournment? Under what circumstances will it typically not?

11. What is a "stay of proceedings"? Under what circumstances might a party request a stay of proceedings, and under what circumstances might a tribunal grant a stay?

12. In what circumstances is it appropriate for the tribunal panel to question witnesses? If the panel does ask questions, what is an appropriate way of doing this?

13. What is the purpose of closing arguments, and what are the main components of those arguments?

EXERCISES

1. Ontario's Environmental Review Tribunal (ERT) (<http://elto.gov.on.ca/ert>) holds hearings under the *Environmental Protection Act*, the Ontario *Water Resources Act*, the *Environmental Bill of Rights*, and the *Environmental Assessment Act*.

   a. In what documents on the ERT website will you find the procedures that the Tribunal will follow during its hearings?

   b. What do these documents tell you about each of the following?

      - the role of parties at hearings
      - the role of intervenors at hearings
      - the use of court reporters at hearings
      - the role of tribunal counsel at hearings
      - the role of expert witnesses at hearings
      - opening statements by parties
      - the use of documents as evidence at oral hearings
      - the procedures for filing evidence in written hearings under the *Environmental Bill of Rights, 1993*
      - what factors the tribunal will consider in determining whether to hold oral, written, or electronic hearings
      - when the tribunal will use a combined hearing format
      - the purpose of making site visits or inspections, and the procedure for doing this.

2. Identify a tribunal that permits oral, electronic, and written hearings. Using the rules of procedure for its jurisdiction (for example, in Ontario, the *Statutory Powers Procedure Act*), determine the pros and cons of having an oral, electronic, or written hearing for the tribunal. Create a comparative chart that shows why one form of hearing is advantageous over the other options.

3. Choose a tribunal and identify the steps that must be undertaken to prepare and present an oral, electronic, or written case in front of the tribunal. List the hearing stages that would occur during the type of tribunal proceeding you have chosen.

Further Reading

Robert Macaulay & James Sprague, *Practice and Procedure Before Administrative Tribunals* (Toronto: Carswell, 1991) (loose-leaf) ch 12–16, 21, 21A.

Murray Rankin & Leah Greathead, "Advising the Board: The Scope of Counsel's Role in Advising Administrative Tribunals" (1993–94) 7 Can J Admin L & Prac 29.

Graham Steele, "Tribunal Counsel" (1997–98) 11 Can J Admin L & Prac 57.

Presenting Evidence at a Hearing

LEARNING OUTCOMES

After reading this chapter, you will understand

- what kinds of information a tribunal will and will not receive from parties in a dispute;

- how a tribunal determines whether information is admissible as evidence at a hearing;

- what makes evidence relevant, reliable, necessary, and fair;

- what elements are considered in assessing the reliability of evidence;

- what the difference is between direct evidence and circumstantial evidence, between fact and opinion, and between direct observation and hearsay;

- how the credibility of witnesses is assessed;

- what the order is of presentation of evidence;

- what procedures are followed in examining witnesses; and

- in what circumstances a tribunal may collect its own evidence, by calling its own expert witnesses or by visiting the site that is the subject of the dispute.

Administrative tribunals exist to administer the social, economic, environmental and public policies of elected politicians. Achieving the goals of these policies must not be impeded by technical evidentiary rules pressed by lawyers who argue from common law precedent rather than from logic or public policy.

There is a good reason why tribunals should not be bound by the common law rules of evidence: most of these rules are troublesome and no source of pride for lawyers.

Ian Blue, "Common Evidentiary Issues Before Administrative Tribunals
and Suggested Approaches" (January 1993) 4:4 Adv Q 385

Differences in the Use of Information by Departments, Agencies, and Tribunals

When a person applies for a government benefit, tax relief, a licence, or approval, or seeks a decision on some other matter that affects his or her interests, the decision-maker will refer to the law setting out the circumstances in which the application will succeed or fail. However, before applying the law, the decision-maker must determine the facts of the case. The form in which the necessary information will be received and the manner in which it will be assessed will depend on whether the decision-maker is an official of a government department or agency or a member of a tribunal.

Departments and Agencies

Unless there is a law or a rule of practice specific to the department or agency restricting the information that a public official may consider, the official may receive any information in any form. In general, there is no difference between the information that the official may consider and the information that he or she may rely on in making the decision. However, the official must decide which parts of the information received are both relevant to the decision and reliable. In a department or an agency, the task of weighing information and discarding what is irrelevant or unreliable is carried out at the back end of the decision-making process rather than at the front end. In contrast, in some tribunals, information is screened at the outset to determine whether it should be received.

While there is no legal requirement for advance screening of the information that a department or an agency official may consider, the concept of jurisdiction provides safeguards against the use of inappropriate information. If it can be shown that an official refused to consider relevant information, or that the official's decision was based on irrelevant or unreliable information, a court may find that the official acted outside his or her jurisdiction and may strike down the decision.

However, when a regulator is considering a matter, there is no formal, systematic, transparent way to test the relevance and reliability of the information that was used by an official to make his or her decision. This systematic approach to testing information arises only when the matter comes before a tribunal.

Tribunals

Some tribunals have the same latitude as officials to receive and consider any information in any form, while others are required by law to restrict the information that they will receive. All tribunals must ultimately base their decisions on information that is both relevant and reliable.

Although there may be no statutory limitations on the kind of information that a tribunal may receive, common law principles of procedural fairness require most tribunals to place some restrictions on the kind of information they will consider, the form the information should take, and the manner in which the information is presented to them. The information put before tribunals is called "evidence."

> *If administrative systems are much less predictable [than courts] (even while being more rigid), it's not because bureaucrats are necessarily less fair, benevolent, or intelligent than judges or lawyers. Nor is it because they care less about the public interest, or about the welfare of the human beings in their charge. The sole reason is institutional: it is because officials operate behind closed doors and with an almost unfettered discretion. Compared to the courts, any bureaucracy will be—and will also appear to be—unfair and capricious.*
>
> Edward L Greenspan & George Jonas, *Greenspan: The Case for the Defence* (Toronto: Macmillan, 1987) at 354

What Is Evidence?

Evidence is information that a party seeks to use in a legal proceeding to prove or disprove a contention or allegation. **Relevant evidence** is evidence that is helpful in determining the answer to a question that a tribunal must address in making a decision. That is, evidence is relevant if it tends to prove or disprove the matter in issue, or if it can reasonably and fairly influence the tribunal's belief about that matter.

Evidence is "admissible"—that is, the tribunal will consider it (though not necessarily accept it as true)—if it meets this test of relevance as well as three other tests:

1. it appears to be reliable;
2. it is necessary to prove a point; and
3. receiving it appears to be fair to other parties.

These considerations are described in more detail below.

Evidence presented in an oral or electronic hearing may consist of oral or written statements, photographs, maps, charts, drawings, or physical objects, or a combination of these. Evidence used in a written hearing is necessarily restricted to information that can be presented in writing or in readily reproducible form (such as photocopies of charts and documents).

Determining Admissibility

What Is Admissibility?

The information that a court or a tribunal is permitted to consider is called **admissible evidence**. **Admissibility** is determined in the courts by a set of **rules of evidence**, made up of a combination of common law principles, statutory provisions, and constitutional principles. The rules that determine what will be considered evidence—and therefore what can be put before the court—are complicated. Even lawyers have difficulty understanding them, and the courts spend much of their time listening to arguments about whether various pieces of information are admissible evidence.

For purposes of this discussion, the important point about court rules of evidence is that they are based on four fundamental principles. In order to be admissible, evidence must be

1. relevant,
2. reliable,
3. necessary, and
4. fair.

Courts and legal scholars have often stated that tribunals are not required to follow the complex rules of evidence used in court. This is true in the sense that tribunals have greater latitude than courts (but less latitude than government officials) to consider information that may not comply with court rules of evidence. However, tribunals are required to respect principles of procedural fairness. In the treatment of evidence, a tribunal has two choices:

1. unlike a court, it can listen to a wide range of information without preliminary screening and then base its decision on selected parts of that information; or
2. like a court, it can place limits on the information it will hear.

In practice, many tribunals use both approaches.

Tribunals that do not follow a set of rules to screen out potentially inadmissible evidence must still ensure that they do not rely, or appear to rely, on information that is irrelevant, unreliable, unnecessary, or unfair. Where a tribunal has wide latitude to receive information, in presenting its decision at the conclusion of the hearing the tribunal should state what evidence it relied on and what evidence it excluded in reaching its decision. For example, if the tribunal received unreliable information, it should demonstrate to the parties that it did not use that information.

Again, in accordance with principles of procedural fairness, tribunals should follow a consistent approach in deciding what evidence may be presented to them and what weight that evidence should be given. It is neither practical nor necessary for tribunal members to learn the complex rules of evidence used in the courts. An alternative approach is to apply the four principles underlying the rules to the available information in a particular case, in order to decide which parts of the information are admissible as evidence and which are not.[1] This process of review and selection involves four steps:

- *Step 1: Determine whether the information is relevant*   Evidence is relevant if it helps answer a question that the tribunal must address in making its decision.

- *Step 2: Determine whether the information is reliable*   Court rules of evidence are designed to weed out any information that might mislead the court because it is unreliable. Information presented to a tribunal may be relevant to the issues to be decided, but it may be unreliable because it is unlikely to be true or because no reliable method of testing its truth or accuracy is available to the tribunal. The reliability of evidence depends largely on its source and on the form in which it is communicated. Two of the most important considerations in determining reliability are (1) whether the evidence is first-hand observation or "hearsay," and (2) whether the evidence is fact or opinion. First-hand observation is inherently more reliable than hearsay and opinion. Since hearsay evidence and opinion evidence are often unreliable, special rules apply to them. These rules are discussed below, under the heading "Reliability of Evidence."

- *Step 3: Determine whether the information is necessary*   A tribunal may decide not to receive information that is relevant and reliable if, for example, it duplicates earlier evidence that is not in dispute. Alternatively, if the information is relevant but there are questions about its reliability, a tribunal may nevertheless be inclined to accept it if it is the only evidence available to a party. For example, hearsay evidence may be admissible where a party cannot refer to first-hand observation or factual evidence to prove his or her case.

- *Step 4: Determine whether it would be fair to hear the evidence*   Public policy or the public interest may rule out the use of information that would otherwise be admissible as evidence. If the information appears to be relevant, reliable, and necessary, the tribunal should consider whether there is any reason why it would be unfair to receive the information—that is, whether some social or personal harm is likely to arise from admitting the information that outweighs the value of the information in proving a party's case. Through the application of this test, evidence may be excluded because, even though it may be true, it was obtained in an improper manner. For example, when a confession has been coerced or tricked out of a person charged with an offence in a manner that contravenes the person's constitutional right to remain silent, the confession may be unreliable, but, more importantly, even if it is reliable, it would be unfair for the tribunal to use it in deciding the case. Other instances in which evidence that is relevant, reliable, and necessary is

---

1 For a more detailed discussion of this approach, see Ed Ratushny, "Rules of Evidence and Procedural Problems Before Administrative Tribunals" (1988–89) 2 Can J Admin L & Prac 157; and James Sprague, "Evidence Before Administrative Agencies: Let's All Forget the 'Rules' and Just Concentrate on What We're Doing" (1994–95) 8 Can J Admin L & Prac 263.

inadmissible for public policy reasons are situations where the prejudicial effect of the information outweighs its usefulness in proving a point in dispute (its **probative value**) or where the information is subject to some form of **privilege,** or protection from disclosure (discussed under the heading "Privileged Information").

Our labour relations statutes generally contain a provision which astonishes many newcomers to the field, such as: "The Board may receive and accept such evidence and information on oath, affidavit or otherwise as in its discretion it considers proper, whether or not the evidence is admissible in a court of law." (My emphasis.)

Conceptually, this type of legislative provision has always astonished me. The implications are that the statutory and common law rules of admissibility, weight and probative value that have been hammered out on the anvil of over 500 years of experience can be disregarded on an ad hoc basis. Visions of the Star Chamber can spring into your mind, while echoes of the saying in the days of the Star Chamber that "The quality of justice is measured by the length of the Chancellor's foot" can start ringing in your ears. While such legislative provisions contain the seeds of an enormous potential for both intellectual and procedural abuse by Labour Board decision-makers, I am happy to say that in over twenty years of labour relations practice, my encounters with such abuse have been rare. In only a handful of cases can I say, mustering as much objectivity as possible, that the decision turned on evidence which was improperly admitted.

Benjamin B Trevino, "Advocacy Before Labour Relations Boards and in Labour Negotiations" in Franklin R Moskoff, ed, Administrative Tribunals: A Practice Handbook for Legal Counsel (Aurora, Ont: Canada Law Book, 1989) 1 at 7–8

Although a tribunal may be permitted to hear evidence that would not be admissible under court rules of evidence, representatives of parties should apply the four-step process outlined above before they ask the tribunal to admit information as evidence. That is, representatives should ask themselves whether the information is relevant to the issues the tribunal must decide, whether the information is inherently reliable, and whether it is likely to be necessary for the tribunal to receive the information. If the information is not inherently reliable, representatives should ask themselves whether a degree of reliability can be established during the hearing, using procedures such as cross-examination or corroboration through the testimony of other witnesses. Finally, if the information appears to be relevant, reliable, and necessary, representatives should ask themselves whether it would be fair to hear the evidence.

By asking these questions, representatives can make logical and appropriate decisions about whether to ask the tribunal to admit certain pieces of information as evidence or to attempt to prove the case by some other means.

Tribunals do not always rule correctly on the admissibility of evidence. For example, a tribunal may refuse evidence that should have been admitted, or it may admit and base its decision on evidence that should have been excluded. In this situation, the representative of the party who is negatively affected by the exclusion or use of the evidence may request a remedy from the tribunal, or ultimately from the courts, to ensure a fair outcome in the case.

Challenging a Tribunal's Ruling on Admissibility

If the tribunal has ruled against the admission of a piece of evidence that you submitted because it did not appear at the time to be relevant, and its relevance later becomes apparent, you may ask the tribunal to reconsider its ruling and hear the evidence. The tribunal may reverse its ruling, provided that it gives all parties an opportunity to challenge the new evidence, through cross-examination or possibly by calling further evidence.

Conversely, if the tribunal admits evidence that is harmful to your client and that evidence is later shown to be irrelevant or unreliable, you should ask the tribunal to disregard the evidence. When the tribunal issues its decision, it should state in its reasons that it did not rely on the evidence, and why. If the tribunal does not do this and there is doubt as to whether the tribunal excluded the evidence in reaching its decision, you may apply to a court to overturn the tribunal's decision.

Reliability of Evidence

The reliability of the evidence on which a tribunal bases its decision is critical to the determination of a fair outcome for the parties to the proceeding. Generally, the reliability of evidence is measured along five dimensions:

- The first dimension is the means by which the information was obtained. Direct personal knowledge obtained by a witness through observation, physical examination, or testing is at the most reliable end of the spectrum, while information that a witness was told by others is at the opposite end.

- The second dimension relates to a witness's motivation. Where a witness has a strong incentive to be truthful, the evidence is more likely to be inherently reliable. At the other end of the spectrum, where a witness has strong reasons to fabricate evidence (as in the case of an accomplice in the matter in dispute, who expects to receive lenient treatment in return for testifying against the respondent), the information is more likely to be unreliable.

- The third dimension is the extent to which specialized knowledge or training is necessary to correctly interpret information. There is a fine line between what a person has observed and that person's interpretation of those observations. The observations themselves are facts; their interpretation is opinion. Opinions are less reliable than facts because they are subjective. Evidence of a witness whose opinion is informed is more reliable than evidence of an uninformed witness.

- The fourth dimension is the extent to which the evidence points directly to the fact to be proved, or does not support the fact directly but invites the drawing of an inference about that fact.

- The fifth dimension is the degree of **corroboration**. The more strongly evidence is corroborated (confirmed or supported) by other evidence, the more likely it is to be reliable.

The degree of reliability of a particular piece of evidence along each of these dimensions will determine the **weight** that the tribunal gives the evidence in arriving at its decision. Specific aspects of evidence that tribunals may consider in establishing reliability and assigning weight are discussed in more detail below.

Direct Evidence and Circumstantial Evidence

Direct evidence is evidence given by a person who actually observed the occurrence of the event in question. **Circumstantial evidence** is evidence of circumstances that suggest the manner in which the event occurred. If a person is accused of murder, the fact that a witness saw the accused person pull the trigger is direct evidence of the identity of the killer. If the witness saw the accused running away from the building a few minutes after the time of death, this is circumstantial evidence of identity.

Direct evidence carries the greatest weight in the assessment of evidence presented in a proceeding. Circumstantial evidence is not as inherently reliable as direct evidence, but it is often the only kind of evidence available. Circumstantial evidence may be enough to prove a case if it is of sufficient quality and quantity.

Opinion Evidence

One of the basic rules of evidence applied by courts is that a witness may testify only to facts within his or her own knowledge. In general, "facts within his or her own knowledge" means acts that the witness has performed himself or herself and things that the witness has observed through his or her primary senses of sight, hearing, touch, smell, and taste.

Other evidence is often excluded either because it is inherently unreliable or because its reliability cannot be determined through methods available to the court, such as cross-examination or the testimony of other witnesses. Testimony based on a witness's opinion is one example of this kind of evidence; another is hearsay evidence, discussed in the next section.

Tribunals have greater leeway than courts to listen to **opinion evidence**, but, if they do, they should be aware of its limitations. Some parties will argue that the adjudicator should not allow a witness to give opinion evidence because such evidence would be inadmissible in court. Other parties will argue that, because a tribunal has the power to hear opinion evidence, it is obliged to do so. Neither argument is correct. The tribunal has discretion whether to hear opinion evidence, and it should exercise that discretion according to the principles discussed below under the heading "Expert Evidence." It can be appropriate for tribunals to admit evidence that courts would not listen to provided that the adjudicators state clearly in their final decision what weight they gave such evidence. However, sometimes the degree of unreliability or unfairness of evidence is so great that even hearing the evidence would be a legal error because it would offend the principles of procedural fairness.[2]

---

2 *Re B and Catholic Children's Aid Society of Metropolitan Toronto* (1987), 59 OR (2d) 417 (H Ct J); *Re Girvin and Consumers' Gas Co*, [1973] 1 OR (2d) 421 (H Ct J).

Hearsay Evidence

When a witness provides information to a court that he or she did not receive directly through personal observation but was told by someone else, the testimony is generally not admissible as evidence. Because the witness has no first-hand knowledge of the truth of the information, the court is unable, through examination of the witness, to test whether the information is correct.

If Joe says he saw something happen, the truth of his statement can be tested by asking him questions designed to test his powers of observation, his opportunity to make accurate observations, and his memory. However, if Joe says that Susan told him something, it is impossible to test the truth and accuracy of Susan's statement by questioning Joe.

Similarly, statements in documents generally are inadmissible in a court because the accuracy of the statements cannot be tested, unless the person who wrote them down is present to testify to the truth of the contents of the document.

Statements made by someone who is not available for cross-examination are known as **hearsay evidence**, whether they are found in documents or passed on by a witness to whom they were told.

Tribunals generally may accept hearsay evidence, but, in considering whether to do so and in weighing the value of hearsay evidence that has been admitted, adjudicators should consider the following questions:

- Is it likely that this information is reliable?
- To what extent may it be unfair and prejudicial to admit the information if its reliability cannot be tested?
- Would it be easy or difficult for the party who wishes to rely on the evidence to produce the person who can give first-hand evidence or provide the same evidence in a form more likely to be reliable—for example, by producing an original document instead of a copy?

Some documents are safer to admit than others because the circumstances in which the statements were written down make it likely that the statements are true—for example, where the person who wrote down the information had an incentive to be truthful and is unlikely to have had a motive to lie, where the documents are of a routine nature, and where the information recorded is inherently likely to be accurate. Examples of inherently reliable documents are government documents such as deeds to land, articles of incorporation, weather records, and birth certificates, as well as many routine business records such as invoices, purchase orders, and receipts.

> [T]he approach to hearsay evidence generally has been the subject of change in recent years. Nowadays, rather than being the subject of a rule of prohibition with a variety of exceptions, it is said that the admissibility of hearsay should be determined in each instance through a principled approach. ...
>
> In my view, the concern ought to be less about the admissibility of hearsay evidence per se and more about the quality of the hearsay evidence that is offered and received. ...

[E]ven if hearsay is admitted, it does not obviate the need to ensure that the hearsay evidence is as reliable and trustworthy as it can be.

Nordheimer J in *R v Allan* (2003), 64 OR (3d) 610 at 616–17

Expert Evidence

WHEN SHOULD A TRIBUNAL HEAR EXPERT EVIDENCE?

As discussed, generally witnesses in court may only testify to what they have observed; they are not allowed to offer their opinions except with regard to matters within their own knowledge. The reason for this is that if the witness has no special knowledge or expertise to bring to bear in interpreting facts or observations, the judge is in as good a position as the witness to form opinions as to the meaning or significance of the evidence, and the witness's opinions therefore are of no value to the court. In a tribunal proceeding, opinion evidence is often harmless, because an experienced adjudicator will appreciate its limitations and exclude the evidence from the final decision. However, as a precaution, the representative of the opposing party will likely object if an ordinary witness is allowed to offer an opinion.

Under court rules of evidence, an exception may be made for opinions provided by an expert witness. An **expert witness** is a person who, because of education or experience in a field, has an understanding of the subject on which he or she is testifying beyond that of the general public. Whether the person's knowledge and understanding are sufficient to justify admissibility of the opinion depends on the circumstances of each case. Therefore, courts generally hold a **qualification hearing** before deciding whether to permit an expert to give his or her opinion. Although they are not required to do so, many tribunals also use qualification hearings in deciding whether to listen to expert opinions.

Qualification Hearing Procedures

In a qualification hearing, the representative of the party who has called the expert witness informs the tribunal of the nature of the opinions that will be offered and the issues to which they relate. The representative then questions the witness about his or her education and experience in order to demonstrate that the witness has the necessary knowledge on which to base his or her opinion. The opposing party may accept the qualifications and agree that the witness may give his or her opinion on the specified issues, or it may argue that the representative has not established that the witness is qualified to give an expert opinion. If the opposing party intends to argue that the witness is not qualified, the party or the party's representative may cross-examine the witness to bring out weaknesses in the witness's qualifications before making this argument.

After examination and cross-examination, both parties submit their arguments. The adjudicator then rules either that the witness is qualified to give his or her opinion on the issues in question, or that the witness lacks the necessary knowledge or experience to provide a reliable opinion and therefore may not give the evidence.

Because tribunals are free to accept evidence that would be inadmissible in court, adjudicators may listen to opinions of witnesses who are not qualified, or they may modify or dispense with a qualification hearing. However, they must make it clear in their decisions that they have accepted only evidence that is reliable and have rejected opinions based on insufficient expert knowledge.

WHAT ARE THE OBLIGATIONS OF AN EXPERT WITNESS?

Tribunals allow experts to testify on scientific or technical issues because such evidence assists them in understanding complex matters. Two obligations follow from this reason for hearing expert opinions:

1. Expert witnesses should be called to testify only in areas where their evidence is needed. Representatives increasingly attempt to lend weight to their cases by finding "experts" on issues that require no special expertise. For example, when an expert is called to explain English grammar and syntax in supporting the interpretation of a clause in a legal document, the evidence may be rejected as superfluous because the average person has a sufficient understanding of grammar and syntax to form his or her own opinion.

2. If the expert is to assist, he or she must participate as an independent professional rather than as an advocate for the client.

Even though the expert may have specialized knowledge beyond that of an ordinary person and the expert's testimony may meet the "necessity" test, the fact that the expert is paid by one of the parties or is defending his or her own work for a party will affect the reliability of the expert's evidence.

To be a helpful, neutral professional whose primary purpose is to assist the tribunal in finding the truth rather than to act as a hired gun, the expert should disclose all the facts and assumptions underlying the opinion, acknowledge any limitations and qualifications in the opinion, and fully disclose his or her relationship to the party on whose behalf he or she is testifying.

Expert witnesses should also provide the tribunal with written reports or witness statements, give oral evidence in plain English, and avoid using technical jargon except as necessary to properly explain a concept. Increasingly, tribunals—as well as courts—are demanding this kind of candour and clarity from expert witnesses, and they are criticizing in their decisions those who do not meet these requirements. Some tribunals and courts have gone so far as to enunciate standards of conduct for expert witnesses. The practice directions promulgated by the Environmental Review Tribunal are contained in the Environment and Lands Tribunals Ontario Rules of Practice and the Practice Directions of the Environmental Review Tribunal. The ERT's Practice Direction for Technical and Opinion Evidence is reproduced in Appendix D.

HOW CAN A TRIBUNAL EVALUATE THE RELIABILITY OF EXPERT EVIDENCE?

Expert evidence consists of opinions that are needed by an adjudicator because he or she lacks the specialized knowledge, training, or experience to resolve an issue without such assistance. How, then, is a court or tribunal supposed to decide which evidence to accept when expert witnesses give conflicting opinions?

The answer lies partly in the application of the standard of proof. Often, the opinions of expert witnesses differ because the facts are uncertain. Therefore, the adjudicator may be unable to determine with certainty which opinion is correct. The problem can be resolved by clearly identifying the causes of uncertainty, the nature of the uncertainty, and the degree of uncertainty, and then applying the standard of proof to the witnesses' testimony. Remember that the party that has the burden of proof must establish the facts to the standard, or the degree of certainty, required by law. If that party's expert evidence is not sufficiently convincing—that is, if the opinions of the opposing expert are sufficiently persuasive to cast the requisite level of doubt on the evidence of the party who has the burden of proof—the standard of proof will not be met. It is not necessary for the adjudicator to determine which expert is correct, but only to determine which of the conflicting opinions achieves the higher degree of certainty.

Adjudicators can use a variety of approaches in determining the sources, kinds, and degrees of uncertainty inherent in a scientific issue and evaluating the reliability of scientific evidence. In *R v Johnston*, one Ontario judge listed 14 factors that should be considered,[3] including

- the potential rate of error,
- the existence and maintenance of standards,
- the care with which the scientific technique has been employed and whether it is susceptible to abuse,
- the presence of fail-safe characteristics,
- whether the technique has generally been accepted by experts in the field,
- the clarity with which the technique may be explained,
- the nature and breadth of the inference drawn from the data, and
- the expert's qualifications and stature.

MAY A TRIBUNAL OBTAIN ITS OWN EXPERT EVIDENCE?

Some tribunal members find it frustrating to listen to opposing experts, each of whom claims a high degree of certainty for his or her opinion and neither of whom explains the basis of that opinion clearly. Some tribunals are given the authority by their statutes to obtain their own expert evidence. For example, the Workplace Safety and Insurance Appeals Tribunal may appoint a roster of "medical assessors" to assist hearing panels by providing expert evidence. The advantage of such evidence is that it may be more impartial than evidence provided at the request of a party.

Tribunals that can retain their own experts often have rules to ensure that they do not unfairly favour these experts over the witnesses called by the parties. For example, the parties may be invited to participate in choosing the tribunal's expert, the expert's report may be made available to the parties, and the parties may be

---

3   *R v Johnston* (1992), [1992] OJ No 147, 69 CCC (3d) 395 (Gen Div).

given an opportunity to cross-examine the tribunal's expert and to call their own evidence to contradict the expert's testimony.

Physical Evidence

Physical evidence includes test results, documents, photographs, video recordings, motion pictures, and other objects. The key to establishing the reliability of physical evidence is to demonstrate that the object in question is authentic and has not been altered or tampered with. The most effective way to do this is to ask the person who collected or created the object to appear as a witness and verify that the object has not been changed from the time of its collection or creation to the time of its presentation to the tribunal. Alternatively, a witness may be called who is familiar with the object and who can testify that it has not been changed since the events in question. Where a substance such as a sample of a liquid has been handled by several people or subjected to testing procedures, the integrity of the process is demonstrated by establishing a "chain of custody" (see below).

DOCUMENTS

The best way to prove the reliability of documents is to have the person who prepared the document identify it and testify to its authenticity. However, this is often impractical. Other indications of reliability include whether the documents were routinely created in the course of business and whether they were created by a person who had no motive to falsify them. In addition, an original is more reliable than a copy. However, if copies have been given to more than one person, comparing two copies can reveal whether one of them has been altered.

TEST RESULTS

The results of tests and analyses (of substances, for example) are used as evidence in many proceedings. They may include analyses of blood or urine samples, or of water or air quality; tests of the structural integrity of objects; assessment of the source of harm or damage; or measurement of the extent of harm or damage to individuals or objects. The integrity of test results is usually proved by verifying that accepted testing methods were used and by establishing the **chain of custody**, or continuity of possession, of the object tested. Protection of the chain of custody requires each person who handles a test sample to prevent others from having unsupervised access to the sample and to document from whom the sample was received, how it was maintained, who had access to it, and to whom it was transferred.

PHOTOGRAPHS, VIDEO RECORDINGS, AND MOTION PICTURES

Photographs are generally admissible as evidence if the person who took the photograph or a person who was present at that time describes when and how the photograph was taken, and testifies that it accurately depicts the scene or event in question.

The same conditions apply to video recordings and motion pictures; however, the photographer must also be prepared to state whether the tape or film has been edited and to be cross-examined about any material that has been deleted. While the images may be admissible, admissibility of the sound portion of the tape or film is subject to further conditions. If people shown are heard speaking or if there is voice-over narration of what is shown, the speakers must be prepared to testify to the truth of the recorded statements and the authenticity of the recording, and to be cross-examined on those statements. If this testimony cannot be provided, the tribunal may choose to exclude the entire sound recording. In this situation, it may be possible to use the visual portion of the evidence by playing the tape or film with the sound turned off.

The admissibility of information recorded by modern methods such as laptop computers, smartphones, electronic tablets, digital cameras, and media players may also be admissible evidence, although the means of proving the information to be accurate and complete may differ from those used to authenticate information recorded by traditional cameras and videotape recorders. The *Evidence Acts* of Canada and several provinces have been amended in recent years to deal with the admissibility of electronic data.[4]

Weighing Evidence and Assessing Credibility

While a tribunal may refuse to admit some evidence because it is inherently unreliable, it must still assess the reliability of the evidence that is admitted. Representatives can assist the tribunal in making this assessment through cross-examination, which is designed to reveal any aspects of the evidence that may raise questions about its reliability. Ultimately, however, it is the adjudicator's task to determine the reliability of each piece of evidence. This procedure is called "weighing the evidence." The assessment of the evidence of a particular witness is often referred to as "assessing credibility."

When witnesses give conflicting evidence, the adjudicator must determine which evidence is more likely to be accurate. However, accuracy is not a simple matter of truthfulness. Assessment of the credibility of a witness involves many factors, including the opportunities of different witnesses to observe the same events; the prior knowledge and understanding that a witness has brought to his or her observations of the events; and the witness's intelligence, powers of observation, and exposure and susceptibility to suggestions about his or her interpretation of the events.

Demeanour

Adjudicators often consider the "demeanour," or outward behaviour, of a witness in deciding whether the witness is telling the truth. They must be cautious, however, in using demeanour as a measure of credibility, since a witness's manner in presenting testimony may reflect considerations unrelated to truthfulness. An adjudicator might, for example, ask himself or herself, "Is this witness hesitant in answering because the witness is fabricating evidence, or because he or she is thoughtful and wants to provide the most complete factual information? Or might the hesitancy be due to cultural or other factors?"

---

4 See, for example, s 31 of the *Canada Evidence Act*, RSC 1985, c C-5.

Another important factor in assessing a witness's credibility is the internal consistency of the witness's statements and the consistency of the witness's statements with other evidence that is clearly true. However, inconsistency in itself is not necessarily an indication that the witness is not credible. A degree of forgetfulness and inconsistency is normal, and for this reason can even enhance a witness's credibility. In fact, testimony that is excessively polished or glib may be a warning sign. Refusal of a witness to acknowledge obvious facts is also a sign of resistance to the truth.

> In cross-examination, the prosecutor challenged the evidence given by the accused:
>
> "Do you understand that you are on trial for murder?" she asked.
>
> "Yes," replied the accused.
>
> "Do you understand the penalty for perjury?"
>
> "I certainly do," said the accused, "and it's a lot less than the penalty for murder."

When witnesses give conflicting versions of events and both versions appear plausible, it can be very difficult to decide which evidence to accept. There is no magic formula for assessing credibility. The adjudicator may compare both scenarios with all the available evidence in order to determine which one is more compatible with the evidence as a whole. However, in the end, the adjudicator must rely on his or her own knowledge and observations in determining which of the two scenarios is more inherently plausible. In doing this, adjudicators must be willing to recognize their own limitations, including their personal biases and preconceptions, and must do their best to set them aside.

While it is desirable to determine which version of events is correct, it is not always necessary. If, in the end, the adjudicator does not have sufficient information to establish the facts, the case may be decided on the burden and standard of proof. In a tribunal that relies on an adversarial process, the party who has the onus of proving the facts in dispute will lose the case if the evidence that party presents does not establish those facts to the degree of probability required by the applicable standard of proof. In a tribunal that follows an inquisitorial process, the situation may be different. The tribunal itself may have the onus of collecting sufficient evidence to answer the question before it.

Privileged Information

Even though it may be relevant and reliable, some information is not admissible as evidence either because it is privileged at common law or because it is protected by statute. **Privileged information** is information that might be relevant, but nevertheless is protected from disclosure to protect a relationship of confidentiality deemed by society to be worth preserving. Two important types of privileged information are the contents of communications between a lawyer (solicitor) and the lawyer's client, and statements made during settlement discussions. Other information that is protected from disclosure as a matter of public policy includes discussions between a doctor and the doctor's patient about the patient's health, and the identity of informants when offences are alleged to have been committed.

A detailed description of the law of privilege is beyond the scope of this book. However, it is useful to know that the privilege for solicitor–client communications belongs to the client rather than to the lawyer. A lawyer may not disclose the information without the client's consent; however, the client can "waive" his or her privilege by disclosing or authorizing the lawyer to disclose the information. If the client discloses the information or otherwise acts in a manner that is inconsistent with the presumed confidentiality of the information, in some circumstances the client will be deemed to have waived the privilege, even without intending to authorize disclosure.

Impact of Information Access and Privacy Laws

The federal *Access to Information Act*[5] and *Privacy Act*[6] and the various provincial freedom-of-information and protection-of-privacy acts have two fundamental purposes:

1. to require governments, and, in some provinces, hospitals and universities, to provide the public with information that need not be kept confidential; and

2. to ensure that governments do not give out information about a person that would invade his or her privacy, without first obtaining that person's consent.

How do these statutes affect tribunal proceedings? The main issue is whether witnesses who are government employees have a right to withhold from the tribunal relevant documents in their custody because of the confidentiality requirements of freedom-of-information and protection-of-privacy statutes. Under some statutes, it is an offence for a government employee to deliberately disclose information that violates a person's privacy without obtaining that person's prior consent. Consequently, some witnesses or representatives will object to the witness's answering questions at a hearing when the witness's knowledge was gained from government documents. Witnesses also may object to providing the documents themselves, on the grounds that doing so would violate their duties of confidentiality under access and privacy laws.

In some cases, it is not clear whether these objections are valid. However, in several provinces (for example, Alberta, British Columbia, Ontario, and Saskatchewan), the access and privacy statutes specifically state that their confidentiality provisions do not prevent parties from presenting evidence to a court or tribunal and do not affect the power of a court or tribunal to compel (require) a witness to testify or compel the production of a document.[7]

---

5 RSC 1985, c A-1, s 2.

6 RSC 1985, c P-21, s 2.

7 See, for example, *Freedom of Information and Protection of Privacy Act*, RSA 2000, c F-25, ss 56(3) and 69(2).

In order to decide whether documentary evidence must be provided when questions of confidentiality are raised, the tribunal should review the document to determine whether it contains information that justifies its exclusion from the proceeding. If it does, the solution is not to allow the witness to withhold testimony, but to arrange for the evidence to be given in a closed hearing, provided that this procedure is permitted under the tribunal's governing statute.[8]

Presenting Evidence

Order of Presentation

The order in which the parties will present their case is usually set out in the tribunal's rules or guidelines. Otherwise, it is determined on a case-by-case basis by a procedural ruling made at a pre-hearing conference or at the start of the hearing.

In a hearing with only two parties, the party who initiated the proceeding or who has the burden of proof is usually the first to call witnesses. After the opposing party (the respondent) has called its witnesses, the first party may be given the opportunity to present further evidence in response. This is called **rebuttal** or **reply evidence**.

In most cases, no further evidence may be called after rebuttal. However, on rare occasions the rebuttal will raise an issue that is so significant that the tribunal will allow the other party to refute that evidence. This reply to a reply is known as **sur-rebuttal**, and it should be permitted only in exceptional circumstances.

In a hearing with several parties and intervenors, the order of presentation is similar but more complex. The party who initiated the process or who has the burden of proof usually calls its witnesses first. Then any other parties whose interest or position is similar call their evidence.

Next, the opposing party calls its witnesses, followed by any other parties whose interest or position is similar.

Intervenors usually present evidence after the evidence of the parties whose position they support.

Again, the leading parties (and sometimes intervenors as well) have the opportunity to present reply evidence in response to the evidence of the opposing party's witnesses.

Some tribunals may follow a different order of presentation, depending on the nature of the case. If a tribunal often begins with the evidence of a party other than the party who initiated the proceeding or who has the burden of proof, the tribunal may explain the rationale for this practice in its procedural rules or practice directions. Alternatively, the rationale may be set out in an earlier decision of the tribunal.

---

8 In Ontario, the circumstances in which a tribunal may hold a closed hearing are set out in section 9 of the *Statutory Powers Procedure Act*, RSO 1990, c S.22. Similar criteria are set out in section 41 of British Columbia's *Administrative Tribunals Act*, SBC 2004, c 45 and section 131 of Quebec's *Administrative Justice Act*, CLRQ c J-3.

Swearing In the Witness

In Ontario, tribunals may accept evidence without requiring witnesses to affirm or swear to its truth. If the tribunal's practice is to "swear in" witnesses, it will be the job of the adjudicator, the court reporter, or a tribunal staff member to carry out this procedure. In recognition of Canada's religious and cultural diversity, the tribunal should offer the witness the opportunity to choose the form of oath or affirmation that will bind his or her conscience, such as solemnly promising to tell the truth or referring to a religious text or sacred artifact.

Usually, the person administering the oath or affirmation begins by asking the witness to state her name. If there is no written witness list, the person may ask the witness to spell her name as well. The witness is then asked whether she wishes to swear an oath or whether she would prefer to make a solemn affirmation that she will tell only the truth.

If the witness chooses to swear an oath, she is asked to put her right hand on the religious text or sacred object she has chosen and to swear to the truth of her testimony. When the Bible is used for the oath, the witness is usually asked, "Do you solemnly swear that the evidence you will give will be the truth, the whole truth, and nothing but the truth, so help you God?" If the witness chooses instead to make a solemn affirmation, she is usually asked, "Do you solemnly affirm that the evidence you will give will be the truth, the whole truth, and nothing but the truth?"

In some tribunals, the person swearing in the witness will also ask whether she understands that it is an offence to deliberately fail to tell the truth.

Witness Examination

Each witness is first examined—that is, asked questions—by the party or representative who called him or her to give evidence. This is called **examination-in-chief** or **direct examination**. The witness may then be questioned by other parties whose interest or position is similar.

Next, the main opposing party questions the witness, followed by other parties whose interest or position is similar. This stage of questioning is called **cross-examination**. (Some tribunals, such as the Workplace Safety and Insurance Appeals Tribunal, use the term **cross-questioning**.) Cross-examination is one of the primary methods of determining the reliability of evidence provided by a witness. A skilled cross-examiner will ask questions that reveal inconsistencies, uncertainties, or inaccuracies in the witness's testimony and also bring out additional evidence helpful to his or her own case.

After the witness has been cross-examined, the party who called the witness may ask him or her further questions to clarify answers the witness provided or to address new issues that arose during the cross-examination. Other parties who have already questioned the witness may also ask further questions arising out of the witness's examination by other parties. This procedure is called **re-examination**.

Finally, after the witnesses of all the parties have been questioned, in the reply or rebuttal stage of the proceeding, parties are sometimes given an opportunity to recall witnesses or call additional witnesses for the purpose of rebutting testimony given in subsequent questioning by the opposing party.

Many tribunals require parties questioning witnesses to follow, to a greater or lesser degree, certain rules used by the courts governing the form in which questions may be asked. Parties are generally more restricted in the kinds of questions they may ask when questioning their own witnesses, whether during examination-in-chief or in reply, than when they are cross-examining another party's witnesses.

In examination-in-chief, parties are expected to ask "open" rather than "closed" questions on any matters of substance. In legal jargon, **closed questions** are called **leading questions**. An **open question** invites the witness to provide an independent response. It does not suggest the answer that the questioner is looking for or contain crucial facts or conclusions that the questioner wants the witness to confirm. In other words, it does not put words in the witness's mouth. In contrast, a leading question does suggest the expected answer; it contains crucial information with which the witness is asked to agree or disagree. In examination-in-chief, parties are expected to ask leading questions only on matters that are not controversial, such as undisputed background facts, or on points that the witness clearly has not understood and that need clarification.

Open Questions and Leading Questions

One way to tell a leading question from an open question is that leading questions can usually be answered with "yes" or "no."

The following question would be leading on uncontroversial matters (the witness's name and job; the fact that he was on duty on March 15, 2008; and the fact that he attended at 15 Marchmount Road), but open on matters that may be in dispute (what the witness observed at 15 Marchmount Road):

> Mr. Noseworthy, you are a constable with the Toronto Police Service and were on duty on March 15, 2008. In that capacity, you attended at 15 Marchmount Road in response to information that had been provided to you. Is that correct? Please tell the tribunal at what time you arrived there, and what you observed.

Typical open questions to elicit further information would be, "And what happened next?" or "What was the next thing you did?"

A leading question such as the following would likely cause the opposing party's representative to object:

> Mr. Noseworthy, I understand that in your capacity as a constable with the Toronto Police Service, you attended at 15 Marchmount Road on March 15, 2008, and at that time you observed the accused leaving the house through a broken window. You read him his rights and asked him what he was doing, and he admitted that he had broken into the house. Is that correct?

In this case, it is the questioner rather than the witness who is providing all the evidence of what supposedly happened. This denies the opposing party and the tribunal members the opportunity to assess how well the witness himself remembers the events.

There are good reasons to place some limits on the use of leading questions, particularly in examination-in-chief. The problem with leading questions is that it is the person questioning the witness, rather than the witness himself or herself, who provides the answers. As a result, neither the opposing parties nor the adjudicator can form a fair assessment of the witness's evidence. If instead the witness volunteered the information in his or her own words, the witness's answer might convey a very different impression from the prepackaged response offered by the examining party, who naturally wants to present the information in the light most favourable to its case.

A sequence of open-ended questions, taken from an actual court record:

Crown attorney:	*Then what did you do?*
Police officer:	*I began kicking the door.*
Crown attorney:	*What kind of footwear did you have on?*
Police officer:	*Size 12 boots.*
Crown attorney:	*How many times did you kick the door?*
Police officer:	*About ten.*
Crown attorney:	*What was Sergeant Harp doing while you were kicking the door?*
Police officer:	*Laughing at me.*

In cross-examination, the examining parties are not restricted to asking open questions on points of substance. They may attempt to put words in the witness's mouth, and often do so. However, they may not browbeat the witness or distort the facts. The party who originally called the witness may object if another party asks the witness to contradict the evidence given by the principal witness in the case or by other witnesses.

Cross-examination is beyond any doubt the greatest legal engine ever invented for the discovery of truth.

John H Wigmore, *Evidence in Trials at Common Law,* rev by James
H Chadbourn (Boston: Little, Brown, 1974) vol 5 at 32

In hearings involving several parties, it may not be clear whether all parties are entitled to cross-examine witnesses other than their own, particularly when either the witness or the party who called the witness has an interest or position that is favourable to the party seeking to cross-examine. In such situations, questioning of the witness may not be aimed at attacking his or her evidence or credibility, as is the usual purpose of cross-examination, but rather at strengthening them. Some adjudicators therefore limit the "friendly" cross-examination that may occur or ask the examining party to carry out an examination-in-chief rather than a cross-examination (which will avoid leading questions) so that the adjudicator can better assess the credibility of the witness and the weight to be given to the witness's answers.

Witness Panels

Usually, each witness is fully examined and cross-examined before the next begins to testify. However, it is sometimes more efficient for a party to present the testimony of two or more witnesses at the same time and then make the witnesses available simultaneously for cross-examination, especially where their testimony covers similar or overlapping subjects. This format is called a **witness panel**. Some governing statutes specifically allow tribunals to use this procedure under certain conditions.[9]

When a panel of witnesses gives evidence, the person cross-examining is often given the option of addressing his or her questions either to the panel as a whole, in which case any of the witnesses can choose to answer, or to a specific witness on the panel. The adjudicator has a duty to allow the questioner to cross-examine on a topic as thoroughly as if each witness had testified separately. However, adjudicators also have the right to prevent unnecessary repetition of questions and answers, since one of the purposes of using a witness panel is to avoid overlap and duplication of evidence.

If witnesses are testifying separately rather than in a panel, a witness may sometimes avoid answering a question by suggesting that another witness is better qualified to provide the answer. This risk can also arise with a witness panel, where a more knowledgeable witness may defer to a less qualified or less credible witness. Another risk with witness panels is that witnesses may collude in providing consistent answers to questions so as to avoid revealing weaknesses in their testimony.

Objecting to Questions

Representatives at a hearing are entitled to object to questions that other representatives ask witnesses, whether these are directed to their own witnesses or to other witnesses in cross-examination. To object, a representative should stand up quickly, before the witness has an opportunity to answer, and state loudly and clearly that he or she objects to the question.

Common grounds for objection are that

- the information sought does not meet one of the criteria for admissibility— that is, it is irrelevant, unreliable, unnecessary, or unfair;

- the question is repetitive or stated in a bullying manner;

- the answer would be unreliable (for example, based on hearsay or speculation);

---

9 For example, section 15.2 of Ontario's SPPA permits a tribunal to hear evidence from witness panels as long as the parties have first been given an opportunity to make submissions as to whether this procedure is appropriate.

- the answer is outside the witness's knowledge (as when a question asks an ordinary witness to provide an expert opinion);
- an expert witness is being asked to give opinions on a matter outside his or her area of expertise; or
- the examiner is asking leading questions.

It is good practice not to object except when necessary. Frequent objections waste time and annoy adjudicators. A representative should trust the adjudicator to decide when a question is unacceptable—up to a point. If the information sought offends a rule of evidence but is relatively harmless, it is better to allow the witness to answer the question. However, if the questioning will seriously mislead the tribunal or unduly lengthen the proceeding, the representative should interject.

> *From actual court records:*
>
> *Defence counsel:* *I object to the prosecutor objecting to my objecting to standard legal objections.*

Keeping Track of Documentary and Physical Evidence

In many hearings, much of the evidence submitted consists of documents. Occasionally, the evidence will also include an object, such as a sample of blood, a machine part, or a video recording. Although documents may not be admitted as evidence without proof of their authenticity, they are generally accepted once a person who is sufficiently knowledgeable about their contents identifies them and testifies to their accuracy. Similarly, objects are admitted as evidence once they have been identified. These documents and objects are made part of the formal hearing record by **marking** them as **exhibits**.

Typically, once a party feels that it has laid sufficient groundwork for the document or object to be admitted as evidence, the party will tender (offer or submit) the document as an exhibit. If there is no objection, or if the tribunal accepts the document or object despite objections, the adjudicator gives the document or object a number. It is advisable to mark on each exhibit, in addition to its number, the name or file number of the case. The adjudicator or tribunal staff may write this on the document or on a tag to attach to the object, but usually they will use a stamp bearing the tribunal's name and providing space for other identifying information.

The adjudicator and each representative (or party) should keep a list of the exhibits and record on it the party who provided the exhibit, as well as the title or description of the document or object. This list will help the representatives and the adjudicator keep track of the exhibits when they are referred to during the hearing. It will also be helpful to tribunal staff after the hearing, when the exhibits will be returned to the parties who provided them or forwarded to a court for reference in an appeal or a judicial review of the tribunal's decision.

A pre-printed form such as the one in Appendix E can be useful for keeping a record of exhibits.

Site Visits

If objects are readily movable, a party who wants to present them as evidence usually brings them to the hearing. If they are not movable, a photograph or video recording may suffice. However, in some circumstances, it may be necessary for the tribunal to examine a large and cumbersome object or to visit a site that is central to the matter in dispute, as in cases involving land-use planning, environmental issues, or the cause of a traffic accident. A site visit is usually called **taking a view**.

It is not clear whether tribunals have an inherent power to take a view or whether they can do so only if expressly permitted to by statute. Assuming that a tribunal has this power and wishes to exercise it during a hearing, all parties and their representatives must be given the opportunity to participate in the site visit. If taking a view is a common practice of the tribunal, there may be rules or practice directions governing the procedure. In the absence of such rules, the adjudicator should invite submissions from the parties as to whether the tribunal should take a view and, if so, what procedures should be followed in doing so.

During the site visit, the parties and their representatives should remain within sight and earshot of each other and of the tribunal members at all times. If the hearings are being recorded, it is advisable to have the reporter attend and record all discussion that takes place during the visit.

Following the site visit, the adjudicator should request further submissions from the parties as to whether information received during the visit should be treated as evidence and what weight it should be given. The adjudicator may also hear evidence from the persons who attended, describing what they observed and their view of its significance. If the adjudicator observed something that he or she considers significant, the adjudicator will tell the parties and invite them to make submissions or call evidence regarding the interpretation of these observations.

The difficulty with determining what is usable as evidence after a site visit is that the participants, including the tribunal members, may observe different things or have different interpretations of the meaning or significance of what they observed. For this reason, Ontario courts have ruled that the observations of a hearing panel during a site visit do not constitute evidence from which inferences may be drawn, but can be used only to clarify (that is, to confirm or contradict) evidence given in the hearing room by witnesses.[10]

---

10 Note, however, that these cases deal with courts rather than tribunals and that the use that can be made of a "view" is different in other provinces (see John Sopinka, Sidney Lederman & Alan Bryant, *The Law of Evidence in Canada* (Toronto: Butterworths, 1992) at 18). In the context of administrative law, Blake states that the purpose of a site visit by a tribunal is to allow the tribunal better to appreciate the evidence, not to gather evidence (Sara Blake, *Administrative Law in Canada*, 5th ed (Toronto: LexisNexis Butterworths, 2011) at 65).

CHAPTER SUMMARY

While decision-makers in most government departments and agencies can receive any information provided to them and decide, within the limits of their jurisdiction, what use to make of it, tribunals are more restricted in the information they can receive and how they can use it. Information provided to a tribunal is known as evidence. Evidence may take a variety of forms, including oral statements, documents, sound or visual recordings, and objects.

The courts have developed strict and complex rules to determine the kind of evidence they will receive. Tribunals are not required to follow these rules, but they must still ensure that the evidence they accept is relevant, reliable, necessary, and fair. Tribunals and courts place the greatest weight on first-hand evidence—that is, information obtained by direct observation. Information received from another source is called hearsay, and tribunals accept it with caution. Hearsay is inherently unreliable, since the witness who reports it has no personal knowledge of whether it is true. For a similar reason, tribunals usually allow witnesses only to present facts, and not opinions. An exception is sometimes made for expert witnesses, who may be permitted to offer opinions on scientific or technical matters about which they have specialized knowledge or experience.

Tribunals generally follow a standard procedure for receiving the evidence of witnesses. Typically, the party who initiated the proceeding or who has the burden of proof is the first to call witnesses, followed by other parties with a similar interest, then the main opposing party and other parties with a similar interest, and finally any intervenors. Sometimes, witnesses give evidence in panels rather than individually.

The first stage of witness examination is questioning by the party who called the witness, known as examination-in-chief or direct examination. In examination-in-chief, information is brought forward by open questions; leading questions, which contain or suggest the desired answers, are discouraged.

The second stage of questioning is cross-examination, in which the other party tests the reliability of the witness's evidence by asking questions designed to reveal any weaknesses in the witness's testimony. In cross-examination, leading questions are acceptable. Once a witness has been cross-examined, the party who called the witness may be allowed to ask further questions designed to clarify any answers given in cross-examination. This stage of questioning is called re-examination.

In most proceedings, the final stage of questioning is rebuttal or reply, in which the party who first called witnesses may call additional evidence to respond to the evidence presented by the opposing party.

The overall purpose of these procedures is to ensure that the tribunal's decision is based on information that is relevant, reliable, necessary, and fair, and to ensure that all parties have a fair opportunity to present their evidence at the hearing.

KEY TERMS

admissibility: the qualification of information to be received as evidence in a proceeding as determined by the tests of relevance, reliability, necessity, and fairness; *see also* admissible evidence

admissible evidence: information that a court or tribunal will receive as evidence in a proceeding because it meets the tests of relevance, reliability, necessity, and fairness

chain of custody: documented proof that physical evidence has not been tampered with, by showing "continuity of possession"; involves keeping the object under lock and key or otherwise secure, and ensuring that a record is kept of each person who handled or transported the object from the time it was received until the date of the proceeding

circumstantial evidence: evidence that tends to show that something is likely to be a fact even though no witness directly observed the event in question; evidence from which inferences about other facts can be drawn; *see also* direct evidence

closed question: *see* leading question

corroboration: confirmation or support of evidence in a case provided by other evidence

cross-examination: questioning of a witness by an opposing party or representative for the purpose of casting doubt on the reliability of the witness's testimony or bringing out additional evidence supporting the position of the opposing party; *see also* examination-in-chief

cross-questioning: *see* cross-examination

direct evidence: evidence relating to an event that is given by a witness who directly observed the occurrence of the event; *see also* circumstantial evidence

direct examination: *see* examination-in-chief

examination-in-chief: initial evidence given by a witness in response to questions asked by the party or representative who called the witness to testify; *see also* cross-examination

exhibit: a document or other form of physical evidence accepted by a tribunal

expert evidence: opinions provided by an expert witness, which are required by an adjudicator who lacks the specialized knowledge, training, or experience to resolve an issue without such assistance; *see also* expert witness

expert witness: a witness who is permitted, as a result of a competence acquired through study or experience in a specialized field, to give opinions on matters related to that field as evidence before a court or tribunal; *see also* expert evidence

hearsay evidence: information provided by a witness who did not obtain the information through direct observation but heard it from another person or read it in a document written by another person

leading question: a question put to a witness that contains the crucial facts or conclusions that the questioner wants the witness to confirm, and with which the witness is merely required to agree or disagree; generally, a question that can be answered simply "yes" or "no"; also called a "closed question"; *see also* open question

marking: the procedure by which documents and other forms of physical evidence are entered into the hearing record as evidence; involves assigning an exhibit number and usually stamping or otherwise marking on the item the name or file number of the case

open question: a question put to a witness that invites an independent response; a question that does not suggest the answer that is sought or contain crucial information that the questioner wants the witness to confirm; a question that does not put words in the witness's mouth; *see also* leading question

opinion evidence: evidence that is the product of a witness's belief or conclusion about a fact, rather than the product of direct observation of a fact through the witness's primary senses of touch, sight, hearing, taste, or smell

physical evidence: any object produced before a court or tribunal as evidence that a judge or adjudicator may observe with his or her own senses—for example, a weapon alleged to have been used in committing an offence or a product alleged to be defective; also called "real evidence" or "demonstrative evidence"

privilege: an exception to a general right or duty; in the case of evidentiary privilege, the right or duty of a person to withhold otherwise admissible evidence from a court or tribunal to preserve its confidentiality; *see also* privileged information

privileged information: information that a court or tribunal cannot compel a person to disclose because of the need to protect its confidentiality even though it may otherwise be admissible; *see also* privilege

probative value: the usefulness of information in proving a point in dispute

qualification hearing: a hearing held by a court or tribunal for the purpose of deciding whether to admit opinion evidence of an expert witness

rebuttal: *see* reply evidence

re-examination: further questioning of a witness by the party or representative who called him or her for the purpose of clarifying any answers given by the witness during cross-examination

relevant evidence: evidence that helps to answer a question that a court or tribunal must address in making a decision

reply evidence: evidence called to rebut or refute the evidence presented by an opposing party; *see also* surrebuttal

rules of evidence: rules used by the courts to determine the admissibility of evidence, composed of a combination of common law principles, statutory provisions, and constitutional principles, and requiring that evidence presented in court be relevant, reliable, necessary, and fair

surrebuttal: presentation of further evidence in response to an issue raised in rebuttal; also called "surreply"; *see also* reply evidence

taking a view: a site visit by the adjudicator and other participants in a proceeding for the purpose of examining immovable evidence that is central to the matter in dispute

weight: the extent or degree to which evidence is reliable in deciding the issues before a court or tribunal

witness panel: a format used in a proceeding to permit simultaneous examination and cross-examination of two or more witnesses

REVIEW QUESTIONS

1. What is "evidence"?

2. What forms may evidence take?

3. List and briefly describe the four tests that a court or tribunal applies when determining whether to receive evidence. What term is used to describe information that meets these four tests?

4. Why are courts and tribunals reluctant to listen to the opinions of most witnesses?

5. What is an "expert witness," and why are expert witnesses permitted to express opinions when other witnesses are not?

6. What are the obligations of an expert witness to the party who called him or her and to the tribunal?

7. If the opinions of two expert witnesses conflict, how does a tribunal determine which opinion to accept?

8. What is "privileged information," and why are tribunals not permitted to receive such information as evidence? Give three examples of information that is privileged.

9. Describe the order in which parties call their witnesses.

10. What is the difference between examination-in-chief, cross-examination, and re-examination?

11. What is a witness panel, and what are the advantages and disadvantages of this format for presenting evidence?

12. Explain what an exhibit is, and how and why tribunals "mark" exhibits.

13. What is a "site visit"? What is the purpose of "taking a view," and what steps can a tribunal take to ensure that the information it receives during a site visit is reliable and is shared with all the parties?

FACT SCENARIOS

Scenario 1

The Hogtown Licensing Commission is an agency of the city of Hogtown. Under the municipal business licensing bylaw, the Commission regulates the taxicab industry by issuing licences to own and drive taxis, setting standards, and holding hearings regarding the suspension or revocation of the licences of taxi owners and drivers.

Mr. W. owns and drives a taxi. Two months ago, he drove a woman from her home to her doctor's office. The following day, she complained to the Commission that Mr. W. made sexual advances toward her. After investigating, the Commission proposed to revoke Mr. W.'s licence to drive a taxi.

At the hearing subsequently held by the Commissioner, the Commission staff attempt to introduce evidence of three previous infractions of standards in support of their request to revoke the licence. Mr. W.'s representative challenges the admissibility of this evidence. The evidence that the Commission staff want to introduce is as follows:

- Seven years ago, a passenger complained that Mr. W. used profane language while driving her to a hairdressing appointment. The evidence consists of an inspector's report in Mr. W.'s file, stating that the inspector interviewed both the passenger and Mr. W., and that Mr. W. denied the allegations. The file also contains a letter from the passenger setting out her complaint. The Commission staff intend to call the inspector as a witness, but not the complainant.

- Five years ago, a taxi owned and driven by Mr. W. had a broken trunk door, causing discomfort and inconvenience to a group of passengers. The evidence consists of an inspector's report found in Mr. W.'s file. According to the report, the inspector received a complaint from a passenger stating that, because the trunk would not open, the passenger could not put his luggage in the trunk and had to put it in the back seat, crowding himself and another passenger. There is no written or signed statement from the passenger, and no evidence that anyone from the Commission inspected the vehicle, notified Mr. W. of the complaint, or took any disciplinary action. The Commission staff do not intend to call the inspector or the complainant to testify.

- Three years ago, Mr. W. allowed another driver to drive a taxi he owned when the brakes were worn and needed replacing. The evidence consists of a report prepared and signed by a mechanic employed by the Commission to carry out safety checks on taxis, stating that she inspected the vehicle and found that the brakes were worn to the point that it was dangerous to operate the vehicle.

1. Is any of this evidence admissible? Why, or why not?

2. If the evidence is admissible, what considerations should the Commission take into account in deciding what weight it should be given?

Scenario 2

A valve was left open at the Hideous Chemical Company plant, and a clear, colourless, odourless chemical flowed into the roadside ditch. The chemical ran down the ditch toward a pond in which a neighbouring farmer was raising trout for sale to upscale restaurants. Shortly after this incident, all the fish in the pond died.

Mr. B., an inspector for the Ministry of the Environment, investigated. Mr. B. is a technician who is trained to investigate pollution incidents, including the taking of samples for toxicity analysis. As a result of the investigation, the Ministry gave Hideous notice that

- it would suspend the company's licence to produce chemicals at the location for three months, and
- it would issue an order for the company to replace the fish in the farmer's pond and compensate him for lost profits.

Hideous appealed the licence revocation and the order to replace the fish. The company argued that the amount of chemical spilled was insufficient to reach the pond and, moreover, that the chemical in question is not toxic to fish.

At the hearing, the Ministry's representative asked Mr. B. how he knew that the toxic chemical entered the water and killed the fish. Mr. B. testified that, while he did not take any samples of the water in the pond to determine the presence of the chemical, he saw the fish rising to the surface and "gulping for air, which is a sign that they are being affected by a chemical."

1. Is this evidence admissible? Why, or why not?

2. If you were representing Hideous, would you raise an objection, and if so, on what basis?

3. If you were the adjudicator, how would you respond to the objection?

Further Reading

Ian Blue, "Common Evidentiary Issues Before Administrative Tribunals and Suggested Approaches" (January 1993) 4:4 Adv Q 385.

P Brad Limpert, "Beyond the Rule in Mohan: A New Model for Assessing the Reliability of Scientific Evidence" (1996) 54 UT Fac L Rev 65.

Robert Macaulay & James Sprague, *Practice and Procedure Before Administrative Tribunals* (Toronto: Carswell) (loose-leaf) ch 17, 18, 20.

Ed Ratushny, "Rules of Evidence and Procedural Problems Before Administrative Tribunals" (1988-89) 2 Can J Admin L & Prac 157.

James Sprague, "Evidence Before Administrative Agencies: Let's All Forget the 'Rules' and Just Concentrate on What We're Doing" (1994–95) 8 Can J Admin L & Prac 263.

John Swaigen & Alan Levy, "The Expert's Duty to the Tribunal" (1998) 11 Can J Admin L & Prac 277.

Management and Control of the Hearing Process

12

LEARNING OUTCOMES

After reading this chapter, you will understand

- the source and scope of a tribunal's authority to manage anc control the conduct of hearings;

- the kinds of conduct at a hearing that are considered unusual or unacceptable;

- the steps that a tribunal can take to deal with unusual or unacceptable conduct;

- why a tribunal may consider it necessary to exclude members of the public from a hearing;

- why a tribunal may choose to exclude parties, and perhaps their representatives as well, from a hearing; and

- to what extent a tribunal can restrict the presence and conduct of the media at a hearing.

Most agencies are intended to be oriented towards a single purpose and to operate informally, openly and expeditiously. Their members are intended to be specialists in particular fields, one of which is not necessarily the law, and to be masters of special skills, one of which is not necessarily procedure. At the same time, the technical drafting of statutes and regulations makes it more difficult for those who are not lawyers to serve as agency members.

One might expect that, where a task is to be performed by individuals not trained in any procedural process, some care would be taken in assisting them in the conduct of this task by a detailed delineation of expected procedure in a way that will be comprehensible to them. This is not the rule, however, in our current federal administrative system. … A statutory statement that a decision-maker has all the powers of a superior court of record is not of much assistance to a decision-maker who is unaware that some courts are "of record" while others are not (let alone that some are "superior"). … Today's administrative system commonly expects non-legally trained individuals not only to conduct themselves in accordance with all of the complex and subtle principles of administrative law but to instruct those who appear before them in these principles as well.

Martin Freeman & James Sprague, "The Case for a Federal Administrative Powers and Procedures Act" in Philip Anisman & Robert F Reid, eds, *Administrative Law Issues and Practice* (Scarborough, Ont: Carswell, 1995) 127 at 135

Authority to Manage the Hearing Process

The principle of procedural fairness, combined with the objective of efficiency in the conduct of hearings, requires that tribunals have both the authority and the tools to manage and control the hearing process. A tribunal's authority to manage hearings may be set out in a statute of general application or in the tribunal's own enabling statute, in the form of provisions allowing the tribunal to make its own procedural rules.[1] Therefore, the first step in the management of a hearing is for the tribunal to develop a set of procedures that contribute to a fair and smooth hearing process. The tribunal should make sure that these procedures are explained clearly and made available to tribunal members, parties, other participants, and the general public.

In developing and applying hearing procedures, a tribunal should aim for a balance between certainty, consistency, and sufficient flexibility to allow the adjudicator to depart from usual practice in unusual situations. The adjudicator should also have the flexibility, within the requirements of correct procedure, to take into account the concerns and motives of participants. For example, an aggressive representative who seems to be disregarding the rules of the tribunal may sincerely believe that he or she is simply defending the interests of her client, while a party

---

1   See, for example, British Columbia's *Administrative Tribunals Act*, SBC 2004, c 45 (ATA), ss 11–13; Quebec's *Administrative Justice Act*, CQLR c J-3 (AJA), s 11; and Ontario's *Statutory Powers Procedure Act*, RSO 1990, c S.22 (SPPA), s 25.1.

whose manner is abrasive may feel that "the system" is stacked against him or her and may see the tribunal as a component of that system. In such cases, the adjudicator may be given discretion to respond as the circumstances seem to require, instead of automatically imposing procedural restrictions or penalties.

Authority to Control the Conduct of Hearings

All tribunals have an inherent right under common law to take any steps necessary to control their process. This right may be codified in a statute of general application[2] or in a specific enabling statute. Statutes may also set out certain specific powers of tribunals relating to the conduct of hearings. For example, some statutes give tribunals the power

- to ask a court to inquire into and, if necessary, punish conduct amounting to "contempt" of the tribunal (*Statutory Powers Procedure Act*[3] (SPPA), s 13; *Administrative Tribunals Act*[4] (ATA), s 49);

- to bar an incompetent representative, other than a lawyer (and, in Ontario, a licensed paralegal), from a hearing (SPPA, s 23; ATA, s 48);

- to ask a judge to issue a warrant or an order requiring the attendance and testimony of a witness (SPPA, s 12(4); ATA, s 49);

- to issue orders or directions to prevent abuse of the tribunal's processes (SPPA, s 23(1));

- to issue orders or directions for the maintenance of order at the hearing and, if necessary, to call on a police officer for assistance in maintaining order (SPPA, s 9(2); ATA, s 48);

- to award costs to a party where the conduct of another party has been unreasonable, frivolous, or vexatious, or the party has acted in bad faith (SPPA, s 17.1; ATA, s 47); and

- to require a party whose conduct has been improper to pay part of the tribunal's expenses in connection with the hearing (ATA, s 47).

These powers are discussed in more detail below.

Power to Deal with Contempt

Tribunals have limited powers to deal directly with behaviour that shows disrespect for the tribunal's authority or that tends to interfere with (that is, that tends to

---

2 See, for example, s 11(1) of the ATA and s 25.0.1 of the SPPA, *supra* note 1.

3 RSO 1990, c S.22.

4 SBC 2004, c 45.

obstruct) the administration of justice. Examples of behaviour that would fall into this category include:

- disruption of the proceeding by a participant or by a member of the public who is attending the hearing;
- failure of a participant to carry out a promise (an **undertaking**) made to the tribunal;
- failure of a witness to obey a summons to attend and give evidence;
- failure of a party or representative to comply with a valid order of the tribunal; and
- provision of statements by parties or their representatives to the media intended to influence the outcome of the hearing.

Such conduct may constitute **contempt** of the tribunal, equivalent to the offence of contempt of a court. Since contempt is considered a criminal offence in some circumstances, tribunals do not have the authority to impose formal sanctions (or punishment) on the person behaving in such a manner. However, under some statutes, including the SPPA and the ATA, tribunals do have the power to refer the matter to a court for review and a decision on punishment.

Before taking this step, the adjudicator may halt the proceeding, point out the offensive behaviour, and provide the person with an opportunity to show why the tribunal should not refer the matter to a court. At this "show cause" hearing, the person may attempt to explain and justify the behaviour, or may admit that it was inappropriate and apologize, in the hope that this will be acceptable to the adjudicator. If the person does not wish to provide an explanation, the tribunal may not have the authority to require him or her to do so.

If no explanation or apology is given, or if the explanation or apology is unsatisfactory, the adjudicator may ask a court to commence formal contempt proceedings. However, this remedy should be sought only in the most serious cases. Courts will exercise their contempt powers only when the rule of law is challenged. Moreover, deciding a case of contempt is a cumbersome and time-consuming process. The tribunal must prepare a written statement of facts for the court, witnesses may be called, and the person charged may present a defence. Therefore, tribunals rarely ask courts to impose punishment for conduct amounting to contempt.

If the person responsible for the objectionable behaviour is a lawyer, an alternative remedy available to the tribunal is to report the conduct to the provincial law society. Law societies require all practising lawyers in the province to comply with strict rules of professional conduct, and have the authority to discipline any member who breaches those rules. One of the rules is that lawyers must show appropriate respect to courts and tribunals. In Ontario, paralegals can also be disciplined by the law society—the Law Society of Upper Canada (LSUC)—as all professional paralegals are licensed by the LSUC and are required to comply with rules of conduct similar to those governing lawyers.

It is trite observation that certain litigation can bring out the worst in legal counsel. This was one such matter in which the behaviour of counsel was so disruptive to the proper conduct of the hearing that the [Ontario Labour Relations] Board feels compelled to make several comments regarding the behaviour of counsel. ... It should be stressed that none of the comments which follow are directed towards Mr. Stout, who represented his client before the Board in an entirely professional manner throughout the course of his participation in this proceeding.

Mr. Tarasuk and Mr. Abbass were, on numerous occasions, rude, interruptive, and disrespectful of other counsel appearing at the hearing, of me, as the Vice-Chair of the Board assigned to hear this matter, and of the Ontario Labour Relations Board, as an institution. Mr. Abbass, in particular, seemed to take pleasure in continually disrupting the course of this proceeding. Both Mr. Abbass and Mr. Tarasuk appear to hold the view that each has the unqualified right to interject personal opinions or snide commentary at will during opposing counsel's argument. On innumerable occasions I directed each of Mr. Abbass and Mr. Tarasuk to refrain from such conduct. Each was advised that he would have an opportunity, at the appropriate time, to respond to opposing counsel's argument. However, my directions were regularly ignored or challenged by counsel and more often than not caused Mr. Abbass and Mr. Tarasuk to more vigorously interject, resulting, on occasion, in the need for me to raise my voice above theirs in order to maintain some semblance of order in the hearing room.

UFCWIU Local 175 v Vic Murai Holdings Ltd, [1996]
OLRB Rep 106 at 148 (Shouldice)

If the behaviour of the representative does not make it impossible for the hearing to proceed, or if it would be impractical to expect the affected party to find another representative at this point in the hearing, the adjudicator may decide to wait until the hearing is finished and a decision has been rendered before instituting formal contempt proceedings or making a complaint to the law society. The reason for waiting to take action is that if this action is taken while the hearing is in progress, the representative concerned will likely request an adjournment until the proceedings before the court or the law society are complete, thereby delaying the hearing indefinitely. An adjudicator who continues the hearing in these circumstances risks allegations that his or her decision cannot be impartial.

Even if the adjudicator delays any action until after the decision has been rendered, if the adjudicator does not forewarn the representative concerned of his or her intention to file a complaint or institute formal contempt proceedings, the representative or the party he or she represented may argue that the adjudicator was biased throughout the hearing and that the decision should therefore be struck down (assuming that the representative lost the case). On the other hand, if the adjudicator tells the representative that the tribunal may take action following the hearing, this knowledge may make it more difficult for the representative to pursue his or her client's case as vigorously as he or she might otherwise have pursued it.

These concerns make it difficult for an adjudicator to decide whether to take action and, if so, when to do so.

Power to Bar a Representative

One aspect of the fairness of a proceeding is that the parties must have responsible representatives. The SPPA reinforces this requirement by giving a tribunal the power to bar a representative (other than a lawyer or a paralegal licensed by the LSUC) from participating in the hearing if the representative is incompetent or does not understand and carry out his or her duties and responsibilities as his or her client's advocate. In the event that the representative is a lawyer or a licensed paralegal, the tribunal can make a complaint to the LSUC, as it can in cases of conduct constituting contempt. The ATA permits a tribunal to eject any person (including a lawyer) from a hearing if he or she disobeys an order or direction of the tribunal (s 48).

Power to Compel Witnesses

Under the SPPA, if a witness has been served with a summons and either has failed to attend or refuses to provide the evidence required by the summons, the tribunal can ask a judge to issue a warrant to arrest the witness and, if necessary, detain him or her until he or she testifies. Tribunals have similar powers under the ATA.

In general, witnesses are required to answer all questions put to them by the party who calls them. In cross-examination, if an objection is to be made to a question posed to a witness, the party or representative who called the witness should make the objection, not the witness. A witness may not object to or refuse to answer a question unless the party or representative who called the witness has made an objection and the tribunal has upheld the objection.

However, there may be exceptions. In some cases, the party who has called a witness may not be prepared to protect legitimate interests in confidentiality raised by the witness, either because the party and the witness have competing interests or because the party's representative does not have access to information needed to determine whether an objection should be made. In such cases, it may be appropriate for the witness to raise the objection and to request an adjournment so that the witness can arrange for the attendance and assistance of his or her own counsel. Section 11 of the SPPA provides for a limited right of witnesses to be advised of their rights by their own counsel or agent. The witness's representative can take no other part in the proceeding unless the tribunal gives permission.

Power to Prevent Abuse of Process

The inherent common law right of tribunals to control their process gives rise to the power to act to prevent an abuse of that process, even without specific statutory authority. **Abuse of process** is a term used by courts and tribunals to refer to conduct by a participant in a proceeding involving a flagrant and serious violation of the rules of procedure or other reasonable expectations of the court or tribunal. The ATA authorizes BC tribunals to dismiss cases that give rise to an abuse of process (s 31), while the SPPA permits tribunals to make orders to prevent abuse of process (s 23(1)). For example, if the same representative represents two parties whose interests may conflict, a tribunal may prohibit the representative from acting, as this would be an abuse of the tribunal's process.

Power to Maintain Order

Occasionally, a tribunal may be confronted with disorderly conduct or behaviour that seriously disrupts the proceeding. The SPPA and ATA provide certain Ontario and BC tribunals with a broad power to deal with such conduct, first by ordering or directing the offending person(s) to obey the tribunal's rules of procedure, and second, if the conduct continues, by calling on the police to maintain order.

Generally, police intervention should be a last resort. However, sometimes disorderly conduct may be a sign of possible violence. A tribunal member who feels that a person's behaviour is threatening or potentially dangerous should take preventive action, such as halting the proceeding and calling the police, in order to remove the risk of harm to others present at the hearing.

Power to Award Costs

As mentioned, tribunals generally do not have the power to award costs at a hearing. However, some enabling statutes authorize individual tribunals to award costs. In addition, a trend appears to be developing to provide for costs, at least under limited circumstances, in statutes of general application. Ontario's SPPA was amended in 1999 to permit tribunals to award costs to a party where another party has behaved unreasonably or in other ways considered improper, or has acted in bad faith. This power can serve to deter parties from engaging in disruptive or obstructive conduct at a hearing. In contrast, tribunals subject to BC's ATA have a general power to award costs in accordance with regulations that may be made, and, in addition, may demand reimbursement of their own expenses incurred as a result of a party's improper conduct.

Represented Versus Unrepresented Parties

In responding to an unruly or uncooperative party, an adjudicator must often consider whether the party is represented at the hearing or is acting for himself or herself. If the party is represented, the adjudicator is entitled to make the representative responsible for his or her client's conduct. Representatives—and lawyers in particular—are expected to have a basic understanding of the hearing process and the tribunal's rules of procedure, and to follow those rules, as well as to keep their clients' and witnesses' behaviour under reasonable control.

If, on the other hand, the party is unrepresented, it is sometimes better for the adjudicator to give the party an opportunity to express his or her anger or frustration rather than deal with the party strictly according to the tribunal's standards of practice and procedure. The individual may simply need to let off steam for a moment and will then settle down for the remainder of the hearing.

It is important to keep in mind that parties to a dispute are often upset and distrustful, particularly if they are unrepresented. An adjudicator can earn the respect and cooperation of the parties, and of the other participants, by treating them all with respect.

Protesters

Occasionally, a hearing that deals with issues of concern to the broader community will attract protesters. In such cases, the protesters may demonstrate outside or even bring signs and banners into the hearing room. If they are present while the hearing is under way, they may cheer statements that support their position and boo or laugh at statements for which they have contempt. Their behaviour may make it difficult for the adjudicator to keep control of the hearing, maintain decorum, and preserve the integrity of the tribunal. In dealing with situations of this nature, the adjudicator and other members of the tribunal must try to achieve a balance between respect for the protesters' constitutional right to freedom of expression and the need to protect the rule of law.

Abusive Participants

There is a fine line between venting or letting off steam and being abusive. As mentioned, it is often reasonable for an adjudicator to permit a party to vent, provided that this behaviour does not seriously interfere with the progress of the hearing. Abuse is a different matter. If a participant behaves abusively toward the tribunal or other participants, this conduct should be quickly stopped. Threats, unfounded or irrelevant accusations of wrongdoing, and discriminatory remarks of any kind are unacceptable.

Dealing with Abusive Behaviour

Laurel Cropley, a former immigration adjudicator with the federal government, suggests a "three strikes and you're out" rule for abusive behaviour:

- Stop the individual who is speaking, remind him or her that this is a formal administrative hearing, and tell the individual that the behaviour is unacceptable and will not be tolerated.

- If the behaviour continues, warn the individual that unless it ceases, the individual will be asked to leave and the tribunal will reach its decision without his or her input.

- Follow through. If the individual ignores the warning, ask him or her to leave the hearing. If the individual refuses to leave, it may be necessary to adjourn the hearing. If a party is asked to leave, arrangements may be made for him or her to participate from a distance—for example, by sending the party transcripts of evidence and allowing him or her to make submissions in writing.

Closed (In Camera) Hearings

Section 2(b) of the *Canadian Charter of Rights and Freedoms*[5] has been interpreted to require that court proceedings be held in public except in exceptional circumstances where publicity may cause serious harm.[6] It is clear that this ruling applies to some tribunals as well. The integrity and credibility of the administrative justice system are founded on the principle that hearings should generally be held in public. This principle has been codified in the SPPA, the ATA, and in Quebec's *Administrative Justice Act*[7] (AJA).

Section 9 of the SPPA requires tribunals to hold hearings that are open to the public unless the requirement of confidentiality for matters involving public security or information of an intimate personal or financial nature outweighs the public interest in an open hearing. Even an electronic hearing must be open to the public (except in these circumstances) unless arranging for this is impractical. In a written hearing, openness is achieved by providing the public with the ability to access the documents submitted where requested. Section 41 of the ATA requires that oral hearings be open except under circumstances similar to those outlined in section 9 of the SPPA. The ATA is silent as to whether electronic or written hearings must be open, except to state in section 41(3) that in all hearings the documents submitted must be accessible to the public except where private or public interests in confidentiality override the public interest in open hearings. Section 10 of Quebec's AJA requires that hearings must generally be held in public but permits a private or "closed" hearing where this is necessary to maintain public order—for example, where protesters in the audience are heckling witnesses and refuse to stop.

Generally, a **closed hearing** (or an *in camera* **hearing**, to use the Latin phrase) is attended by all parties, their representatives, and any other individuals whose presence is necessary, such as expert witnesses. Apart from tribunal members, staff, and a court reporter (if required), no one else is permitted to be present. In some cases (discussed below), it is necessary to close only part of the hearing. To ensure procedural fairness, tribunal members should hear the submissions of all parties before deciding whether and to what extent the hearing should be closed.

When all or part of a hearing is closed, arrangements must be made to protect the confidentiality of information disclosed during the private proceeding. For a fully closed hearing, the record of the proceeding will be sealed and unavailable to the public. For a partially closed hearing, only those portions of the documented record that relate to the closed part of the proceeding will be sealed. In addition, the tribunal should apply procedural rules requiring the persons who attend the hearing to maintain the privacy of information disclosed in their presence. (Samples of such

---

5   Part I of the *Constitution Act, 1982*, being Schedule B to the *Canada Act 1982* (UK), 1982, c 11.

6   See *Re Southam Inc and The Queen (No 1)* (1983), 41 OR (2d) 113.

7   *Supra* note 1.

rules are set out in the model rules of procedure published by the Society of Ontario Adjudicators and Regulators.)[8]

Exclusion of the Media from a Hearing

Hearings that are open to the public are also open to the media. Hearings that are closed to the public may or may not be closed to the media, depending on the governing statute that applies to the tribunal. For example, in Ontario, tribunals subject to the SPPA may exclude the media from a hearing only by closing the hearing to the public.

Protecting the Confidentiality of Information in a Closed Hearing

To ensure that information disclosed in the course of a closed proceeding remains confidential, the parties and their representatives and witnesses are often required to sign an undertaking, before the closed session begins, that they will not reveal the oral evidence given or show anyone the documentary evidence received. They may also be required

- to keep any notes they may take confidential,
- not to make copies of documents or notes, and
- to return all documents to the party who tendered them or to the tribunal when the hearing is over.

An example of such an undertaking is included in Appendix F.

A tribunal may also order that documentary evidence provided by the participants and any transcript or audiotape of oral evidence be sealed and kept separate from the public hearing record. Tribunal staff may be instructed to return the documents to the party whose privacy is to be protected after the hearing is over and the deadline for any appeal has passed.

As it may not be necessary to keep confidential *all* the evidence heard during the closed hearing, after consulting the parties the tribunal may order the release of any portions of the documentary evidence or of the transcript of oral evidence that are not sensitive. This information will then be available to the public.

By contrast, in Quebec, section 130 of the AJA gives the Administrative Tribunal of Quebec (ATQ) the authority to allow journalists to attend a closed hearing unless the tribunal considers that their presence may prejudice a person whose interests may be affected by the proceeding. However, a journalist who is granted access to a closed hearing is prohibited from publishing anything that would identify "a person concerned" unless otherwise authorized to do so by law or by the tribunal. ("Publishing" in this context is used in the broad sense of making information available to

---

8   David B Braund & Carole A Prest, *Ontario Rules: A Model for Administrative Justice Agencies* (Courtice, Ont: Society for Ontario Adjudicators and Regulators, 2000).

the public, whether by radio or television broadcasting, posting on the Internet, or by publication in a newspaper, magazine, book, or other form.)

A tribunal (or court) order prohibiting the publication of information disclosed in a proceeding is called a **publication ban**. It appears that as a general rule, if the media are allowed to attend a hearing, a tribunal cannot forbid the publication of information disclosed in the proceeding unless it is specifically authorized to do so by statute. For example, as described, the AJA provides for a partial publication ban in the case of a journalist attending a closed hearing. Section 131 of the AJA also gives the ATQ a broader authority to ban the publication of information where necessary either to maintain public order or, in the case of confidential information, "to ensure the proper administration of justice." At this time, the SPPA provides no specific authority for a tribunal to issue a publication ban.

The inherent authority of tribunals to control their proceedings allows them to impose reasonable requirements on the conduct of representatives of the media (including reporters, camera operators, and sound recorders) during the hearing. For example, the tribunal may require camera technicians or photographers to station their equipment in a part of the hearing room that is out of the line of vision of participants and other observers, may prohibit movement of equipment except during breaks in the hearing, and may prohibit the use of noisy equipment and distracting lighting. For certainty and consistency, it is helpful for a tribunal to set out these conditions in its rules of procedure; however, some tribunals may prefer to issue orders governing the conduct of media representatives on a case-by-case basis.

Exclusion of Parties from a Hearing

One of the fundamental principles of fairness is the right of a party to be present throughout a hearing. However, in the rare case where it is necessary to keep information confidential even from a party, a tribunal may deny the party the right to be present during the time when that information will be revealed or discussed. For example, a party may refuse on principle to sign a confidentiality undertaking, or the party's past behaviour may provide evidence that the party cannot be trusted to comply with such an undertaking. In such cases, the party—and, in some circumstances, the party's representative (as well as witnesses)—may be required to leave the hearing room while testimony involving the information that must be kept confidential is being given, and may be denied the opportunity to examine documents or other evidence concerning that information. British Columbia's ATA explicitly permits exclusion of parties and intervenors where necessary to ensure the proper administration of justice (s 42).

> *If a valid reason exists for refusing to disclose information to a party, counsel representing the party may be permitted to peruse the information on an undertaking not to disclose any information to the client and to use the information only for the purpose of the proceeding. However, in some cases, the information is so sensitive that disclosure even to counsel is not permitted.*
>
> Sara Blake, *Administrative Law in Canada*, 2nd ed
> (Toronto: Butterworths, 1997) at 38

CHAPTER SUMMARY

Tribunals have the authority under common law to control their process. This authority may be codified in statutes granting tribunals specific powers for managing and controlling their hearings. Some tribunals have more powers than others. These powers may include the power to make rules of procedure, to ask a court to punish for contempt, to expel or refuse to hear obstructive or incompetent agents, to require witnesses to testify, to call for the assistance of police, and to award costs for improper conduct.

Although tribunals generally must hold public hearings, most have a limited power to hold closed hearings. This allows them to exclude the public from attending and from having access to a record of the proceeding, and often allows them to exclude the media as well. A closed hearing may be held in order to protect confidential information, or to preserve public security or public order. Under rare circumstances, a party may be excluded from part of a hearing or denied access to certain evidence.

Because conduct in the course of a hearing that appears unreasonable to tribunal members or to another party may be reasonable from the point of view of the participant engaging in the conduct as well as others, the tribunal should exercise its powers of control with restraint. The adjudicator should aim to balance the need to keep order and maintain respect for the process against the experience and motivation of the participant whose behaviour does not conform to the tribunal's rules.

KEY TERMS

abuse of process: conduct by a participant in a proceeding involving a flagrant and serious violation of the rules of procedure or of other reasonable expectations of the court or tribunal

closed hearing: a hearing held behind closed doors (in private), in which the only persons permitted to attend are those directly involved in the case, such as parties, their representatives, and necessary witnesses; also called an "*in camera*" hearing

contempt: conduct that shows disrespect for the authority of a court or tribunal or that tends to interfere with (obstruct) the administration of justice; examples include the disruption of a proceeding by a participant or by a member of the public, the failure of a participant to carry out an undertaking made to the court or tribunal, the failure of a witness to obey a summons, the failure of a party or representative to comply with a valid order of the court or tribunal, and the provision of statements by a participant to the media intended to influence the outcome of a proceeding

in camera **hearing:** *see* closed hearing

publication ban: an order issued by a court or tribunal prohibiting the publication of evidence and other information disclosed in a proceeding

undertaking: a promise made to a court or tribunal by a party or his or her representative to fulfill a specific obligation, such as producing a document or other evidence relevant to a proceeding

CASES TO CONSIDER

Contempt

Re West End Development Corp (1994), 29 Admin LR (2d) 71 (Ont EAB)

FACTS: Counsel failed to appear at a pre-hearing conference before Ontario's Environmental Appeal Board (now the Environmental Review Tribunal) on a date and time that had been confirmed in writing by the counsel's office. Her failure to appear was due to a misunderstanding at her office as to which person in the office was responsible for the file. Section 23(1) of the *Statutory Powers Procedure Act* provides that "[a] tribunal may make such orders or give such directions in proceedings before it as it considers proper to prevent abuse of its processes."

ISSUE: Was there a case for contempt under section 23(1) of the *Statutory Powers Procedure Act*?

DECISION: An order under section 23(1) of the SPPA was not appropriate. There was an innocent explanation that was reasonable and acceptable. This was not a case of contempt.

The Tribunal's Contempt Powers

Canadian Broadcasting Corporation v Quebec (Police Commission) (1979), 101 DLR (3d) 24 (SCC)

FACTS: The Canadian Broadcasting Corporation (CBC) allegedly broadcast a picture of a witness at an inquiry into organized crime that was conducted by the Quebec Police Commission. Broadcasting of the picture was contrary to an order by the Commission that the photograph not be published. The CBC was summoned to appear before the Commission on charges of contempt.

ISSUE: Did the provincial legislature have jurisdiction to confer on an administrative tribunal the power to punish for contempt *ex facie* (that is, "not in the face of" the tribunal but outside of a hearing)?

DECISION: Administrative tribunals such as the Quebec Police Commission do not have an inherent power to punish for contempt; therefore, such power must be conferred by statute or it does not exist. The authority of the provincial legislature to confer this power in a statute is also limited. The legislature may not give the Police Commission the power to investigate or punish contempt committed *ex facie*. The legislation should be interpreted narrowly on the assumption that the legislature did not intend to exceed its authority. Interpreting the relevant legislation strictly, there was no intention to confer broad *ex facie* contempt powers to the Commission. The allegation against the CBC was for contempt *ex facie*, and the Commission had no jurisdiction to inquire into it.

The Tribunal's Power to Manage and Control the Hearing Process

Chrysler Canada Ltd v Canada (Competition Tribunal), [1992] 2 SCR 394

FACTS: The Competition Tribunal issued an order against Chrysler Canada Ltd. under part VIII of the *Competition Act* (RSC 1985, c C-34) requiring Chrysler to resume supplying car parts to a customer. The director of investigation and research, having reason to believe that Chrysler failed to comply, filed a motion with the Tribunal initiating contempt proceedings. Chrysler argued that the Tribunal lacked jurisdiction to hear contempt proceedings.

ISSUE: Did the Competition Tribunal have jurisdiction over civil contempt for breaches of its orders under part VIII of the *Competition Act*?

DECISION: At common law, only superior courts have the power to punish for contempt. However, clear statutory language can override the common law and confer contempt powers on an inferior tribunal. In this case, section 8(1) of the *Competition Tribunal Act* (RSC 1985, c 19 (2nd Supp)) is the basis of the Tribunal's jurisdiction. It provides that the Tribunal has jurisdiction "to hear and dispose of all applications made under … Part VIII of the *Competition Act* and any related matters."

Section 8(2) of the *Competition Tribunal Act* confirms the Tribunal's jurisdiction. It expressly confers powers on the Tribunal, with respect to enforcement of the Tribunal's orders, including contempt for breach of its orders.

REVIEW QUESTIONS

1. What rules of procedure or practice directions can a tribunal make under British Columbia's *Administrative Tribunals Act* to help its members maintain control of a proceeding and prevent unnecessary delay or disruption of the hearing?

2. Apart from rule-making powers, list the powers given to Ontario tribunals under the *Statutory Powers Procedure Act* and to the ATQ under the *Administrative Justice Act* that can assist them in maintaining order and avoiding unnecessary delay.

3. What steps can a tribunal take if a lawyer or other representative is incompetent? What if the problem is not incompetence but disrespect for the tribunal or for other parties or their representatives or witnesses?

4. In what circumstances can a tribunal close its hearings to

   a. the public, and

   b. the media?

5. When can a tribunal

   a. exclude a party from a hearing, or

   b. prevent a party from examining evidence?

FACT SCENARIOS

Scenario 1

You are representing a party at a hearing that will last several weeks. The lawyer representing one of the other parties frequently arrives half an hour to an hour late. The tribunal has criticized this conduct, but it continues.

Your client suggests that you should ask the tribunal to impose a penalty on the lawyer for being late.

1. What action do you ask the tribunal to take?

2. What arguments do you make in support of your request?

3. What is the statutory or common law basis for your arguments?

Scenario 2

You are representing a neighbourhood association at a hearing to determine whether to approve a waste disposal site in the area. The residents are worried that the facility will result in heavy traffic, air pollution, water pollution, noise, odours, and dust. The tribunal panel has made comments that lead your client to believe that the tribunal is not sympathetic to these concerns and is likely to approve the facility.

As a result of these comments, your client feels that the tribunal is biased and that withdrawing from the hearing and denouncing the panel is a more effective way of communicating its concerns about the proposal than continuing to participate in the hearing process. Your client has instructed you to announce to the tribunal that its members consider the tribunal to be biased and are withdrawing from the proceeding. All the members present at the hearing will then stand up and walk out of the hearing room, and you will follow them. Outside the building, the neighbourhood association's executive will hold a press conference and denounce the tribunal as a kangaroo court.

You tell your client that you need to consider this plan. After researching the law and reviewing your client's strategic options, what course of action do you advise?

EXERCISES

1. For the following powers, find a relevant case, and for each case, prepare a report containing a summary of the case: facts, issues, decision, and rationale for the decision.

   - powers of a tribunal to deal with contempt,

   - powers of a tribunal to bar a party or representative,

   - powers of a tribunal to compel witnesses,

   - powers of a tribunal to deal with abuse of process,

   - powers of a tribunal to maintain order, and

   - powers of a tribunal to award costs.

2. Find a journal article, news article, or paper that discusses one of the following issues that can arise at a hearing before a court or tribunal: dealing with unrepresented parties; dealing with protesters; dealing with abusive participants; holding closed (*in camera*) hearings; exclusion of media from hearings; or exclusion of parties.

   Prepare a summary of the following:

   - a description and explanation of the issue as it arises in hearings, and

   - a discussion of how this issue is (or should be) dealt with in the context of a hearing.

FURTHER READING

David B Braund & Carole A Prest, *Ontario Rules: A Model for Administrative Justice Agencies* (Courtice, Ont: Society of Ontario Adjudicators and Regulators, 2000).

Paul Lordon, "Administrative Tribunals and the Control of Their Processes" (1997–98) 11 Can J Admin L & Prac 179.

Robert Macaulay & James Sprague, *Practice and Procedure Before Administrative Tribunals* (Toronto: Carswell) (loose-leaf) ch 9.

Jeffrey Miller, *The Law of Contempt in Canada* (Scarborough, Ont: Carswell, 1997).

Conduct Outside the Hearing

13

LEARNING OUTCOMES

After reading this chapter, you will understand

- why participants in a hearing should not discuss any aspect of the case with the adjudicator or another member of the tribunal unless all other participants are also present;

- why tribunal members should limit their social contact with participants in a hearing and with individuals and organizations that are likely to appear before the tribunal;

- whether participants and tribunal members should talk to the media about a case that is under way;

- why tribunal members should not comment publicly on decisions of the tribunal; and

- whether tribunal members may make public statements on issues that the tribunal has ruled on in the past or may decide in the future.

In the ordinary course, decisions of this Court, as with any other court, must speak for themselves without further elaboration by any member of the court, except through the medium of a later decision of the Court. However, in a circumstance where misstatement of a decision is substantial and the potential consequences of the misstatement are significant, the unusual step of indicating the existence and extent of the misstatement has to be considered, lest silence be taken to be confirmation of the misstated position.

Clyde Wells, chief justice of Newfoundland, in a letter to
Globe and Mail reporter Kirk Makin, December 2002

Introduction

In addition to rules of conduct and procedure for the hearing of a case, there are standards of conduct that participants and tribunal members must observe outside the hearing room before, during, and after the hearing. This chapter describes the standards that apply to conduct in the following contexts:

- communication outside the hearing between participants and tribunal members;
- social contact between tribunal members and individuals or organizations that may appear before the tribunal in future proceedings;
- contact with the media by participants and tribunal members; and
- public statements by adjudicators about previous decisions of the tribunal or about issues that may come before the tribunal in the future.

The Society of Ontario Adjudicators and Regulators has published a model code of conduct for consideration by tribunals that addresses how adjudicators should deal with the matters above.[1]

Codes of conduct for lawyers and paralegals may also address some of the issues above. For example, rule 6 of the *Paralegal Rules of Conduct* adopted by the Law Society of Upper Canada states that a paralegal must not communicate information to the media or make public statements about a matter before a tribunal if the paralegal knows or ought to know that the information or statement will have a substantial likelihood of materially prejudicing a party's right to a fair trial or hearing.[2]

Ex Parte Communication

Ex parte communication (in Latin, meaning communication "on one side only") refers to communication between a party in a proceeding and the adjudicator or

---

1 Society of Ontario Adjudicators and Regulators, *Code of Professional and Ethical Responsibilities for Members of Adjudicative Tribunals—A Model* (Courtice, Ont: Society of Ontario Adjudicators and Regulators, 1996), online: <https://soar.on.ca/sites/soar.ca/files/code-of-conduct.pdf>.

2 Law Society of Upper Canada, *Paralegal Rules of Conduct* (Toronto: LSUC, 2014, as amended), online: <http://www.lsuc.on.ca/paralegal-conduct-rules>.

other members of the tribunal from which other parties and panel members are excluded. The principle of procedural fairness—and, in particular, the obligation of impartiality—prohibits *ex parte* communication in tribunal proceedings.

Accordingly, a participant in a hearing should never attempt to discuss any aspect of the case with an adjudicator—or, generally, with other members of the tribunal—unless all other members of the panel and all other participants are present. Similarly, an adjudicator should not ask for or receive written or oral communications from any party about a proceeding that either has not yet begun or is under way, or about a potential proceeding, unless all other parties and panel members are fully informed and involved. These restrictions mirror the standard of conduct expected of judges regarding communication with participants in a case over which they are presiding outside the courtroom.

The tribunal's procedures should ensure that participants do not have direct access to tribunal members outside the hearing room. Telephone calls and correspondence from parties should be channelled through tribunal staff, who can accept inquiries and provide the information requested either independently or after consulting the adjudicator and perhaps other members of the tribunal. Staff are generally trained to screen information received from parties before passing it on to panel members, so as to eliminate any information that may lead to bias or create an appearance of bias. Staff can also ensure that any communication from one of the parties is made available to all panel members and other participants as well. Without the full involvement of all parties, even the most innocent inquiry from one of the participants may be viewed by the others as an improper attempt to influence the adjudicator. Similarly, if a tribunal member wants to inform the parties about a procedural matter—for example, the fact that a hearing must be postponed because of a death in the adjudicator's family—the tribunal staff, not the tribunal member or adjudicator, should make the telephone call or sign the letter. Procedures such as these can ensure that no issue will be decided, or appear to have been decided, without all parties being given an opportunity to contribute to the decision.

> *No judge should talk with one counsel about any case in the absence of other counsel. Discussions with all counsel involved in a case out of a courtroom and in the absence of a court reporter, ought, in general, to be avoided. All proceedings in a trial are matters of record and it is improper that agreements or rulings should be made and not recorded. There also exists the danger that such agreements or rulings may be misunderstood, or, in rare cases, deliberately misrepresented in a courtroom before a jury. Litigants must have a natural and proper distrust of any proceedings in the case which are not open to their hearing.*
>
> JO Wilson, *A Book for Judges* (Ottawa: Supply and Services, 1980) at 52

In addition, adjudicators and panel members should generally avoid casual conversations with any of the participants outside the hearing room during hearings, as this may raise concerns among the parties. In the case of long hearings or hearings in small communities with a limited range of facilities for accommodation and meals, it may not be practical for adjudicators and participants to avoid having any contact with each other outside the hearing. In addition, in brief encounters near the hearing room, a failure to engage in everyday exchanges—such as remarking on the weather or the previous night's hockey game, for example—may be interpreted as arrogance. However, participants and adjudicators must realize that even the most harmless conversation from which some parties are excluded can raise the possibility of an apprehension of bias. At the very least, adjudicators should attempt to have any conversation with a participant in full view of the other participants, and should ensure that any casual remarks exchanged with one party are balanced by similar treatment of other parties over the course of the hearing. (See the box feature "The Dangers of Fraternization.")

The Dangers of Fraternization

It is clearly inappropriate for an adjudicator or tribunal member to have social contact with participants in a hearing that is under way. But how should an adjudicator or member handle social situations involving individuals or organizations that are likely to appear at future hearings? This is a difficult question. In such cases, **fraternization** (friendly social interaction) can be a problem.

One of the most useful discussions of fraternization is found in a book written by American administrative law judge Merritt Ruhlen. In the United States, administrative law judges play a similar role to adjudicators in many Canadian tribunals.

> Public attitudes about judicial conduct have become stricter in recent years, and judges should be sensitive to this change. A judge should limit social activities with friends or colleagues if there is any likelihood of their being involved in matters coming before the judge. It is not enough merely to avoid discussing pending matters; a judge should shun situations that might lead anxious litigants or worried lawyers to think that the judge might favour or accept the views of friends more readily than those of unknown parties.
>
> One approach is for judges to maintain their personal ties but disqualify themselves in any case in which a friend appears. If the bar is small this may be unfair to counsel and their clients, and impractical as well. An alternative course is to describe publicly the relationships whenever a friend or associate is involved and offer to disqualify oneself if so requested. This puts an unfair burden on objecting counsel by requiring him to imply publicly that the judge may be biased; also, if done frequently, it may seem to be avoidance of the judge's own responsibility. In any event, a judge must avoid the appearance of impropriety. Thus the judge should not regularly play bridge or golf or dine with lawyers whose firms may appear before him, nor should he actively participate in politics or political meetings.
>
> Judges must accept a certain amount of loneliness. They needn't become recluses, but they should realize they are no longer "one of the boys," and that they live in a critical and suspicious world.

— Merritt Ruhlen, *Manual for Administrative Law Judges* (Washington, DC: Administrative Conference of the United States, 1982).

Contact with the Media

A party's strategy for raising money to pay expert witnesses and lawyers, for increasing public awareness of an issue, or even for obtaining a favourable decision, may include creating public interest in the case through publicity in newspapers and/or on the radio, on television, or the Internet. The representative of a party who wishes to use such a strategy should be prepared to provide advice on the advantages and disadvantages of such publicity and, if the party decides to proceed, to suggest how to go about making these arrangements. The representative may also be called upon to act as a spokesperson in interviews with the media.

The guarantee of freedom of expression in the *Canadian Charter of Rights and Freedoms* (s 2(b))[3] gives parties and their representatives wide latitude to publicize their views. However, it is important that they not argue their case in the media. Statements made outside the hearing room that are intended to influence the outcome of the hearing may constitute contempt of the tribunal. It is also important to ensure that information provided to the media is consistent with evidence given at the hearing. Remember that tribunal members read and listen to the news, too. If other parties become aware of details about the case in the newspaper or on the Internet that do not appear in the evidence in the hearing, they may be concerned that the tribunal will be influenced by information that is incorrect or at least not subject to challenge through cross-examination.

Tribunal members should not discuss with the media any case that is in progress or is expected to come before them. Even a casual comment may be interpreted as a member showing bias toward or against a party or prejudging the issue. As discussed in the next section, even after a case has been decided, it is only in exceptional circumstances that an adjudicator or other member of the tribunal should issue public statements on the decision.

Comments on the Tribunal's Decisions

As a general rule, adjudicators will not defend, explain, or comment on decisions of the tribunal in the media or in other public forums. Again, a similar constraint applies to judges with respect to decisions of the courts.

A tribunal's rulings will not be immune from criticism—by the media, by politicians, by the academic community, or by unsuccessful parties. However, adjudicators will generally not respond to such criticism, even if they feel it is unfair. The risk with public comments is that they create uncertainty about the tribunal's reasons for the decision. For the parties in the case and as a matter of public record, it will not be clear whether the reasons for the decision are the ones provided when the decision was rendered at the conclusion of the hearing, or the further explanations reported in the media.

The decisions of a tribunal should speak for themselves. To ensure that they do, the adjudicator in a case will make every effort to state the reasons for the decision

---

3   Part I of the *Constitution Act, 1982*, being Schedule B to the *Canada Act 1982* (UK), 1982, c 11.

as clearly and as fully as possible. Only in exceptional circumstances will an adjudicator respond to requests by the media or persons other than the parties in a hearing to explain or defend a decision. Even then, any statements on the case will generally be provided by the tribunal chair, registrar, or counsel, rather than directly by the adjudicator.

Explanation or Defence of a Ruling: Exceptional Circumstances?

In an article published in *The Globe and Mail* on December 12, 2002, journalist Kirk Makin reported that a unanimous ruling that had just been made by a panel of three judges of the Newfoundland Court of Appeal appeared to criticize the Supreme Court of Canada by saying that judicial activism had gone too far. This ruling caused quite a stir because in the legal community it is not considered proper for the lower courts to criticize the rulings of the Supreme Court. In fact, although all three judges agreed on the outcome of the case, only one of the judges made the comments about activism.

On the day that Makin's article was published, Clyde Wells, the chief justice of Newfoundland, wrote a letter to Makin in response, saying that the statement that judicial activism had gone too far was only the opinion of the judge who wrote the decision, Justice Marshall, and was not shared by the other two judges who had agreed with the result. Wells wrote that many of the opinions expressed by Justice Marshall "reflect *only* the opinions and comments of one of the three judges sitting on that appeal." The chief justice's letter to Makin was written with the consent of the other two judges responsible for the decision. The following day, *The Globe and Mail* published an article reporting on the chief justice's letter. Was it appropriate for the chief justice to comment in public about the judgment?

John Crosbie, a former federal minister of justice, didn't think so. He made a formal complaint against the chief justice to the Canadian Judicial Council. The council is responsible for investigating complaints about the conduct of judges and making rulings about whether their conduct is proper. In Mr. Crosbie's view, the decision should speak for itself and it was improper for the chief justice to attempt to clarify the judgments of other judges. Mr. Crosbie believed that the intervention of the chief justice interfered with the independence of the two judges who had not commented on the question of judicial activism.

On March 12, 2003, the Judicial Conduct Committee exonerated the chief justice. The chair of the Committee said that Wells was right to write the letter because "a Council policy endorses a role for chief justices in correcting errors in public reports of judicial decisions." However, he added, "The principle of judicial independence and the perception of judicial impartiality are usually best served when judges refrain from commenting on their judgments. ... [A] lesson to all of us in this matter is the abundant caution that must prevail when taking the initiative to correct perceived errors in relation to judgments."

Who was right: former justice minister Crosbie or the Canadian Judicial Council?

What if, instead of the chief justice, it had been one of the judges on the panel that had made the ruling who had written to *The Globe and Mail* to explain the comments about judicial activism?

The constraints outlined above do not apply where it is found that there are errors or ambiguities in a decision. In this situation, the adjudicator, on his or her own initiative or at the request of a party, may issue a written statement correcting the errors or clarifying the reasons, provided that all parties are first consulted if there is any doubt about whether a change should be made.[4]

Criticism of Decisions by Representatives

If you represent the losing party in a case, there is nothing to prevent you from criticizing the tribunal's decision in the media or in some other public forum. You are entitled to say that you believe the decision is wrong and to explain why. However, your criticisms should be restrained and well founded. Avoid targeting individual tribunal members, who, like judges, are prohibited from speaking out in their own defence.

If a tribunal's processes and decisions are frequently unfair, representatives can seek a remedy by, for example, documenting trends, lobbying the tribunal to improve its attitude and practices, and lobbying the government to appoint better qualified or more empathetic tribunal members.

Public Statements by Adjudicators

The last question addressed here is whether adjudicators may speak in public or write about issues that may come before them. In general, the fact that an adjudicator, before appointment to a tribunal, expressed views on issues that may be the subject of subsequent hearings does not prevent the adjudicator from serving on the tribunal—although it may disqualify him or her from deciding cases involving those issues. However, once appointed, the adjudicator must avoid taking any position in public that may lead parties to believe that the adjudicator will not approach the issues before him or her with an open mind.

---

4 *Chandler v Alberta Association of Architects* (1989), 62 DLR (4th) 577 (SCC). See also *Statutory Powers Procedure Act*, RSO 1990, c S.22, s 21.1; *Administrative Tribunals Act*, SBC 2004, c 45, s 53; and *Administrative Procedures and Jurisdiction Act*, RSA 2000, c A-3, ss 153, 154. A former version of the *Human Rights Code*, RSO 1990, c H.19, s 39(6), stated: "A member of the Tribunal hearing a complaint ... shall not communicate directly or indirectly in relation to the subject-matter of the inquiry with any person or with any party or any party's representative except upon notice to and opportunity for all parties to participate."

CHAPTER SUMMARY

In addition to rules of conduct for adjudicators and participants at the hearing itself, there are standards of conduct that participants and tribunal members must observe outside the hearing room before, during, and after the hearing. Generally, participants must avoid actions that may be seen as attempts to influence the tribunal panel. Similarly, adjudicators and other tribunal members must avoid any conduct that may suggest that they are open to influence or that they are biased for or against any party.

In particular, during the hearing, there should be no communication regarding any aspect of the case between a participant and a tribunal member unless all other participants and members are also present or otherwise fully informed and involved. Outside the hearing room, casual exchanges between participants and tribunal members should be limited, and any suggestion of favouritism should be avoided. Similar constraints apply to social relations between tribunal members and individuals or organizations that may appear at future hearings.

Parties should exercise caution in making public statements about the case while the hearing is in progress. After the tribunal has issued its ruling, the losing party may criticize the decision in public, within reasonable limits. There are tighter restrictions on public statements by tribunal members, particularly with respect to cases currently under consideration, but also regarding previous decisions of the tribunal and positions on issues that may be the subject of future hearings. These constraints reinforce the principle of procedural fairness and the tribunal's obligation to remain impartial in arriving at its decisions.

KEY TERMS

ex parte: "on one side only"; refers to a statement or application made to an adjudicator or panel member by a party to a proceeding in the absence of other parties or panel members

fraternization: friendly social interaction; refers to social relations between tribunal members and actual or potential participants in a proceeding

CASES TO CONSIDER

Ex Parte Communications

Kane v Bd of Governors of UBC, [1980] 1 SCR 1105

FACTS: Kane, a university professor, was found to have been making unauthorized personal use of university computers. The University of British Columbia (UBC) suspended him for three months without pay and ordered him to pay restitution to the university. Kane appealed the suspension to UBC's Board of Governors. The BC *Universities Act* provided that the university president was a member of the Board "and shall attend its regular meetings." Therefore, the president attended Kane's hearing before the Board. The president responded to questions from the Board, but did not pose any questions to Kane. At the end of the hearing, Kane was asked to leave so that the Board could deliberate. The president, however, remained throughout the deliberations, and although he did not participate in the discussions or vote on the final decision, he did answer questions directed to him by members of the Board. The Board approved the three-month suspension without pay and the order for restitution. Kane sought judicial review of the Board's decision.

ISSUE: Were the Board's *ex parte* discussions with the president improper?

DECISION: The principles of natural justice were breached because the president had answered questions after the hearing and in Kane's absence. A tribunal must listen fairly to both sides, giving the parties a fair opportunity to correct or contradict any relevant statement prejudicial to their position. The tribunal must also refrain from holding private interviews with witnesses or hearing evidence in the absence of a party subject to discipline. It did not matter whether the evidence given in Kane's absence actually influenced the Board's decision, as long as it was capable of doing so. If the Board required further information, it should have waited until Kane was present and asked the questions in his presence. Or, at the very least, it should have informed Kane of the additional information it had received from the president and given him an opportunity to respond.

Reasonable Apprehension of Bias: Multiple Roles of Participants

Bailey v Saskatchewan Registered Nurses' Association, 1996 CanLII 6670, 137 DLR (4th) 224 (Sask QB)

FACTS: Three registered nurses were dismissed by their Director after a hearing before a disciplinary panel of the Saskatchewan Registered Nurses' Association. Their Director was also the president-elect of the nurses' association at the time of the investigation and hearing. The prosecutor at the discipline hearing had been counsel for the investigation committee when the nurses were investigated. His firm was general counsel for the nurses' association, and was responsible for training discipline committee members; in fact, the prosecutor had personally trained the chair of the discipline committee. In addition, the prosecutor's law firm regularly advertised in the nurses' association magazine and had contributed $5,000 to the association's building fund prior to the hearing. During the hearing, there was a noticeable degree of familiarity between the panel and the prosecutor.

ISSUE: Was there a reasonable apprehension of bias, particularly with respect to the prosecutor's familiarity with the panel?

DECISION: The process was flawed from the beginning of the investigation to the conclusion by the discipline committee. The discipline committee did not appear to have understood that issues of fairness and bias were involved. The nurses would understandably have perceived bias when they tried to raise a defence challenging the management practices of their Director, who also happened to be president-elect of the nurses' association. Ordinarily it was not objectionable for counsel to hold multiple roles, especially in administrative practice. In this case, however, the relationship between the committee and the prosecutor raised a reasonable apprehension of bias because of its degree and because of all of the surrounding factors that raised concerns of unfairness and bias. These factors included the familiarity between the prosecutor and members of the discipline committee; that the committee chair had been trained by the prosecutor; that the prosecutor's law firm had provided training for the committee; that the law firm regularly advertised in the nurses' association magazine; and that the law firm had contributed $5,000 to the association's building fund. Together, these factors created a relationship between the discipline committee and the prosecutor sufficient to raise a reasonable apprehension of bias.

Social Contact Between Adjudicators and Parties

United Enterprises Ltd v Saskatchewan (Liquor and Gaming Licensing Commission), [1997] 3 WWR 497 (Sask QB)

FACTS: United Enterprises operated a tavern. Its liquor licence was suspended by the licensing authority, and it appealed the suspension to the licensing commission. At the hearing, lawyers for the licensing authority and members of the commission referred to each other by their first names. They walked to and from the hearing room together, and the licensing authority lawyer was invited to a barbecue by the commission chair on the evening after the hearing. In contrast, the lawyer for United Enterprises was referred to by his last name and had no contact with commission members outside the hearing. The commission ultimately upheld the suspension. United Enterprises appealed the decision, arguing that the friendly relations between counsel for the licensing authority and members of the commission raised a reasonable apprehension of bias. United sought reinstatement of its licence on the ground that it was no longer possible to have a fair hearing.

ISSUE: Did the familiarity between the authority's lawyer and members of the commission create a reasonable apprehension of bias?

DECISION: The familiarity between the licensing authority's lawyer and members of the commission raised a reasonable apprehension of bias. However, the court could not substitute its own decision for the decision of the licensing authority to suspend the liquor licence. A new hearing before different members of the commission was ordered.

REVIEW QUESTIONS

1. Should a party's representative call a tribunal member to find out when the hearing of his or her case is likely to be held? Explain.

2. Should a tribunal member call a party's representative to inform the representative that another party has asked for an adjournment and to ask whether the adjournment is acceptable to the representative's client? Explain.

3. How should a tribunal handle social relations between tribunal members and individuals or groups that frequently appear before the tribunal?

4. To what extent are tribunal members free to write or speak about issues that the tribunal has decided in the past or may decide in the future?

5. What factors should a party consider in deciding whether to comment publicly on the tribunal's decision? If a party chooses to comment, what guidelines or rules should the party follow or observe?

FACT SCENARIOS

Scenario 1

You represent a party in a hearing. During a recess, a reporter comes up to you and comments that some of the panel's questions suggest that the tribunal is biased against your party's case. How do you reply?

Scenario 2

You are a representative for a party at a hearing held out of town. You enter the hotel dining room and see the adjudicator eating breakfast alone. Do you join her? What if she invites you to join her? What if the lawyers representing two of the three other parties are already at the table?

Scenario 3

You appear frequently before a tribunal that hears appeals from decisions of the government when it refuses applications for social assistance. This tribunal often decides in favour of the government and against applicants. You have just received a decision that does not take into account much of the evidence that you put before the tribunal. A reporter asks you to comment on the decision. What do you do? What if the reporter asks you to comment on the overall conduct of the tribunal as well as the specific decision?

Scenario 4

You are at a hearing before the Landlord and Tenant Board. The party you represent faces eviction for having a noisy dog. During a recess, when you are in a cubicle in the washroom, you hear two people enter the washroom. One of them says to the other that he hates dogs. You peek and see that it is the adjudicator talking to the court reporter.

1. Do you take any action, and, if so, what and when?

2. Suppose you are the adjudicator who made this comment and the appellant's representative questions your conduct in the hearing room later that day. What do you do?

3. Suppose the hearing panel in this case consists of three adjudicators. The person in the washroom cubicle who overhears this conversation is not the appellant's representative but one of the other panel members. What, if anything, should that panel member do?

FURTHER READING

Canadian Judicial Council, *Canadian Ethical Principles for Judges* (Ottawa: Canadian Judicial Council, 2004, online: <http://www.cjc-ccm.gc.ca/cmslib/general/news_pub_judicial conduct_Principles_en.pdf>.

John Swaigen, *A Manual for Ontario Adjudicators*, revised ed (Courtice, Ont: Society of Ontario Adjudicators and Regulators, 2000) ch 14.

Tribunal Decision-Making Procedures

14

LEARNING OUTCOMES

After reading this chapter, you will understand

- the degree of consensus among adjudicators that is required for a tribunal's decision in a case;

- the kind of information that a tribunal's decision must be based on;

- permissible sources of assistance to a tribunal in making its decision and drafting its reasons;

- a tribunal's obligation to consult parties when relying on legal authorities not included in evidence at the hearing;

- the kinds of remedies that may be granted in tribunal decisions;

- the requirement that tribunals give reasons for their decisions in certain situations, and what a tribunal's reasons should set out;

- solutions to the problem of delay in the release of a decision;

- who are the first persons to be informed of the tribunal's decision; and

- how the requirement of procedural fairness affects the way the decision is communicated.

The mischief of penetrating the decision process of a tribunal member is exactly the same as the mischief of penetrating the decision process of a judge.

Apart from the practical consideration that tribunal members and judges would spend more time testifying about their decisions than making them, their compellability would be inconsistent with any system of finality of decisions. No decision ... would be really final until the judge or tribunal member had been cross-examined about his decision. Instead of appeal or extraordinary remedy [judicial review], a system would grow up of review by cross-examination. In the case of a specialized tribunal representing different interests the mischief would be even greater because the process of discussion and compromise among different points of view would not work if stripped of its confidentiality.

Agnew v Ontario Assn of Architects (1987), 64 OR (2d) 8 (Div Ct) at 14

Overview of the Decision-Making Process

The decision-making process of tribunals is more rigorous than that of other government agencies. To reach a decision, decision-makers in administrative agencies

1. identify the issue(s) to be settled;
2. obtain relevant information from the person who will be directly affected by the decision;
3. apply the agency's policies, guidelines, or criteria to the facts; and
4. consult other persons whose interests may be affected by the decision.

Usually, the agency issues its decision in a letter, often using a standard form. As a general rule, there is no statutory requirement for an agency to give reasons for its decision, but procedural fairness may sometimes require reasons.

The adjudicator of a tribunal makes the decision in a case on the basis of information provided at a formal hearing. Following the hearing, the adjudicator

- identifies the issue(s) raised by the parties in the course of the hearing;
- reviews and weighs the evidence related to the issue(s) that the parties presented at the hearing;
- reviews the arguments of the parties in support of their respective positions on the issue(s);
- makes findings of fact based on the evidence;
- determines the law and any administrative policies or guidelines that apply to the facts;
- applies the law, policies, and guidelines to the facts in order to reach a decision; and
- writes the decision and the reasons for the decision.

Where a panel of adjudicators conducts the hearing, an additional stage may be the negotiation of a consensus, or agreement, on the decision among the members of the panel.

Often, a tribunal reaches its decision immediately after the hearing. It then communicates the decision to the parties, either orally or in writing, at the hearing. In more complex cases, the tribunal may conclude that it needs more time to consider the issues, and it will inform the parties that it is **reserving** its decision. It will then continue its review of the case and release a written decision at some future date. When a tribunal issues a written decision, it may be required to issue written reasons as well.

Several important elements of the decision-making process are discussed in more detail in the following sections.

Rules of Consensus and Dissent

When a case is decided by a panel rather than by a single adjudicator, there must be a minimum level of consensus, or agreement, on the decision among the panel members. If the panel has an odd number of members, the general rule is that the decision of the majority is the decision of the tribunal. This rule is sometimes stated explicitly in a tribunal's enabling statute or in a statute of general application.[1]

If the panel has an even number of members and there is no majority—that is, there is a tie—there are three possible solutions:

1. in the case of a two-member panel, the governing statute may require a unanimous decision;[2]
2. the governing statute may provide for a tie-breaking vote;[3] or
3. if the first two solutions do not apply, the hearing must be held again.

If one or more members disagree with the majority decision, most tribunals permit the minority to write their reasons for disagreeing, called a **dissent**, and issue the dissent along with the tribunal's decision and reasons. Generally, governing statutes do not state whether a tribunal must issue a dissent with its decision,[4] and the right of parties to be provided with dissenting reasons has not been clearly established as an aspect of procedural fairness.

---

1 See, for example, s 4.2(3) of the *Statutory Powers Procedure Act*, RSO 1990, c S.22 and s 145 of the *Administrative Justice Act*, CQLR c J-3.

2 *Ibid.*

3 For example, s 145 of Quebec's *Administrative Justice Act* (*supra* note 1) states that, where opinions are equally divided, the president or vice-president of the Administrative Tribunal of Quebec, or his delegate, has the right to make the decision. Ontario's *Statutory Powers Procedure Act* (*supra* note 1) does not contain a tie-breaking provision.

4 An exception is s 145 of Quebec's *Administrative Justice Act* (*supra* note 1), which specifies that if a member of a panel dissents, the grounds for dissent must be recorded in the decision.

Basis for the Decision

Tribunals differ from administrative agencies with respect to the kind of information they may rely on in making a decision. Decision-makers in government agencies may receive information from many sources and in many forms. They may rely on any of this information that is relevant to the decision; however, procedural fairness may require them to disclose the basis for their decision and to give the persons affected an opportunity to challenge it.

As a general rule, tribunal adjudicators may base their decisions only on information obtained during the hearing in the form of evidence presented by the parties. There are two exceptions to this rule that are recognized in common law and in some statutes. These exceptions are explained below.

Facts That May Be Accepted Without Proof

The first exception relates to two categories of facts that a tribunal may accept without proof—in legal language, facts of which it may take official notice (also known as "judicial notice" or "administrative notice"). Both Ontario's *Statutory Powers Procedure Act*[5] (SPPA) and Quebec's *Administrative Justice Act*[6] (AJA) refer specifically to these two categories of facts.

The first category consists of facts that are so commonly known that they are not disputed by reasonable people. Such facts are referred to in section 16(a) of the SPPA as "facts that may be judicially noticed" and in section 140 of the AJA as "facts so well-known as to not reasonably be questionable." Obvious examples are the statement that a horse is a mammal or that the normal length of a human pregnancy is about nine months. In the context of a hearing, an adjudicator who is familiar with local geography, for example, may take notice of the location of a street within a municipality, even if no evidence has been presented as proof of this fact.

> *Mr. Justice Cartwright … was a member of a panel of the Supreme Court of Canada sitting on an appeal from an expropriation assessment of a garden nursery. One of the comparable properties used in evidence was the Sheridan Nursery on Yonge Street in Toronto which was located within a few blocks of the house in which Mr. Justice Cartwright lived before moving to Ottawa. He asked whether it could be usefully used as a comparable property since it was as he well knew a corner property and had two frontages. Counsel answered that there was no evidence that the property was a corner property. "Well then," he replied, "I shall wipe it from my mind." Counsel all knew that he would.*
>
> The Law Society *Gazette*

---

5 *Supra* note 1.

6 *Ibid.*

The second category of facts that may be accepted without proof consists of facts that can be immediately and accurately demonstrated by reference to readily accessible and reliable sources. Section 16(b) of the SPPA refers to facts in this category as "any generally recognized scientific or technical facts, information or opinions within [the tribunal's] scientific or specialized knowledge." Section 141 of the AJA refers to "facts that are generally recognized and ... opinions and information which fall within [the adjudicator's] area of specialization or that of the division [of the tribunal] to which he is assigned."

Tribunal members sometimes find it frustrating that they are appointed to a tribunal because of their specialized knowledge of the subject matter of its hearings, yet they are limited in the extent to which they can apply that knowledge or verify evidence by conducting their own research. The second exception to the general rule allows adjudicators to apply their knowledge in their own field, but only to matters that are inherently uncontroversial.

Canada's leading text on evidence contains statements about judicial notice that appear difficult to reconcile. On the one hand, it states that no practical purpose is served by allowing evidence to be led to contradict a judicially noticed fact because if the process is carried out correctly, the judge or adjudicator will already have had the benefit of all available information on the subject. On the other hand, it states that before taking judicial notice, a judge should give counsel an opportunity to lead evidence and/or make argument as to the appropriateness of taking judicial notice of the particular fact in question.[7] Regardless of which explanation is correct, the practical view is that if an adjudicator intends to take notice of a fact, it is advisable for the adjudicator to inform the parties of his or her intention to do so and to give the parties an opportunity to make submissions on this point, even if the adjudicator believes that the facts are so obvious that there is no need of proof. In this way, fairness and the appearance of fairness will be upheld.

Reliance on Legal Authority

While it is clear that adjudicators have this limited ability to rely on facts for which there is no need of proof, it is less clear whether they may consider legal authorities not included in the information presented at the hearing.

The general rule is that if, in the course of writing the decision, the adjudicator finds a judgment of a court or a statutory provision that is relevant to an issue raised at the hearing but was not referred to by the parties, the adjudicator may rely on that authority without informing the parties of his or her intention to do so. However, an adjudicator should not rely on a legal authority that addresses an issue that was not raised at the hearing without first giving the parties an opportunity to make submissions and, where appropriate, provide evidence. This common law rule[8] is spelled out

---

7   Sidney Lederman, Alan Bryant & Michelle Fuerst, *The Law of Evidence in Canada*, 4th ed (Toronto: LexisNexis, 2014) at 1334–35.

8   *Consolidated-Bathurst Packaging Ltd v International Woodworkers of America, Local 2-69* (1986), 56 OR (2d) 513 (CA) at 517, aff'd 68 DLR (4th) 524 (SCC) at 565; *Ellis-Don Ltd v Ontario (Labour Relations Board)* (1994), 16 OR (3d) 698 (Div Ct), leave to appeal to CA and SCC refused.

in section 142 of Quebec's AJA: "The Tribunal may not base its decision on grounds of law … if it has not first given the parties, other than parties who have waived their right to state their allegations, an opportunity to present their observations."

Orders and Remedies

A tribunal's decision often includes **orders** for specific measures to be taken to redress or compensate for the wrong at issue in the case, or to relieve or prevent recurrence of the situation that gave rise to the dispute. These orders are sometimes referred to as **remedies**.

Generally, the remedies that a tribunal may grant are limited to those specifically authorized by the tribunal's governing statute. If a remedy is not provided by statute, the tribunal probably cannot grant it. For example, in the absence of a statutory power, a tribunal may not award costs. (See the box feature "Examples of Remedies That Tribunals May Grant.")

Examples of Remedies That Tribunals May Grant

Remedies that tribunals are authorized to grant reflect the purpose of the proceeding.

In regulatory proceedings involving an application for approval of an activity, the remedy is usually to grant approval with or without terms or conditions, or to refuse approval.

In regulatory proceedings involving non-compliance with standards of service or performance, remedies may include

- a reduction of rates for services provided to the complainant,
- an order to upgrade the service for certain classes of consumers,
- an order to provide service in ways that are less intrusive on rights such as privacy or that are more user friendly, or
- an order to provide service in ways that conserve energy or protect the environment.

Some regulatory tribunals have authority to order payment of compensation to victims of incompetent or dishonest work, although this usually requires a separate proceeding in court.

In disciplinary proceedings, remedies may include

- a reprimand,
- a fine,
- suspension or revocation of an individual's licence,
- the imposition of conditions or limits on an individual's right to practise, or
- the imposition of requirements on an individual to upgrade his or her qualifications.

Tribunal decisions are usually forward-looking; that is, they result in orders for individuals or organizations to carry out or cease some activity in the future, rather than punish their past conduct or require compensation or restitution for harm caused. Even remedies such as suspension or revocation of a licence are intended primarily to protect the public and improve future conduct rather than to punish past wrongdoing. However, when a hearing involves charges of professional misconduct, the tribunal's governing statute usually provides that if the individual involved is found guilty, he or she may also be required to contribute to the cost of the investigation and prosecution.

Assistance in Making the Decision or Drafting the Reasons

As a general rule, the person who hears a case is the only person who may decide it. In other words, only the tribunal members who heard a case may make the decision. In some instances, a statute may provide authority for the tribunal as a whole to substitute its decision for that of the hearing panel—for example, when past tribunal decisions on an issue conflict and the tribunal wants to achieve consensus, or when a decision will raise a significant policy question for the tribunal. However, tribunals rarely make use of such provisions.[9]

The general rule does not prevent individuals associated with the tribunal, such as tribunal counsel or the tribunal's chair, from providing the adjudicator with limited assistance in reaching the decision or drafting the reasons for it. However, in providing such assistance, no one may put pressure on the adjudicator or hearing panel to decide for or against a particular party.

Adjudicators may ask for suggestions or advice, or obtain clerical assistance, from other tribunal members and tribunal staff. In addition, when tribunal counsel or outside counsel engaged by the tribunal has acted as a neutral adviser during the hearing, the adjudicator may also consult counsel at the decision-making stage. Again, it must be emphasized that the ultimate decision remains the adjudicator's alone; adjudicators may not delegate their decision-making authority to counsel.

When an adjudicator obtains legal advice about a case in progress, the question arises whether this advice must be shared with the parties. Some statutes specifically include this requirement.[10] Where the statute is silent, it now appears that the parties have no right to be informed. In *Pritchard v Ontario (Human Rights Commission)*,[11] the Supreme Court of Canada ruled that unless a statute specifies that a regulator must share the advice received from counsel with the parties, a regulator

---

9   See, for example, s 39(6) of a former version of Ontario's *Human Rights Code*, RSO 1990, c H.19, which provided that "the Tribunal may seek legal advice from an advisor independent of the parties and in such case the nature of the advice shall be made known to the parties in order that they may make submissions as to the law."

10   *Ibid.*

11   (2003), 63 OR (3d) 97 (CA), aff'd 2004 SCC 31, [2004] 1 SCR 809.

has no duty to do so. This ruling has been interpreted to apply to legal advice given to tribunals.

Requirement to Give Reasons

Until 1999, when the Supreme Court of Canada issued its decision in *Baker v Canada (Minister of Citizenship and Immigration)*,[12] it was not clear whether tribunals had a duty to give written reasons for their decisions. The ruling in *Baker* established that in cases where the outcome will seriously affect the rights or privileges of an individual or there is a statutory right of appeal, procedural fairness requires tribunals as well as other statutory decision-makers to give reasons for the decision.

Regardless of whether the law requires an adjudicator or other statutory decision-maker to give clear and understandable reasons for the decision that he or she has reached, there are several reasons why an adjudicator should do so:

- to help himself or herself clarify his or her thinking, which often results in a better decision;
- to demonstrate respect for the parties;
- to permit parties to make an informed decision whether they have grounds to appeal or seek judicial review of the decision;
- if there is an appeal or judicial review of the decision, to permit the court or reviewing body to assess the correctness or reasonableness of the decision;
- to enhance the likelihood that the decision will be upheld if appealed or judicially reviewed;
- to provide guidance to regulated communities and their advisers as to the appropriate standards of conduct;
- to provide certainty and predictability to individuals and businesses whose interests may be affected by the tribunal or agency's decisions; and
- to bolster the credibility of the tribunal or administrative agency.

> *The giving of reasons is required by the ordinary man's sense of justice. It is also a healthy discipline for all who exercise power over others.*
>
> HWR Wade, *Administrative Law*, 6th ed (London: Oxford University Press, 1988)

Section 13 of Quebec's AJA, section 51 of British Columbia's *Administrative Tribunals Act*,[13] and section 7 of Alberta's *Administrative Procedures and Jurisdiction Act*[14] require that when an authority exercises a statutory power in a way that adversely affects a person's rights, the authority must provide written decisions with

---

12   [1999] 2 SCR 817 [*Baker*].

13   SBC 2004, c 45.

14   RSA 2000, c A-3.

reasons. Under section 17(1) of the SPPA, a tribunal must give its final decision or order in writing, but it is required to provide written reasons only if a party requests them. This rule does not apply to other statutory decision-makers.

> *In my opinion, it is now appropriate to recognize that, in certain circumstances, the duty of procedural fairness will require the provision of a written explanation for a decision. The strong arguments demonstrating the advantages of written reasons suggest that, in cases such as this where the decision has important significance for the individual, when there is a statutory right of appeal, or in other circumstances, some form of reasons should be required. This requirement has been developing in the common law elsewhere.*
>
> L'Heureux-Dubé J in *Baker v Canada (Minister of Citizenship and Immigration)*, [1999] 2 SCR 817 at 848

Writing the Reasons

While the Supreme Court in *Baker* established a requirement that statutory decision-makers must give reasons for certain decisions, it did not specify what must be included in those reasons. Because the decision-making process is more rigorous for tribunals than for administrative agencies, it is likely that the reasons of tribunals should also be more detailed.

The sequence of stages in a tribunal's decision-making process was outlined at the beginning of this chapter. The tribunal's reasons should reflect the fact that the adjudicator has thought through what the decision should be by following that process. A person reading the decision should be able to understand how the tribunal reached its conclusions. Those conclusions should be supported by the facts found by the adjudicator and the application of laws and policies to those facts.

Although much more could be said about the art of decision writing, at a minimum, the reasons should set out

- the issue(s) addressed in the case;
- a summary of the evidence, indicating not only the evidence that the adjudicator relied on but also the evidence that the adjudicator rejected, and the reasons why he or she accepted or did not accept evidence;
- findings of fact based on the evidence considered relevant; and
- a statement of the law, and any applicable policies and guidelines, that determined the adjudicator's decision.

If a panel heard the case and the decision was not unanimous, the reasons may also include a statement of dissent, with reasons.

The reasons and the decision should be written in clear and concise language. There should be no confusion or uncertainty about either the ruling in the case or the facts and analysis on which it is based.

Tribunal members and officials should consider the audience for their decisions and should write their decisions, and the reasons, in a way that will meet the needs of that audience. The primary audience is the parties to the proceeding—most importantly, the person who has been denied what he or she is seeking. The decision should explain to that person as clearly, persuasively, and diplomatically as possible why he or she was unsuccessful. There are often other audiences to keep in mind, including the legal community, who look for guidance on how to prepare and present future cases; the decision-makers' colleagues and superiors; the media, if the situation is newsworthy; and politicians, academics, and the general public.

Release of the Decision

Dealing with Delay

Parties often complain about delays in the release of tribunal decisions. A person subject to an administrative action, whether before a tribunal or by a bureaucrat, has a common law right to completion of proceedings and receipt of a decision without undue delay. However, in practice, there is little that a party can do to speed resolution of the case short of applying to a court to order the tribunal to make a decision. Adjudicators will seldom take offence to a politely phrased inquiry several months after the hearing as to when the decision may be expected. In many cases, this will cause them to give higher priority to that decision. Most representatives are reluctant to make repeated inquiries because these may only serve to annoy the adjudicator. If the delay becomes unreasonable, a party can apply for judicial review, asking a court to order the tribunal to produce a decision or order a new hearing before a different panel. However, this is a costly way to obtain a remedy.

Some legislators have attempted to solve the problem of delay by including provisions in statutes that require a tribunal to produce a decision within a specified time after the conclusion of the hearing. Ontario's SPPA leaves the setting of deadlines to the individual tribunal, requiring only that tribunals establish guidelines for completing their proceedings (s. 16.2). Quebec's AJA goes further. Section 146 requires the tribunal to render its decision within three months unless the president of the tribunal has granted an extension to the hearing panel. If there is excessive delay, the president of the tribunal can withdraw the decision from a member of the panel. The decision of the other members will then be binding, as long as there is a quorum. If there is no quorum after one member is disqualified, the case must be heard again—presumably by a different panel.

Communication of the Decision

All parties in a proceeding have a right to receive the tribunal's decision. As discussed, in many cases, they also have a right to receive written reasons. Fairness requires that all parties receive the decision at the same time, or as close to the same time as methods of communication permit. Fairness also requires that the parties be informed of the final decision before it is made available to any other person (excluding tribunal members, staff, or counsel involved in the preparation of the decision).

In the most straightforward hearings, the adjudicator may deliver an oral decision at the end of the hearing, with all parties or their representatives present. In the case of a written decision, including a reserved decision, the procedure may be more complicated. For example, it may be necessary to fax or email the decision or to deliver it by courier, particularly if one or more parties live out of town. If a party does not have access to a fax machine or email account, the tribunal may deliver the decision to that party orally, by telephone, at the same time as the other parties are receiving it by fax or email.

If a reserved decision involves a matter of public interest, subject to cost considerations, the tribunal may choose to announce its decision at a public meeting. The tribunal will notify the parties and the public of the location, date, and time of the announcement. At the meeting, the adjudicators or other tribunal members, or their representatives, will deliver the decision, often reading it aloud along with the reasons for it. Copies of the decision will be made available to those in attendance.

CHAPTER SUMMARY

Tribunals and other agencies, as well as administrators, have a duty, when an application or request is made to them to grant a right or benefit or confer a privilege, to make a decision in a timely manner, to provide reasons for the decision, and to communicate the decision and reasons to the relevant parties.

For administrators and agencies other than tribunals, the process of making a decision may be fairly informal. A wide variety of information may be used and a variety of officials may be involved in making the decision. Although reasons must be provided, they need not describe in detail the considerations that went into making the decision.

In contrast, tribunals are restricted in the kinds of information they can take into account, and they must follow more restrictive procedures than administrators and other agencies in reaching their decision. Often, their reasons must be more detailed and must be communicated to all the parties, preferably at the same time.

When a tribunal consists of more than one member, the majority's decision is usually the tribunal's decision. When a tribunal has an even number of members, the statute governing the tribunal dictates what happens in the event of a tie. However, tribunal members generally work together to achieve consensus and try to avoid ties or dissenting decisions.

Tribunals generally must base their decisions on facts proven by the parties, but there are exceptions for information so obvious or well known that it needs no proof. Tribunals should not base their decisions on legal grounds or policy considerations that were not advanced by the parties without first advising the parties and hearing their views.

Only the adjudicators who heard the case and who were present throughout the entire proceedings are entitled to participate in a tribunal's decision. However, adjudicators can obtain limited assistance from tribunal staff and other members of their tribunal in reaching their decision and writing the reasons, provided that they make the decision themselves and do not delegate the decision-making to others or allow others to pressure them.

A well-reasoned decision is one that sets out the issues, evidence, facts, law, and applicable policies and guidelines, and that explains the reasons in clear, concise language. Decisions should also clearly state what remedy the tribunal is providing and what, if anything, a person is ordered to do.

An administrator, agency, or tribunal can only provide remedies or make orders that are permitted by statute. The remedies available to tribunals are generally forward-looking—that is, they usually require someone to do or refrain from doing something in the future. Generally, tribunals cannot punish someone for past behaviour, and in most cases they cannot order compensation or award costs, although there are exceptions.

When the decision is released, all parties should receive the decision at the same time or as close to the same time as possible, to avoid any appearance of bias.

KEY TERMS

dissent: a written statement of an adjudicator's disagreement with the decision of the majority of adjudicators on a court or tribunal panel, usually setting out the reasons why the adjudicator would have reached a different decision

order: a legally enforceable remedial measure issued by a government official, tribunal, or court; sometimes used to refer to the decision of a tribunal; *see also* remedy

remedy: a measure that an authority such as a government official, court, or tribunal can take to prevent, redress, punish, or compensate for a wrong, or to relieve, cure, or correct a condition

reserve: to reserve a decision is to hold back a decision following a proceeding to allow for further consideration of the matter by the court or tribunal and the release of the decision at a later time

CASES TO CONSIDER

Delay in Making a Decision

Ramsay v Toronto (City) Commissioners of Police (1988), 66 OR (2d) 99 (Div Ct)

FACTS: Ramsay was allegedly beaten by three police officers. He made a complaint, which led to an internal investigation. Ramsay then sued the police officers and named the chief of police as a defendant. The report of the public complaints officer was completed and forwarded to the chief of police. According to the governing legislation, the chief of police was required to review the report and decide whether any further action should be taken. The chief refused to review the report until the civil action concluded, arguing that the review would place him in a conflict of interest with his officers. Ramsay applied for judicial review seeking an order requiring the chief of police to review the final report and refer it to the complaints commission for a hearing.

ISSUE: Could the police chief refuse to review the report until the conclusion of the civil suit?

DECISION: The purpose of the complaints procedure was to provide inexpensive, quick, and effective action in dealing with complaints against police. The police chief's refusal to review the final report of the complaint until the conclusion of the civil suit would frustrate the purposes of the complaints process. The court ordered the chief to review the final report and make a decision. However, since the chief ultimately had discretion as to whether he would act on the report by referring it to the commission, the court could not order him to refer the complaint or to carry out any other action.

Scope of Tribunals' Right to Consult Before Deciding

Ellis-Don Ltd v Ontario (Labour Relations Board) (2001), 194 DLR (4th) 385 (SCC)

FACTS: A union filed a grievance with the Ontario Labour Relations Board alleging that the employer, Ellis-Don, had subcontracted work to non-union subcontractors contrary to the collective agreement. The first draft of the panel's decision dismissed the grievance. However, when the draft decision was reviewed by the full Board in accordance with its standard practice, the Board determined that, although the panel's reasoning was not incorrect, the reason for dismissing the grievance was not necessarily sufficient or determinative. The panel decided to change its ruling and uphold the grievance. Ellis-Don sought judicial review of the decision.

ISSUE: Are adjudicators allowed to change their decisions after consultation?

DECISION: Adjudicators may alter their draft decisions if certain rules are respected. The consultation must be restricted to questions of policy and law, and not touch on questions of fact. The decision-makers must arrive at their own conclusions. The change in the panel's decision in this case concerned a matter of law and policy. The panel did not appear to have changed its understanding or assessment of the facts, and therefore the change in decision did not breach any rules of natural justice.

Scope of Tribunals' Right to Consult Before Deciding

International Woodworkers of America, Local 2-69 v Consolidated-Bathurst Packaging Ltd, [1990] 1 SCR 282

FACTS: A three-member panel of the Ontario Labour Relations Board ruled that Consolidated-Bathurst had failed to bargain in good faith by not disclosing its plans to close a plant during negotiations for a collective agreement. During the panel's deliberations, the full Board met to discuss the policy implications of the panel's draft decision. The findings of fact made by the three-member panel were accepted by the full Board. Consolidated-Bathurst sought judicial review of the panel's decision.

ISSUE: Were the discussions by the full Board appropriate?

DECISION: Full board meetings are a practical means of calling upon the experience of all board members when deciding important matters of policy. This helps achieve consistency and coherence by avoiding the possibility that different panels will decide similar issues in a different way. The Board must be allowed to consider the broader policy implications of its decisions. Factual matters concerning the actual parties may only be examined and discussed by the panel members who heard the evidence, and the parties must be given a fair opportunity to present their case before the panel. The participation by other Board members at the full Board meeting did not amount to "participation" in the final decision. Discussions between panel members and other members who did not hear the evidence was not necessarily a problem because it did not prevent the panel members from making an independent decision. The full Board meeting was an important element of a legitimate process and did not constitute "participation" by members who had not heard the parties. The discussions were limited to policy matters, and the panel members ultimately come to their own decision based on the evidence they heard and the law and policy as discussed in the meeting of the full Board.

Scope of Tribunals' Right to Consult Before Deciding

Tremblay v Quebec (Commission des affaires sociales), [1992] 1 SCR 952

FACTS: Quebec refused to reimburse the cost of bandages to Tremblay, a social assistance recipient. Tremblay appealed this decision to the Commission des affaires sociales. The appeal was heard by two commissioners, and a draft decision favourable to Tremblay was signed by the commissioners and sent to the Commission's lawyer for verification and consultation, according to the established practice at the Commission. Since the lawyer was on vacation, the president of the Commission reviewed the draft. He then sent the two commissioners a memo in which he disagreed with their decision on a point of law. At the request of one commissioner, the issue was submitted to a "consensus table" for consideration. At that meeting, a majority of members disagreed with the draft decision and one of the commissioners changed her mind and wrote an opinion unfavourable to Tremblay. The commissioners were then divided on the question and the matter was submitted to the president of the Commission for resolution. He decided the matter as he had indicated in his earlier memo.

ISSUE: Did the process used by the Commission contravene the rules of natural justice?

DECISION: The consultative process adopted by the Commission was not consistent with the rules of natural justice. A consultative process that includes a meeting by the whole board, designed to promote consistency in decision-making, is generally acceptable. However, that process must not limit the freedom of the panel to decide according to its own conscience, and it must not create an appearance of bias in the minds of the parties. The "consensus tables" held by the Commission, although optional in theory, were in practice compulsory when legal counsel determined that the draft decision was contrary to previous decisions. The fact that the president of the Commission expressed his contrary opinion to the commissioners and then became the "tie-breaker" was also a breach of the rules of natural justice.

REVIEW QUESTIONS

1. If a panel of three adjudicators holds a hearing and one of them disagrees with the decision of the other two, how will the tribunal deal with this situation?

2. In making a decision, may an adjudicator take into account information other than evidence presented during the hearing?

3. If an adjudicator is considering relying on facts not presented at the hearing, what procedures should the adjudicator follow?

4. May adjudicators consult others when making decisions? If so, what kinds of assistance may they seek and from whom, and what are the limits on the participation of others in this process?

5. In what circumstances are tribunals and other agencies required to give reasons for their decisions?

6. What are the characteristics of a well-reasoned decision?

7. Do adjudicators have a duty to reach a decision within a reasonable time? Explain. What can parties do if there is excessive delay in the release of a decision?

8. How should a tribunal's decision be communicated to the parties?

9. Who is the "audience" for a tribunal decision? That is, with whom should the adjudicator try to communicate when writing the decision?

10. List the reasons why a tribunal adjudicator or other statutory decision-maker should give clear and understandable reasons for the decision that he or she has reached.

EXERCISES

1. Zoning bylaws regulate the use of land and the use, siting, and many other characteristics of buildings erected on land, including density, height, bulk, setbacks, and parking. 95 Apple Avenue is a house in a residential area of Winnipeg. The municipal zoning bylaw designates this property as "R2," one of six categories within the "single family residence" zone. In an R2 zone, residence is limited to a single family, whether owners or tenants, but up to 700 square feet may be a separate apartment as long as the rest of the house is occupied by no more than one family. The official plan for this area of Winnipeg designates the area in which this home is located as "residential." (An official plan is a formal set of principles and policies concerning the nature, pattern, extent, and scheduling of future growth and change within the municipality.)

    Planning legislation permits uses of land that vary from the requirements of the zoning bylaw, but only if they are minor changes. To apply for such a "minor variance," a homeowner must apply to the Committee of Adjustment, a municipal tribunal.

    The house at 95 Apple Avenue is sold after having been owned and occupied by a family of four for the past 20 years. The purchaser applies to the Committee of Adjustment for a minor variance to permit him to convert the space in the house into three self-contained rental apartments. He does not plan to live in the house himself.

    At the Committee hearing, five neighbours object. They are concerned that if a trend toward higher density develops, this may lead to traffic and parking problems. They also believe that as a result of a trend toward absentee landlords, quality of life in the neighbourhood will deteriorate, as tenants do not have as great a stake in maintaining the property as owners do and tend not to be as involved in the community.

    The Committee refuses the application. Its reasons consist of two handwritten notations: "does not comply with official plan" and "variation not minor."

    What is wrong with these reasons for the decision?

2. Regulations made pursuant to section 114(2) of the former *Immigration Act*, RSC 1985, c I-2 empower the minister of citizenship and immigration to facilitate the admission to Canada of a person where the minister is satisfied, owing to humanitarian and compassionate considerations, that admission should be facilitated or that an exemption from the regulations made under the Act requiring applicants for permanent resident status to apply from outside Canada should be granted.

    In the Supreme Court of Canada decision in *Baker v Canada (Minister of Citizenship and Immigration*, [1999] 2 SCR 817, the Court considered the reasonableness of an immigration officer's decision to refuse Mavis Baker's application for an exemption from the requirement to apply for permanent residence from outside Canada, based on humanitarian and compassionate considerations, pursuant to section 114(2) of the former *Immigration Act*.

    The immigration officer's written reasons for refusing Ms. Baker's application are set out in paragraph 5 of the Court's decision. Given the facts of this case set out at paragraphs 2 and 3 of the decision, how would you modify the reasons set out in paragraph 5 to turn them into a well-reasoned decision issued by a tribunal?

FACT SCENARIO

Your province's health insurance plan will reimburse individuals for the cost of drugs that have been approved for payment by the Ministry of Health but not for other drugs. A Ministry decision not to add a drug to the list of approved drugs may be appealed to a tribunal. A patient for whom a doctor has prescribed this drug or the pharmaceutical company that manufactures the drug has standing to launch such an appeal. In deciding whether to approve a drug, the Ministry is required to have regard to both effectiveness and cost.

You are a member of the tribunal that hears these appeals. You have just completed a lengthy hearing of an appeal from the Ministry's refusal to approve a new antidepressant drug. The manufacturer and several individuals who want access to this drug are parties. The hearing involved complex and contradictory scientific evidence about the drug's effectiveness.

The Ministry provided evidence that the drug is very costly to purchase and that reimbursement of patients for this drug would put a strain on the Ministry's budget. If the drug is funded, the Ministry will not have the money to fund certain other drugs. However, the tribunal also heard evidence that without reimbursement by the provincial drug insurance plan, many individuals will not be able to afford the drug.

The tribunal heard conflicting evidence about whether the drug is as effective in treating depression as other drugs that are less costly to buy. However, the experts called as witnesses by all parties agreed that the drug does not cause suicidal thoughts—a side effect that many other antidepressants cause or are believed to cause. The experts called as witnesses, however, disagreed as to how likely other drugs are to cause suicidal ideation.

The hearing also raised serious issues about the interpretation and application of the Ministry's policies, the fairness of the Ministry's decision-making process, the fairness of the tribunal's procedures, and the interpretation of a regulation under the statute that governs the provincial health insurance scheme.

You begin to write your decision.

a. You want to write a clear and well-reasoned decision that will be useful to the audience. Who would you expect to be the audience for this decision, and why?

b. Writing a clear and well-reasoned decision will take time—possibly several months. The case raises several factual, policy, procedural, and statutory interpretation issues. You believe it would be worthwhile to discuss the possible outcomes and reasons with the full tribunal, as this decision will affect how the tribunal handles similar issues in the future. However, it is not possible to convene a meeting of all the members of the tribunal in the next three months. The parties have all suggested that if they do not like the decision, they will appeal it to a court. However, some parties have argued at the hearing that lack of access to this drug will result in suicides, and therefore an early decision is needed.

Assume that releasing a decision now with reasons to follow at some future date is not an option. Do you take the time to produce a clear and well-reasoned decision even if this will take several months? Or do you attempt to produce a "quick and dirty" decision, in which you do not explain your reasoning in regard to each of the issues in much detail? Explain.

FURTHER READING

Edward Berry, *Writing Reasons: A Handbook for Judges* (Victoria, BC: E-M Press, 2007).

Lisa Braverman, *Administrative Tribunals: A Legal Handbook* (Aurora, Ont: Canada Law Book, 2001) ch 4.

Canadian Judicial Council, *Ethical Principles for Judges*, online: <http://www.cjc-ccm.gc.ca/cmslib/general/news_pub_judicialconduct_Principles_en.pdf>.

SR Ellis, Carole Trethewey & Frederika Rotter, "Tribunals—Reasons, and Reasons for Reasons" (1990–91) 4 Can J Admin L & Prac 105.

Robert Macaulay & James Sprague, *Practice and Procedure Before Administrative Tribunals* (Toronto: Carswell) (loose-leaf) ch 22.

RA Macdonald & David Lametti, "Reasons for Decision in Administrative Law" (1989–90) 3 Can J Admin L & Prac 123.

Louise Mailhot & James Carnwath, *Decision, Decisions—A Handbook for Judicial Writing* (Cowansville, Que: Yvon Blais, 1998).

Michael H Morris, "Administrative Decision-Makers and the Duty to Give Reasons: An Emerging Debate" (1997–98) 11 Can J Admin L & Prac 155.

Society of Ontario Adjudicators and Regulators, *Code of Professional and Ethical Responsibilities for Members of Adjudicative Tribunals—A Model*, online: <https://soar.on.ca/sites/soar.ca/files/code-of-conduct.pdf>.

Lee Stuesser, *An Advocacy Primer*, 3rd ed (Toronto: Carswell, 2005).

Selected Administrative Agencies: Their Mandates, Powers, and Procedures

LEARNING OUTCOMES

After reading this chapter, you will understand

- the mandates, practices, and procedures of certain regulatory agencies and tribunals;

- the regulatory frameworks into which these agencies and tribunals fit;

- where to find additional information about the powers and procedures of these tribunals.

The proliferation of these many tribunals means that there is an onus on lawyers to become familiar with them in order to preserve the rule of law, and also to assist their clients. Matters of procedure, that is how to present a case before these tribunals, are, in my view, more crucial than matters of substance. It is, in fact, the practical process by which a tribunal functions, which will enable a given applicant to achieve or not achieve that ultimate, desired result.

Franklin R Moskoff, ed, *Administrative Tribunals: A Practice Handbook for Legal Counsel* (Aurora, Ont: Canada Law Book, 1989) at x.

Before making an application to a department or agency or appearing before a tribunal for the first time, an advocate must become familiar with the statutes, regulations, and policies under which the agency and the tribunal operate; with the tribunal's rules of procedure and practice guidelines; and with decisions that the agency or the tribunal has made in cases that are similar to the case the advocate is preparing to present. Much of this information can be found on department, agency, and tribunal websites. In addition, advocates can often find other information about the agency or tribunal that may help them prepare and present a case effectively in the agency or tribunal's annual reports, in textbooks, and in papers (usually found in conference proceedings or law journals) written by tribunal members or agency staff and advocates familiar with the agency or tribunal.

The descriptions in this chapter of the operation of various stand-alone tribunals, as well as regulatory agencies and tribunals that operate in conjunction with each other, are constructed from such sources. You should consult these sources for any tribunal before which you are preparing to appear in order to develop an understanding of the tribunal's mandate, practices, and procedures that is clear enough to allow you to represent a party effectively and to avoid serious errors—for example, missing a limitation period, failing to serve a necessary party, or failing to bring forward evidence needed to support your case. The regulatory regimes described below have been selected because they are ones in which paralegals or law clerks frequently represent clients, with one exception—the Patented Medicine Prices Review Board. It is included to illustrate how wide the range of regulatory agencies is.

The Canadian Human Rights Commission and the Canadian Human Rights Tribunal

The *Canadian Human Rights Act*[1] implements government policy through a commission and a tribunal in relation to a single subject matter—the prevention of discrimination by the federal government and in industries regulated by the federal government, such as banks, telecommunications, railways, and airlines. (Businesses

---

1   RSC 1985, c H-6.

regulated by the provincial governments are subject to similar commissions and tribunals established by provincial governments.)

The Act accomplishes its goals by creating two separate agencies: the Canadian Human Rights Commission (CHRC—a regulatory agency) and the Canadian Human Rights Tribunal (CHRT). The creation of two separate agencies is an attempt to separate investigatory, prosecutorial, and adjudicative functions because these may conflict when carried out within a single agency.

The CHRC

The CHRC is part of a legislative scheme for identifying, preventing, and remedying discrimination based on sex, sexual orientation, marital status, family status, race, national or ethnic origin, colour, age, disability, conviction for an offence that has been pardoned, and religion. It is responsible for, among other things, maintaining close liaison with similar bodies in the provinces, for considering recommendations from public interest groups and any other bodies, and for developing programs for public education.

Although the CHRC and the CHRT are designed to be relatively independent of each other, Parliament has delegated a law-making function to the CHRC, which appears as a party before the CHRT. The *Canadian Human Rights Act* authorizes the Commission to issue "guidelines"—in reality, binding regulations—that dictate to the Tribunal how it must interpret the Act in specific classes of cases. The regulations must be consistent with the Act. For example, the Equal Wages Guidelines issued by the Commission tell the Tribunal how it must interpret certain provisions of the Act relating to pay equity.

When establishing policies to implement the Act, the CHRC issues a draft, then carries out a formal consultation with interested parties, such as human rights advocacy groups and industry associations. It then revises the draft policies, taking into account the feedback it has received, and issues a final version that is adopted as a binding regulation.

The CHRC also employs investigators, who investigate complaints of discrimination and report their findings to the CHRC. The Commission will attempt to negotiate a settlement between the complainant and the alleged discriminator. Most complaints are either dismissed by the CHRC for lack of evidence or resolved through mediation or conciliation by CHRC staff, rather than being referred to the CHRT for a hearing.

The CHRT

If the alleged discriminator denies the allegations and refuses to provide redress but the CRHC finds that there is sufficient evidence supporting the allegations to require further inquiry, it makes a request to the president of the CHRT to appoint a panel of tribunal members to hold a hearing and determine whether there has been discrimination and, if so, what sanctions should be imposed. A complainant cannot require the Tribunal to hear his or her case; the case must be referred to the Tribunal by the Commission.

As mentioned, the Tribunal is largely independent of the Commission and of the government. It has a different president from the Commission and different members. The CHRT has no policy-making function—its function is purely adjudicative. It conducts hearings into complaints that have been referred to it by the CHRC. It is empowered to find facts; to interpret and apply the law to the facts; and to award appropriate remedies, such as ordering federally regulated companies to pay women the same salaries as men for work of equal value.

The CHRT operates in a manner similar to a court. The parties present evidence, call and cross-examine witnesses, and make submissions on how the law should be applied to the facts.

The complainant and the subject of the complaint (the respondent) are parties to the hearing. They may represent themselves or be represented by lawyers or other representatives.

The CHRC is entitled to participate in the hearing as a party. If it chooses to do so—for example, where the case raises important issues of law or policy—its role is to represent the public interest rather than to represent the complainant. However, often, the public interest and the interests of the complainant coincide or overlap. The Commission's staff lawyers may call the Commission's investigators as witnesses to prove the allegations of discrimination, but they may put forward different arguments or request different remedies than the complainant.

Practice Tip: Determining Whether the Commission Supports the Complainant's Position

Sometimes [the public interest and the interests of the complainant] overlap. At other times, they do not. Therefore, if you are a complainant and if the Commission plans to participate in your hearing, it is important that you confer with the Commission's lawyer as soon as possible to determine whether you agree with the Commission's choice of evidence and remedy. If you do not, you may wish to exercise your option to retain your own lawyer or to represent yourself.

Canadian Human Rights Tribunal, *What Happens Next? A Guide to the Tribunal Process*, online: <http://chrt-tcdp.gc.ca/NS/pdf/layguide-e.pdf> at 4.

CHRT Procedures

When the Tribunal receives a referral from the Commission, its staff send a letter to the complainant, the respondent, and the Commission asking whether they agree to participate in a one-day mediation of the complaint by a Tribunal member. If all parties agree, the Tribunal contacts the parties to arrange a date for mediation, usually within a few weeks.

If mediation resolves the complaint, all parties sign a binding settlement agreement and the Tribunal closes the file.

If the complaint is not resolved, the Tribunal sets up three to four "case management" conference calls with the parties; the **case management conference** is similar to what other tribunals call a pre-hearing conference (PHC). During these calls, a Tribunal member will address matters such as whether the parties will be represented by a lawyer or other representative at the hearing, how many witnesses each party intends to call at the hearing and who they are, how many hours or days each party's evidence will take to present, whether parties want to raise any preliminary matters, what remedy each party is seeking, what deadlines should be established for filing particulars of the complaint and completing disclosure of evidence, whether an agreed statement of facts is possible, and where and when the parties would like the hearing to be held.

Matters that cannot be resolved through a case management conference—for example, a challenge to the Tribunal's jurisdiction—can be addressed by the party who wants to raise them or the party's representative by filing a motion with the Tribunal requesting a ruling and serving it on the other parties.

The Tribunal's disclosure rules require the parties to exchange in advance of the hearing all the documents they intend to put forward as evidence at the hearing as well as other documents that are relevant but will not be relied on. The parties must also exchange lists of documents that are relevant to the case but whose contents will not be disclosed because they are privileged; a summary of the topics they intend to address at the hearing, the facts they intend to prove, and the arguments they intend to present; and, where applicable, the remedy they seek, a statement of particulars, a list of their witnesses, witness statements, and written reports of expert witnesses. All this information, except copies of the documents in a party's possession that may be submitted as evidence, must also be filed with the Tribunal within the time limit determined at the case management conference. Documents that may be evidence will be filed when they are referred to by a witness and accepted as exhibits at the hearing.

The Tribunal's rules of procedure provide for service of documents by fax, email, ordinary or registered mail, courier, in person, or by a process server. Parties can prove service to the Tribunal by filing a letter from the person who served the document with the Tribunal confirming that the document was served, swearing before the Tribunal that the document was served, filing an affidavit of service, providing the Tribunal with a fax machine printout showing that transmission of the document to a particular fax number was completed, providing a registered mail receipt, or providing an admission or acknowledgment of service from the party who received the document.

Practice Tip: Consequences of Failure to Disclose Information

If you fail to disclose a document, you may not be allowed to introduce it into evidence at the hearing. Similarly, you may not be permitted to examine witnesses or raise legal issues (including remedy sought) that you have failed to identify in advance. The Tribunal will allow a party to rely on evidence not disclosed before the hearing only in exceptional circumstances. You also have an ongoing duty to disclose any new relevant document as soon as it comes into your possession and any new witness or legal issue as soon as it comes to your attention.

Canadian Human Rights Tribunal, *What Happens Next? A Guide to the Tribunal Process*, online: <http://chrt-tcdp.gc.ca/NS/pdf/layguide-e.pdf> at 18.

Once the hearing is scheduled, Tribunal staff send all parties a notice of hearing, usually well before the hearing date. About one month before the hearing, the

Tribunal sends all parties a letter telling them how many copies of each document they must bring to the hearing.

At the hearing, the issues may be whether the respondent actually did what the complainant claims he or she did; if the act occurred, whether it was discriminatory; whether the complainant suffered any harm; and what is the appropriate remedy. The evidence usually consists of documents and testimony of witnesses, particularly those who witnessed the events in issue.

' At the end of the hearing, the Tribunal usually reserves its decision, which it attempts to complete within four months (as set out in the Tribunal's practice note regarding timeliness of hearings and decisions). A party who is dissatisfied with the decision may make an application for judicial review of the decision to the Federal Court within 30 days of the release of the decision.

Information about the mandate and procedures of the CHRC, including the text of memoranda of understanding signed by the Commission and major federal employers, such as Bell Canada and Canadian Pacific Railway, is found on the Commission's website at <http://www.chrc-ccdp.ca>. The website of the CHRT at <http://www.chrt-tcdp.gc.ca> contains the full text of the *Canadian Human Rights Act*; a description of the Tribunal's jurisdiction and a guide to its process; a list of cases most often referred to in hearings before the Tribunal; the Tribunal's rules of procedure, practice notes, and mediation procedures; and the full text of all the Tribunal's decisions, searchable by key word.

The Ontario Human Rights Commission and the Human Rights Tribunal of Ontario

The Ontario Human Rights Commission (OHRC) and the Human Rights Tribunal of Ontario (HRTO) are jointly responsible for enforcing the Ontario *Human Rights Code*.[2] The third important player in this scheme is the Human Rights Legal Support Centre, which provides legal assistance to people who believe they have experienced discrimination contrary to the Ontario *Human Rights Code*.

The Ontario Human Rights Code and the Role of the OHRC

The Code guarantees every person in Ontario the right to equal treatment and equal opportunities in five "social areas": employment; housing; goods, services, and facilities; contracts; and membership in trade and vocational associations such as unions. It does not apply to federal government departments and agencies or businesses that are federally regulated, such as banks, airlines, television and radio stations, and telephone companies. However, the OHRC and the HRTO have jurisdiction over the provincial government, municipalities, individuals, and any business or other organization that is provincially regulated.

On June 30, 2008, extensive amendments to the *Human Rights Code* came into effect that dramatically changed the human rights system in Ontario. Before that,

---

2 RSO 1990, c H.19.

the OHRC was responsible for investigating complaints of discrimination and trying to resolve them. If a complaint was not resolved through discussions and mediation services provided by the Commission, the Commission could decide to refer the case to the HRTO for adjudication or it could refuse to refer the case if it felt the case did not warrant a hearing. If the Commission referred a case to the Tribunal, the Commission usually presented the complainant's case to the Tribunal (not formally representing the complainant, but rather acting in the public interest to address the issues raised by the applicant). In reality, the Commission referred only a small percentage of the complaints to the Tribunal. If it did not refer a case, the complainant had no access to a tribunal unless he or she could convince a court that the Commission had acted unfairly.

The system described above led to complaints that investigations took too long and that the Commission sometimes vetoed hearings in meritorious cases. Several studies recommended reforms, and as a result of these the Code was revised.

Under the revised Code, the Commission no longer investigates complaints and is no longer the "gatekeeper" to the Tribunal. Instead, it plays a stronger role in preventing discrimination and in promoting and advancing human rights. The OHRC has an increased role in promoting a culture of human rights in the province by taking proactive measures to prevent discrimination through public education, policy development, research, and analysis. The Commission may also

- conduct public inquiries (on its own initiative or when a matter is referred to it by the Tribunal);
- initiate its own applications to the Tribunal (for example, on behalf of an individual who alleges that he or she was harmed and the case raises important issues);
- intervene in proceedings at the Tribunal (for example, where the Commission is concerned that the applicant and respondent may not address a policy issued by the Commission in a way that will provide guidance on how one of the grounds for discrimination listed in the Act should be interpreted); and
- where the Commission feels that a decision of the Tribunal is not consistent with the Commission's policies, apply to the Tribunal to state a case to the Divisional Court, requesting the court's opinion as to whether the Tribunal's decision complies with the Code.

The Commission also reviews Ontario statutes, regulations, and municipal bylaws, as well as provincial and municipal programs and policies, to ensure that they are consistent with the intent of the Code.

HRTO Procedures

The HRTO is a member of the Social Justice Tribunals cluster, which brings together the HRTO and seven other tribunals: the Social Benefits Tribunal (discussed later in this chapter), the Custody Review Board, the Child and Family Services Review Board, the Criminal Injuries Compensation Board, the Landlord and Tenant Board, and the Special Education Tribunals (English and French).

Applications and Responses

Under the revised Code, an individual who believes he or she has experienced discrimination or harassment may make an application directly to the HRTO. An organization such as a union may also file an application on behalf of an individual claiming discrimination or harassment with that individual's consent. The Commission may also make an application, with or without the allegedly harmed individual's consent, if it believes that doing so is in the public interest (for example, where there have been media reports about an employer sexually harassing employees but the affected employees have been unwilling to pursue their rights).

An application must be filed within one year of the occurrence of the alleged incident or, if there was a series of incidents, within one year of the last alleged incident. However, if the Tribunal is satisfied that a delay in filing was incurred in good faith and no one will be harmed by the delay, the Tribunal may extend the time for making an application beyond the one-year period.

The application must be made on forms approved by the Tribunal. Application forms are available on the Tribunal's website at <http://www.sjto.gov.on.ca/hrto>. In addition to the main application form, applicants are required to fill out supplementary forms eliciting further details relating to the social area to which their application applies—for example, there is a supplementary form for a housing complaint, an employment complaint, a services complaint, a contract complaint, or a complaint about discrimination by a union or other vocational association.

The application forms require the complainant to provide personal information and information about the respondent, including contact information for the applicant and the respondent, the ground or grounds of discrimination, the area of discrimination, facts that support the application (what happened, where and when it happened, and who was involved), the effect of the conduct on the complainant, the remedy sought, whether mediation is desired, whether there are any ongoing or completed legal proceedings relating to the same events, a list of documents that support the application, and a confidential list of witnesses who have information that will support the application as well as a description of their evidence.

The Human Rights Legal Support Centre

The publicly funded Human Rights Legal Support Centre, established under the Ontario *Human Rights Code*, provides assistance to individuals who believe they have experienced discrimination contrary to the Code at various stages of the complaint process.

The Centre provides a broad range of services, including assisting individuals with filling out applications and assembling the documentation in support of an application, assisting in mediation, providing representation at the hearing, and helping to enforce tribunal orders by applying to the Superior Court for an order requiring compliance with the tribunal's order.

Anyone who feels he or she has been the victim of discrimination or harassment in violation of the Code may apply for assistance from the Centre. There are no needs-based eligibility criteria.

The Centre's website at <http://www.hrlsc.on.ca> contains information about how to contact and obtain assistance from the Centre.

When the Tribunal has reviewed the application and determined that it is complete, and has determined that it has jurisdiction, the Tribunal sends a copy of the application (not including the witness list or the applicant's contact information) and a response form to the respondent. The respondent is asked to complete and return the response form to the Tribunal within 35 days; the Tribunal shares the response with the applicant. If the respondent has raised any new matters in his or her response, the Tribunal gives the applicant an opportunity to file a reply to the response.

Practice Tip: Duty to Provide a Complete Response

As with applicants, respondents must take care to provide a reasonably complete description of facts and issues and a reasonably complete list of documents and witnesses with their response. The Tribunal may refuse to allow a respondent to present evidence or make submissions with respect to any fact or issue that was not raised in the response unless it is satisfied that there would be no substantial prejudice or undue delay to the proceedings.

Mary Cornish, Fay Faraday & Jo-Anne Pickel, *Enforcing Human Rights in Ontario* (Aurora, Ont: Canada Law Book, 2009) at 97.

The HRTO's rules of procedure provide for filing of applications, responses, and other documents with the Tribunal by fax, email, hand delivery, courier, regular mail, registered mail, certified mail, or in any other manner approved by the Tribunal. The party filing a document is usually required to deliver it to all the parties as well, and to verify that they have delivered it by filing a "statement of delivery" setting out how and when the party delivered the document.

Pre-Hearing Procedures

Before holding a hearing, the HRTO often follows procedures similar to the PHCs held by other tribunals. Within 45 days of receiving the respondent's response to the application, the Tribunal convenes a **case conference** with all the parties and affected persons to discuss the conduct of the proceedings. As a result of this conference, or later in the proceedings, the Tribunal may issue a **case assessment direction**. This direction may address any matter that the Tribunal feels will facilitate the fair and expeditious resolution of the case—for example, it may identify the main issues, facts on which the parties agree, procedural issues that need to be decided before the hearing, and any witnesses who should attend the hearing.

Applicants who require assistance filling out the forms as well as other help during the tribunal process can contact the Human Rights Legal Support Centre; community legal clinics; and community organizations such as the Centre for Equality Rights in Accommodation, which focuses on discrimination in housing.

The Tribunal will usually attempt to help the parties settle the claim. The application and response forms ask the parties to check a box indicating whether they would like to participate in mediation. Where both parties indicate a willingness to participate, the Tribunal attempts to schedule a mediation session within six months of a completed application having been accepted for processing.

Although mediation is voluntary, the Tribunal may contact the parties to discuss the possibility of mediation even when the parties have not indicated a willingness to participate. If the parties agree to participate, the Tribunal sends them a notice of mediation setting out a date, time, and location for the mediation. Mediation is conducted by a tribunal member, who can make any signed agreement arising out of the mediation into a binding order if the parties consent.

Hearings

When mediation has been declined or is unsuccessful, the HRTO will hold a hearing to decide whether discrimination or harassment took place, and, if so, to determine the appropriate remedy. If mediation has taken place, a different member of the Tribunal than the member who conducted the mediation will be assigned to conduct the hearing.

The Tribunal uses the material filed with it to estimate how many days the hearing will take. It then sends all the parties a confirmation of hearing, which includes the dates for the hearing (usually four to five months later), the starting time, and the location.

Within 21 days of a confirmation of hearing being sent out, the parties must exchange copies of all "arguably relevant" documents in their possession except those for which privilege is claimed. In addition, no less than 45 days before the hearing, the parties must exchange a list of their witnesses, witnesses' "will say" statements, a list of documents on which the parties intend to rely at the hearing, and a statement of any additional facts on which they intend to rely. This material must also be filed with the Tribunal.

If a party is not available on the date set out in the confirmation of hearing, it must contact the tribunal **registrar** within five days and provide five other dates when it is available. The Tribunal will contact the other parties to arrange a different date. The Tribunal aims to complete its hearings within 22 weeks of the date on which it sends out the confirmation of hearing.

The parties in a hearing are always the applicant (the person who allegedly suffered the discrimination, an organization applying on that person's behalf, or the Commission) and the respondent. Where the applicant is an organization that has applied on behalf of someone who allegedly has suffered discrimination, the latter is also a party. The Tribunal may add any other person as a party, including the Commission.

Where the Commission is not a party, it may apply to be an intervenor. The Tribunal may also grant intervenor status to any other individual or organization that files a request to intervene and serves it on all the other parties. A request to intervene must answer several questions, including

- what issue or issues the person wishes to address;
- the person's interest and expertise in relation to that issue;
- the person's position, if any, on the issue; and
- any facts on which the person will rely.

Before deciding whether to grant an individual intervenor status, the Tribunal gives the other parties an opportunity to support or oppose the application.

Parties may represent themselves before the HRTO, or retain a lawyer or a paralegal licensed by the Law Society of Upper Canada (LSUC) to represent them. They may also be represented by certain individuals who are exempt from the Law Society's licensing requirements, such as unpaid friends or family members, trade union employees or volunteers, employees of the Human Rights Legal Support Centre, and employees or representatives of legal aid clinics. The Tribunal has published a policy setting out its expectations for appropriate conduct of representatives.

The provisions of the *Statutory Powers Procedure Act*[3] (SPPA) apply to hearings. However, section 42 of the Code states that if the SPPA requirements conflict with the Tribunal's rules of procedure, the rules prevail. Section 41 permits the Tribunal to adopt practices and procedures that will facilitate fair, just, and expeditious resolution of cases, including "alternatives to traditional adjudicative or adversarial procedures" (such as mediation).

Orders, Reconsideration, and Judicial Review

Following the hearing, the Tribunal will decide whether the alleged conduct took place, whether it amounted to discrimination or harassment, and what remedy is appropriate.

The orders that the Tribunal can make include financial compensation for losses such as lost wages and benefits, increased rent, and moving expenses; damages for loss of dignity and hurt feelings; reinstatement in a job; work modification to accommodate a disability; and orders to prevent further human rights violations, such as a requirement to apologize for discriminatory conduct, change hiring practices, or provide staff with human rights training.

On its own initiative or at the request of a party, the Tribunal may reconsider its decision under very limited circumstances—for example, where there are new facts or evidence that might have changed the decision but were not available earlier, where the objecting party was entitled to but did not receive notice of the hearing, or where the decision conflicts with other tribunal decisions and raises a matter of public interest.

There is no appeal from the Tribunal's decisions. Like all tribunals, the HRTO is subject to judicial review, but the Code states that a court may not reverse the Tribunal's decision unless it is patently unreasonable. (Because this is a statutory standard of review, it applies despite the ruling of the Supreme Court in *Dunsmuir* that the only standards of review at common law are reasonableness *simpliciter* and correctness; see the discussion of standard of review in Chapter 16.)

The OHRC's website at <http://www.ohrc.on.ca> contains information about the Commission's mandate and how to file an application with the Tribunal. The HRTO's website at <http://www.sjto.gov.on.ca/hrto> contains a link to the *Ontario Human Rights Code*. CanLII also has a link for the Code: <http://www.canlii.org/en/on/

---

3 RSO 1990, c S.22.

laws/stat/rso-1990-c-h19/latest/rso-1990-c-h19.html> and for the regulation made under the code: <http://www.canlii.org/en/on/laws/regu/o-reg-290-98/latest/o-reg -290-98.html>. The Tribunal's rules of procedure, practice directions, forms, users' guides, and FAQs can be found on the website. The Tribunal's decisions can also be accessed online free of charge from CanLII, for a fee or by subscription from the *Canadian Human Rights Reporter* and on Quicklaw, and in hard copy from the Ontario Workplace Tribunals Library.

The Financial Services Commission of Ontario

The Financial Services Commission of Ontario (FSCO) is an arm's-length agency of the Ontario Ministry of Finance. It carries out several functions previously performed by the Ontario Insurance Commission, the Pension Commission of Ontario, and the Deposit Institutions Division of the Ministry of Finance. FSCO administers 11 statutes regulating automobile insurers, co-operatives, credit unions, loan and trust companies, mortgage brokers, and pension plans. In these sectors, FSCO licenses operators, monitors their financial health, investigates complaints, and enforces compliance with standards. In some cases, such as motor vehicle accident benefits claims, FSCO also operates as a tribunal, deciding disputes between businesses and their clients.

Statutory Accident Benefits Schedule Claims

Ontario's *Statutory Accident Benefits Schedule*[4] (SABS) is a regulation under the *Insurance Act*[5] that establishes the benefits that a person injured in a motor vehicle accident and others affected by the injury can claim from an automobile insurance company; these benefits may be available regardless of whose fault the accident was.

Under the SABS, both a person injured in a motor vehicle accident and a person suffering certain losses because a friend or relative was injured in a motor vehicle accident (see below) may apply to the injured person's automobile insurance company to receive certain benefits. The benefits available to the injured person may include medical, hospital, and nursing care; chiropractic, psychological, occupational therapy, and physiotherapy services; medication, prescription eyeglasses, dentures, and other dental devices; and medical devices such as wheelchairs, prostheses, and orthotics. Rehabilitation benefits are also available, including measures to reduce or eliminate the effects of any disability. In addition, the SABS will sometimes provide coverage for home renovations, vehicle modifications, and attendant care required as a result of an accident, and compensation for lost income.

---

4 O Reg 403/96.

5 RSO 1990, c I.8.

Certain individuals who are affected by the insured individual's injury may also apply to the insurer for benefits under the SABS. For example, if the injured person was an unpaid caregiver or provided housekeeping and home maintenance to a disabled family member, the family member may claim benefits for loss of these services. If the accident results in the insured person's death, family members may claim death and funeral benefits.

Under the SABS, a claimant must notify the insurer of his or her intention to make a claim within 7 days of the accident and must complete an application for benefits within 30 days of receiving an application form from the insurer (unless there is a reasonable explanation for the delay, such as an inability to apply because of the severity of the injuries).

To claim benefits, a claimant must submit an application to the insurer together with medical evidence and evidence of, among other things, loss of income. The forms to be filled out and the information to be provided depend on the benefits claimed, but they may include an application for accident benefits, the employer's confirmation of the claimant's income before the accident, the claimant's declaration of his or her income since the accident, a disability certificate, the claimant's permission to allow doctors to disclose health information to the insurer on request, an assessment by a qualified health practitioner of attendant care needs if such care will be required, and a treatment plan if the claimant is requesting payment for ongoing medical treatment. Where the accident results in the death of the insured person, a family member must submit a death and funeral benefits application.

Practice Tip: Don't Wait to Send in Forms Until All Information Is Available

The [Accident Benefit] Application contains a number of forms, which require completion by a number of sources. The forms should be completed and sent in as they are received. Often, clients will wait until they receive all of the forms before sending anything [but completed forms should be submitted to the insurer] as quickly as possible. This will allow the insurer to get the application process underway, and hopefully avoid any unnecessary delays. Often, when we are assisting the client with completing the forms, we will forward the Accident Benefit Application OCF-1 to the insurer and advise that the remainder of the forms have been provided to the insured's doctor, employer, etc., and that these outstanding forms will be provided to the insurer as soon as possible.

Raymond Watt, "Best Practices in Handling Accident Benefit Claims" in *Best Practices for Paralegals—An Introduction to Accident Benefits Cases at FSCO* (Donald Lamont Learning Centre, The Law Society of Upper Canada, 4 November 2008) (Toronto: Law Society of Upper Canada, 2008) at 3–50.

When the injured person or the individual who claims to be deprived of the injured person's services makes a claim to the insurer, an adjuster representing the insurance company investigates whether the claim is legitimate, determines whether the benefits sought are ones that are available under the statutory benefits scheme, and decides what benefits are payable.

Before deciding whether to accept a claim, the insurer has a right to question the claimant under oath about his or her injuries. The insurance company also may require the claimant to submit to an independent medical examination conducted by a health care practitioner chosen by the insurer. The claimant has a similar right to a medical assessment by a doctor of his or her choice, at the insurance company's expense, provided that he or she submits the request for an assessment to the insurer in advance.

A benefit claimed may be refused for various reasons. For example, the benefit claimed may be covered by some other insurance policy; the claim may not have been submitted within the prescribed time limit; or the adjuster may believe that the injury is less serious than claimed, that it was not caused by the accident, or that the treatment requested is unnecessary or would be ineffective.

Appeals

When an insurance company refuses to provide benefits for losses arising from motor vehicle accidents under the SABS, the claimant can appeal the refusal. As of July 2015, this appeal is to FSCO, which functions as a tribunal as well as a regulator. However, to increase the separation between these functions, the Ontario Government has decided to transfer these appeals, starting in April 2016, to a stand-alone tribunal, the Licence Appeal Tribunal (LAT). This change was mandated in the *Fighting Fraud and Reducing Automobile Insurance Rates Act*.[6]

The LAT is an independent adjudicative tribunal created under the *Licence Appeal Tribunal Act, 1999*[7] to hear appeals and render decisions respecting compensation claims and licensing activities regulated by various administrative agencies. LAT is a member of the Safety, Licensing Appeals and Standards Tribunals of Ontario "cluster" (SLASTO).

The information below describes the process in effect as of July 2015.

Before a claimant may appeal to a FSCO **arbitrator**, the claimant must apply to FSCO's Dispute Resolution Services branch to mediate the dispute; a claimant may not apply for a hearing before a FSCO arbitrator without first attempting mediation. The application for mediation must be made within two years of the refusal of the claim by the insurance adjuster.

If mediation is unsuccessful, the claimant has the choice of applying to FSCO for arbitration or suing in court. **Arbitration** is an adjudication in which one or more neutral third parties makes a binding decision after holding a hearing. (Although the term usually refers to an adjudication in which the adjudicator is chosen by the parties, FSCO arbitrators are assigned by FSCO rather than selected by the parties.)

The claimant must apply to FSCO or a court the later of two years after the insurance company's refusal or 90 days after the mediator issues his or her report. The

---

6 SO 2014, c 9.

7 SO 1999, c 12, Schedule G.

claimant initiates an arbitration by filing an application for arbitration with FSCO. FSCO will serve the application on the insurer within 20 days of receiving it.

FSCO will usually hold a PHC, which it calls a pre-hearing discussion, within six to eight weeks after a request for arbitration or neutral evaluation has been filed. The PHC procedures are set out in FSCO's rules (available on its website at <http://www.fsco.gov.on.ca/en/drs/DRP-Code/Pages/sectiona-part3.aspx#prehearingdiscussion>). As discussed, PHCs aim to explore possible settlement of issues; identify and clarify issues; determine facts or evidence that may be agreed upon; identify witnesses to be called at the hearing; estimate the length of the hearing; and determine the time, date, and location of the hearing. Claimants can represent themselves at PHCs or be represented by a lawyer or licensed paralegal.

The Role of Paralegals in SABS proceedings at FSCO

Paralegals may perform a variety of services for motor vehicle accident benefits claimants, including advising claimants about their rights under the SABS, assisting in completing application forms, negotiating with an insurance adjuster, participating in dispute resolution proceedings at FSCO, and representing claimants at FSCO arbitration hearings. To participate in FSCO proceedings, paralegals must be licensed by the LSUC. They must register with FSCO before representing a claimant, and must pass a criminal record check, adhere to the LSUC's *Paralegal Rules of Conduct* as well as the Code of Conduct for Statutory Accident Benefit Representatives established by FSCO, (found at <http://www.fsco.gov.on.ca/en/auto/auto-bulletins/2003/Documents/a-06_03-1.pdf>), and carry errors and omissions liability insurance of $1 million. Paralegals may not charge a contingency fee, or accept or pay referral fees.

Hearings

The arbitration hearing usually begins within six months of the date of the PHC.

The evidence submitted by the parties will usually include assessments by professionals of the nature and extent of the injuries and the treatment and support needed as a result of the accident, and opinions regarding whether the claimant's injuries were caused by the accident or were pre-existing conditions. Documents relating to these issues may include ambulance call reports, hospital records, the family doctor's clinical notes and records, workers' compensation files, and assessment reports. Evidence in relation to income loss claims may include information from the claimant's employment file, and income tax returns filed for several years before and after the accident. The insurer may also present the evidence of investigators who have conducted surveillance to determine whether claims of disability are exaggerated (for example, where a claimant says she is bedridden but is observed engaging in physical activities inconsistent with this claim).

FSCO arbitrators may uphold or reject the claim in whole or in part. Where the arbitrator upholds a claim, he or she may order the insurer to provide the requested benefits to the claimant. However, FSCO arbitrators also have the authority to award additional monetary compensation where they find that an insurer unreasonably withheld or delayed a benefit. FSCO arbitrators cannot award benefits that are expected to be required in the future but are not yet required. As a result, a single accident may result in several claims and hearings as an injured person becomes eligible for additional benefits with the passage of time.

The Ontario Workplace Safety and Insurance Board and the Workplace Safety and Insurance Appeals Tribunal

The Ontario Workplace Safety and Insurance Board (WSIB) and the Workplace Safety and Insurance Appeals Tribunal (WSIAT) are two agencies established under Ontario's *Workplace Safety and Insurance Act, 1997*.[8] The Act creates a regime that is intended to provide a regular (although reduced) income to workers who have been injured in the workplace or who suffer from a work-related illness, and to provide such workers with medical and other forms of treatment (known as "rehabilitation services") that will help them recover from their illness or injury and return to work.

This benefits system (better known by its former name—"workers' compensation") operates as an insurance scheme. The WSIB, which acts both as a regulatory agency with a public education component and as a tribunal, is funded by premiums paid by employers. Like property insurance or car insurance premiums, these premiums vary according to the risk level in each industry and the safety record of the individual company.

WSIB Claims

When a worker makes a claim for income support or rehabilitation services, WSIB staff investigate the validity of the claim and make an initial decision whether to allow or deny it. If assistance is denied, the worker can request a review by different agency staff. Conversely, employers have the right to challenge the claim on the basis that the injury or illness is minimal or non-existent, or resulted from an activity or exposure that is unrelated to the worker's employment (for example, a pre-existing condition). Employers can contest claims because successful claims may raise an employer's insurance rate.

When a worker suffers a work-related accident or illness, employers have three days to file a Form 7, the employer's report of injury or disease, with the WSIB. The form documents the employer's account of the type of accident or illness and its onset, the treatment received by the worker, work time lost, and wage information. If the employer anticipates a WSIB claim and intends to dispute the claim, the employer will include in this form information that will contradict the position the worker is expected to take.

---

8 SO 1997, c 16, Schedule A.

To make a claim, injured workers must file a Form 6 within six months. This form addresses the same information as Form 7, but from the worker's perspective. Both forms can be found on the WSIB's website at <http://www.wsib.on.ca>. Electronic forms (eForm 6 and eForm 7) can be submitted electronically.

The WSIB does not hold formal hearings unless a formal hearing is requested during the appeal process. Rather, the WSIB usually collects medical information from the worker's doctors and may have its own doctors examine the worker. It communicates with the employer and receives workplace documentation from the employer, as well as written submissions and documentation from both the worker and the employer. In addition, the WSIB may obtain information about other insurance or government benefits that may be available to the worker. The WSIB may ask its investigators to make inquiries, question witnesses and others, undertake tasks such as examining the workplace where the worker was allegedly injured, and report the results to the WSIB staff member carrying out the review.

Internal Appeals and Requests for Reconsideration

Within the WSIB, an appeal of the initial WSIB decision is available to the WSIB's Appeals Services Division. An appeal to an appeals resolution officer (ARO) in the Appeals Services Division is launched by filing a notice of appeal. The Appeals Services Division will then send the appellant an objection form on which the appellant should explain why he or she believes the decision is wrong or incomplete and indicate the remedy desired.

At the same time as appealing to the Appeals Services Division, an unsuccessful applicant may request the decision-maker to reconsider his or her decision, a step that may result in a more timely resolution than proceeding with the appeal to the Appeals Services Division. However, if a reconsideration request is unsuccessful, the ARO will then decide the case, usually without a formal hearing, by reading the material filed (such as medical reports) and consulting with the worker and employer. Formal hearings are generally held only where there are factual disputes, including credibility issues.

Since the WSIB and the WSIAT deal with issues similar to FSCO, the evidence presented to them is often similar to the evidence presented to FSCO—for example, medical history; diagnoses of the causes of illness and injury, and prognoses for recovery; employment history; vocational assessments; rehabilitation plans; and investigators' reports.

Issues that are adjudicated in both the internal appeal process within the WSIB and the appeal of the WSIB's final decision to the WSIAT may include

- the worker's initial entitlement to benefits (that is, whether the injury or illness is work related);
- the areas of injury;
- the duration of benefits (which may be reduced or eliminated in some circumstances);
- whether compensation should be paid for non-economic loss (for example, for permanent impairment);

- whether there has been a loss of earnings, and, if so, whether it is likely to be permanent or temporary (future economic loss);
- the availability of benefits from other sources, especially insurance and government programs; and
- whether the worker is capable of returning to work, especially if offered work that is modified to accommodate his or her disabilities.

WSIAT Appeals

Once all the decision-making levels within the WSIB have been exhausted, the worker or the employer may appeal the WSIB's decision to the WSIAT. In most cases, the worker has six months to appeal a WSIB refusal, but some limitation periods are shorter. For example, a WSIB decision that a worker must attend a course to upgrade his or her skills rather than simply continue to receive financial benefits must be appealed within 30 days. Missing a time limit may result in the loss of the right to appeal.

Practice Tip: Prepare a Chronology of Events

If the file is over 100 pages, do a time line of events. How is one ever to remember what is going on in a claim when you next pick up the file to work on if you don't have some facts (including medical findings) in sequential order to place the claim back into its litigation context.

Richard Fink, "The Workers' Compensation Procedure—The Workers' Perspective" in Law Society of Upper Canada, *Best Practices for Paralegals Before the WSIB and WSIAT* (Donald Lamont Learning Centre, The Law Society of Upper Canada, 5 December 2008) (Toronto: Law Society of Upper Canada, 2008) at 1–3.

An appeal to the WSIAT is launched by filing a notice of appeal. When the appellant is ready for the Tribunal to schedule a hearing, the appellant files a confirmation of appeal. (For example, an appellant may have several different benefits claims at different stages of consideration; an appeal is not ready for a hearing by the WSIAT if there are still related matters unresolved at the WSIB level.)

Although employers and injured workers have standing to participate in proceedings before both the WSIB and the WSIAT, often either the employer or the worker will not appear because their interests will not be affected by the decision. For example, workers rarely participate in an employer's appeal related to cost relief under the WSIB's second injury and enhancement fund (SIEF) because cost relief for the employer would have no effect on the benefits to which the worker is entitled.

Although the WSIAT holds court-like hearings, it is not bound by the *Statutory Powers Procedure Act*[9] (SPPA), and its hearings have both inquisitorial and adversarial aspects. That is, the worker and the employer are parties to the appeal and may present evidence and cross-examine witnesses, but some of the evidence may be collected and presented by WSIAT staff. Another reason that the process may

---

9 *Supra* note 3.

have an inquisitorial rather than adversarial component is that there is often only one party. When a worker claims entitlement that has been refused by the WSIB, the employer often does not participate. In some cases, the employer is no longer in business. Although the WSIB made the decision that is being appealed, the WSIB is rarely a party before the WSIAT, although it has the right to appear.

WSIAT appeal hearings typically last a half day. If a worker notifies the WSIAT that he or she does not speak English well, the WSIAT will provide a professional translator at no cost to the party.

The WSIAT is largely independent of the WSIB, but the *Workplace Safety and Insurance Act, 1997* requires the WSIAT to follow WSIB policies where applicable. For example, if the WSIB forms a policy that illnesses that arise purely from stress rather than from any physical act or exposure to some noxious substance are compensable only under certain narrow circumstances (for example, where the worker suffered stress as a result of seeing the death of another worker in an industrial accident), the WSIAT may not broaden the circumstances in which it will compensate for stress. This is a change from the previous practice, which permitted the WSIAT—which does not share the WSIB's interest in reducing employers' premiums—to recognize types of illnesses or injuries that the WSIB refused to recognize.

Practice Tip: Obtain New Information

Often, the representative will need to obtain additional information not found in the claim file. This may include medical reports, witness statements, educational records, job search records or earning documentation, depending on the issues.

Medical reports are the most common new information. It may simply be a matter of obtaining a copy of an existing medical report from a treating health care practitioner which is not in the claim file for some reason. On other occasions, the representative will require a medico–legal opinion from a treating doctor or from a doctor whom the representative refers the worker to. The medico–legal referral letter to the doctor is an important document, and must be carefully crafted to ensure that it is unbiased in its wording and that all relevant documents are provided to the doctor. The referral letter must be provided to the Board or Appeals Tribunal, along with the medico–legal opinion, and you can be sure that biased wording in the referral letter will be noticed by your opponent and the decision-maker.

Michael S Green, "Preparing for and Attending at a Hearing Before the Appeals Resolution Officer or the Workplace Safety and Insurance Appeals Tribunal" in *Best Practices for Paralegals Before the WSIB and WSIAT* (Donald Lamont Learning Centre, The Law Society of Upper Canada, 5 December 2008) (Toronto: Law Society of Upper Canada, 2008) at 7–3.

The WSIAT's website at <http://www.wsiat.on.ca> contains extensive information about WSIAT pre-hearing and hearing processes, and a number of medical and legal resources. Parties and their representatives can search the WSIAT decision database using a full text search on CanLII.

Challenging WSIAT Decisions

A party unsatisfied with a WSIAT decision may challenge it in two ways. First, the WSIAT has a reconsideration power, and reconsiderations are frequently requested.

Second, WSIAT decisions are subject to judicial review, and there are a substantial number of applications for such review to the Divisional Court.

Representation Before the WSIB and the WSIAT

Workers and employers may represent themselves in dealing with the WSIB and the WSIAT; however, the issues are usually sufficiently complex that this is generally unwise. Workers may seek advice, assistance, and representation from lawyers; from "consultants" who are licensed paralegals; from family members and friends; and from the Office of the Worker Adviser (OWA), an agency of the Ministry of Labour. However, due to its limited staff, the OWA must reject many requests for assistance.

Employers may seek assistance and representation from lawyers, licensed paralegals, and from the Office of the Employer Adviser (OEA). The OEA provides advice and representation to employers with fewer than 100 employees; larger employers must represent themselves, hire their own representatives, or rely on the results of WSIB and WSIAT investigations. In rare cases, they may be able to have their case presented by WSIB or OEA staff before the WSIAT. The websites of the OWA and the OEA can be accessed at <http://www.owa.gov.on.ca> and <http://www.employeradvisor.ca>.

The WSIB has an internal code of conduct for representatives, which allows it to bar representatives for repeated misconduct. The code prohibits representatives from making false or misleading statements about the WSIB, providing false or misleading information to the WSIB, and speaking or writing to WSIB staff in an abusive or threatening manner. Where WSIB staff believe a representative has violated the code, they may make a report to their manager. The WSIB has a process for deciding whether the code has been violated, issuing warnings, and refusing to allow individuals to continue acting as a representative if repeated violations are found.

As they must be when appearing before most other Ontario tribunals, most paid paralegals must be licensed by the LSUC to appear before the WSIB or the WSIAT. Representatives who appear before the WSIAT, whether lawyers or paralegals, and whether licensed by the LSUC or not licensed, are bound by the WSIAT's *Code of Conduct for Representatives*. Paralegals licensed by the Law Society are also subject to the LSUC's *Paralegal Rules of Conduct*.

The Municipal Property Assessment Corporation and the Assessment Review Board

MPAC

In Ontario, the Municipal Property Assessment Corporation (MPAC), established under the *Municipal Property Assessment Corporation Act, 1997*,[10] is responsible for

---

10   SO 1997, c 43, Schedule G.

assessing the value of all property in Ontario. Since property values rise and fall, MPAC reassesses properties periodically every four years.

MPAC arrives at an assessment for each property by looking at a variety of factors such as the lot size, location, and square footage; the age of the building and the quality of construction; any major renovations, additions, and improvements—such as additional bathrooms, fireplaces, and swimming pools; the number of stories; and by comparing the property with the values established for similar properties (informally referred to as "comparables").

MPAC provides these assessments to municipalities on annual assessment rolls. Municipalities use these values to calculate municipal taxes and education taxes. The assessment alone does not determine the property tax that property owners must pay. Different tax rates apply to different types of property—for example, residential properties may be subject to a different tax rate than industrial or commercial properties. To determine the amount of tax payable on an individual property, the municipality multiplies the assessed value of each property by a tax rate (formerly known as the "mill rate") of its own choosing that applies to all properties in that class of property. By raising or lowering the tax rate, the municipality can affect the individual tax bill for all the properties in the same class, even though the assessed value of any specific property does not change.

The choice of tax rate is a political decision that cannot be appealed; therefore, in most cases, the only method for attempting to lower a tax bill is to challenge the property's assessed value or, in a few cases, to challenge the classification of the property. By successfully appealing an assessment, a property owner can lower his or her tax liability. In limited circumstances, applications for tax refunds may be filed with a municipality, with a right to appeal the municipality's decision to the Assessment Review Board (discussed below).

Requests for Reconsideration and Appeals to the Assessment Review Board

All provinces have a process for reviewing property assessments. In Ontario, a property owner who believes his or her assessment is too high may challenge the assessment in two ways:

1. by requesting MPAC to reconsider the assessment, and/or
2. by appealing MPAC's decision to the Assessment Review Board (ARB).

MPAC sends property owners a notice of assessment in the fall of each year that will be used for property taxation in the following year unless there has been no change in value since the previous notice. The notice states the assessed value of the property and the time limit for filing a request for reconsideration (RFR) or appealing the assessment to the ARB. An owner of industrial or commercial property has the option of first requesting a reconsideration by MPAC or appealing directly to the ARB. An owner of residential, farm, managed forest, or conservation land property must file an RFR with MPAC and obtain a decision on the RFR before filing an appeal to the ARB.

The ARB is a tribunal established under the *Assessment Act*.[11] Its role is to determine whether the methodology used by MPAC to value property produced a correct current (market) value for a particular property; if the evidence supports an adjustment, the ARB has the power to lower or increase the assessment. Because assessment appeals constitute the vast majority of appeals heard by the ARB, they are the only appeals discussed here.

An owner who either bypasses the RFR process or is not satisfied with the RFR decision may file an appeal to the ARB by sending the ARB a notice of appeal together with an appeal fee. If the owner has filed an RFR, the notice of appeal must be sent within 90 days of the date MPAC mailed its RFR decision. If the owner is appealing an assessment of commercial or industrial property directly to the ARB without having first filed an RFR, the deadline is March 31 of the year for which the property is assessed. For supplementary or omitted assessments, the deadline is the later of 90 days after the notice was mailed or March 31 of the taxation year.

The appellant must notify the ARB of his or her appeal, but need not notify MPAC or the municipality. The notice of appeal may be given to the ARB in a letter or on the appeal form provided by the ARB on its website (<http://elto.gov.on.ca/arb>), but it must contain the information required by the ARB's rules of practice and procedure. The notice of appeal can be filed by mail, hand delivery, fax, or through the ARB's website.

The parties to an appeal are specified by the *Assessment Act* to be MPAC; all persons appealing and all persons whose assessment is the subject of the appeal; and the municipality in which the land is located, or, if the land is not within a municipality, the minister of finance.

Since the appellant is not required to notify MPAC or the municipality of an appeal, there is no need for the appellant to provide the ARB with any proof of service of the notice of appeal, except in the case of "stranger" or "third-party" appeals. These are usually appeals by a ratepayer that the property assessment of another person is too low and should be raised. Although unusual, stranger appeals could also allege that the assessment is too high or the classification of the property is wrong. In those cases, the appellant must confirm to the ARB in writing that he or she has served the owner of the property in question with a copy of the notice of appeal.

When the ARB receives the appeal notice and fee, it sends the appellant a letter acknowledging receipt of the appeal. The *Assessment Act* requires the ARB to give MPAC a copy of every notice of appeal; there is no similar provision requiring the ARB to notify the municipality of the appeal before the hearing is scheduled. When the ARB is ready to schedule a hearing, it mails the appellant, the owner of the property in a third-party appeal, the municipality, and MPAC a notice of hearing. The ARB must give reasonable notice of the hearing to allow adequate time for preparation. In practice, the ARB usually gives at least 28 days' notice.

Property owners may represent themselves before the ARB or have a friend or family member, a lawyer, or a paralegal licensed by the LSUC represent them.

---

11   RSO 1990, c A.31.

Pre-Hearing Conferences, Mediation, and Hearings

At formal hearings, the ARB follows a court-like adversarial procedure, with both the property owner and MPAC giving evidence, calling witnesses, and making submissions. However, the ARB's rules of practice and procedure provide for preliminary procedures that are less adversarial. PHCs may be held to attempt to settle issues without a hearing or to discuss procedures for the hearing. In addition, the ARB provides parties with alternative dispute resolution services, such as mediation, to help them reach a settlement. Recently the ARB has begun to place greater emphasis on the use of ADR.

The *Assessment Act* provides that at a hearing, MPAC has the burden of proving that its assessment is correct; however, if the appellant has failed to give MPAC a reasonable opportunity to inspect the property or has not complied with a request by MPAC for additional information or documentation, the burden of proof shifts to the appellant. The ARB has decided that this change to the burden of proof only applies if the refusal to allow inspection or provide information or documentation occurs when MPAC is making the assessment, not during the ARB proceeding.

The following kinds of evidence are often useful in challenging an assessment:

- detailed information about the property (such as the location, lot size, square footage, age of the building, the number of stories, and so on);
- detailed information of the same kind about comparable properties in the same area as the property in question;
- the sale prices of the property in question and comparable properties;
- the assessed values of the property in question and comparable properties;
- photographs of the property in question and comparable properties.

All the parties receive copies of the ARB's decisions. If the ARB reduces the assessment, the clerk of the municipality is required to change the tax roll to state the revised value and recalculate the property tax based on that value. If the property is not within a municipality, the ARB sends its decision to the minister, who will change the assessment roll and recalculate the tax.

The *Assessment Act* provides for appeals from the ARB to the Divisional Court, but only on questions of law, and only if the court gives leave to appeal. An application for leave to appeal must be made within 30 days of the date the ARB mailed its decision.

The text of the *Municipal Property Assessment Corporation Act, 1997* and the *Assessment Act* are available on the Ontario government's e-Laws website at <http://www.ontario.ca/laws>. The MPAC website also contains information about how MPAC assesses property and how to resolve assessment concerns through the internal review process and appeals to the ARB. Much of the information that a property owner or owner's representative needs in order to determine whether the assessed value of the property is correct and equitable with the assessments of neighbours and to prepare for an appeal hearing can be obtained by visiting the "AboutMyProperty" section on MPAC's website (under "Products and Services") and using the user ID and password on the property assessment notice. In addition to the reports available in that section, requests for comparable property reports can be made through the inquiry form. Detailed information about the mandate, practices, and procedures of the ARB can be found on the ARB's website.

The Landlord and Tenant Board

The *Residential Tenancies Act, 2006*[12] (RTA) sets the rules for most residential rental housing in Ontario. The Ontario Landlord and Tenant Board (LTB), established under the RTA, provides information about the RTA and resolves disputes between most residential landlords and tenants. Both landlords and tenants can make applications to the Board, which is part of the Social Justice Tribunals cluster.

Information about the RTA and the LTB can be found in the RTA and regulations, as well as on the Board's website at <http://www.sjto.gov.on.ca/ltb>. Additional information can be found in the "Housing Law" section of Community Legal Education Ontario's website (<http://yourlegalrights.on.ca>) and on the website of the Advocacy Centre for Tenants Ontario (<http://www.acto.ca>), a community legal clinic funded by Legal Aid Ontario. The LTB publishes some of its most important decisions; these can be found in online legal search services such as Quicklaw, eCarswell, and CanLII.

Common Applications

Landlords may terminate a tenancy because of a tenant's failure to pay rent, because of inappropriate behaviour that damaged the property or that interferes with other tenants or neighbours, because of a tenant's refusal to leave after giving notice or agreeing to vacate, or because they wish to perform major renovations or repairs. One of the most frequent applications to the LTB is an application by a landlord to evict a tenant for not paying rent.

To evict the tenant, a landlord must give the tenant proper notice in accordance with the requirements of the RTA. If the tenant fails to comply with the notice to vacate the premises, the landlord may apply to the LTB for an eviction order. Landlords may also apply to the Board for an order that a tenant pay arrears of rent or compensation for damage; produce a key for a lock that the tenant changed without permission; or for a remedy for an unauthorized sublet or assignment of the rented premises.

Tenants may apply to the LTB for a reduction in rent as a result of inadequate maintenance of the rented premises; for a rent rebate if the landlord failed to pay interest on the last month's rent that was paid in advance; for a remedy for the landlord improperly interfering with the tenant's use and enjoyment of the rented premises; for a remedy because the landlord terminated the tenancy in bad faith; or

---

12   SO 2006, c 17.

for an order requiring the landlord to allow a tenant to assign or sublet, where the landlord has no justification for denying the tenant this opportunity.

The RTA also controls the amount of rent that a landlord may charge. Where there is a dispute as to whether a rent increase is allowed under the Act, the LTB may hear an application by a tenant to lower the rent or an application by the landlord to raise it.

LTB Practices and Procedures

Applications, Notice of Application, Notice of Hearing, and Proof of Service of Notices

Section 69 of the RTA provides that a landlord may apply to the Board for an order terminating a tenancy and evicting a tenant if the landlord has first given the tenant notice of his or her intent to terminate the tenancy under the Act. An application to the Board for an order of eviction must be filed with the Board in the form approved by the Board, and accompanied by a copy of the notice of termination and a certificate of service of the notice of termination.

The information to be included in the application form includes the landlord's name and contact information; the address of the rental unit; the names and contact information of the tenant(s); the file numbers of any other applications to the Board that relate to the same rental unit; the amount of rent or other money owed by the tenant and the reason it is owed (for example, because the tenant failed to pay rent or stayed in the rental unit without paying after the termination date, or for NSF cheque charges); and the landlord or agent's signature, the date the application was signed, and, if the applicant is an officer or agent of a corporation, the company's name and contact information.

The Board sends the tenant a notice that an application has been filed, which includes the necessary details, but does not send a copy of the application itself.

When the Board establishes a date for the hearing, the Board gives the applicant a notice of hearing. If the hearing is an oral hearing, the notice must include a statement of the time, place, and purpose of the hearing and a statement that if the party notified does not attend at the hearing, the tribunal may proceed in the party's absence and the party will not be entitled to any further notice. For written and electronic hearings, the contents of a notice of hearing are similar, with any necessary modifications. The notice must include a reference to the statutory authority (generally, the name of the statute and the appropriate section number) under which the hearing is held.

The applicant must give a copy of the application and the notice of hearing to each of the other parties. The parties to an application are the landlord and any tenants or other persons directly affected by the application; for example, if the landlord applies to evict more than one tenant from a unit, each of the tenants must be given a copy of the notice of hearing. If the party has a representative, the application and notice of hearing may be served on the representative. The application and hearing notice must be served as soon as possible, but not less than ten days before the hearing date.

Section 191(1) of the RTA lists the means by which the application and notice of hearing are considered to have been sufficiently given to a person other than the Board:

(a)   by handing it to the person;

(b)   if the person is a landlord, by handing it to an employee of the landlord exercising authority in respect of the residential complex to which the notice or document relates;

(c)   if the person is a tenant, subtenant or occupant, by handing it to an apparently adult person in the rental unit;

(d)   by leaving it in the mailbox where mail is ordinarily delivered to the person;

(e)   if there is no mailbox, by leaving it at the place where mail is ordinarily delivered to the person;

(f)   by sending it by mail to the last known address where the person resides or carries on business; or

(g)   by any other means allowed in the Board's rules.

Rule 5 of the *Landlord and Tenant Board's Rules of Practice* (available on the Board's website) outlines other permitted methods of service. These include notice by courier; by fax, if the person has a fax machine at home or where he or she carries on business; by placing it under the door or through the mail slot in the door of the rental unit; by hand delivery, mail, courier, or fax to the tenant's representative; or by any other method directed or permitted by the Board in writing.

A party serving an application and notice of hearing is required to satisfy the Board that everyone entitled to receive them has been served by filing with the Board a certificate of service, signed by the individual who gave the application and notice to another party, regardless of who actually files it. Filing the certificate will ensure that the Board will have a complete file on the hearing date.

The certificate of service must be in the form approved by the Board. It must be filed within five days of serving the application and notice of hearing. The certificate of service form can be found on the Board's website under the tab "Forms, Filing, Fees." To find the form, look under "Forms for Landlords," which has a subsection called "Other forms for landlords."

Section 192(1) of the RTA lists the means considered sufficient with respect to notice to the Board:

(a)   by hand delivering it to the Board at the appropriate office as set out in the Board's Rules;

(b)   by sending it by mail to the appropriate office as set out in the Board's Rules; or

(c)   by any other means allowed in the Board's Rules.

Mediation, Hearings, and Review of Decisions

Before holding a hearing, the Board will offer the services of a mediator, who may help the parties settle the case. The Board usually provides this service on the day of the hearing, but if a party requests it, the Board may schedule a mediation in person or by telephone conference call at an earlier date. Mediation may result in a compromise—for example, in an application to evict a tenant for non-payment of rent, a landlord may agree that the tenant can stay if he or she agrees to pay the current rent and pay off the arrears over time. This settlement is made legally binding by the parties signing an agreement or by an order of the Board without the need for a hearing. If the tenant does not comply with the agreement or order, the Board has an expedited process for ordering the eviction of the tenant quickly without further notice to the tenant.

Although the Board can hold written and electronic hearings, it usually conducts oral hearings in person. It follows a court-like adversarial process, in which each of the parties gives evidence, calls witnesses, and cross-examines the other parties' witnesses. However, the Board also may make its own inquiries and consider the information obtained, as long as it informs the parties of the additional information it has collected and gives them an opportunity to explain or refute it. A party may object to another party's questions to a witness on grounds such as irrelevance or because a party is asking his or her witnesses leading questions.

On an application for eviction and payment of arrears of rent, the Board may order termination of the tenancy and full payment, particularly if the tenant has broken agreements or failed to comply with Board orders to pay arrears of rent on other occasions. However, if the Board is convinced that the tenant is likely to repay what he or she owes over time, the Board may permit the continuance of the tenancy and order a repayment schedule. The Board will usually order the unsuccessful party to pay the out-of-pocket expenses of the successful party; however, it will usually not award representatives' fees against an unsuccessful party unless that party behaved inappropriately in the proceedings (for example, by bringing a frivolous or vexatious application or motion) or the party has been unsuccessful in a hearing to review the order.

The Board has the power to review its decisions. Parties also have the right to appeal Board decisions to the Divisional Court on questions of law. The decisions are subject to judicial review for errors of jurisdiction or breaches of procedural fairness.

The Social Benefits Tribunal

In Ontario, two programs make "social assistance" (sometimes known as "welfare") from the provincial government available to individuals who are unable to support themselves: the Ontario Works program (OW) and the Ontario Disability Support Program (ODSP). Both of these programs have two components: financial assistance and employment assistance.

Under the *Ontario Works Act, 1997*,[13] the Ontario government established the Ontario Works program (OW). Administered by the Ministry of Community and Social Services, OW provides financial assistance to unemployed individuals who

---

13   SO 1997, c 25, Schedule A.

demonstrate that they need financial assistance and are attempting to obtain employment. The government also provides such individuals with help finding and keeping a job, including skills upgrading.

The *Ontario Disability Support Program Act, 1997*,[14] also administered by the Ministry, provides income support from the provincial government for individuals with disabilities. Under the Ontario Disability Support Program (ODSP), the provincial government also helps individuals with disabilities find and keep work.

These two statutes and the regulations made under them set out the following:

- which individuals are eligible for assistance, and the kinds of assistance for which they are eligible;
- the obligations of individuals receiving assistance to cooperate in government efforts to help them find work, such as participating in retraining programs;
- the application process that individuals seeking financial assistance must follow;
- the method of calculating the amount of financial assistance available to particular individuals;
- the amount and types of income and assets that are considered in determining whether an individual is eligible for financial assistance;
- the reasons why an administrator may refuse, cancel, or reduce assistance;
- the right to appeal to the Social Benefits Tribunal and the process for appealing; and
- the right to appeal from the Tribunal to the Divisional Court.

Administration of OW and ODSP

The *Ontario Works Act, 1997* and the *Ontario Disability Support Program Act* are administered by the Ministry of Community and Social Services. The ODSP is administered by Ministry staff, and OW is administered by service providers designated by the Ministry—typically, local municipalities or district social services area boards that represent several municipalities. The Ministry or these local agencies decide whether applicants are eligible for financial and employment support programs, and make decisions regarding new and continuing assistance.

Eligibility for OW financial benefits is based on the applicant's need and the applicant's willingness to take part in activities that will help him or her find a job. To be eligible for the ODSP, an applicant must be in financial need and must also meet the definition of "person with a disability," which requires a substantial physical or mental impairment that is expected to be continuous or recurrent and last at least a year and that substantially restricts the applicant's ability to work, take care of himself or herself, or take part in community life. In determining the amount of money an applicant may receive from OW or ODSP, the administrator will take into account family size, income, assets, and housing costs.

---

14 SO 1997, c 25, Schedule B.

Financial support under both programs is intended to pay for basic living expenses, such as food and housing, as well as for other benefits such as prescription drug and dental coverage, eye glasses, and moving or eviction costs. Employment support may include access to basic education; workshops on looking for work, resumé writing, and preparing for an interview; referrals to job counselling; job-specific training programs; information about who is hiring; and access to telephones, fax machines, computers, and job banks.

Information about eligibility criteria for OW and ODSP, how to apply, the benefits that may be available, answers to frequently asked questions about the programs, and the numerous provincial policy directives that guide the administration of the programs is available on the Ministry's website at <http://www.mcss.gov.on.ca/en/mcss/programs/social/index.aspx>.

Internal Reviews and Appeals of Benefits Decisions

An individual who is refused financial assistance or whose financial assistance has been cancelled, revoked, or put on hold, or who is not satisfied with the amount of financial assistance granted, must first apply for an internal review. Section 27(2) of the *Ontario Works Act, 1997* together with section 69 of Ontario Regulation 134/98 provide that requests for internal reviews must be made within 30 days from the day the decision was received. Similarly, section 22(2) of the *Ontario Disability Support Program Act, 1997* together with section 58(1) of Ontario Regulation 222/98 provide that requests for internal reviews must be made within 30 days from the day the decision was received. The internal review must be requested within ten days of an individual having received an unfavourable decision. A different staff member in the office that made the unfavourable decision conducts this review.

Thirty days after an unfavourable internal review decision, or 40 days later if no decision has been made within 10 days of the review request, the individual may appeal the official's decision to the Social Benefits Tribunal (SBT) established under the *Ontario Works Act, 1997*. (Some decisions to refuse, revoke, or reduce employment support and other discretionary benefits, such as funeral expenses, cannot be appealed to the SBT.) The appeal is launched using an appeal form available from the office that made the unfavourable decision, from the SBT's website at <http://www.sjto.gov.on.ca/sbt>, or from community legal clinics.

The SBT is an independent adjudicative tribunal that is separate from the Ministry of Community and Social Services and the local agencies that administer these financial support programs. It is part of the Social Justice Tribunals Ontario cluster that was formed in 2011, along with other tribunals such as the Human Rights Tribunal of Ontario (HRTO) and the LTB. The main offices are in Toronto, but there are several regional offices. The Tribunal members are from different parts of the province, and they travel to hold hearings wherever appellants live. The SPPA applies to the SBT's hearings, which are similar to those of a court but are less formal.

SBT Hearings

The parties in an SBT hearing are the appellant and the office that made the unfavourable decision. The vast majority of appeals deal with the ODSP and the issue of whether the appellant meets the definition of a person with a disability. Parties are entitled to be represented by lawyers or paralegals licensed by the LSUC, but a representative may not also be a witness. Many appellants are represented by staff lawyers and community legal workers (paralegals) employed by community legal clinics established to provide legal assistance to those who cannot afford it.

Appellants are required to send any documents on which they intend to rely to both the SBT and the agency that made the unfavourable decision no less than 20 days before the hearing. These documents often include medical and psychiatric reports, drug lists, prescriptions and drug receipts, doctors' letters, separation and child custody agreements, immigration papers, and job search lists. In an appeal of a decision that a person is not a person with a disability, the regulations do not permit the Tribunal to adjourn a hearing date to permit an appellant to obtain further medical reports.

At the hearing, the appellant and the respondent OW or ODSP decision-maker may both testify, call witnesses, and cross-examine witnesses. In the vast majority of ODSP appeals, the ODSP office does not send any representative to the hearing, but relies on its written evidence and submissions. Most hearings last only about an hour.

If an appellant notifies the SBT that he or she does not speak or understand English well, the Tribunal will provide a professional translator. In some cases, the Tribunal may allow friends or relatives to translate.

Following the hearing, the Tribunal will decide whether to grant the appeal or uphold the respondent agency's decision, in whole or in part.

Requests for Reconsideration and Appeals to the Divisional Court

The appellant or the respondent may request that the SBT reconsider its decision by submitting an application for reconsideration, including reasons why the Tribunal should change its decision or hear the appeal again, within 30 days of the Tribunal's decision.

Reconsideration is a two-step process. First, the Tribunal will consider whether it should grant a reconsideration hearing, taking into account such factors as whether the Tribunal acted outside its jurisdiction, violated the rules of procedural fairness, made a serious error of law, or did not have access to important new evidence that would have affected its decision. If the Tribunal finds that any of these factors are present, it will hold a reconsideration hearing after notifying all the parties to the original hearing of the date, time, and place of the hearing. Usually, the Tribunal will assign a member other than the member who heard the original appeal to hold the reconsideration hearing.

The statutes provide for an appeal to the Divisional Court on questions of law.

The SJTO's website contains a link to the SBT website, which has links to the text of the *Ontario Works Act* and the *Ontario Disability Support Program Act*, descriptions of the SBT's process, appeal forms, SBT practice directions, and procedures for complaining about the conduct of tribunal members. The SJTO's annual report contains a report on the SBT (<http://www.sjto.gov.on.ca/en/reports-plans-standards>). Further information about ODSP, Ontario Works, and the SBT can be found in the

"Social Assistance and Pensions" section of the "Resources" page on the website of Community Legal Education Ontario (<http://www.cleo.on.ca>). The Income Security Advocacy Centre, a legal clinic funded by Legal Aid Ontario, also has relevant information on its website at <http://incomesecurity.org>.

The Immigration, Refugee Protection, and Citizenship Process

The rules governing who is entitled to come to Canada as an immigrant or refugee and who is entitled to become a Canadian citizen are lengthy, complex, and subject to frequent change. The decisions whether to permit a Canadian resident to sponsor a relative, whether people who are not Canadian citizens will be removed from the country, whether individuals are entitled to enter or remain in Canada as refugees from persecution in their homeland, whether immigrants may be detained by the government, and whether citizenship should be granted to applicants are governed primarily by two statutes: the *Immigration and Refugee Protection Act*[15] (IRPA) and the *Citizenship Act*.[16] Under the IRPA, immigration and refugee decisions are divided among the minister of citizenship and immigration, the minister of public safety and emergency preparedness (who is responsible for the Canada Border Services Agency [CBSA]), and the Immigration and Refugee Board (IRB) (an independent tribunal).

The minister of citizenship and immigration's responsibilities include developing immigration policy, determining targets each year for how many immigrants will be permitted to enter Canada, facilitating the settlement and integration of newcomers, facilitating the resettlement of refugees, and developing policies related to admissibility. Under the *Citizenship Act*, this minister may grant citizenship to foreign nationals[17] who are eligible; decide applications to renounce or restore Canadian citizenship; and revoke citizenship that was obtained through fraud or misrepresentation.

The minister of public safety is primarily responsible for enforcement of immigration rules and policies, largely through the operation of the CBSA. The CBSA's functions include examining people at points of entry, arrest, detention, removal of people who are inadmissible to Canada, and investigation of suspected smuggling of goods. Certain officers have the power to arrest a permanent resident or foreign national whom they believe has breached or may breach the IRPA and may detain the person if he or she poses a danger to the public, his or her identity is in question, or there is reason to believe the person will not appear for a hearing or for removal from Canada.

---

15   SC 2001, c 27.

16   RSC 1985, c C-29.

17   Under the IRPA, a "foreign national" is a person who is neither a Canadian citizen nor a permanent resident. Unless an applicant for citizenship is born in Canada, a prerequisite for Canadian citizenship is that the applicant be a "permanent resident."

Citizenship and Immigration Canada (CIC) officers process applications for temporary residence, permanent residence, refugee status, and citizenship; provide settlement and integration assistance to newcomers; conduct research; and develop immigration policy and programs.

The two ministers may designate any members of their departments' staff or any category of staff members as "officers" under the IRPA. The ministers may delegate the authority to carry out most of their duties, such as the power to question, arrest, detain, and remove individuals from Canada, to such officers. There is a variety of such officers, including visa officers, examining officers, senior immigration officers, immigration officers and CBSA officers.

Practice Tip: How to Determine Whether You Are Submitting a Request to the Right Official

The specific delegation structure is outlined in the Citizenship and Immigration Canada Instrument of Designation and Delegation, which is published online. …

Practitioners should consult this document to ensure they are addressing any requests or applications to the appropriate office and if there is any question as to the jurisdiction of a particular Officer. [Emphasis in original.]

Chantal Desloges, "Administrative Decision-Making in Immigration and Refugee Law Matters," presented at Administrative Law Practice Basics 2014 (Donald Lamont Learning Centre, The Law Society of Upper Canada, 14 May 2014) (Toronto: Law Society of Upper Canada, 2014).

To understand which officers have been delegated the authority to carry out a particular function and what principles and procedures they will follow in making their decisions, it is necessary to look at the IRPA for a high-level overview of their functions, as well as the *Immigration and Refugee Protection Regulations*[18] for a more precise and detailed description. However, most of the policies and procedures that immigration and enforcement officers will follow are not set out in statutes or regulations, but are contained in a number of Ministerial Instructions, Operational Bulletins, and Operational Manuals. The Ministerial Instructions and Operational Bulletins are available online, as are some (but not all) of the Operational Manuals.

The Immigration and Refugee Board

If an officer makes a decision that is adverse to an individual, such as refusing entry to Canada, ordering the person removed from the country or detaining him or her, or refusing to permit a Canadian citizen or permanent resident to sponsor a family class member to immigrate to Canada, the decision can be appealed in some cases to the IRB, which is a quasi-judicial tribunal established by the IRPA. However, not everyone subject to an adverse decision has a right of appeal to the IRB. For example, only permanent residents and some foreign nationals (Convention refugees and visa holders) can appeal a decision of inadmissibility to the IRB. The remedy

18 SOR/2002-227.

available to those who do not have access to the IRB is an application to the Federal Court for judicial review.

The IRB is the largest tribunal in Canada. It consists of four Divisions: the Refugee Protection Division (RPD); the Refugee Appeal Division (RAD); the Immigration Division (ID); and the Immigration Appeal Division (IAD).

Rules of Procedure Common to All Four IRB Divisions

Sections 162 to 169 of the IRPA set out rules that must be followed by all four IRB Divisions in conducting their hearings and making decisions. These rules

- require each Division to deal with all proceedings as "informally and quickly" as is consistent with fairness;
- authorize the Division to do whatever is necessary where there is no rule dealing with a matter;
- determine whether a hearing will be open or closed to the public;
- give persons appearing before the Board a right to counsel; and
- require the Board to give reasons for its decisions.

Each of these Divisions, in addition to the common rules, has its own procedural rules in the form of a regulation under the IRPA.

In addition to the requirements and guidance provided by the IRPA and formal rules of procedure, the IRB publishes on its website several other kinds of guidance documents intended to be followed by tribunal members and staff, and, where applicable, by parties and their representatives. They include the documents listed here.

- Chairperson's Guidelines, which are provided for in the IRPA, provide guiding principles for adjudicating and managing cases and making decisions. While the Guidelines are not mandatory, decision-makers are expected to apply them or provide a reasoned justification for not doing so. There are currently eight Guidelines, including guidelines for dealing with gender-based refugee claims, vulnerable claimants, and child claimants.
- Chairperson's Instructions, which provide formal direction to IRB personnel to take or avoid specific actions, such as instructions on how members should maintain the confidentiality of legal advice to tribunal members from the IRB's staff lawyers.
- Policy Notes, which are used to address areas of concern, such as the use of "persuasive decisions" to encourage consistent decisions from one member to the next and between IRB Divisions, and the consistent use of Canada's two official languages by the four divisions.
- Persuasive Decisions, which are decisions that have been identified by a division head (deputy chairperson of an IRB division) as being of persuasive value in developing the jurisprudence of a particular division. Members are encouraged (but not required) to rely on these decisions in the interests of consistency and high-quality decision-making.

- A series of Legal References, which include a "Designated Representative's Guide," a guide to weighing evidence, a guide to removal order appeals, and a guide to sponsorship appeals.

The Refugee Protection Division

The Refugee Protection Division (RPD) hears claims for refugee protection made inside Canada. Once an officer has determined that a person is eligible to have his or her claim referred to the RPD under section 100 of the IRPA, the RPD then decides whether the person is a "Convention refugee" or a "person in need of protection" and so entitled to stay in Canada.[19] Convention refugees are people who are outside their home country or the country where they normally live, and who are unwilling to return because of a well-founded fear of persecution based on race, religion, nationality, membership in a particular social group, or political opinions. Persons in need of protection are individuals who face a danger of torture or would risk their lives or face cruel and unusual treatment or punishment if returned to their homeland.

The RPD also hears applications by the minister to declare that the person granted refugee status is no longer in need of protection or that refugee status granted to an individual should be vacated because the claimant obtained a favourable decision as a result of misrepresenting or withholding material facts.

RPD RULES OF PROCEDURE

The rules of procedure of the RPD that are not common to all the IRB divisions are set out in a regulation, the *Refugee Protection Division Rules*. They include requirements that the tribunal question witnesses before the claimant's representative where the minister is not a party and rules governing the disclosure and use of documents, as well as rules setting out the procedure that must be followed to request an adjournment and the factors the tribunal will take into account in deciding whether to grant one.[20]

The Refugee Appeal Division

Section 110 of the IRPA provides that either the minister or the claimant may appeal the decision of the RPD to the Refugee Appeal Division. The statutory grounds for the appeal are alleged errors of law, fact, or mixed law and fact (wider grounds than those on which decisions can generally be appealed to courts).

The IRPA prohibits certain appeals; for example, there is no appeal from

- a decision of the RPD that a refugee protection claim has been withdrawn or abandoned;

---

19 The circumstances in which a claim is not eligible to be referred to the RPD are set out in s 101 of the IRPA.

20 Note that there is a different procedure for claims made after December 15, 2012 than for claims made before that date (known as "legacy claims").

- a decision stating that the claim has no credible basis;
- a decision where the issue decided by the RPD was whether refugee protection has ceased; or
- a decision where the issue before the RPD was whether to vacate a decision to grant refugee protection.

In an appeal from the RPD, the RAD has authority to confirm the RAD's decision, set it aside and substitute its own decision; or refer the matter to the RPD to be reconsidered. In most cases, the RAD will proceed without a hearing, on the basis of the documents provided by the parties and the RPD record.

Important RAD procedural rules include deadlines for filing an appeal as well as a provision in the IRPA itself that restricts the admission of new evidence in an RAD appeal.

The Immigration Division

The Immigration Division (ID) has jurisdiction to conduct two types of hearings: admissibility hearings and detention review hearings.

An admissibility hearing is a review of the opinion of an immigration officer that a permanent resident or a foreign citizen who is in Canada is not entitled to enter Canada or remain here. Where the immigration officer comes to this conclusion, the minister may refer the matter to the ID for a ruling on admissibility in some circumstances, but may make a removal order without referring the case to the ID in other cases.

Detention reviews are reviews of administrative decisions to detain foreign nationals or permanent residents because an officer believes they are a danger to the public, unlikely to appear at an admissibility hearing, a threat to national security, or have provided false identities. The minister may arrest and detain someone, but if detained, the person is entitled to a detention review by the ID within 48 hours. The minister must apply to the ID for an order authorizing the detention.

The ID is required to order the release of detained individuals unless it is satisfied that they fit into one of the above categories. It can order release subject to conditions such as payment of a deposit or posting of a guarantee by a bondsperson.

ID PROCEDURAL RULES

The procedural rules of the ID are set out in the IRPA, as well as in a regulation, the *Immigration Division Rules*.[21] The rules applicable to all ID hearings include

---

21 SOR/2002-229.

requirements governing the use and disclosure of documents. Rules that apply only to detention reviews include section 57 of the IRPA, requiring that an initial review of a detention order must be conducted within 48 hours of detention, at least once more in the next seven days, and at least once every 30 days after that. Rule 9 of the ID Rules permits a detained person to apply for an early detention review, and allows the ID to hold an early review if the person provides new evidence that justifies this. There are three sets of rules in the regulation. In Part 1, sections 3 to 7 are rules for admissibility hearings only; in Part 2, section 8 to 11 are rules for detention reviews only; and in Part 3, sections 12 to 52 are rules for both kinds of hearings.

A detailed *Guide to Proceedings Before the Immigration Division*, written by the IRB's staff lawyers to assist the ID members, is available to the public and can be found on the IRB's website.[22]

The Immigration Appeal Division

The Immigration Appeal Division (IAD) hears

- appeals by individuals whose applications to sponsor a family member to come to Canada have been refused;
- appeals by permanent residents, protected persons, or permanent resident visa holders of removal orders made against them in an inadmissibility hearing before the ID or by an enforcement officer;
- appeals by the minister against decisions of the ID at inadmissibility hearings; and
- appeals by permanent residents against decisions made by officers outside Canada that they have not complied with the residency requirements in the IRPA.

The IRPA prohibits a number of appeals, including appeals by:

- foreign nationals who are not protected persons or holders of permanent resident visas;
- persons found to be inadmissible on security grounds, for violating human rights, for participation in organized crime, or for serious crime (which is defined to include a criminal offence with a punishment of six months or more in jail—this was changed from two years by the 2013 *Faster Removal of Foreign Criminals Act*);[23] and
- applicants for sponsorship who received a negative decision because of inadmissibility or misrepresentation.

---

22 The Guide can be found online at <http://www.irb-cisr.gc.ca/Eng/BoaCom/references/LegJur/Pages/GuideIdSiAboPro.aspx> and it can be downloaded as a PDF as well: <http://www.irb-cisr.gc.ca/Eng/BoaCom/references/LegJur/Documents/GuideIdSi_e.pdf>.

23 SC 2013, c 16.

Section 66 of the IRPA sets out the remedies that the IAD can grant. They include allowing the appeal, staying a removal order, and dismissing the appeal. However, the IAD can allow an appeal only where it finds that the decision appealed is wrong in law or fact or mixed law and fact; where a principle of natural justice was not followed; or on humanitarian or compassionate grounds. Humanitarian and compassionate grounds are not available in some cases, such as sponsorship appeals where the sponsored person is found to be not a member of the family class.

The IAD rules of procedure are also found in a regulation made under the IRPA.[24] They include timelines for the various classes of appeal, procedures for serving notices of appeal, requirements for the contents of the "appeal record" and for its service, rules governing the use and disclosure of documents, and the requirement to identify witnesses to be called to testify (including expert witnesses). The rules provide that if a party does not provide this information within the specified time, the witness may not be permitted to testify.

The Federal Court

There is no statutory right of appeal from the IRB to the Federal Court. However, the Federal Court has jurisdiction to hear judicial review applications challenging decisions of immigration officers as well as some divisions of the IRB. In fact, immigration and refugee decisions are the matters most frequently judicially reviewed by the Federal Court.

The *Federal Courts Act* states that the Federal Court has jurisdiction to order federal boards, commissions, and other tribunals to do anything they have unlawfully failed or refused to do or have unreasonably delayed in doing.[25] "Federal Board, commission or other tribunal" is defined in the Act to include "any body, person or persons having, exercising or purporting to exercise jurisdiction or powers conferred by or under an Act of Parliament or by or under an order made pursuant to a prerogative of the Crown,"[26] with certain listed exceptions. The bodies and persons captured by this definition include the IRB as well as the ministers responsible for enforcement and administration of the IRPA and the *Citizenship Act* and the officers to whom they have delegated their responsibilities.

The right to apply to the Federal Court for judicial review is not automatic. The applicant must obtain the court's permission (called "leave").

The Patented Medicine Prices Review Board

Regulating the prices that manufactures may charge for drugs is a very different function from those of the agencies and tribunals discussed above. However, the Patented

---

24   *Immigration Appeal Division Rules*, SOR/2002-230.

25   RSC 1985, c F-7, s 18.1(3).

26   *Ibid*, s 2(1).

Medicine Prices Review Board (PMPRB) also has similar functions to those bodies. As stated earlier, the PMPRB is included here for comparison and contrast and to illustrate how wide the spectrum of administrative decision-making is.

To improve the likelihood that Canadians will be able to afford the prescription drugs that they require, the Government of Canada, through the PMPRB, sets limits on the prices that the persons or companies who hold patents on drugs (called "patentees") may charge to wholesalers, hospitals, and pharmacies for these drugs.

Established in 1987 under Canada's *Patent Act*,[27] the Board consists of five members who are appointed by the federal Cabinet but nominated by the federal minister of health. Under the Act, the minister may appoint an advisory panel consisting of representatives of provincial health ministers, representatives of consumer groups, and representatives of the pharmaceutical industry to recommend suitable candidates for the Board. The Board operates at arm's length from the Health Canada. It has authority to hire staff as well as to retain experts with technical or specialized knowledge.

The Board's mandate is to ensure that the prices charged by patentees (usually, the manufacturers) for patented drugs sold in Canada are not excessive. To this end, Board staff periodically review the prices of drugs available in Canada to determine whether the prices are excessive and, if so, what orders to make to correct this. The Board may order the patentee to reduce the price to offset any excessive revenue it may have received.

The Role of Board Staff

Once a drug has been shown to be safe and effective, it is approved for sale in Canada by Health Canada. Manufacturers are required to inform the Board of their intention to sell a patented medicine, but are not required to obtain approval of the price of a patented medicine from the Board before they begin to sell it. If the Board requests this information, the manufacturer must provide information about intended pricing before introducing the product.

The patentee must notify the Board of the introductory prices and sales of a new patented medicine within 60 days of the first sale of the drug in Canada. The patentee must continue to file detailed information about prices and sales of the drug twice per year until the patent expires.

Board staff review the price and sale information provided by manufacturers periodically and monitor pricing practices. If they believe that the price of a drug exceeds the amount considered reasonable under guidelines developed by the Board, they will conduct an investigation. As part of this investigation, they may require the patentee to provide information about the costs of making and marketing the drug and, if applicable, its selling price in other countries; the company's revenues from selling other medicines in Canada; and its Canadian expenditures on research and development of medicines, as these are considered relevant factors in determining a fair profit for the drug.

---

27 RSC 1985, c P-4.

If the investigation supports the staff's concern that the price in any market is excessive, negotiations begin between the patentee and the Board staff over what price the patentee will be permitted to charge for the drug. These negotiations may result in a voluntary compliance undertaking by the manufacturer to reduce the price and/or take other measures to comply with the guidelines, such as offsetting the excess revenues obtained. This offset may be achieved through an additional price reduction beyond the reduction needed to comply with the guidelines, by a reduction in the price of other drugs sold by the manufacturer, or by a payment to the government of Canada.

If the patentee and the board staff cannot agree on a solution, the staff prepare a report setting out their findings and recommending a hearing. They submit this report to the chair of the Board, who decides whether it is in the public interest to hold a hearing into any allegations of excessive pricing.

The Hearing Process

The Board is not permitted to make an order for a remedy (for example, that the patentee reduce the price of a drug or pay the government money to offset excessive profits it may have received) unless it first holds a hearing at which the patentee is given the opportunity to challenge the proposed order. The hearing must be open to the public, except where disclosure of information would cause the patent holder or others "specific, direct and substantial harm."[28] The Board must give notice of the hearing to the federal minister of industry and provincial health ministers, all of whom are entitled to participate in the hearing.

If the chair of the Board determines that a hearing is warranted, he or she convenes a panel of board members to adjudicate the matter. Under the Board's rules of practice and procedure, the Board staff are responsible for presenting the case for a price reduction or offset order to the hearing panel. The staff have a lawyer to present their case, and the hearing panel has its own lawyer to provide it with independent legal advice.

Through their lawyer, board staff call witnesses and present documentary evidence, cross-examine witnesses for the patentee, and make arguments on procedural issues as well as on what the outcome of the hearing should be. The patentee's lawyer will call witnesses to give evidence that the price is reasonable.

In deciding whether the price of a drug is excessive, the Board is permitted to consider the following factors set out in the *Patent Act*:

- the prices at which the drug has been sold;
- how the current price compares with the price of comparable medicines in the same market;
- the price at which the drug and comparable drugs have been sold in other countries;

---

28   *Ibid*, s 86(1).

- changes in the consumer price index; and
- any other factors specified by regulations.[29]

In reviewing these factors, the Board has guidelines to determine whether the price is excessive. For example, if the price of a new drug is higher than the highest-priced existing drug used to treat the same disease, it will be considered excessive, and the Board will reduce the price of the new drug to a price similar to that of the existing drug. The Board also tries to price drugs at prices that are no higher than the median charged for the same drug in other industrialized countries. Drug companies may apply to the Board for annual price increases, but these are limited to increases in the consumer price index.

Board Orders and Review of Board Proceedings and Orders

If the Board decides that the price of an existing drug is excessive, it can order the drug company to reduce the price of the drug, or to reduce the price of another drug to offset the higher price of the drug in question. The Board can also order the company to pay money to the government to offset its profits above those it would have seen had the drug been correctly priced.

The Act does not provide for an appeal of the Board's orders but, at common law, judicial review would be available to a party who alleges that the Board has exceeded its jurisdiction or followed unfair procedures.

---

29 *Ibid*, ss 85(1), (2).

CHAPTER SUMMARY

Despite some similarities—for example, having processes for receiving applications or appeals, identifying issues, providing opportunities for mediation, determining the date(s) and duration of a hearing, notifying the parties of the hearing, serving documents, filing proof of service, conducting hearings, and so on—all tribunals are unique in certain ways. For this reason, it is important for representatives to familiarize themselves with the mandate, powers, and procedures of any tribunal before which they are preparing to appear. This may include researching the tribunal's governing statute and regulations; the background of the tribunal members who will hold the hearing; the tribunal's rules of procedure, procedural guidelines, and practice directions; and past rulings of the tribunal and the courts on the issues that will be heard. While some tribunals are "stand-alone" tribunals (such as the LTB), others operate as part of a regulatory process that includes both a regulator and a tribunal (for example, the WSIAT and the WSIB, or the CHRC and the CHRT).

The CHRC and the CHRT are part of a legislative scheme for identifying, preventing, and remedying discrimination under the *Canadian Human Rights Act*. The Act addresses discrimination by the federal government and by businesses that are federally regulated. The Ontario *Human Rights Code* addresses discrimination by the Ontario government, municipalities, and provincially regulated businesses. This regulatory scheme includes a policy body (the OHRC), a tribunal (the HRTO), and an agency (the Human Rights Legal Support Centre) that provides legal advice and assistance to applicants to the Tribunal.

FSCO regulates several business sectors, including insurance companies, co-operatives, credit unions, loan and trust companies, mortgage brokers, and pension plans. It also acts as a tribunal to hear appeals from decisions of automobile insurance companies to pay motor vehicle accident benefits claims.

The WSIB provides income support and rehabilitation services to workers who are injured on the job. A decision to grant or deny benefits can be appealed to the WSIAT.

MPAC and the ARB are components of Ontario's system for determining property values for the purpose of collecting property taxes. MPAC is responsible for assessing the value of all property in Ontario. Property owners, and in some cases municipalities, who disagree with their assessments may appeal them to the ARB.

The *Residential Tenancies Act, 2006* governs the relationship between tenants and landlords for most residential rental housing in Ontario. Landlords and tenants may apply to the LTB, established under the Act, to resolve disputes between them.

In Ontario, the *Ontario Works Act* and the *Ontario Disability Support Program Act* make financial and other assistance available from the government to individuals who are unable to support themselves. These benefits are administered by the Ministry of Community and Social Services and by local service providers delegated by the Ontario government. An applicant who is not satisfied with a benefits decision may appeal it to the SBT.

The IRB is the largest federal tribunal in Canada. It oversees the implementation of laws, procedures, and policies that determine who can migrate to Canada for work or seek refuge in Canada from persecution in their homeland. This area of administrative law and practice is influenced heavily by the government's economic, social, and cultural priorities. Chief among these priorities are economic growth and prosperity; safety and security concerns; and the overall development of Canada as a nation. The IRB adjudicates appeals from immigration applications; first-instance refugee applications and appeals of refugee claimants; admissibility hearings; and detention reviews. When appointed to the IRB, members become paid federal employees.

The PMPRB's mandate is to set and enforce limits on the prices that drug manufacturers may charge in order to improve the likelihood that Canadians will be able to afford the prescription drugs that they require. Board staff monitor the prices charged by patentees for their drugs and analyze information about matters such as the cost of research, development, and production. If they believe a drug's price is excessive, they report their findings to the Board, which holds a hearing and may issue orders.

KEY TERMS

arbitration: an adjudication in which one or more neutral third parties makes a binding decision after holding a hearing; usually refers to an adjudication in which the adjudicator, sometimes called an "arbitrator," is chosen by the parties; *see also* arbitrator

arbitrator: sometimes used instead of the term "adjudicator" to refer to members of tribunals in which the members are appointed by the government or a regulatory body, or chosen by the parties themselves

case assessment direction: in a proceeding before the HRTO, a direction issued by the Tribunal before a hearing that may address any matter that the Tribunal feels will facilitate the fair and expeditious resolution of the case—for example, identifying the main issues, facts on which the parties agree, procedural issues that need to be decided before the hearing, and any witnesses who should attend the hearing; *see also* case conference

case conference: in a case before the HRTO, a meeting of all the parties and affected persons convened by the Tribunal to discuss the conduct of the proceedings, often leading to the issuance of a case assessment direction; *see also* case assessment direction

case management conference: a procedure of the CHRT, similar to the pre-hearing conferences of other tribunals, at which a tribunal member addresses matters such as whether the parties will be represented by a lawyer or other representative, how many witnesses each party intends to call at the hearing, how long each party's evidence will take to present, and so on

registrar: the head of the tribunal staff; responsible for processing applications or appeals and handling related issues and procedures, such as providing parties with information about the tribunal's procedures; scheduling motions, pre-hearing conferences and hearings; and sending out notices and decisions

CASES TO CONSIDER

FSCO's Mandate: Interpreting Benefits Available Under the SABS

B(G) v Pilot Insurance Co (2008), 89 OR (3d) 228 (Div Ct)

FACTS: In 1998, when she was 22, single, and childless, GB sustained serious injuries. She later married and, in April 2004, gave birth to a daughter. In October 2001, a future care costs report commissioned by her insurer recognized that in the future GB might need the services of a nanny to help her care for a child, since she was unable to perform some of the physical activities that would be required.

In November 2004, GB submitted a treatment plan prepared by a nurse to the insurer. The plan included nanny services to help GB care for her child. The insurer rejected the proposal on the ground that GB was not entitled to nanny services under the language of the *Statutory Accident Benefits Schedule* (SABS) (O Reg 403/96). GB appealed to an FSCO arbitrator, who ruled that she was entitled to this benefit. The insurer appealed the arbitrator's decision to an FSCO Director's delegate. The delegate overturned the arbitrator's decision, ruling that the language of the SABS does not permit the provision of nanny care as a rehabilitation benefit because nanny care is covered by a provision dealing with caregiver benefits, to which GB was not entitled. GB applied to the Divisional Court for judicial review of the delegate's decision.

ISSUE: Can nanny expenses be recovered as a rehabilitation benefit under section 15(5)(1)of the SABS, which deals with eligibility for rehabilitation benefits, when child care is addressed by section 13 of the SABS and GB is not eligible for those child care benefits?

DECISION: It was undisputed that provision of a nanny would meet all the requirements of section 15—namely, an independent assessor had found the expenses to be reasonable and necessary, and the purpose was to reduce or eliminate the disability resulting from the accident and to facilitate GB's reintegration into her family. The fact that section 13 also dealt with child care did not prevent childcare benefits from being awarded under section 15 if they met the criteria in section 15. Section 13 should not be interpreted as being the exclusive basis for caregiver funding. Section 15 contains an express exclusion of services provided by a case manager, but no other exclusion limiting the broad language "other goods and services that the insured person requires," a requirement that the independent needs assessment supported.

The WSIAT: Procedural Issues and Assessment of Credibility

Workplace Safety and Insurance Appeals Tribunal, Decision No 1854/99

FACTS: A seaman suffered a back injury when he slipped and fell in the course of his work in July 1991. In July 1997, he fell and suffered a left knee injury. He claimed that the 1997 fall occurred because his leg gave way as a result of the earlier back injury. The WSIB granted the worker financial benefits and provided access to medical rehabilitation and vocational rehabilitation programs until the summer of 1999. However, despite these rehabilitation programs and a back operation, except for a brief trial period, the worker never returned to work, claiming he continued to be in pain that prevented him from working.

Several reports were obtained from doctors over the years. Some claimed that the worker had ongoing pain; others stated that no physiological cause for the pain could be found. The worker gave several explanations besides his pain as to why he had not applied himself more diligently to return to the same work or seek alternative work, and why he had missed appointments with his neurosurgeon and delayed his back surgery. His reasons included transportation problems as a result of losing his driver's licence; preoccupation with ongoing court proceedings for custody of his child; and his inability to pay the union dues required in order for him to maintain his eligibility for seafaring jobs.

Three decisions of the WSIB granted benefits to the worker for the back injury as well as the 1997 left knee injury. In 1998, the seaman's employer appealed the WSIB decisions to continue benefits after December 30, 1991 to the WSIAT. The employer argued that the worker should not have received benefits beyond that date on the grounds that he was capable of returning to work after that date. This was based on the findings of a report that stated the worker had a soft tissue injury and was expected to fully recover.

Believing that the evidence of a WSIB caseworker who assisted the worker and of the worker's treating orthopaedic surgeon would support the position that the worker no longer needed to be off work after December 1991, the employer requested the WSIAT to subpoena them to give evidence of their dealings with the worker.

ISSUES: Should the WSIAT accede to the employer's request to subpoena a WSIB caseworker and the worker's treating orthopaedic surgeon to testify at the hearing? Should the benefits have stopped by December 1991 because the worker was capable of returning to work after that date?

DECISION: Following the hearing, the WSIAT found that it had sufficient evidence to make its decision without subpoenaing the caseworker and doctor. Instead of requiring the doctor to appear as a witness, the WSIAT required its staff to request him to provide a further written medical report addressing certain issues. The Tribunal ruled that the caseworker's written reports prepared at the time of her dealings with the worker were sufficient for its purposes, and it was not clear that the caseworker could provide any additional evidence as she had not been involved in the worker's claim for several years.

The WSIAT upheld the payment of benefits to June 1, 1992, but denied benefits after that date based on evidence that the original back injury had resolved by that time. The Tribunal accepted the evidence of a doctor that the 1997 knee injury was unrelated to the earlier back injury. There were inconsistencies between the worker's oral evidence as to what occurred when he damaged his knee and the written record of his earlier explanations to doctors. His testimony about the cause of his knee injury also changed when he was questioned by tribunal counsel and by the employer's representative. In addition, the Tribunal was not convinced that the worker intended to return to work for the employer, since he terminated his Seafarers' Union dues shortly after the accident. Surveillance video of the worker taken in 1998 and 1999 showed him with a full range of motion in his back and knee. Although there was medical evidence of a bulging disc, there was also evidence that it would not have prevented the worker from working as a seaman after May or June of 1992. There was also evidence that the worker had spent more time working on shore than on ships, casting doubt on whether his chosen trade was seaman. The panel found that the worker was not motivated to return to work. He was motivated by what the panel called "secondary gain factors"—namely, receiving a stable monthly income while on compensation that potentially exceeded what he could earn as a seasonal ship worker, and his focus on ongoing family litigation rather than on returning to work.

The ARB: The Standard for Serving a Notice of Appeal

Toronto (City) v Wolf, [2008] 169 ACWS (3d) 943 (Ont Sup Ct J, Div Ct)

FACTS: Annette Wolf was the assessed owner of two properties on the Toronto assessment roll for the taxation year 2005, one at 761 King Street West and one at 771 King Street West in Toronto. The mailing address on the assessment roll for those properties was 775 King Street West, Toronto. On February 25, 2005 Wolf, sold the properties to 2027330 Ontario Inc. (Ontario Inc.). The City believed that MPAC's assessment of the properties was too low because they sold for $3.5 million more than the assessed value.

Section 40 of the *Assessment Act* (RSO 1990, c A.31) allows a municipality to complain to the Assessment Review Board (ARB) that MPAC's assessment of a property is lower than its true value. To appeal the assessment, the municipality must deliver a notice of appeal to both the person assessed and to MPAC. Section 40.4(3) requires that the notice of appeal must "state a name and address where notices can be given to the person [whose assessment is appealed.]"

On March 31, 2005, the last day for mailing a notice of appeal, the City mailed copies of the notice of appeal to both Wolf and Ontario Inc. at 775 King Street West, the address for service shown on the assessment roll. Wolf had provided the City with this address when she purchased the properties many years earlier.

At the hearing of the City's appeal before the ARB, Wolf and Ontario Inc. submitted that they had not received the notice of appeal before receiving the notice of hearing from the ARB. They argued that the ARB had no jurisdiction to hold a hearing because they had not received a notice of appeal that complied with section 40(3) of the Act. They argued that nothing in section 40(3) authorizes the use of the mailing address on the assessment roll for purposes of sufficient notice. The sale document that the City relied on to launch the appeal showed a different address for Wolf, and the City should have used that address rather than the one on the assessment roll.

The ARB agreed that the City had no power under section 40(3) to rely on the address on the assessment roll when it had knowledge that the address on the roll might be wrong—that is, it ought to have known that a mailing sent to that address would likely not reach the intended recipient. The ARB dismissed the City's appeal. The City appealed to the Divisional Court.

ISSUES: Does section 40(3) of the *Assessment Act* allow the City to send a notice of appeal to the address on the assessment roll or does it require the City to send the notice to the "best" address known to the City—that is, to the address where receipt is most likely? If the service did not comply with section 40(3), does this render the appeal void, or is it a curable defect (that is, a defect that can be cured by steps such as re-serving Wolf and Ontario Inc. at a different address or by granting an adjournment)?

DECISION: Section 40(3) does not specify a particular address to which the notice of appeal must be sent, nor does it require personal service or actual receipt of the notice by the assessed person. The section appears to contemplate more than one address to which the appeal notice may be sent, when it uses the words "*a* name and address" rather than "*the* name and address." An appellant meets the notice requirements if he or she acts reasonably and in good faith in selecting an address for service. In this case, the City acted reasonably and in good faith in sending the notices to Wolf and Ontario Inc. at the address listed for service on the assessment roll. The ARB erred in requiring the City to meet a higher standard for service of the notices than section 40(3) requires. The court set aside the Board's decision and required the Board to hold a hearing on the merits of the appeal.

NOTE: The *Assessment Act* has been updated since this case was reported. For example, section 40(3) is now section 40(9).

REVIEW QUESTIONS

1. What is the mandate of each of the following bodies, and what remedies can each provide to claimants?

   a. the Canadian Human Rights Commission

   b. the Financial Services Commission of Ontario *[Note that this is changing in April 2016 because there will be new legislation to transfer the dispute resolution function to the Licence Appeal Tribunal.]*

   c. the Workplace Safety and Insurance Board

   d. the Immigration and Refugee Board.

2. Which of the tribunals discussed in this chapter require a party to file evidence that documents have been served on the other parties, and what methods of proving service are acceptable?

3. What are the consequences of failing to disclose evidence to other parties in a hearing before the Canadian Human Rights Tribunal?

4. Which of the regulatory regimes discussed in this chapter require a person dissatisfied with an agency's decision to make additional efforts to ask the agency to review its decision internally before he or she may request a hearing before a tribunal? Describe the process required in each case.

5. Who has standing as a party in the following?

   a. proceedings before the Workplace Safety and Insurance Board

   b. proceedings before the Workplace Safety and Insurance Appeals Tribunal

   c. an assessment appeal before the Assessment Review Board

   d. an eviction appeal before the Landlord and Tenant Board.

6. Once an appeal to the Landlord and Tenant Board is ready for a hearing, who is responsible for notifying the parties, and what information does the notice of hearing contain?

7. What are the deadlines for filing the following?

   a. an application to the Human Rights Tribunal of Ontario

   b. an appeal to the Social Benefits Tribunal

   c. an appeal to the Assessment Review Board

   d. an appeal to the Workplace Safety and Insurance Appeals Tribunal.

8. How does a person apply for intervenor status before the Human Rights Tribunal of Ontario?

9. Which of the tribunals discussed in this chapter hold inquisitorial rather than adversarial hearings?

10. Which of the tribunals discussed in this chapter are required to follow policies established by the agencies whose decisions are appealed to them?

11. What recourse is available to a party who is dissatisfied with the tribunal's decision in a hearing before the following boards and tribunals?

    a. the Canadian Human Rights Tribunal

    b. the Human Rights Tribunal of Ontario

    c. the Assessment Review Board

    d. the Landlord and Tenant Board.

12. In what circumstances is the Human Rights Tribunal of Ontario willing to reconsider a decision that it has made?

EXERCISES

1. The mandate, powers, and procedures of Ontario's Municipal Property Assessment Corporation and Assessment Review Board are discussed in this chapter. Provide the authority for ten of the statements made about these bodies where no source has been cited in this chapter. The authority may be a provision of a statute, a section of a regulation made under a statute, a common law doctrine (such as procedural fairness), a rule of procedure or practice direction issued by the body, and so on.

    For example, the text states: "The *Assessment Act* requires the ARB to give MPAC a copy of every notice of appeal." The authority for this statement is section 40(10) of the *Assessment Act*.

2. The Workplace Safety and Insurance Appeals Tribunal has jurisdiction to uphold or disallow benefits for an individual who claims to have a temporary total disability as a result of an injury sustained before January 1, 1998. What is a "temporary total disability"? Where is it defined?

FURTHER READING

Canadian Human Rights Tribunal, *What Happens Next? A Guide to the Tribunal Process*, 2006, online: <http://chrt-tcdp.gc.ca/NS/pdf/layguide-e.pdf>.

Mary Cornish, Fay Faraday & Jo-Anne Pickel, *Enforcing Human Rights in Ontario* (Aurora, Ont: Canada Law Book, 2009).

John Dickie & David Lyman, *Working with the Residential Tenancies Act*, 3rd ed (Toronto: Emond Montgomery, 2011).

Jack Fleming, *Ontario Landlord and Tenant Law Practice, 2016 Edition* (Toronto: LexisNexis, 2015).

Lynn Fournier-Ruggles, *Canadian Immigration and Refugee Law for Legal Professionals*, 3rd ed (Toronto: Emond Montgomery, 2016).

Law Society of Upper Canada, *Best Practices for Paralegals—An Introduction to Accident Benefits Cases at FSCO* (Donald Lamont Learning Centre, The Law Society of Upper Canada, 4 November 2008) (Toronto: Law Society of Upper Canada, 2008).

Law Society of Upper Canada, *Best Practices for Paralegals Before the WSIB and WSIAT* (Donald Lamont Learning Centre, The Law Society of Upper Canada, 5 December 2008) (Toronto: Law Society of Upper Canada, 2008).

Jack Allen Walker & Andy Anstett, *Ontario Assessment Legislation, 2015–2016 Edition* (Scarborough, Ont: Carswell, 2015).

Challenging Decisions of Tribunals and Administrative Agencies

16

LEARNING OUTCOMES

After reading this chapter, you will understand

- the most common reasons for challenging decisions of tribunals and administrative agencies;

- the methods, or review mechanisms, available for challenging decisions;

- who is entitled to make use of these review mechanisms;

- in what circumstances these review mechanisms are available;

- the time limits for raising a challenge;

- the effect of a challenge on a party's duty to comply with the agency's decision;

- the available grounds for appeal and judicial review;

- the standards that the courts apply in reviewing decisions; and

- the remedies available in the case of a successful challenge.

Given the courts' constant demands that [the system of administrative justice] remake itself, it is questionable if it is a system at all. Dr. Johnson might have said that, as with "a dog walking on its hinder legs," the wonder is not that the "system" works badly, it is that it works at all. Judicial review is a poor way to run a railroad. . . .

[T]he courts have shown only a dim perception of the lives and times of the tribunals. I am quick to add that this is not the fault of the judges. They do their best. But lacking, as most do, hands-on experience in the administrative law system, they can hardly be expected to display greater understanding of it.

This raises the question whether supervision by the courts is not the cause, rather than the solution, of the problems. I read most of the administrative law decisions of Canadian courts, or summaries of them, and they are all over the lot. They are lamentably inconsistent, contradictory, and inscrutable. The system is sick, but are we going to the right doctor?

> Justice Robert F Reid, "Judicial Review: A Poor Way to Run a Railroad"
> in Law Society of Upper Canada, *Administrative Law: Principles, Practice
> and Pluralism* (Scarborough, Ont: Carswell, 1993) 455 at 458–59

In an article on advocacy before administrative tribunals, Willard Estey, a former justice of the Supreme Court of Canada, perhaps with tongue planted firmly in cheek, gave the following general rule for effective advocacy: "Never seek to quash an administrative board to which you must one day inevitably return."[1]

Good advice, no doubt, but sometimes there is no choice but to challenge the procedures and rulings of agencies. Moreover, doing so need not be a career-ending move. Agencies will often understand that challenges are sometimes in their interests. Appeals, petitions, and other forms of review of agency decisions provide opportunities to clarify the law and to achieve consistency where agency members have different interpretations of law or policy. Because panels of a tribunal cannot bind each other, external reviews provide an opportunity for final and binding rulings on issues about which panels disagree. A well-founded challenge can be viewed as an opportunity to validate sound practices and decisions and to strengthen the agency's performance by indicating areas for improvement.

Common Grounds for Challenging Decisions

A decision of an administrator, an administrative department or agency, or a tribunal (collectively, "an agency") may be challenged by a person affected by the decision—usually, the person or party directly involved, but in some cases by a third party, such as a person or group in the community. The purpose of the challenge is

---

1   Philip Anisman & Robert F Reid, *Administrative Law: Issues and Practice* (Scarborough, Ont: Carswell, 1995) at 190.

to have the decision reviewed and overturned by the agency itself or by an external authority such as a court.

For a request for review to be accepted, there must be valid grounds for objecting to the decision. The following are among the most common grounds for challenging the decisions of agencies:

- The agency acted outside its jurisdiction. (For example, a tribunal applied a law that it has no authority to apply or granted a remedy that it has no statutory authority to grant.)

- The agency failed to take action that it was under a legal obligation to take. (For example, where the agency is required to make a decision and fails to do so or makes a decision without notifying those who have a right to be consulted.)

- The agency improperly delegated a decision that it was obliged to make itself. (For example, a tribunal allowed counsel or tribunal members not present at the hearing to make the decision in a case.)

- In exercising its discretion, the agency failed to consider options or factors that it was obliged to take into account, or took into account irrelevant factors. (For example, a tribunal based its decision on evidence that had no bearing on the issues in the case.)

- The agency misinterpreted the applicable law.

- The agency acted in bad faith. (For example, an adjudicator heard and decided a case knowing that he or she had a conflict of interest.)

- The agency failed to follow fair procedures. (For example, a tribunal failed to give adequate notice of a hearing to a party, an adjudicator failed to grant a necessary adjournment, or a panel of adjudicators exhibited bias in favour of one of the parties.)

Broadly speaking, the grounds for a judicial review application can generally be characterized as acting outside the administrator or agency's jurisdiction, or following an unfair process.

The grounds for a statutory appeal, on the other hand, are usually limited to those set out explicitly in a statute. The permitted grounds are usually either questions of law alone (the narrowest grounds), questions of fact, or questions of mixed fact and law. In some cases, both questions of law and questions of fact may be allowed (the broadest grounds). The differences between questions of law, questions of fact, and questions of mixed fact and law are described below.

Avenues for Review of Decisions

Review of Decisions Made by Administrative Agencies Other Than Tribunals

Most government decisions that directly affect the rights, interests, and privileges of citizens are subject to some form of review by a higher authority. Decisions made by officials of a department or an administrative agency are often initially reviewed by specialized units or by superiors within the department or agency. Even where an agency has no formal review process, in some situations a non-adjudicative administrative official may have discretion to reconsider his or her decision on request. Depending on the circumstances, such an administrator may have jurisdiction to do this even in the absence of an explicit statutory power to reconsider decisions.

In addition, several mechanisms may be available to persons affected by the decision to initiate a review by an independent authority.

In some cases, the agency's enabling statute provides a right to **appeal** to an independent tribunal. Alternatively, unless the decision deals strictly with matters of legislation or policy, the complainant may be able to apply for judicial review of the decision. However, the courts have discretion whether to accept applications for judicial review. If the agency's legislation provides for a review by a tribunal, a court will usually insist that the individual first seek a remedy through this route before asking a court to review the decision. If the tribunal upholds the agency's decision and the individual believes the decision of the tribunal is also incorrect, generally a court appeal or judicial review of the tribunal's decision is available.

A review by an internal or external monitoring official or agency may also be available. Most governments have officials who monitor the operations and programs of departments and agencies to ensure that they are operating effectively, efficiently, and fairly; spending public funds prudently; and accounting properly for these expenditures. Some of these watchdogs are quasi-independent officials within a department or agency (such as the Fair Practices Commissioner within Ontario's Workplace Safety and Insurance Board or the City of Toronto's Ethics Commissioner), while others are independent officers of the legislature who report to the legislature as a whole rather than to the government.

The best-known independent watchdogs are the **ombudsmen**, who have authority to investigate complaints from citizens about almost any form of unfair treatment by government officials. An ombudsman cannot overturn a decision but can recommend a different result in an individual case, as well as recommending fairer practices generally.

There are various other officials who conduct reviews of government programs and in some cases investigate individual complaints. They include

- provincial auditors and the federal auditor general, who review the effectiveness and efficiency of government programs and spending;
- environmental commissioners, who comment on the fairness and effectiveness of environmental programs;
- ethics or integrity commissioners, who ensure that politicians do not engage in activities that constitute a conflict of interest or violate codes of ethics;
- provincial and federal information and privacy commissioners; and
- federal government officials who monitor the implementation of official languages legislation, the treatment of prisoners in federal penitentiaries, and matters related to air travel.

While these officials fulfill important roles in ensuring that government officials act responsibly and within their jurisdiction, this chapter focuses on the principal authorities to which a challenge of an agency's decision may be addressed—tribunals, courts, and ombudsmen.

Review of Decisions Made by Tribunals

Many decisions made by bureaucrats are subject to review by a tribunal. A party that is dissatisfied with a tribunal's decision may have one or more avenues to challenge it. Most tribunal decisions are open to review by the tribunal itself (often called "reconsideration," "reopening," or "rehearing"), by a court, or by both.

When a complainant wishes to challenge a decision, it is often quicker and cheaper to ask the tribunal to conduct an internal review or reconsideration where this option is available before seeking a remedy from the courts. If that solution fails or is unavailable, the complainant may apply to a court by way of either appeal, if this is authorized by the tribunal's governing statute, or judicial review. Generally, a court will not undertake judicial review if there is a statutory right to an appeal and the complainant has not exercised that right. A second restriction on the availability of judicial review of a tribunal's proceedings is that a court will rarely entertain an application for judicial review of the fairness of the tribunal's procedures or of its jurisdiction before the tribunal has rendered its decision. Such judicial review applications will usually be rejected as premature.

There are two different routes to challenging a tribunal decision before a court—appeal and judicial review. The similarities and differences between these procedures are explained below, under the subheadings "Appeals" and "Judicial Review."

In some cases, the tribunal's decisions may be reviewed by another tribunal, but this is unusual. In addition, ombudsmen may have a limited power to review the decisions of tribunals and recommend remedies.

Time Limits for Raising a Challenge

Complainants and their representatives must be aware that there may be a deadline for raising a challenge to an agency's decision.

Generally, in the case of reconsideration of a decision by a tribunal, the tribunal will specify in its rules of procedure any time limit for the conduct of the review. However, the timing of the review may also be subject to a requirement under the tribunal's governing statute. For example, section 21.2(2) of Ontario's *Statutory Powers Procedure Act*[2] (SPPA) states that the review must take place "within a reasonable time" after the decision was made, while section 53(3) of British Columbia's *Administrative Tribunals Act*[3] (ATA) requires parties to apply for clarification of tribunal decisions within 30 days. Internal departmental reviews of staff decisions may also have time limits.

---

2 RSO 1990, c S.22.

3 SBC 2000, c 45.

For an appeal of a tribunal's decision to a court, there is usually a statutory time limit requiring the complainant to file the appeal within a relatively short time (often 30 days) of receiving the tribunal's decision.[4]

The time limits for applying for judicial review of an agency's or an official's decision may vary from province to province. Some provinces—including Ontario, British Columbia, and Prince Edward Island—have legislation governing judicial review procedures. In Ontario, there are no specified time limits; however, as a matter of practice, if the court considers that there is excessive delay, it may deny the application. The *Federal Courts Act*,[5] which governs judicial review of federal departments, boards, commissions, and tribunals, provides for a 30-day time limit.

Effect of a Challenge on Compliance with the Decision

Application to "Stay" the Decision

A person challenging a tribunal's decision or order either through a request for reconsideration, an application for judicial review, or an appeal does not want to comply with the order before its validity has been decided. The procedure for stopping a decision from taking effect is called an application to "stay" the decision. A **stay** is an order issued by a tribunal or court suspending the decision that is being challenged, usually until the challenge has been either decided or abandoned. However, in some circumstances, the tribunal or court that is hearing the challenge may lift the stay before it has completed its review—for example, if it finds that the complainant is deliberately delaying further proceedings.

Normally, a request to the tribunal to reconsider its decision does not automatically stay the operation of the order, unless the tribunal's rules of practice state that it does. In most cases, a request for reconsideration must be accompanied by a separate application to the tribunal for a stay until the tribunal has completed its review of the decision.

In Ontario, an appeal of a tribunal's decision to a court generally results in an automatic stay of the tribunal's decision.[6] In contrast, an application for judicial review in Ontario does not itself stay the decision; however, a party may apply separately for a stay.[7] Depending on the governing statute, in an appeal or judicial review application the stay request may be made to the tribunal, to the court conducting the appeal or review, or in some cases to either the tribunal or the court.

---

4   For example, s 145.6(1) of Ontario's *Environmental Protection Act*, RSO 1990, c E.19 in combination with rule 61.04(1) of Ontario's *Rules of Civil Procedure*.

5   RSC 1985, c F-7.

6   SPPA, *supra* note 2, s 25(1).

7   *Courts of Justice Act*, RSO 1990, c C.43, s 106.

Test for Granting a Stay

The accepted test for granting a stay is set out in *RJR-MacDonald Inc v Canada (Attorney General)*.[8] The party seeking the stay must convince the decision-maker that:

1. There is a serious issue to be determined.

   Generally, the threshold for meeting this requirement is low. All that is required is that the court or tribunal conduct a preliminary assessment of the merits of the case. If the case appears to have any merit, the test will be met unless the effect of granting the stay would be to nullify the tribunal's order—for example, where the rights granted by the order that is being challenged cannot be exercised at all unless they are exercised immediately. In such a case, the court should conduct a more probing examination of the merits of the case.

2. The party seeking the stay will suffer irreparable harm if a stay is not granted.

   "Irreparable harm" is harm that cannot be quantified in money terms or cannot be rectified by payment of compensation for the harm suffered— for example, where compliance with the challenged order will put the applicant out of business, cause permanent injury to health, or destroy the environment.

3. The balance of convenience favours granting a stay.

   If the party seeking the stay will suffer greater harm if the stay is refused than the party that benefits from the tribunal's order will suffer if the stay is granted, the balance favours a stay. Where one party will suffer irreparable harm from the decision whether to stay an order and the other will not, the balance usually favours the party who will suffer irreparable harm. However, if both parties will suffer irreparable harm from staying or not staying an order, in deciding the balance of convenience the court or tribunal will consider which party will suffer more irreparable harm.

Specific Review Mechanisms

Reconsideration by the Tribunal Itself

Tribunals have a limited power to review and change their decisions even without any statutory authority to conduct such a review, and a much broader authority to do so where the statute establishing the tribunal or some other statute authorizes this practice. As mentioned, this review procedure is known as **reconsideration**, **reopening**, or **rehearing**.

In Ontario, section 21.2(1) of the SPPA authorizes tribunals to review their decisions if they consider it "advisable" to do so and if they have made rules governing the conduct of such reviews. The same provision gives tribunals wide discretion in

---

8   [1994] 1 SCR 311 at paras 43–81.

determining the consequences of a review. Specifically, they may "confirm, vary, suspend or cancel" the decision.

In Quebec, section 154 of the *Administrative Justice Act*[9] (AJA) authorizes the Administrative Tribunal of Quebec to review its decisions where a new fact is discovered that might result in a different decision, where a party who should have been heard was not heard, or where a defect in the procedure or decision is sufficiently serious that it could render the decision invalid. The procedure for conducting a review is set out in the AJA.

The above provisions in the SPPA and the AJA reflect an important change in the law. Traditionally, at common law, the rule known as **functus officio** applied when a court or tribunal rendered a decision. This Latin term means "having discharged its duty" and implies that a court or tribunal has exhausted its authority once it has made a decision. In the past, unless a statute expressly provided otherwise, a court or tribunal could not change its decision except to correct minor errors (such as clerical errors and errors of calculation) or to clarify ambiguities.

In its 1989 decision in *Chandler v Alberta Association of Architects*,[10] the Supreme Court of Canada ruled that tribunals have a broader power to amend their decisions. The Court said that even without explicit statutory authority, "if the tribunal has failed to dispose of an issue which is fairly raised by the proceedings and of which the tribunal is empowered by its enabling statute to dispose, it ought to be allowed to complete its statutory task."[11] Other court decisions have permitted—and even required—tribunals to reconsider their decisions in cases where it is clear that a factual error influenced the decision of an adjudicator[12] and where a tribunal's order inaccurately reflected a settlement made by the parties.[13]

Chandler was a case involving the finality of a decision made by a tribunal. It affirmed that the *functus officio* doctrine continues to apply to tribunals, but in a much more flexible fashion than previously believed. However, *Chandler* did not address whether *functus officio* applied at all to informal, non-adjudicative administrative decisions. In other words, once a non-adjudicative administrator makes a decision to grant or refuse a licence or benefit, is he or she prohibited by the *functus officio* doctrine from changing his or her mind? The courts are divided as to whether *functus officio* has any application under these circumstances.[14] Some courts have ruled that officials cannot reconsider their decisions unless the statute governing their decision-making power expressly permits reconsideration. Other courts

---

9   CQLR c J-3.

10   [1989] 2 SCR 848.

11   *Ibid* at 862.

12   *Grier v Metro International Trucks Ltd*, [1996] 28 OR (3d) 67 (Div Ct).

13   *Re City of Kingston and Mining and Lands Commissioner* (1977), 18 OR (2d) 166 (Div Ct).

14   For a good survey of the cases dealing with this question in the immigration context, see *Kurukkal v Canada (Minister of Citizenship and Immigration)*, 2009 FC 695, aff'd in part by the Federal Court of Appeal, 2010 FCA 230.

have ruled that officials can reconsider their decisions unless the statute forbids reconsideration.

In Ontario, under the SPPA, tribunals may have even greater power to reopen and reconsider their decisions as long as they make rules governing the exercise of this power. Usually, the rules define a two-stage process. The first stage consists of evaluating requests for review against specific criteria to determine whether the tribunal should undertake such a review. If the answer is "yes," the rules then specify who should conduct the review and how it should be conducted. The Society of Ontario Adjudicators and Regulators has prepared model rules that can be adopted or modified for this purpose.[15]

Appeals and Applications for Judicial Review

Appeals

A person may appeal a decision of an official or a tribunal to a court or other independent authority only when this alternative is set out in a statute—usually, the agency's governing statute. The statute may provide for an appeal on questions of law alone, on questions of law and jurisdiction, or on questions of fact or law. In some cases, the statute will provide for an appeal on questions of law to a court and on questions of fact, policy, or the public interest to a government official, Cabinet minister, or Cabinet.[16]

The Supreme Court has described the difference between a question of law, a question of fact, and a question of mixed fact and law:

> In making a factual inference, the trial judge must sift through the relevant facts, decide on their weight, and draw a factual conclusion. ...
>
> At the outset, it is important to distinguish questions of mixed fact and law from factual findings (whether direct findings or inferences). Questions of mixed fact and law involve applying a legal standard to a set of facts ... . On the other hand, factual findings or inferences require making a conclusion of fact based on a set of facts. Both mixed fact and law and fact findings often involve drawing inferences; the difference lies in whether the inference drawn is legal or factual. Because of this similarity, the two types of questions are sometimes confounded. ...
>
> [A] finding of negligence by a trial judge involves applying a legal standard to a set of facts, and thus is a question of mixed fact and law. Matters of mixed fact and law lie along a spectrum. Where ... an error ... can be attributed to the

---

15   Society of Ontario Adjudicators and Regulators, *Ontario Rules: A Model for Administrative Justice Agencies* (Courtice, Ont: Society of Ontario Adjudicators and Regulators, 2000).

16   For example, s 145.6 of Ontario's *Environmental Protection Act*, *supra* note 4, provides for an appeal from the Environmental Review Tribunal to the Divisional Court on questions of law, and to the minister of the environment on any matter other than a question of law (for example, questions of fact or interpretation or application of policies). Section 95 of the *Ontario Municipal Board Act*, RSO 1990, c O.28 provided for a petition to Cabinet from decisions of the Ontario Municipal Board until 2007, when this provision was repealed.

application of an incorrect standard, a failure to consider a required element of a legal test, or similar error in principle, such an error can be characterized as an error of law ... . [I]t is often difficult to extricate the legal questions from the factual. It is for this reason that these matters are referred to as questions of "mixed law and fact." Where the legal principle is not readily extricable, then the matter is one of "mixed law and fact."[17]

When the appeal is to a court, usually the only evidence that can be put before the court is the evidence that was put before the tribunal. The parties cannot present additional evidence.

Sometimes the appeal is "as of right," meaning that no permission is needed. However, some statutes provide for an appeal only "with leave," which means that the party who wants to appeal must persuade the court to grant permission. The criteria for obtaining leave are either set out in a statute or in the court's rules of procedure, or are part of the common law. These criteria often involve convincing the court that the appeal raises an important legal issue and has reasonable prospects for success.

Usually, only the tribunal's final decision can be appealed. A party who wants to challenge a procedural ruling of the tribunal or argue that the tribunal does not have jurisdiction *before* the final decision is rendered must seek judicial review rather than launch an appeal. However, as stated earlier, courts are reluctant to permit judicial review applications partway through a proceeding, and will often refuse to permit parties to interrupt proceedings.

In addition to providing a right to appeal, governing statutes generally specify the procedures a court must follow in hearing the appeal and the remedies available to the court. In judicial review applications, the procedures and remedies are more likely to be determined by common law or found in a general statute governing judicial review applications.

When an appeal is available, the complainant is usually required to seek a remedy through this mechanism before applying for judicial review. Where there is no statutory right to appeal, application for judicial review is the only means of bringing a challenge of a decision before the courts. (See the box feature "Petitions to Cabinet.")

Judicial Review

In the past, the legislature that created a tribunal often wanted the tribunal's decisions to be final and not subject to review by a court, so it provided for no right of appeal. Seeing how unfair this lack of opportunity to appeal could be, the courts created their own limited form of "appeal," known as judicial review, available in cases where there was no statutory right of appeal. Judicial review refers to a review of an agency's or an official's decision by a court that has an inherent authority to

---

17   *Housen v Nikolaisen*, [2002] 2 SCR 235. Although *Housen* was a civil action for negligence, its characterization of errors of law and errors of mixed fact and law has been adopted in the field of administrative law. See, for example, *X (Re)*, 2014 CanLII 66630 (Can IRB).

ensure that the department or agency has not acted outside its jurisdiction. The person seeking a remedy must apply to the court for judicial review, and acceptance of the application is granted at the discretion of the court. The fact that access to a judicial review is discretionary contrasts to the right to appeal provided by the authority of a statute.

Petitions to Cabinet

Instead of providing a right to appeal, the governing statutes of certain agencies provide a right to challenge an agency's decision by submission of a petition to Cabinet. There are some important differences between these two ways of challenging a decision.

- In reviewing a petition, Cabinet has greater power to take political considerations into account than is the case for a court or other authority hearing an appeal.

- Cabinet's decision on a petition may not be appealed to a court or other authority.

- An application for judicial review cannot be made regarding Cabinet's decision on a petition.

- Cabinet is not bound to follow rules of natural justice or procedural fairness. It can obtain any information and advice from government staff, including information not put before the agency that made the original decision, and need not reveal what information it considered in reaching its decision.

- Cabinet is not required to make a decision. If it does make a decision, it is not required to give reasons for the decision.

- Because there are often no fixed rules of procedure, individuals or organizations who did not participate in the tribunal proceedings may be allowed to make representations to Cabinet.

- Cabinet may consider issues or base its decision on grounds not raised before the tribunal.

The procedures for making applications for judicial review of decisions by provincial and municipal departments, agencies, and tribunals, and the remedies that may be granted by judicial review, may be set out in a provincial judicial review procedure statute; in the rules of civil procedure under the Ontario *Courts of Justice Act* and similar acts across the provinces and territories; or determined by the common law. The *Federal Courts Act*[18] governs judicial review of federal departments and tribunals such as the Immigration and Refugee Board of Canada.

A party to a tribunal proceeding or a person directly affected by a decision of a government official can seek judicial review of the decision on the grounds that the tribunal or official exceeded its jurisdiction. Exceeding jurisdiction can consist of acting outside the powers provided by statute, failing to follow the requirements of

---

18 *Supra* note 5.

a statute, or following an unfair procedure. However, the courts have ruled that a decision that is clearly not supported by the evidence is also a jurisdictional error and subject to judicial review. Because this is the kind of error that would normally be addressed in an appeal, by treating this as a matter of jurisdiction, the courts have given themselves a power of review almost as broad as if an appeal were available.

In its 1979 decision in *CUPE v NB Liquor Corporation*,[19] the Supreme Court of Canada changed the justification of the courts' power to review errors such as evidentiary errors. Instead of branding such issues as jurisdictional, the Court decided that where a specialized tribunal with particular expertise that has been given the protection of a privative clause (see below) is alleged to have made an error in weighing evidence or interpreting law while acting within its jurisdiction, the tribunal's interpretation of its enabling statute would be allowed to stand unless the interpretation is "so patently unreasonable that its construction cannot be rationally supported by the relevant legislation."[20] This was the beginning of a new approach to judicial review in which the courts would sometimes defer to the views of a tribunal even if they did not agree with them (see the box feature "Deference").

When the legislature does not want to provide an appeal mechanism and wants to prevent the courts from conducting a review of a decision despite the absence of an appeal right, or when there is a statutory right to appeal and the legislature is concerned that a court may conduct a broader review than is available through the appeal mechanism, the legislature will insert a privative clause into the agency's governing statute. A **privative clause** attempts to restrict or prevent review by a court of the actions or decisions of an agency.

Privative Clauses

The following example of a privative clause is from the Ontario *Labour Relations Act, 1995* (SO 1995, c 1, Schedule A, s 116):

> No decision, order, direction, declaration or ruling of the Board shall be questioned or reviewed in any court, and no order shall be made or process entered, or proceedings taken in any court, whether by way of injunction, declaratory judgment, certiorari, mandamus, prohibition, quo warranto, or otherwise, to question, review, prohibit or restrain the Board or any of its proceedings.

In practice, because the courts have ruled that privative clauses are inapplicable to matters of jurisdiction, such clauses have had little success in preventing judicial review. With respect to privative clauses in provincial statutes, the Supreme Court of Canada has ruled that any law that prohibits the courts from considering whether a tribunal has exceeded its jurisdiction is unconstitutional.[21] In addition, as

---

19 [1979] 2 SCR 227.

20 *Ibid* at 237.

21 *Crevier v AG (Quebec)*, [1981] 2 SCR 220; *Dunsmuir v New Brunswick*, 2008 SCC 9, [2008] 1 SCR 190.

mentioned, the courts generally have interpreted errors of jurisdiction to include almost any substantial error of fact or law. This leaves little room for privative clauses to insulate agency decisions from judicial review. (Privative clauses have had some effect, however, in influencing how critically a court will scrutinize an agency's decision; this point is discussed in more detail in the sections on "Standards of Review.")

ADMISSIBLE EVIDENCE

Like an appeal, a judicial review hearing is generally limited to a review of the facts and information in the tribunal's "record" (that is, the material that was put before the tribunal during its hearing). In a judicial review hearing, parties may supplement this evidence with affidavits containing additional evidence only in exceptional circumstances—for example, to demonstrate that there was a complete absence of evidence before the tribunal on an essential point, to show that the tribunal followed an unfair procedure, or when the evidence was unavailable during the original proceeding and is practically conclusive of the issue before the court.[22]

Who May Appeal or Seek Judicial Review

Because appeals are available only when provided for in a statute, the only persons who have the right to appeal an agency's decision are those specifically authorized by the section of the statute establishing that right. In most cases, the relevant legislation is the enabling statute governing the particular agency. Neither Alberta's *Administrative Procedures and Jurisdiction Act*[23] nor Ontario's SPPA contains a right of appeal, although the SPPA does recognize that a decision of a tribunal may be appealed to a court or other authority.[24] Quebec's AJA provides for appeals in certain cases but not in others.[25] Usually, statutes give only a party or a person directly affected a right to appeal. However, if the appeal is to a superior court, the court may have authority under its rules of practice to permit intervenors to participate.

For judicial review applications, the common law determines who may initiate proceedings. Provincial statutes governing judicial review procedures do not address this question.

The parties in a tribunal hearing generally have a right—also known as "standing" or *locus standi*—to apply for judicial review of the tribunal's decision. Intervenors do not automatically have standing, but they may be permitted to apply at the discretion of the court. In the case of decisions of officials and agencies other than tribunals, the applicant for judicial review usually must have a direct and substantial interest in the decision. Generally, this means a property right or financial interest.

---

22 *Re Keeprite Workers' Independent Union and Keeprite Products Ltd* (1980), 114 DLR (3d) 162 at 170 (Ont CA); *Canadiana Towers Ltd v Fawcett* (1978), 90 DLR (3d) 758 at 763 (Ont CA).

23 RSA 2000, c A-3.

24 As mentioned, s 25(1) of the SPPA provides that an appeal effectively stays a decision of a tribunal.

25 *Supra* note 9, s 159.

Traditionally, the courts have refused to accept applications for judicial review when a public right or interest is involved except in the following circumstances:

- where the attorney general consents to the applicant being granted standing;
- where the applicant will suffer some special damage peculiar to himself or herself as a result of interference with a public right; or
- where the applicant will suffer no greater damage or harm than the rest of the public but qualifies for public interest standing.

To decide that a person qualifies for public interest standing outside of the circumstances above, for several decades the courts had to find the following:

1. that the issue that the applicant wants to raise is serious or important;
2. that the issue is **justiciable** (that is, it is an issue that a court can decide);
3. that the applicant has a genuine interest in the issue; and
4. that there is no other reasonable and effective way for the applicant to bring the issue before the court.

Regarding the third point, the kind of interest required for public interest standing need not be a financial or property interest. For example, a demonstrated history of educating the public about an issue or promoting the values involved may be sufficient.

This was a test that evolved over several decades. The liberalization of standing requirements for persons seeking to challenge governmental decisions began with *Thorson v Attorney General of Canada*,[26] which first accepted the concept of "public interest" standing in constitutional cases. The fourth component of the test was most clearly articulated in 1981 in *Minister of Justice of Canada v Borowski*.[27] The Supreme Court of Canada revisited the *Borowski* formulation in 2012 in *Downtown Eastside Sex Workers*.[28] In *Downtown*, a society whose objectives include improving conditions for female sex workers in the Downtown Eastside of Vancouver, and K, who had formerly worked as a sex worker, launched a Charter challenge with regard to the prostitution provisions of the *Criminal Code*.[29] The British Columbia government argued that the Society and the former prostitute did not qualify for public interest standing because they did not meet the fourth part of the *Borowski* test.

The Supreme Court made a small but meaningful change to the fourth component of the test. The Court ruled that an applicant for public interest standing need not prove that there is no other reasonable and effective means to bring the case to court, but only that the application before the court is a reasonable and effective means to bring the case to court. This should make it easier for public interest

---

26   [1975] 1 SCR 138.

27   [1981] 2 SCR 575.

28   *Canada (Attorney General) v Downtown Eastside Sex Workers United Against Violence Society*, 2012 SCC 45, [2012] 2 SCR 524.

29   RSC 1985, c C-46.

litigants to obtain standing not only in Charter challenges but also in other judicial review applications, because it is easier for an applicant to show that an application to the court is *one* reasonable way to have the issue heard rather than to show that it is the *most* reasonable way or the *only* way.

The Court also ruled that the other elements identified in *Borowski*, particularly the third one, are not to be viewed as rigid requirements, but rather as considerations to be weighed cumulatively in exercising judicial discretion in a "flexible and generous"[30] way.

Standards of Review

In reviewing agencies' decisions, the courts apply different standards of review depending on various factors. In this context, **standard of review** refers to the degree of rigour with which a court will scrutinize an agency's decision, and the degree of error or the level of uncertainty about the reasonableness or correctness of an agency's decision that a court will tolerate in deciding whether to accept or overturn the decision.

In the past, the courts would sometimes give a tribunal more latitude for error on a decision brought for judicial review than one brought on appeal. To pass on appeal, the standard of review was **correctness** and the requirement was strictly applied. If a decision contained a legal or factual error that affected the outcome of the case, the decision was usually overturned. In appeals, the courts did not recognize that in some cases, rather than there being a single "correct" interpretation of the law or the facts, there might be more than one reasonable interpretation, which could result in two or more equally valid decisions.

In judicial review proceedings, the rule was different. Although the courts did not permit legislatures to completely immunize tribunal decisions from court review, they recognized that, because of the special expertise of some tribunals or because the legislature made it clear that it did not want the tribunal's decisions reviewed, in some circumstances the courts should not second-guess the tribunal's reasoning and conclusions if the decision was reasonable. Consequently, on judicial review, the standard of review was either correctness or patent unreasonableness. Where the standard was **patent unreasonableness**, the tribunal did not have to be correct, only reasonable, and the court would not overturn its decision unless it was obviously ("patently") unreasonable on its face. However, in certain other circumstances—for example, where the tribunal had no special expertise or there was no privative clause to indicate that the legislature wanted to limit the power of the courts—the courts applied the standard of correctness.

In 1997, the Supreme Court introduced a third standard of review in judicial review proceedings: **reasonableness** *simpliciter*, or simple reasonableness.[31] In applying this standard, a court had to determine whether the agency's interpretation of the law or the facts, or both, was reasonable.

---

30 *Supra* note 28 at paras 20 and 53.

31 *Canada (Director of Investigation and Research) v Southam Inc*, [1997] 1 SCR 748.

Deference

The basis for having more than one standard of review is the idea of **deference** to the judgment of an agency. The courts formulated three different standards of review because it seemed appropriate that in some circumstances they should show respect to the legislature's choice to delegate certain decisions to specialized tribunals rather than to courts. Courts show this respect by deferring to the tribunal in certain cases—that is, by accepting its decision even if they disagree with it.

For example, when a tribunal has made a decision that is clearly within its jurisdiction—such as weighing evidence and making findings of fact, or deciding a matter where it has greater expertise than a court, or where it is interpreting its enabling statute—the court should not substitute its own views even if it disagrees with the tribunal's decision, as long as the tribunal's decision is a reasonable one. However, if the issue decided by the tribunal is closer to the special expertise and central mandate of a court—for example, if the tribunal is determining the limits of its jurisdiction (a purely legal question) or applying a statute that deals with an area of law that is different than the area with which the tribunal's enabling statute deals—the courts feel that they should be free to pay less deference to the tribunal and have more leeway to substitute their own decisions for those of the tribunal.

In 2003, in its decisions in *Dr Q v College of Physicians and Surgeons of British Columbia*[32] and *Law Society of New Brunswick v Ryan*,[33] the Supreme Court of Canada declared that, although the issue of whether a court was conducting an appeal or a judicial review would be a factor in determining which standard of review applied in a particular case, any of the three standards *might* apply to a case, regardless of whether it was an appeal or a judicial review, depending on which standard the court judged most appropriate. This removed an important area of inconsistency between appeals and judicial reviews; however, it did not make the question of whether the court was conducting an appeal or a judicial review irrelevant, as this would still be a factor in determining which standard of review applied in a particular case.

Although it was now clear that the same three standards of review could apply in judicial reviews and in appeals, how to decide which standard applied in a particular case remained confusing except where a statute stated what standard should apply.[34] In *Dr Q* and *Ryan*, the Supreme Court sought to clarify the differences between the three standards of review and presented guidelines to aid courts in deciding which standard to apply in a particular case; these are discussed below, under the heading "Determining the Standard of Review Before *Dunsmuir*: The Pragmatic and Functional Approach."

---

32   *Dr Q v College of Physicians and Surgeons of British Columbia*, [2003] 1 SCR 226 [*Dr Q*].

33   *Law Society of New Brunswick v Ryan*, 2003 SCC 20, [2003] 1 SCR 247 [*Ryan*].

34   For example, s 58 of British Columbia's ATA (*supra* note 3) sets out the standards of review for tribunals whose enabling statutes contain a privative clause, while s 59 sets out the standards of review for those that do not have such a clause.

CORRECTNESS

In a case in which there is only one right answer, a decision is correct if the tribunal gave that answer; it is incorrect if the tribunal gave any other answer. For example, if the issue is one on which a tribunal has less expertise than the court (such as a question of interpretation of a statute that the tribunal is not usually called on to apply) and the court disagrees with the tribunal's conclusion, the court will generally overturn the tribunal's decision.

In such cases, the court is said to "owe no deference" to the tribunal.

REASONABLENESS SIMPLICITER

"Reasonableness *simpliciter*" means simple reasonableness. As the expression implies, this standard allows a court to accept a tribunal's decision that is based on a reasonable interpretation of the facts or the law as opposed to a single correct answer. To apply this standard, the courts determine whether the tribunal has given reasons for its decision and, if so, whether they show a logical connection between the evidence and the tribunal's conclusions. A court may find a decision to be reasonable even if a relevant issue is not dealt with in the reasons, as long as there is recorded evidence on the issue that is consistent with the tribunal's overall findings.

When the standard was simple reasonableness, the courts were required to give the tribunal's decision considerable deference, but not as much deference as when the standard of review was patent unreasonableness.

> *A decision will be unreasonable only if there is no line of analysis within the given reasons that could reasonably lead the tribunal from the evidence before it to the conclusion at which it arrived. If any of the reasons that are sufficient to support the conclusion are tenable in the sense that they can stand up to a somewhat probing examination, then the decision will not be unreasonable and a reviewing court must not interfere . . . . This means that a decision may satisfy the reasonableness standard if it is supported by a tenable explanation even if this explanation is not one that the reviewing court finds compelling.*
>
> Iacobucci J in *Law Society of New Brunswick v Ryan*,
> 2003 SCC 20, [2003] 1 SCR 247 at para 55

PATENT UNREASONABLENESS

In *Ryan*, the Supreme Court described a patently unreasonable decision as one containing a defect so obvious that there could be no doubt that the decision itself was defective. The decision is "clearly irrational" or "evidently not in accordance with reason," and so flawed that "no amount of curial deference can justify letting it stand."[35] Unless a decision could be characterized as irrational, the courts had to defer to the tribunal even if they did not agree with its decision.

---

35   *Law Society of New Brunswick v Ryan, supra* note 33 at para 52.

Of the three standards, patent unreasonableness implied the highest degree of deference to the tribunal. Even if the court found that the tribunal's conclusions were incomplete or poorly reasoned, it would overturn the decision only if no court could possibly agree with it.

> *When asked to explain "standard of review" to non-lawyers, I say that it is the degree of rigour that a court applies in reviewing the decision of an administrative tribunal. This sometimes prompts the question, "Well, wouldn't the court want to do its best every time?"*
>
> *At the risk of causing administrative law scholars to throw up when they read this, here is a summary of my usual explanation. The court applies a complex legal analysis (the functional and pragmatic approach—another wondrously mind-numbing phrase) to determine how much deference or respect it will give the tribunal's decision.*
>
> *At one end is correctness, where the court applies the test: Do I agree with you? ("You" being the tribunal.) In the middle is reasonableness simpliciter, or I don't agree with you, but I can see where you're coming from. Finally, at the other end of the scale is patently unreasonable, which means You're crazy.*
>
> Douglas Mah, "Think Latin Is Hard to Learn? Try
> Administrative Law" (June–July 2003) *National* at 46

Standards of Review After Dunsmuir

In its 2008 decision in *Dunsmuir v New Brunswick*,[36] the Supreme Court eliminated the standard of patent unreasonableness from the standards that a reviewing court may choose to apply, leaving only those of reasonableness and correctness. The Court reasoned that it was illogical to have a standard of review of patent unreasonableness for some tribunals, as this implied that these tribunals were allowed to be unreasonable, as long as their unreasonableness was not obvious.

Patent unreasonableness remains as a standard of review only where a statute explicitly states that it applies. Some statutes continue to require a patent unreasonableness standard despite *Dunsmuir*—for example, British Columbia's ATA prescribes a standard of patent unreasonableness for certain types of tribunal decisions,[37] and Ontario's 2008 amendments to the *Human Rights Code*,[38] passed after *Dunsmuir*, state that a decision of the Human Rights Tribunal of Ontario may not be set aside unless the decision is patently unreasonable.[39]

---

36 2008 SCC 9, [2008] 1 SCR 190 [*Dunsmuir*].

37 *Supra* note 3, ss 58–59.

38 RSO 1990, c H.19.

39 *Ibid* at s 45.8.

REASONABLENESS

In *Dunsmuir*, the Court explained that the reason some decisions need only be "reasonable" rather than "correct" is that certain questions that come before administrative tribunals do not lend themselves to just one acceptable answer. Instead, they may give rise to a number of possible, reasonable conclusions. In those circumstances, the appropriate standard of review is reasonableness.

The Court also revised its explanation in cases such as *Ryan* and *Dr Q* of what makes a decision reasonable. A decision is reasonable if it falls within a range of possible, acceptable outcomes that are defensible in relation to both the facts and the law.

CORRECTNESS

Dunsmuir did not change the meaning of "correctness" articulated in *Ryan* and *Dr Q*. However, the Court explained that when applying the correctness standard, a reviewing court will not show *any* deference to the decision-maker's reasoning process. Rather, it will undertake its own analysis of the question, which will lead it to decide whether it agrees with the determination of the decision-maker. If the court disagrees, it will substitute its own view and provide the correct answer.

Determining the Standard of Review Before Dunsmuir: The Pragmatic and Functional Approach

> *In attempting to follow the court's distinctions between "patently unreasonable," "reasonable," and "correct," one feels at times as though one is watching a juggler juggle three transparent objects. Depending on which way the light falls, sometimes one thinks one can see the objects. Other times one cannot and, indeed, wonders whether there are really three distinct objects there at all.*
>
> *Miller v Workers' Compensation Commission (Nfld)* (1997),
> 154 Nfld & PEIR 52 at 57–58 (Nfld SCTD)

The Supreme Court has provided direction to the courts to assist them in deciding which standard of review to apply in a particular case. Before *Dunsmuir*, and even before the decisions in *Dr Q* and *Ryan*, the Supreme Court directed the courts to use a "pragmatic and functional approach"[40] in reviewing tribunal decisions. In this approach, a reviewing court was to ask whether the issue before the tribunal was one that the legislators intended to be left to the exclusive jurisdiction of the tribunal. If the answer was "yes," the court was not to substitute its view of what was right for the tribunal's view unless the tribunal's decision was patently unreasonable.

The Supreme Court elaborated on the pragmatic and functional approach in *Dr Q* and *Ryan*. In this approach, the overall aim of the courts was to discern the intent of the legislators in enacting the particular statute that the tribunal was

---

40 *Pushpanathan v Canada (Minister of Citizenship and Immigration)*, [1998] 1 SCR 982, 160 DLR
   (4th) 193 at 209.

applying or interpreting, keeping in mind the constitutional role of the courts in maintaining the rule of law. The courts were not to view this process of discerning the legislative intent as "an empty ritual"[41] or to apply the process mechanically.

Discerning the intent of the legislators required the courts to consider the following four factors in every case:

1. the presence or absence of a statutory right of appeal or a privative clause in the tribunal's governing statute;

2. the expertise of the tribunal relative to that of the court reviewing the decision in question;

3. the purpose of the legislation and, in particular, of the provision the tribunal was applying or interpreting; and

4. the nature of the question—for example, whether it was one of fact, law, or mixed fact and law.

The Supreme Court stressed that none of these factors was conclusive and that the four factors may overlap. Therefore, they must be considered together. In addition, different factors may be given different weight in different circumstances.

The court went on to provide more specific guidance on how the four factors were to be used in determining the appropriate standard of review. These suggestions are summarized in the following sections.

RIGHT TO APPEAL VERSUS PRIVATIVE CLAUSE

According to the Court, a statute that provided for a right of appeal was an indication that the legislature welcomed close scrutiny of the tribunal's decisions and was therefore an invitation to the courts to give less deference to those decisions. A court's approach in this case would lean toward the correctness standard. On the other hand, a statute that contained a privative clause was an indication that the legislature did not want the courts to interfere with the tribunal's decisions and therefore suggested a more deferential standard of review. When there was a privative clause, a court's approach would lean toward the standard of reasonableness *simpliciter* or patent unreasonableness. If the statute contained neither a privative clause nor a right of appeal, the legislature's position was neutral and did not suggest any particular standard of review.

THE AGENCY'S EXPERTISE

The expertise of the tribunal relative to that of the reviewing court was usually considered the most important of the four factors. The court should look at the issue that the tribunal addressed in the decision and ask itself whether the tribunal or the court was in a better position to address the particular issue. The court could then consider questions such as

- whether the work of the tribunal involved specialized knowledge,

---

41   *Dr Q, supra* note 32 at 238.

- whether tribunal members had experience and expertise in the area of activity regulated through the tribunal, and
- whether individual tribunal members were assigned to cases that draw upon their particular area of knowledge.

Generally, the court would have more expertise in answering legal questions. However, the degree to which the court would defer to the tribunal depended to some extent on the kind of legal question addressed in the decision. For example:

- A tribunal would generally be given more deference on a question of law that arose within its jurisdiction than on one that limited its jurisdiction.
- A tribunal would often be given more deference in interpreting the statute that governed its area of activity than in interpreting some other statute.
- A tribunal's interpretation of the Constitution would be given no deference.

Thus, even though the standard of review applicable to a legal interpretation was frequently correctness, in some cases the court would accept that reasonableness *simpliciter* was the more appropriate standard.

Apart from matters of legal interpretation, a tribunal was sometimes considered to have greater expertise than the court when its governing statute required decision-makers to have expert qualifications or experience in a particular area, or to play a particular role in policy development. If a tribunal was frequently called on to make findings of fact in a distinctive legislative context—for example, determining the appropriate standards of conduct or rules of practice for lawyers, doctors, or plumbers—the court might defer to the tribunal's judgment in those areas, applying the reasonableness *simpliciter* or patent unreasonableness standard rather than the standard of correctness.

PURPOSE OF THE STATUTE AND PROVISION

Because the primary aim of the pragmatic and functional approach was to reveal the intent of the legislature, the purpose of the statute the tribunal was applying or interpreting was relevant in deciding how much deference a court should give a tribunal. For example, if one of the purposes of the statute in question was to give the public a right to an independent review of a government department's decisions, this would suggest that the court should give deference to an agency set up specifically to provide such a review when the agency, in its decision, was considering the issues delegated to it by the legislature. If the statute dealt with complex issues that required a tribunal to balance competing considerations (such as deciding between the government's need to keep certain information confidential and the public's right of access to government information), this would suggest that the court should be reluctant to substitute its view of the appropriate balance for that of the tribunal.

A statutory purpose that requires a tribunal to select from a range of remedial choices or administrative responses, is concerned with the protection of the public, engages policy issues, or involves the balancing of multiple

*sets of interests or considerations will demand greater deference from a
reviewing court.*

McLachlin CJ in *Dr Q v College of Physicians and Surgeons of
British Columbia*, 2003 SCC 19, [2003] 1 SCR 226 at para 31

NATURE OF THE QUESTION

Finally, the court had to consider the nature of the question under review: was it a
question of fact, law, or mixed fact and law? In deciding on the appropriate standard
of review, the court was supposed to determine whether the question involved, for
example, the application or interpretation of government policies or guidelines; the
interpretation of standards or practices in an industry, trade, or profession regulated
by the tribunal; or a determination of the public interest. These considerations would
generally indicate questions of fact or mixed fact and law. On the other hand, a
question involving the interpretation of a statute would clearly be a question of law.

The determination of the standard of review and the degree of deference on a
particular decision was sometimes particularly difficult in relation to the nature of
the question under review. Questions of law were the simplest to deal with because
the standard of correctness often applied. For questions of fact, the court generally
gave the agency more deference, but might be less inclined to accept an agency's
decision where the facts did not relate to the agency's area of expertise. Some questions of fact—for example, those relating to matters of interpretation or subjects on
which the facts are far from clear—may involve a greater degree of subjectivity in
arriving at a decision. In these cases, the appropriate degree of deference was more
uncertain.

*When the finding being reviewed is one of pure fact, this factor will militate in
favour of showing more deference towards the tribunal's decision. Conversely,
an issue of pure law counsels in favour of a more searching review. This is
particularly so where the decision will be one of general importance or great
precedential value.*

McLachlin CJ in *Dr Q v College of Physicians and Surgeons of
British Columbia*, 2003 SCC 19, [2003] 1 SCR 226 at para 34

Determining the Standard of Review After Dunsmuir: Standard-of-Review Analysis

Instead of using the pragmatic and functional approach to determine the appropriate standard of review, the Supreme Court in *Dunsmuir* directed the courts to
conduct a "standard-of-review analysis." In this contextual approach, for a court
to decide whether the appropriate standard is reasonableness or correctness it
must first ascertain whether previous court decisions have already determined
"in a satisfactory manner" the degree of deference to be accorded to a decision-
maker in regard to a particular category of questions. If so, then there is no need
to re-analyze the situation—the standard of review established by past decisions
will apply. However, what will be considered a "satisfactory manner" remains to be
determined.

If previous decisions have not determined the standard of review or have not determined it in a satisfactory manner, the court must carry out a standard-of-review analysis. The "standard-of-review analysis" appears to be the "functional and pragmatic" analysis by another name. The court looks at the same factors post-*Dunsmuir* as it did pre-*Dunsmuir*. Whether the appropriate standard is reasonableness or correctness depends on a number of factors, including:

- the presence or absence of a privative clause,

- the purpose of the tribunal as determined by an interpretation of its enabling legislation (for example, whether the legislation requires the tribunal to administer a complex regulatory regime or balance many competing interests);

- the nature of the question at issue (for example, whether it is a question of law, fact, or mixed fact and law, and in the case of a question of law, whether it involves interpreting the tribunal's enabling statute, some other statute, or the Constitution); and

- the expertise of the tribunal in dealing with the matter at issue (for example, whether special expertise beyond an ability to interpret a statute is required to interpret and apply the regulatory regime).

Factors pointing to a reasonableness standard include:

- the existence of a privative clause in the tribunal's governing statute;

- a specialized administrative regime that gives rise to expertise by the decision-maker; and

- an initial decision where the decision-maker

  - answered questions involving fact, discretion, or policy, or questions where legal and factual issues are interrelated and cannot be readily separated;

  - interpreted its own statute or another statute or statutes that are closely connected to the tribunal's functions and with which the tribunal is familiar;

  - answered questions that invoke the decision-maker's expertise in applying general common law or civil law in a statutory context; or

  - answered questions that are not of central importance to the legal system and that are within the tribunal's area of expertise.

In a later decision, the Supreme Court elevated interpreting a tribunal's home statute or closely related statute from merely a factor pointing to a reasonableness standard to a presumption that the appropriate standard is reasonableness.[42]

Factors pointing to a correctness standard include:

- a decision in which the decision-maker interpreted the Constitution;

---

42   *Alberta (Information and Privacy Commissioner) v Alberta Teachers' Association*, 2011 SCC 61, [2011] 3 SCR 654.

- an initial decision where the decision-maker answered a true question of jurisdiction—that is, a question of whether the statute authorizes the decision-maker to decide a particular question;

- an answer by a decision-maker to a question that is of central importance to the legal system as a whole and is outside the decision-maker's area of expertise; and

- a decision by a decision-maker regarding which of two or more specialized tribunals had jurisdiction over a matter.

It is not always necessary to consider all the factors because some of them may conclusively determine the appropriate standard. For example, if the question is the validity of a tribunal's interpretation of the Constitution, it will not be necessary to consider whether the tribunal's enabling statute contains a privative clause or whether the tribunal interprets a discrete and special administrative regime, as the standard with regard to this issue is *always* correctness.

The Role of Statutory Standards of Review and Statutory Grounds for Review

Soon after *Dunsmuir*, in *Canada (Citizenship and Immigration) v Khosa*,[43] the Supreme Court was faced with the questions of whether the *Dunsmuir* analysis applies if the standard of review is set out in a statute and whether statutory grounds for review should be treated as determining the standard of review. The Court ruled that a legislature is free to specify a standard of review if it shows a clear intention to do so, but the *Dunsmuir* factors will still be relevant in interpreting the legislature's intent where the language of the statute is unclear as to whether the legislature is specifying a standard of review.

The Court also considered whether the grounds for appeal set out in a statute are determinative of the standard of review for decisions under that statute. For example, section 18 of the *Federal Court Act*[44] states that the decisions of federal government decision-makers may be overturned on several specified grounds, such as the decision-maker having acted without jurisdiction, having failed to observe a principle of procedural fairness, having made an error of law or fact, or having acted in any other way that is contrary to law.

In *Khosa*, the minister of citizenship and immigration argued that these grounds constituted a legislated standard of review that replaced the common law standards of reasonableness and correctness. However, the Court found that unless the legislative language requires a court to treat grounds of review as standards of review, a court will not do so, but the grounds set out may be useful in determining the appropriate standard where this is not specified in the statute.

The Supreme Court of Canada has interpreted and reinterpreted what *Dunsmuir* requires in several decisions. They cannot find agreement among themselves as to

---

43   2009 SCC 12, [2009] 1 SCR 339.

44   *Supra* note 5.

what *Dunsmuir* means and how it is to be applied. Even when they agree on the result, they disagree on the reasons for reaching the conclusion.[45] Future decisions may clarify the *Dunsmuir* requirements.

Procedural Fairness and the Standard of Review

It is not necessary to determine the appropriate standard of review when a decision is attacked for procedural unfairness. In such cases, the question for the court to ask is simply whether the principles of procedural fairness were violated. If so, the agency has acted outside its jurisdiction and its decision must be overturned.[46]

Who May Represent the Party in an Appeal or Judicial Review?

In an appeal to a tribunal, government official, minister, or Cabinet, a party may represent himself or herself or be represented by a lawyer or an agent.

In a court proceeding, representation is determined by the rules of the court in the particular jurisdiction. In Ontario, most appeals to courts and all applications for judicial review relating to provincial and municipal government decisions are heard by the Divisional Court, a branch of the Superior Court of Ontario. The level of court will vary from province to province. In proceedings of the Divisional Court or other courts at this level (known as the "superior courts" or "courts of inherent jurisdiction"), an individual who was a party to a tribunal decision may represent himself or herself or be represented by a lawyer, but may not be represented by an individual who is not a lawyer. A corporation must either hire a lawyer or obtain permission from the court for one of its officers or directors to represent it.

Can the Agency Defend Its Decision?

Although the agency's decision will be defended in a court proceeding by the party or person favoured by the decision, the agency may not want to rely entirely on that defence, particularly if the party or person represents himself or herself instead of

---

45 See e.g. *Smith v Alliance Pipeline Ltd*, 2011 SCC 7, [2011] 1 SCR 160; *Canada (Canadian Human Rights Commission) v Canada (Attorney General)*, 2011 SCC 53, [2011] 3 SCR 471; *Alberta (Information and Privacy Commissioner) v Alberta Teachers' Association*, 2011 SCC 61, [2011] 3 SCR 654; *Doré v Barreau du Québec*, 2012 SCC 12, [2012] 1 SCR 395; *Rogers Communications Inc v Society of Composers, Authors and Music Publishers of Canada*, 2012 SCC 35, [2012] 2 SCR 283; *Martin v Alberta Workers' Compensation Board*, 2014 SCC 25, [2014] 1 SCR 546.

An exception is *Ontario (Community Safety and Correctional Services) v Ontario (Information and Privacy Commissioner)*, 2014 SCC 31, [2014] 1 SCR 674, in which the Supreme Court unanimously disagreed with the Ontario Court of Appeal that a correctness standard should apply to the Commissioner's interpretation of *Christopher's Law (Sex Offender Registry), 2000*, SO 2000, c 1. The Supreme Court held that the standard was reasonableness since the Commissioner's interpretation of *Christopher's Law* was for the narrow purpose of determining whether it contained an applicable confidentiality provision, this was "intimately connected to her core functions under [the *Freedom of Information and Protection of Privacy Act*]" and involved interpreting provisions of *Christopher's Law* "closely connected" to her functions.

46 *Baker v Canada (Minister of Citizenship and Immigration)*, [1999] 2 SCR 817.

retaining a legal adviser. Members or officials of the agency may have a better understanding of the issues on both sides of the case, and they can usually offer a more complete explanation of the reasons for their decision. However, agencies do not have an inherent right to appear in a court proceeding. Practice varies for different agencies and in different jurisdictions.

In the case of tribunals, some governing statutes explicitly permit the tribunal to participate in a court proceeding. In the absence of a statutory right, the tribunal may apply to the court for permission to participate. Some courts provide a limited right to participate where the issue concerns the tribunal's jurisdiction. For example, if a person under investigation by the Canadian Human Rights Commission challenges the Commission's right to investigate through a judicial review application, the Federal Court will allow the Commission to participate in the proceedings if the grounds for the challenge are that the Commission had no authority to investigate, but not if the grounds are that the investigative process lacked procedural fairness. Other courts grant a tribunal the right to defend the merits of its decision as well. Some tribunals routinely ask the court for permission to intervene for that purpose, while others generally leave it to one of the parties to defend the decision.

Remedies Available from the Court

Generally, in an appeal or judicial review proceeding, when the court decides to overturn the decision of an agency, the court may choose to substitute its own decision or it may inform the agency of its error and send the case back to the agency, asking it to make the decision again. If the original proceeding of a tribunal did not provide sufficient evidence to support a correct or reasonable decision, the court may order the tribunal to hold further hearings, listen to any additional evidence the parties may produce, and make a new ruling based on that evidence.

In an appeal, the court may rule that the agency made an error of law, or sometimes an error of fact. In a judicial review, the court may rule that the agency acted unfairly or outside its jurisdiction. Depending on the ruling, the court may order the agency to do anything that it was required, and failed, to do; prohibit it from doing anything that it was not authorized to do; or declare that what it did was not in accordance with the law.

More specifically, the court may

- order the agency to make the decision it should have made;
- substitute the decision the agency should have made for the decision it did make;
- declare that an action taken or a decision made by the agency is invalid and has no effect;
- order the agency to take some action that is a step on the road to making its decision (for example, to give notice to affected persons who should have been notified of the hearing or provide a party with an opportunity to make final arguments if that was not provided at the hearing);

- order the agency not to take some action it intended to take (for example, prohibiting a decision-maker from granting a remedy it has no authority to grant); or
- exercise the discretion that the agency should have exercised.

Unlike the civil courts, the court reviewing a tribunal's decision cannot usually award damages to a party that was harmed by the decision. However, in some cases—for example, where an agency has been negligent or has acted in bad faith—a party may claim damages in a separate civil suit.

Stating a Case

To avoid making errors in their decisions, some tribunals are permitted to make use of a procedure called "stating a case." A tribunal **states a case** by asking a court to clarify or resolve an important point of law that is being raised before the tribunal. In contrast to most judicial proceedings—which seek to correct an error *after* it has been made, and usually after the tribunal has issued its decision—the right to state a case permits a tribunal to formulate a legal question and ask the court for its opinion on that question *at any time* during the hearing process. The formulated question given to the court for its consideration is known as a **stated case**.

Not all tribunals have access to this preventive mechanism; a tribunal's entitlement to state a case must be expressly provided for in its governing statute. In general, agencies other than tribunals may not state a case.

A tribunal may state a case on its own initiative or at the request of a party, although it is generally the tribunal that has the right to decide whether to refer a question to the court. The tribunal also usually decides the content of the question, although tribunals often confer with the parties before submitting the question to the court.

Because the stated case procedure is a privilege, tribunals should exercise discretion in using it. Courts will not look favourably on tribunals that submit non-essential questions or questions on which a court's opinion is not required.

> *A tribunal should not state a case unless the opinion is essential to the board's ability to deal with the matter before it.*
>
> Robert Macaulay & James Sprague, *Practice and Procedure Before Administrative Tribunals* (Toronto: Carswell) (loose-leaf) at 24.2

Review by the Ombudsman

In some cases, a person or a party affected by an agency's decision may submit a complaint to the provincial ombudsman or one of the specialized federal ombudsman-like officials, such as the Official Languages Commissioner or the Privacy Commissioner, regarding the decision itself or a procedure that the agency followed in making the decision. The ombudsman may respond by conducting a review and making a recommendation; however, he or she may be more constrained in reviewing the decisions of tribunals than in scrutinizing those of other agencies and government officials.

While it may be reasonable for an ombudsman to scrutinize the fairness of the procedures or practices followed by a tribunal, it is less appropriate for an ombudsman to challenge the *findings* of a tribunal. If a tribunal has held a hearing following the requirements of procedural fairness and has issued a decision based on the evidence presented, it may be inappropriate for someone who has not heard the evidence to express his or her own views on whether the decision itself is correct or reasonable. (Remember the rule that the person who hears a case is the only person who may decide it.) Although the Ontario Ombudsman's Fairness Standards once provided assurance that "[a]ppropriate respect for the independence and expertise of decision-makers is shown to agencies, boards, commissions and tribunals,"[47] some tribunals have questioned whether the ombudsman may properly evaluate the merits of a tribunal decision, as distinguished from the fairness of the procedures used to reach that decision.

---

47 Ombudsman Ontario, *Ombudsman Fairness Standards for Decision-Making by Government Organizations* (Toronto: Ombudsman Ontario, 2000). These are standards that the ombudsman formerly used in reviewing the fairness of government actions.

CHAPTER SUMMARY

Occasional reviews of an agency's decisions, whether internally or by external authorities such as the courts or the ombudsman, should be welcomed by the agency's decision-makers. Reviews provide an opportunity to validate sound decisions and to strengthen the agency's performance by indicating areas for improvement.

In addition, since panels of a tribunal cannot bind each other, external reviews provide a forum where final and binding rulings can be made on issues about which panels may not agree.

Agency decisions are usually open to review on the basis of a serious error of law or fact, an unfair procedure, an improper exercise of discretion, or an action that is outside the agency's jurisdiction. Reviews are often initiated by the parties or persons directly affected by the decision, through the submission of a formal complaint about the decision itself or the procedures followed in reaching the decision.

In an appeal or judicial review of a tribunal's decision, the reviewing court may apply different standards of review depending on the circumstances. In some cases, the court will require the tribunal's decision to be "correct," while in others it will accept the decision as long as it is "reasonable." Whether the court will apply a reasonableness standard or a correctness standard in reviewing a tribunal's decision depends on factors such as whether the enabling statute contains a privative clause, the expertise of the tribunal, the purpose of the tribunal, and the nature of the question at issue.

There are several mechanisms for conducting reviews of agency decisions. Some are available for decisions of any agency and some are tailored specifically to decisions of a tribunal. These mechanisms include reconsideration of a decision by the tribunal itself, statutory appeal, application for judicial review, and review by a watchdog agency such as an ombudsman. In some cases, certain tribunals may also ask a court's opinion on a question of law that the tribunal is considering during a hearing.

In many cases, the reviewing authority has the power to overturn an agency's decision and substitute or order a different one. Some authorities—such as senior officials, Cabinet ministers, or the ombudsman—may only make a recommendation.

KEY TERMS

appeal: a request for a review of an agency's decision by a higher authority such as a court or a senior government official or body; a right that is available only when provided by statute; distinguished from judicial review

correctness: standard applied by a court to an agency's decision where there is only one correct answer to the question addressed; one of three standards of review historically applied by the courts in an appeal or judicial review proceeding; *see also* patent unreasonableness, reasonableness *simpliciter*

deference: a court's willingness to accept a decision of an agency rather than substitute a decision of its own despite the fact that the court may not agree with the decision; referred to in the context of standards of review in appeal or judicial review proceedings, often implying a duty or obligation of the court to the agency (to whom the court is said to "owe deference")

functus officio: Latin term meaning "having discharged its duty"; having made its decision, the tribunal has exhausted its authority and cannot change the decision except where a statute expressly provides otherwise or in certain exceptional circumstances permitted by the courts

justiciable: falling into the category of subjects that are appropriate for examination by a court of justice

ombudsman: an independent official reporting to the legislature with authority to investigate complaints of unfair treatment and to recommend a different decision in an individual case, as well as recommending fairer practices generally

patent unreasonableness: a defect or error in an agency's decision of such significance that a court is left in no doubt that the decision must be overturned; formerly, one of three standards of review to be applied by the courts in an appeal or judicial review proceeding, but as a result of the Supreme Court's decision in *Dunsmuir* now only a standard of review where specified by a statute; *see also* correctness, reasonableness *simpliciter*

privative clause: a provision included in an agency's governing statute for the purpose of restricting or preventing judicial review of specified actions or decisions of the agency; intended to preserve the distinction between matters that are the subject of an appeal and matters that may be addressed by judicial review

reasonableness *simpliciter*: simple reasonableness; an alternative to correctness as a standard for accepting an agency's decision in an appeal or judicial review, based on a determination that the agency's interpretation of the law or the facts, or both, is reasonable; used when a question does not lend itself to just one "correct" answer, but rather several different answers may each be reasonable; *see also* correctness, patent unreasonableness

reconsideration: the procedure established by a tribunal to review its decision when a party provides evidence or argument that the decision may be wrong or unreasonable; also called "rehearing" or "reopening"

rehearing: *see* reconsideration

reopening: *see* reconsideration

standard of review: the degree of rigour with which a court will scrutinize an agency's decision, and the degree of error or the level of uncertainty about the reasonableness or correctness of an agency's decision that a court will tolerate in deciding whether to accept or overturn the decision

stated case: a request by a tribunal to a court to give its opinion on a question of law formulated by the tribunal, together with any facts that the tribunal considers necessary for answering the question

state a case: a process by which a tribunal requests a court to give its opinion on a question of law formulated by the tribunal

stay: an order issued by a tribunal or court suspending the decision that is being challenged until the challenge has been decided or abandoned

CASES TO CONSIDER

The Scope of Judicial Review

Ottawa (City of) v Ontario (Attorney General) (2002), 64 OR (3d) 703 (CA)

FACTS: Hydro One applied to the Ontario Energy Board for approval to build a transmission line. The Board heard the case on the merits, and at the same time as it released its decision, the Board, pursuant to section 32 of the *Ontario Energy Board Act* (SO 1998, c 15), stated a case on a question of law for the opinion of the Divisional Court. The Board approved the transmission line, and the Divisional Court quashed the stated case without considering it on the merits. Since the Board had been able to render its decision in the original application, the court concluded that the Board was *functus officio* and unable to state the case. The city appealed to the Court of Appeal.

ISSUE: Was the Board *functus officio* after the application was decided on the merits, or could it still state a case on a question of law for the opinion of the Divisional Court?

DECISION: The Court of Appeal ruled that the Board could state a case under the Act and was not limited to stating a case based only on an issue in a particular application. The question stated had general application. The opinion of the Divisional Court would be useful to the Board in fulfilling its statutory mandate.

Scope of Judicial Review

Service Employees' International Union, Local No 333 v Nipawin District Staff Nurses Association, [1975] 1 SCR 382, 41 DLR (3d) 6

FACTS: The Nipawin District Staff Nurses Association applied to the Labour Relations Board to determine that the nurses association was an appropriate bargaining unit for collective bargaining with the employer. The Service Employees' International Union opposed the application, arguing that the nurses association was not a "trade union," but was a "company-dominated organization." The Labour Relations Board agreed that the nurses association was a "company-dominated organization" within the meaning of section 2(e) of *The Trade Union Act* (RSS 1972, c 137) and was therefore not a trade union. However, it failed to make a specific finding that the nurses association was an "employer or employer's agent," an element of the definition of "company-dominated organization."

ISSUES: Did the Labour Relations Board make a proper inquiry under *The Trade Union Act*? Did it act beyond its powers as conferred on it under the legislation by failing to make a specific finding that the association was an "employer or employer's agent"?

DECISION: The court upheld the Board. The question was whether or not the nurses association was a trade union, and the Labour Relations Board found that it was not. It was not required to make an explicit finding on each element of the definition. It acted in good faith and its decision could be rationally supported by a reasonable interpretation of the statute.

Standard of Review

Dr Q v College of Physicians and Surgeons of British Columbia, 2003 SCC 19, [2003] 1 SCR 226

FACTS: An inquiry committee of the College of Physicians and Surgeons found that Dr Q was guilty of infamous conduct. A patient, who had sought help for depression, alleged a sexual relationship with Dr Q, who denied the allegations. The committee accepted the patient's evidence over that of Dr Q, and the Council of the College suspended Dr Q from practising medicine. On an appeal under the *Medical Practitioners Act*, RSBC 1996, c 285, the reviewing judge set aside the inquiry committee's decision, disagreeing with its findings as to credibility. The Court of Appeal dismissed the college's appeal because it could not conclude that the reviewing judge was "clearly wrong."

ISSUE: Did the judge apply too strict a standard of review by reconsidering the committee's findings on credibility? Did the Court of Appeal apply an inappropriate test in assessing the decision of the reviewing judge?

DECISION: The reviewing judge applied too strict a standard of review and wrongly substituted her own view of the evidence for that of the committee. The standard of "clear and cogent evidence" did not permit the reviewing judge to re-evaluate the evidence. The reviewing judge failed to determine the appropriate standard of review, and inappropriately applied a correctness standard where the standard should have been reasonableness. She failed to address the need for deference to the committee that actually heard the evidence, especially with respect to determinations of credibility.

The Court of Appeal applied an inappropriate test. It wrongly determined that the standard for assessing the reviewing judge's decision was whether, in her re-evaluation of the evidence, she was clearly wrong. This was not a judicial review of an administrative decision, but an appellate review of a subordinate court. Therefore, the question of the right standard was a question of law and was to be answered correctly. The Court of Appeal should have corrected the reviewing judge's error. It should have assessed the committee's decision based on the appropriate standard of reasonableness.

Standard of Review

Law Society of New Brunswick v Ryan, 2003 SCC 20, [2003] 1 SCR 247

FACTS: A complaint against a lawyer practising in New Brunswick was filed by two of his clients. The clients had hired the lawyer to represent them in a wrongful dismissal claim. For over five years, the lawyer did nothing with the file, and lied repeatedly about it. At one point he gave the clients a forged court decision dealing with their case. Eventually, he admitted that the "whole thing was a lie," and the clients filed a complaint with the Law Society. The Law Society's Discipline Committee decided that the lawyer should be disbarred. The lawyer appealed, arguing that he suffered from a mental disability. After considering medical and psychiatric evidence, the Discipline Committee confirmed that disbarment was appropriate. The New Brunswick Court of Appeal disagreed, and substituted a penalty of indefinite suspension with the possibility of being able to practise law again.

ISSUE: Was reasonableness *simpliciter* the appropriate standard of review, and was it properly applied by the New Brunswick Court of Appeal?

DECISION: The Supreme Court of Canada overturned the decision of the Court of Appeal, and restored the order for disbarment of the Discipline Committee. There are only three standards for judicial review of administrative decisions: correctness, reasonableness *simpliciter*, and patent unreasonableness. Although the statute permitted an appeal from decisions of the Discipline Committee, the expertise of the Committee, the purpose of its enabling statute, and the nature of the question in dispute all suggested a more deferential standard of review than correctness. The appropriate standard was reasonableness *simpliciter*.

Where the appropriate standard is reasonableness *simpliciter*, a court must not interfere unless the decision, taken as a whole, is unreasonable. The decision need not be supported by a compelling explanation—a tenable explanation is sufficient. There was nothing unreasonable about the Discipline Committee's decision to disbar a member when his repeated conduct was so egregious. The Committee provided reasons for disbarment that were tenable and grounded in the evidence.

Standing in Applications for Judicial Review

Finlay v Canada (Minister of Finance), [1986] 2 SCR 607

FACTS: Finlay was a "person in need" within the meaning of the Canada Assistance Plan, and sought a declaration that cost-sharing payments by Canada to Manitoba pursuant to the plan were illegal. In accordance with the cost-sharing arrangement, an amount was deducted from his monthly social allowance for a period of 46 months. This had the effect of reducing the amount of a social allowance payment below the cost of his basic requirements. He also sought an injunction to stop the deductions because of provincial non-compliance with the conditions and undertakings imposed by the plan. He claimed to be prejudiced by the provincial non-compliance.

ISSUE: Did Finlay have standing to seek the declaratory and injunctive relief?

DECISION: While Finlay did not have a sufficiently direct and personal interest in the legality of the federal cost-sharing payments to bring him within the general requirement for standing, he should be recognized, as a matter of judicial discretion, as having public interest standing to bring his action. Finlay met the criteria for public interest standing. His action raised justiciable issues, which were serious issues, and he had a genuine interest in them. If Finlay were denied standing, there would be no other way to bring these issues before a court.

REVIEW QUESTIONS

1. List as many grounds as you can for challenging the decisions of bureaucrats and tribunals in the courts.

2. List five kinds of officials who conduct reviews of the procedures or decisions of a tribunal or government official.

3. How can a party who has challenged a tribunal's decision stop the decision from taking effect while it is under review? What factors will a court or tribunal consider when deciding whether to temporarily suspend the effect of a tribunal decision?

4. When does a party have the right to appeal a decision, and when is it necessary instead for the party to make an application for judicial review?

5. Who may appeal or seek judicial review of a tribunal's decision? For each person you listed, what criteria must be met for the courts to permit a right to appeal or to seek judicial review?

6. What three standards of review were used by the courts before the Supreme Court's decision in *Dunsmuir*? Explain how these standards differ from each other.

7. Since *Dunsmuir*, in what circumstances will the court apply each of the three standards of review?

8. List the remedies a court can grant in an appeal or judicial review of an agency's decision.

9. What is a "stated case" and how does a stated case come before a court?

EXERCISE

Using a database of provincial statutes, list the tribunals in your province that fall into the following categories and the related statutory provisions:

1. The tribunal is

   a. not subject to any statutory appeal

   b. subject to an appeal only on questions of law

   c. subject to an appeal on questions of fact or law

   d. subject to an appeal on policy or public interest grounds.

2. The parties in a hearing of the tribunal

   a. always have a right to appeal

   b. have a right to appeal only with the permission of a court.

3. Where there is a right to appeal, the appeal is

   a. to a court

   b. to some other person or body.

4. Where the appeal is to a court, the appeal is

   a. to a court of inferior (statutory) jurisdiction

   b. to a superior court.

5. Decisions of the tribunal are subject to a privative clause.

6. The tribunal's governing statute authorizes the tribunal to reconsider its own decision.

FURTHER READING

Sara Blake, *Administrative Law in Canada*, 5th ed (Markham, Ont: LexisNexis, 2011).

Lisa Braverman, *Administrative Tribunals: A Legal Handbook* (Aurora, Ont: Canada Law Book, 2001) ch 5.

Donald Brown & John Evans, *Judicial Review of Administrative Action in Canada* (Toronto: Carswell) (loose-leaf).

Michael Bryant & Lorne Sossin, *Public Law* (Toronto: Carswell, 2002) ch 4.

Colleen Flood & Lorne Sossin, *Administrative Law in Context*, 2nd ed (Toronto: Emond Montgomery, 2013).

Robert Macaulay & James Sprague, *Practice and Procedure Before Administrative Tribunals* (Toronto: Carswell) (loose-leaf) ch 24, 27A, 28.

Beverley McLachlin, "Administrative Tribunals and the Courts: An Evolutionary Relationship" (27 May 2013), Supreme Court of Canada, online: <http://scc-csc.gc.ca/court-cour/judges-juges/spe-dis/bm-2013-05-27-eng.aspx>.

Enforcement of Tribunal Orders

17

LEARNING OUTCOMES

After reading this chapter, you will understand

- the source of the authority to enforce orders of a tribunal;

- who may apply for enforcement of a tribunal's order;

- the various methods of enforcing tribunal orders and the circumstances in which a particular enforcement mechanism may be used; and

- the remedies that are available from a court once it has been established that an order of a tribunal has not been followed.

In some instances, enforcement of an order is up to the parties themselves and the tribunal has no role to play. … The notion that the intervention of the court is necessary to enforce agency orders is offensive to some public regulators because it undercuts the principle that each agency is the master of its own proceedings. This tug of war between agencies and courts has crystallized over the exercise of the power to commit for contempt.

John I Laskin, "Enforcement Powers of Administrative Agencies" in *Special Lectures of the Law Society of Upper Canada 1992: Administrative Law—Principles, Practice and Pluralism* (Scarborough, Ont: Carswell, 1992) 191 at 223

Authority to Enforce a Tribunal Order

Tribunals rarely enforce their own decisions (referred to here as "orders"). Unless a statute specifically provides for the tribunal to enforce its orders, it is unlikely that the tribunal has this authority.

For most tribunals, the authority for compelling enforcement of an order and the procedures to be followed are set out in the tribunal's governing statute. In Ontario, section 19 of the *Statutory Powers Procedure Act*[1] (SPPA) and section 54 of British Columbia's *Administrative Tribunals Act*[2] (ATA) contain such enforcement provisions for tribunals governed by those Acts. In the absence of a statutory right, the common law determines enforcement authority. Section 156 of Quebec's *Administrative Justice Act*[3] (AJA) makes decisions of the Administrative Tribunal of Quebec enforceable when deposited with a court.

Who May Apply for Enforcement of an Order

If a party in a tribunal proceeding fails to comply with an order issued by the tribunal in its final decision, it is usually up to the party who will benefit from the decision to take action to enforce the order. In some cases (discussed below, under the heading "Enforcement Mechanisms and Remedies"), other persons who were not parties in the proceeding also may be entitled to take action.

Enforcement Mechanisms and Remedies

Statutes and the common law provide three main mechanisms for enforcement of tribunal orders:

---

1   RSO 1990, c S.22.

2   SBC 2004, c 45.

3   CQLR c J-3.

1. treating the order as an order of a civil court and using civil court procedures to obtain compliance;

2. treating the violation of the order as an offence and prosecuting the violator in a criminal court proceeding; and

3. treating the violation as contempt and initiating contempt proceedings in a superior court.

In some cases, it may also be possible to seek enforcement through a civil action for an injunction or through judicial review by a superior court.

The circumstances in which each of these mechanisms is available are discussed in the following sections.

Civil Court Order

In Ontario, the most common enforcement mechanism is to give the tribunal's order the status of an order issued by a civil court. In some cases, a statute deems the tribunal's order to be a court order[4] and it is not necessary to apply for such treatment. Otherwise, the injured party or the tribunal must apply to register the tribunal's order with a civil court. An order that is deemed to be an order of the court or registered as a court order can be enforced in the same way as an order issued by that court. Giving the order the status of a civil court order also permits the court to find the violator in contempt (discussed below).

If the order requires a person ("the debtor") to pay money to another person ("the creditor"), the creditor will request a court official to seize the bank account, wages, or other property of the debtor and pay the creditor the amount specified in the order. If the order requires a person to take some action other than paying money or to refrain from taking some action, it is usually necessary to obtain an order from a judge compelling compliance.

Prosecution as an Offence

If a statute provides that failure to obey a tribunal's order is an **offence**, the party who will benefit from the order, the government, and often others (such as public interest groups concerned with an issue) who may not be directly affected by the violation may prosecute the violator. **Prosecution** involves laying a charge and proving the violation in a criminal court. An advantage of prosecution is that the right to prosecute is usually not limited to parties in the tribunal's proceeding. However, some statutes restrict the right to prosecute to the attorney general or a government department or agency.[5]

---

4 For example, s 19(1) of the SPPA provides that, where a certified copy of the decision or order is filed with the court, the order is deemed to be an order of the court at the time it is filed.

5 Section 61(1) of the *Freedom of Information and Protection of Privacy Act* (RSO 1990, c F.31) makes it an offence to wilfully disobey an order of the Information and Privacy Commissioner. Section 61(3) prohibits prosecution of this offence without the consent of the attorney general.

Most statutes provide that the penalty on conviction is a fine. Where this is the case, the court may not have the power to order compliance. However, some statutes provide for other remedies, such as probation, remedial orders, or even imprisonment.[6]

Contempt Proceedings

The availability of contempt proceedings in a particular case may arise in one of three ways:

1. through treating the violation of the order as a breach of a civil court order (as described above);
2. through a statutory provision stating that contempt is an available remedy for violation of a tribunal order; or
3. through the inherent common law right of superior courts to protect the integrity of tribunal decisions.

A tribunal's governing statute may explicitly provide that failure to comply with an order of the tribunal constitutes contempt of the tribunal or of court. Tribunals usually do not have the authority to punish a person for contempt. Statutes generally permit the injured party either to apply directly to a court or to ask the tribunal to apply to a court to find the violator in contempt. A person may apply to a lower ("inferior") court for a remedy for contempt of a tribunal's order only where the court has statutory authority to punish for contempt. The superior courts, on the other hand, have the *inherent* authority to find the violator of a tribunal order in contempt, meaning that they may do so even without a statutory provision permitting them to hear contempt applications.

The court will automatically grant the injured party standing to seek a remedy for contempt. It also has discretion to grant standing to others who are affected by the violation or who may be affected by an order that the court may make to remedy the violation. However, it is doubtful that the tribunal itself would have standing to apply to a court to find someone in contempt of its order without explicit statutory authority to do so. Tribunal powers are limited to those provided by statute, and courts are reluctant to interpret those powers to imply this kind of power.

Depending on the circumstances, contempt of a tribunal's order may be a civil wrongdoing or it may be a criminal offence. Where a tribunal's order has been filed with a court—thus making it an order of the court itself—a party who publicly defies the order in a way that the party should know is likely to hold the court up to public scorn and undermine the court's authority may be guilty of a criminal offence. In other circumstances, the failure to comply is merely a civil offence, and the penalties for disobeying the order are likely to be less severe.

---

6   Provisions that provide for prosecution for breach of a tribunal order include breach of an order of the Alberta Public Health Board under s 73 of the *Public Health Act*, RSA 2000, c P-37; other remedies: *Environmental Protection Act*, RSO 1990, c E.19, ss 183(2), 190, 190.1.

Courts have broad powers to punish for contempt. They can order a wide range of remedies, including a reprimand, a fine, an order to carry out the tribunal's order, or imprisonment of the violator until he or she agrees to comply with the tribunal's order.

Injunctions, Prohibition Orders, Mandamus, and Declarations

Although such cases are rare, it is possible that an injured party could also launch a civil action for an injunction or apply to a superior court for judicial review to compel compliance with a tribunal's order.

Where the person violating an order of a tribunal is not a government decision-maker, a civil action for an injunction is the appropriate procedure, as judicial review is only available against governmental authorities. An **injunction** is an order requiring the violator to cease an activity that violates the tribunal's order. Where the violator is a government agency, an injunction may be available through either a civil action or an application for judicial review. In the context of judicial review, the order to cease and desist may be called either a **prohibition** or an injunction.

In addition, an application for judicial review may result in an order requiring the violator to take positive steps to comply with the tribunal's order (known in Latin as "*mandamus*"). **Mandamus** is available to require a municipality—and sometimes federal or provincial government officials, departments, and agencies—to obey a tribunal's order. However, it is not available against the federal or provincial governments in some circumstances. In cases where *mandamus* is not available, the applicant will request a **declaration** that the government is violating the order. A declaration of violation by the court does not require the government to cease violating the order; however, it is usually effective because governments generally respect court declarations.

CHAPTER SUMMARY

Tribunals generally do not have the authority to enforce their own orders. If a party fails to comply with an order, it is usually the responsibility of the injured party to take legal action to obtain enforcement of the order.

The authority for affected parties to compel compliance with a tribunal's order is often set out in the tribunal's governing statute. The most common mechanisms for enforcing orders are to treat the order as equivalent to an order of a civil court and provide for enforcement in the same manner as for an order of that court; to treat the violation of the order as an offence and prosecute the violator in a criminal court proceeding; or to treat the violation as equivalent to contempt of court and seek a ruling of contempt from a superior court. The remedies available under these mechanisms include an order to comply, a fine, seizure of assets, and even imprisonment, depending on the method of enforcement applied.

In addition to the three main mechanisms, in some circumstances an injured party can launch a civil action for an injunction against continued violation of the order or apply to a superior court for judicial review. The latter could result in an order of *mandamus* or prohibition, an injunction compelling compliance, or a declaration that the activity is illegal.

KEY TERMS

declaration: a judgment issued by a court stating that a government authority is violating the law

injunction: an order issued by a court requiring a person (usually a party to a civil action) to perform some act or refrain from some conduct that is harmful to the party who seeks relief

mandamus: Latin term referring to an order of a court to a governmental official, department, or agency compelling the performance of a public duty

offence: violation of a statutory provision, regulation, or bylaw that requires a person to carry out a specified act or refrain from specified conduct, such as a requirement to meet a standard or to comply with a duty specified by the enactment

prohibition: an order issued by a court in an application for judicial review requiring a person to refrain from some conduct harmful to the party who seeks relief

prosecution: the laying of a charge and proving of an offence against an alleged offender

CASES TO CONSIDER

The Courts' Power to Punish for Contempt

MacMillan Bloedel Ltd v Simpson, [1995] 4 SCR 725

Although this decision does not deal with contempt of an order of a tribunal, it illustrates the distinction between the powers of superior courts and those of inferior courts to deal with contempt.

FACTS: A logging company, MacMillan Bloedel, had obtained an injunction from the British Columbia Supreme Court prohibiting protest activities interfering with its operations in Clayoquot Sound. Seventeen-year-old J.P. was charged with contempt of court after he ignored the injunction and continued his protest activities. Although the contempt application was brought before the British Columbia Supreme Court (since the injunction originated in that court), the *Young Offenders Act* (RSC 1985, c Y-1), in force at the time, stated that the British Columbia Youth Court had exclusive jurisdiction over every contempt of court committed by a young person against any court outside that court. Based on this provision, J.P. applied to be tried in youth court; his application was denied, and he was tried in the BC Supreme Court instead. J.P. was convicted of contempt and sentenced to 45 days' imprisonment and a fine. He appealed his conviction to the Court of Appeal on the grounds that the BC Supreme Court had no jurisdiction to hear the case, since the provision in the *Young Offenders Act* gave the youth court exclusive jurisdiction over youths accused of committing this form of contempt. The Court of Appeal struck down the provision as unconstitutional because Parliament or a legislature has no authority to make a law that deprives a superior court of the right to take actions that are within its inherent jurisdiction. J.P. appealed to the Supreme Court of Canada.

ISSUE: Was the provision of the *Young Offenders Act* that required charges of contempt against youth to be heard by the youth court unconstitutional?

DECISION: The section of the *Young Offenders Act* granting exclusive jurisdiction over contempt proceedings to the youth court was unconstitutional. Although giving the youth court the power to try youth for contempt is permissible, the transfer of *exclusive* jurisdiction to the youth court is not, because it deprives the superior court of an inherent power—in other words, it attempts to remove a power that cannot be removed except by constitutional amendment. The rule of law requires that courts be able to enforce their orders and ensure that their processes are respected. Removing the power to punish contempt by youths would affect the court's ability to enforce its own orders. Short of a constitutional amendment, Parliament has no jurisdiction to pass laws that take away the inherent jurisdiction of superior courts, which is constitutional in nature. Given the youth court's expertise in dealing with young people, it will be preferable in most instances for the youth court to try to punish a youth for contempt of a superior court order, but the superior court must still retain its jurisdiction.

The Courts' Power to Punish for Contempt of a Tribunal's Order

United Nurses of Alberta v Alberta (Attorney General), [1992] 1 SCR 901

FACTS: The Alberta Labour Relations Board filed directives with the court of Queen's Bench forbidding strike action by the province's nurses. In violation of these directives, the nurses went on strike anyway. The nurses' union was found to be in contempt of the directives by a court in which the Board's order had been filed and was fined $25,000. The union appealed to the Alberta Court of Appeal, which upheld the decision. The union appealed this decision to the Supreme Court of Canada.

ISSUES: Can a union be found in contempt? When is non-compliance with a tribunal's order a civil contempt and when is it a criminal contempt? Can non-compliance with a directive of a provincial board give rise to criminal contempt, or is contempt of such an order necessarily civil in nature because a provincial government cannot make criminal laws?

DECISION: A union can be held liable for contempt. Although unions are unincorporated associations and may not have legal status for some purposes because they have been given legal status for collective bargaining purposes under labour relations statutes they should be accountable to a court if they violate those statutes. Board orders filed with a court have the same force as orders of the court. Therefore, the directive filed by the Board could provide a basis for the union's contempt conviction even though the directive did not originate with the court. If a person accused of contempt breached a directive in a manner that amounted to public defiance of the court's authority in circumstances that they knew or should have known would hold the court up to public scorn, the court could find the accused in criminal contempt. Finally, even though the directive could provide the basis for a contempt conviction, the Board was not enacting criminal law when it issued the directive. The directive itself was not criminal in nature, and superior courts have authority to enforce the orders of provincial tribunals.

REVIEW QUESTIONS

1. Can a tribunal enforce its own orders or must a party take action to require enforcement? Explain.

2. What are the three main methods for enforcing a tribunal's order?

3. Are other methods of enforcement available? Explain.

4. How can a party find out what methods of enforcement are available for orders of a particular tribunal?

5. What are the sources of the authority for punishing a person for violating a tribunal's order?

6. If the injured party is successful in proving that another party has violated a tribunal's order and that the order should be enforced, what remedies may the court or the tribunal provide?

EXERCISE

What remedies are available for an order that was violated and was issued by:

a. the Canadian Human Rights Commission or the Canadian Human Rights Tribunal,

b. the Saskatchewan Labour Relations Board,

c. an official or body established under the Quebec *Police Act*,

d. the Canadian Dairy Commission,

e. Ontario's Licence Appeal Tribunal,

f. Ontario's Environmental Review Tribunal

　i. in a hearing under the *Environmental Protection Act*,

　ii. in a hearing under the *Environmental Assessment Act*,

　iii. in a hearing under the *Environmental Bill of Rights*?

FACT SCENARIO

A journalist makes a request to the Ontario Ministry of the Environment for records relating to inspections of a waste disposal site. The Ministry refuses to disclose these records and the journalist appeals the refusal to the Ontario Information and Privacy Commissioner. The Commissioner orders the Ministry to disclose the records within 15 days.

One month later, the journalist still does not have the records. She writes to the minister asking him to comply with the Commissioner's order. There is no answer. She writes again two weeks later and again receives no answer. Finally, the journalist writes to the Commissioner asking her to enforce the order.

1. What remedies may be available to the journalist, and what is the statutory authority for your answer? Does the journalist have standing to apply for a remedy? Why, or why not?

2. Does the Commissioner have the power to enforce her rulings? Explain.

3. What remedies may be available to the Commissioner from a court? Explain.

FURTHER READING

John I Laskin, "Enforcement Powers of Administrative Agencies" in *Special Lectures of the Law Society of Upper Canada 1992: Administrative Law—Principles, Practice and Pluralism* (Scarborough, Ont: Carswell, 1992) 191.

Robert Macaulay & James Sprague, *Practice and Procedure Before Administrative Tribunals* (Toronto: Carswell) (loose-leaf) ch 29, 29A, 42.

Appendixes

Interpreting Statutes, Regulations, and Bylaws

LEARNING OUTCOMES

After reading this appendix, you will understand

- why it is necessary to interpret statutes, regulations, and bylaws;

- the difference between traditional and modern approaches to statutory interpretation;

- the meaning of purposive, contextual, and consequential analysis of statutes;

- the difference between a strict and a liberal interpretation of a statute; and

- the tools available for interpreting statutes.

There is no better way to exercise the imagination than the study of law. No artist ever interpreted nature as freely as a lawyer interprets the truth.

Jean Giradoux

Whether the law entitles a person to some right, benefit, or privilege, imposes a duty, restricts a person's freedom, or requires that a particular procedure be followed sometimes depends on how the law is interpreted. For example, if a law says a pension benefit is available to the "spouse" of a deceased person, does the law include only a partner in a traditional, state-sanctioned marriage between a man and a woman, or does it also include a partner in a common law marriage (often referred to as a "common law spouse") or a partner in a same-sex marriage? The answer depends on how one interprets the word "spouse."

The Role of Statutory Interpretation in Effective Advocacy and Decision-Making

Those who represent individuals or groups in dealing with the government start with a set of facts. They must find out what law applies to these facts. They may be called on to persuade a decision-maker that a law should be interpreted in a way that advances the interests of the client.

If a law can be interpreted in more than one way, the decision-maker has to determine which interpretation is correct. If a person and a government agency disagree about whether the law permits the person to receive a benefit or privilege or imposes on him or her some obligation, a tribunal will often be authorized to resolve the question. Then, both the person (or his or her representative) and the decision-making agency will try to persuade the tribunal to adopt their interpretation of the law. The representative may argue that his or her client—for example, a woman in a same-sex relationship—is a "spouse" within the meaning of the statute, while the agency may argue that only members of heterosexual unions are "spouses."

A court or tribunal always applies law to the facts of the case. However, if the opposing parties argue for different meanings of a word, phrase, or provision, the court or tribunal must decide which interpretation of the law is correct before it can apply the law. Even where the legislation gives government officials or tribunal members broad discretion in deciding what course of action to take, the exercise of this discretion may involve the interpretation of laws in accordance with the spirit and intent of the law that governs the process or proceeding.

The interpretation of laws passed by elected assemblies—whether those laws are statutes, regulations, or municipal bylaws—is known as **statutory interpretation**, and the principles used in interpreting laws are known as **rules of statutory interpretation**. These are not really "rules," but a set of principles or guidelines that flow from the rules of grammar and syntax, logic, and common sense. These rules have been developed by the courts as part of the common law, and, while some remain only within the common law, many are now codified in statutes. Each province, as well as the government of Canada, has passed a statute called the *Interpretation Act*,[1] which sets out some of the rules to be used for interpreting the statutes of that jurisdiction.

The Traditional Approach to Statutory Interpretation

A number of different approaches to statutory interpretation were developed by the courts: the plain meaning rule, the golden rule, and the mischief rule.

The Plain Meaning Rule

The plain meaning rule was often used as a starting point in the interpretation of a law. A court or tribunal looked only at the words of the statute to be interpreted; if they were clear, the court or tribunal had to give effect to them, regardless of the consequences. However, this approach often did not provide a definitive answer, because if the meaning of a law were perfectly clear, there would be no need to interpret it. Interpretation is necessary only when the wording of a statute has more than one potential meaning.

An example of the plain meaning approach is the rule that every word in a statute must be deemed to have a meaning. A word cannot be ignored, even if it appears to be redundant, inconsistent with other language in the statute, or inserted by mistake.

The Golden Rule

An Example of the Plain Meaning Approach?

One day at the law office one lawyer said to the other, "You really look terrible this morning." The other lawyer replied, "I woke up this morning with a splitting headache, and whatever I do, I can't get rid of it." The first lawyer told him, "When that happens to me, I take a few hours off work, go home to my den, and watch an old movie while enjoying a small drink from my bottle of rare cognac. That always works for me."

The other lawyer answered, "That sounds great. Just give me your house keys and I'll head right there."

The golden rule was a variation on the plain meaning rule. A court or tribunal was permitted to ignore the plain or literal meaning of the words of a statute only if adherence to the plain or literal meaning would lead to an absurd result. An absurd result is one that the legislature could not possibly have intended because it is clearly inconsistent with the spirit and intent of the law. For example, if a statute deals with

---

1   Ontario's *Interpretation Act* has been renamed. It is now called the *Legislation Act*.

a specialized field and a word in that specialized field has a different meaning from its ordinary meaning, and it is apparent from the context that the specialized meaning is intended, the court or tribunal may interpret the word as having the specialized meaning.

The plain meaning and golden rule approaches to statutory interpretation were based on the premise that the legislators meant exactly what they said, and that this original intent should guide a tribunal's or a court's interpretation unless it would lead to an absurd result or a result that was contrary to the obvious spirit and intent of the law. If the legislation said something that the individual or body interpreting it did not think it should say, or if it failed to say something that the individual or body thought it should say, the individual or body could not change the meaning or supply the missing pieces. They were to assume—even though this assumption may have been wrong—that the legislators, in the words of Horton the elephant, "said what they meant and meant what they said."

Since these approaches assumed that the words in question have a plain or literal meaning, they disallowed or discouraged the use of external aids to interpretation. For example, a plain meaning approach would not consider the headings within a statute or the preamble to the statute, because these are technically not part of the provisions that impose legally binding requirements. Similarly, it was generally considered improper to look at earlier drafts of a statute, discussion papers produced by governments before introduction of a bill, or statements made by politicians during debates on the bill.

The Mischief Rule

The mischief rule was developed in an attempt to avoid the overly strict and literal interpretation of statutes that results from using a plain meaning approach. The mischief rule required a court or tribunal to determine the "mischief" the legislature was trying to prevent by making the law. In other words, the court or tribunal sought to recognize the problem that the legislature was trying to solve or the good that it was trying to do, and then interpreted provisions in a way that achieved this goal. The mischief rule has been incorporated into most interpretation acts. For example, Nova Scotia's *Interpretation Act* states:

> 9(5) Every enactment shall be deemed remedial and interpreted to insure the attainment of its objects by considering among other matters
> (a) the occasion and necessity for the enactment;
> (b) the circumstances existing at the time it was passed;
> (c) the mischief to be remedied;
> (d) the object to be attained;
> (e) the former law, including other enactments upon the same or similar subjects;
> (f) the consequences of a particular interpretation; and
> (g) the history of legislation on the subject.[2]

---

2 RSNS 1989, c 235.

This approach is closer to the modern approach to interpreting statutes, but, like all approaches, it has its limitations. Who can be sure, for example, whether all the members of a legislature had the same goal when they voted for a statute, or what problem the government really intended to address when it introduced the statute? Moreover, the problem to be solved may often be defined broadly or narrowly. Imagine, for example, the following scenario. Your province's *Highway Traffic Act*, which sets the rules for the road, contains the following definition: "Motor vehicle includes an automobile, motorcycle, and motor-assisted bicycle, unless otherwise indicated in this Act." The Act says that motor vehicles must be driven on the right side of the road; it was passed before snowmobiles were invented and has not been updated. The police stop a driver of a snowmobile and charge her with driving on the left side of the road. She argues that her snowmobile is not a "motor vehicle" as defined in the Act, so she is guilty of no offence.

In determining the correct interpretation of "motor vehicle," the court must consider whether the intent of the legislature was

- to regulate the conduct of drivers only of cars and other existing types of vehicles;
- to regulate all motorized devices with wheels, such as cars and motorized bicycles; or
- to ensure the safety of all users of the road, and therefore to regulate any device driven on the road, whether it has wheels or tracks and whether or not it existed at the time the term "motor vehicle" was defined.

The Modern Approach to Statutory Interpretation

The approach to statutory interpretation currently favoured by courts and legal scholars does not focus to the same extent on the literal words of the statute or attempt to read the minds of the legislators. The modern approach, as it is usually called, assumes that where the meaning of a provision is disputed, the words of the provision probably have no single plain meaning. If they did, the parties would not likely invest time and money trying to convince a court or tribunal of their different interpretations. The modern approach also does not assume that sufficient evidence is available to discern what the legislators had in mind when they passed the law.

The modern rule has been described as follows:

Courts are obliged to determine the meaning of legislation in its total context, having regard to the purpose of the legislation, the consequences of proposed interpretations, the presumptions and special rules of interpretation, as well as admissible external aids. In other words, the courts must consider and take into account all relevant and admissible indicators of legislative meaning. After taking these into account, the court must then adopt an interpretation that is appropriate. An appropriate interpretation is one that can be justified in terms of (a) its plausibility, that is, its compliance with the legislative text; (b) its efficacy, that is, its promotion of the legislative purpose; and (c) its acceptability, that is, the outcome is reasonable and just.[3]

The modern approach is often described as a "contextual and purposive" analysis.

Using this approach to interpreting a statute, one looks first at the specific words, phrases, or provisions that are to be interpreted. If they are not clear on their face—or, if their meaning is clear but results in consequences that are contrary to accepted norms of justice or reasonableness—then one looks at the neighbouring parts of the statute to see whether their meaning becomes clear or whether they have a more acceptable meaning in this context. If there is still any ambiguity or if the consequences of giving the words their plain meaning continue to be unacceptable, one looks at the statute as a whole for clues. In this "contextual analysis," one looks at the context in which the word, phrase, or provision is found for clues to its meaning, and may also consider how the statute relates to or compares with other statutes that deal with similar subject matter.

"Purposive analysis" is closely related to, and overlaps with, contextual analysis. If the meaning of a word, phrase, or provision is not clear on its own, or if it is clear but is unacceptable, one looks at the statute as a whole and the background to the statute and tries to determine what problem the statute was intended to solve and by what means. If the word, phrase, or provision has two equally possible interpretations, the purpose of the statute may indicate which of the two meanings is more consistent with the goal of the statute. The theory is that the interpretation that fulfills the purpose of the statute must be the one that the legislators intended.

Closely related to purposive analysis is "consequential analysis." A court or tribunal may reject the plain meaning of a word, phrase, or provision where the consequence of giving it that meaning are clearly unintended and unacceptable—for example, where giving a word a particular interpretation would defeat the purpose of the statute.

Contextual, purposive, and consequential analyses are very subjective. They can be used creatively to glean the hidden meaning of legislation and prevent unreasonable or unfair results, but they can also be abused by decision-makers, who may use this kind of analysis to substitute a meaning that reflects their own values for the plain meaning of the wording of a statute. Generally, it is not the adjudicator's role to fix the legislature's mistakes. If an unclear provision can be made clearer through intellectual honesty and rigour, the decision-maker should seek to clarify it in this way. But if the legislature has simply not done its job, the adjudicator should not twist or torture language or logic to fix the problem, as tempting as this may be; nor should a professional or responsible representative promote this. Rather, in all but the most exceptional circumstances, the adjudicator should apply the law as written, even if doing so leads to an unpalatable result.

---

3   Ruth Sullivan, *Driedger on the Construction of Statutes*, 3rd ed (Toronto: Butterworths, 1994) at 151. The leading case adopting Driedger's "modern approach" is *Rizzo & Rizzo Shoes Ltd (Re)*, [1998] 1 SCR 27.

An Example of Contextual Analysis?

The judge said to the prisoner in the dock, "You look familiar. Have you ever been up before me?"

"I don't know," said the prisoner. "What time do you get up?"

Strict and Liberal Interpretation

An example of purposive analysis is the rule that laws that encroach on the rights and freedoms of individuals are to be interpreted strictly (narrowly). These laws include statutes whose purpose is to prohibit conduct, punish violations, or impose taxes. Such laws should be interpreted in the manner most favourable to the person affected by them.

For example, the *Criminal Code*[4] contains many offences involving the illegal possession or use of a firearm. "Firearm" is defined as a barrelled weapon from which a projectile can be discharged and which is capable of causing serious injury, and also includes "anything that can be adapted for use as a firearm" (s 2). A liberal, or broad, interpretation of the phrase "anything that can be adapted for use as a firearm" could bring within the definition any object that can possibly be converted to a working firearm, no matter how difficult it would be to accomplish this or how long it would take. However, the narrower, or "strict," interpretation given to this phrase by the courts is that it includes only those objects capable of conversion to a working firearm in a relatively short period of time with relative ease.

In contrast, statutes that grant individuals rights or freedoms or that are intended to be preventive or remedial should be interpreted more liberally or expansively—that is, they should be interpreted in a manner that helps solve the problem the statute was intended to address, with less concern given to the impact that doing so may have on the individuals who will be affected. Using the example above of whether a snowmobile fits within the definition of "motor vehicle" under the *Highway Traffic Act*, a strict interpretation of the phrase "motor vehicle" might exclude snowmobiles from regulation under the Act. However, a court may adopt a liberal interpretation that includes snowmobiles because such an interpretation better serves the remedial purpose of the Act, which is to prevent harm to users of the road.

Tools for Interpreting Statutes

When researching the meaning of a statutory provision, use the tools provided by the Act itself before looking at external sources of information. Look for definitions of the word or phrase in question in the statute, and at how the word or phrase is used in other parts of the statute. Is it used consistently throughout the statute or

---

4 RSC 1985, c C-46.

does it have different meanings in different parts of the statute? Also consider any explanations of the purpose of the statute or provision. These may be found in the preamble to the statute, in headings, or in marginal notes. Next, determine whether courts or tribunals have interpreted the provision in question.

If this does not resolve the question, move to external sources, such as dictionary definitions of the words or phrases in question; definitions of the same words or phrases in other statutes; and court and tribunal decisions that have interpreted similar words, phrases, or provisions in other statutes.

Finally, you may turn to statements of general principles, such as interpretation acts, drafting conventions, maxims, and presumptions. These are rarely definitive, but they provide guidance.

Legislative History and Legislative Evolution

If one wants to look at the full context of a statute, it is sometimes necessary to go beyond the words of the statute to look at how the statute was developed and how it evolved over time through amendments after it was passed.

Legislative history is the process of development of a statute, from the identification of a problem and proposed solutions by the legislators to the final wording passed by the elected assembly or approved by the executive branch of government. This historical context can include study papers (often referred to as "white papers") or commission reports and statements made by politicians in the legislative assembly or municipal council, as well as wording changes made after a law was introduced as a bill but before it was finally passed as a law. In the past, courts frowned on the use of legislative history as an interpretive aid, but they are more receptive toward it today.

Legislative evolution refers to amendments made to a law after it came into effect. Over the years, a law may be amended many times. If one wants to understand a provision in the current version of a statute, the similarities and differences between this version and past versions may shed light on whether an amendment was intended to continue an idea expressed in a previous version or whether it was meant to modify the original concept.

Interpretation Acts

In determining the meaning of a provision, one can turn to several sources of information. As mentioned, every province has a statute (usually called the *Interpretation Act*), which addresses some questions that commonly arise in interpreting statutes. For example, section 87 of Ontario's *Legislation Act, 2006*[5] defines a range of words and terms, from "Act" to "rules of court." The Act provides that when any of these words or terms is used in any Ontario act or regulation, it should be given the same meaning as its definition in the *Legislation Act* unless the context requires that it be given a different meaning. Thus, a "person" is defined to include a corporation any

---

5 SO 2006, c 21, Schedule F.

time this word is found in any Ontario law, unless the context requires a broader or narrower interpretation.

Definition Sections

Most statutes, regulations, and bylaws (collectively known as **enactments**) contain a list of definitions of terms used in the enactment. If one is attempting to determine the meaning of a word or phrase in an enactment, the definition section may resolve any possible ambiguity about the meaning of the word or phrase in that enactment.

If a word is not defined in the enactment itself, one may look at how it is defined in other enactments. The closer the purpose of the other enactment is to the purpose of the enactment in question, the more persuasive the argument will be that the word or phrase in the enactment one is interpreting should be interpreted as it is defined in the other enactment.

Dictionaries and Textbooks

If a word or phrase is not defined in the statute in question, one may look at the definitions in ordinary dictionaries. Dictionaries often contain several definitions for a word, some of which support the interpretation one favours and some of which do not.

Whether the ordinary dictionary definition will apply may depend on whether the word or phrase is to be given its ordinary meaning or whether it is a technical term. For example, "instrument" has several different meanings. In ordinary usage, it means a tool or implement. In the context of a law dealing with music, however, it may mean only a musical instrument, while in a law dealing with health it may mean only a medical instrument. "Instrument" also has a specialized legal meaning. In the legal context, an instrument is a document, usually one with some binding legal effect.

If a statute deals with a specialized area, it may also be useful to look at books in that field, such as textbooks or specialized dictionaries, to determine the meaning of a term. For example, there are medical, scientific, and engineering dictionaries.

Court and Tribunal Decisions

If a word or phrase is not defined in a statute or in an *Interpretation Act*, the most conclusive way to determine its correct interpretation is to find out how the courts have interpreted it in other parts of the statute, or in statutes intended to cover similar ground in the same jurisdiction or in other jurisdictions. The answer can be sought in case law reporters, case digests, textbooks, legal dictionaries, and, where they exist, annotated versions of the statute. (See Appendix B.)

It is also useful to look for provisions in other statutes that are worded in a way that is similar to the one in question and find out how courts have interpreted those provisions. One might then argue that the same interpretation should be given in the statute in question because the statutes are similar in structure and purpose, or that a different interpretation would be more reasonable because of differences in the purposes or subject matter of the statutes or in the wording of the provisions.

If a superior court has interpreted the provision in question in the same statute, this interpretation is binding on a tribunal in the same jurisdiction. If, however, there is no existing judicial interpretation of the provision, or if there are conflicting interpretations, it may be necessary to use a variety of tools in combination.

English and French Versions

A Canadian rule of statutory interpretation is that the English and French versions of laws have equal weight and should be interpreted in a way that, wherever possible, gives them the same meaning. One may thus compare the English and French versions of a statute to resolve ambiguity. For example, if a word in the English version has more than one meaning, the French version may offer a clue as to which meaning is most similar to the word used in French.

Preambles, Purpose Sections, Marginal Notes, and Headings

Statutes often have a preamble or "purpose section," and marginal notes or headings for each section. The preamble and headings or marginal notes are not considered part of the wording of the statute itself, but they may be used with caution to shed some light on the meaning of a provision. Purpose sections and definitions, which are considered an integral part of the statute, have greater weight.

Drafting Conventions, Maxims, and Presumptions

Courts and tribunals recognize that drafters of legislation have developed standard ways of expressing ideas. They know that if a particular construction is used, it is likely to convey a particular meaning, and they tend to give it that meaning. For example, legislative drafters generally use the word "shall" to indicate that an act is mandatory, and "may" to signify that it is discretionary. Therefore, if a provision states that "the applicant shall file a notice of appeal within 10 days," the court will interpret this to mean that the notice must be filed, and if it is not, there may be legal consequences. However, this rule is not determinative (that is, it does not conclusively decide the issue). Where the context requires a different interpretation, the court will interpret a provision containing "shall" as only directing, rather than requiring, an action.

The courts have developed a number of maxims, usually expressed in Latin, as guidelines for interpretation based on these conventions of legislative drafting.

Two commonly cited maxims deal with the interpretation of lists. The kind of word used to begin or end a list may be a clue, for example, as to whether the list is exhaustive (complete) or whether the provision is intended to cover not only the things in the list but also anything similar.

Ejusdem generis ("of the same kind") says that a general word that follows particular and specific words of a similar nature takes its meaning from those words and is considered to be limited to the same class.

For example, if a statute provides that horses, cows, sheep, pigs, and other farm animals must be kept enclosed behind a high fence, one might interpret "other farm animals" using the *ejusdem generis* rule as meaning animals raised for sale or for use in farming operations, but as not meaning barn cats, field mice, or barn swallows, even though these animals are also found on farms.

Expressio unius est exclusio alterius ("to express one thing is to exclude another") says that the inclusion of one thing in a statute, but not other things that one would expect to find included when that particular thing is mentioned, is the legislature's way of indicating that it intends to exclude those other things.

For example, section 6 of the *Winnipeg General Hospital Act*[6] exempted "property used for hospital purposes" from certain kinds of tax. The section stated that hospital property included "property used … for necessary parking facilities, interns' quarters, school of nursing, nurses' residence, power house or laundry." The Manitoba court had to decide whether the term "hospital property" included two apartment buildings owned by the hospital and rented to hospital staff. Applying the *expressio unius* rule, the court held that the legislature, in making such a long and detailed list, would have included apartment buildings rented to staff if it meant to. Because the apartment buildings were not included in the list of property exempt from taxation, the buildings were subject to tax.[7]

An Example of *Expressio Unius Est Exclusio Alterius*?

Two lawyers went to a restaurant and ordered drinks. When the drinks arrived, each lawyer took a sandwich from his briefcase and began to eat.

The owner rushed over to the table and exclaimed, "You can't eat your own sandwich here!"

The lawyers looked at each other, shrugged, and exchanged sandwiches.

Two other commonly cited maxims are:

- *Verba ita sunt intelligenda ut res magis valeat quam pereat*   Words are to be understood to carry out the object of the enactment and not to have the object fail. Thus, if a word can be interpreted in a way that supports the purpose of an enactment and in a way that defeats that purpose, it should be given the former interpretation.

- *Verba quae aliquid operari possunt non debent esse superflua*   Words that can have some effect should not be treated as superfluous. For example, "sanction" and "punish" are often used as synonyms. But "sanction" can also mean the opposite of "punish"; it has other meanings such as "endorse" or "legitimize." Therefore, if an enactment contained the phrase "punish or sanction conduct," following this maxim a tribunal would interpret "sanction" in this

---

6   RSM 1968, c 103.

7   *Re Medical Centre Apartments Ltd v City of Winnipeg* (1969), 3 DLR (3d) 525 (Man CA).

context to mean "endorse" rather than "punish," because the phrase "or sanction" would be superfluous if it has the same meaning as "punish."

A **presumption** is a legal inference or assumption that a fact exists, based on the known or proven existence of some other fact or group of facts. Courts and tribunals will apply certain presumptions to assist them when interpreting statutes. However, these presumptions are generally rebuttable. That is, if the presumption does not lead to an appropriate result, the court or tribunal need not apply it.

One of the most important presumptions is the presumption against retroactive operation of statutes. In interpreting a statute, unless the statute explicitly states that it applies to events that took place before it was passed, a court or tribunal will generally assume that the statute only imposes consequences for actions taken after the statute was enacted. In the words of former Chief Justice Dickson, a statute should not "reach into the past and declare that the law or the rights of parties as of an earlier date shall be taken to be something other than they were as of that earlier date."[8]

The presumption of compliance with constitutional norms requires that where legislation is open to two interpretations, one of which would render the law invalid, the court or tribunal should choose the interpretation that avoids invalidity, even though it may limit the scope or effectiveness of the provision.

The presumption of stability provides that in interpreting amendments to laws, the legislature must not be presumed to have intended the amended law to depart from the previous law any further than it expressly stated.

---

8   *Gustavson Drilling (1964) Ltd v Minister of National Revenue*, [1977] 1 SCR 271.

APPENDIX SUMMARY

Government decision-making often requires the decision-maker to choose between two or more possible meanings of a law or policy. The advocate's job is to persuade the decision-maker to choose a reasonable interpretation that reflects his or her client's interests. Over the decades, courts have developed principles of statutory interpretation that are derived from logic, rules of grammar and syntax, and common sense. Legislatures have also helped by including definition sections in statutes and passing statutes like the *Interpretation Act* or the *Legislation Act* that set out principles for interpreting all laws within their jurisdiction.

The traditional approach to statutory interpretation started with a search for the plain meaning of provisions. Courts seldom looked outside the statute itself for clues. This approach was gradually eclipsed by approaches that focus more on the purpose of provisions and what they are intended to accomplish. Today, courts and tribunals attempt to give provisions a meaning that is in harmony with the legislators' intent by looking at the purpose of the statute as a whole and the context in which the disputed words appear as well as considering whether the consequences of an interpretation are acceptable. They are also much more willing to consider external sources of information, such as debates in the legislature, white papers, and ministerial statements.

KEY TERMS

enactment: a law enacted by an elected legislative body—for example, a statute, regulation, or bylaw

legislative evolution: the amendments made to an enactment over time after it has been passed

legislative history: the background and events leading to the enactment of a law, including matters such as study papers, statements by ministers, debates in the Legislative Assembly, and changes to an enactment made between its introduction and its final passage

presumption: a legal inference or assumption that a fact exists, based on the known or proven existence of some other fact or group of facts

rules of statutory interpretation: the principles used in interpreting laws; *see also* statutory interpretation

statutory interpretation: the process of interpreting laws passed by elected assemblies, whether those laws are statutes, regulations, or municipal bylaws; also known as "statutory construction"

REVIEW QUESTIONS

1. Why do laws require interpretation?

2. When will a court or tribunal depart from the plain meaning of a provision in interpreting a law?

3. When the meaning of a law is unclear, what approaches will a court or tribunal use to ascertain its meaning?

4. What is "contextual analysis"?

5. In what ways are the modern and traditional approaches to statutory interpretation different? In what ways are they similar?

6. Where would you look to find the meaning of a word if it is not defined in a statute?

7. If the meanings of the English and French versions of a provision are different, how is the correct meaning determined?

8. Can the preamble or internal headings in a statute be used to assist in interpreting the statute's provisions? If so, what is their value as interpretive tools compared with the value of a definition or purpose section within the statute?

9. If a provision contains a list, how would you determine whether the list is intended to be exhaustive or whether items not in the list are also covered by the provision?

EXERCISES

1. Section 18 of Ontario's *Environmental Protection Act* (RSO 1990, c E.19) permits a Director of the Ministry of the Environment under certain circumstances to make an order requiring the owner of property to "monitor" the discharge of a contaminant into the natural environment.

   The Act states:

   Order by Director re preventive measures

   18(1) The Director, in the circumstances mentioned in subsection (2), by a written order may require a person who owns or owned or who has or had management or control of an undertaking or property to do any one or more of the following:

   1. To have available at all times, or during such periods of time as are specified in the order, the equipment, material and personnel specified in the order at the locations specified in the order.

   2. To obtain, construct and install or modify the devices, equipment and facilities specified in the order at the locations and in the manner specified in the order.

   3. To implement procedures specified in the order.

   4. To take all steps necessary so that procedures specified in the order will be implemented in the event that a contaminant is discharged into the natural environment from the undertaking or property.

   5. To monitor and record the presence or discharge of a contaminant specified in the order and to report thereon to the Director.

   6. To study and to report to the Director on,

      i. the presence or discharge of a contaminant specified in the order,

      ii. the effects of the presence or discharge of a contaminant specified in the order,

iii. measures to control the presence or discharge of a contaminant specified in the order,

iv. the natural environment into which a contaminant specified in the order may be discharged.

7. To develop and implement plans to,

i. reduce the amount of a contaminant that is discharged into the natural environment,

ii. prevent or reduce the risk of a spill of a pollutant within the meaning of Part X, or

iii. prevent, decrease or eliminate any adverse effects that result or may result from a spill of a pollutant within the meaning of Part X or from any other discharge of a contaminant into the natural environment, including,

A. plans to notify the Ministry, other public authorities and members of the public who may be affected by a discharge, and

B. plans to ensure that appropriate equipment, material and personnel are available to respond to a discharge.

8. To amend a plan developed under paragraph 7 or section 91.1 in the manner specified in the order.

Grounds for order

(2) The Director may make an order under this section if the Director is of the opinion, on reasonable and probable grounds, that the requirements specified in the order are necessary or advisable so as,

(a) to prevent or reduce the risk of a discharge of a contaminant into the natural environment from the undertaking or property; or

(b) to prevent, decrease or eliminate an adverse effect that may result from,

(i) the discharge of a contaminant from the undertaking, or

(ii) the presence or discharge of a contaminant in, on or under the property.

There are a variety of chemicals in the groundwater surrounding your client's factory and the Ministry is having difficulty determining what they are and whether they are dangerous. Under section 18, the Director orders your client to pump the water out of the ground and store it in large tanks for an indefinite period, and to take samples and have them analyzed by the laboratory. Using the tools described in this appendix, answer the following questions:

a. What does the term "monitor" mean in this context?

b. Is pumping and storing the water "monitoring"?

c. Is collecting and analyzing water samples "monitoring"?

2. Consider the following scenario. A province's *Land Use Planning Act* states, "Any person may appeal a municipal zoning bylaw to the Planning Review Board." The statute does not define "person." However, the provincial *Interpretation Act* defines "person" as follows:

In every Act, unless the context otherwise requires,

"person" includes a corporation and the heirs, executors, administrators or other legal representatives of a person to whom the context can apply according to law.

The municipality has passed a zoning bylaw rezoning a tract of land to permit an oil company, Petrocon, to establish a gasoline refinery. Save Our Soil (SOS), an unincorporated association of local residents and naturalists, appeals the zoning bylaw to the Board on the grounds that air emissions, discharges of effluent into a local watercourse, and possible spills and leaks of petroleum products and other chemicals will interfere with residents' use and enjoyment of their homes and will contaminate the soil and groundwater in a nearby woods and wetland.

Before the Board, Petrocon argues that SOS has no standing to bring an appeal because it is not a "person." Is SOS a "person" for the purposes of this section of the *Land Use Planning Act*?

3. Section 21 of the British Columbia *Freedom of Information and Protection of Privacy Act* (RSBC 1996, c 165) provides in part:

21(1) The head of a public body must refuse to disclose to an applicant information

(a) that would reveal ...

(ii) commercial, financial, labour relations, scientific or technical information of or about a third party,

(b) that is supplied, implicitly or explicitly, in confidence, and

(c) the disclosure of which could reasonably be expected to

(i) harm significantly the competitive position or interfere significantly with the negotiating position of the third party,

(ii) result in similar information no longer being supplied to the public body when it is in the public interest that similar information continue to be supplied,

(iii) result in undue financial loss or gain to any person or organization, or

(iv) reveal information supplied to, or the report of, an arbitrator, mediator, labour relations officer or other person or body appointed to resolve or inquire into a labour relations dispute.

Lawyers who provide legal aid to those who cannot afford it are paid for their services by the Ministry of Justice, which is a public body subject to the *Freedom of Information and Protection of Privacy Act*. The rates at which lawyers are paid are determined by negotiations between the Ministry and the British Columbia Bar Association (BCBA). In fact, a statute provides that the BCBA will act as the bargaining agent for all the lawyers in the province and the lawyers will be bound by the agreement between the Ministry of Justice and the BCBA.

On behalf of your client, you make a request to the Ministry of Justice for memoranda and correspondence relating to the most recent negotiations between the BCBA and the Department.

The Ministry refuses access to the information on the grounds that this is "labour relations" information under section 21(1)(a)(ii) of the *Freedom of Information and Protection of Privacy Act*.

You believe that this is a misinterpretation of the statute. You argue that the term "labour relations" refers to negotiations between an employer and a labour union representing employees, not negotiations between a government agency and an independent association representing professionals.

What light do the following shed on the proper interpretation of "labour relations" in section 21(1)(a)(ii) of the *Freedom of Information and Protection of Privacy Act*?

a. the preamble or purpose section of the *Freedom of Information and Protection of Privacy Act*;

b. any other provisions of the *Freedom of Information and Protection of Privacy Act* that use the phrase "labour relations";

c. the definitions, if any, of the term "labour relations" in other BC statutes; and

d. the definitions, if any, or usage of the term "labour relations" in other Canadian freedom-of-information statutes.

FURTHER READING

Peter Butt, *Modern Legal Drafting: A Guide to Using Clearer Language*, 3rd ed (Cambridge: Cambridge University Press, 2013).

Pierre Côté, Stephane Beaulac & Mathieu Devinat, *The Interpretation of Legislation in Canada*, 4th ed (Cowansville, Que: Les Éditions Yvon Blais, 2011).

Robert C Dick, *Legal Drafting in Plain Language*, 3rd ed (Toronto: Carswell, 1995).

David Keeshan & Valerie Steeves, *The 1996 Annotated Federal and Ontario Interpretation Acts* (Scarborough, Ont: Carswell, 1996).

Julie Maciura & Richard Steinecke, *The Annotated Statutory Powers Procedure Act* (Aurora, Ont: Canada Law Book, 1998).

Ruth Sullivan, "Statutory Interpretation in a New Nutshell" (2003) 82 Can Bar Rev 51.

Ruth Sullivan, *Sullivan on the Construction of Statutes*, 6th ed (Toronto: LexisNexis, 2014).

Research Tools and Procedures

B

LEARNING OUTCOMES

After reading this appendix, you will understand

- what kinds of documents to look for when preparing to represent a client before a tribunal or other agency, and what kinds of publications contain these documents;

- what other sources of information can be accessed;

- how to obtain pertinent information from libraries and the Internet; and

- the financial considerations in accessing some sources of information as opposed to others.

Cases by the million! Libraries so labyrinthine as to require a guide! The leaves of the books like the leaves of the trees! Who can now read all the reports of cases dealing with the law of consideration for informal promises, stating the reasons deemed sufficient for enforcing such promises, laying down the doctrines and constructing the definitions? Certainly not the writer of this volume.

Arthur L Corbin, *Corbin on Contracts*, vol 1 (St Paul, Minn: West Publishing, 1963) at 489

Categories of Useful Information

Whether one is helping a client apply for a benefit, recommending to a regulatory agency what practices it should allow in an industry or profession, or appearing before a tribunal, one may need to find the following categories of records:

- Laws of general application that apply to the activities of the agency. Such laws may be statutes, regulations, or municipal bylaws. Laws of general application that may affect the jurisdiction or procedures of agencies include the *Statutes Act*, the *Regulations Act*, and the *Interpretation Act* of Canada and of various provinces. In the case of municipalities, these laws include the *Planning Act* and the *Municipal Act*. For most departments, agencies, and tribunals, the province's *Judicial Review Procedure Act*, or, in the case of federal government tribunals, the *Federal Courts Act*, sets out procedures for challenging the decision of an official or tribunal in court. In Quebec, Ontario, British Columbia, and Alberta, there are general statutes that set out minimum rules of procedure for a variety of tribunals and sometimes other statutory decision-makers.

- Statutes, regulations, or bylaws that establish the agency or set out its jurisdiction and procedures. For example, the Ontario Municipal Board is established by the *Ontario Municipal Board Act*, but it derives some of its powers from other statutes such as the *Planning Act*.

- Court decisions that interpret laws of general application that apply to the agency.

- Court decisions that interpret laws that govern the agency.

- Court decisions that interpret administrative law concepts such as jurisdiction, discretion, delegation, procedural fairness, and natural justice.

- Decisions and rulings of the agency in question.

- Decisions and rulings of agencies in other jurisdictions that carry out functions similar to the agency in question or that are governed by statutes that are similar in wording.

- Rules and regulations made by the agency to govern the processing of requests and applications or to govern the conduct of proceedings before it.

- Guidelines and policies that the agency uses in making its decisions.
- Forms used by the agency and by the public in applications to the agency or in proceedings before the agency (for example, application forms, statutory declarations, and summonses to witnesses).

Sources for Obtaining This Information

Primary Sources and Secondary Sources

Sources of information can be divided into primary sources and secondary sources.

Primary sources are publications that contain the full text of documents such as laws, cases, rules, guidelines, policies, and forms.

Secondary sources are publications that summarize, analyze, interpret, or explain the primary records. They include case digests; legal encyclopedias; dictionaries of legal words and phrases as these have been interpreted by the courts; textbooks; **law journals**, newsletters, and blogs, which contain articles about various topics or areas of law or practice; and brochures or pamphlets published by an agency to assist the public in using its services.

Some publications are a combination of primary and secondary material. For example, **annotated** statutes contain the full text of the statute, but they also contain analysis of the overall purpose and operation of the statute, as well as analysis of each section of the statute and a description of court or tribunal cases that have interpreted that section. Similarly, casebooks are a kind of legal textbook that often combine court or tribunal decisions or excerpts from these decisions with commentary and explanations of the legal principles established by these cases.

General Publications and Topical Publications

Sources of information may also be described as general or topical. General publications contain all the laws of a province or all the decisions of a specific court or selected decisions of all courts on a variety of issues.

Topical publications deal with specific subject matters such as labour relations, environmental protection, occupational health and safety, torts, or administrative law.

Media in Which Legal Information Is Recorded

The publications described above can be found in several media. They include paper documents such as books, periodicals, and pamphlets; Internet websites, blogs, search engines, directories, and newsletters/listservs; CD-ROMs; and videotapes, audiotapes, podcasts, and other recorded media. Although some publications are available in just one medium (for example, only online or only in hard copy), legal publications are increasingly available both electronically and on paper.

Locating Primary Sources of Administrative Law

The full, unedited text of bills, statutes, regulations, and bylaws; court and tribunal decisions; and court and agency rules, guidelines, and policies can be found in the ways described below.

Finding Bills, Statutes, and Regulations

The powers and duties of any body established by a statute can be found in the statute or in regulations made under the statute. This applies to ministries of government, government agencies, boards and commissions, universities, and the governing bodies of self-regulating trades and professions.

A **bill** is a version of a statute that has been introduced in Parliament or a provincial or territorial legislature but has not yet been passed. The original bill may be amended by the legislature or its committees, sometimes more than once, before it is passed. The contents of a bill and its status (whether it has been given first, second, or third reading; whether it has been referred to a committee; whether it has been passed; and whether it is in effect) may be ascertained by subscribing to a bills subscription service operated by the government or a private publisher. Some government websites also provide this information. For example, the text of federal bills is available on LEGISinfo (<http://www.parl.gc.ca/LEGISINFO>). Federal bills and the bills of all provinces and territories are also available online from Lexis Advance Quicklaw.

The contents of statutes and regulations may be found in three media: paper, CD-ROM, and online. The federal government and the provincial governments periodically publish compilations of all the statutes and regulations that are in force in their jurisdiction. New regulations are found in the *Canada Gazette*, published by the federal government (<http://www.gazette.gc.ca>), and in the gazettes published weekly or biweekly by provincial and territorial governments. Governments also often produce bound versions of individual statutes soon after they are passed, and compile in a single volume all the statutes passed each year. All federal statutes are available on the Internet, either through free websites (such as <http://laws.justice.gc.ca>) or through commercial services.

The statutes of several provinces and territories are available on the government's website. For example, all Ontario public statutes and regulations are available on the Ontario government's website at <http://www.ontario.ca/laws>. The government aims to add amendments within two business days after each change is made. All laws on the site are searchable—for example, by word or phrase. The site also includes reference tables that allow users to check for recent changes in the law.

The statutes and regulations of Canada and the provinces and territories can also be found on the website of the Canadian Legal Information Institute (CanLII) (<http://www.canlii.org>), on Lexis Advance Quicklaw (<http://www.lexisnexis.ca>), and in WestlawNext's LawSource directory (<http://www.westlawnextcanada.com/

westlaw-products/lawsource>). Access to CanLII is free; access to LexisNexis Quicklaw and LawSource is by paid subscription.

As mentioned above, federal and provincial/territorial statutes and regulations are available on the Internet. They are also available on CD-ROM. The *Ontario Statute Citator* and the *Canada Statute Citator* can be accessed as weekly PDF bulletins or installed on a computer (CD-ROM updates are published several times per year). These **statute citators**, also called **citators**, contain all public statutes that are in effect; the text of all regulations made under these statutes; and the history of the statutes and regulations, including the date of the law's passage and, on a section-by-section basis, the date of passage of every amendment and sometimes the text of each amendment. The statutes and regulations are searchable by statute name, section number, or keyword. The citators also list recent court decisions that have interpreted particular sections of statutes. For a more complete list of cases, it is necessary to look elsewhere.

Finding Bylaws, Resolutions, and Other Information of Municipal Agencies

Where a municipal body is created by a bylaw or resolution of the municipal council, at least some of its powers and responsibilities will be set out in the resolution or bylaw. (The functions might be found partly in a statute such as the *Municipal Act* and partly in bylaws or resolutions.)

Resolutions and bylaws are generally not published and must be obtained from the clerk of the municipality or a department head or other official who may have a copy. However, some of the larger Ontario municipalities post their bylaws on their websites. For example, Toronto's bylaws are available at <http://www.toronto.ca/legdocs/bylaws/lawhome.htm>.

Finding Court and Tribunal Decisions

The text of a court or tribunal decision can be located in two ways: by reference to its case name (for example, "*Doe v Joe*" or "*Re Wigle Estate*") or by its **citation** (or, colloquially, its **cite**). The citation for a case is a combination of the year the case was decided (or sometimes, the year it was published in a law report), the abbreviated name of the law report, the volume and/or series of the law report, the first page of the decision (its number), and the abbreviated name of the court (if the court is not apparent from the name of the law report). (See below for information on neutral citations.)

A typical case name and citation looks like this:

Re Knowles (1997), 26 CELR (NS) 71 (Ont EAB)

In the example above, "*Re Knowles*" is the case name (also known as the "title of proceedings" or "style of cause"); "(1997)" is the year the case was decided; "26" is the volume number; "CELR" stands for *Canadian Environmental Law Reports*; "(NS)" means "New Series"; "71" is the first page of the decision; and "(Ont EAB)" stands for the Ontario Environmental Appeal Board. So this citation tells you that the decision in the case of *Re Knowles* was made by the Environmental Appeal Board, released in 1997, and is published in volume 26 of the new series of the *Canadian Environmental Law Reports*, starting at page 71.

The first problem one faces with a case citation is finding out what the abbreviation of the name of the publication stands for, if one is not familiar with it. For example, if you do not know that CELR stands for *Canadian Environmental Law Reports*, you will have difficulty locating the case even though you have all the relevant information. Lists of abbreviations of the names of law reporters and law journals are found at the front of several publications, including the *Index to Canadian Legal Literature* and the *Canadian Law Dictionary*. A list of abbreviations can also be found at the back of the *Canadian Guide to Uniform Legal Citation* (the McGill Guide).

Neutral citations serve as unique case identifiers, but they do not contain the necessary information to locate the text of the case. They consist of the year of the decision, an abbreviation that identifies the court, and a number that corresponds to the number of decisions released by that court to date during the year. For example, in the citation *Newfoundland and Labrador Nurses' Union v Newfoundland and Labrador (Treasury Board)*, 2011 SCC 62, the neutral citation shows that the case was the 62nd decision of the Supreme Court of Canada in 2011.

Electronic databases have their own citation systems. For example, in a case citation that gives the law report as "OJ," the law report is *Ontario Judgments*, which is a computerized publication of Ontario decisions on LexisNexis Quicklaw. The decision may or may not also be available in a print publication such as the CELR.

The three primary ways of finding decisions of courts and tribunals are to look

- in law reporters,
- on the website of the court or tribunal in question, or
- at a database or electronic directory in which decisions are collected.

Law reporters, also called **law reports** or **reporters**, are collections of court and tribunal decisions deemed by experts in the field to be significant because they shed new light on the interpretation of the law. Most law reports periodically publish a cumulative index of cases, in which a case can be located either by name or by subject matter.

Some electronic databases also include only cases selected for their significance from the vast number of court and tribunal decisions rendered each year. Other databases contain all the decisions of a particular court or tribunal, regardless of their legal importance.

Law reports and databases of cases may be regional (for example, the *Western Weekly Reports*, which publishes important decisions of the courts of Manitoba, Saskatchewan, Alberta, and British Columbia, and the *Alberta Law Reports*); topical (the *Canadian Environmental Law Reports*, the *Canadian Human Rights Reporter*, and the *Canadian Labour Relations Boards Reports*); or may represent the collected decisions of a particular court (the *Supreme Court Reports* and the *Federal Courts Reports*).

Decisions of Courts That Interpret Statutes Governing Agencies

On paper as well as online, there are several general-purpose law reporting services that publish court decisions considered to be significant because they shed new light on the interpretation of the law. They include the *Ontario Reports*, which publishes decisions of all levels of the Ontario courts, and the *Dominion Law Reports*, which publishes decisions of courts across Canada. Some of these decisions interpret the statutes that govern administrative bodies.

There are also law reports that are restricted to the decisions of a particular court. For example, the *Federal Courts Reports* carries decisions of the Federal Court of Canada and the Federal Court of Appeal. These courts interpret statutes passed by the government of Canada, including statutes under which federal government agencies operate. There are two law reporters that carry only the decisions of the Supreme Court of Canada: the *Supreme Court Reports* and the *National Reporter*.

Administrative Law Court Decisions

Decisions of courts that have interpreted the application of common law principles of administrative law—such as natural justice, procedural fairness, and the rule against subdelegation—in relation to specific administrative bodies can be found in the general law reporters and annotation services listed above.

Procedural Law Court and Tribunal Decisions

SPECIFIC TRIBUNALS OR CATEGORIES OF TRIBUNALS

There are several commercially published law reporters devoted to specific tribunals or categories of tribunals. These law reporters usually publish decisions of the tribunal that the editors deem to be significant, as well as court decisions that interpret the powers of the tribunal or its procedures. For example, the *Canadian Human Rights Reporter* includes court decisions that interpret federal and provincial human rights statutes as well as significant decisions of the Canadian Human Rights Commission, the Canadian Human Rights Tribunal, and provincial human rights commissions and tribunals. The *Canadian Environmental Law Reports* compiles decisions of courts across Canada that interpret environmental laws, but it also includes significant decisions by environmental tribunals such as the Alberta and British Columbia environmental appeal boards and the Ontario Environmental Review Tribunal. Occasionally, CELR will also include a summary of a royal commission report on an environmental concern.

Law reporters on paper and online that are devoted to the decisions of an individual tribunal and court decisions interpreting the powers of that tribunal include the *Ontario Municipal Board Reports*, produced by a commercial publisher, and the *Ontario Labour Relations Board Reports*, published by the OLRB.

ADMINISTRATIVE LAW CASE REPORTING SERVICES

There is one commercial law reporter devoted solely to administrative law decisions from across Canada that is available both on paper and through a commercial

Internet service. The *Administrative Law Reports* includes significant decisions of individual tribunals as well as administrative law decisions of all levels of courts throughout Canada.

Although there are relatively few paper publications devoted to collecting the decisions of individual tribunals, comprehensive collections of the decisions of many tribunals are available on the Internet from a number of sources: CanLII, Lexis Advance Quicklaw, and the websites of the tribunals themselves. In some cases, such as the Appeals Commission for Alberta Workers' Compensation, the tribunal publishes its decisions to CanLII.

On the Internet, one can also compare how tribunals in different jurisdictions have dealt with the same problem or interpreted similar statutes. For example, CanLII has databases for decisions of the Labour Relations Board of Canada, Alberta, British Columbia, Nova Scotia, Newfoundland and Labrador, Ontario, Prince Edward Island, and Saskatchewan.

Tribunals that maintain websites with all their decisions include the federal Privacy Commissioner; the information and privacy commissioners of Alberta, British Columbia, and Ontario; and Ontario's Environmental Review Tribunal. Tribunal websites are often accessible through the website of the provincial or federal government that established the tribunal. Additionally, some services offer specialized collections of tribunal decisions; the Ontario Workplace Tribunals Library, for example, makes available hard copies of the decisions of the Ontario Labour Relations Board, the Workplace Safety and Insurance Appeals Tribunal, and the Pay Equity Hearings Tribunal.

Locating Secondary Sources of Administrative Law

Descriptions, summaries, analysis, and commentary regarding particular statutes; regulations; bylaws; court and tribunal decisions; and agency rules, guidelines, and policies can be found using the sources and methods described below.

Textbooks

There are numerous Canadian, American, and British textbooks that deal with administrative law as a whole or with specific areas of administrative law, such as bias, subordinate legislation, and disciplinary proceedings. For a selection of Canadian texts, most of which are available only in paper form, see the list under "Selected Resources" at the end of this appendix.

Law Journals and Newsletters

General law journals, such as those published by bar associations and university law faculties, contain articles on a variety of topics, including administrative law. (For example, Laverne A Jacobs & Thomas S Kuttner, "Discovering What Tribunals Do:

Tribunals Before the Courts" (2002) 81 Can Bar Rev 616). In addition, a few law journals are devoted exclusively to administrative law topics. The *Canadian Journal of Administrative Law and Practice* is published by Carswell and is available through Carswell's commercial website. The American Bar Association publishes the *Administrative Law Review*, which covers more esoteric and specialized issues than those covered by Canadian publications.

Many law journals are available on the Internet, although some are still only available on paper. Law journals published by a university or non-profit association may be available on the university's or association's website. Some law journals that are published on paper by commercial publishers are also available online through the publishers' electronic research facilities (see below).

Carswell's comprehensive *Index to Canadian Legal Literature* is available both on paper and online. It is possible to locate articles in most Canadian law journals through the Index. Articles are listed by author, title, and subject matter; one of the listed topics is administrative law. There is also an administrative justice bibliography (AJB) online at <http://www.law-lib.utoronto.ca/Conferences/Administrative_Justice_Bibliography/AJB.HTM>. The AJB is a categorized and annotated bibliography of articles, chapters of books, text and treatise sections, reports, press clippings, theses, conference presentations, jurisprudence, and other materials of interest to those working in the field of administrative justice tribunal design and reform.

Lexis Advance Quicklaw's Administrative Law Commentary (AMPA) is a collection of journal articles, papers, and newsletters related to administrative law. Bulletin LexisNexis Droit administratif (BADQ) deals with current events in administrative justice in Quebec, while the bimonthly *Harper Grey Administrative Law Observer* newsletter covers new cases on the powers of administrative bodies, conduct of hearings, and judicial review of administrative decisions.

Legal Encyclopedias

Legal encyclopedias are legal textbooks that cover a wide variety of areas of law, from A (abandonment, administrative law) to Y and Z (young offenders, zoning). For each subject, they provide a summary of the law in the jurisdiction they cover, as well as case citations supporting each rule or principle described. At least one legal encyclopedia, the *Canadian Encyclopedic Digest*, is available on paper as well as through WestlawNext.

Case Law Digests

Case law digests are regularly updated collections of summaries of significant court or tribunal decisions arranged alphabetically by subject matter. There are case law digests for specific areas of law as well as case law digests that are encyclopedic—that is, they cover a wide variety of areas of law. The *Canadian Abridgment* is one digest that is available on paper and through WestlawNext. It contains summaries of significant court decisions, grouped by subject matter. One of the subject areas is administrative law.

Case Citators

Once a case has been considered significant enough to report, it is important to determine when the courts have followed the decision and when they have rejected it, or found that it does not apply to the case before them. Publications that list significant court decisions and track how they are applied in subsequent cases are called **case citators** or "case citations."

These publications do not contain the text of the court decision; rather, they simply identify the law reports in which the decision is reported. *Canadian Case Citations*, which is part of the *Canadian Abridgment* series, is published by Carswell. It contains citations for cases decided by courts throughout Canada from 1867 to the present.

Case citations are available on paper, on CD-ROM, and through online commercial and free research facilities. For example, CanLII tracks how each of the cases it has published has been treated in subsequent decisions in other court cases.

Legal Dictionaries

Legal dictionaries are usually general in nature, although there are a few topical legal dictionaries, such as the *Dictionary of Environmental Law and Science*, published by the Environmental Law Centre in Alberta. There does not appear to be a legal dictionary devoted to administrative law, but general legal dictionaries such as *Black's Law Dictionary*, the *Dictionary of Canadian Law*, the *Canadian Law Dictionary*, and *Words and Phrases Legally Defined* explain administrative law concepts such as natural justice, procedural fairness, jurisdiction, and subdelegation, as well as relevant Latin phrases like *audi alteram partem*. Online dictionaries include the 'Lectric Law Library's dictionary at <http://www.lectlaw.com/def.htm> and Emond's glossary at <http://www.emond.ca/higher-education/glossary-of-legal-terms.html>.

Conference Proceedings

For topics that are too specific, narrow, or new to be given detailed treatment in more permanent form, papers presented at topical conferences are a useful source of information. Papers are often provided to conference participants in printed form or electronically (for example, as PDFs). Conference organizers often tape the oral presentations and sell the resulting videos or audio recordings. A narrow topic such as a lawyer's perspective on practice before a specific tribunal, or the tribunal chair's description of recent developments, may be the subject of a conference presentation that is recorded and available on paper or electronically as an audio or video recording.

Blogs

Blogs often contain commentary on recent developments in the law, and many are written by leading academics and practitioners. One current blog on administrative law, *Administrative Law Matters*, is maintained by law professor Paul Daly (<http://

www.administrativelawmatters.com/blog>). Other blogs may contain more general commentary that includes administrative law material, such as the *Canadian Appeals Monitor* (<http://www.canadianappeals.com>), published by McCarthy Tétrault LLP.

Combined Primary and Secondary Sources

Annotated statutes and statute annotators, statute citators, and legal casebooks combine primary and secondary sources.

Annotated Statutes and Statute Annotators

An annotated statute is a book that contains the full text of a statute as well as section-by-section commentary on the meaning of that particular statute and citations of court or tribunal decisions that have interpreted each section of the statute (see the list under "Selected Resources" at the end of this appendix).

A statute annotator, although similar in name, is somewhat different from an annotated statute. It contains all the statutes of a particular jurisdiction such as a province, with a list of cases that have interpreted each provision of each of the statutes.

Statute Citators

Statute citators list cases that have interpreted provisions of statutes. *Canadian Statute Citations*, part of Carswell's *Canadian Abridgment* series, lists every section of each federal statute and all provincial statutes, together with the citations of court decisions that have interpreted each of them. CanLII has a similar online service.

Citations for recent cases that have interpreted provisions in statutes of Canada are in the *Canada Statute Citator*, while recent cases that have interpreted Ontario statutes are in the *Ontario Statute Citator*. For federal and Ontario decisions before 1990, it is necessary to look in earlier paper editions of the citators.

Casebooks

Casebooks contain lengthy extracts from important court decisions together with commentary on them and references to related cases. They are generally more useful as a teaching tool than as a research tool. Emond has published a casebook on administrative law entitled *Administrative Law: Cases, Text, and Materials*, 7th ed (Toronto: Emond Montgomery, 2015).

Web-Based Research

The primary and secondary sources of legal information described above can all be found in print, and in some cases on CD-ROM, but most of the same information can now be found much faster—and sometimes at less expense—on the Internet.

Search Engines and Directories

If you know the URL of a particular website that contains the kind of information you are looking for, you may access the site on your computer. However, if you know the topic you want to research but not which websites contain the information, you can find relevant sites through search engines and directories; you type in the keywords or phrases you are looking for, and the search engine or directory produces links to the pages of websites that contain these words or phrases.

General Search Engines

General search engines that produce good results are Google (<http://www.google.com>), Bing (<http://www.bing.com>), and Yahoo (<http://www.yahoo.com>).

Google has an advanced search option that allows users to search, among other options, within a specific site or domain (for example, ".gc.ca" or ".edu"). Additionally, Google Scholar (<https://scholar.google.ca>) can be used to locate American case law and articles.

Legal Search Engines, Directories, and Websites

There are two kinds of legal directories, search engines, and websites: commercial services to which users must subscribe and pay a fee, and free search services.

COMMERCIAL SEARCH ENGINES AND DIRECTORIES

Among the most comprehensive and established commercial database directories are Lexis Advance Quicklaw and WestlawNext Canada's LawSource. Subscribers to these online legal research services pay a fee for access. In some cases, subscribers can choose between a monthly flat rate or an hourly rate for actual search time. Rates vary according to the number of users in the law firm or company that subscribes.

◇ Lexis Advance Quicklaw

Lexis Advance Quicklaw (<http://www.lexisnexis.ca>) focuses on Canadian information sources, although it also contains some foreign information, particularly from the United States and the United Kingdom. It has hundreds of legal databases containing court and tribunal decisions, statutes and regulations, newsletters, law journals, papers, articles, legal texts, and legal directories.

LexisNexis (<http://www.lexisnexis.com>) is similar, but with a focus on US law, although it also contains some Canadian information.

◇ WestlawNext

WestlawNext (<http://www.westlawnextcanada.com>) offers topical case law databases integrated with legislation and commentary, including case citations and statute citations, as well as the *Canadian Encyclopedic Digests*, the *Canadian Abridgment Digests*, and the *Index to Canadian Legal Literature*.

FREE LEGAL SEARCH ENGINES, DIRECTORIES, AND WEBSITES

Much of the information available on commercial websites is also available on free websites, so it is often possible to avoid paying fees for information such as court and tribunal decisions, legislation, and some law journal articles.

Some websites consist mainly of links to other websites and have very little information. Other websites contain a wide variety of legal information, including statutes, case law, and law journal articles.

The following search engines and directories link to a variety of legal websites:

- World Legal Information Institute (WorldLII; <http://www.worldlii.org>) contains links to over 1,700 databases of case law, legislation, and other legal materials from 123 jurisdictions via 14 legal information institutes, including:

  - The Canadian Legal Information Institute (CanLII; <http://www.canlii.org>). CanLII contains the full text of Canadian federal, provincial, and territorial statutes and regulations, and almost 300 case law databases containing more than 500,000 court decisions, tribunal decisions, and administrative agency rulings, including the decisions of the appeal courts of each of the provinces and territories and the Federal Court of Appeal as well as the decisions of the lower courts of many of the provinces and territories. The information is organized by jurisdiction with hyperlinks between case law and legislation.

  - The Australasian Legal Information Institute (AustLII; <http://www.austlii.edu.au>). AustLII provides access to primary legal materials such as decisions of Australian courts and tribunals, and most Australian state and federal legislation, as well as secondary Australian legal materials.

  - The New Zealand Legal Information Institute (NZLII; <http://www.nzlii.org>). NZLII contains New Zealand court and tribunal cases, legislation, and law journals.

  - The British and Irish Legal Information Institute (BAILII; <http://www.bailii.org>). BAILII is a source of British and Irish cases and legislation with links to free full-text legal journals and other journal article abstracts. It also contains links to other world collections, including resources from Asia, some European countries, some African countries, and the Pacific Islands.

- Cornell University's Legal Information Institute (<http://www.law.cornell.edu/uscode>) provides searchable full-text access to the *United States Code*, a compilation of all federal statutes passed by Congress and signed by the president (or passed over the president's veto). This includes the *Administrative Procedures Act*, which codifies rules that federal agencies must follow for rule making and holding hearings.

- Office of the Law Revision Counsel (<http://uscode.house.gov>) also provies access to the *United States Code*, and allows you to search by title, section, or key term.

- Justia (<https://www.justia.com>) is a comprehensive American website that contains case law, federal and state legislation, codes, and regulations.
- Court websites: Some courts maintain websites containing all their decisions as well as other information such as their rules of practice and their practice directions.

Supreme Court websites:
- The Supreme Court of Canada (<http://www.scc-csc.gc.ca>) provides access to hundreds of decisions, the progress of cases currently before the court, and instant email updates as new decisions are released.
- The US Supreme Court (<http://www.supremecourt.gov>) provides information about the court, its procedures, and recent opinions.

Federal Court of Canada and provincial and territorial court websites:
- Federal Court of Appeal: <http://decisions.fca-caf.gc.ca/fca-caf/en/nav.do>
- Alberta: <https://albertacourts.ca>
- British Columbia: <http://www.courts.gov.bc.ca>
- Manitoba: <http://www.manitobacourts.mb.ca>
- New Brunswick: <http://www.gnb.ca/cour/03COA1/index-e.asp>
- Newfoundland and Labrador: <http://www.court.nl.ca>
- Northwest Territories: <https://www.justice.gov.nt.ca/en>
- Nova Scotia: <http://www.courts.ns.ca>
- Nunavut: <http://www.nucj.ca>
- Ontario: <http://www.ontariocourts.on.ca>
- Prince Edward Island: <http://www.gov.pe.ca/courts>
- Quebec: <http://citoyens.soquij.qc.ca>
- Saskatchewan: <http://www.sasklawcourts.ca>
- Yukon: <http://www.yukoncourts.ca>
- Guide to Law Online (<http://www.loc.gov/law/help/guide.php>), prepared by the US Law Library of Congress, is an annotated guide to sources of information on government and law available online. The site includes links to other sites for legal information.
- FindLaw (<http://lp.findlaw.com>) contains legal news; US federal legislation and Supreme Court decisions; US state legislation and state court decisions; and information on legal subjects such as constitutional law, patents and trademarks, criminal law, and labour law.
- Lawrunner is a legal research tool offered by the Internet Legal Resource Group website (<http://www.ilrg.com>), FindLaw (<http://lp.findlaw.com>), and Lexum (discussed below). It provides access to the websites of government bodies, courts, and bar associations of all 50 US states and more than 200 nations.

- Lexum (<https://lexum.com/en>) contains statutes and regulations, case law from courts and tribunals, periodicals, Canada–US treaties, and other international law resources.

- PublicLegal (<http://www.ilrg.com>), a product of the Internet Legal Research Group (ILRG), is an index of more than 4,000 websites in more than 200 nations. Established to serve as a comprehensive resource of the information available on the Internet concerning law and the legal profession, the site contains web pages, legal forms, and downloadable files. It lists legal indexes and search engines as well as law journals and publications available online.

APPENDIX SUMMARY

Understanding the functions and structures of administrative bodies, and preparing to advocate a position before them, involves finding rules, policies, and guidelines that the bodies have published and the decisions they have issued. It also requires finding decisions of the courts that have interpreted the powers and duties of these agencies.

This information is available in a variety of places, ranging from agency offices to the Internet, and in primary as well as secondary sources. It is often available from governments, from agencies, and from commercial publishers of legal materials, and may be found on paper, on the Internet, on audiotapes and videotapes, and on CD-ROM. Obtaining the information you need may be costly, but it is often available free of charge online.

KEY TERMS

annotated: of a court or tribunal decision or a provision of a statute, regulation, or other rule or guideline, a version containing notes or comments intended to explain its meaning

bill: in parliamentary and legislative practice, a version of a statute (or in municipal practice, a version of a bylaw) introduced in the legislative assembly to be passed as a law

case citator: a publication that lists significant court decisions and tracks how they are applied in subsequent cases

citation: information identifying where a statute, regulation, bylaw, court or tribunal decision, or article is published; also called a "cite"

citator: *see* case citator, statute citator

cite: as a noun, colloquial for "citation"; as a verb, refers to the use of a case or a law as an authority for a proposition, such as a particular interpretation of a law

law journal: a periodic publication containing scholarly articles about legal issues, often discussing the significance of laws and decisions of courts and tribunals

law report: *see* law reporter

law reporter: a periodic publication containing either the full text or a summary of decisions of courts and tribunals as they are released; also called a "law report" or "reporter"

reporter: *see* law reporter

statute citator: a publication that lists all the provisions of a statute and for each provision, sets out amendments that have been made, and sometimes court decisions that have interpreted the provisions; also called a citator

REVIEW QUESTIONS

1. Explain the difference between a primary source and a secondary source of information about the law.

2. What information is found in the citation for a court or tribunal decision?

3. Where would you look for the full text of a statute, regulation, or court or tribunal decision other than a paper publication?

4. What is the difference between a law journal and a law reporter?

5. Name a law journal and a law reporter that specialize in publishing information about administrative law.

6. What is the difference between a case citator and a statute citator?

7. What is the difference between an annotated statute and a statute annotator?

8. If you want to know how courts or tribunals have interpreted a specific word or phrase in a statute, where should you look?

EXERCISES

1. Using any of the sources discussed in this appendix, list the statutes under which the Ontario Municipal Board operates. Describe in one paragraph for each statute the functions the Board carries out under that statute.

2. Find the following cases on paper and electronically, and explain how you located them without a citation:

   a. *Spy Hill v Bradshaw*

   b. *Crocock v Orion Insurance Co*

   c. *Morisette v The Maggie*

3. Ontario's *Crown Agency Act* contains the following definition of "Crown agency":

   In this Act, "Crown agency" means a board, commission, railway, public utility, university, manufactory, company or agency, owned, controlled or operated by Her Majesty in right of Ontario, or by the Government of Ontario, or under the authority of the Legislature or the Lieutenant Governor in Council.

   Find three court or tribunal decisions that have considered whether a particular body falls within this definition, and list them, including their case name and citation. Explain where you looked for this information and where you found these cases.

4. List five law journals that have published articles dealing with administrative law in the past five years, and record the full bibliographic information of five articles.

5. The word "control" is used in many legal contexts—for example, statutes provide that it is an offence to have "care or control" of a vehicle while impaired, and insurance policies sometimes provide that the insurance coverage is in effect only while property or premises are "under the custody or control" of the insured person.

   Find five cases that interpret the meaning of "control" in different legal contexts. For each, list the case name and citation and explain how you located the case.

SELECTED RESOURCES

Annotated Statutes

Edward L Greenspan & Marc Rosenberg, *Martin's Annual Criminal Code* (Aurora, Ont: Canada Law Book, 2016).

M David Keeshan & Valerie M Steeves, *The 1996 Annotated Federal and Ontario Interpretation Acts* (Scarborough, Ont: Carswell, 1995).

Rick Libman, *The Annotated Contraventions Act* (Toronto: Carswell, 2015).

Julie Maciura & Richard Steinecke, *The Annotated Statutory Powers Procedure Act* (Aurora, Ont: Canada Law Book, 1998).

Law Journals

Canadian Journal of Administrative Law and Practice (Carswell).

Legal Dictionaries

Daphne Dukelow, *The Dictionary of Canadian Law*, 4th ed (Toronto: Carswell, 2011).

John D Gardner & Karen Gardner, *Sanagan's Encyclopedia of Words and Phrases, Legal Maxims*, 5th ed (Toronto: Carswell) (loose-leaf).

BA Garner, ed, *Black's Law Dictionary*, 10th ed (St Paul, Minn: West Group, 2014).

David Hay, *Words and Phrases Legally Defined*, 4th ed (London: LexisNexis, 2007).

William A Tilleman, ed, *Dictionary of Environmental Law and Science*, 2nd ed (Edmonton: Environmental Law Centre, 2005).

John A Yogis, Stephan Gerard Coughlan, Catherine Cotter & Steven H Gifis, *Canadian Law Dictionary*, 7th ed (Hauppauge, NY: Barrons, 2013).

Textbooks

Sara Blake, *Administrative Law in Canada*, 5th ed (Toronto: LexisNexis Canada, 2011).

Donald JM Brown & John M Evans, *Judicial Review of Administrative Action in Canada* (Toronto: Canvasback, 2009) (loose-leaf).

Michael J Bryant & Lorne Sossin, *Public Law* (Toronto: Carswell, 2002).

Colleen M Flood & Lorne Sossin, *Administrative Law in Context*, 2nd ed (Toronto: Emond Montgomery, 2013).

Denys C Holland & John McGowan, *Delegated Legislation in Canada* (Toronto: Carswell, 1989).

David P Jones & Anne S deVillars, *Principles of Administrative Law*, 6th ed (Toronto: Carswell, 2014).

John Mark Keyes, *Executive Legislation*, 2nd ed (Toronto: LexisNexis Canada, 2010).

Robert Macaulay & James Sprague, *Practice and Procedure Before Administrative Tribunals* (Toronto: Carswell, 1991) (loose-leaf).

William J Manuel & Christina Donszelmann, *Law of Administrative Investigations and Prosecutions* (Aurora, Ont: Canada Law Book, 1999).

Guy Régimbald, *Canadian Administrative Law*, 2nd ed (Toronto: LexisNexis Canada, 2015).

Gus Van Harten, Gerald Heckman, David Mullan & Janna Promislow, *Administrative Law*, 7th ed (Toronto: Emond Montgomery, 2015).

Websites for Legal Research Techniques and Tips

Best Guide to Canadian Legal Research: <http://www.legalresearch.org>.

Doing Legal Research in Canada: <http://www.llrx.com>.

Internet Legal Resource Group: <http://www.ilrg.com>.

LawGuru: <http://www.lawguru.com.>

Quebec Law: The French text of Denis Le May and Dominique Goubau's guide to researching law, *La Recherche Documentaire en Droit*, is found on the website of the library of Laval University at <https://www.fd.ulaval.ca/sites/default/files/recherche/recherche-doc-droit-6-v2012.pdf>. It includes a chapter on researching Quebec law.

FURTHER READING

Shelley Kierstead, Suzanne Gordon & Sherifa Elkhadem, *The Law Workbook: Developing Skills for Legal Research and Writing*, 2nd ed (Toronto: Emond Montgomery, 2012).

Margaret Kerr, JoAnn Kurtz & Arlene Blatt, *Legal Research: Step by Step*, 4th ed (Toronto: Emond Montgomery, 2015).

Moira McCarney, Ruth Kuras, Annette Demers & Shelly Kierstead, *The Comprehensive Guide to Legal Research, Writing & Analysis*, 2nd ed (Toronto: Emond Montgomery, 2016).

McGill Law Journal, *Canadian Guide to Uniform Legal Citation*, 8th ed (Toronto: Carswell, 2014).

Sample Tribunal Opening Statement

[Note: The words in italics are for direction of the chair and are not to be spoken.]

Good morning/afternoon, this is a hearing by the [Tribunal] under the [relevant Act].

The subject matter of this hearing is an application …

(Read the second paragraph of the title of proceedings in the notice for hearing.)

(Introduce the Tribunal members.)

On my right is … , and on my left is … , who are members of the [Tribunal]. My name is … , and I will be chairing this hearing today.

(Independence of the Tribunal)

For those of you who have not appeared before the [Tribunal] on a previous occasion, I wish to advise you that we are an independent tribunal that is required to hear applications under various [type—e.g., environmental] Acts. Although the members of this tribunal are appointed by the Government of [province or territory], we are not employees of the [related government ministries] or any other government department. We have no knowledge of the matters in issue in this application except for the decision that is being appealed, the applicant's notice of appeal setting out the grounds for the appeal, and [any other information provided to the hearing panel].

The Tribunal can uphold the [initial decision-maker's] decision/order, amend it, revoke it, or substitute a different decision/order.

(Parties to the proceedings)

The Tribunal will now address the matter of parties. The [initial decision-maker] and the applicant, *(name the applicant)*, are automatically parties to this proceeding. The Tribunal has the authority to specify additional persons as parties to this hearing. Any person may give testimony under oath or affirmation that is relevant to the hearing, but this person does not need to be specified as a party to do so.

A person who is made a party has the additional right to cross-examine witnesses, to call other people as witnesses, and to make statements and arguments. In addition, parties have a right to appeal the Tribunal's decision to the [applicable tribunal or court].

First, may I please have the name and address of counsel or the agent representing the applicant.

(The panel chair should make sure that counsel or the agent states on the record that he/she is representing the applicant.)

*(Where the applicant is **not represented** by a lawyer or an agent, state the following:)*

Madam/Sir: You do not need to have a lawyer or agent to represent you at this hearing, but I would like to know if you intend to represent yourself or if a lawyer or agent is representing you.

(If the applicant responds that he or she has a lawyer (or agent),
ask why that lawyer (or agent) is not present today. If the applicant states
that he or she wishes to be represented by a lawyer (or agent),
ask why he or she does not have a lawyer or agent present.)

Now, who is representing [initial decision-maker] at this hearing? Would you please give us your name and address and the name of the [decision-maker] you act for in this matter. Thank you very much.

Are there any other people here today who wish to testify or be specified as parties at this hearing? All persons who have not been called as witnesses by either the applicant or [initial decision-maker] and who wish to testify, or wish to file documents, or to cross-examine witnesses, or to make a statement should identify themselves now please ...

(As each person responds, ask:)

Would you please state your name and address. Do you wish to be named as a party? Why?

(When each person has given you their reason to be a party, ask the re-
spondent and the applicant if they have any objection to this person being
named a party. You should obtain their consent, if possible, before naming any
person as a party. If either the respondent or the applicant objects, you—as the
Tribunal—have authority under [relevant Act and section] to specify parties.)

The Tribunal recognizes Ms/Miss/Mrs./Mr. ... as a party to these proceedings.

The procedure for this hearing will be as follows:

All parties will be requested to make an opening statement. It would be beneficial if the parties could outline what they think will be the issues in this case and make a brief summary of the evidence they intend to call and any other matters they think will assist the Tribunal in conducting this hearing. It may be helpful if you advise the Tribunal of the names of the witnesses you wish to call and give some estimation of the time required to present your case.

All witnesses must give their evidence under oath or affirmation.

The [initial decision-maker] will present its case first. The applicant and any other parties will be allowed to cross-examine any witnesses called by [initial decision-maker]. Upon completion of the cross-examination of each witness, [initial decision-maker] shall be entitled to re-examine the witness on matters that arose for the first time during the cross-examination of the witness.

Environmental Review Tribunal Practice Direction for Technical and Opinion Evidence

I. Practice Direction for Technical and Opinion Evidence

Purpose

1. Technical staff, advisers, consultants and "expert" witnesses routinely give scientific and technical information and their professional opinions in reports and testimony on important issues that the Tribunal must resolve. The opinions given usually purport to be the independent professional judgment of the adviser or witness, based on his or her considerable experience and training. The Tribunal relies on the professional integrity and ethics of these witnesses.

2. The purpose of this Practice Direction is to assist Parties, their representatives, and their witnesses who will give scientific, technical, and opinion evidence to prepare for the Hearing and to present evidence to the Tribunal. The Tribunal seeks to ensure the reliability of scientific and technical evidence and opinion evidence provided to it. Comprehensive and reliable evidence will promote efficiency and fairness in the Tribunal's process, decrease cost and delay, and make the Hearing process less adversarial.

Technical and Scientific Evidence

3. Many witnesses, particularly government employees, appear before the Tribunal to give evidence of scientific and technical observations, tests, measurements, and estimates. While these witnesses are often not considered "experts" who interpret scientific and technical evidence and provide opinions, they collect, compile, and to some extent interpret, information that is essential to the Tribunal's understanding of the issues and often forms the basis for expert opinion evidence. In this Practice Direction, these witnesses are referred to as "technical witnesses" and the scientific and technical information they convey is referred to as "technical evidence."

Opinion Evidence

4. Generally, lay witnesses, including technical staff of companies and government agencies may only state facts—that is, observations made with their physical senses, or in the case of person with appropriate training, observations made with specialized equipment; for example, taking samples and analyzing them in a laboratory and recording the results. They may not give opinions about the significance of the results of such measurements for environmental quality or human health.

5. To give opinion evidence, a witness must have specialized education, training, or experience that qualified him or her to reliably interpret scientific or technical information or to express opinions about matters for which an untrained or inexperienced person cannot provide reliable opinions. Such matters often include whether pollution has caused or is likely to cause significant harm to the environment. Such witnesses are often called "expert witnesses" or "opinion witnesses."

The Role of the Technical Witness

6. The Tribunal expects the witness giving technical or scientific evidence to remain within his or her area of competence. The witness should not attempt to interpret the meaning or significance of tests, observations and measurements unless qualified to do so. The witness should disclose in advance to the other Parties all measurements, tests, observations, and data relating to the issues about which he or she will give evidence, and disclose in examination-in-chief all information relevant to the issues before the Tribunal. Observations, tests, or measurements that do not appear to support the position of the Party for whom the witness is testifying should also be stated.

The Role of Expert or Opinion Witnesses

7. Opinion evidence from a properly qualified "expert" witness should be based on accurate facts, reliable estimates, and accepted or tested techniques or methods of investigation, measurement, and analysis. Expert witnesses must present evidence in an unbiased manner and not act as an advocate. The same obligations applicable to technical witnesses apply to expert or opinion witnesses.

The Role of the Tribunal

8. The decisions that the Tribunal must make involve the public interest and may have serious and far-reaching environmental consequences. These decisions must be based on a balanced record, composed of accurate and reliable technical information and professional opinions. All Parties and their representatives and witnesses have a responsibility to contribute to such a balanced record to assist the Tribunal to fulfill its duty. They are expected to make every effort to comply fully with this Practice Direction. The Tribunal expects that lawyers and other representatives will provide appropriate direction to witnesses to achieve this result.

9. (a) The Tribunal expects the opinion witness to provide it with assistance by way of qualified, relevant opinions and accurate information in relation to matters within his or her expertise. Objectivity and impartiality are necessary to assist the Tribunal in making its decision.

   (b) Evidence that is influenced by the special interests of a Party may be received and considered, but the Tribunal may give this evidence little or no weight.

   (c) The witness should express an opinion to the Tribunal only when the opinion is based on adequate knowledge and sound conviction. The witness should be reluctant to accept an assignment to provide evidence for use by the Tribunal if the terms of reference of the assignment do not allow the witness to carry out the investigations and obtain the information necessary to provide such an opinion. A witness who accepts an assignment under these circumstances should advise the Tribunal of the limitations that the terms of reference place on his or her ability to provide the information necessary to assist the Tribunal in making a sound decision.

(d) Technical evidence and opinion evidence should be, and should be seen to be, the independent product of the witness uninfluenced by the interests of any Party and should, therefore, be fair, objective and non-partisan.

(e) The witness must never assume the role of an advocate for a Party. Argument and advocacy should be left to counsel or other representatives presenting the Party's case. This does not preclude the vigorous advancement of strongly held scientific or other professional opinions or prevent a duly qualified witness who is also a Party from advancing technical and opinion evidence.

(f) The witness has a duty to change his or her opinion where circumstances, such as the receipt of new information, require it. If at any time before the Tribunal issues its final decision, the witness changes his or her view on a material matter for any reason, particularly after having read the reports or listened to the evidence of witnesses for other Parties, the change in the information and/or opinion should be communicated to the other Parties and the Tribunal without delay. Where reports or documents prepared by the witness contain errors or information which has changed, this must be promptly identified. However, the witness must not change his or her opinion or change or withhold information to suit the position taken by any Party.

Preparing Reports

10. In preparing reports to be used by the witness's employer or client in determining the issues to be raised and the employer or client's position on those issues and for use as evidence, and in testifying before the Tribunal, the witness has the following disclosure duties:

(a) It is the responsibility of the witness to make fair and full disclosure.

(b) The witness should make it clear when a particular question or issue falls outside his or her expertise.

(c) To provide enough information on the assumptions made, procedures used, and conclusions drawn to allow comprehension of the report as it stands, and to permit fair and efficient cross-examination.

(d) When the witness is providing an opinion or giving evidence on an issue for which there are differences of professional or scientific opinion he or she has an obligation to make such differences clearly known to the Tribunal and all Parties. The witness should make reasonable efforts to be fully informed of those differences.

(e) The witness should state all the material facts and assumptions upon which his or her opinion is based. He or she should consider and acknowledge material facts which could detract from the opinion. Where the facts are in dispute, the Tribunal expects that the witness will give his or her view of the facts and the proof relied upon before giving the opinion.

(f) Where the opinion and evidence are based on information contained in other documents, detailed references should be provided in any report prepared by the expert, and copies of those documents made available on request before and during the Hearing.

(g) The witness is expected to disclose to the Tribunal and to the other Parties all significant information and opinions, and errors, shortcomings and limiting factors even if no one has asked for them.

(h) The witness should give direct answers to questions and should not be evasive while giving testimony. Any effort to avoid answering direct questions could adversely affect the weight assigned to the witness's evidence on the issue or the evidence as a whole.

Giving an Opinion

11. (a) When giving an opinion, the witness should provide a resume of the witness's qualifications and should state and explain the degree of certainty of the opinion or the level of probability that it is correct. The degree of uncertainty and the reasons for uncertainty should be candidly acknowledged. Uncertainties and assumptions inherent in measurement, estimates, projections and predictions should be clearly identified. The level of confidence or the sensitivity to error must be explained.

(b) Where there is a lack of consensus with respect to the use of a particular model or formula, the rationale for the chosen approach should be identified.

(c) If the witness's opinion is not properly researched because insufficient data are available, this shortcoming must be stated. Any limiting qualifications to the opinion should be identified. The Tribunal expects to be told when a lack of factual information or experience will increase the probability of inaccurate conclusions or predictions. The witness should avoid speculation where data are insufficient.

(d) Where an estimate falls within a range of reasonable possibilities, based on the same data, the variance within that range should be thoroughly disclosed. Where a prediction can lead to a range of potential impacts, that range should be fully described.

Plain Language

12. (a) In preparing reports and giving testimony, the witness should take into account that the Hearing process is a public process in which reports and testimony must be understood by participants and observers who

may not have any significant technical knowledge. Therefore, the language and writing style should be simple and direct and scientific or technical terms and concepts should be explained in clear, simple language.

(b) Where specialized language is necessary to accurately convey information, the witness should use it rather than risk misleading or over-simplifying. However, the witness should avoid the use of scientific terms and jargon and unfamiliar acronyms, or at least fully explain those terms, so that the technical information and opinion can be easily understood.

Issue Resolution

13. (a) The Tribunal expects that the witness will attempt to adequately address, well in advance of the Hearing, the concerns raised by other Parties in an effort to resolve issues, shorten the Hearing, and save time and expense.

(b) The Tribunal may order the Parties' consultants (including independent consultants, technical or professional staff and advisers) to have one or more meetings and, where appropriate, communicate directly with each other outside of meetings in order to expedite the proceeding. The purposes of the meeting are to:

   (i) exchange all relevant information and documentation related to facts or opinions in dispute;

   (ii) discuss all facts or opinions in dispute with a view to reducing or eliminating areas of controversy;

   (iii) arrange for a site visit if this may assist the consultants to obtain more complete information;

   (iv) reach consensus on facts, issues and opinions that do not require a determination by the Tribunal;

   (v) clarify differences of opinion and to consider whether further studies or information are required;

   (vi) where applicable, develop conditions of approval acceptable to all Parties; and

   (vii) explore any other means of resolving areas of dispute between the Parties.

Efficiency

14. (a) Reports, witness statements, and information should be produced in a timely fashion to all Parties.

(b) All reasonable requests for answers to written questions (often referred to as "interrogatories") must be answered promptly and thoroughly by the witness.

(c) Notwithstanding the requirements for full disclosure, the witness should make every effort to give succinct answers (while at the same time ensuring that they are direct and complete) to questions put to him or her in writing, in examination in-chief, in cross-examination and in re-examination and by the Tribunal. Answers should be concise, responsive and focused on the most essential issues.

(d) During his or her testimony a witness should not be called upon to review the minutia of fundamental techniques, and to read correspondence and other reports line-by-line, unless it is clear that the purpose of such elaboration warrants this expenditure of time.

Compliance

15. If this Practice Direction is not complied with, the Tribunal may:

(a) decline to accept the opinions or evidence of an otherwise qualified witness;

(b) admit the evidence, but accord it little weight;

(c) adjourn the date of the Hearing until such time as this Practice Direction is complied with;

(d) note the conduct of the witness and subject the witness to adverse comment in its decision;

(e) report a breach of professional standards of conduct, an attempt to mislead, incompetence or negligence, extensive violation of this Practice Direction, or serious interference with the Tribunal's process to the professional association or licensing body responsible for compliance with standards of conduct; and/or

(f) order that costs be paid forthwith by the Party who retained or employed the witness.

Sample Exhibit Log

Case No.: _____

EXHIBIT LIST

[Name of Hearing]

EX. #	DESCRIPTION	FILED BY	DATE
1.			
2.			
3.			
4.			
5.			
6.			
7.			
8.			
9.			
10.			
11.			
12.			
13.			
14.			
15.			
16.			
17.			
18.			
19.			
20.			
21.			
22.			
23.			

Date: _____

Sample Tribunal Declaration and Undertaking

F

DECLARATION AND UNDERTAKING

I _____ am _____ for

         (name)   (witness, counsel/agent, consultant, etc.)

_____

I hereby declare:

1. THAT I am ordinarily resident in Canada and am not an employee, officer, director, or major shareholder of the party for which I act or of any other person known by me to be a participant in this hearing;

2. THAT I have read the [Tribunal]'s Rules of Practice and Procedure and the Order of the Tribunal dated _____ that relate(s) to the release of confidential information, and I understand that this Order may be filed with [relevant court]. I further understand that any breach of the terms of the Rule and the Order could be the subject of contempt proceedings in [relevant court].

I hereby undertake:

1. THAT I will maintain the confidentiality of any information or evidence that I receive pursuant to the above Rules and the Order, and will not disclose any of this information;

2. THAT I will not reproduce in any manner, without the prior written approval of the Tribunal, any information, notes, evidence, transcripts, or written submissions dealing with the evidence taken and submissions made in relation to the information that is subject to the above Rule and the Order;

3. THAT within [number of days] days after the Tribunal releases its final decision or order, I will personally deliver to [person submitting the confidential information] all information provided to me pursuant to the above Order, and will destroy or safeguard the confidentiality of any notes taken by me with respect to that evidence or information.

DATED AT _____, [province] this ____ day of _____, 20____ .

Signature: _____

Name: _____

Firm/Company: _____

Glossary

A

abuse of process: conduct by a participant in a proceeding involving a flagrant and serious violation of the rules of procedure or of other reasonable expectations of the court or tribunal

accommodation: *see* duty of reasonable accommodation

act: *see* statute

adjudication: the process of receiving and considering the evidence and arguments presented by both sides in a dispute and making a binding decision by applying relevant law to the issues in the case

adjudicator: the tribunal member or panel of tribunal members responsible for conducting a hearing and deciding the matter in dispute

administrative agency: *see* agency

administrative law: law that governs the organization, duties, and quasi-judicial and judicial powers of the executive branch of government, including both central departments and agencies; a branch of public law

administrative notice: *see* judicial notice

administrative tribunal: *see* tribunal

admissibility: the qualification of information to be received as evidence in a proceeding as determined by the tests of relevance, reliability, necessity, and fairness; *see also* admissible evidence

admissible evidence: information that a court or tribunal will receive as evidence in a proceeding because it meets the tests of relevance, reliability, necessity, and fairness

adversarial system: a system of resolving disputes by holding a hearing in which the judge or adjudicator does not actively seek out the truth or investigate but relies on opposing parties or their representatives to present evidence and challenge each other's evidence; the adjudicator's decision is based on the evidence presented, regardless of how complete or incomplete the evidence is

adverse effect discrimination: the act of imposing an apparently neutral requirement that disproportionately affects a particular individual or group in a negative way based on a ground of discrimination prohibited under a human rights code

advocacy: the act of pleading for or supporting a position or viewpoint

advocate: a person who pleads for or represents the position or viewpoint of another; also called a "representative"

affidavit: a statement, sworn before an authorized person such as a lawyer, in which the person signing the statement sets out facts that he or she affirms to be true

agency: any body, such as a board, commission, or tribunal, established by government and subject to government control to carry out a specialized function that is not an integral part of a government ministry or department

agent: a person appointed by a participant in a proceeding to represent him or her; usually distinguished from counsel; also called a "representative" or "advocate"

alternative dispute resolution: methods of resolving disputes without adjudication, such as conciliation or mediation, in which a facilitator seeks to assist the parties in reaching an agreement without a formal hearing

annotated: of a court or tribunal decision or a provision of a statute, regulation, or other rule or guideline, a version containing notes or comments intended to explain its meaning

appeal: a request for a review of an agency's decision by a higher authority such as a court or a senior government official or body; a right that is available only when provided by statute; distinguished from judicial review

appellant: a person who appeals a decision of a government official, a tribunal, or a court

applicant: a person who applies for a hearing before a tribunal to obtain a decision on a matter in dispute; *see also* appellant

arbitration: an adjudication in which one or more neutral third parties makes a binding decision after holding a hearing; usually refers to an adjudication in which the adjudicator, sometimes called an "arbitrator," is chosen by the parties; *see also* arbitrator

arbitrator: sometimes used instead of the term "adjudicator" to refer to members of tribunals in which the members are appointed by the government or a regulatory body, or chosen by the parties themselves

arguments: presentation to a court or tribunal of reasons to accept a party's point of view, including a summary of the evidence and the law that support this point of view; also called "submissions"

B

bias: an interest, attitude, relationship, or action that leads a decision-maker to favour one party over another

bill: in parliamentary and legislative practice, a version of a statute (or in municipal practice, a version of a bylaw) introduced in the legislative assembly to be passed as a law

bona fide occupational requirement: a requirement or qualification for employment that is essential to the successful carrying out of the duties of a position, and therefore justifies discriminating against an individual who cannot meet the requirement based on one of the grounds of discrimination prohibited under a human rights code; also called a "BFOR"

book of authorities: a binder containing the cases, statutory provisions, and excerpts from legal texts that a representative will rely on in support of his or her position before a court or tribunal

burden of proof: the obligation to provide sufficient evidence to prove a point in dispute; also called "onus of proof"; *see also* standard of proof

bylaw: law enacted by a subordinate legislative body, such as a municipality, under the authority of a statute

C

Cabinet: a committee of members of Parliament or the provincial legislature appointed by the prime minister, in the case of the federal government, or the premier of a province to preside over government departments (also known as the "governor in council" federally and the "lieutenant governor in council" provincially)

case assessment direction: in a proceeding before the HRTO, a direction issued by the Tribunal before a hearing that may address any matter that the Tribunal feels will facilitate the fair and expeditious resolution of the case—for example, identifying the main issues, facts on which the parties agree, procedural issues that need to be decided before the hearing, and any witnesses who should attend the hearing; *see also* case conference

case citator: a publication that lists significant court decisions and tracks how they are applied in subsequent cases

case conference: in a case before the HRTO, a meeting of all the parties and affected persons convened by the Tribunal to discuss the conduct of the proceedings, often leading to the issuance of a case assessment direction; *see also* case assessment direction

case management conference: a procedure of the CHRT, similar to the pre-hearing conferences of other tribunals, at which a tribunal member addresses matters such as whether the parties will be represented by a lawyer or other representative, how many witnesses each party intends to call at the hearing, how long each party's evidence will take to present, and so on

chain of custody: documented proof that physical evidence has not been tampered with, by showing "continuity of possession"; involves keeping the object under lock and key or otherwise secure, and ensuring that a record is kept of each person who handled or transported the object from the time it was received until the date of the proceeding

Charter principles: *see* Charter values

Charter values: the values that underlie the specific rights and freedoms set out in the Charter; for example, the value "privacy" underlies the right to be free from unreasonable search and seizure in section 8 of the Charter; also called "Charter principles"

circumstantial evidence: evidence that tends to show that something is likely to be a fact even though no witness directly observed the event in question; evidence from which inferences about other facts can be drawn; *see also* direct evidence

citation: information identifying where a statute, regulation, bylaw, court or tribunal decision, or article is published; also called a "cite"

citator: *see* case citator, statute citator

cite: as a noun, colloquial for "citation"; as a verb, refers to the use of a case or a law as an authority for a proposition, such as a particular interpretation of a law

closed hearing: a hearing held behind closed doors (in private), in which the only persons permitted to attend are those directly involved in the case, such as parties, their representatives, and necessary witnesses; also called an "*in camera*" hearing

closed question: *see* leading question

codification: the collection of the principles of a system or subject of law into a single statute or set of statutes

common law: a body of law set out in court decisions; derives its authority from the recognition given by the courts to principles, standards, customs, and rules of conduct (generally reflecting those accepted in society) in deciding disputes; distinguished from statute law

concurrent jurisdiction: two or more courts or tribunals having authority over the same matters

conflict of interest: a situation in which a decision-maker has a personal or financial interest in the outcome of the proceeding that can affect his or her ability to make a fair decision

Constitution: the body of binding fundamental rules that govern the exercise of power by government; to be valid, all other laws must conform to this set of fundamental rules

constructive discrimination: *see* adverse effect discrimination

contempt: conduct that shows disrespect for the authority of a court or tribunal or that tends to interfere with (obstruct) the administration of justice; examples include the disruption of a proceeding by a participant or by a member of the public, the failure of a participant to carry out an undertaking made to the court or tribunal, the failure of a witness to obey a summons, the failure of a party or representative to comply with a valid order of the court or tribunal, and the provision of statements by a participant to the media intended to influence the outcome of a proceeding

convention: an agreement among nations, such as a multilateral treaty

correctness: standard applied by a court to an agency's decision where there is only one correct answer to the question addressed; one of three standards of review historically applied by the courts in an appeal or judicial review proceeding; *see also* patent unreasonableness, reasonableness *simpliciter*

corroboration: confirmation or support of evidence in a case provided by other evidence

counsel: a lawyer who represents and advises a participant in a proceeding; usually distinguished from an agent; also called a "representative" or "advocate"

court of competent jurisdiction: in respect to the power to grant a remedy under section 24 of the Charter, a body that (a) possesses jurisdiction over the parties, (b) possesses jurisdiction over the subject matter, and (c) has jurisdiction to grant the remedy requested

cross-examination: questioning of a witness by an opposing party or representative for the purpose of casting doubt on the reliability of the witness's testimony or bringing out additional evidence supporting the position of the opposing party; *see also* examination-in-chief

cross-questioning: *see* cross-examination

D

damages: a sum of money awarded by a court as compensation for harm or loss caused by a violation of the law

declaration: a judgment issued by a court stating that a government authority is violating the law

declining jurisdiction: failure of an official or agency to carry out a statutory function that it has a duty to perform

deference: a court's willingness to accept a decision of an agency rather than substitute a decision of its own despite the fact that the court may not agree with the decision; referred to in the context of standards of review in appeal or judicial review proceedings, often implying a duty or obligation of the court to the agency (to whom the court is said to "owe deference")

delegate: entrust a person or body to act in another's place

delegated legislation: *see* subordinate legislation

department: a unit of the executive branch of government over which a minister presides; usually established to administer a specific set of laws and programs relating to a particular subject area, such as health, protection of the environment, government finance, or stimulation of business activity

direct discrimination: discrimination resulting from a standard that is discriminatory on its face, rather than from a standard that is neutral on its face but has a discriminatory effect; *see also* adverse effect discrimination

direct evidence: evidence relating to an event that is given by a witness who directly observed the occurrence of the event; *see also* circumstantial evidence

direct examination: *see* examination-in-chief

disclosure: a pre-hearing procedure in which parties are required to present evidence relevant to the proceeding to each other (and sometimes to the tribunal) for use in preparing their cases and, in some cases, to be used as evidence at the hearing

discretion: the power of a government official or agency to choose a course of action from among a variety of options available under the law

dissent: a written statement of an adjudicator's disagreement with the decision of the majority of adjudicators on a court or tribunal panel, usually setting out the reasons why the adjudicator would have reached a different decision

duty of reasonable accommodation: where a requirement or qualification has a disproportionately negative effect on an individual because of a ground prohibited by human rights legislation, the duty of an employer to take all reasonable steps to the point of undue hardship to accommodate the special needs of that individual

E

electronic hearing: a hearing held through a teleconference or video conference

employment equity: the elimination of the underrepresentation of individuals in designated groups—such as women, Aboriginals, members of visible minority groups, and people with disabilities—in the workplace

enabling legislation: a statute that sets out the powers of an agency; it is often, but not always, the statute that establishes the agency; some agencies are established by one statute but carry out functions under several statutes, each of which may give it powers for the purpose of the functions governed by that statute

enactment: a law enacted by an elected legislative body—for example, a statute, regulation, or bylaw

equity program: program designed to "level the playing field" for disadvantaged groups—for example, an employment, educational, or pay equity program

evidence: information that a party seeks to use in a legal proceeding to prove or disprove a contention or allegation

ex parte: "on one side only"; refers to a statement or application made to an adjudicator or panel member by a party to a proceeding in the absence of other parties or panel members

examination for discovery: a form of disclosure in which one party orally questions another party under oath or affirmation

examination-in-chief: initial evidence given by a witness in response to questions asked by the party or representative who called the witness to testify; *see also* cross-examination

exhibit: a document or other form of physical evidence accepted by a tribunal

expert evidence: opinions provided by an expert witness, which are required by an adjudicator who lacks the specialized knowledge, training, or experience to resolve an issue without such assistance; *see also* expert witness

expert witness: a witness who is permitted, as a result of a competence acquired through study or experience in a specialized field, to give opinions on matters related to that field as evidence before a court or tribunal; *see also* expert evidence

F

fettering discretion: in relation to the actions of a statutory decision-maker, refusing to consider an option that is available under the law, or refusing to consider any factor that is relevant to the choice of an option, when making a decision that affects a person's rights or interests

fraternization: friendly social interaction; refers to social relations between tribunal members and actual or potential participants in a proceeding

functus officio: Latin term meaning "having discharged its duty"; having made its decision, the tribunal has exhausted its authority and cannot change the decision except where a statute expressly provides otherwise or in certain exceptional circumstances permitted by the courts

fundamental justice: the basic tenets of the legal system; includes the right to procedural fairness in criminal proceedings and administrative decision-making, as well as certain substantive principles of fairness

H

harassment: vexatious comments or conduct directed at a person because of his or her race, ancestry, or other prohibited ground of discrimination under a human rights code

hearing: refers both to the opportunity to be "heard" by an administrative decision-maker, in the sense of being notified of an intended decision and given an opportunity to respond, and to the more formal hearing required when the decision-maker is a tribunal, including the various procedural safeguards that are appropriate given the nature and complexity of the issues involved and the seriousness of the consequences of the decision to the parties and the public

hearsay evidence: information provided by a witness who did not obtain the information through direct observation but heard it from another person or read it in a document written by another person

human rights: the freedoms, immunities, and benefits generally recognized nationally as well as internationally as rights to which all individuals should be entitled in the society in which they live

I

implied powers doctrine: the common law rule that agencies have whatever additional powers are necessarily incidental to their explicit powers; a court will find these powers by necessary implication only where the jurisdiction sought is necessary to accomplish the objectives of the legislative scheme and is essential to the body fulfilling its mandate; *see* necessary implication

***in camera* hearing:** *see* closed hearing

inherent powers doctrine: the common law rule that an agency has an inherent power to utilize a procedure that is reasonably necessary to carry out its statutory functions even if that power is not explicitly set out in a statute

injunction: an order issued by a court requiring a person (usually a party to a civil action) to perform some act or refrain from some conduct that is harmful to the party who seeks relief

inquisitorial system: a system of resolving disputes through holding a hearing in which the judge or adjudicator plays an active role in investigating, collecting facts, putting forward evidence, and questioning witnesses

institutional bias: bias or the appearance of bias on the part of a group of decision-makers in an agency, or of the agency as a whole, arising from aspects of the agency's structure or functions that suggest a lack of independence from a government official or body affected by a decision of the agency

interrogatory: a form of disclosure in which one party submits written questions to another party; that party is required to answer the questions in writing

intervenor: a person who, because he or she may be adversely affected by the outcome or can provide assistance to the tribunal in deciding the dispute, is granted the right to participate in a proceeding, but without the full range of rights granted to a party

intervenor status: the right of a person to participate in a proceeding without the full range of rights usually granted to a party; a tribunal's power to grant individuals such status may be authorized by statute or provided for in a tribunal's procedural rules

issues: matters that are in dispute in a hearing; the questions that a court or tribunal must answer in order to make a decision; may be questions of fact, questions of what law applies, or of how to apply or interpret the law in the circumstances of the case, or questions of what is the correct policy to apply, or of how to interpret or apply the policy

J

judicial notice: the exception to the rule that an adjudicator must rely solely on the facts established at the hearing in making a decision; the acceptance by a court or tribunal of certain facts that would be known to a well-informed member of the community or by a well-informed member of a professional group; also called "administrative notice" or "official notice"

judicial review: the exercise by a superior court or other court granted authority by statute of its supervisory authority over ministries and other government agencies by reviewing whether they have carried out their functions in accordance with the principles of administrative law

jurisdiction: the scope of the authority or powers conferred on a government body or official by legislation or by common law

justiciable: falling into the category of subjects that are appropriate for examination by a court of justice

L

law: a rule made by a body of elected representatives or their delegates or by a court, using procedures that are also prescribed by law

law journal: a periodic publication containing scholarly articles about legal issues, often discussing the significance of laws and decisions of courts and tribunals

law report: *see* law reporter

law reporter: a periodic publication containing either the full text or a summary of decisions of courts and tribunals as they are released; also called a "law report" or "reporter"

leading question: a question put to a witness that contains the crucial facts or conclusions that the questioner wants the witness to confirm, and with which the witness is merely required to agree or disagree;

generally, a question that can be answered simply "yes" or "no"; also called a "closed question"; *see also* open question

legislate: pass statutes and bylaws, and make regulations

legislation: the creation of law; the statutes, regulations, and bylaws passed by bodies of elected representatives or their delegates

Legislative Assembly: the body of elected representatives constituting the legislative branch of a provincial government; in Quebec, known as the "National Assembly"; also called the "legislature" or "provincial parliament"

legislative evolution: the amendments made to an enactment over time after it has been passed

legislative history: the background and events leading to the enactment of a law, including matters such as study papers, statements by ministers, debates in the Legislative Assembly, and changes to an enactment made between its introduction and its final passage

legislature: in Canada, the body of elected representatives constituting the legislative branch of the federal or a provincial government; *see also* Legislative Assembly, Parliament

legitimate expectations: the principle that public officials who create the expectation of a certain result, or an expectation that a certain practice or procedure will be followed, should not be able to change that result, practice, or procedure where the change will have an adverse effect without first notifying those who will be affected and giving them an opportunity to comment on the proposed change

locus standi: *see* party status

M

mandamus: Latin term referring to an order of a court to a governmental official, department, or agency compelling the performance of a public duty

marking: the procedure by which documents and other forms of physical evidence are entered into the hearing record as evidence; involves assigning an exhibit number and usually stamping or otherwise marking on the item the name or file number of the case

mediation: a method of alternative dispute resolution in which an impartial person who has no decision-making authority intervenes in a dispute in order to assist the parties in reaching a settlement

ministry: *see* department

motion: an oral or written application to a court or tribunal to rule on an issue in a proceeding

moving party: a party who brings a motion; *see also* responding party

N

natural justice: a body of rules or set of principles of fair procedure that tribunals must follow; *see* procedural fairness

necessary implication: an implication so probable that it would be unreasonable to draw any other inference from the facts; *see* implied powers doctrine

notice: a document that informs a person of a legal proceeding that may affect the person's interests or in which the person may have a right to participate

notwithstanding clause: a clause in a statute that states expressly that a provision of the statute continues to operate notwithstanding that it violates a right or freedom guaranteed by section 2 or sections 7 to 15 of the Charter

O

offence: violation of a statutory provision, regulation, or bylaw that requires a person to carry out a specified act or refrain from specified conduct, such as a requirement to meet a standard or to comply with a duty specified by the enactment

ombudsman: an independent official reporting to the legislature with authority to investigate complaints of unfair treatment and to recommend a different decision in an individual case, as well as recommending fairer practices generally

onus of proof: *see* burden of proof

open question: a question put to a witness that invites an independent response; a question that does not suggest the answer that is sought or contain crucial information that the questioner wants the witness to confirm; a question that does not put words in the witness's mouth; *see also* leading question

opinion evidence: evidence that is the product of a witness's belief or conclusion about a fact, rather than the product of direct observation of a fact through the witness's primary senses of touch, sight, hearing, taste, or smell

oral hearing: a hearing in which all the participants are physically present in the same place, receiving the same information at the same time

order: a legally enforceable remedial measure issued by a government official, tribunal, or court; sometimes used to refer to the decision of a tribunal; *see also* remedy

ordinances: laws enacted by the northern territories, similar in content to provincial and federal statutes

P

Parliament: the body of elected representatives constituting the legislative branch of Canada's federal government; also called the "legislature"

particulars: details that explain or clarify matters related to evidence, arguments, or remedies disclosed before or in the course of a proceeding—for example, details and clarifications of allegations made by one party against another, or, where the tribunal staff presents the case, details of allegations made by the tribunal staff against a party

party: a person who has a right to participate fully in a legal proceeding

party status: usually, the right of a person to participate fully in a proceeding; may be granted by statute or at the discretion of the tribunal; also called "standing" or "*locus standi*"

patent unreasonableness: a defect or error in an agency's decision of such significance that a court is left in no doubt that the decision must be overturned; formerly, one of three standards of review to be applied by the courts in an appeal or judicial review proceeding, but as a result of the Supreme Court's decision in *Dunsmuir* now only a standard of review where specified by a statute; *see also* correctness, reasonableness *simpliciter*

pay equity: the right of women to receive the same pay as men for work of equal value

physical evidence: any object produced before a court or tribunal as evidence that a judge or adjudicator may observe with his or her own senses—for example, a weapon alleged to have been used in committing an offence or a product alleged to be defective; also called "real evidence" or "demonstrative evidence"

pre-hearing conference (PHC): an informal meeting or formal hearing in advance of the main hearing in a proceeding for the purpose of making procedural decisions or resolving issues

precedent: a decision or judgment of a court of law that is cited as the authority for deciding a similar situation in the same manner, on the same principle, or by analogy; see also stare decisis

preliminary hearing: see pre-hearing conference (PHC)

presumption: a legal inference or assumption that a fact exists, based on the known or proven existence of some other fact or group of facts

private law: law that governs the conduct of persons other than government; distinguished from public law

privative clause: a provision included in an agency's governing statute for the purpose of restricting or preventing judicial review of specified actions or decisions of the agency; intended to preserve the distinction between matters that are the subject of an appeal and matters that may be addressed by judicial review

privilege: an exception to a general right or duty; in the case of evidentiary privilege, the right or duty of a person to withhold otherwise admissible evidence from a court or tribunal to preserve its confidentiality; see also privileged information

privileged information: information that a court or tribunal cannot compel a person to disclose because of the need to protect its confidentiality even though it may otherwise be admissible; see also privilege

probative value: the usefulness of information in proving a point in dispute

procedural fairness: the requirement that a decision-maker acting under a statutory power of decision must give any person whose rights, privileges, or interests may be affected by a decision reasonable notice of the intended decision and the reasons for it, and an opportunity to respond, and must be impartial, even if the function of the decision-maker is not quasi-judicial in nature; see natural justice

procedural law: law that prescribes methods of administration, application, or enforcement of a law—for example, the provisions of the Criminal Code that specify the procedures to be followed when a person is believed to have committed an offence; distinguished from substantive law

prohibition: an order issued by a court in an application for judicial review requiring a person to refrain from some conduct harmful to the party who seeks relief

proof of service: a written statement affirming that a notice of motion has been served on all parties to a proceeding and indicating how and when the notice was served

prosecution: the laying of a charge and proving of an offence against an alleged offender

public law: law that deals with the structure and operation of government; governs the relationship between individuals or private organizations and the government, between governments, and between departments and agencies within a government; includes administrative law; distinguished from private law

publication ban: an order issued by a court or tribunal prohibiting the publication of evidence and other information disclosed in a proceeding

Q

qualification hearing: a hearing held by a court or tribunal for the purpose of deciding whether to admit opinion evidence of an expert witness

quasi-constitutional: in relation to a law, a law that is below a country's Constitution but above ordinary laws in the hierarchy of laws because it protects rights that, although they may not be explicitly recognized in the Constitution, are very important to society

quasi-judicial: similar to that of a judge; often used to describe the functions of a tribunal when it must make a decision regarding the substantive rights of a person

question of fact: a question that is not answered by determining what the law is on a given point

question of law: a question of what law applies, or how to apply or interpret the law in the circumstances of a case

question of mixed fact and law: a question of how to apply a legal standard to a set of facts

R

re-examination: further questioning of a witness by the party or representative who called him or her for the purpose of clarifying any answers given by the witness during cross-examination

reasonable apprehension of bias: the appearance of bias to a reasonable and well-informed observer; also called an "appearance of bias" or "perception of bias"

reasonableness *simpliciter*: simple reasonableness; an alternative to correctness as a standard for accepting an agency's decision in an appeal or judicial review, based on a determination that the agency's interpretation of the law or the facts, or both, is reasonable; used when a question does not lend itself to just one "correct" answer, but rather several different answers may each be reasonable; *see also* correctness, patent unreasonableness

rebuttal: *see* reply evidence

reconsideration: the procedure established by a tribunal to review its decision when a party provides evidence or argument that the decision may be wrong or unreasonable; also called "rehearing" or "reopening"

registrar: the head of the tribunal staff; responsible for processing applications or appeals and handling related issues and procedures, such as providing parties with information about the tribunal's procedures; scheduling motions, pre-hearing conferences and hearings; and sending out notices and decisions

regulations: detailed rules that flesh out the meaning and requirements of a statute; made under the authority of a statute, either by Cabinet or by a body to which this power is delegated; also called "subordinate legislation" or "delegated legislation"

rehearing: *see* reconsideration

relevant evidence: evidence that helps to answer a question that a court or tribunal must address in making a decision

remedy: a measure that an authority such as a government official, court, or tribunal can take to prevent, redress, punish, or compensate for a wrong, or to relieve, cure, or correct a condition

reopening: *see* reconsideration

reply evidence: evidence called to rebut or refute the evidence presented by an opposing party; *see also* surrebuttal

reporter: *see* law reporter

representative: *see* advocate

reserve: to reserve a decision is to hold back a decision following a proceeding to allow for further consideration of the matter by the court or tribunal and the release of the decision at a later time

respondent: the party against whom a claim is brought or who is required to respond to an application, allegation, or appeal by another party

responding party: a party who is required to respond to a motion brought by another party; *see also* moving party

rule of law: the principle that governments, as well as individuals and corporations, must follow the law; in particular, governments may take actions that limit the activities of citizens or their access to rights or benefits only in accordance with substantive and procedural requirements prescribed by law

rules of evidence: rules used by the courts to determine the admissibility of evidence, composed of a combination of common law principles, statutory provisions, and constitutional principles, and requiring that evidence presented in court be relevant, reliable, necessary, and fair

rules of statutory interpretation: the principles used in interpreting laws; *see also* statutory interpretation

S

sexual harassment: any unwelcome sexual solicitation or advance either by someone in a position of power in relation to the victim (such as an employer or landlord) or by someone whose conduct a person in a position of power has the ability to control (such as a co-worker or fellow tenant of the victim) *sine die* **adjournment:** adjournment for an indefinite period

standard of proof: the quantity and kind of evidence that will be considered sufficient to prove a point that is in dispute; *see also* burden of proof

standard of review: the degree of rigour with which a court will scrutinize an agency's decision, and the degree of error or the level of uncertainty about the reasonableness or correctness of an agency's decision that a court will tolerate in deciding whether to accept or overturn the decision

standing: *see* party status

stare decisis: Latin term referring to the principle that courts should decide similar cases in the same way unless there is good reason for them to do otherwise; the rule that courts must follow previous decisions made by higher courts; *see also* precedent

state a case: a process by which a tribunal requests a court to give its opinion on a question of law formulated by the tribunal

stated case: a request by a tribunal to a court to give its opinion on a question of law formulated by the tribunal, together with any facts that the tribunal considers necessary for answering the question

statute: law passed by Parliament or a provincial legislature; also called an "act"; often specifically provides for the authority to make regulations or to delegate this power; distinguished from subordinate legislation; *see also* statute law

statute citator: a publication that lists all the provisions of a statute and for each provision, sets out amendments that have been made, and sometimes court decisions that have interpreted the provisions; also called a citator

statute law: in Canada, the body of laws passed by Parliament or a provincial legislature; generally, the body of laws passed by an assembly of elected representatives of the public; distinguished from common law

statutory interpretation: the process of interpreting laws passed by elected assemblies, whether those laws are statutes, regulations, or municipal bylaws; also known as "statutory construction"

stay: an order issued by a tribunal or court suspending the decision that is being challenged until the challenge has been decided or abandoned

stay of proceedings: the temporary or permanent suspension of proceedings before a court or tribunal by order of that court or tribunal or of a higher court

subdelegation: in relation to a power or authority that a statute has delegated to a particular person, the act of delegating that power or authority to another person

submissions: *see* arguments

subordinate legislation: legislation made by a body other than Parliament or a provincial legislature (such as Cabinet, a Cabinet minister, an agency, or a municipal council), as authorized by statute; generally includes regulations, proclamations, rules, orders, bylaws, or other instruments; also called "delegated legislation"; distinguished from statutes

substantive law: law that is concerned with the substance of a problem or the legal issue that the law is designed to address; for example, the provisions of the *Criminal Code* setting out the elements of the offence of theft; distinguished from procedural law

summons: a document issued to a witness by a tribunal or court that requires the witness to attend the hearing, bring relevant documents, and present evidence; sometimes called a "subpoena"

surrebuttal: presentation of further evidence in response to an issue raised in rebuttal; also called "surreply"; *see also* reply evidence

T

taking a view: a site visit by the adjudicator and other participants in a proceeding for the purpose of examining immovable evidence that is central to the matter in dispute

tort: a wrongful act or omission causing an injury, other than a breach of contract, for which recovery of damages is permitted by law

tribunal: a type of agency that is not a court but operates like a court in deciding disputes between individuals and/or companies, or between individuals or companies and the government, over statute-based rights, entitlements, and duties

U

undertaking: a promise made to a court or tribunal by a party or his or her representative to fulfill a specific obligation, such as producing a document or other evidence relevant to a proceeding

W

weight: the extent or degree to which evidence is reliable in deciding the issues before a court or tribunal

witness panel: a format used in a proceeding to permit simultaneous examination and cross-examination of two or more witnesses

witness statement: a written statement provided by a party to other parties or to a court or tribunal, or both, setting out the expected evidence of a person the party expects to call as a witness; also known informally as a "will say"

written hearing: a hearing conducted through the exchange of written evidence and arguments

Index